RICHARD HELLIE

Enserfment and Military Change in Muscovy

The University of Chicago Press

CHICAGO AND LONDON

THE UNIVERSITY OF CHICAGO PRESS, CHICAGO 60637
THE UNIVERSITY OF CHICAGO PRESS, LTD., LONDON

© 1971 by The University of Chicago
All rights reserved
Published 1971
Printed in the United States of America

International Standard Book Number: 0–226–32645–4
Library of Congress Catalog Card Number: 74–160839

Enserfment
and Military Change
in Muscovy

To my wife, Jean

Contents

Acknowledgments

The idea for this monograph can be traced to the 1965 defense of my doctoral dissertation, "Muscovite Law and Society: The *Ulozhenie* of 1649 as a Reflection of the Political and Social Development of Russia Since the *Sudebnik* of 1589." William McNeill asked how I could explain the enserfment of the Russian peasantry in light of the fact that the group demanding it, the middle service class cavalry archers, was displaced soon after 1649 as the major military force of Muscovy by a semistanding infantry armed with guns. In 1967 I decided that the problem of the interaction between military-technological and social change was more interesting than the relationship between law and social change and began working on the problem. I must again thank Mr. McNeill for his stimulating queries and his remarks on this work.

My study has benefited immeasurably from the comments of the many people who have taken the time to criticize it: Samuel Baron, Sumner Benson, Philip Burno, Michael Confino, Robert Crummey, Ole Hellie, Arcadius Kahan, Emile Karafiol, Lawrence Langer, Benjamin Nadel, David Ransell, Benjamin Uroff, Charles Wilmot, and Richard Wortman. Each reader contributed something different, and my listing of their names is insufficient to acknowledge the help of their sharp criticism and valuable suggestions. I also must thank Terry Clark for his advice on sociological literature.

I owe a lasting debt to Leopold Haimson, who introduced me to Russian history as a subject worthy of continuing investigation.

I am most obligated to the University of Chicago. I received all my formal education after the eleventh grade at that institution and have had the privilege of teaching in it since 1966. The environment of stimulating colleagues and demanding students increases my desire to work. The university library has a fine Russian-language collection, thanks in large part to the tireless efforts of the Slavic bibliographer Vaclav Laska, who also obtained from Moscow microfilms of the military-history materials cited in the bibliography. Interlibrary-loan librarian Helen Smith found items in other libraries. Grants from the university's Social Science Research Committee financed the research and typing.

Lastly, I am grateful to the University of Chicago Press for stimulating me to write this work with a letter of intent to publish it.

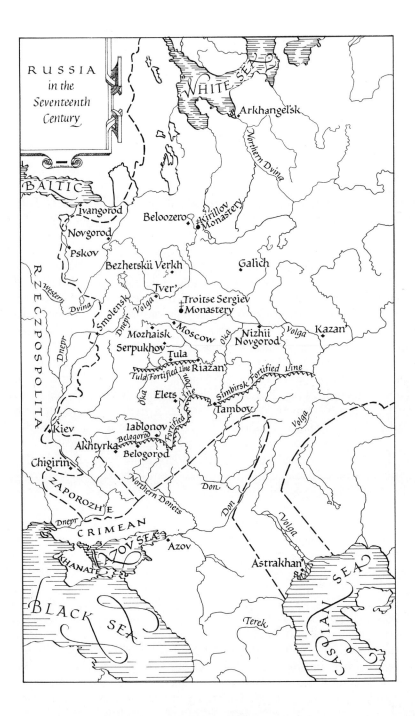

RUSSIA
in the
Seventeenth
Century

WHITE SEA

BALTIC

Arkhangel'sk

Northern Dvina

Ivangorod

Beloozero   Kirillov
Monastery

Novgorod

Pskov

Bezhetskii Verkh   Galich

R Z E C Z P O S P O L I T A

Western Dvina

Tver'

Smolensk   Dnepr   Volga

Troitse Sergiev
Monastery

Mozhaisk   Moscow   Oka   Nizhii   Volga   Kazan'
Novgorod

Serpukhov

Tula

Tula Fortified Line   Riazan'   Simbirsk Fortified Line

Dnepr   Oka   Don   Elets   Line   Tambov

Kiev   Iablonov   Fortified   Volga

Akhtyrka   Belogorod

Chigirin   Belogorod

ZAPOROZH'E   Northern Donets   Don

Dnepr   Don

CRIMEAN   Volga

AZOV SEA   Azov

KHANATE   Astrakhan

BLACK   CASPIAN SEA
SEA   Terek

1.

Introduction

The evolution of serfdom has been the most significant, the most studied, and the most controversial problem of Russian history.[1] Although a wealth of material on this topic has been unearthed and published, fruitful archival work is still in progress. The results of this work already permit more precise generalizations about the causes of this fundamental institution of Russian history than were possible even a decade ago.[2]

Historians have attributed the origin of serfdom to diverse causes and times, from the supposed conquest by the Varangians in the ninth century[3] to the reforms by Peter the Great in the first quarter of the eighteenth century.[4] Two well-known interpretations of the evolution of serfdom have emerged from more than a century of study. They can be summarized under the headings of the "decree" interpretation and the "nondecree" interpretation. Since a definitive historiography of the views on the enserfment of the Russian peasantry has not been written, the following review will present the context in which the present study has been undertaken.[5] I shall also indicate those interpretations which the available evidence seems to prove are no longer tenable.

Adherents of the legal, or decree, interpretation hold that the peasants, as a mass, were not effectively enserfed (either in law or in fact) until the promulgation of the *Ulozhenie* (law code) of 1649, and that the binding of the peasantry was achieved only after a series of conscious actions taken by the state power over the course of about two centuries. V. N. Tatishchev began this interpretation in the eighteenth century by examining laws of 1550, 1597, 1601, 1602, and 1607 and concluding that a law must have been promulgated in 1592 which forbade peasants to move.[6] N. M. Karamzin took the decree interpretation from Tatishchev more or less as proved fact.[7] The question re-

1

mained at this stage from the 1820s until the late 1850s, when it was opened for discussion by the government preparatory to the Emancipation of 1861. The decree view can be found in the monumental general history of S. M. Solov'ev[8] as well as in the special studies of B. N. Chicherin,[9] N. I. Kostomarov,[10] and I. D. Beliaev.[11] The arguments of Beliaev and Kostomarov became part of the Emancipation debate: if the state had enserfed the peasants, then the state should free them.[12]

In the period between the Emancipation era and the turn of the century the decree interpretation steadily lost favor and nearly disappeared from the historical literature. The failure to find any solid evidence of governmental action made this position increasingly difficult to hold in face of the argument that the state power had taken no role in the enserfment of the peasantry. Nevertheless, the legal historian V. I. Sergeevich and his student N. N. Debol'skii, basing their contentions on Tatishchev's documents and others, continued to hold essentially to the old position. Sergeevich opted for an earlier date, 1584 or 1585, for the putative state decree enserfing the peasants,[13] while Debol'skii chose the period 1589-95.[14] The position of these men was that the peasants were free in all respects until the state promulgated the putative decree, which was then followed by other edicts. These state actions, culminating in the *Ulozhenie* of 1649, were viewed as having been dictated by state needs, primarily that of supporting the army.[15] A decree interpretation seems to be correct in light of the evidence currently available.[16]

The alternative[17] nondecree interpretation consists of several parts, the merits of which not all adherents of the general nondecree theory will agree to. This interpretation, which denies that the state played a major role in the enserfment of the peasantry, was initiated by M. M. Speranskii, a leading government servant in the first third of the nineteenth century. Prior to the Emancipation this conception was adopted by the conservative M. P. Pogodin—some say to absolve the state of blame for the enserfment of the peasantry and, conceivably, even of the need to do anything about the peasants' plight.[18] In his 1858 article "Should Boris Godunov Be Considered the Founder of Serfdom?" Pogodin gave a negative answer and declared that Boris issued no decree binding peasants to the land. "Circumstances," the "life process," and most of all the "national character" were responsible for the development of serfdom. This article was followed by Kostomarov's Emancipation-debate answer, and the discussion that still continues was launched. Pogodin was considered the originator of the nondecree (or "environmental") interpretation by some historians in the nineteenth century, but later study has shown that he knew Speranskii's work.[19]

2

The interpretation, in more refined form, was taken up by most of the pre-Soviet historians, such as V. O. Kliuchevskii,[20] P. N. Miliukov,[21] M. A. D'iakonov,[22] A. S. Lappo-Danilevskii,[23] S. F. Platonov,[24] and A. E. Presniakov.[25]

Pogodin's claim for the absence of state involvement in the enserfment of the peasantry won few adherents among serious students of the problem,[26] but ensuing refinements of his argument did. These refinements began with a book published in 1863, in Kiev, by F. I. Leontovich on the status of the southwestern Russian peasantry in Lithuanian law of the fifteenth and sixteenth centuries. Subsequently, his conclusion that the Lithuanian enserfment resulted from a combination of indebtedness and "long-time residency" (*starozhil'stvo*) was applied to the Muscovite peasant. This sparked an intellectually fruitful but, in the end, disappointing search for the causes of the enserfment, a search which should serve as an object lesson for advocates of comparative history.[27] Analogies may offer seemingly valid explanations in the absence of data, but interpretations based on such analogies must yield when facts are found.

In 1880, however, before Russian scholars set to work seriously on Leontovich's Lithuanian example, the Dorpat University professor of Russian law, I. E. Engelman, published his treatise *Entstehung und Aufhebung der Leibeigenschaft in Russland*. Engelman said that in the late sixteenth century land cadastres bound the peasant so that the treasury's interest in its taxpayers would be protected. He added that throughout the sixteenth century lords had the right to sue for the return of peasants who were registered in the cadastres and who had fled. In the seventeenth century a whole series of private measures combined gradually to enserf the peasant, a process which culminated in the *Ulozhenie* of 1649.[28]

A precedent-setting interpretation was made in a work published in 1885 by V. O. Kliuchevskii. Traces of Engelman's ideas are evident in this work, but the major innovation can be attributed to Leontovich's observation that indebtedness played a major role in the enserfment of the southwestern Russian peasantry in Lithuania. For Kliuchevskii indebtedness became the key to the enserfment of the Great Russian peasantry, and thus binding was largely a personal matter. Serfdom in Russia was not created by the state, but only with the participation of the state. Economic difficulties in the second half of the sixteenth century forced the traditionally nomadic Russian peasants, particularly in the center of the Muscovite state, to borrow from landowners in order to continue their agricultural pursuits. By the end of the sixteenth century (if not earlier) inability to repay the loans bound the indebted peasants to their lords. In the first half of the seventeenth century, the status of the indebted peasant merged with that of the limited-service contract slave (*habal'nyi kholop*), and the laws which followed only legalized what was already a fact of life.[29] This new variation of the nondecree interpretation of enserfment has remained a part of Russian historiography with which all students have had to contend. Below I shall advance some of the arguments against the indebtedness interpretation.

Another major part of Leontovich's thesis was that "long-time residency" (*starozhil'stvo*) was responsible for the enserfment of the Lithuanian-Russian peasantry. Article 13 of chapter 12 of the *Lithuanian Statute* of 1588, a law code known to have had a significant impact on Russia, defined a "long-time resident" (*starozhilets*) as a person who had lived in the same place for ten years or more; such a person lost the right to move through disuse of the right. The Russians frequently borrowed from Lithuanian practice in life as well as in law. Leontovich proposed that somehow the status of the Muscovite peasant merged with that of the Lithuanian peasant.[30] The student of Russian and Lithuanian law, M. F. Vladimirskii-Budanov, first noted the category of "long-time residents" among the Russian peasantry, but did not state that this alone enserfed the mass of the peasantry.[31] Russian *starozhil'tsy* were present in the fifteenth century and, according to this interpretation, they did not move for a long time.[32] By custom they came to be viewed as belonging where they lived.[33] Thus the Muscovite peasant lost the right to move by not using it, and in time the de facto situation became de jure. This form of serfdom is viewed as having spread to the lands which were being incorporated into the Muscovite state in the second half of the fifteenth century and later.[34] In response to petitions from landowners (mostly monasteries) the government would decree that these peasants, bound already by custom, were formally prohibited from moving.[35] Later, A. S. Lappo-Danilevskii summed up the factors which might make a person a "long-time resident": prolonged residence in one place; using land a long time, being born in a peasant family which had already lived in a place a long time, being born a peasant and moving from one landowner to another on the basis of a private contract between lords; paying taxes in a place for a long time.[36] This long-time residency variant of the nondecree interpretation has also proved very persistent, and has even been used by some Soviet historians, though with little success.[37]

As might be expected, attempts were soon made to combine Kliuchevskii's indebtedness theory with Vladimirskii-Budanov's long-time residency hypothesis. This role fell to the institutional historian M. A.

D'iakonov. He developed Kliuchevskii's theory and Vladimirskii-Budanov's into an interesting combination.[38] M. K. Liubavskii, considered by some the greatest prerevolutionary synthesizer of early Russian history, adopted this interpretation.[39]

P. N. Miliukov amalgamated the theories of Engelman, Kliuchevskii, and D'iakonov and attributed serfdom to three phenomena: the binding of the peasants to their tax status; long-time residency; and the growth of indebtedness, which landlords used "to entangle" the peasants.[40] This was a good summary of the nondecree interpretation.

This interpretation, however, has not survived close scrutiny. Students of the indebtedness theory of the enserfment of the Russian peasantry have noted that never was it stated in any Muscovite primary source that repayment of debt was always the invariable precondition for moving (otkaz), whether the peasants repaid by themselves (vykhod) or with some kind of outside assistance (vyvoz). Indeed the recently discovered Novgorod birchbark documents, like the Pskov Judicial Charter, state that indebted peasants could move the year around.[41] Moreover, no one has proved that the average landlord had any claim on an indebted peasant for anything other than the loan: the creditor could sue for the money, but not for the person of the peasant.[42] Furthermore, at the end of the 1570s peasants everywhere in Russia (and even later in some places) were still moving about freely.[43] When the government reassigned lands from one person to another, no mention was made about indebtedness of the peasants living on the land. Had debts been of large-scale significance, presumably some provision would have been made for their repayment before the creditor lost all contact with those in his debt.[44] This raises the question of how universal the practice of taking loans was—a point which has never been discussed thoroughly.[45] Finally, S. B. Veselovskii observed that there is no proof of an increase in peasant indebtedness during this period, as one would assume should have happened if the indebtedness had been an agent of change in the condition of the Muscovite primary producers.[46]

V. I. Sergeevich, commenting on Kliuchevskii's theory, noted long ago that Muscovite legislation strictly distinguished limited-service contract slaves (kabal'nye kholopy) from peasants and in principle did not allow the latter to become the former.[47] Therefore the fusion of the two because of debt alone would have been very difficult. Recent research by V. M. Paneiakh casts doubt on whether peasants who took loans from their lords were even of the same category as people who became limited-service contract slaves.[48] If Paneiakh is correct, Kliuchevskii's theory that, in the first half of the seventeenth century, the peasants merged with this type of slave because of similarity in their status as debtors is further weakened. (There is no doubt that the status of peasant and slave did merge in certain respects in the seventeenth century, as will be shown in chapter 6.)

A very cogent argument can be made for the case that much of the peasant indebtedness resulted from enserfment rather than caused it.[49] S. I. Tkhorzhevskii summed up the minimum conclusion to be drawn from the arguments against the indebtedness interpretation: either peasant indebtedness was a comparatively rare phenomenon, or it was no obstacle to the movement of peasants and hence was hardly a significant factor in their enserfment.[50] A final weakness of the indebtedness theory is that, in the last analysis, it is a description of the process of the binding of the peasantry, rather than an analysis of the ultimate causes of this binding.[51]

The long-time residency theory also was subjected to withering criticism. Some skeptics undermined the theory by asking if the concept was effective everywhere or if, instead, it was applicable only to specific lords.[52] Sergeevich, in a caustic review of D'iakonov's 1898 synthesis *Ocherki iz" istorii sel'skago naseleniia,* denied that *starozhil'stvo* was a legal concept or institution applicable in determining the status of the peasantry.[53] A recent scholar has convincingly denied the validity of the entire theory and has shown that a "long-time resident" was little more than a person whose testimony, because of his knowledge, was suitable for use as evidence in trials in the absence of documents.[54]

Taking cognizance of obvious weaknesses in the non-decree interpretation, some scholars attempted to correct or revise the D'iakonov synthesis. One of the most valiant efforts was made by the young pre-revolutionary scholar P. E. Mikhailov. He convincingly refuted D'iakonov's "guess" that long-time residency and indebtedness were related.[55] Mikhailov doubted that the landowners of Muscovy were or could have been as generous with loans as D'iakonov had assumed.[56] Moreover, he said that the debtors in Muscovy were not the long-time residents, but the new settlers just commencing their farming and therefore needing aid from a lord.[57]

Under the influence of Fustel de Coulanges's *Le colonat romain,* Mikhailov agreed with Vladimirskii-Budanov, D'iakonov, and Lappo-Danilevskii that long-time residents had been restricted in their right of movement before other categories of peasants had been so restricted.[58] Mikhailov viewed long-time residents as successful renters, and the institution of "long-time residency" as the product of the "good life."[59] The institution did not arise, as D'iakonov believed, from a defense of private interests by landowners. Under the influence of the legal writer and theoretician Lev Petrazycki, Mikhailov portrayed the institution of *starozhil'stvo* as arising out of a sense by the peasants of a greater interest in a popular social and legal economic order which motivated even "educated" people to remain settled, even in difficult times, and to work diligently on the land to maintain life and develop culture.[60]

In spite of its obvious drawbacks, the non-decree interpretation was generally recognized as the "correct" one among prerevolutionary historians.[61] This interpretation, particularly its emphasis on indebtedness, has tended to dominate American knowledge of the process of enserfment in Russia, largely because of the prestige and accessibility of Kliuchevskii's *Course in Russian History*.[62]

The fundamental shortcoming of the non-decree interpretation was that its proponents were at first unaware of and later minimized the "Forbidden Years" (*zapovednye leta*)—those times when peasants were prohibited from moving by governmental decree. The first relevant document on this point was published in 1894, others appeared later (see chapter 5). This was an apparent state action which holders of the non-decree interpretation could not ignore. A few attempts were made prior to 1917 to work the new discoveries into the history of serfdom. It was at this time that D. M. Odynets initiated the interpretation that the Forbidden Years repealed the right of peasants to move.[63]

In spite of the new evidence, most authors remained true to the prevailing non-decree interpretation. The first author of an article on the Forbidden Years, S. A. Adrianov, attempted to tie them in with D'iakonov's long-time resident hypothesis.[64] Nearly twenty years later P. E. Mikhailov tried to work the new documents in with his new interpretation of long-time residency. Denying that there was any real, meaningful decree, he stated that the interdiction on moving was popularly believed to have originated from the tsar long before 1582 (sic), whereas in fact it had originated from common practice. Furthermore, there could not have been a governmental decree, for "legislative creativity was entirely outside the capacity of the laws of those days."[65] M. A. D'iakonov demolished this argument, pointing out that the interdiction was a conscious prohibition against moving and that nothing linked the prohibition with long-time residency. But after reviewing all the literature and sources on the Forbidden Years, D'iakonov incredibly concluded that the right of the peasant to move had died without a legal repeal.[66]

After the Revolution the conservative historian S. F. Platonov worked the Forbidden Years into his histories, partially adopting a decree interpretation in which the state—responding to the chaos in the second half of the sixteenth century by binding the peasantry in the interests of the fisc and the military class—had a major role.[67] He speculated that temporary decrees were used for such a long time that the right to move died out without a general legal repeal. He did not deny, however, that such a general repeal might have existed, and he said that the major historical task was to find such a decree. Platonov was the first historian to focus sharply on the conditions which led to state intervention in the peasant question. Giving a new twist to old interpretations and combining the results with obvious facts, Platonov conjectured that long-term residence on both peasant and seignorial lands arose juridically because of the binding of the peasants to the tax rolls through registration in the cadastres, not because of indebtedness or any civil obligations.[68]

Platonov's lead was only partially followed by the historians active in the 1920s.[69] Iu. V. Got'e took note of peasant indebtedness, but assigned to the state the prohibition of peasant mobility. Elsewhere, he in essence ignored the meaning of the Forbidden Years and concluded that Boris Godunov had not enserfed the peasants.[70] S. I. Tkhorzhevskii noted the Forbidden Years and assigned to them the goal of preserving the land fund for the military service class. The years were not "decisive" in the enserfment, for they were only temporary, and were operative only in connection with the land cadastres compiled to bind the peasants to a taxpaying status. He concluded that the right of the peasant to move was never formally repealed by a general law.[71]

The economic historian I. M. Kulisher, relying heavily on Western European analogies, insisted that the Kliuchevskii-D'iakonov indebtedness thesis, "universally recognized as correct," was still viable. The peasant had not been enserfed by any specific state law, but rather by a series of economic conditions. These conditions created and then strengthened the power of the military service landholder over the peasant largely through indebtedness, which bound the peasant to the creditor. Simultaneously, long-time residence bound the peasant to the land by common law, so that the right to move died of itself, without any direct or indirect legislative repeal.[72]

Hardly more original was the interpretation of the declared Marxist N. A. Rozhkov. He denied that any law had been promulgated at the end of the sixteenth century binding the peasants, and stated that they still enjoyed the legal right to move freely from one lord to another. They were restrained by debts they could not pay, but this did not destroy the right to move and it did not enserf them. However, the binding to tax status in the cadastres, longevity of residency, and indebtedness combined to put long-time residents in a serf status, if only conditionally. These developments in the second half of the sixteenth century provided only sporadic legal precedents. In the first half of the seventeenth century serfdom was finally established juridically: the peasants signed away their freedom in contracts with their lords, indebtedness rose, and the fusion of the status of slave and peasant occurred. As Kliuchevskii had written long before, all this was finally sanctioned in law in the *Ulozhenie* of 1649.[73]

On the issue of serfdom M. N. Pokrovskii, the Marxist "dean" of early Soviet historians, was strikingly unoriginal. He was under the influence of the Kliuchevskii thesis of the extralegal confluence of the status of the indebted peasant and the status of the slave, and said that peasants were forbidden to move simply to curtail disputes over them.[74] This was one of the many futile attempts which have been made to combine the uncombinable. In other works he attempted to create a "materialist" explanation of the enserfment, which he viewed sometimes as a consequence of the introduction of the three-field system of agriculture, elsewhere as a consequence of "merchant capitalism." Finally, at the end of his career, after the launching of the industrialization drive and the collectivization of agriculture, he attached considerable significance to the "direct intervention of the state" in the enserfment of the peasantry.[75]

The most interesting analysis of the enserfment of the peasantry in the 1920s was made by B. D. Grekov, soon to replace Pokrovskii as the dean of Soviet historians. He formed a combined materialist and decree interpretation of the enserfment. On the one hand, said Grekov, changes were taking place in agriculture. In the fifteenth and early sixteenth centuries Russian landowners had hardly any land under cultivation for their own use; they were satisfied in collecting rent, largely in kind, from peasants on their lands. But in the first half of the sixteenth century landowners began to farm more of their own land themselves, at the expense of the peasant-rented land; they also began to demand corvée from their peasants and to collect more rent in cash. By the 1580s an extremely exploitative corvée system was in operation. Out of his desire to get cash to buy luxury goods and other market items, "the lord declared economic war on his peasant." This new system, coupled with external forces, reduced vast numbers of peasants to the level of a rural proletariat. These *bobyli* were subject to a lord and thus were in his economic and extraeconomic power. All of these events combined to undermine the position of the peasant, to reduce him to a status close to that of a serf.[76]

But if this was not enough, Ivan's Livonian War (1558–83) caused an economic crisis "which sharpened and complicated the generally developing economic process." As a result the state intervened by forbidding all peasants to move, in order to save the military service class.

The state action coincided with the "natural economic process," and after 1581 the Russian peasant was a serf.[77] After he became the leading Stalinist historian, Grekov changed his approach to a considerable degree, as we shall see below. In the second half of Grekov's essay on the enserfment, much of which is devoted to refuting D'iakonov's objections to the efficacy of the Forbidden Years, we find a strong swing away from the nondecree interpretation back to the old view that indeed the state played a crucial role in the enserfment of the peasantry.

There are other interpretations of the enserfment besides the decree and nondecree theories. They can be summarized in the assertion that, for one reason or another, the Russian peasant throughout nearly all of recorded history was a serf. Thus D. Ia. Samokvasov wrote that in Russia, as in the West, there were no laws binding the peasants. The peasants became serfs because of conquest[78] (in this case, the Varangian conquest), which led to the taxation of the conquered communes in 946, in Kiev, and in 1034, in Novgorod. This "enserfment," embodied in the fact that the peasants had to pay taxes, was continued by the Mongol censuses and then the Muscovite censuses, on the basis of which registered peasants had to pay taxes and render services. Samokvasov considered this obligation a form of serfdom. The legislation of the fifteenth and sixteenth centuries was applicable only to free people—those who had been manumitted, those who immigrated to Russia from abroad, and *izgois*. The masses had never enjoyed the right of movement.[79]

Views on the omnipresence of serfdom throughout most of Russian history have been prevalent in much of Soviet historical writing, especially since the beginning of the 1930s, when Soviet historiography "transferred to new Marxist rails."[80] Already in 1924, however, I. M. Kulisher noted Samokvasov's interpretation (which he rejected), and himself declared that there were not two periods in the history of the Russian peasantry as most historians had supposed, one of freedom and one of serfdom; rather, the latter condition had been the real situation of the Russian peasant throughout history.[81] Soviet scholars are prone to dismiss both the decree and the nondecree interpretations as simply untenable.[82]

Many Soviet historicists[83] and their followers abroad claim that all of recorded Russian history up to 1861 was a "feudal" period; that an essential, constituent part of feudalism is serfdom; and therefore that the Russian peasant up to 1861 was always a serf. This syllogism has been the fundamental premise of Soviet historiography for nearly forty years, and is worthy of more detailed examination.

All Soviet discussions of feudalism are based on the Lenin canon, particularly on remarks in the attack on the Populists, "Who are the 'Friends of the People,'" written when the revolutionary was twenty-four years old.[84] In 1912 Lenin defined feudalism as "land ownership and the privileges of lords over serfs."[85] This 1912 remark was part of a political tirade prior to the Revolution, but every Soviet historian now has to take it into account.

Currently, attempts to define feudalism are more sophisticated. Feudalism is the third stage in the history of mankind, a necessary social and economic formation, a universal stage of historical development encompassing legal, political, economic, and social relationships. It is a form of organization of production and distribution, and a condition of the human spirit. Rent relationships are seen as the cornerstone of feudalism. Soviet Marxist medieval study views feudalism as a means of production based on large landed property and dependent small peasant economies owned by the peasants themselves and exploited by the nominal owners of land through methods of extraeconomic compulsion based on patrimonial forms of state organization. Handicraft production, in which the means of production are owned by the artisans themselves, is also a feature of the feudal economy. Another distinguishing mark of feudalism is the fact that the productive forces are fully enough developed to ensure producers enough to live on as well as to satisfy the demands of exploiters, thus passing the grosser exploitation of the slavery stage. Under the conditions of "primordial" hegemony of the private, large-estate system of property (antedating capitalistic private property), there are two basic phases: first, the dominance of a system of universal ties of personal dependence between those who perform public functions—the vassal-fief system (monarchy-suzerainty); next, the system of "universal citizenship" (absolute monarchy). The transitional boundary between the two is marked by the development of towns and economic exchange.[86]

N. P. Pavlov-Sil'vanskii was the first historian to posit the presence of feudalism in Russia.[87] After the Revolution, M. N. Pokrovskii, following Pavlov-Sil'vanskii, first worked out a Soviet Marxist understanding of Russian feudalism and traced its origin and major cause (large landownership) to the thirteenth century.[88] The leading advocate in Soviet historiography of the presence of feudalism in Russia was S. V. Iushkov, another follower of Pavlov-Sil'vanskii.[89] (In 1938 Iushkov tried to update the Kliuchevskii-D'iakonov indebtedness theory which has been discussed above.)[90]

In the 1920s Soviet scholars toyed with the idea of a natural feudal economy yielding to a capitalistic, money economy in the late fifteenth and the sixteenth centuries.[91] The subject of "Russian feudalism" was hardly studied in the early years of Soviet power, however, and the views of Pokrovskii were accepted without question.[92]

Great debates on feudalism took place in the years 1929-34, and Pokrovskii's conception of periods of "merchant" and "industrial" capitalism (the second half of the sixteenth century to the Emancipation) was rejected in favor of extending the feudal period up to 1861.[93] Thus "capitalism" was postponed for about three centuries in Russia. The origins of feudalism in Russia were discussed in debates in 1932 and 1933, and B. D. Grekov's position that a slave-owning period, the second Marxist stage (Kiev Rus'), was succeeded by feudalism was discarded in favor of the present dogma, laid down by M. M. Tsvibak, that Russia had bypassed the slave-owning period entirely.[94] Grekov subsequently incorporated the prescribed dogma into all of his works. (Russia's leading specialist on slavery, A. I. Iakovlev, had written earlier that serfdom had developed out of the law of slavery, from the ownership rights of lords over slaves already formulated in the tenth and eleventh centuries.) [95] In the 1960s one of the problems most agitating Soviet medievalists was the transition from a primordial or slave-holding social system to a feudal one, and a number of interesting theories were developed.[96]

Currently "feudalism" is thought to have originated in Russia at some time in the second half of the first millennium A.D.[97] This is an even earlier origin than that found by some of the Stalinist historians. For example, I. I. Smirnov observed the genesis of feudalism about the eleventh century, and then claimed that the twelfth and thirteenth centuries were the period of "developed feudal society."[98] No Soviet historian, to my knowledge, now questions the premise that all of early Russian history (the Kievan period) was part of the feudal epoch.

D. P. Makovskii has recently raised the issue of whether feudalism may have been yielding to capitalism at the end of the fifteenth and in the first half of the sixteenth centuries—a throwback to the interpretation of the 1920s.[99] A conference held in Moscow in July, 1965, once again rejected such suggestions and decided that the period from the end of the fifteenth to the second half of the eighteenth centuries should not be included in a transitional epoch from the feudal method of production to the capitalistic, but rather should be called the period of "progressive feudalism."[100]

Soviet historiography has seen more debate on the issue of whether serfdom is a necessary constituent part of a feudal period.[101] In 1929 the critic of the "Asiatic means of production," S. M. Dubrovskii, raised the issue by stating that feudalism and serfdom were two different sociopolitical formations. A. I. Malyshev, criticizing Dubrovskii, began the Soviet tradition that serfdom and feudalism were identical.[102] Thus L. V. Danilova writes that it is now "absolutely clear" that the division proposed by Dubrovskii is unscientific (nepravomernyi).[103] Elsewhere she has written that feudalism "could not possibly exist without a class of dependent peasantry."[104] (As we shall see below, a "dependent peasant" is another way of saying "serf.") Danilova's statements are reminiscent of similar ones in the 1940s, when it was said that serfdom was simply the juridical expression of the productive relationships of feudal society. "Without serfdom there is no feudalism."[105] Some Soviet historians who believe that the Russian peasants were always enserfed have been wont to apply the term "second enserfment" to the events under review in this work.[106]

I. Ia. Froianov attributes the hegemony of the standard Soviet interpretation to a 1946 remark by Stalin. Citing Marx, he "proves" that ideologically this interpretation is in fact not necessary, that it is a distortion of Marx, that serfdom is in fact not a synonym for feudalism.[107] A. G. Man'kov has also left the issue open by noting that serfdom was not the basis of feudalism, but rather a superstructural phenomenon— the implication being that feudalism might be possible without serfdom.[108] N. E. Nosov, in observing that the new twelve-volume history of the USSR published under the auspices of the Academy of Sciences still hews to this traditional line, remarked that the basic thing wrong with such a view is that it cannot be supported by the facts because the Russian peasants were not enserfed en masse until the sixteenth century.[109]

The axiom that the Russian peasant was always a serf stems from the Leninist canon, for Lenin once remarked that serfdom existed in the ninth century. In 1932 B. N. Tikhomirov proposed that the basic mass of the peasantry in Kievan Rus' was unfree, that seignorial relations eased a bit at the end of the fifteenth century, and that the "second enserfment"—simply a new stage in the development of serfdom—occurred in the second half of the sixteenth century. In 1933 he was joined in this position by B. D. Grekov.[110] According to I. I. Smirnov, the fact that the peasant of the fifteenth century had the right of movement (perekhod) was not, as claimed by bourgeois scholars, a sign that the peasant was free, but was an expression of the process of the destruction of the peasant commune and the enserfment of the communal peasants by "feudal landowners.[111]

The movement away from Stalinist historiography has witnessed some change in the assertion that the Russian peasant was always a serf. In 1956 L. V. Cherepnin declared that some Kievan smerdy were state peasants, while others were "dependent" directly on the prince as a landowner.[112] More recently the acknowledgment has been made that, at least in the tenth to twelfth centuries, the majority of the peasants were personally free and owned their land.[113]

The problem of the peasants in the fifteenth and sixteenth centuries is more complex. A. G. Man'kov, an official Soviet spokesman on these matters in the 1950s, claimed that all peasants in the fifteenth and beginning of the sixteenth centuries were feudally dependent, and that those on privately-owned land were bound to that land.[114] G. E. Kochin, on the other hand, has said that some peasants were free and were not serfs.[115] The issue of "black peasants" (taxpayers living on land which was either their own or belonged to the state) and their freedom or dependence in this period is currently one of the most lively issues of Soviet historiography.[116]

Orthodox Soviet historians determine that the Russian peasant was always a serf by examining not laws, but "the relationships of production." For example, B. D. Grekov, in periodizing peasant history, offered the following three forms of exploitative relationships as successively characterizing recorded pre-Petrine Russian history: (1) primitive labor rent, similar to French *mains mortales,* from the middle of the first millennium A.D. to about the twelfth century; (2) rent paid in kind in a natural economy—from the twelfth and thirteenth to the mid-sixteenth centuries (based largely on data extant from the Galicia-Volynia and Novgorod-Pskov regions); (3) rent paid in cash plus a considerable amount of corvée, and a rise of exploitation connected with the developing internal market from the end of the sixteenth through the middle of the seventeenth century.[117] This interpretation is connected with the discovery that the Russian peasant, after the founding of the Kievan state, always farmed land belonging to someone else.[118] He was not the owner of the means of production and therefore was "dependent" upon a lord, that is, he was a serf.[119] (In 1924 I. M. Kulisher offered a slightly different version by saying that peasants who had to pay unspecified quitrent and render unlimited corvée were "dependent" on their lords.[120] In 1930 A. I. Malyshev expressed the situation in yet another way: during a feudal period the peasant, in practice, owned his tools and means of production, the land, but nevertheless was personally dependent on a lord.) [121] Those who advance this line say that the developments of the Muscovite period caused a slight difference in the form of serfdom, but that the essence of the peasant's position, his "feudal obligations," remained unchanged. Something as fundamental as serfdom must be rooted in the sphere of production, not in the sphere of superstructural legal norms.[122]

Occasionally Soviet scholars account for the observable changes which occurred in the Muscovite period by noting that until, say, 1581 the peasant living on a lord's land was feudally dependent, but not bound. Peasants who had their own land were not feudally dependent.[123] N. E. Nosov has gone so far as to put aside the ideological blinkers and has written that actually, as well as legally, serfdom began only at the end of the sixteenth century. While recognizing the positive role B. D. Grekov played in the development of Soviet historiography, Nosov says that Stalin's court historian was wrong in maintaining that serfdom was a long and complex process which began in Kiev Rus' and only became intensified at the end of the sixteenth century.[124] Thus serfdom is once again attributed to the Forbidden Years. Once again serfdom is seen largely as a "decree" phenomenon.

Many Soviet historians have devoted serious effort to the study of the legal enserfment of the peasantry, and significant contributions in this field are still being made by them at the present time. Certainly the most notable is V. I. Koretskii's 1968 publication of state documents on events at the beginning of the 1590s.[125] This publication largely meets Platonov's desideratum of the 1920s.

Much of the disagreement on the issue of enserfment stems from differing definitions of "serf." The Soviet view, based on the presumption of the presence of "feudalism," has been mentioned. For others, as has been noted, "serfdom" has meant the obligation to pay taxes, or the necessity to render services or to pay dues to a lord. For the purposes of this essay, however, a serf will be considered the individual peasant who is (1) legally bound to a plot of land, (2) legally bound to the person of his lord and who continues to pay taxes, or (3) who is subject in a meaningful way to the administrative and judicial authority of his lord rather than the crown.[126] Significant changes occurred in these areas during the Muscovite period of Russian history, with the most important taking place as the peasant's legal ties to the land became increasingly unseverable. The serf differed from the slave in Russia in that the serf, as a peasant, was nearly always subject to taxation whereas the slave was not. The slave was largely an object of the law, whereas the peasant was, in varying degrees, its subject.[127]

Two preconditions were necessary for the enserfment of the Russian peasant. The country had to be fairly well unified politically and a powerful special group consciously interested in curtailing peasant mobility had to be present.

The Kievan state in the eleventh century unified to some extent the lands of the Eastern Slavs (the lands from the Gulf of Finland to the confluence of the Vorskla and Dnepr rivers and outposts on the Black Sea, from the Pripiat Marshes to the Volga-Oka triangle), but by the second half of the century the country had fallen into a number of feuding principalities ("appanages"). This process of disintegration was not halted by the Mongol conquest of Russia in 1237–40. While "appanage Russia" was in this fragmented condition there was little reason for a Russian prince to attempt to limit the mobility of the peasants within his realm, for another labor-short principality was not far distant.[128] Occasional attempts were made by various princes to halt recruiting of labor in one another's domains or to return peasants who had moved from one principality to another, but the consensus is that these were paper agreements only and not enforced.[129] Most princes seem to have been willing to gamble that any potential net labor flow would be in the direction of their particular principalities, and so they were not interested in enforcing an agreement which might work to their potential (or actual) disadvantage. Consequently curtailment of peasant mobility waited upon the consolidation of the Russian lands into a unified state and an administration willing to decree and enforce such curtailment.[130]

The second necessary factor was a desire to limit peasant mobility. For example, the state might desire to bind each individual to a given spot to facilitate the collection of taxes and to enforce the rendering of state obligations.[131] Or, a particular institution or group in society might conclude that peasant mobility in its present form was not in its favor and consequently might ask the government to curtail this mobility. Such a possiblity presupposes the existence of institutions or groups which were aware that they relied on peasant labor for their survival; furthermore these institutions or groups had to be influential enough to convince the state to curtail a mobility which might well be working at the moment to the advantage of other segments of society. That all groups and institutions, including the state itself, desired the enserfment of the peasantry in Muscovy can be demonstrated to be patently false. Some groups did desire this, were vociferous about wanting to bind the peasantry, and eventually achieved their goal; others emphatically did not want this goal.

Both necessary factors, a politically unified state and influential forces desiring a limitation of peasant mobility, appeared on the east European plain in the fifteenth century. It is not accidental that the beginning of the process of the enserfment of the peasantry can be traced back to this time. The immediate cause, the enzymatic trigger, of this process was the civil war during the reign of Vasilii II (1425–62).

16

The enserfment of the Russian peasant culminated in the *Ulozhenie* of 1649, which added effective sanctions to decrees binding him to the land. This culmination was the result of pressure put on the government by the middle service class—the members of the Muscovite cavalry who were dependent for financial support on the peasants who lived on their landholdings. This middle service class cavalry finally was abolished because of technological obsolescence in 1682, the year which began a new era in Russian history by witnessing the abolition of the "system of places" (*mestnichestvo*) and the inauguration of Peter I.

The history of the rise of the middle service class and of the military changes which made it obsolete is not as controversial as that of the enserfment of the peasantry. Controversy, where it exists, is usually over details rather than over the general course and causation of events. It would be fair to say that the major research in both areas was done by prerevolutionary scholars. Soviet scholars, reacting against previous concentration on the study of the upper class and military history, have largely ignored both areas.[132] As a result, much Soviet writing on the middle service class and military subjects is derivative, lacks historiographic interest, and in general is inferior to pre-Soviet efforts. This result is unfortunate, for, as this work will attempt to show, the fate of the peasantry cannot be understood without knowledge of both areas—the state of the military art as well as the economic needs, the social position, the psychological condition, and the political status of the men who bore arms.

This is not a new idea. A century ago the historian of the gentry, A. V. Romanovich-Slavatinskii, in essence following N. M. Karamzin, attributed the enserfment of the peasantry to an attempt by the state power to provide for the needs of the military servitors.[133] This view lost favor during the hegemony of the nondecree interpretation of the enserfment. After the Revolution, S. F. Platonov and particularly A. E. Presniakov and S. I. Tkhorzhevskii observed that the peasants were enserfed to satisfy the interests of the landholders. This theme became a topic of scholarly interest to some subsequent Soviet historians,[134] but Soviet ideology has made detached consideration of this issue difficult. As we have seen, the peasants were decreed to have been always serfs, and the events of the sixteenth century were considered to be relatively insignificant, sometimes part of a "second enserfment." Many Soviet historians have been reluctant to see any divergence of interest among the various landed elements of Muscovite society.[135] The discovery of much new archival material in the last century makes worthwhile a reexamination of the enserfment, the interests of the landholders, and their utility to the state power.

17

The story of the enserfment of the peasantry occupies approximately a quarter of a millennium, slightly less than one-fourth of the time that Russia has existed as a political entity. I am not attempting to tell the whole story of the peasantry in this period, but only the factors relating to the enserfment (a juridical process), many of which lie entirely outside the history of the peasantry per se.[136] The story will be told through highlights, not stopping for every known fact and development, and will demonstrate the immediate and perhaps some of the ultimate causes of the enserfment of the peasantry. From time to time comparisons will be made with developments elsewhere, although this essay, because of the author's limitations, does not pretend to be nor can it be the final comparative history of the problems under review.

Part I

The Rise of the
Middle Service Class

2.

The Creation of the
Middle Service Class

War was the major preoccupation of the Muscovite state. The expansion of the territory ruled from Moscow testifies to the fact that, on balance, Muscovite arms were more successful than those of Moscow's rivals and neighbors. At the beginning of the fourteenth century the Muscovite principality was quite small, less than the 47,000 square kilometers of Moscow oblast' today. This principality expanded to roughly 430,000 square kilometers in 1462, 2,800,000 square kilometers in 1533, 5,400,000 square kilometers at the end of the sixteenth century, and finally 15,280,000 square kilometers by 1688.[1] While the rise and territorial aggrandizement of Moscow was a complex phenomenon, there is no question that its military forces played a major role in this development. The demands of the military forces required by Muscovy's strategic situation played a decisive role in the enserfment.

The Muscovite army was made up of diverse elements. Of these, the major military figure from the end of the fifteenth century through the middle of the seventeenth century was the middle service class cavalryman. The cavalryman was essential to Muscovy because of the nature of the enemies it faced. In all recorded history up to the reign of Ivan III (1462-1503) Russia had to contend with foes on three sides —east, south, and west. In the Muscovite period these can be reduced to two basic frontiers, a Kazan', Nogai, and Crimean Tatar frontier in the east and south, and a Swedish, Polish, and Lithuanian one in the west. The Tatars presented the greatest continuous danger to Muscovy, at least until the end of the sixteenth century, and the Russian military forces had to be structured to meet this threat. The member of the middle service class was cut out to be a match for the Tatar warrior, whose counterpart he was, on horseback, in every feature except race. He was successful in holding, defending reasonably adequately, and even advancing the Russian frontier at Tatar expense until the steppe no

21

longer threatened the forest zone of Russia. This should be sufficient to demonstrate the usefulness and efficacy of the middle service class cavalry while the threat lasted. The problem of the western frontier will be discussed in chapters 9–11.[2]

During the period of its hegemony the middle service class gained many privileges. But before we continue we must define precisely what is meant by the term "middle service class."

For the sake of discussion and analysis the military and civil service cadres of the Muscovite state can be grouped into three categories— upper, middle, and lower service classes. The major characteristics of the upper service class were geographic concentration in Moscow and compensation largely by hereditary and service land-grants from the government. These people, about two thousand individuals in the first half of the seventeenth century, comprised the "power elite" of Muscovy. They can be subdivided into two groups, the upper upper-service class and the lower upper-service class. The members of the former were the boyars, *okol'nichie,* and *dumnye dvoriane* and had the right to sit in the Boyar Council (*Boiarskaia Duma*). This was the body which, along with the great prince-tsar, was responsible for making policy, centralizing administration, and serving as a supreme court.[3] Its members also served as heads of, and as judges in, important central governmental chancelleries, as generals in the army, as ambassadors, and as governors sent out from Moscow to run provincial administrations in most of the period under review (the exception was the second half of the sixteenth century).[4] Historically these persons had formed the ruling class in Moscow and in the other principalities annexed, largely in the fifteenth century, by Moscow. Many of them were nobles descended from ancient princely lines, but some were commoners who had worked their way up by serving the rulers. These people did not harbor separatist aspirations, for they quickly adapted themselves to the new order of the consolidated Muscovite state. Even before the Oprichnina (Ivan IV's mad state within the state, 1565–72) was formed, supposedly to combat "treason," most of the magnates, who had a right to serve in government, had accommodated themselves to the reality of vying for places in the central administration, and did not dream of being heads of independent principalities.[5] This was even more true after the Time of Troubles at the beginning of the seventeenth century, when the upper service class became completely remolded into an officialdom connected with service interests.[6] The members of these families vied for control of the government during periods of weak rulers. In 1668 sixty-two people held the ranks of *boiarin, okol'nichii,* and *dumnyi dvorianin.* Most of them had been raised to these ranks fairly recently, for only twenty-eight of them had families that had been in the Boyar Council even as recently as during the reign of Tsar Mikhail Fedorovich (1613–1645).[7] A few of the magnates had thousands of peasants living on their lands, but in 1637–38 each of the forty-one members of the Boyar Council had an average of 520 peasant households outside of the immediate Moscow area (*podmoskov'e*).[8] Many of them also had tens of thousands of acres of land, but some had as little as a thousand acres.[9] At the end of the 1670s they had an average of 480 peasant households each as their numbers increased to ninety-seven.[10]

The members of the lower upper-service class had the following ranks: *pechatnik, koniushii, oruzheinichii, lovchii, stol'nik, striapchii, spal'nik,* and Moscow *dvorianin.* Of these, the titles of *okruzheinichii, lovchii, komnatnyi stol'nik,* and *komnatnyi striapchii* were court ranks. The *ploshchadnye stol'niki* and *striapchie,* Moscow *dvoriane,* and *zhil'tsy* served in Moscow, but not at court.[11] The *Boiarskaia kniga* of 1627 listed 236 *stol'niki,* 94 *striapchie,* and 826 Moscow *dvoriane.*[12] On an average in 1638 each *stol'nik* had seventy-eight peasant households. By Tsar Aleksei Mikhailovich's reign (1645–76) their numbers had risen to over five hundred. In 1638 the average *striapchii* had twenty-four peasant households. By the middle of the century their numbers had risen to eight hundred. In 1638 each of the 997 Moscow *dvoriane* had an average of twenty-nine peasant households.[13] They all had lands in Moscow province, and lived on them when not in service. They served in lower capacities in the same jobs as did the members of the Duma: they were battalion and company commanders; they presided over important provincial judicial cases; they ran second-level chancelleries; and they were governors of second-level towns.[14] They also made up the "tsar's regiment" on military campaigns.[15] However, it should be noted that service at court carried much higher prestige than service in the army.[16] In 1630 an official count of all Moscow ranks (boyar down through Moscow *dvorianin*) totalled 2,642 men.[17]

A transitional group were the *zhil'tsy,* who did not necessarily have lands close to Moscow but lived and served in Moscow in shifts a quarter of the year at a time, and made up part of the tsar's regiment also.[18] Members of the *zhilets* stratum could join the "Moscow register" (*moskovskii spisok*) by petition, after having rendered service of sufficient length or quality.[19] The *zhil'tsy* were either members of the middle service class who were being promoted (three hundred were appointed from the *vybornye dvoriane* to serve for a term of three years as an honorary convoy for the tsar) or were the children of members of the upper service class just beginning their service careers. By the middle of the seventeenth century there were about 1,500 *zhil'tsy.*[20]

In 1681, due to population growth, promotions, and other factors, there were 6,385 members of the upper service class. Of these, 3,761 were officers in the regiments of provincial gentry; 2,624 were in the tsar's regiment and brought with them over 21,000 armed slaves, or about 9 slaves each.[21] Members of the upper service class protected their positions against outsiders by the *mestnichestvo* system, a device which regulated the inheritance of service relationships among families in the network. Parvenus were effectively barred from the top service posts because they had no position in the network of relationships, which was jealously preserved by the status-conscious Muscovites.[22] The titles associated with the upper service class (*boiarin, okol'nichii, stol'nik, striapchii, dvorianin,* and *zhilets*) were phased out in the first half of the reign of Peter the Great.[23]

The middle service class was based in the provinces, lived primarily on the basis of land grants (*pomest'ia*) from the government, and had the right to use peasant labor. Members of the middle service class were assigned a small annual cash salary rate, but it was not always paid, even when needed to outfit the serviceman for an impending campaign. The middle service class, about 25,000 strong during the period of their major influence (c. 1550–c. 1650) had the ranks of *dvorianin* (plural, *dvoriane*) and *syn boiarskii* (plural, *deti boiarskie*).[24] They constituted the major military force of the consolidated Muscovite state until the completion of the gunpowder revolution in the second half of the seventeenth century. The average member of the middle service class had only five to six peasant households for his support.[25] A member of the middle service class rose from one rank to the next upon petition. Ranks were rarely skipped. Ranks also were not skipped by those going down —for example those who did not perform the required service.[26]

Social distinctions between the upper and middle service classes were apparent even in the criminal law of the seventeenth century. For example, the compilers of the law code (*Ulozhenie*) of 1649 must have felt that members of the elite were incapable of committing certain crimes which *dvoriane* and *deti boiarskie* might commit. The latter, in turn, were less suspect than peasants and slaves.[27] In real life the gap between the upper and middle service classes was also great. A boyar looked upon the rank and file military servitors as a "sovereign on his subjects."[28]

The lower service class (*sliuzhilye liudi po priboru*) differed from the higher classes primarily in the fact that its members lived off annual salaries paid by the treasury and were explicitly denied the right to exploit peasant labor.[29] They were recruited from poor *deti boiarskie,* townsmen, and peasants; after society became rigidly stratified in the mid-seventeenth century, their numbers were maintained by hereditary succession. They were usually garrisoned for training in settlements outside of both Moscow and the provincial towns, where they were collectively granted large plots of land for individual use as gardens. Members of the lower service class were musketeers (*strel'tsy*), gunners (*pushkari*) and cossacks in government service. After the military reforms of the 1630s–1650s period, they were joined (and ultimately replaced) by soldiers (*soldaty*), dragoons, lancers, and cavalrymen (*reitary*) —the subject of chapters 9–11.

These were the major service classes of Muscovy. Of course there were transitional groups such as the previously discussed *zhil'tsy* and the commanders of lower service regiments who had land and peasants. Each group had its definite interests and place in the political and social structure of the Muscovite state.

Having defined our subject, we shall now discuss the creation, functions, and problems of the middle service class, then the elevation of the group's status in the reign of Ivan IV.

In the Kievan period the Russian army had consisted of large contingents of infantry recruited from the urban population. Until the eleventh century the Russians hired foreign mercenaries when they needed cavalrymen. The Mongol attacks of the thirteenth century destroyed the towns, and this may have been partly responsible for the conversion of the Russian forces to cavalry in the ensuing era. Later the Russians were influenced to a lesser extent by the glamor of the Polish cavalry. Russia always borrowed militarily from its enemies, so it was only natural that it copied the Mongol-Tatar military style and to a lesser degree, that of the Poles. Throughout the "Mongol period" the Russian forces were predominantly cavalry.[30] The townsmen and peasantry played only a secondary role in the army. They built fortifications, worked in engineering battalions, and perhaps performed supply functions, but as a rule they were not part of the combat forces.[31] Throughout most of the Muscovite period the peasantry played a secondary role in the country's armed forces.[32]

Prior to the reign of Ivan III there seems to have been no centralized direction of the armies of Russia. Each prince had his own court (*dvor*) and small cadre of retainers. These retainers were boyars and their offspring, other free people, and slaves. The term "dvorianin," which is first found in the chronicle under the year 1175, meant "courtier," a retainer in a prince's *dvor*.[33] There was no particular concept of citizenship or loyalty, and every prince's servitors (except the slaves) were free to leave when and as they thought fit. These private armies were very small, probably most of them numbering no more than a few hundred men at most. Servitors were paid with cash, when it was available, the booty they could plunder on campaigns, and fees gathered from administration while they were not in the army. In this era the Russian army was a collection of such small groups under individual princes. Some princes retained their private armies well into the first half of the sixteenth century.[34]

Much of this was changed with the rapid centralization of the Russian state around Moscow during the reign of Ivan III. Most of the independent princes came to Moscow and joined the court of the great prince. Many of their boyars came with them. Their lesser retainers remained behind in the provinces as local garrison forces which could be summoned by Moscow in time of need. Until the middle of the sixteenth century these forces remaining in the provinces probably constituted the majority of the troops of Muscovy. When war broke out, each prince brought his own regiments from his own *dvor*.[35] As Muscovy gathered the Russian lands, these princes and boyars took their places in the Moscow hierarchy (the *mestnichestvo* system) and gained their incomes from their old lands and from posts in the central and provincial administration. This period also saw the creation, in about 1475, of the Military Chancellery (or at least its immediate ancestor), which began to direct in a systematic way, and to keep records of, the ever growing army of Muscovy.[36]

All of these conditions were prerequisites for the creation of the middle service class, an event which can be linked with the annexation of Novgorod, when numerous lands were confiscated from Novgorod boyars, merchants, and church institutions and subsequently distributed to individuals loyal to Moscow. These lands, known as *pomest'e* lands (service lands), were granted to military men who had the right of usufruct as long as they served the Moscow prince, but lost that right when they ceased to render such service. The *pomest'e*, in some respects analogous to the Western medieval fief, was a new type of arrangement.[37]

Earlier, conditional land grants had occasionally been made to servitors and administrators in a prince's household or economy; these grants had to be surrendered upon leaving service.[38] The earliest known *pomest'e* grant in northeastern Russia was made prior to 1328 by Ivan Kalita, who granted Bogoroditskoe Selo in Rostov to Borisko Vorkov on the condition that he serve one of Ivan's sons. The type of service to be rendered (military, court, or economic) was not spelled out.[39] Grants for military service prior to the annexation of Novgorod had usually been allodial grants (*votchiny*, hereditary estates) for service already rendered; ownership of these lands was not conditional upon present or future service. Moreover, the owning of land was not highly esteemed. There were few markets which small producers could utilize to convert surplus agricultural goods into cash. Land was abundant, so owning a relatively free commodity was not profitable. More valued was service at court with its attendant perquisites and in the army with its possibilities for "foraging." For all these reasons land and its possession was never a basis of power from which outside elements could challenge the government.[40]

Significant progress in putting land to state use was made during the reign of Ivan III, who can justly be called the father of the *pomest'e* system.[41] This was a period of considerable economic upsurge, when land became more valuable. Thousands of grants of unknown size were made at the time of the annexation of Novgorod. In 1488, 8,000 men were deported from Novgorod to areas nearer Moscow (Vladimir, Nizhnii, Murom, Pereiaslavl', Iur'ev, Rostov, Kostroma provinces). They were replaced in Novgorod by over 2,000 servicemen from Moscow, including over fifty families of slaves manumitted by their boyars by state order and settled in the Novgorod region. A total of around 150 boyar slaves were converted into service landholders (*pomeshchiki*) in the Novgorod area at this time, and simultaneously 230 princes and Moscow boyars were transferred to the newly-annexed region. Most of the 2,000 *pomeshchiki* had been provincial *deti boiarskie*, fairly prosperous provincial landowners with small estates.[42]

The new system, which lasted for over two centuries, served a variety of purposes. It assured that the landholders of the region would be loyal to Moscow. (It was unfortunate, as will be shown in chapter 14, that Moscow settled upon this device to guarantee the reliability of newly-annexed areas.) It also permitted expansion of an army loyal to Moscow. Each serviceman was beholden solely to Moscow for his land, so Moscow was sure of his service. Also, it probably permitted the creation of an army of a nearly maximum size given the primitive economic and taxation systems.[43]

Additional *pomest'e* grants were made after the subsequent annexation of other principalities and, in fact, throughout the sixteenth century, largely out of court lands and lands confiscated from peasants ("black lands"), "treasonous" boyars, and others.[44] The *pomest'e* system never reached the northern part of Muscovy. This area was far from the usual combat zones, so that sending troops to the front annually from such a distance would have made little sense.[45]

Initially the *pomest'e* system was in some ways similar to a provincial administrative-judicial assignment from Moscow (a *kormlenie*, or "feeding"). How much each *pomeshchik* was to receive from each piece of land and each village or portion of a village was registered in the land cadastres. The formula in the cadastres said that such a village (or part

27

of one) was a *pomest'e* and *kormlenie* for such and such a *pomeshchik*. The serviceman could not meddle in the lives of the peasants ascribed to him, and perhaps did not even himself collect the income from the *pomest'e*. This was done by an official of the great prince. Government officials, obviously using set formulas, determined the obligations of the peasants, which were kept at about the traditional levels.[46] The system continued to be run this way into the 1550s.[47] However, neither at this time nor later did gaining one's income from a service landholding carry the prestige of a *kormlenie*, which was considered the most respectable form of compensation.[48] No doubt the authority and dominance implicit in a *kormlenie*, added to its greater profitability, made it more attractive than the simple *pomest'e*, which produced a fixed income.

The change to the *pomest'e* system was made for financial considerations and was a method of vastly enlarging the size of the fundamentally traditional military forces of rapidly expanding Muscovy; it was not a change that reflected any new or dramatic change in military technology or technique. (Russia adapted to the new military technology of the era quite independently of the *pomest'e* system by introducing new taxes in cash and in kind to finance the support of other military personnel; see chapters 9–11.) The precise effectiveness of the *pomest'e* system in enlarging the cavalry cannot be determined because no exact figures about the size of the army in the early period are available. Most of the numbers given are preposterously large. In the 1510s and 1520s the Austrian diplomat Sigismund Herberstein reported seeing 20,000 middle service class troops stationed on the southern frontier to stop attacks and looting by the Crimean Tatars. This estimate is credible.[49] By the middle of the sixteenth century there were at least 17,000 members of the middle service class (see Appendix).

The origin of these *dvoriane* and *deti boiarskie* is still unclear, but it seems as though they came from three sources: genuine sons of boyars[50] (*deti boiarskie*) who did not go with their fathers to Moscow when the latter accompanied their princes to the capital; free and probably slave retainers from the courts (*dvory*) of the extinct *udel* princes; and others (petty landowners, children of clergymen, peasants,[51] cossacks,[52] and manumitted slaves)[53] who were permitted to join the rather fluid manpower-short middle service class at the end of the fifteenth and during the course of the sixteenth century.[54] Prior to the sixteenth century, service was voluntary, but then lifelong service became mandatory.[55]

The Russian army of this time was relatively unsophisticated, but in theory, at least, before the field of combat was reached, it had five main regiments: advance, right, left, rear guard, and center or main. The center grouping, which often was called the "tsar's regiment" when he was on campaign, was divided into units of one hundred. There were separate units of *stol'niki,* Moscow *dvoriane,* and *zhil'tsy.* Tsar Ivan IV (1547–1584) favored the units of *zhil'tsy,* who were selected from the provincial *dvoriane* and *deti boiarskie* and given service lands near Moscow. The artillery was also in the center regiment. There were other units, the one of chief interest being the light cavalry reconnaissance detachment introduced by Ivan III which went out several days ahead of the main army; behind the reconnaissance regiment went an engineering battalion of peasants on foot which prepared the road for the main army. This was the fundamental organization of the Russian army from the reign of Ivan III through the reign of Aleksei Mikhailovich.[56]

This five-regiment army usually fought by using age-old echelon tactics, with masses of cavalrymen first shooting a volley of arrows and then swinging sabres in hand-to-hand combat to overwhelm the enemy. Because the Russian cavalry forces did not maneuver together, the tactic of forming a phalanx with lances was not used.[57] This form of "organization," this horde-like overwhelming of opposition, was doomed to extinction in the gunpowder era, when strategically placed artillery fire or concentrated small-arms fire was able to rout such an army even prior to contact with its front line. Some change in Russian tactics was noticeable in the second half of the sixteenth century, after Russia began to concentrate more attention on the western frontier: the deep formations, so susceptible to artillery fire, began to shorten as the line stretched out along the front.[58]

Another characteristic of the army was that it reported only on call; it was not a standing army. Usually one half was called up in the spring, to await an expected Tatar invasion on the frontier, and served to mid-summer. Then it was replaced by the other half, which served until late autumn. During either offensive or defensive emergencies, which were frequent throughout this period, both "halves" were summoned simultaneously, usually considerably in advance of an expected invasion and always well in advance of a planned offensive.[59] Rather detailed battle plans with alternatives were sometimes drafted, outlining how an invader should be met or an offensive campaign conducted.[60] Gathering this army took a long time and the rate of absenteeism and desertion was often very high. The success of any mobilization call was highly dependent on the condition of agriculture at the moment of the summons. If a serviceman's lands could not provide the wherewithal for his service, he would not report for duty. After a dramatic change in lord-peasant relations in the 1560s, when the serviceman was given the right to control his peasant tenants, the rate of absenteeism rose

29

because calling a member of the middle service class to arms disrupted his economy.[61]

The Tatars, Russia's main enemy until at least the 1560s and perhaps even to the end of the century, were skilled horsemen armed with bows and arrows, sabres, and spears. Each warrior carried a knife, a piece of steel to kindle a fire, an awl, and a length of rope for tying up the captives carried off from Russia by the tens of thousands. The slaves thus taken were sold in the great slave market of the Crimea—Kafa, the present Feodosiia.[62]

The *pomeshchik* cavalry was adapted to cope with such an enemy. The Austrian diplomat Baron Sigismund Herberstein, who was in Russia in 1517 and 1526, noted how unlike Western cavalrymen the Russians were. They rode their small shoeless horses, which they purchased from the Nogai Tatars by the thousands, high in the stirrups. They also used spurs only rarely, relying rather on a small lash around the little finger of the right hand to get the horse to move faster. Long reins were tied to the little finger of the left hand so that the horseman would be free to shoot his bow in any direction.[63] In the sixteenth century the Russian cavalry continued to use the Eastern saddle with short stirrups, a Tatar model. In the seventeenth century they switched to another Eastern model, this time Persian. Both saddles were so constructed that the rider could turn around to shoot. They had the drawback, noted by Herberstein, that the horseman could be knocked out of the saddle with a light blow. But in the south against the Tatars, where this cavalry was effective, maneuverability was crucial.[64]

The middle service class cavalryman went to war armed much as the military forces of Kiev had been.[65] In the sixteenth century he had bow and arrows (*saadak*), a sabre (*sablia*), and occasionally a spear (*rogatina*) or a lance (*kop'ia*). For example, all the 279 cavalrymen from Kolomna province (*uezd*) in 1577 had bows and arrows, none had firearms.[66] Even at the end of the sixteenth century the sabre was the dominant middle service class weapon, having replaced the heavier sword considerably earlier. The Russians came to appreciate the sabre, of Eastern origin, earlier than did the West.[67] A Persian damask sabre blade cost 3 rubles, and when mounted 5 to 6 rubles. Only the wealthy had such costly weapons, the rank and file *pomeshchiki* having to rely on sabres of Russian manufacture.[68] According to the late Soviet military historian A. V. Chernov, the extraordinary ineffectiveness of the armament of the Russian cavalry—reflecting the near absence of technological change—was one of the basic causes of the frequent defeats of the Muscovite army in field warfare.[69]

30

The so-called "Boyar Book'" (*Boiarskaia kniga*) of 1556 provides an excellent record of the armor of a middle service class cavalryman, armor which was valued at 4 rubles 50 kopeks. The cavalryman was protected by a conic, spiked iron helmet, chain-mail armor with chain-mail sleeves (*pantsyr'*), and knee plates. This Eastern-type armor provided good protection against arrows and cold weapons. It should be noted that Russians never wore the solid armor used by knights in the West, as this would have hindered their mobility. A less prosperous cavalryman might wear, instead of chain mail, a *tegiliai*, a short-sleeved, high-collared densely quilted coat of hemp or flax tow, sometimes with iron bands sewed inside, often with armor plate underneath. Another type of armor, which was very ancient but lasted to the end of the seventeenth century, was called a *kuiak*: a garment of cloth or leather with metal strips sewed on. Instead of an iron helmet, a poorer cavalryman might occasionally wear a cloth hat made of hemp, flax, and cotton, with a metal nosepiece which served as some protection against a transverse sword blow. Here we see almost no reflection of the presence of firearms, the only exception being the conic spiked helmet, which by the middle of the sixteenth century became somewhat flattened in the process of being converted into a spherical helmet of the modern type.[70] When a cavalryman did not appear for service in the full armor described, he was fined: one man in 1556 had to pay a ruble fine because he did not have a helmet.[71]

Several types of military service were required of the middle service class. These included appearance at annual reviews where military preparedness was verified and shortcomings in horses and hardware corrected; appearance in shifts on the frontier, on the routes followed by the nomads (*shliakhi*), in anticipation of Tatar raids;[72] and actual service when invasion was anticipated from or aggression contemplated against any quarter.[73] The average serviceman could expect his life to be so patterned from the age of fifteen to his death, or until illness, wounds, or old age had incapacitated him to the extent that he could no longer go out on horseback and was relegated to relatively easy defensive service inside a fortress, known as "siege service."[74] There was also a separate service along the southern frontier to watch for invasions and to guard the fortified lines. Muscovites considered service along the Oka frontier to be unworthy of them. The small service landholders of Riazan', Tula, Orel, and Seversk uezdy were poorly born and poverty-stricken.[75] Their interests often diverged from those of their brethren living off peasant labor in the older parts of the state.

There is considerable dispute in the literature over how much training, if any, the *pomest'e* cavalry received in the first century of its existence. Available evidence indicates that the Russians were good horsemen and fairly good shots with the bow and arrow, with which they practiced. What other forms of practice or drill they had is unknown. Probably there was none. The review was an important feature of the military life of the middle service class cavalry, for there each cavalryman was checked regularly to determine whether he was adequately equipped for combat. The fact that the serviceman lost part (or, in 1556, all) of his *pomest'e* for neglecting to appear is an indication of the importance attached to the review.[76] The Russian army was becoming something more than a horde relying on superior numbers to win its military conflicts. This regimentation was a prerequisite for the introduction of more technologically advanced weapons and tactics. However, there was no division of labor in the *pomest'e* cavalry. There was neither any pretension to expertise, any permanence of rank, position, or appointment, nor even the slightest degree of specialization.[77]

One of the greatest problems facing the Russian army while it relied on the *pomest'e* cavalry was discipline. In the first place, the commanders themselves often engaged in disputes over officer assignments (*mestnichestvo*) and would refuse to fight when placed under someone "lower" than themselves, no matter what the ability, age, or experience of the person was. Each of the main army regiments had within it definite prestige positions. Considerations of place, rather than military preoccupations, were uppermost in the minds of the officers. This led to innumerable disputes and probably hampered considerably the effectiveness of the middle service class cavalry. Ivan attempted to remedy this weakness in his 1549 campaign against Kazan', and in 1550 he ordered that all campaigns "be fought without resort to consideration of places." Subsequent rulers repeated the attempt to rid Russia of this vicious system, but disputes lasted in the native officer corps until, and even beyond, the abolition of *mestnichestvo* in 1682.[78]

There was also the problem of discipline among the rank-and-file cavalrymen; getting them to report for service was a continuous headache, and convincing them not to desert from service (either out of cowardice or out of a desire to have a look at the home estate) was an even bigger problem.[79] Finally, there was the problem of battle discipline, the task of coordinating largely untrained forces to fight as a body rather than acting simply as a mass. The level of martial discipline was never very high in the Russian cavalry, a phenomenon frequently noted by foreign observers. The problem was aggravated by the fact that the major goal of warfare was booty. The state did not provide for the cavalrymen, so they were particularly sensitive to every possibility for supplementing their income by looting—at which opportunity martial discipline disappeared.[80] So long as the middle service class was the major fighting force of the Russian army, there was really nothing which could be done to raise the level of discipline.

Here it is necessary to emphasize that the middle service class cavalry was the creation of the Muscovite state power and remained its creature until the seventeenth century. It was not a landed gentry which voluntarily came to the aid of the government when asked, but rather a group of landholders existing at the sufferance of the state.[81] Even the value of the serviceman's honor, something akin to the Old English wergild, depended entirely on the individual's government-determined position and pay in service.[82] This meant that the *pomest'e* cavalry was not a class or estate with recognized common interests at the time of its formation by Ivan III; those interests which its members did come to have in common developed only after decades of government-enforced companionship in the army. Article 45 of chapter 16 of the *Ulozhenie* of 1649, dating from 1633–36, summarized the intentions of the *pomest'e* system by declaring that, if *dvoriane* and *deti boiarskie* did not want to be in service and gave away their service lands or hereditary lands, or sold or mortgaged them, then the lands were to be confiscated from the person in whose favor the serviceman had alienated them and returned to the person who was required to render the service. The serviceman himself was to be beaten with a knout and returned to service. It would be fallacious to maintain that the middle service class was in any sense a "ruling class."

On the other hand, while the middle service class was the creature of the state power, the latter, after the consolidation of the Muscovite state and while the Tatar threat lasted, could not get along without this class.[83] The middle service class had no independent existence of its own, but the government had to rely on it for its military power (and at times its existence, although the legitimacy of the government was never threatened); it was this symbiotic relationship that enabled the government to dominate the middle service class while the latter was accumulating enormous privileges. The relationship proved disastrous for the free peasantry, as will be shown in Part 2 below.

Very little is known about the middle service class during its formative years before the reign of Ivan IV. Presumably the entrance upon the scene of the new service class must have evoked cries of dismay and acts of resistance, but there is no record of such things. What thoughts ran through the heads of the people whose lands were confiscated to make the early *pomest'e* grants can only be surmised. The same holds true for the peasants who labored on the lands as well as for the troops who were either displaced by or converted into *pomeshchiki.*

By the reign of Ivan IV the middle service class had become the backbone of the Russian army. This was a trying period for the mounted cavalry, as well as one of many rewards. Major campaigns were launched and carried out against the Tatars from the time Ivan acceded to the throne in 1547 until the capture of Astrakhan' in 1556. Russia then carried on a twenty-five-year war, first successful, then disastrous, against its western neighbors.[84] All of this, plus the practical disappearance of the peasant agricultural labor force from the central and Novgorod areas of the Muscovite state,[85] was hard on the middle service class.

The Marxist historian N. A. Rozhkov dated the beginning of what he termed "the gentry revolution" to the reign of Ivan IV.[86] Not only did the middle service class (which evolved into the gentry) begin to formulate its interests and delineate its position vis-à-vis other segments of society at that time, but the government of Ivan IV, led by Adashev, Kurbskii, Metropolitan Makarii, and others, began to formalize the cavalry militia's position, rights, and obligations much more explicitly than had been done previously.[87]

Several issues of interest to the middle service class arose during Ivan's reign. A major matter of concern was the relationship of this class to the monarch and the upper service class. Problems concerning the functions, obligations, and remuneration of the servicemen were raised and clarified. Landholding, along with the peasant question, also became a major issue.

During Ivan's minority some of the magnates running the government had decided that they could enhance their own positions by abusing members of the middle service class. However, in February, 1549, at what has come to be known as the "Assembly of Reconciliation" (a meeting of the leaders of the church and the Boyar Council), Ivan IV defended the *deti boiarskie* and their peasants from offenses they were suffering at the hands of the boyars and their slaves in legal cases involving land, slaves, and other matters.[88] I assume this first Assembly of the Land in Russian history was convoked in an attempt to convey to the aggrieved servicemen the government's concern for their well-being on the eve of the Kazan' campaign. Ivan declared that provincial judges (*namestniki*, often boyars) were henceforth not to try *deti boiarskie* in any cases except murder, robbery, and theft. Presumably in these matters self-interest was hard to manipulate. All other cases involving members of the middle service class were to be tried in Moscow before the Tsar.[89] This was the first major victory of the middle service class at the expense of other political and social forces of the Muscovite state.[90]

The 1549 Assembly of the Land prepared the way for the 1555–56 repeal of the "feeding" (*kormlenie*) system of administering the provinces from Moscow that had been the major source of income for the boyars and other magnates.[91] The rapacious "lieutenants" (*namestniki*)[92] were replaced by a Moscow-directed provincial self-administration (the *guba* and *zemskaia* systems) dominated by the middle service class.[93] The areas of jurisdiction of the *namestniki* had been gradually whittled away since the end of the fifteenth or the beginning of the sixteenth century. First they yielded their authority over the construction of fortifications to special officials, usually members of the middle service class, the *gorodovye prikazchiki*, whose jurisdiction was subsequently enlarged. Initially the *gorodovye prikazchiki* were appointed by the central power, but in the 1550s they were elected by their peers.[94] Beginning in the 1530s, minor offenses were gradually turned over to local authorities chosen by and from the peasants and townsmen (the *zemskaia reforma*), and major offenses were dealt with by the *guba* authorities. Land disputes were also adjudicated locally. No doubt the reform appealed to advocates of efficiency, who sought to instil more honesty, order, and rationality into the administration of the Muscovite state.[95] To attribute all the change simply to power politics and highly rational machinations would be a gross oversimplification. Nevertheless, what may have had administrative or fiscal origins had political consequences. While the reform lasted, through the second half of the sixteenth century, the middle service class reigned supreme in the provinces where servicemen lived, and the power of the old provincial nobility was weakened.

This series of events often has been viewed as a setback for the magnates, and rightly so. However, it was not part of a grand design to undermine the power of the boyars in order to strengthen the monarchy. The measures of 1549 and 1555–56, continuing a process begun earlier, were unquestionably attempts primarily to rectify the situation caused by the criminal behavior of certain magnates by releasing from their grasp those they had abused and transferring some of the magnates' functions to those who had been abused during the period of Ivan's minority.[96] The magnates were not accused of having threatened the newly consolidated state or the institution of the autocratic monarchy, and the ensuing administrative actions of Ivan's early years on the throne were directed at criminal acts, not political ones.[97] The decrees of 1549 and 1555–56 removed significant sources of income, dominance, and social prestige from the magnates and, one would assume, increased their interest in landownership. Thus the stage was being set for the bitter struggle for labor which led to the Forbidden Years.[98] Finally, as a side effect, these efforts to control the capricious criminality of the magnates unintentionally raised the social position and prestige of the middle service class.

Ivan IV made an attempt to grant lands according to systematic norms in 1550 when, building on earlier practice, he created the "selected thousand."[99] Before that time the Moscow government had at its immediate disposal no more than five or six hundred men.[100] The additional thousand were to be ready for instant service. Each of the chosen boyars and *okolnichie* was to be granted 200 *chetverti* of land in Moscow province; *deti boiarskie* of the first rank also were to receive 200 *chetverti,* those of the second rank 150 *chetverti;* and those of the third rank 100 *chetverti* within 67 to 70 kilometers of Moscow.[101] Those who had new lands within 50 to 60 kilometers of Moscow were not to be granted new *pomestia.* They were to be granted the same number of haystacks (*kopny*) as *chetverti* of arable land, in addition to the hay they could collect from their peasants. When one of the thousand died, he was to be replaced by his son or, if the son was not suited for service, by someone else. According to the decree, 1071 men were to be granted 118,200 *chetverti* of land. Most of the "selected thousand" were members of the middle service class whose proximity to the capital gave them added political influence.[102]

Also in the 1550s, in connection with measures formalizing service requirements, a regular compensation scale was set up for the armed forces of Muscovy. At this time there were twenty-five grades, a number reduced to around six at the end of the century. Each grade received a certain amount of land and cash pay.[103] (See table 1.)

TABLE 1

COMPENSATION SCALE, END OF SIXTEENTH CENTURY[104]

GRADE	LAND	CASH
1	350 *chetverti* of land in one field	12 rubles
2	300 "	10 "
3	250 "	8 "
4	200 "	7 "
5	150 "	6 "
6	100 "	5 "

A serviceman's rank depended on four criteria: the state of his health, his material position (both important for rendering service), his social origin (it was assumed those with high-ranking fathers would already possess military knowledge), and past service. The amount of land the serviceman was entitled to depended on his rank; the amount of service he had to render, at least after 1556, depended on how much land he actually had. His initial status, such as *syn boiarskii*, would entitle him to a place in the hierarchy, a specific grade (*stat'ia*), with its cash and land compensation equivalents. After serving for a while, or after performing a notable deed, the soldier would ask for a raise.[105] If the parsimonious central government felt he deserved it, the raise would be granted. This high degree of centralization and lack of discretionary authority for the field commander was typical of the Muscovite army.

Neither enough land nor enough cash was available to give each man his due. In fact, only from 25 to 60 percent of the demand for inhabited land created by the nominal grants could be satisfied.[106] (To have a high compensation scale [*oklad*] was advantageous, as will be shown later, even though to attain it was in reality close to impossible.) During the Oprichnina the size of the average *pomest'e* holding was drastically reduced.[107]

The land fund was managed by the Service Land Chancellery (*Pomestnyi Prikaz*), and the servicemen devoted much effort to seeking free land and asking the government to assign it to them. There was no waiting line for land, so it was always "first come, first served." The servicemen spent much of their time on law suits in an attempt to gain more land. Moreover, the government encouraged informers to denounce those holding service land illegally.[108] These features of the compensation system tended to weaken the cohesion of the middle service class by creating a jungle-like atmosphere in which each serviceman was always at war with every other one in a struggle for survival. This atmosphere in turn permitted the government to exercise more control over, and to be more independent of, the members of the middle service class than one might expect, given their military value to the state power.

Cash was paid, when the treasury had any, prior to a campaign so the serviceman could buy needed items in the market. Frequently servicemen got no pay in cash for years on end. Except for items which had to be purchased for cash (armor, weapons, perhaps a horse), the *pomeschchik* was expected to get all his war materiel (food, transport, sometimes even his weapons) from his assigned estate. In peacetime he depended totally on the support his peasants could render him.[109] This support was not always regular, and collecting it was difficult. Many people with connections at court refused service lands and demanded all their compensation in cash. However, the successive governments never had the means to pay everyone solely in currency.[110]

An important innovation both for holders of *pomest'e* land and owners of *votchina* estates was the 1556 Decree on Service (*Ulozhenie o sluzhbe*) which regularized service requirements.[111] It is doubtful whether prior to this statute the state knew how much service it could expect or landholders knew how much they were required to render. Prior to 1556 all old *votchinniki* enjoyed at least the theoretical right of departure. Thus in 1539 Prince Belskii had gone to serve Lithuania without suffering confiscation of his estates, even for treason. While his case may have been an exception, there almost certainly was no formal service requirement for such people.

After 1556, service requirements depended not on who one was, but how much land one had. For every 100 populated *chetverti* of land (located in one field in the prevailing three-field agricultural system, which amounted to a total of 300 *chetverti* in all three fields, or about 400 acres), the lord was to provide one man equipped for service on a horse. If the campaign was to be a long one, two horses had to be provided.[112] The horsemen had to be in full armor, and the lord was fined if he or any of his retainers did not appear for service fully equipped.[113] If the lord provided extra troops (usually slaves), over and above his norm, he was usually paid two and one-half times the compensation for the one required man.[114] If for some reason a lord could not supply the required men, he had to send cash instead.[115] If he desired, he could send a substitute for himself. For not appearing for service or for deserting, the serviceman lost part or all of his land grant. In the last quarter of the sixteenth century this provision was extended to hereditary lands as well.[116] No doubt the 1556 decree attracted both those who desired to rationalize governmental and military operations and the members of the middle service class, who must have rejoiced that the magnates were being forced to bear a proportionally equal load.[117]

In the 1550s, still fairly prosperous times, landholders often appeared for service with more than the required complement of men and fully armed retainers. For example, a man required to come to service with four men might come with six, someone supposed to come with seven might bring twenty, and so on. One man who had 400 *chetverti* of land in one field was supposed to provide for service three additional men in armor besides himself, but he brought with him four men in armor and three in *tegiliai* and received seventeen rubles for the extra men.[118] The Soviet historian A. A. Zimin has claimed that as high as three-quarters of the entire cavalry in the 1550s was made up of slaves.[119] No doubt the lord had to calculate how he could most profitably put his slaves to work for him; for many lords the most profitable course was to bring the slaves into the army. It should also be noted that at this time the rate of absenteeism among members of the middle service class themselves was very low. Out of 174 cavalrymen in one 1556 list, only two were unaccountably and inexcusably absent.[120]

Required reporting for service diminished as Russia became impoverished in the 1560s and especially in the 1570s. In 1577, of 279 members of the middle service class from Kolomna only 163 (59%) had full armor. This is one of the indicators that the material condition of the middle service class was worsening, and helps to explain why its members may have asked the government to do something to halt the flight of the peasants from their landholdings.[121]

When members of the middle service class became impoverished, for whatever reason, there were several courses open to them. They could complain and beg for relief, which probably did little good. They could show up for service unequipped, which they did in ever-mounting numbers. This practice was likely to be suicidal, and obviously benefited the armed forces little. Another possibility was to opt out of the middle service class completely by selling oneself into slavery. As a slave, the impoverished former *syn boiarskii* might remain in the armed forces, but only as a better-equipped retainer of a more prosperous serviceman, often of the upper service class. The price for such a slave was perhaps five times higher than for an ordinary one, which the member of the middle service class might also become.[122]

Leaving the service class by selling oneself into slavery became a matter of considerable concern both to its members and to the government. There were at least two reasons why the servicemen were disturbed by such an act. For one, in theory it cost them money because the government forced them to guarantee financially each other's performance (the *krugovaia poruka*).[123] However, I know of no instance where this sanction was applied. More important must have been the servicemen's sense of corporate interest. In opposing the practice of members leaving the ranks to become slaves, the *deti boiarskie* must have been motivated by a collective feeling of insecurity—the feeling of "there but for the grace of God go I."

The government had some interest in this matter too, although its attitude varied from time to time as the issue came up repeatedly from 1550 to 1650. One may suspect that when the issue was raised initially in 1550 and 1558[124] it was part of the attempt by Adashev to strengthen the state interest at the expense of the magnates, with whom poor *deti boiarskie* lived under the name of *znakomtsy*,[125] by cutting off the flow of recruits into the magnates' private armies. For the same reason servicemen who had become debtors in 1558 were granted five years (from Christmas 1557 to Christmas 1562) in which to settle with their creditors without the payment of past or future interest, rather than fall into slavery. During that period they could contract no new debts; later they could do so at 20 percent interest. They had to pay the debt off in equal installments, except while in service, after which it was due upon return.[126] In 1560 servicemen were again exempted from paying interest when they repaid their debts.[127] The *Sudebnik* of 1589 decreed that *deti boiarskie,* unless discharged from service, could not borrow money at interest because they could not repay their debts by personal servitude should they default on the loans.[128]

In the second half of the sixteenth century the issue of members of the middle service class selling themselves into slavery was raised but not resolved. At this time the problem seems to have been largely of concern to the state, and much less so, if at all, to the collective consciousness of the servicemen themselves. The issue became a matter of concern to the collective middle service class only after the Time of Troubles.

The interests of the government and the middle service class coincided on the issue of land ownership. Both desired to regulate ownership so as to minimize the amount of land held privately while maximizing the quantity of populated land in the *pomest'e* network. State action in this sphere, initiated already by Vasilii III, can be witnessed in laws of 1551, 1562, and 1572, which limited the rights of hereditary landowners (*votchinniki*) to alienate ancestral estates. Only the sons of serving princes had the unconditional right to inherit estates. Selling, exchanging, and giving estates as a dowry or to a monastery were forbidden.[129] Laws of 1550 and 1557 regulated the right of heirs to redeem clan estates which had been alienated in any way.[130] These laws were part of an attempt to curb the growth of land ownership by monasteries as well as to redress the outrages committed by the magnates during Ivan IV's minority. At that time the population had been fairly stable, so the magnates enriched themselves by plundering land with peasants on it. This had led to numerous conflicts between the magnates and the *pomeshchiki.*[131] The goal of the laws was to maximize the amount of land from which military service was owed and perhaps also to promote the return of lands to the state fund, which then could be apportioned out again to the middle service class.[132]

The Oprichnina expropriated many boyar estates in favor of members of the middle service class, and as a result service landholding became the predominant form of tenure; it appeared as though hereditary land ownership might expire by the 1580s.[133] Ivan's actions were not, as has been argued by some apologists for the Oprichnina, a deliberate attempt to elevate the middle service class by destroying the magnates.[134] As S. B. Veselovskii and others have conclusively shown, not all the boyars were Ivan's enemies and not all the members of the middle service class were his supporters.[135] Ivan's paranoid choice of "enemies" resulted in the execution of numerous boyars and the temporary turning over of their lands to the largely middle service class *oprichniki*. Even at the height of the Oprichnina, however, some boyar estates were not touched,[136] and many members of the middle service class suffered everything from expropriation to execution along with the magnates.[137]

Thus it would seem that the Soviet historians I. I. Polosin and I. I. Smirnov were in error in saying that the reforms and other governmental activities of the mid-sixteenth century were consciously motivated to satisfy the middle service class. Others, such as S. V. Bakhrushin, A. A. Zimin, and S. O. Shmidt have been closer to the mark with the conclusion that most developments were in favor of the state, which required a general leveling of privileges of the upper and middle service classes. The privileges of the magnates were not taken away (even though some of their activities were restricted), and these privileges were frequently extended to the middle service class.[138] Nowhere was this trend of elevating the status of the middle service class more evident than in the new institution of the Assembly of the Land, which was created to sanction intentions of the government. The middle service class delegates to the Zemskii Sobor were asked to consider and consent to matters which previously had been the prerogatives of the upper upper-service class.[139]

The result of these institutional changes—the creation of the Assembly of the Land along with the *guba* administrative network—was the weakening of the Boyar Council, the focus of power of the magnates in the Muscovite state. R. G. Skrynnikov has demonstrated that this also was one of the consequences, although an unintentional one, of the Oprichnina.[140] The net impact was to increase the relative weight of the centralized state power and the middle service class at the expense of the magnates.[141] It is crucial to stress once again that there was no campaign directed against the upper service class itself, most of whose members were quite content to pursue their own enrichment within the framework of the centralized state, which they would not have wanted to see fragmented.[142]

In this regard, the extant evidence shows that the concerns of the middle service class were not always uppermost in the mind of the government. This can be witnessed in a post-Oprichnina decree of 1572–73 permitting the sale of vacant service lands in Moscow province to any civilian buyers, including boyars, but not to monasteries.[143] Such a measure hardly favored the middle service class, but was in the interest of the government, which may have desired to raise money to carry on the Livonian War; or, as has been suggested, the measure may have been designed to line the pockets of government officials and to reward favorites by "selling" them lands close to Moscow.[144]

We have already noticed several times the issue of church land-ownership. A major concession by Ivan's government to the middle service class was the limitation placed on the acquisition of land by church establishments. Because the amount of land was limited, the question of monastery land-ownership was closely linked to the *pomest'e* system which supported the middle service class. Land owned by the church was automatically denied to the civilian army. Much confiscated Novgorod church land had been included in the initial *pomest'e* system. However, the church land fund emerged undiminished from the controversy over the role of the church in the world between the Possessors (Josephites) and Non-possessors (Trans-Volga Elders) at the beginning of the sixteenth century—in spite of the apparent desire by Ivan III to support the Non-possessors in order to gain additional lands to distribute as *pomest'ia* to his new middle service class.[145] At the church council of 1503 Ivan III had gone so far as to propose a minor secularization of church lands. His son, Vasilii III, also tried to, and at times did, check the growth of monastery land-ownership.[146] Under Ivan's grandson, when over four hundred monasteries possessed estates embracing over one-third of the populated seignorial land of Muscovy, the church did not fare so well.[147] Decrees of 1551,[148] 1572,[149] 1580,[150] and 1584[151] forbade completely additional land acquisition by monasteries. This was done in favor of the middle service class, which noted that it was finding service difficult because of the ever-increasing size of the church land fund and the attraction which living on these lands held for the peasantry.[152] Living on monastery lands was the rational choice for peasants because of the frequently more advanced economic level of operation on such properties, more enlightened "personnel policies," and, probably, lower rents. Many monasteries were not dependent solely on exploiting peasants for income, but received large cash donations. Others derived over half of their incomes from trade, and may have been willing to collect slightly less from their peasant tenants in order to gain marketable commodities.[153] Finally, upon occasion, the government freed from taxation peasants living on monastery land so that the monks could collect part of the tax money for their own purposes.[154]

In light of the rational restraint in the government's land policy, I find little evidence for the contention that "Ivan strove to subject the church to himself with the aid of the most ferocious, despotic measures" or for the comparison of Ivan with the French Louis XI or Henry VIII in England.[155] Ivan undoubtedly was an "abominable despot," but his general policy toward the church and its lands was not despotic. In fact the attack by the government of Ivan IV on church privileges was rather moderate, with the result that no lands were secularized and the church's landed expansion was simply curtailed to areas such as the north, where the army could not use lands. It was for this reason, for example, that monasteries did not, in general, follow Russia's southward expansion, where the land was considered desirable by the service class.[156]

In 1551 Ivan tried to confiscate some property belonging to the metropolitan to hand out as service lands. However, the church primate protested, and no action was taken.[157] At times during the chaotic reign of Ivan IV, particularly in the Oprichnina, members of the middle service class simply seized monastery lands. Later, however, such properties were restored.[158] When church lands were taken in the Oprichnina, the institutions affected usually were given other lands elsewhere, and sometimes lucrative privileges were thrown into the deal as well.[159] Some monasteries cooperated actively with Ivan, and during the Oprichnina the monastery land-fund probably grew in size.[160] Moreover, no steps were taken by the government which would have limited royal grants of peasant "black" lands to monasteries.[161]

A related measure was the temporary ("until the land recovers") abolition of church tax-exemption privileges (*tarkhany*) in 1584, adopted "because the servicemen suffer great losses from them [the tax exemptions enjoyed by monasteries and high church officials]."[162] During Ivan's reign few new privileges in this sphere were granted, although many of the old ones had been confirmed during a review of 1551.[163] A certain amount of backsliding had occurred in 1563 and later, when the paranoid Ivan felt he could gain church support against his "enemies" by giving more liberal tax privileges to monasteries.[164] This modest reversal of 1584 probably made little difference to contemporaries. As a rule, the interests of all magnates, ecclesiastical as well as lay, were preserved by the fact that the *tarkhany* were not repealed.[165] The 1584 measure soon lapsed.

The Russian church was not exempt from taxation; however, a tax exemption sometimes could be purchased. As a rule, monastery peasants paid higher taxes than did seigneurial peasants. The monasteries were called upon to share their resources with the state or to help carry out state functions in both war and peace. For example, in 1574–75 the monasteries were forced to help pay for the Livonian War.[166] They also contributed troops which the government knew were paid for largely out of the proceeds of tax-exempt enterprises.[167] Olearius in the 1630s observed a monastery which had an abbot, 60 monks, and 400 peasants, and maintained 100 royal servicemen as well.[168] Nikon told Patriarch Macarius of Antioch that he had furnished 10,000 soldiers for the war with Poland in the 1650s.[169]

In spite of the fact that there was no real threat to the church, there can be hardly any doubt that monasteries, probably aware of the dissolution of their English counterparts in 1536 and 1539, were made uneasy by the attack upon their privileges during the second half of Ivan's reign. This is evident, for example, in a forgery of about 1586 or 1587 by the famous Troitse Sergiev monastery. The monastery itself had been losing land suits for two decades, and, in addition, it was one of the major targets of the legislation directed against spiritual corporations. It tried to improve its position by drawing up a document "to prove" that the privileges which seemed threatened had been given to its founder, Sergei of Radonezh, by his prince, Dmitrii Donskoi.[170] The Muscovites had, as a rule, great respect for antiquity, and any relations which could be shown to be of long duration were less likely to be attacked than those of recent origin. Another monastery, the Spaso Efim'ev, lost some property to purported peasant usurpers. During the reign of Ivan the monastery, in several attempts, was unable to get a trial to determine ownership of the settlement. Only in 1589 was a trial granted. The land was given back to the monastery.[171]

In retrospect the fears of the Troitse Sergiev seem exaggerated. The Spaso Efim'ev case was only a passing incident. As a matter of state policy, no legally acquired monastery lands were touched in the sixteenth century, for the secularizing spirit was not yet of age in Russia. Ivan IV was not Henry VIII. The Russians had too much awe of the church to carry out an attack against it. The government only dared to aid the army by attempting to restrict further ecclesiastical acquisitions of land and privileges, not by whittling away its established position.

In closing, one atypical development of 1592–93 is of interest. At that time, precisely when Boris Godunov, regent for the feeble Tsar Fedor Ivanovich, issued a decree binding all peasants to the land, some lands were confiscated from the Troitse Sergiev monastery. These properties had been acquired in violation of the decrees discussed earlier.[172] This action must be viewed as a demagogic move by Boris to win the support of the servicemen in his drive for the throne. The measure was analogous to modern governmental measures against great corporations. The corporate wrist is slapped, the headlines blaze, the public is impressed, and things continue as before. Obviously Godunov's confiscation hardly hurt the Troitse Sergiev at all, and did the servicemen little good either.

While the church was not really losing any privileges, members of the middle service class were gaining some. One of the most valued privileges in Muscovy was the right to trade duty-free, or to pay less than the customary fees connected with mercantile activity. Such privileges were granted to some *pomeshchiki* during the Oprichnina.[173] The privilege did not, however, become a general norm at this time.

One of the most crucial privileges Ivan gave the members of the middle service class was the right to control directly their service lands. During the Oprichnina, Ivan, in some of the documents issued to landholders ordering peasants to pay their rent and so on (*poslushnye*), permitted the *pomeshchiki* themselves to set the level of the rent (*obrok*). This privilege violated the customary relations between peasant and serviceman which had been part of the *pomest'e* system since its inception.[174] Ivan also gave the members of the middle service class the right to collect the rent in person from the peasantry, further undermining the *pomest'e* as a *kormlenie*-type source of income. We shall see in chapter 6 how this led to increased exploitation of the peasants and increased peasant flights.[175] Giving the service landholder control over his lands and the right to collect rents elevated his status closer to that of the hereditary landowner and constituted a crucial step in the rise of the middle service class.

This was one of the greatest mistakes Ivan made in his long reign. On the one hand, it gave the serviceman the opportunity to plunder, and thereby destroy, his service lands—lands he did not care about because they were not his and could not be passed legally to his heirs.[176] The government tried to punish servicemen who devastated their villages, but to little avail. Only the eventual conversion of the service lands into heritable property curtailed the predatory conduct of the middle service class.[177] Giving the *pomeshchik* control over his lands meant that the demands imposed by state service contradicted the interests of his own economy. Each *pomeshchik* acquired a personal interest in the peasants on *his own* land, setting the stage for putative appeals to cancel the peasants' right to move on St. George's Day. In time the landed status of the middle service class became more important than its service status.[178] This was one reason why the state in the course of the next century looked to an element not dependent on land for its military service. In the meantime the landholding cavalrymen used all means to escape service. In turn the state resorted to brutal and degrading means (public beatings and widespread use of informers) to enforce service. The servicemen, who could not afford stewards to mange their estates, devised ever more ingenious ways of avoiding service and being absent without leave became customary. Because of its attachment to the land,

45

the middle service class could never be any kind of a standing army. The state could not keep the *pomeshchiki* in service. "On return from service it was necessary to discharge them to look after their economies. Had it been otherwise, giving them service lands would have lost all sense."[179]

A number of other developments stemmed from the personal control over the lands assigned to them that Ivan gave to members of the middle service class. When an agent collected the rents and turned them over to the serviceman, the fact that the lands assigned to the serviceman were not contiguous, but were scattered in five or six widely separated provinces, made little difference. When the serviceman became a lord, he liked to have the lands near at hand for easy supervision. This was made possible by a decree of 1576 that servicemen were to get lands only in the districts of the towns from which they served. While this was of unquestionable benefit to the servicemen, it also benefited the government: with the landholder in one place, the authorities knew where to find him when a military call-up was issued. The decree may have been promulgated with a 1577 campaign in mind. It is not known when, if ever, this provision was formally abolished. The principle was alluded to in a verdict on a private case in 1634, but by that time the principle had been long abandoned in practice.[180] The desire to have contiguous parcels of land also led to a body of law and practice on how land could be exchanged (*pomest'e* land could not be sold) to effect this desideratum.[181]

There can be little doubt that many of the reforms and changes of the second half of the reign of Ivan IV were made "in response to the needs of the middle service class."[182] This is, nevertheless, a rather ambiguous statement, for it does not tell us who perceived these needs and how and why they were transmitted to governmental policy-makers. The surviving evidence does not permit the formulation of precise answers. One can speculate, however, that the level of group consciousness of the middle service class was not yet high by the end of the reign of Ivan IV, although the peasant question was the type of issue around which a middle service class collective consciousness might have begun to coalesce. The middle service class was still very much the creature of the government and had a relatively fluid membership. The annual military call-ups and reviews provided suitable settings for the formulation of group needs and interests, which could have been conveyed to the government. The *guba* system, whose officials had to come to Moscow every year, provided another potential vehicle to relay class desires to the government. There is no evidence that either the military or the civil institution was used to present collective petitions to the government, as occurred in the seventeenth century. This does not prove that such

Weberian "communal actions" did not exist, but it seems unlikely that they did. Moreover, the Assembly of the Land was not yet the type of institution which it was to become after the Time of Troubles, one in which group interests could be formulated and pressed.[183]

The system probably worked in another way. Rather than outright lobbying by the middle service class, individual members certainly must have used petitions to and personal interviews with leading officials (even the tsar) to inform the government of their needs.[184] These communications contributed to the formulation of the views of policy-makers, who also relied on other channels for information on the state of the country. The result was that the middle service class received an increasingly exalted status in the Muscovite state. This was not because either the servicemen or the government intentionally desired or willed in advance that such a situation should result, but rather this was the result of the development of the Muscovite state by the end of the reign of Ivan IV. The outcome certainly was by no means inevitable, and nearly an infinite number of counterfactual arguments could be constructed to show what might have happened had something been different. Nevertheless, the following were essential elements in the in-deliberate, unconscious rise of the middle service class during its first century of existence: the desire of the rulers to have a cavalry army as large as possible and directly responsive to their control; a population insufficient to support an army as large as the authorities deemed essential; government solicitation for the welfare of the army; the presence of groups—the church and the old magnates—with privileges which could be envied and emulated; hypertrophy of state power and economic hypotrophy; Ivan's mad Oprichnina; costly wars; and a general absence of human rights respected by all. These natural conditions and historical phenomena combined to create within the course of a century an ascendant body of 25,000 military servitors with a privileged legal and social position in Muscovy. In spite of these gains, the position of the middle service class was by no means secure. Membership was open to anyone, the status of members was not high, and the servicemen had to contest with other groups for the land and labor that provided their livelihood. Finally, while the eventful reign of Ivan IV effected change, his military reforms probably had no profound, immediate impact on the daily life of the average member of the middle service class.

3.

The Conscious Rise of the
Middle Service Class

A definite qualitative change occurred in the nature and self-image of the middle service class between the reigns of Ivan IV and Mikhail Romanov. This was a change that permitted the class to go on to acquire and consolidate further privileges not only in lord-peasant relationships, but also in matters of land tenure, compensation, service obligations, rights of survivors, tax status, relations with the courts, and in other areas of life. On the peasant question, Boris Godunov tried to follow a policy aimed primarily at consolidating and maintaining his own power position. Following his mentor, Ivan IV, he tended to favor the middle service class, occasionally trimming his course to meet the demands of the magnates. Besides repealing completely in 1592 or 1593 the right of all peasants to move on St. George's Day, he freed from taxation, about 1591, the land personally cultivated by *pomeshchiki*. This, coupled with the binding of the peasants to the land, stimulated a considerable increase in the amount of peasant corvée on middle service class lands.[1]

In another move to gain the support of the middle service class, Boris halved the service requirement in 1604 by revising the law to read that one mounted cavalryman had to be supplied from each 300, rather than 150, *desiatiny* of arable land. The law was also less demanding in other ways than its 1556 predecessor. The landholder could send a slave substitute for himself if he had no son and was himself too old to serve or was ill or was working in the Moscow or provincial administration. He was given two years off from service if he had been wounded or had just returned from captivity. A two-year wait was prescribed before demanding service from the lands belonging to widows and minors whose husbands and fathers had been killed in war or captured.[2]

During the brief reign of Boris Godunov the first signs of a trend toward a closed service class, something akin to a warrior caste, became apparent. A law of 1601 decreed that children of slaves, peasants, and clergymen could not become members of the middle service class.[3] (A law of 1606 added children of townsmen to the list.) [4] Such measures helped to create a rigidly stratified society in Muscovy. The laws were a "logical," but not necessary, sequel to the binding of the peasants to the land. With the peasantry officially and legally subordinate, only time and favorable circumstances were required to elevate further the privileged' middle service class. After the measures concerning the peasantry, these were Boris's most demagogic enactments. They specifically set the middle service class apart as a distinct entity and paved the road for further developments after the Time of Troubles.[5]

The first False Dmitrii, one of the few really enlightened rulers Russia has ever had, also tried to win the middle service class to his side. He did this in the more traditional ways, by raising the compensation scales for both cash and land. The Pretender did not have time to increase the amount of land actually held by the servicemen, but his actions during his brief tenure indicate that in time he might have secularized some church property. He did deliver the money—by "borrowing" from the monasteries. All of his actions reflected the modernizing, rationalizing tendencies which led to his early murder and rendered his months in office generally without impact on the broad course of Russian history.[6] (More on this subject will be said in chapter 10.)

The middle service class, like the upper service class, did not distinguish itself during the Time of Troubles. Many members of the class fought on the side of the slaves and peasants against the government during the Bolotnikov uprising.[7] Many were destroyed, and many of those who survived were demoralized.[8] The country had to resort to the local militia in order to drive out the invading Poles and Swedes and to restore order. But while many of the members of the old upper service class were exterminated during the Time of Troubles (crowning the process begun by the Oprichnina) and were subsequently replaced by a new group of magnates, the middle service class came out victorious.[9]

The military reality of the era after the Time of Troubles and the actual functional utility of the middle service class will be discussed at length in chapter 12. For the moment, we shall note merely that the military requirements for each serviceman after the Time of Troubles were never made known in a general decree comparable to those of 1556 and 1604. The service requirements were prescribed by the *okladchik,* an individual the cavalrymen elected locally from among themselves, on the basis of his "subjective whim."[10] As a general rule service seems to have been no longer based so much on land, which was plentiful, but according to the number of peasants, who were scarce. The general notion seems to have been that one serviceman should be provided for every fifteen peasant households, although servicemen felt that, unless they had fifty peasant households,[11] they could not go to war without cash payment from the state. In cases where a land standard was still used, as in 1633, peasant recruits were collected at the rate of one per three hundred *chetverti* of land for every landowner in Russia who himself was not serving personally in the war. The recruits had to be mounted on good horses (worth at least ten rubles) and fully armed (with general armor—*sbrui*, cuirasses—*laty*, helmets—*shishaki*, chain mail —*pantsyri*, and plate mail—*bekhtertsy*). If a lord did not have three hundred *chetverti* of land, then he had to pay to the government, in lieu of service, a percentage of thirty rubles equal to the portion of the three hundred *chetverti* he held. In this instance, no recruits were requested from Moscow *uezd*, a typical favor to the upper service class.[12]

Members of the middle service class frequently were assigned tasks in addition to their traditional responsibilities; these tasks, when performed, must have enhanced the value of the members in the eyes of the state power. For example, on March 8, 1627, soldiers, *deti boiarskie,* and cossacks were appointed to man the saltpeter boilers in Romanovo. They were to be there personally, armed and with horses, and were not to hire substitutes or send their relatives or children. The commanders were to make sure that the *sluzhilye liudi* served out their full terms.[13] They also were required to work in the new iron industry. On January 2, 1644, the Treasury sent a memorandum to the Military Chancellery about the appointment of a *dvorianin* and a *d'iak* to the Tula iron business.[14] Members of the middle service class also were sent out on intelligence-gathering missions. On June 12, 1638, the *dvoriane* and *deti boiarskie* of Riazan' petitioned the tsar to be released from an order which had decreed that they were to go out after "news" beyond distant border towns. They claimed that they were too poor to bear this added burden and that the regular spies were able to do the job. The central government left the decision up to the local military commander, Boiarin Prince I. B. Cherkasskii.[15] Others participated in the exploration and plunder of Siberia.[16]

One of the obligations of the *dvoriane* and *deti boiarskie* was the building and maintaining of the *zaseka,* the combination forest-belt, log-fence, moat-and-rampart defensive fortification system (see chapter 10 below) against the Tatars along the southern frontier.[17] In 1638 the Riazan' *dvoriane* and *deti boiarskie* asked to be relieved of their normal responsibilities for building the *zaseka* (that year they were scheduled to build a fortress in it) because of their poverty. They suggested that the local peasants be made to fill in for them. The government granted the substantive part of this petition, but drafted members of the Moscow province lower service class—soldiers and musketeers (*strel'tsy*)—to build the fortress in their stead. A willingness to exempt members of the middle service class from their responsibilities was quite common in the seventeenth century.[18] Such exemptions must have lowered the value of these servicemen in the eyes of higher state officials.

The compensation scale of the seventeenth century was much the same as that of the end of the previous century. There were five to ten grades with corresponding theoretical rates of land and cash compensation. As earlier, few received what they were entitled to, and the situation actually deteriorated; the middle service class itself was increasing in size, and the government tended to increase each individual's compensation for every trifling service. Neither the cash nor the land supplies could keep pace with these grants.[19]

Service usually began between the ages of fifteen and eighteen, but sometimes began as young as fourteen.[20] Skipping no ranks, the man rose after petitioning either on the basis of his own service or on the basis of how the rest of his family was doing—"my father has . . . , so grant me. . . ."[21] Service lasted for life. This reflected both the general shortage of people in Muscovy and the inability of the *pomest'e* system to cope systematically with the problem of superannuation. Occasionally a serviceman could obtain a discharge after he convinced the government in Moscow that he was so old, sick, or wounded that his further presence in the army would be of no possible military use.[22] Sometimes commanders insisted that discharged servicemen report for active duty; this led to much correspondence between Moscow and the provinces. The discharged serviceman received as a pension a percentage of the land he was entitled to (his *oklad*). A veteran granted 20 percent of his theoretical compensation of 600 *chetverti* could keep all the land he actually possessed if he had only 120 *chetverti*. The same mechanism operated in determining the size of subsistence grants to widows and orphans, and, beginning in 1610, for rewarding servicemen for exceptional feats of valor and the like. In the case of rewards, usually 20 percent of the hero's compensation scale could be converted from service land into his own hereditary estate.[23] As a result, servicemen valued a high theoretical compensation scale, even though it could never be obtained in full while they were in the army.

One of the major causes of the Time of Troubles, the extinction of the seven-century-old Riurikovich dynasty, in 1598, was liquidated in 1613 with the election of the new Romanov dynasty. Mikhail Romanov, of an important boyar family, was chosen because personally he was a near nonentity. From 1613 to 1619, known as the "non-tsar period," or "period of sons-in-law, brothers-in-law, and nephews," the leading families were the Romanovs and Saltykovs, and their Sheremetev, Cherkasskii, Lykov, Troekurov, Katyrev, and lesser relatives, who concentrated their efforts on an orgy of land grants to themselves and their supporters and monasteries.[24] The court was run by Mikhail's mother, Kseniia Shestova (the nun Marfa).[25] She and her favorites stopped at absolutely nothing to enrich themselves, including the appropriating of others' property.[26] It was obviously much more rewarding to appropriate land than simply to draw off the labor power from it. A traditional magnate practice during the reigns of weak monarchs, this appropriation unquestionably became more attractive after the repeal of *kormlenie* had reduced the access of the powerful to governmental income posts and thus made such persons more dependent for their wealth on the exploitation of peasants. This dependence, in turn, increased the competition between the upper and middle service classes for populated land.

The middle service class shared (on the short end) with those related to the new dynasty in a massive distribution of lands in 1613. Its members played an active role in the Assembly of the Land until Filaret returned and put a stop to the Sobor.[27] It may well be that a certain middle service class esprit de corps, a strong sense of common identity, was forged during the Smuta crisis and the ensuing sessions of the Zemskii Sobor. But in spite of the apparent triumph of the middle service class in 1613, its members were soon pushed away from the locus of power by the new magnates at the Romanov court. Nevertheless, during the initial years of the new dynasty the middle service class achieved some significant concessions, at least on paper. A major one was the 1619 commission to investigate abuses by the "strong people" (*Prikaz prikaznykh del* or *Prikaz, chto na sil'nykh liudei chelom b'iut*) during the non-tsar period.[28] The commission, however, proved to be ineffectual.

While little relief was attainable against the machinations of the "strong people," other areas of concern received more favorable consideration. This was particularly likely to occur during the reign of Filaret, who in essence solicited petitions from various groups and rendered his decision on the basis of the position with the most pressure behind it.[29] No doubt this contributed to the further formulation of the group identity as well as to the rise of the middle service class.

Reflecting the chaos caused by the Smuta, special review land cadastres were compiled which benefited the middle service class by cutting tax assessments down to the level of actual ability to pay, a privilege not granted to other sectors of society. To have done otherwise would have ruined the servicemen, who then would have been unable to meet any of their military obligations.[30] In 1620 Filaret commenced a massive distribution of peasant black lands to the service class, a distribution which was to continue until mid-century. The purpose initially was to enable more cavalrymen to render service, though in time many of the grants served simply to enrich the "strong people."[31]

In 1616 the *dvoriane* and *deti boiarskie* got the government to issue orders closing access to the middle service class to outsiders; the tsar issued an order that service lands and cash should not be given to sons whose parents had not been or were not in service.[32] This order was repeated throughout the seventeenth century. For example, a similar order was sent in the name of the tsar to the Post Chancellery (*Iamskoi Prikaz*) in 1641; the order itself was a general memorandum about who could be taken into service.[33] Nevertheless, from time to time the strictures were violated, especially on the southern frontier, where generals would even recruit peasants into the *deti boiarskie*. This practice went to such lengths that by the middle of the seventeenth century the southern frontier *deti boiarskie* who had no peasants were very distinct from those of old Muscovy who were still living off peasant labor.[34]

These laws served to limit the potential competition for the available labor supply while ushering in the formation of a closed service group. There were cases of slaves and peasants serving as members of the middle service class, but they were usually expelled from service upon detection.[35] In 1647 a man was expelled from the ranks of the *deti boiarskie* because his father had not been a *syn boiarskii*, but a monastery servant.[36] By the time of the *Ulozhenie,* even on the southern frontier the striving for a closed service class was successful. There was a strict order: "Do not give service land grants to children of nonservice fathers, slaves, and peasants."[37] However, it was still possible to rise from the lower into the middle service class. In 1650 Tsar Aleksei gave some cossacks and musketeers the rank of *syn boiarskii.*[38]

Decrees of October 20, 1652, and January 31, 1660, again forbade specifically priests' children from entering the middle service class.[39] In 1661 a decree prescribed that ranks in the middle service class could be granted only to children of *deti boiarskie* who had served in the army.[40] In 1675 and 1678 peasants, slaves, townsmen, and in general all children whose fathers were not servicemen were again formally excluded.[41]

Once the middle service class had become a relatively closed caste, the stage was set for the formulation of privileges which might be assumed to be part of the perquisites natural to membership in such an exclusive group, the well-being of which might be considered crucial to the survival of the Muscovite state after the harrowing experience of the Time of Troubles.

A major objective of the members of the middle service class was to obtain and then keep a monopoly on the use of land for its members, excepting, necessarily, the holdings of the church and upper service class. As a result of grants by the contesting sides during the Smuta and the first Romanov administrations, service landholding increased markedly at the expense of peasant black lands and from expropriated boyar possessions. The cavalrymen, who came out of the Time of Troubles with devastated service lands, could hope thereby to maximize the labor force at their disposal: peasants would be able to live only on lands belonging to *pomeshchiki*.[42] In the sixteenth century the principle was established that service lands could be granted only to members of the middle service class. In 1626 this principle was extended to hereditary lands also, with the notice that nonservice people such as priests, peasants engaged in trade, monastery employees, and slaves could own neither *votchiny* nor *pomest'ia*.[43]

In 1627–28 a person who served in the town night-patrol service, and thus was not considered a member of the service class, was not permitted to have service lands. Such a person who held service lands had two alternatives: he could keep the lands by quitting the night patrol and joining the service class, or he could stay in the night patrol and see his lands confiscated for distribution to the *sluzhilye liudi*.[44] The same choice was offered to laymen (often troops) in the church service: they either had to quit serving the church, join the tsar's service, and keep the lands they had purchased or were using as the result of a mortgage; or they could remain in the service of the church but lose their lands.[45] A decree of 1642 again stated that slaves could no longer own lands. (At the same time a law expelled slaves from the service class.) The person who denounced landowning slaves to the government was given their lands.[46] In a society in which increasing prestige was attached to ownership of land, a symbiotic relationship between the upper and middle service classes could be achieved by such a measure: the slave-owning magnates would get direct ownership of their slaves' property, while the poor rank-and-file cavalrymen would find psychic satisfaction in the fact that people in the social hierachy lower than they were deprived of a major status symbol—land-ownership. The principle was being established that only the wellborn could own land.

Depriving slaves of the right to own land would appear to be a victory of some significance, yet it may have been largely a hollow one, for such properties could simply be transferred to the magnates who owned the slaves. The middle service class got none of the land, but no doubt got some of the satisfaction that segregation of American Negroes gave poor whites. A larger issue was that of the lands owned by the magnates themselves. (The question of monastery property will be discussed below.) While members of the upper service class succeeded, as a rule, in resisting middle service class pressure, this was not always true. Under pressure from the servicemen in the frontier regions, a decree of 1637 forbade the granting of frontier and steppe service lands (which were just then being secured) to the members of the service class who were based in Moscow—the boyars, *okolnichie*, and Moscow *dvoriane*. Furthermore, they could not buy lands there.[47] This decree was broadened in 1639 to include service lands and a clause was added against the exchange of all types of land by members of these groups all over Russia.[48] It has to be noted that this measure was not enacted until after the Cherkasskii-Sheremetev clique, ruling for Tsar Mikhail after the 1633 death of Patriarch Filaret, had had adequate opportunity to enrich themselves. The decree of 1637 was repealed in 1647, probably so that the Morozov-Miloslavskii clique, ruling from 1645 in the name of minor Tsar Aleksei, could steal legally.[49] An attempt was made in 1647–48, however, to enforce the law of 1637, and in several frontier regions the government confiscated service and hereditary lands held by people of higher service ranks living in Moscow.[50] These laws represented an attempt by the smaller provincial service class members to hold off land grabbing by the more influential people based in Moscow. The reality was, however, that these prohibitions had little effect.[51] More efficacious, often, were laws of opposite intent such as that of 1628 which essentially allowed magnates—those with cash reserves—to buy court and escheated and unclaimed state land from the government at a ridiculously low price.[52]

A measure of considerable significance was the provision in the *Ulozhenie* that when someone found service lands which had been uninhabited for a long time, and belonged to no one, and were wanted by no one as service lands, then that person could buy such lands from the government. They became hereditary lands, but only on the condition that the purchasers were *dvoriane* and *deti boiarskie* who had service ranks and were serving from the regions of the vacant lands.[53] This was a concession of great significance to the provincial servicemen, who were constantly struggling against absentee ownership by the strong people.

The middle service class struggle for a monopoly on land was given unexpected support by seemingly extraneous circumstances. The first half of the seventeenth century was one of the most xenophobic periods in Russian history. Right after the Time of Troubles a special pool of lands was, in essence, set aside for foreign servicemen. These lands could not be given to anyone besides foreigners, and foreigners could not enlarge their holdings at the expense of lands which had belonged to Russians. Much of this xenophobia, which was a response to the defeats in the Time of Troubles, took a religious cast. The middle service class benefited when the government decreed that non-Slavs in Russian service (Tatars, Mordva, and the like) could expand their service land-holdings only by becoming Orthodox. The trend of limiting service lands to Russians and Orthodox became particularly pronounced at the time of the Smolensk War (1632–34), which, as will be shown in chapter 10, began to challenge the very existence of the native middle service class. There can hardly be any question that the *deti boiarskie* and *dvoriane* welcomed, if they did not in fact encourage, Orthodox xenophobia with its consequence of restricting the land fund for their own use. The government needed the service of non-Orthodox warriors and foreign mercenaries, so it compromised with its own citizens by limiting the granting of additional lands to non-Slavs who were willing to abandon their own faiths.[54]

A logical consequence of the right to control service lands which was given to *pomeshichiki* by Ivan IV was the right to own them—a direct contradiction of the principle of service landholding. One of the major thrusts of the middle service class in the course of the seventeenth century was to convert the service *pomest'e* into a *votchina,* an hereditary estate. After 1556 it probably made little difference to the government whether lands were *votchiny* or *pomest'ia,* for, at least in theory, equal service was required from both types of lands. Moreover, alienating a *votchina* by giving it to a party who would not render service from it was made increasingly more difficult by successive governmental decrees.

The government may have realized that the cavalryman was less likely to plunder his own estate for a short-run gain than he would a service landholding, but there is no evidence which would indicate that the government did understand this or act accordingly. Nevertheless, all sixteenth-century rulers, including Boris Godunov, supported the service land principle. Only during the Time of Troubles did the contesting sides begin to distribute lands with the right of hereditary tenure.[55]

To the servicemen there was considerable difference, for the *votchina* could be sold and otherwise alienated, whereas the *pomest'e* could not. This was the major reason why the serviceman who had both types of land was tempted to move his peasants from the latter to the former, a tendency against which the government began to legislate at least as early as 1621.[56] The hereditary estate obviously had much higher status connotations than the lowly service landholding. Hard-pressed rulers and would-be rulers could gain support from the servicemen by pandering to these desires for higher status. When the desire of the middle service class was satisfied, the Muscovite state witnessed within a century a complete reversal of its land tenure policy—from the dominance of the *pomest'e* at the expense of the *votchina* in the second half of the sixteenth century to the near extermination of the *pomest'e* by the *votchina* a hundred years later. This reversal contributed to the conversion of the cavalrymen into a sometimes parasitic class of landlords in the same period.[57]

Perhaps the most important step in the conversion of the *pomest'e* into a *votchina* was to make it the permanent property of the service landholder himself.[58] Decrees of 1621 and 1634, repeated in the *Ulozhenie*, stated that no service lands were to be given to someone else while the holder lived.[59] Furthermore, a decree of 1636 stated that while a service landholder was in captivity, his service lands could not pass to his sons.[60] The captive had the right to get his service lands back no matter how long his captivity lasted—even if it was twenty-five years or more.[61] Thus, except for cases when the holder fell into beggary and was totally unable to serve, grants once made were usually good for life.[62]

Another step in this reversal of policy was to permit *pomest'e* lands to pass to direct heirs. This already had become custom in the second half of the sixteenth century. As a result of the desires of the middle service class, laws of 1611, 1613, 1614, and 1618 forbade the transfer of service lands to anyone besides relatives. Only if no relatives survived, could service land go back into the general fund for redistribution.[63] This was the period in which the government was daily under the influence of the Assembly of the Land, which was dominated by the middle service class.

By the time of the compilation of the *Ulozhenie* of 1649, it was accepted practice for sons to inherit their fathers' fragmented service landholdings.[64] This, it was hoped, would provide for the education of a new soldier.[65] The earliest source for these articles I could find dates from 1636, but the practice was considerably older. Decrees of 1634 and 1638 spoke of "familial service lands," an obvious contradiction of the service land principle.[66] In some regions the officials did not even distinguish between hereditary and service landholding, but gave only combined figures for both in their reports to the central government.[67] In the second half of the century, service lands nearly everywhere were a lesser percentage of the total than were hereditary lands. In 1678, in the center of the Muscovite state (*Zamoskovnyi krai*), 59 percent of the members of the middle service class owned land under the rules of hereditary tenure.[68]

The near consummation of the conversion of the *pomest'e* into the alienable *votchina* occurred in the last third of the century. A law of 1674 permitted a discharged *pomeshchik* to sell or mortgage his service lands.[69] In laws of 1676 and 1677 the government recognized the reality of the situation and essentially abolished the *pomest'e* in favor of the *votchina*.[70] In 1690 the free transfer of peasants between the two types of landholding was legalized. Earlier, only transfer to the service holding from a familial estate had been legal. This further equalized the rights of *votchinniki* and *pomeshchiki*.[71] Peter revived the service principle, but in 1714, in response to the historical trend and perhaps the Bulavin peasant uprising of 1707–9 and its aftermath, he enacted an important measure which equated the *pomest'e* with the *votchina* by making the former into hereditary property. In 1731 Anna combined the service landholding and the hereditary estate and gave all *pomeshchiki* the rights which *votchinniki* had in relation to their lands.[72]

Members of the middle service class also had provisions enacted into law in the 1630s and 1640s extending the provisions providing for the care of surviving children and widows out of *pomest'e* lands.[73] This furthered the confluence of the service and hereditary types of land tenure. Laws of 1666 and 1679 made it difficult even for leading merchants to buy lands, thus compartmentalizing Russian life further while strengthening the monopoly position of the upper and middle service classes.[74]

The dramatic reversal in the basic form of land tenure in Muscovy which occurred, roughly, between the middle of the sixteenth and the middle of the seventeenth century should hardly be a surprise, either in and of itself or in the context within which it occurred. For a rigorous service landholding system to endure over a long period of time, would have required a regenerative élan at odds with the sluggish, survival-oriented Muscovite nature—or human nature in general, for that matter. Moreover, the degeneration which occurred fits in perfectly with what was happening to the middle service class anyway. One may doubt whether each step was consciously viewed as another privilege or concession to the mass of service landholders, but the aggregate result of squeezing out the *pomest'e* in favor of the *votchina* was ultimately the creation of a landed gentry. In turn this contributed to the decline of the *pomest'e* cavalry, the subject of chapter 12.[75]

The theory of the service landholding system demanded that a person who ceased to serve lose his lands, regardless of whether the lack of service was because of desertion, retirement, or refusal to serve at all. However, as the seventeenth century progressed, the government became increasingly reluctant to enforce the rule. As a result, the service landholding increasingly became the personal property of the holder. Even when lands were taken away in whole or in part because of failure to report for service or desertion, they were usually restored upon petition by the offending serviceman.[76]

In the first half of the seventeenth century land remained essential for service. Particularly after the Time of Troubles the economy was in such bad shape that an army could be supported only by relying essentially on those fruits which a near-natural, nonexchange economy could provide. Just having the land was not enough; it had to be inhabited and worked to be of any utility. With this in mind, the middle service class argued that its members should not have to fight unless they had populated service lands. The government conceded that under normal conditions, if they had no populated lands, they only should have to render service in a fortress ("siege service").[77] This helps to explain why the land question was so important to the *dvoriane* and *deti boiarskie;* not only was it an issue of prestige, it was also crucial for fulfilling their role in society. The reality of the situation was graphically spelled out in a 1630 petition requesting additional land. The writer noted that his colleagues were uneasy over their low pay and felt that somebody was concealing land from them. He recommended a census of all land and peasants to determine the facts. He offered to work on the task himself—a curious proposition, considering the fact that an elaborate cadastre had just been compiled. Nothing was done to check on the land seized during the Time of Troubles by the "strong people," however, until the Smolensk War gave rise to a need for funds and thus forced a more careful look into the holdings of the magnates.[78]

Undoubtedly in response to pressure by the middle service class, the government decreed that lords who had fewer than twenty peasants on their lands did not have to furnish these peasants as workers (as official assistants—*tseloval'niki,* guards—*storozhi,* and clerks—*pod'iachie*) for the *guba* administration.[79] This decree should have applied to nearly all the *deti boiarskie* and probably most of the *dvoriane,* whose peasants' obligations were reduced to paying taxes and supporting them. Moreover, no seignorial peasants had to work in the customs service, as toll collectors, or as alcohol revenue agents in the taverns.[80] Landholders had requested this privilege numerous times after the Time of Troubles, but received an answer only in 1649. Henceforth these tasks were turned over to officials of the central government.[81] This increased the middle service class monopoly on peasant labor.

Another privilege granted to the middle service class was preferential access to the grain market in time of shortage. For example, in 1622 (when Russia was at peace on all frontiers) merchants were forbidden to buy grain in the town of Verkhotur'e because the servicemen could not buy any grain at a reasonable price.[82] Another privilege was a general exemption from the liability of billeting troops. In 1629 the military commander of Tula reported that there were not sufficient houses for billeting the troops. He tried to billet them on the local servicemen, but they refused, showing him documents that exempted them from this duty. The tsar supported the *sluzhilye liudi* in this dispute and said that they had the right not to be forced to billet troops.[83]

The members of the middle service class did not have to pay taxes to ransom captives, unlike the members of the lower service class, townsmen, and peasants.[84] These taxes violated all the modern actuarial concepts of insurance based on risk, and those who paid the least were the greatest potential gainers from this legislation. The higher a person was in society, the less of the "captive ransom tax" the person paid and the more the government was willing to pay to ransom him. The 1649 rate was fifteen rubles for peasants and slaves, but twenty rubles per one hundred *chetverti* of land *oklad* for *dvoriane* and *deti boiarskie*.[85]

In October, 1647, when the government was hunting fugitive peasants in the Novgorod area, it did not penalize *dvoriane* and *deti boiarskie* who had harbored them, in contrast to the fact that monasteries and high church officials who had done the same thing were required to compensate the peasants' lords for their losses.[86] This was a typical favor for the middle service class. Another explicit favor to the *pomesh-chiki* was the fact that their peasants paid lower taxes than did those living on church or nonseigniorial lands.

As one might expect from the foregoing, a whole series of rights enjoyed by the *sluzhilye liudi* while they were in service evolved in this period. Most of them relate to the years of the Smolensk War (1632–34), the last war of the middle service class and the period when the central government most needed the services of that class. One nearly always expects this type of thing—a rash of wartime laws in favor of the serviceman—but the crucial point is that some of these concessions were retained in subsequent legislation. Thus to curtail profiteering, in 1631 the government ordered provisioners to sell at prices set by the state.[87] The following year the state established the prices to be paid for food products by those active in the Smolensk campaign.[88] This was followed by a decree authorizing for the servicemen the free use of hay growing along the roadside.[89] The government agreed to pay for the "medicine" to cure those injured in the war.[90] In 1634 people were discharged from service so they could try to catch their fugitive slaves and peasants.[91]

Other rights, some of them probably dating from this period, were codified for people in service. They could buy horses without going through the usual procedures, ones which called for a number of documents and witnesses so that it could be proved that the animal had not been stolen. A trial had to be granted when servicemen were accused of stealing horses and had no documents proving ownership.[92] Servicemen also had the right to free use of fodder in unenclosed fields on the way to service,[93] the right not to be charged more than the current market price for products while on the way to service,[94] and the right to buy firewood and building materials.[95] In the historical literature these provisions are attributed to chapter 2 of the *Lithuanian Statute* of 1588. Most, if not all, of these borrowings, which amounted to privileges for the middle service class, were first promulgated during the Smolensk War.

This interpretation is supported by the circumstances of the Smolensk War. Russia had, as it were, a fifth column in its rear. Not only was it necessary to contend with the Poles and the Tatars, but the government had to suppress the Balash movement, a series of disorders caused by peasants and Smolensk deserters. All of these simultaneous developments prompted the government to take measures—which proved to be successful—to undermine potential dissatisfaction in the middle service class. In addition to the more permanent measures just mentioned, the government in November and December of 1633, a particularly difficult time, paid cash to its troops at Smolensk, offered sick pay to those wounded in the war, and exempted war widows from the obligation to furnish troops from their lands.[96] This situation is analogous to the events of 1648, which led to the repeal of the time limit on the recovery of fugitives and to the consummation of the enserfment of the peasantry. In fact, the following generalization can be made about the political behavior of the early Romanov governments: concessions to the middle service class were granted by the magnates only when they felt seriously threatened.

Perhaps the major service-connected privilege demanded by the servicemen (next to compensation in its various forms) was the postponement of trials scheduled for times when the men were in service. A law of 1619, reflecting the highly centralized nature of the Muscovite judicial system, had established for most parties with immunity charters (basically monasteries and boyars) three general court dates in Moscow for answering suits, and sometimes for initiating them:[97] Trinity Day (in the spring, fifty days after Easter),[98] St. Simeon's Day (September 1, or New Year's Day according to the Russian calendar of the seventeenth century), and Christmas. The problem was that on the first two of these days the servicemen were usually in service; this left only one day a year when they were able to come to court.[99] (The demand for the postponement of trials while they were in service contradicted another insistent demand of the *sluzhilye liudi,* the right to prompt justice). The demand for the postponement of trial dates that fell during military service was made and granted many times.[100] The *Ulozhenie* codified the granting of delays in the holding of trials for several situations involving the *sluzhilye liudi:* if a person petitioned for some concealed vacant service land as he was about to go into service, the case was not to be decided until he returned from service. In this interval the land in question could not be disposed of.[101]

Furthermore, if a person was sued while he was in service, he did not automatically lose the case if he did not show up at the trial by the third summons (as was the general rule). In such cases an extension after the completion of service was allowed.[102] At the Assembly of the Land of 1648–49 a new law was drafted permitting servicemen residing in far-off places such as Siberia, Astrakhan', or the Terek River in the foothills of the Caucasus, and those in the tsar's service in the army on the frontier or anywhere else not to have to answer suits until their service terms had expired. This was such a lively issue that the Odoevskii legislative commission, which compiled the new law code, not only copied the 1628 version found in the Statute Book of the Moscow Administrative Chancellery (*Ukaznaia kniga zemskago prikaza*) [103] and the Statute Book of the Robbery Chancellery (*Ukaznaia kniga razboinogo prikaza*),[104] the version went into article 118 of chapter 10 of the *Ulozhenie,* but compiled another new article of essentially the same content to satisfy the insistent demands of the middle service class at the Assembly of the Land.

Another related problem was the recurrent demand for court reform. In a petition of February, 1637, on the problem of fugitive peasants, the *sluzhilye liudi* added that their legal defenses were to no avail because of the shortcomings of the court system.[105] Using special privileges, the "strong people"—magnates and others who violated the laws with impunity—sued for huge sums because they did not have to pay any court fees.[106] They did not post bond when required. Many of the members of the middle service class could not come to court for trials in Moscow because, they claimed, "we are so poor, the distances are so great, and we have been ruined by the 'strong people.' " If they did not appear in court, they lost their peasants "not on the basis of a legal case, but because [of the technicality] of the trial dates." If they did come to Moscow, the cases would go on forever: "They hinder us . . . with Moscow red tape and delay, hoping for the tsar's five years [to elapse]."[107] Furthermore, the "strong people" would not show up at the Christmas court sessions nor would they bring the peasants and slaves who were in dispute. The conclusions of the members of the middle service class were that the time limit for hunting down fugitive peasants should be repealed and that the court should be reformed by moving it out of Moscow, where the "strong people" were the dominant group, to the provincial towns where the members of the middle service class had more influence.[108] Even when the court decisions were favorable, said these *sluzhilye liudi* in their petition, their peasants were given to the "strong people" anyway. The members of the middle service class asked that trials be held at any time in the towns and that the judges be selected from the local middle service class and peasantry, a sort of elected local court.[109] In 1638 a similar petition about red tape and delays in court cases was filed, but to no avail.[110] The question of the local court was raised again at the Assembly of the Land of 1642, but nothing came of this either.[111]

In the summer of 1641 the *dvoriane* and *deti boiarskie* assembled in Moscow to meet the threat of a Turk-Tatar invasion in the south. Again they petitioned the tsar for court reform. They wanted trials granted without any time limit in cases involving fugitive peasants. They also wanted the oath to be substituted for the casting of lots in the trial procedure in cases involving those affiliated with church institutions other than the monks or clergymen themselves. They had some limited success: the length of time for suits was extended and oaths were substituted for lots involving fugitive peasants and church personnel. The members of the middle service class also claimed that the military governors and local chancellery officials refused to grant trials against the "strong people" and claimed that the local officials lacked jurisdiction to try such cases—charges which, in the majority of cases, were true. Local authorities lacked jurisdiction because so many cases were preempted by the Moscow chancelleries or because one of the parties had so-called "privilege charters"—documents which permitted the parties having them to try cases themselves or else in "joint courts" and thereby removed them from complete governmental jurisdiction in all cases other than felonies.[112] The petition of 1637 had also complained that "in the towns they do not grant us trials against high church officials, monasteries, and Moscow 'strong people' of all civil ranks,"[113]—precisely the people who had the "privilege charters." The government sidestepped this issue and decreed instead that tolls not be collected from *sluzhilye liudi* going about state business. One of the desired court reforms was granted, however: trials were to be held at any time from October 1 to April 1, rather than only three times a year.[114]

On January 2, 1645, perhaps in response to pressure by those assembled in Moscow for the general court sessions, a law was promulgated requiring persons who held up court cases to pay the other party one ruble per day of unnecessary delay.[115] This law should have been a significant victory for the members of the middle service class, but we do not know whether it was ever enforced.

The issue of court reform—or what amounted to decentralization—also came up in petitions of the *deti boiarskie* of the southern town of Elets in 1646 and 1648. They asked for permission to elect the entire local administration "so that they will listen to us in all cases and not oppress us in anything and we shall not have to give them bribes."[116] The request, a throwback to the sixteenth century, was not granted.

The middle service class lost its struggle to decentralize the government because the time was too late. The middle service class, as will be shown below, had by this time opted out of both central and provincial administration. In the sixteenth century *dvoriane* and *deti boiarskie* had played an important role in running the country, but in the seventeenth century a bureaucracy had taken their place. The frequent request to replace the bureaucratic administration with what would have been in essence a gentry administration was fifty years too late. The government could and did ignore all such requests to turn the clock back.

The *sluzhilye liudi* suffered on the one hand from the fact that justice could be delayed so long by the "strong people" and on the other hand because the time available in which they could obtain justice was not long enough. In general, however, the middle service class felt that it was to its advantage to have speedy trials, for constant postponements were very expensive. The only two exceptions were while they were in service and when their subjects ran away.

The triumph of the middle service class on the issue of speedy justice can be found in the *Ulozhenie* of 1649, which decreed that no one, with certain exceptions, could hold up cases, and that the person who did would be fined, beaten, jailed, and have the army sent after him.[117] Civil military governors (who very frequently oppressed the local *dvoriane* and *deti boiarskie*), except those in very distant places, had to respond immediately to suits against them.[118] These laws were promulgated in 1648. Their impact is unknown.

In addition, a limit of three was placed on petitions for permission to divide up lands (*razdel'nye gramoty*), "so that in such matters no one will suffer excessive travel costs, delay, and losses."[119] No more than a six-month illness could be claimed in delaying a case involving a suit for hereditary lands or concealed service lands.[120] A three-month limit was placed on dragging out the settlement of vacant land disputes.[121]

An attempt was made to cut down delay in slavery cases by limiting time-consuming appeals to distant places.[122] And finally, the *Ulozhenie* declared that judicial decisions had to be handed down rapidly.[123] The origin of these last articles from the *Ulozhenie* is unknown, but in spirit they belong to the 1640s, the period of the ascendancy of the middle service class.

This streamlining of legal procedure was opposed by the "strong people" who profited by manipulation of legal procedure at the expense of the vast majority of the rest of the population.[124] The "strong people" had the means to have someone (usually a slave) stand in for them at endless trials, or just to sit and wait if necessary, whereas the rank-and-file servicemen were not so affluent and had to come to trials themselves or send someone else at considerable expense. The former alternative was almost out of the question while the serviceman was on duty, and the latter practically prohibitive because of the lack of means. During the summer of 1648, while the "strong people" stayed out of sight, measures inimical to their vested interests were advanced by the middle service class and incorporated into the law of the land. Whether these laws were subsequently enforced is a matter for further study.[125]

In another area, the government was even willing to go so far as to violate international treaties to placate the middle service class. In 1634, after the Smolensk War was over and in violation of the Polianovka "Eternal Peace" with Poland, the government granted the servicemen of Chernigov and Putivl' the right to keep as slaves the women, girls, and small boys they had taken captive during the war. This was to compensate them for their service and the fact that they had been "ruined."[126]

This period after the Time of Troubles was not simply one of unending triumphs by the middle service class. Amid the triumphs there were setbacks, the most crucial of which centered around the peasant question. The tribulations this ultimately caused the members of the middle service class will be detailed in chapter 7.

In spite of the law, impoverished members of the middle service class continued to sell themselves as slaves to magnates to escape starvation, onerous taxation, and military service. During the chaos of the Time of Troubles, selling oneself into bondage, especially by *deti boiarskie,* became a common phenomenon.[127] In 1620, after some order had been restored, a decree proclaimed that *deti boiarskie* no longer could sell themselves into bondage.[128] In 1621 the *okladchiki* were ordered to search out *deti boiarskie* and cossacks who had abandoned their lands and become slaves and "to take them from the boyars' houses into service and register them from service and hereditary lands."[129] Why the members of the middle service class opposed a lessening of their numbers is, at first, not apparent. One might imagine that there would be a general rejoicing over a decrease in the number of competitors in the vicious struggle for the limited quantity of available populated land. A vigorous campaign to lessen the competition from the side of the church for the available land fund was pushed vigorously, so why should there be any complaint when competition within the ranks of the service class itself was diminished?

The members of the middle service class did not like their colleagues to shirk their duty by leaving the service class to become slaves. This aspect of middle service class solidarity probably was motivated, as has been said, by the feeling "that there but for the grace of God go I" and by the desire by the generally impoverished mass of *deti boiarskie* not to see the bottom of their corporation disappear; if this happened, those remaining would, of course, be that much closer to the bottom themselves. There was in Muscovy also a general notion of primitive equality which was violated when a serviceman became a slave. This notion is evident in the usual equal division of property among heirs and the avoidance of primogeniture in such instances. Moreover, the descent into slavery violated the belief, which was crystallizing at the time, in rigidly closed estates.

And finally, the *mestnichestvo* "system of places" must not be omitted from consideration. Initially the provincial *dvoriane* were the lowest rank to have the right to participate in the system of places, but by the 1640s all groups were worrying about their honor.[130] This is yet another symptom of the fact that the middle service class was forming a higher opinion of its members' dignity and social status—while the status of the peasants was falling. According to the *mestnichestvo* calculation, each person's "honor" was dependent to some extent on the "place" of his relatives, so that when one person fell in status (as when he went into slavery), all his relatives fell with him. This was probably a real fear among numerous *deti boiarskie*. The *sluzhilye liudi* petitioned the central government at least five times—in 1636, 1638, 1641, 1642, and 1645[131]—for the curtailment of the practice of their members' going into slavery.

But decree as it might, the government was not heeded on this matter. Each time, the prohibition was repeated by the government in a new law—which was not enforced.[132] It may be imagined that the law was not enforced because of conflicting interests in the central government apparatus which dealt with such matters: on the one hand, when servicemen became slaves they ceased to render service directly to the state (although a number of them went to war under their boyars) ; but on the other hand they became the slaves of precisely the wealthy "strong people" who controlled the government most of the time and directed the running of the apparatus. In 1648 the members of the middle service class were again in a position to force concessions from the government, and so the prohibition on the assumption of bondage by *deti boiarskie* was included in the *Ulozhenie* in substantially the same form as it had appeared in 1620.[133] The law was not made retroactive and consequently did not remove from slavery those *deti boiarskie* who had not been in service, had no compensation, and in 1648 belonged to boyars; but in the future no *deti boiarskie* were to become slaves for any reason, as had been decreed in 1641. The *Ulozhenie* further decreed that members of the middle service class could not be forced into slavery against their will even if they could not pay their debts.[134]

The magnates usurped middle service class lands,[135] sued servicemen falsely in court and refused to respond to countersuits, awarded verdicts against them unjustly, and in general treated them badly.[136] Filaret in 1627 forbade the members of the court to acquire additional lands, but his successors, the Cherkasskii-Sheremetev clique, initiated great distributions of land to the court nobility.[137] After they had sated themselves, they enacted a law in 1644 which forbade the upper service class specifically and other servicemen and chancellery officials in general to buy vacant lands in Moscow province intended for distribution to petitioners who had little or no *pomest'e* land.[138] There is no evidence that, after the fright engendered by the 1648 riots had passed, the magnates who ran the government heeded this law.

The middle service class, as has been noted, wanted more local government at the expense of the military governors, a resurrection of the supposed power and influence the local *guba* institutions had at the time of Ivan IV.[139] This concession—a return to the importance of the autonomous local *guba* institutions at the time of Ivan IV—was not granted. This was because the "strong people" and the upper service class as a whole preferred that the real power remain in their own hands, either in the Moscow chancelleries or in the jurisdiction of the military governor (*voevoda*) sent to the provinces from Moscow. *Guba* institutions, usually run by superannuated servicemen, became simply tools in the hands of the military governor.[140]

Another concern of the middle service class was the continued existence of the privilege charters (discussed in chapter 6 below) held by church magnates, which took many court cases out of local jurisdiction.[141] These judicial immunities covered not only the church institutions themselves and church officials and agents, but also all the peasants who lived on church lands. Under the prevailing court rules of the period, defendants had the right to be tried by the body to which they were subject—a particular town, one of the chancelleries in Moscow, or one of the church institutions. In cases initiated by laymen against clergymen or those under church jurisdiction the matters were decided by the church body, and most of the time the servicemen felt that the layman was at a distinct disadvantage in such situations. The solution adopted in the sixteenth century to resolve these jurisdictional problems was the so-called "mixed court": instead of the usual one judge, there were two, one from each of the jurisdictions of the litigants.[142] Some of the people who were actually subjects of the church were placed under the legal jurisdiction of the civil authorities.[143] The *Ulozhenie* tried to solve this problem by denying the legitimacy of all judicial immunity charters outstanding and by ordering that no more were to be granted "because they cause people great losses, expense, and insult."[144] Nevertheless, such documents continued to exist and be recognized until some were repealed in 1672, and the rest in 1677.[145] Members of the lower upper-service class, the middle service class, and townsmen were not satisfied with the *Ulozhenie* limitations on church judicial immunities. At their request most church institutions and personnel were transferred from the jurisdiction of the tsar's Chancellery of the Great Court to the state system; this move was accomplished with the establishment in 1649 of the Monastery Chancellery, a combined judicial, administrative, and financial organ. Those in the patriarch's domain were exempted from the Monastery Chancellery's jurisdiction.[146]

Despite the spate of legislation directed toward the limitation of church land-ownership in Ivan's reign, the monasteries annexed a great quantity of land during the Time of Troubles.[147] After the Time of Troubles, in 1619, the government reviewed the land titles held by church institutions, but nothing was done about the recent illegal acquisitions. However, in 1620 or 1621 Filaret's administration did take away once again the tax exemption from almost all monasteries and collected the heavy post and musketeer taxes nearly universally.[148] Nevertheless, some monasteries continued to enjoy privileges exempting them from the full payment of customs and duties.[149]

During Filaret's patriarchate (1619–33) church landholding grew rapidly.[150] A law of 1622 recognized all acquisitions prior to 1612, regardless of the 1581 law.[151] In 1623 the church owned 43.7 percent (93,000 *desiatiny*) of all the cultivated land in Moscow province.[152] In 1628 owners of hereditary estates which had been granted for meritorious service were permitted to alienate them as they pleased, including giving them to monasteries.[153] (However, another law of 1628 stated that lands which had been purchased from the treasury could not be willed to a monastery;[154] in 1634 provisions were established for forced repurchase by the state of donations to monasteries under the 1628 law.)[155] After full recovery from the consequences of the Time of Troubles, the church owned about 16 percent of all the cultivated land in Russia.[156] The monasteries had a large cash flow, and they did not stint when they wanted to purchase a parcel of land. Service landholders even noted that monasteries paid such high prices that "no one else can buy estates except them."[157] Resentment at this state of affairs came out at the 1648–49 Assembly of the Land, a time when laymen in general felt little love for the clergy.[158]

Because of his alliance with Patriarch Iosif, Boris Morozov, Tsar Aleksei's former tutor and the real ruler after 1645, was unable in 1648 to grant the middle service class demand for the confiscation and redistribution to them of church lands acquired since 1580.[159] All the law could do was to mouth the 1580–81 prohibitions against further acquisitions by church institutions.[160] The *Ulozhenie* did, however, as noted above, specify that the state land fund could not be used to support the church's military servitors and that the patriarch would have to give his *deti boiarskie* part of his own lands.[161]

In general one must conclude that the middle service class desire to curtail church landholding failed to be realized. Throughout the second half of the seventeenth century land grants continued to be made to monasteries and other church institutions, even by the state. An active purchasing campaign was also maintained.[162] In the late 1660s the Englishman Samuel Collins estimated that the church owned nearly two-thirds of all the land in Russia.[163] This estimate was a gross exaggeration, but the fact that it was made gives an indication of the impression the extent of church land-ownership must have had on Russians as well. (In reality, about 13.3 percent of all peasant households were on church lands in the late 1670s.[164] This amounted to roughly a quarter of the enserfed peasantry or 16 percent of the entire population.) [165] These peasants were supporting an establishment of about 25,000 persons in monastic orders at the beginning of the eighteenth century.[166] Foreigners also commented on the excessive number of monks in Russia. From a secular point of view, these resources would have been better spent on the army.

The middle service class lost this battle because of the nearly continuous symbiotic relationship between church and state since 988. This relationship was renewed and reinforced by the controversies in the first half of the sixteenth century, then by the personality of Filaret in the seventeenth century. It should not be surprising that the state, many of whose leading figures were personally related to the rulers of the church, never took action against church land-ownership in the countryside. The middle service class campaigns against this landholding may have curtailed its growth, but little more. It took a massive wave of secularization in the eighteenth century to resolve the issue. In Muscovy there was never a tendency toward such a dramatic resolution of the conflict between spiritual interests and military needs.[167]

The Muscovite government in the middle third of the seventeenth century was frequently able to disregard the needs of the middle service class, except in moments of crisis. The middle service class was well aware of this, as was revealed in a 1647 trial of a *syn boiarskii*. He noted that little heed was paid to the petitions of the servicemen and that even submitting complaints was difficult. He blamed the tsar for not defending the servicemen. The boyars ordered the man executed for the crime of speaking ill of the tsar. The tsar commuted the sentence to a merciless beating with the knout, after a mock execution.[168] In such ways the government used a mixture of terror and calculated concessions to keep the middle service class in line.

During their rise, the *dvoriane* and *deti boiarskie* cast off many of the obligations which would have made them indispensable to the government.[169] They were not essential, as they had been in the sixteenth century, in the central chancelleries,[170] a fact the government demonstrated in the 1658–63 period when it drafted those in the central government apparatus into the army.[171] The top jobs in the chancelleries generally were a preserve of the upper service class, although it was often necessary to rise through the ranks—no doubt to gain experience—to obtain the top positions in the government. Thus 90 percent of all chancellery secretaries (*d'iaki*) had once been clerks (*pod'iachie*). Kotoshikhin noted that some *d'iaki* came directly from the ranks of the upper service class without this apprenticeship. Of the fifty persons appointed directly as chancellery secretaries in the seventeenth century, thirty-nine came from the upper service class and eight from the top merchant corporation (*gosti*).[172] Thus mobility into the upper circles of government service was fairly well confined to members of the upper service class and the leading merchants.[173] The approximately two thousand clerks in the central chancelleries were by and large a self-perpetuating caste.[174] Of the 278 clerks in the Service Land Chancellery at the beginning of the eighteenth century (when data are available), 86 were children of chancellery employees, 73 children of clergy, 43 of servicemen (hereditary and drafted), 29 of townsmen, and so on. Sometimes even fugitive peasants became clerks.[175] The bulk of the available evidence

70

indicates strongly that the *dvoriane* and *deti boiarskie* had no significant role in the central administration. Working there was not even regarded as service; such work, in fact, was considered harmful to a family's social standing. The petitions reveal that the middle service class, far from identifying in any way with the bureaucracy, despised and opposed it.[176]

One might think that these servicemen were essential to the government in the provincial administration. After the subordination of the *guba* administration to the *voevoda* in the seventeenth century this was no longer the case, as it had been in the sixteenth century. Evidence for 1686–87 from the Military Chancellery, which also doubled as the central government personnel office, shows that among the provincial *voevody* were 3 boyars, 2 *okol'nichie*, 27 *stolniki*, 8 *striapchie*, 9 *zhil'tsy*, 52 Moscow *dvoriane*, and only 31 provincial *dvoriane*.[177] All of these people, by a law of 1661, were no longer fit for military service.[178] Service as Moscow-appointed head of the provincial administration (*voevoda*) came to be viewed as a short-term (usually three years) opportunity for favorites of the elite to enrich themselves, somewhat like the old *namestnik* who had been abolished in 1556. These favorites petitioned for the jobs, submitting requests to be discharged to "feed" (*opustit' pokormit'sia*).[179] The burden of collecting tolls, tavern revenues, internal tariff duties, and levies such as the salt tax was taken from the servicemen and their peasants and given to the *gosti*.[180] The approximately one thousand clerks in the provinces working for the *voevody* were mainly an hereditary caste also, as in the center. New clerks were hired from among literate cossacks.[181] Thus the middle service class had little leverage even in the provincial bureaucracy and was not essential to the government for its maintenance. As they were not yet a privileged gentry content to live and rule outside the capital, they did not provide the type of stability in the provinces which one would expect from a gentry class.[182]

The role of the *dvoriane* and *deti boiarskie* in minor provincial administration is not clear. The *guba* "elders" continued to be elected, with increasing interference by Moscow, by all classes from among the members of the middle service class when they were available. The lesser *guba* officials were elected from the other categories of the populace, including the peasants.[183] Presumably the *deti boiarskie* did play some role in what was left of the *guba* administration's police work, although the government sometimes drafted them into the army if it felt the need.[184] This would indicate that the government placed minimum priority on *guba* service. The role of lords in minor judicial matters increased in the seventeenth century as peasants became more and more equated with slaves.

71

Members of the middle service class retained only a marginal role in provincial administration. Initially they had served at court and only had service land grants in the countryside. Later, when they moved into the countryside after having been given control of their service landholdings, they themselves were subject largely to the jurisdiction of central chancelleries and chancellery agents in the provinces. The pre-Soviet scholar S. A. Shumakov properly noted that this was one of the major causes of the hypertrophy of the central power at the expense of local government.[185] The influential middle service class was hardly involved in or concerned by provincial institutions, and in fact wanted to escape them, so these institutions withered away and Moscow stepped into the vacuum. The *guba* system became subordinated to the *voevoda* system and to the bureaucrats answerable to the *voevoda* who were sent out from Moscow.[186] The *guba* system was liquidated in 1679.[187]

The evidence on the function of the members of the middle service class in the tax-collecting system is contradictory: did or did they not collect the state taxes from their peasants? In general most peasants in a tax jurisdiction (*sokha*) apportioned the taxes among themselves and then collected them. They turned the revenues over to state agents. Where the lord had a hand in the matter, he was rendering a service which could have been dispensed with readily.[188] The conclusion to be drawn is that the *dvoriane* and *deti boiarskie* performed few extra-military services which were indispensable to the government.

In spite of some setbacks, the middle service class ultimately triumphed. This victory was most evident at the 1648–49 Assembly of the Land.[189] At the request of the members of the middle service class, much of what they considered the burden of local administration was removed from their shoulders. They became something of a closed military caste with many privileges. They could travel relatively freely in Russia.[190] Their service lands became hereditary. And the peasants were enserfed, which was the most important of the privileges garnered by the middle service class. In short, the middle service class in the period between the Time of Troubles and the beginning of the war with Poland for the Dnepr basin in 1654 attained a vast number of concessions and were left with no responsibilities other than the rendering of military service. The *Ulozhenie* of 1649 recognized that the provincial *dvoriane* and *deti boiarskie* did not even have to do that, but could send replacements while they busied themselves with personal matters in Moscow or in the provinces.[191] The process of converting a service class into a wellborn, privileged caste was well on its way to completion.[192]

This rise in position of the *dvoriane* and *deti boiarskie* was a complex phenomenon. Much of the rise followed in the wake of the declining position of the peasantry, and in fact contributed crucially to that decline. Part of the rise involved a reluctant sharing by the magnates of perquisites which had at one time been solely theirs. In the sixteenth century much of the improved status of the middle service class was the product of state necessity, but the era of the Time of Troubles revealed that the cavalry force created by the state power had become an entity which could demand further privileges. Nearly all of the improvement of the position of the middle service class was achieved either by its members individually or as a group consciously pressuring the relatively weak government for concessions. The unprecedented venality of the parvenus running the government—the "strong people"—polarized relations between the middle service class and the magnates,—creating a broad chasm between their interests. This made relations between government and servicemen more openly combative than had been the case in the sixteenth century.[193] In the sixteenth century the seven-hundred-year-old dynasty was sure of itself and was less susceptible to outside pressure than was the fledgling Romanov group after 1613, a group whose very legitimacy was occasionally questioned.

The middle service class did not achieve all its demands because it was not always homogeneous and united. The members' usual state of mind was one of mutual suspicion and enmity brought on by constant law suits and denunciations (which were encouraged by the government) in a frantic search for inhabited land.[194] The situation was aggravated by the fact that the middle service class had no power base or source of sustenance of its own. Its members relied totally on their service lands, which the government could take away from troublesome individuals. These lands, moreover, were fragmented parcels assigned to servicemen on a random basis. Under such conditions the formation of strong local corporate associations able to exert continuous pressure or restraint on the central power was unlikely. What was even worse, the government, at least in theory, was able to force small groups to guarantee the proper conduct of individuals (the *krugovaia poruka*).[195] Had the government been faced by a united group of over twenty-five thousand cavalrymen, it is difficult to conceive that the "strong people" could have had as much leeway as they did.

There is an additional factor to consider. As shown in detail in chapters 11 and 12, the military service which the members of the middle service class were capable of rendering by the 1640s was becoming obsolete. The *dvoriane* and *deti boiarskie* were nearly an anachronism,

73

and the government was highly conscious of this fact. By the end of the 1650s, this class no longer formed the major part of the military forces of the Muscovite state.

The government reacted to this state of affairs as might be expected: it ignored many of the laments of the middle service class. Only under intense pressure, such as the circumstances leading to the consummation of the enserfment of the peasantry in 1648–49, did the magnates reluctantly grant concessions. Later on they began to treat the *deti boiarskie* and *dvoriane* more high-handedly. The government ignored their petitions for the return of fugitive serfs and frequently allowed runaways to remain on the frontier or in the towns. Addressing these servicemen in a tone which would have been unthinkable in the first half of the seventeenth century, the government told them to join the new-type army units or be reduced to peasants.

Nevertheless, in spite of everything, the middle service class retained its privileges. This apparent paradox will be discussed in chapter 14.

Part II

The Enserfment of the
Russian Peasantry

4.

The Introduction of
St. George's Day

Russian peasants were not bound to the land or significantly restricted in their mobility in any way until the reign of Great Prince Vasilii Vasilevich II (1425–62). Until that time there had been no legal prohibition on moving by peasants anywhere, but simply attempts to direct peasant movement "by a definite system of financial stimuli and sanctions."[1]

This is not to say that life was very enjoyable for the average Russian peasant prior to the reign of Vasilii II. It was a short life, about thirty years.[2] It was hard, both because of natural conditions on the East European plain and because of constant enemy attack and plundering by governmental agents.[3] Life also was brutal, and any peasant living on seigneurial lands indubitably had to defer to his landlord. Furthermore, he occasionally had to endure crude exploitation, was charged more than customary or contract rent, and received general abuse.[4] In some cases he was subject to the judicial authority of his landlord.[5] Peasant status and social position were decidedly inferior.

In spite of these factors, the peasant was a free man, in no way bound to a particular class or caste. If conditions did not please him, he could move on. He could even leave his agricultural occupation to become a merchant or artisan, a priest, or a military retainer. These possibilities certainly must have limited caprice by any landowner or official, for unusual abuse would simply cause the peasant to use his right of departure. Labor was scarce, and someone else always would welcome him. He could even farm land belonging to no lord, if he chose to assume the risks, and thus all the means of production could be directly under his personal control. Because of all of these factors the peasant, while of low status, was in every sense free, and in no telling sense was he degraded by being a serf.

In a discussion of the development of serfdom we must bear in mind the size of Muscovy and the equally important sparseness of population. While Rus' was fragmented into many principalities, escaping notice in any particular one would have been difficult for a fugitive peasant; however, a labor-short independent jurisdiction was usually near at hand. But as Moscow gathered the Russian lands, the political refuges for a potential fugitive disappeared; correspondingly the places where he could hide "at home" increased. The Muscovite government, as it came to control an ever-enlarging area, was continuously faced with the task of developing an apparatus and techniques to locate the populace when its support was needed.[6] Foreigners at the end of the seventeenth century marvelled at the centralized government's ability to keep track of its subjects.[7] Nevertheless any really persevering individual, simply by moving elsewhere, could have escaped detection nearly as easily in the middle of the seventeenth century as in the middle of the fourteenth century.[8]

Estimates of the population of Muscovy have varied widely, from two to sixteen millions in the post-Mongol era.[9] For our purposes the exact figures are relatively unimportant. What is crucial is the very low density, which meant that labor was always scarce throughout the quarter of a millennium under review.[10] The scramble for this scarce resource is the major theme in the history of the enserfment of the Russian peasantry.

The enserfment was a political phenomenon as well as a response to economic problems, so an examination of the political circumstances of each cumulative stage is essential for an understanding of the process. The origins of Russian serfdom may be traced to the second quarter of the fifteenth century. When the period began all peasants could and did move freely.[11] However, the reign of ten-year-old Vasilii II opened inauspiciously in 1425 with a serious epidemic, after a three-year famine, both of which reduced the population.[12] There followed, from 1425 to 1432, a relatively insignificant civil war between the boyar government ruling in the name of Vasilii and Vasilii's uncle, Iurii Dmitrievich, prince of Zvenigorod and Galich. Iurii could claim the throne after the death of his brother Vasilii Dmitrievich I on the basis of the perhaps historically obsolete principle of lateral succession. Furthermore, his father, Dmitrii Donskoi, not foreseeing heirs issuing from his oldest son Vasilii I, had stated in his will that the succession should pass to the next son after the death of Vasilii I.[13] The conflict between Vasilii II and Iurii Dmitrievich ended with a truce at the Horde; and the pretexts for civil war logically should have ended with the uncle's death in 1434. According to tradition, the succession had to pass to the oldest son of the oldest brother—in this case Vasilii II.[14]

In 1433 Vasilii II was married to Maria Iaroslavna, sister of Prince Vasilii Iaroslavich of Serpukhov-Brovsk. Among the guests at the marriage ceremony was Vasilii Iur'evich (later Kosoi), cousin of Vasilii II and son of Iurii Dmitrievich. Unfortunately for the future of Russia, Vasilii Iur'evich (Shemiaka) wore at the wedding a golden belt studded with precious stones. According to the fable reported in the chronicle, the belt had been given to Dmitrii Donskoi at his wedding in 1366 as a dowry by his father-in-law, the Suzdal'-Nizhegorod Prince Dmitrii Konstantinovich. Some considered the belt to be part of the great princely regalia. At the 1366 wedding the last Moscow chiliarch (*tysiatskii*), Vasilii Vel'iaminov, had stolen the belt and given it to his son Mikula. Mikula Vel'iaminov in turn had given the belt to I. D. Vsevolozhskii, an "old boyar" opponent of centralization who was embittered by Vasilii II's failure to keep his promise to marry his daughter.[15] He was the one who supposedly passed the fateful object on to Prince Vasilii Iur'evich.[16]

During the 1433 festivities the mother-regent, dowager great princess Sofia Vitovtovna, who was responsible for her son jilting Vsevolozhskii's daughter in favor of Maria Iaroslavna, responded to a provocation arranged by the "old boyar" and caused a scandal by taking the belt from Vasilii Iur'evich.[17] He and his brother Dmitrii Shemiaka, both of whom at the time of the wedding were estranged from their father and opposed his violent efforts to seize the throne, were enraged by the scandal and resolved to take revenge by reopening the civil war. In so doing they broke the truce, which was still on, as signified by the brothers' attendance at the wedding. This began a new stage of the civil war, and, had the belt incident not occurred, the civil war might not have been reopened after the legitimate claimant to the throne, Iurii, died in 1434.[18]

After the belt incident, Vasilii Iur'evich and Dmitrii Shemiaka defeated the sluggish Vasilii II, became accustomed to the idea that the Moscow throne could be captured in war, and thereby began a long and bloody struggle for the throne. Iurii's sons had no legitimate claim at all,[19] and the only reason the civil war lasted almost until Dmitrii Shemiaka's death in 1453 was that the rivals knew, after the belt episode, that the great prince was weak, a poor general, and could be toppled without too much effort. (Unfortunately, however, neither Vasilii Iur'evich nor Shemiaka could hold the throne.)

During the civil war the rival armies (often only bands of several hundred men), assisted by raiding Tatars and Lithuanians, destroyed much of Russia as they pursued one another across the country. Tribute and tax collectors took much of what was left or spared by the armies, fires, and droughts. The property loss and population dislocation were enormous,[20] and those parties with a vested interest in stability took measures in cooperation with the state power to hold together and to restore their economies.[21]

One of the major economic forces in Russia in the fifteenth century was the ever-expanding network of monasteries. During the Kievan period the typical monastery was not an economic behemoth, but an urban center of spiritual retreat. About the middle of the fourteenth century, the monasteries moved into the countryside, altered their structure from idiorhythmic to cenobitic, and became thriving economic enterprises.[22] New monasteries were usually begun with the aid of hired labor, then the laborers often became monks, or monks took over their tasks. Most of the monasteries annexed peasant lands by force or attracted peasants to work on the estates.[23] The monasteries were responsible for some of the intensive breaking in of new land which occurred in northeastern Rus' in the fourteenth and fifteenth centuries.[24] However, as I. U. Budovnits has shown, the monasteries were not the great colonizers some historians assumed they were; the cenobitic institutions often were simply content to expropriate lands which had already been developed by free peasants.[25] By the time of the civil war these institutions were in the process of becoming economic giants with vast landholdings, acquired by donation and purchase, throughout the Muscovite state.[26] Both sides in the civil war sought support from the monasteries, and the monasteries in turn exerted maximum pressure on the authorities for privileges which would enable them to restore their devastated estates.[27]

It is by no means accidental that the surviving records portray the initiation of serfdom in Russia as resulting from governmental grants to monasteries. During the reign of Vasilii II there was no other institution or group which would have been influential enough or interested in limiting labor mobility besides the large monasteries.[28] The lay magnates, enjoying the right of free service in the sundry political jurisdictions of Russia, derived at least as much revenue from high posts in the central government and in the "feeding" (*kormlenie*) system of provincial administration as from revenues from their own estates.[29] The "free servitors" (*slugi vol'nye*) were paid for military service with incomes from second-level, lower administrative-judicial posts.[30] Both the magnates and the free servitors could be given posts wherever there was a population (which was likely to be where security existed) and so were probably relatively unconcerned about movements within a principality. As has been noted, attempts to control mobility among principalities generally failed. Reflecting the Kievan tradition of the prince moving with his retinue from one town to another, service was divorced from land-ownership, even though a prince might give out lands to loyal court servants.[31] Prior to the consolidation of the centralized Russian state by Moscow, many persons served in one principality, yet had land in another. Service was purely personal. The only exception to this rule occurred when a town was under siege: then all lords in the principality were obliged to render aid to the prince to lift the siege.[32] The rank-and-file cavalrymen were not in a position to ask for a limitation of peasant mobility, as they did later, because they did not have lands; they lived at or near a prince's court, subsisting on what the prince paid them plus what they could plunder.[33] Thus, while influential laymen were at best only secondarily interested in populated land, there is abundant evidence that the monasteries were extremely concerned about their peasant labor force.[34]

The first known restriction of peasant mobility was made by the Muscovite Great Prince Vasilii Vasil'evich some time between 1455 and 1462, when he granted the Troitse Sergiev monastery both the right to prevent long-time residents (*starozhil'tsy*) on its estates in Bezhetskii Verkh and Uglich from moving elsewhere, and the right to recover those who had moved.[35] These were unquestionably the wealthier peasants who had fled or might flee because of the unsettled conditions of the area. They were the established inhabitants of the region, the type whose testimony was highly valued in court, the individuals capable of paying rent to the monastery treasury.[36] The rights granted by Vasilii were isolated, extreme measures, a unique favor granted to one institution, reflecting the personal desire of Vasilii to strengthen his favorite religious institution.[37] He must have felt that he had to compete with his rival, Prince Dmitrii Iur'evich Shemiaka of Uglich, who had attempted to woo the same institution with lucrative grants.[38] The Bezhetskii Verkh grant was probably made to assure support for Vasilii in a strategic location between Novgorod and Moscow. The estate to which the grant applied had belonged to Iurii Dmitrievich before his death and had been given by him to the monastery in 1440. The Bezhetskii Verkh principality itself recently had been confiscated by the Muscovite great prince Vasilii II from its ruler.[39] The other extraordinary grant was in Uglich, another civil war battleground, where Vasilii II was sent into exile by Shemiaka after being blinded and reproached for bringing the Tatars into Russia. Shemiaka had held Uglich from the mid-1430s as a gift from Vasilii until he was driven out by the latter's forces in 1447. In 1447 Vasilii exempted the long-time residents of the monastery's Uglich properties from taxes for five years, and any former long-time residents who would come back (*prishlye liudi starozhil'tsy*—or this may mean residents from the monastery's other villages) for seven years. This implies that free movement was possible, that the old system of privileges was being used to encourage some to stay, others to come.[40] Vasilii sent his family to Uglich for protection during the 1451 Tatar attack on Moscow.[41] He probably gave the monastery the grant in gratitude for past services and to ensure loyal support from the area in the future.[42] This step was of great importance in that it initiated the legal enserfment of the peasantry, a step taken by the state power at the request of a particular monastery which was to become the wealthiest in all Rus' by the time all the peasants had become enserfed in 1649.

The far more important step of limiting the right of peasants to move at only one time of year—which did not of itself enserf the peasantry—was also taken at the request of some of the monasteries. This involved limiting the right of peasants to move to a certain period in the autumn after the harvest, St. George's Day (*Iur'ev Den'*), November 26.[43] Unfortunately the documents which survive are not dated accurately enough to determine exactly when and where this process began.[44] The recent consensus has been that the introduction of *Iur'ev Den'* was the result of petitions by the elders of two Beloozero monasteries (Kirillov, which was to become one of the largest in Russia, and Ferapontov, both founded in the 1390s, about 300 miles north of Moscow) to the appanage prince of Beloozero-Vereia, Mikhail Andreevich, in the years 1448–70.[45]

The cause for the granting of these two documents is not difficult to ascertain. Mikhail Andreevich was a faithful ally of Vasilii II in the civil war and possibly made the grants at the behest of the great prince. Vasilii spent time in 1446 and 1447 in both monasteries gaining support from the monks. At a time when much of the church establishment was opposed to Vasilii II, Hegumen Trifon of the Kirillov monastery of Beloozero absolved him from his oath of allegiance to Dmitrii Shemiaka before Vasilii attacked Dmitrii and retook Moscow in February, 1447. In addition, this area had suffered enormous economic dislocation during the period of civil strife.[46]

Both grants can be seen as payoffs for civil-war support with the goal of helping damaged economies by limiting peasant mobility to the period after the harvest. One of these grants concerned only debtors, and was an attempt to limit the right of peasants in debt to move at a time when the loan could be collected; the aim was to force them to pay their debts before moving.[47] (State intervention in lord-peasant debt relationships was an old custom in Russia. According to the expanded version of the *Russkaia Pravda,* article 56, the peasant debtor, the *roleinyi zakup,* became the slave of his lord if he left without paying off a loan. By the fifteenth century the custom was less severe. Sometimes the indebted peasant was returned to his lord until he paid off the loan, sometimes he was given two years to pay it off without interest; but he was not enslaved.) [48] The other decree limited moves by peasants who were not debtors, but definitely did not limit all such peasants.[49] After these decrees, according to the prevailing interpretation, the institution of St. George's Day spread to Muscovy and was applied there to all monastery peasants. Finally, this became a general law for all peasants of the Muscovite state in the law code (Sudebnik) of 1497.[50]

A recent, thorough analysis of these eight documents on the initiation of the St. George's Day mobility limitations by the Moscow University medievalist A. D. Gorskii indicates that the process may have begun in the center and then spread to the periphery of the Muscovite state.[51] Great Prince Vasilii II in the period 1448–62 issued more general documents restricting the right of peasants to move to the Iur'ev Den' period. Those issued by him to the Kirillov monastery at Beloozero, doubtless out of gratitude for the services rendered by Trifon and the monks in 1446–47, hint that the institution of Iur'ev Den' was well known and needed no elaboration.[52] Gorskii supposes that the limitation was first introduced in the center, then was extended by Vasilii II to the possessions of the Kirillov monastery. From here the practice of limiting peasant mobility was borrowed by Mikhail Andreevich.[53] The Beloozero grant of Vasilii II was confirmed twice, in slightly different versions, by his son Andrei Vasil'evich of Vologda.[54] Vasilii's successor, Ivan III (1462–1505), issued several decrees (still extant) for the benefit of the Troitse Sergiev monastery on St. George's Day, each more general than the last. He also added sanctions for flight: the peasant who moved illegally could be returned (as in the Uglich grant by Vasilii mentioned earlier). Once he furnished a state official to help the monastery locate and return its peasants.[55] He established the two-week moving period, one week before and one after St. George's Day, which was to become customary in Russia for the next century. The explicit reasons behind these resolutions of the conflict over the available labor supply in favor of the monastery are not evident, but the documents are consistent with the tendency of the Muscovite princes to aid this powerful institution when called upon to do so.

In a grant (1488–90) concerning the peasants of the Kirillov monastery of Beloozero, Ivan introduced the concept of vyvoz: the debts of a peasant could be paid off by another lord and the debtor moved (the issue of consent was not raised) only during the appointed St. George's Day time limit.[56] It is clear that in the 1470s peasants who were covered by such writs and who took loans had to repay them before they could move. They might be forcibly returned for failure to heed the edicts, but other peasants in the Moscow and Novgorod areas were not bound and could move freely at any time.[57]

On the basis of the evidence now available it is safe to conclude that St. George's Day, the first significant limitation on peasant mobility in Russian history, was introduced during the reign of Vasilii II as a result of labor dislocation caused by the civil war. Arms alone could not resolve the issue. Therefore each side wooed some of the most important monasteries for support. Given the relatively primitive nature of Russia, there were few privileges the contesting forces could offer to supporters. Vasilii II's side struck on the seemingly innocuous device of permitting a few of its supporters to regulate the mobility of their labor force. These grants initiated the enserfment of the Russian peasantry.

The St. George's Day rule became general for all the peasants in the Muscovite state after its codification in the *Sudebnik* of 1497. The right to move was also made contingent upon the payment of a small rent fee. It is well to remember that at least until 1497 there was no universal restriction on mobility for the peasants in Russia, for a 1496 treaty between the two princes of Riazan' equated peasants with people of the upper classes who still had the right to move.[58] Why this limitation was made universally applicable to all peasants in 1497 has never been satisfactorily explained. There seems to have been no noticeable economic dislocation or other turmoil at this time, as there usually was preceding other major steps in the enserfment of the peasantry.

The point has been made that the St. George's Day rule became universal during the reign of Ivan III as a result of the creation of the service land (*pomest'e*) system to support the greatly enlarged army of the now consolidated Muscovite state.[59] It is clear that this could not have happened much before the compilation of the *Sudebnik* of 1497 because the *pomest'e* system was new (Ivan III made massive grants in the years 1484–89). At an earlier time a disgruntled peasant who did not like his current location simply could have fled to another labor-short political jurisdiction where he would have been gratefully received.[60] The consolidation of old Rus' around Moscow made it much more difficult to attain "freedom" by moving to Lithuania.

But how the limitation of peasant mobility could have benefited a member of the middle service class, the service landholder (the *pomeshchik*), after the introduction of the *pomest'e* system, is hard to comprehend.[61] The *pomeshchik* did not have control over the lands (usually parts of widely scattered villages) assigned to him for income, so his personal interest in the peasants on these lands was limited or nonexistent. The traditional dues continued to be collected from the lands confiscated for *pomest'ia* at the time of the *Sudebnik,* so there was no reason for the peasants to flee or for the state to fear that they might.[62]

It is also difficult to imagine that a phenomenon such as the new *pomest'e* system, limited at the time almost exclusively to newly annexed regions, could have had such an immediate and powerful impact on a central government law code. It is possible that the collectors of the dues from the new service lands decided that it was expedient to allow the peasants to move only at one time of the year, immediately after the harvest, so that no one could escape payment of dues and taxes.[63] There is no evidence, however, as there is in abundance for later Muscovite history, that the new military servitor class exerted pressure to force Ivan III to codify restrictions on peasant mobility.

St. George's Day may have been codified in the *Sudebnik* simply because the experience of the large monasteries was found useful for everyone. We do not even know that the peasants objected to being allowed to move at only one time of year.[64] In fact, many peasants continued to move whenever they felt like it, and usually without any difficulty.[65] A number of pre-Soviet historians, including V. O. Kliuchevskii, ascribed the St. George's Day restriction to the "condition of agrarian industry"; it was simply rational to restrict peasants' moving to the time after the harvest had been gathered.[66] Unfortunately there is no evidence to support the further belief of these historians that the intent of the law was to prevent lords from evicting peasants.[67]

The universal restriction on all Russian peasants also might be related to the general economic and population upsurge during the reign of Ivan III, and the rise in the demand for agricultural products as the result of the recovery from the earlier civil war and the end of civil strife in the consolidated Muscovite state.[68] The general good times lasted through the 1550s. One sign was the use of the three-field system (a rotation of winter, summer, and fallow fields) beginning in the 1460s. This use suggests considerable population pressure on the land, with a need for limiting the extremely wasteful assartage (*podseka*) system of agriculture which was inherited from much earlier times and was only significantly limited in Ivan III's reign.[69] With an expansion of the market for agricultural commodities, lords of any sort might well have demanded a limitation on peasant mobility to ensure a regular flow of agricultural commodities, as certainly happened in Poland at this time.[70]

In addition to being deprived of the right to move whenever he pleased, the peasant was required to pay a rent fee to his lord upon departure. The fee was 25 kopeks if he lived on the lord's land a year, prorated up to a ruble if he lived there four years or more.[71] The rent fee was probably prescribed because the peasant who settled on a lord's land was usually exempted from rent or taxes for a term of three or four years.[72] After the expiration of the exemption—about the time it took to exhaust the natural fertility of the soil—the shrewd peasant undoubtedly considered moving on.[73] This would mean that the lord would get no rent at all, and might even be out of pocket had he paid the peasant's taxes, which might be assessed by the government regardless of any arrangements between the lord and peasant. In order to forestall this, the government forced the peasant to pay the rent and taxes before moving.

Cash rent at this time was about 25 kopeks a year.[74] In Novgorod it was 25 kopeks on court land and 17½ kopeks on peasant ("black") lands.[75] The sum of 25 kopeks makes sense in other terms as well. About one-half of the outstanding loans (326 of 670) which the Troitse Sergiev monastery granted its peasants in the year 1532–33 were for 25 kopeks. Another 190 of the loans were for 50 kopeks. Most of the others were for various sums in this general range.[76] The price rise in this period is disputed, but the moving fees remained the same as long as peasant mobility was considered legal by the state power.[77] Therefore paying the fee should have been easier as the century progressed. Even as late as 1615 a peasant settlement contract prescribed a rent of 25 kopeks per year to be paid the monastery owning the land.[78]

I doubt whether the prescribed rent fee was deliberately set at some artificially high, unrealistic, and unpayable level with an eye specifically to detaining the peasant, as is often claimed.[79] If a lord wanted to deny his peasant the right to move, he illegally raised the moving fee to 5 or 10 rubles, as was done in a 1555 case. The government believed that this really denied the peasant his right to move.[80] Had a sum between 25 kopeks and a ruble been a genuine obstacle to moving, no one would have bothered to raise the fee five to forty times the legal amount except as a means of detaining peasants. Finally, peasants could and did pay the moving fee.[81]

Much has been made of the notion that the time selected for moving was disadvantageous and chosen to discourage mobility. Actually the contrary is true, for the period around St. George's Day (November 26) was the best time to move, particularly before the triumph of the three-field system: after the harvest and threshing, immediately after the ground had frozen, the time facilitated travel all over Rus'.[82] St. George was considered by Orthodox Russians to be in charge of the whole growing season, which came between his two holidays, April 23 and November 26.[83] The date chosen for free mobility was in the popular mind the most auspicious time to move—the end of the agricultural season—and was by no means a time to detain the peasant.

Why St. George's Day was universalized in 1497 is a question which could be studied further, but a definitive answer probably is unattainable. The records which might have provided the answer certainly have perished. The most satisfactory answer may be that, in a period of relative prosperity and lingering population shortage, a consensus developed among all landlords that potentially destructive competition for labor should be curtailed by discouraging peasants from moving to another estate after they had lived out the rent-free period which had induced them to settle. This limitation clearly was effected by permitting the peasant to move only after his crop was in and forcing him to part with some of it in the form of the rent payment to compensate for the exemption. This may have resulted in effectively limiting peasant mobility. Be that as it may, the *Sudebnik* of 1497 did not enserf the peasants, but only limited their right to move to one two-week period of the year—the first stage in the enserfment of the peasantry.

The *Sudebnik* of 1550 repeated the provisions of the *Sudebnik* of 1497 that allowed peasants to relocate during the two-week St. George's Day period after paying taxes and the "rent" fee.[84] An interesting clause allowing a peasant who moved to return later to harvest the winter crop was added, reflecting the general change to the three-field system of agriculture; the peasant who moved around November 26 would have already planted his winter crop.[85] The provisions of the *Sudebnik* meant that the peasant was by no means completely enserfed, for he could move to black lands, state or court lands, or seignorial lands if he felt so inclined. There is no doubt that many peasants were moving freely about Russia throughout the first two-thirds of the sixteenth century and that the government, by intervening relatively impartially in the contest for the supply of labor, took measures to ensure this right.[86]

No basic changes were enacted into the law because the demand for labor was fairly well satisfied in what was a general period of prosperity.[87] The Austrian diplomat Baron von Herberstein, in his trips through Russia in the reign of Vasilii III (1505–33), noted a density of population and well-being characteristic of only the best times in Russian history.[88] In 1526 the Russian ambassador to the Pope, one Dmitrii Gerasimov, wrote a Bishop Iovii that the huge town of Moscow lay "in a most populous country."[89] The same was observed by the English travelers Richard Chancellor, Anthony Jenkinson, and Sir Thomas Randolph in the 1550s and even into the 1560s.[90] The available Russian demographic evidence would tend to support the foreigners' views that the population was increasing, at the rate of about 1 percent per year.[91]

The causes and dimensions of this economic upsurge have been well documented by the Soviet historian D. P. Makovskii.[92] Significant factors, which will be simply enumerated here, were demand generated by the gunpowder revolution (see chapter 9 below) ;[93] the rapid growth of towns;[94] the development of urban manufacture divorced from agriculture;[95] rudimentary regional agricultural specialization;[96] the production of religious items to equip the ever-increasing number of churches and monasteries;[97] the removal of many internal customs barriers and the institution of a single system of weights, measures, and coinage (in 1535) by the unified Muscovite state;[98] a favorable legal and social climate (with a minimum of forced labor) ;[99] the curtailment of highway robbery;[100] a booming internal trade;[101] a large and growing foreign trade with both the Occident and Orient;[102] the absence of restrictive monopolistic guilds and corporations which might have curtailed trade and industry;[103] significant capital accumulation which, however, was much too frequently invested in land;[104] and a large supply of available cheap labor.[105] These were the reasons behind the absence of much progress in the enserfment of the peasantry between the law codes of 1497 and 1550.[106]

The *Sudebnik* of 1550 did not specify what should occur when a peasant moved illegally, without paying the taxes and rent, or at the improper time. Practice, borrowed from the institution of slavery, indicates, however, that the lord had to locate his peasant, sue for his return, get a government police agent (*pristav*) to bring the peasant to trial, and then bring back the peasant if the case was won.[107] The rent fee specified in the code prevented peasants unable to pay it from moving legally of their own volition (*vykhod*).. As noted earlier, this fee probably represented the true value of a year's rent. It did not remove the possibility of another lord's paying the fees (*vyvoz*) and certainly did not abolish the right to relocate.[108] The more important thing was that the government was becoming accustomed to the idea that it had the power and the right to limit peasant mobility.

This fact is illustrated in two extraordinary documents promulgated in 1552. After a crime wave—coupled with depredations by governmental agents—had caused a dispersion of the local population, Ivan IV's government issued to peasants in the Dvina basin local government charters removing the agents of the central government, who were to be replaced by officials elected by the citizens of the region. The documents also permitted the recipients of the charters to return without any time limit and without paying any fees (*bezsrochno* and *bezposhlinno*) peasants who had fled during the breakdown of authority. Many of the peasants had moved to monastery lands, which probably were to some degree outside the jurisdiction of the barbarous state officials. One charter was granted to the populace of the Vaga district, in and around the towns of Shenkur'e (Shenkursk) and Vel'sk on the

Vaga River between Vologda and Arkhangel'sk.[109] The other was given to the inhabitants of Malaia Penezhka, Vyia, and Sura of the Dvina district, adjacent on the northeast to the Vaga district, on the other side of the Northern Dvina River.[110] Both were special documents promulgated because of the peculiar circumstances of the districts in question.[111] In this respect they resemble the two documents Vasilii II gave a century earlier to the Troitse Sergiev monastery because of its difficulties. They represent nothing more, however, and were temporary decrees which consciously violated the norms of the *Sudebnik*.[112] They did not represent any change in the overall policy of the Muscovite government on the peasant question for the rest of the country.[113]

A very important factor in addition to the time limit for the recovery of fugitives was the legal control the lord had over the person of the peasant living on his lands. As noted in chapter 1 above, when this control was very strict the peasant living under such a regime might be considered a serf.[114] In the Mongol period lords holding immunity charters had complete judicial and administrative powers over their peasants.[115] In exchange for these privileges, as well as exemption from taxes, the church, particularly, did little to oppose the Mongol-Tatar hegemony. With the consolidation of the Muscovite state, these powers and immunities were gradually reduced. Ivan III limited taxation immunities, issuing them regularly only up to 1480. Very few new ones were issued in the 1480s, and not one is extant for the period 1491–1505. The old ones remained in effect until the compilation of the land cadastres in the second half of Ivan's reign, after which the immunity holders lost most of their exemptions.[116] Judicial immunities were also limited simultaneously. At first the state reserved murder cases for itself. In time it claimed jurisdiction over other felonies, such as robbery, then theft.[117] Monastery hegumens, when sued, were made subject to the prince's court, rather than the metropolitan's.[118] Although some monasteries continued to enjoy immunities until the time of Peter the Great,[119] most of the documents specifying even the major monasteries' privileges were either confiscated completely or greatly reduced in competence in the middle of the sixteenth century.

In his monumental studies of the immunities granted in the period 1492–1548, S. M. Kashtanov analyzed 650 documents. He showed the gradual limiting of privileges throughout the first third of the sixteenth century (particularly after the 1503 attempt to secularize church lands). This was followed by a flood of grants during Ivan IV's minority (particularly to church establishments in the 1540s), which was curtailed once Ivan and his "Selected Council" (*Izbrannaia Rada*) assumed power in 1547; the curtailment culminated in the repeal of tax exemptions by the 1550 *Sudebnik.*[120] (The repeal came only after a series of grants had been made in the central region and Novgorod area to magnates who had aided in the repression of the 1547 rioters.) [121]

Kashtanov had at his disposal only charters issued to great church institutions (usually monasteries) and to petty members of the middle service class on the frontier.[122] No others are extant, and there is a dispute in Soviet historiography as to whether immunity grants to lay magnates do not survive because the documents have perished, or because such favors were never promulgated. The argument that grants to lay magnates do not survive by a quirk of fate is quite persuasive, for the archives of the Moscow and provincial chancelleries, and also those of the lay magnates, have not come down to us, while the archives of some of the monasteries have.[123] It is conceivable that one might "not doubt that great lay lords actually did possess immunity rights and privileges."[124] But it is hard to make a further assumption, as some scholars have, that documents fixing these privileges never existed because lay lords automatically had judicial, administrative, and fiscal powers within their properties which did not need royal sanction.[125] While this may have occurred elsewhere in Europe, it hardly could have been the case in Russia.

The governments of Ivan III, Vasilii III, and Ivan IV did not always make distinctions between church and lay lands. Ivan the Great confiscated church as well as lay lands in Novgorod, and Ivan the Terrible limited monastery acquisitions and unceremoniously exchanged monastery as well as lay lands. The major difference between church and lay land-ownership in this period seems to have been that most church lands were less alienable than civil ones, and the lords of the former had more privileges than those of the latter. Parties holding immunities were zealous to have them confirmed by each new sovereign precisely because they knew that these were privileges which could be (and sometimes were) withdrawn,[126] not because the privileges were mere verbiage setting out rights all landowners enjoyed automatically anyway.[127] Also, unconfirmed privileges lapsed.[128]

For this reason Kashtanov's methodology of analyzing the reasons behind the specific instances of the issuing of the immunity privileges is appropriate—for privileges they were indeed.[129] The Muscovite government was hardly in the habit of confirming the obvious. The situation was comparable to the issuance of the St. George's Day restrictive privileges to selected monasteries in the fifteenth century. The issuing of selective grants was one of the major tools for implementing policy at the disposal of the rulers of Muscovy, and it is clear they made the best use they could of it. The institution of St. George's Day was generalized for all by the *Sudebnik* of 1497. Whether a parallel situation evolved whereby all lords were granted judicial powers over their peasants will be discussed below. There is a major historiographical controversy over what happened after the immunities were cancelled. One school holds that no more judicial immunity charters were issued because the rights contained in them had become customary. The other school claims that the state picked up the charters because it was deliberately limiting the power of the lords once the power of the state had been consolidated; thus the rights formerly possessed by the owner of the immunity charter ceased to exist.[130]

The latter argument is the more convincing. Only the larger church landowners and a few select service landholders ever had immunity charters, and those were gradually limited. (While lay magnates occasionally may have possessed immunities, it is certain that they derived most of their income from government posts and war plunder rather than from peasant agriculture, the sphere in which immunities were profitable.) No immunity charters seem to have been granted to lay lords after 1554. It makes little sense to assume that a government bent on eliminating political fragmentation would give the juridical expression of fragmentation, direct control over citizens, to every petty landowner and return this control to former rulers of independent principalities or their heirs.[131]

The history of sixteenth-century administrative developments, both central and provincial, speaks of increasing direct government contact with all citizens. The development of local institutions under the direction of the state power in the middle third of the century (the *guba* and *zemskii* institutions) recognized the complete citizenship of all free peasants.[132] Even as late as the 1590s communes with their own elective officials (*sotskie*) continued to exist on some seignorial lands.[133] Finally, each immunity charter which still existed (and every customary right a lord may have had over his peasant) contained an implicit self-denying ordinance. Until the state bound the peasant to the land and was willing to enforce such a stricture, no lord who was unwilling to contemplate the loss of his labor force would dare abuse his peasant excessively, for he knew that the victim could (and probably would) simply move somewhere else. Given this fact, the immunity provided the lord with very little extra-economic compulsion over the peasants living on his lands. The lord valued an immunity document, not because it enabled him to make serfs out of his peasants, but because it enabled him to collect monies which otherwise would fall to the state and to entice peasants to his lands (or keep them there) with the prospect of lower rents.

91

The peasant came through the first period of the development of serfdom still a relatively free man. His right to move was restricted only slightly. The initial St. George's Day limitations were political concessions to a few cenobitic monasteries, and the restriction was probably generalized for all peasants for both political and economic reasons. The sparseness of the population, combined with the primitive level of the government, made any more restrictive measures impossible of realization. The peasant was still master of his own person, and, as the government was overcoming the political fragmentation of Russia, more peasants were becoming subject to the central authority. Although the foundations for his abasement had been laid, the peasant was not a serf as late as the 1550s.

5.

The "Forbidden Years"

The next stage of the enserfment involved the middle service class, which was expanding in size and formulating its own special interests. The centralized Muscovite state created by Ivan III needed an expanded military force to ward off attacks by neighboring Swedes, Poles, Lithuanians, Turks, and Tatars and to advance territorial ambitions. This aim was achieved by creating a mounted militia holding conditional land grants from the government and dependent for income almost entirely on the peasants who farmed these lands. Without peasants supporting them, the members of the middle service class were unable to render military service.

Unquestionably the ability of the middle service class to support itself became one of the paramount issues in the last decades of Ivan IV's reign, a time when this class's share of the land fund increased impressively.[1] Intimately linked with this issue was the question of peasant mobility. As specialists such as N. A. Rozhkov and A. A. Zimin have shown, the center of the Muscovite state was becoming more and more depopulated in the late 1560s and 1570s.[2] The economic decline and its accompanying disruption of the peasantry, a situation somewhat analogous to that in the second quarter of the fifteenth century, had many causes: Ivan's mad Oprichnina (1565–72) and its concurrent internal disorder;[3] his twenty-five year Livonian War (1558–83) ;[4] high taxes;[5] Crimean Tatar invasions, droughts, famines, plagues and epidemics;[6] debts;[7] forced labor;[8] and a rise in the level of the exploitation of the peasantry by their lords.[9] The economic progress attained earlier in the century was reversed.[10]

The contemporary German *oprichnik,* Heinrich von Staden, noted that the peasants had a tendency to move away from lands assigned to the middle service class to the estates of the lay and ecclesiastical magnates, who offered greater protection and tax privileges. Without

93

this aid, the peasants would have been completely destitute.[11] Sometimes strong lords simply kidnapped peasants (illegal *vyvoz*) to augment their labor forces.[12] Court peasants also lived considerably better than those on service lands, and undoubtedly peasants moved to take advantage of this opportunity for an easier life.[13] Some peasants became monks, since, at the time, they could not then be returned to the peasantry. Others became beggars, slaves, musketeers (*strel'tsy*), and cossacks.[14]

Ivan's conquest of the Kazan' and Astrakhan' Tatar khanates in the 1550s opened up the whole central and lower Volga region to Russian colonization.[15] Many peasants settled there when life became unpleasant in the center of the Muscovite state.[16] Some peasants moved to the Volga annexations at the urging of government agents (*sadchiki, slobodchiki*), who were instructed to help solidify the conquest by populating the region with Russians.[17] All this resulted in the movement of the population of the Muscovite state from a concentration in the Smolensk-Novgorod, Pskov-Moscow triangle to the Volga basin—a "turn to the East" which was to continue throughout the first half of the seventeenth century.[18]

Other peasants tried to escape the chaos of old Muscovy by moving directly south as the area became safer from Tatar raids after the reorganization of the frontier defense service beginning in 1571.[19] Some peasants even fled abroad, to Sweden, Livonia, Lithuania, and Poland, while others migrated to the White Sea region, the Urals, and Siberia.[20] It is clear, however, that the Russian peasant moved only when forced to by circumstances, that he was not by nature nomadic, and that he frequently remained in the same spot for generations.[21]

The extent of the crisis of the second half of Ivan's reign is by now well known, even though there is considerable disagreement about its causes. As noted by N. A. Rozhkov, the great specialist on the subject, agriculture in the last three decades of the sixteenth century in the central and northwestern areas of the Muscovite state reverted to an extensive fallow type which had disappeared in the first half of the century when population density had become considerable.[22] In the disaster areas the amount of land under cultivation per peasant household underwent a three- to five-fold decline.[23] The 1582 census of the Votskaia piatina of the Novgorod area revealed that only 15 percent of the houses were inhabited. More than 90 percent of the available arable land was not under cultivation. Ten of the fifty *pomeshchiki* registered there had fled because living in a desolate place was impossible. In the Obonezhskaia piatina only 5 percent of the houses were inhabited, with land under cultivation. Worst hit of all was the Derevskaia piatina, where only 1.5 percent of the land remained under cultivation. From 76 to 96 percent of all the settlements of Moscow province were vacant.[24]

Another sign of the chaos of this period was an extraordinarily high turnover of the population. The peasants of the Iosif Volokolamsk monastery were ordinarily very stable, but the chaos of the Oprichnina era caused a complete turnover in their number.[25] One of the major consequences of this turbulence was that population of the Muscovite state barely increased at all in the second half of the sixteenth century, in spite of the fact that the territory under Russian control nearly doubled in the same period.[26]

Another significant factor was the increasing role of slavery.[27] Prior to Ivan's Oprichnina it is clear that the institution of slavery was on the road to extinction in Russia, and was only revived by this man-made calamity.[28] A loophole inserted into article 88 of the *Sudebnik* of 1550 allowed a peasant to sell himself into slavery and leave his lord at any time without the payment of any of the fees or rent.[29] This legal situation, which was to undergo radical change within the next century, largely benefited boyars and some of the most prosperous members of the middle service class, who could thereby add to the numbers of slaves farming their estates, serving in their courts, or accompanying them on military campaigns.[30] Once the specter of hunger began to hang over the Russian countryside, vast numbers of peasants availed themselves of the right to sell themselves into slavery, a phenomenon which reached its peak in the 1580s.[31] The status of slave was not as bad as one might imagine, for, until 1679, the slave always escaped taxation legally, whereas the peasant was usually subject to taxation.[32]

As a result of these developments the members of the middle service class must have been frantic. The drop in the rent-paying population made them unable to render their required onerous military service.[33] Individual monasteries which had suffered devastation and depopulation had the old route open of seeking relief via tax exemption, which they did.[34] This was not a possibility for members of the middle service class, whose members were all suffering nearly equally and collectively in the crisis. Although records do not survive which would serve as definitive proof, one may suppose that the members of the middle service class must have demanded that the government *do something.*[35]

In 1580 Russia was in dire straits. The government was forcing the monasteries to loan it money, nearly always a signal that conditions were bad.[36] It was obvious to everyone that, as was nearly always the case, Russia could not win a long war. Negotiations were opened to end the Livonian War. Some scholars contend that an Assembly of the Land was convoked which called upon the government to end the war,[37] but in all likelihood the only convocation was the well-known Church Council of 1580, which considered nonchurch, political questions (*nekoikh radi tsarskikh veshchei*).[38] The various enemies—the Turks, Crimean Tatars, Nogai Tatars, Lithuanians, Poles, Hungarians, Livonians, Swedes, and others—attacking Russia were mentioned at the council.[39] Probably the issue of the difficulties of the middle service class was raised by someone in connection with these foreign policy considerations.

The government realized the causes and character of the crisis and did the only thing in its power. It decided to try not only to limit peasant mobility to St. George's Day, but to curtail it entirely. Unfortunately, most of the documents which described this development perished in the Moscow fires of 1612 and 1626.[40] Nevertheless, enough of them survive for the following picture to be put together. Beginning in late 1580 or in 1581 the government (perhaps annually) "temporarily" repealed the century-old right of peasants to move on St. George's Day.[41] (Simultaneously the growth of monastery land-ownership was limited, and four years later a temporary measure was enacted curtailing monastery tax privileges.)[42] These were the so-called "forbidden" or "interdicted" years. This measure was not decreed immediately for the entire Muscovite state, but apparently only for those places where land cadastres had been compiled.[43] The repeal of the right to move on St. George's Day probably spread with the compilation of the land cadastres. This project had been initiated by a proposal at the Stoglav Church Council of 1551 and was largely, although not entirely, completed by 1592 or 1593.[44] It is entirely plausible that the legal prohibition on moving spread in this way, for the cadastres served as tangible evidence of peasant residence which would stand up in court should a peasant flee and his lord be forced to sue for his return.[45]

Up to the 1580s the peasant question, perhaps by analogy with the institution of slavery, was largely a civil matter. If a peasant fled or was taken away illegally, it was the concern of his lord to locate, sue for, and return the peasant. During the initial development of the Forbidden Years, however, the first sign of government police intervention in the peasant question appeared. In 1585 an official came from Moscow to the Antonov monastery on the Siia river to take away peasants who had fled there and to collect the tax arrears owed by the peasants.[46] Only later, though, were government sanctions institutionalized.

By the 1580s Ivan's legacy of desolation had reached its peak;[47] in the last decade or so of the sixteenth century Russia recovered to some degree.[48] According to the contemporary visitor Jerome Horsey, "the great tasks, customs, and duties, which were before laid upon the people in the old Emperor's [Ivan's] time, were now abated, and some wholly remitted."[49] Noting that the Russian government was able to loan its allies large sums of money, Horsey said that the Russian state possessed "infinite a treasure, and it was daily increasing."[50] The acute French mercenary captain Jacques Margeret even claimed that Russia was a "very rich" state and spoke of huge cash surpluses in the treasury. He also noted that grain was very cheap.[51]

The blessings of order and prosperity were only superficial, however, and the English diplomat Giles Fletcher noted that Ivan had left the country in an unhealthy state. He correctly predicted that there would soon be a civil war.[52] The available statistics for the time support Fletcher's contention that not all was well as the Riurikovich-Danilovich dynasty was about to expire after over seven centuries of rule. For example, in 1594–95 in Viaz'ma uezd 58 percent of the land was vacant and overgrown with forest. This was somewhat less than the percentages for the central Moscow regions and much less than in the northwest Novgorod area.[53] Only 4 percent of the amount of land the Viaz'ma area servicemen were entitled to according to their compensation scales was under cultivation in the 1590s.[54] By the 1590s two- to three-fold curtailment of land under cultivation per peasant household was observable everywhere—in the presence of vast amounts of vacant land. This curtailment was not related solely to the shift of land from peasant to seignorial registration (for the purposes of escaping taxation and to change the form of rent from quitrent to corvée), a development which was not nearly so widespread. It was rather related to the system of taxation, based on the amount of land under cultivation, and the fact that the *pomeshchik* also collected more when the peasant farmed more. As during similar conditions in the second half of the seventeenth century, the poor peasants tried to make up the deficit by engaging in some form of outside work which was concealed or which was exempt from taxation. Because of the economic dislocation at the end of the sixteenth century, a number of the poorest peasants left the tax rolls and became *bobyli*.[55] Wealthier peasants engaged in usury and invested in trade and industrial enterprises.[56]

The failure of peasant agriculture to return to its pre-Oprichnina level indicated to contemporaries that further action on the question of peasant mobility was in order. They may have reasoned that since partial elimination of mobility had partially restored agriculture, complete elimination of mobility might effect complete restoration. The leading Soviet specialist on the development of serfdom in this period, V. I. Koretskii, has recently discovered and published several interesting documents shedding new light on the legal enserfment of the peasantry in the 1590s. He found numerous references to the right to move (*otkaz,* as in the *Sudebnik's* article 88) right up to the spring of 1592.[57] Those prohibitions which did exist, as in the Forbidden Years, concerned only taxpaying peasants registered in the land cadastres.[58] A careful study of Koretskii's materials leads to the conclusion that there probably was a "temporary" decree (the most crucial decree in Russian history) in 1592 or 1593 binding all Russian peasants with their families to the land, regardless of whether they were registered in land cadastres. This repealed the right to move on St. George's Day. Peasants and *bobyli* no longer enjoyed the right of free movement (*vykhod*).[59]

The right of all peasants to move on St. George's Day must have been deliberately annulled by Boris Godunov (in the name of Tsar Fedor Ivanovich) as a favor to the middle service class. Boris was trying to gain support among these men at a crucial juncture of his struggle with the other boyars for succession to the throne.[60] Soon after the death of Ivan IV in 1584, a noticeable portion of the middle service class had condemned members of the boyar faction supporting Boris, who thereupon had sent a number of them into exile.[61] After Ivan's death, disturbances had broken out in Moscow against Ivan's favorite, Bogdan Bel'skii, a butcher of the Oprichnina, and the heir's uncle, Nikita Romanovich Iur'ev, had come to power. Boris Godunov had gained power by removing this man from his position.[62] Boris, consequently, was well aware from personal experience of what might happen as a result of disorders and the neglect of politically important constituencies.

Another crisis was building up. Toward the end of the 1580s the Englishman Jerome Horsey noted "great syvell decensions growinge emonge the nobility."[63] In the second half of 1591 Boris changed the *intitulatio* in royal charters, certainly with an eye toward seizing the throne. Godunov added his sister's name to that of her husband Tsar Fedor, thus bringing Boris himself closer to royalty and moving toward the establishment of a new dynasty.[64] Certainly a number of the measures Godunov took in the course of these years were intended to win favor with the middle service class.[65] Also, the Russian government's faith in itself had been weakened by its defeat in the Livonian War. The chroniclers felt that the end of the world was near. All of society was conscious of the decline in the government's authority since the peak of Ivan's power.[66]

The timing of the concession to the middle service class was no doubt connected with the extraordinarily high level of prices in 1589, 1590, and especially 1591.[67] The inflation of the preceding 1570s and 1580s is well known. The extraordinary inflationary leap of 1591 may well have been linked with the devastating Tatar invasion by Khan Kazyi-

Girei that year, which was turned back only at the walls of Moscow's Novodevichyi convent; the discontent stemming from the May 15 murder of Tsarevich Dmitrii may also have contributed to the inflation.[68] Some commoners tried to link these events by accusing Boris of inviting the Tatars in order to distract the people from the murder of Dmitrii.[69] Boris in turn tried to curtail the rumors by resort to torture, fire, and sword, with the consequence that many peasant lands became tenantless.[70] These factors caused both peasant unrest and middle service class discontent.

Many of the government's problems at this juncture are outlined in instructions it gave on April 25, 1592, to an official, Ratman Mikhailovich Durov, who was to greet a Lithuanian emissary to Moscow. The document is a bald outline of duplicity and deliberate deception. The government briefed Durov on the questions the Lithuanian might put to him, and told him the responses he should make.[71] The Russian government was concerned that the Crimean Tatars and the Poles might ally with Sweden against it, and wanted the Lithuanian emissary to believe that Russia had especially good relations with the Holy Roman Empire and the Turks. The government was apprehensive about the continuation of the 1582 Iam Zapol'skii armistice which had ended the Polish phase of the Livonian War; it feared that war might break out at any moment with the Rzeczpospolita. (Polish attacks on the frontier became so intense that in October of 1592 the government sent a special embassy to Warsaw to protest the violation of the truce.)[72]

The document reveals considerable anxiety not only about foreign affairs, but internal conditions as well. The official version of the fires which had broken out in Moscow shortly after Dmitrii's death was that the arsonists were agents of the Nagois (Dmitrii's mother's family) and that the claims that Godunov was responsible were deliberate lies.[73] The Crimean Tatar raid was belittled and the failure of the Tatars to capture the capital turned into a victory for Godunov.[74] Boris was credited with setting finances aright, building up the country's fortifications, and reforming the corrupt government. The entire document paints a portrait of an insecure government which was anxious to find support.

In addition to the acknowledged difficulties, there were other troubles. In 1590 there was an uprising of the Cheremisy on the Volga, and the Mordva were restive in the 1590s.[75] Part of the army was engaged in a military encounter with Sweden in an attempt to reverse the 1583 Pliusa truce which had deprived Russia of most of its Baltic outlets (except through the mouth of the Neva). Finally, this was the time when the government was about to annex Siberia, and accordingly wished to consolidate the army's loyalty.[76]

The available evidence indicates that the middle service class had grounds for discontent. Its members had suffered most in the catastrophes of the 1570s and 1580s, and had benefited least from the recovery of the 1590s. The destruction and vacancy rates were especially great in villages belonging to members of the middle service class, those whose compensation scales allotted them one hundred *cheti* of land in one field, or a total of about 375 acres. If Viaz'ma, a district between Moscow and Smolensk, is taken as typical, we find that there were thirty-one such small servicemen in the area. Eleven of them had no peasants or land under cultivation. Fourteen had no peasants or slaves, and only from 1 to 10 percent of the land was under cultivation. Three more had no peasants, but from 11 to 20 percent of their land was under cultivation. Only three had from 21 to 40 percent of their land under cultivation, but two of these had not one peasant or slave. On the other hand, the large boyar estates were in much better condition. In three of the six such estates in the Viaz'ma area, 91 to 97.5 percent of the land was under cultivation; the remaining three had from 40 to 72 percent under cultivation. The six large estates had 554 peasant and *bobyl'* houses, and only thirty, or about 5 percent, of all the homesteads were vacant. About 55 percent of the monastery land in the same district was under cultivation. Or, if the figures for Moscow province for 1585–86 are taken, 6 percent of the land under cultivation belonged to members of the middle service class, 17 percent to lay magnates, and 37 percent to monasteries. These figures are even more striking when compared to the relative amounts of land actually held (but not necessarily under cultivation) by each group: 22 percent belonged to the middle service class, 17 percent to the lay magnates, and about 44 percent to the monasteries. The rest of the land belonged to the tsar and to peasants (black land). These data show that the peasants much preferred to live on the large estates, where the economies were stable and productive.[77] This circumstance was a great source of aggrievement for the middle service class, which favored the prohibition of the movement of peasants.

According to the preamble to a law (which will be discussed below) issued in 1607 by Tsar Vasilii Shuiskii,[78] the right to move on St. George's Day was repealed against the advice of the senior boyar magnates. The latter may well have observed that by the time the law was enacted the labor crisis had passed its peak. Such a law was definitely against the economic interests of the magnates, who were known to favor at least limited peasant mobility.[79] These were the same magnates with whom

Boris was contesting for the throne and whose membership he was breaking up by means of murder, jail sentences, and exile.[80] Boris converted what had been an economic instrument into a political tool. In the crisis of the moment he ordered the binding of all the peasants as the concession which would gain him the most support in the middle service class.

As a consequence of Boris's action, any peasant (with his immediate family) who was registered in a land cadastre after 1592–93 (with the exception of some peasants permitted to move in 1601 and 1602)[81] was for all legal purposes bound to the land, enserfed. No doubt it was this state of affairs which induced the Austrian emissary Martin Shil, sent by Emperor Rudolph II to Boris Godunov, to remark in 1598 that boyars and other lords had come to look upon their peasants as slaves whose rent and labor obligations were formulated by state decree.[82]

The repeal of the right to move on St. George's Day had several ramifications. One of them was the introduction of corvée on some estates. This hotly debated issue in Soviet historiography bears heavy ideological overtones. The assumption is that serfdom and corvée are more or less synonymous institutions. Various Soviet historians have maintained that corvée was always a significant obligation, and most have insisted that it was always increasing throughout the sixteenth century.[83] Much of this certainty stems from the fact that Marx claimed that serfdom usually followed corvée and that corvée rarely arose out of serfdom.[84] As was shown in chapter 1 above, an axiom of most Soviet historiography has been that serfdom existed from the origins of Russian history to 1861. Therefore, obviously, corvée must have existed all this time too. Additional distortion of the history of corvée results from attempts by Soviet dogmatists to extend Lenin's remarks about corvée (which were relevant to the pre-1861 era) back to the sixteenth century, where they had no relevance whatsoever.[85]

The facts of the organization of seignorial landholding in the sixteenth century make one pause before claims of the widespread use of corvée. Even the magnates had small, uncoordinated holdings scattered throughout the country, often only parts of small villages consisting of three to five houses. Members of the middle service class had even smaller scattered holdings, sometimes even fractions of houses. As a consequence, corvée rent would have been neither feasible nor profitable on the majority of seignorial lands.[86] Toward the end of the century, however, measures were taken (as noted in chapter 2) to consolidate middle service class holdings and to exempt from taxation lands farmed on the personal account of servicemen. Perhaps because of these measures, by the end of the sixteenth century one-fifth, one-third, even up to one-half of all *pomest'e* land was under corvée.[87] Large monastery holdings were especially suitable to corvée, and it is on these lands that it was most frequently encountered.

Part of the increased use of corvée may have come from a reversion to a natural economy, completing the reversal of the economic progress achieved prior to Ivan's Oprichnina.[88] This was hard on the urban population, which lost its markets while simultaneously being crushed under an ever-increasing tax burden. Compounding the tragedy was the loss of Russian agricultural markets to the west as a result of the Livonian War and its aftermath. The consequence was a decline of urban life and a fall of exchange between town and countryside.[89] As a result of the downward spiral, estates became increasingly self-sufficient and were based upon the use of corvée.

The binding of the peasants to the land permitted lords to attempt to cope with declining income (inherent in customary cash rent in an inflationary period) by increasing the use of labor rent.[90] The lords could disregard customary levels of rent and introduce whatever forms of exploitation suited them, for legally a peasant could not depart. By the end of the century corvée had become the leading obligation on some estates. Earlier corvée had involved such things as cutting hay and carting wood for a few days. Only after the introduction of the Forbidden Years did a peasant have to take on obligations involving weeks and even months of labor, such as plowing and harvesting. Earlier, such labor had been performed largely by slaves.[91] This accounts for Shil's observation that lords considered the peasants living on their lands to be slaves. There were no penalties for mistreating such peasants, a situation some lords took advantage of.[92] On a few estates there was a real rise of rent following the introduction of corvée.[93]

The introduction of the Forbidden Years had yet another consequence. It began the homogenization of the Russian peasantry. Prior to this time there were many types of peasants, but gradually they were reduced to two, *krest'ianin* and *bobyl'*. The absence of much differentiation in the eighteenth century may be traced to the end of the sixteenth century, although this process really got under way only in the second half of the seventeenth century.[94]

The repeal of the right to move on St. George's Day (unlike the initial restriction) led to peasant resistance. A number of peasant disturbances in the 1580s and 1590s testify to the fact that the Forbidden Years, or their consequences, may have been considered a baneful innovation by the peasant class, which reacted in the only way open to it—by resort to violence.[95] There is some question, however, as to how much of the civil war and general chaos of the Time of Troubles (whose chronological limits vary from the maximum of 1584–1618 to the minimum of 1605–1613) can be attributed to the Forbidden Years. The issue certainly was not apparent to contemporaries, who blamed the Smuta on Providence or the devil and who saw it as an expression of divine wrath for the sins of Ivan IV, Boris Godunov, and the Russian people. They also blamed their own political immaturity, their apathy, indifference, inertia, and cowardice. They did not fully understand the impact of governmental intervention in the social structure.[96] For them the issue was complicated by the fact that representatives of all classes—princes, boyars, rank-and-file servicemen, cossacks, peasants, and slaves—often fought on the "anti-government" side together.[97] Only modern historians have looked at the changed social organization resulting from the economic crisis, the enslavement of thousands of the destitute, and the flight of thousands of peasants to the frontier, where many of them joined the cossacks, as major causes of the Time of Troubles.[98] The slaves and peasants got their revenge (a fleeting one) in the uprisings led by Khlopko, "False Peter," "Tsarevich Ivan-Avgust," Bolotnikov, the pretender "Fed'ka," "False Dmitrii II," I. M. Zarutskii, and others during the Time of Troubles, which crowned the initial protest against the repeal of the right to move on St. George's Day.[99]

The second half of the sixteenth century proved to be disastrous for peasant freedom. To gain support from the middle service class at critical junctures, the government, building on precedents, bound the peasant to the land. The national administration was still relatively undeveloped, so enforcement, both of necessity and by analogy with the institution of slavery, remained a private matter aided by the state's judicial power.[100] The binding of the peasant to the land was accompanied by other assaults on his freedom which practically reduced him to the condition of a slave. The circumstances of the reigns of Ivan IV and Boris Godunov also permitted landowners to ignore the traditional rent structure, and some of them opened economic warfare against the peasantry. The agriculturalists responded to the provocations by resort to flight and violence.

6.
The Statute of Limitations on the Recovery of Fugitive Peasants

The institution of serfdom was not created by the repeal of the right of peasant removal. Contemporaries still had to solve one problem before the peasant could be considered genuinely enserfed: how long could a fugitive peasant be absent from the place where he was registered and still be claimed, if discovered by his lawful lord, and returned? If there were no time limit, all types of abuses might occur, particularly in view of the crude methods of identifying peasants in documents and the weakness of the legal system in general. Without a statute of limitations, courts could become completely congested by litigants claiming the dues and services of a given peasant. On the other hand, if the time limit happened to be too brief, the members of the middle service class would be unable to recover their fugitive peasants, and the whole purpose of the edict annulling the right to move on St. George's Day would be defeated.

At the time Ivan IV first repealed this century-old custom, apparently no limitation was placed on the right of lords to recover their fugitive peasants. This may have been simply an unconscious continuation of the practice of placing no time limit on the recovery of peasants who fled in violation of the St. George's Day regulations.[1] On the other hand, the tsar may have deliberately placed no statute of limitations on the recovery of fugitive peasants to favor the middle service class. Its members needed as extended a time as possible to recover their peasants because of the long periods they spent in military service away from their lands. Another consideration was their lack of means to hire agents to hunt down the fugitive peasants—a matter which the state usually considered, probably by analogy with fugitive slaves, a private affair.

At this time a concept of the desirability of a statute of limitations was developing in many areas of law.[2] Therefore it may not have been

104

unexpected when in the 1590s a statute of limitations was placed on suits for the recovery of fugitive peasants. Lords were given five years from the day the peasants left their estates in which to find them and sue for their return. This time limit came to be known as the "fixed" or "definite" years (*urochnye leta, gody*). If no action was initiated within this time limit, the fugitive peasant became legally free and had the right to settle elsewhere. The source of this five-year limit, known to historians for many years in a law of 1597, has been a mystery widely debated for over a century. Only recently V. I. Koretskii discovered evidence from suits involving peasants that the five-year limit was very probably part of the general decree of 1592–93 which bound all peasants to the land.[3] It is safe to conclude on the basis of Koretskii's evidence that both of these measures were introduced at the beginning of the 1590s. The repeal of the right to move on St. George's Day, as we have seen, was already a decade old (dating from 1580–81) and in the early 1590s was merely extended to the entire Muscovite state. The five-year time limit on the recovery of those who had moved in violation of the repeal of the St. George's Day decree was the new element.[4] At first this time limit for filing suits applied only to questions of who was the lord of a peasant (*vladen'e*), in case the evidence of the cadastres was insufficient, and cases where a peasant had been carried off (*vyvoz*).[5] The decree of 1597 extended this time limit to peasants who fled (*vykhod*).[6]

There are at least two reasons why this measure may have been enacted at this time. The drafters of the laws may have believed that the government lacked the resources to organize recovery operations for fugitive peasants;[7] fearing that the courts would become jammed with suits, they felt some measure had to be enacted to ease congestion.[8] The imposition of a time limit also may have reflected the changed composition of the government and of its policies and difficulties in the 1590s. On the one hand, Boris Godunov is well known as a friend of the middle service class.[9] The general binding of all peasants by the repeal of the right to move on St. George's Day may have been one of his projects to aid the middle service class concentrated in the center of the Muscovite state. But it is also a fact that both the monasteries and the boyar magnates, all of whom had suffered under Ivan IV, made a modest comeback after his death,[10] and the five-year limitation may well reflect their influence. Boris in his drive for the throne may have felt he had to grant a significant concession to the magnates at this moment. Indicative of the discontent in these circles was the fact that after the murder of Dmitrii a number of the most influential figures in Moscow were working on a plan to offer the Russian throne to the Austrian grand duke, Maximilian.[11] Since such a plan would have thwarted Godunov's ambi-

105

tions, he may have enacted the time limit to enhance his appeal with the great landowners.

As a rule, wealthier landowners, both monasteries and lay magnates, preferred a mobile population in this period.[12] They were generally in a better position than members of the middle service class to offer loans and economic concessions (in the form of postponement of payment of dues and frequently taxes too) to peasants who would settle on their estates. But as mobility was curtailed against their wishes, the magnates, both clerical and lay, fell back to another line of defense. They made the recovery of fugitive peasants as difficult as possible—benefiting from the tillage by the fugitives the while—and they did not suffer any penalties in the unlikely event they eventually had to turn over the runaways. Thus there appears to have been a compromise in 1592–93, a form of quid pro quo, between Boris and the middle service class on the one hand and the boyars and the monasteries on the other.[13] The magnates agreed to the permanent binding of the peasantry, that is, to the right to recover those who violated the law by fleeing, with a proviso added for their own benefit: members of the middle service class might recover their peasants if they could find them in a relatively short period of time. A five-year time limit was not nearly so severe a limitation on the magnates as on the members of the middle service class. The wealthy landowners had stewards to supervise their economies who could guard against peasant departures. Peasant flights actually were fewer per capita from larger estates, and the magnates could, and often did, hire agents to track down and return fugitives who had fled from their estates and to see suits for the return of fugitives through the courts. Furthermore, the magnates could conceal fugitives on distant estates, and, after the time limit had expired, return them with impunity, even to an estate next to the one whence they earlier had fled.[14]

This, then, was the situation from the 1590s to 1648: all peasants registered on a parcel of land were to remain there. Initially, only those personally registered were involved, not their relatives. Throughout the 1590s children and relatives of peasants moved where they desired, hired themselves out as workers, joined the cossacks, and became slaves—all of which would be forbidden a half century later.[15] But when someone registered on a plot of land fled, the lord had to recover him within the given time limit or lose his worker.[16] This situation continued to favor the large landowners as against the middle service class. The latter wanted the time limit repealed, with a return to the law of Ivan IV which had no statute of limitations attached. The government, controlled as it was by the magnates, clung to the five-year statutory period.

At the beginning of the seventeenth century Russia experienced one of the worst traumas in its national existence, the Time of Troubles. As the result of a three-year crop failure (1601–3) the price of grain rose manyfold; tens of thousands, maybe even one-third of the total population, died; cannibalism was rampant.[17] This added to the difficulties stemming from the extinction in 1598 of the seven-centuries-old Riurikovich dynasty and presaged a series of pretenders, peasant uprisings, civil war, and finally invasion by the Poles and Swedes. After a decade of chaos, the Russians united to throw out the invaders and to restore order. Russia was left in ruins.[18]

Strange as it may seem, the Time of Troubles did not have a profound impact on the enserfment of the peasantry, leaving aside for a moment the loss of Smolensk to the Poles in 1611. In the 1590s the time limit for the recovery of fugitive peasants had been set at five years.[19] In February, 1606, a decree issued by the pretender Dmitrii I, trying to carry out his promises to his supporters in the lower classes to ease their lot,[20] repeated the five-year limit on suits to recover fugitive peasants.[21] The decree added that peasants who had fled because their lords had refused to feed them during the famine of 1601–3 could not be returned to their former lords against the peasants' will. This concession, made during the Bolotnikov rebellion, was a repetition of a decree made three years earlier for slaves; it may have favored the southern middle service class landholders, in whose direction the peasants were fleeing.[22] According to the 1606 decree, which was an answer to a petition from the boyars and *dvoriane,* the peasant who had fled within the previous five years (and five months), but not because he had been starving, and who had taken a bondage loan contract on himself, was to be returned as a peasant if his former lord sued for his return.[23] This was a measure favored by the lords of the center of the state.[24] This was also the inauguration of the principle that prior obligation as a peasant had precedence over status as a slave, a policy favored by the government for two reasons: the simple rule of precedence; and the fact that the peasant paid taxes while the slave did not. The measure was also favored by the middle service class, whose members had few slaves, and was opposed by magnates, who had many.

Fearing the peasant revolt then going on, the False Dmitrii I, in the spring of 1606, included the right of peasants to change lords on St. George's Day in the so-called Composite Law Code (*Svodnyi Sudebnik*), which was based on the earlier *Sudebniki.*[25] The document was never officially promulgated because in May Dmitrii was murdered. His murder was due partly to the wrath aroused in some landholders by his reissuance of the clause of the *Sudebnik* of 1550 allowing peasants to move.[26] If in fact careful attention was given to the drafting of this law code, as seems to have been the case, then the intention probably was to repeal the Forbidden Years, which the government could not enforce anyway, in an attempt to ward off the Bolotnikov peasant explosion.[27]

One of the most interesting documents in the development of serfdom in Russia was issued in March, 1607, by Tsar Ivan Shuiskii.[28] This law introduced a police element into what previously had been largely a civil matter.[29] The document further reveals that extraordinary events in Muscovy tended to force men to initiate new elements into Russian laws. The preamble or introduction to the law noted that Tsar Fedor Ivanovich, "at the evil urging of Boris Godunov" and against the advice of the boyars,[30] had forbidden the peasants to move and that this had been the cause of great disturbances and many law suits, the like of which there had never been in the reign of Ivan IV. But, according to the preamble, Boris had made an even greater mistake in 1601 and 1602, when he had given the peasants a limited right of transfer.[31] This had been so confusing that even the government officials had not known how to deal with it, and even greater chaos and violence had ensued.[32]

Instead of solving the problem by giving the peasants completely free right of movement, Shuiskii decided to eliminate the right of movement by binding all peasants to their current place of residence. He did not state that the binding was temporary, a fact assumed throughout the first half of the seventeenth century.[33] The step was taken while the Bolotnikov rebellion was being liquidated. The Shuiskii government clearly did not feel solicitous of the peasants; it probably acted out of revenge and at the behest of the members of the service class who wanted to restore their dissipated labor force. The Shuiskii boyar government also extended the time limit to fifteen years to enlist the support of the middle service class in suppressing the Bolotnikov uprising.[34] Many of Shuiskii's norms became a permanent part of Russian serf law after the liquidation of the Troubles.[35]

The decree gave all lords harboring others' peasants until Christmas to return them without having to pay a penalty. The peasants were to live with the lords with whom they had been registered in the land cadastres. If a lord did not petition for his fugitive peasants before September 1, 1607, he would lose claim to them and they would then be registered with the lord with whom they were living.

A fugitive peasant returned to his former lord was to come with his wife, children, and property—a provision similar to those put into practice by the legislation of the 90s.[36] If the peasant had constructed a house on the property of the lord with whom he was living as a fugitive, that lord was to pay him for the house; the house itself was not to be returned with the peasant.[37] The lord who harbored the fugitive had to pay a ten-ruble fine to the state for having violated the law, and a sum of three rubles to the rightful lord of the fugitive peasant for every year he had kept the fugitive.

Peasant women who had fled and were apprehended were to be returned to their rightful lords with their husbands and children, if they had married while in flight. If the husband had had children by a previous marriage, they were to remain with his lord except in those cases where they were under fifteen years of age; if the children had reached the age of fifteen, they presumably were to be returned to the lord on whose property they had lived when they were born. A fifteen-year limit was placed on all future suits for fugitive peasants—the amount of time which had elapsed between this decree of 1607 and the decree of 1592–93 posited by V. I. Koretskii.

An additional police element was interjected by the central state power, which instructed its provincial representatives to learn from local officials about all newcomers and to interrogate the latter to determine whether they were fugitives. If the interrogator learned that a lord had urged the peasant to flee, the lord was to be fined ten rubles, beaten in the market place as a public example, and forced to return the fugitive peasant under bond. Each person who harbored the fugitive for over a week also had to pay a ten-ruble fine to the treasury for each family or single male, and three rubles for a girl or old woman. Local elected officials were held materially responsible for fugitive peasants received by communities on black lands, lands of the tsar, and lands belonging to church institutions. If the representatives of the central government did not carry out their orders, they were supposed to pay a double fine and to be discharged permanently from government service.

Thus the Bolotnikov rebellion, the first large-scale peasant uprising in Muscovite history, evoked a clarification of the law on the peasant serf. While the fifteen-year period for the recovery of fugitives was soon to pass into oblivion,[38] the expanded, harsh provisions of Shuiskii's punitive legislation were to remain for centuries.[39] It well may be that the uprising, because of the fear and desire for revenge it instilled in the ruling elite, injected added life into serfdom, precisely the opposite result the rebels must have hoped for, if the issue of the "temporary" binding of the peasants to the land concerned them. The same was to occur after the Razin uprising several decades later.[40]

In 1610 the second pretender, False Dmitrii II, continued the policy of limiting peasant mobility and forbade both regular peasant movement (*vykhod*) and assisted transference or exportation (*vyvoz*). If peasants left or were carried away, the boyars and military governors were to find them and order them to live where they had lived before.[41] In November,

1610, the Swedish-Russian government in Novgorod also confirmed the binding of the peasants, with the notation that it was only temporary.[42] It may be worthy of note, however, that these "temporary" edicts were becoming chronic.

The interests of the magnates in the peasant question, as the Time of Troubles was nearing its climax, can be seen in the 1610 agreement negotiated with the Poles.[43] It is generally assumed that this treaty reflects the desires of the boyars who drafted it.[44] It forbade peasant *vykhod*, but said nothing about *vyvoz*, or *otkaz*, which would include both.[45] This could hardly have been accidental, especially as the earlier 1610 decree by False Dmitrii II had forbidden both *vykhod* and *vyvoz*.[46] The term *vykhod* was not used in this period to cover both phenomena, as indicated in another contemporary document which preserved the right of a lord to his peasants, protecting him against the depredations of other lords.[47] The treaty with the Poles prohibited free peasant movement (*vykhod*), which might have been random, affecting the magnates as well as members of the middle service class. It allowed, however, transferring of peasants by lords who were willing to pay off a peasant's debts and perhaps the moving ("rent") fee associated with St. George's Day. This was much easier for lay and church magnates with cash reserves than for the hard-pressed *dvoriane* and *deti boiarskie*, the members of the middle service class.

A somewhat different position prevailed in a treaty signed by the boyars of Novgorod and representatives of the Swedish king, Gustavus Adolphus, in late 1612. Peasants living on court lands were not to be permitted to move away, nor were any peasants to move into the court villages until further notice, except in the case of "free people."[48] No doubt here the chaos was so great, especially as the area had never recovered from Ivan IV's raid in 1570, that the sole desire of all parties was to slow things down in an attempt to restore order.

The contemporary attitude of the *deti boiarskie* and *dvoriane* can be observed in the June 30, 1611, decree of the first militia formed by members of the middle service class to drive the Poles out of Russia. Article 23 of this document ordered the return of fugitive and "abducted" peasants to their proper lords without any time limit being specified.[49] The middle service class bias of this first militia was one of the reasons for its failure, for it could not obtain the cooperation of the cossack rebels, made up largely of runaway peasants.[50] The middle service class view continued to prevail at least until the inauguration of Mikhail Romanov as tsar, at which time there seems to have been no notion of a time limit on the recovery of fugitive peasants.[51]

A review of the impact of the Time of Troubles on the course of serfdom in Muscovy indicates that this period contributed to the abasement of the peasants, but actually was responsible for much less change in their status than one might have expected from such a cataclysm.[52] The desolation did, however, lend a major impetus to the binding of the townspeople.

The Time of Troubles did, nevertheless, profoundly affect the Russian peasantry. For one thing, Russia lost the magnificent Smolensk fortress on June 13, 1611, just a few years after the completion of its construction.[53] Russia naturally wanted to recover Smolensk, the gateway both to the lower Dnepr and to the West, and this was attempted during the Smolensk War (1632–34). That war opened the last stage in the enserfment of the peasantry. The other major impact of the Time of Troubles was through its disruption of the peasant labor supply, which led to the reopening of the whole peasant question by select monasteries.

According to one student of the enserfment question, the five-year time limit for recovering fugitive peasants was probably reintroduced in April or May of 1615.[54] Up until that time, for the first two years of the Romanov dynasty, there had been no statute of limitations, as had been the case during the reign of Ivan IV. This situation was evident in July, 1614, when the head of the great Iosif Volokolamsk monastery informed the government that the monastery had been ruined by invading Poles ("Lithuanians") and that all the peasants had been murdered, died of starvation, were taken captive, or fled. The monastery authorities appended a list of missing peasants and their known whereabouts and complained that many of them were living with members of the middle service class. To satisfy the petitioners, the government ordered its local agents to conduct an investigation in the vicinity of the monastery to determine which of the peasants had lived on monastery lands. Those who admitted that they had lived with the monastery were to be returned to its lands, "with their wives, children, standing grain, and planted grain"—a formula which was to be repeated many times in succeeding years. (The returned fugitives had the right to go back later to harvest matured grain.) Nothing was said in the decree about the time limit for returning fugitives. It must be noted that in this petition a monastery was petitioning against members of the middle service class, a situation which was soon to be reversed.[55] The first months of the Romanov dynasty witnessed massive hunts for fugitive peasants with no apparent time limit.[56] Such a policy, which included returning peasants who had fought against the Poles and even served in the musketeers and cossacks, benefited especially the middle service class, which enjoyed considerable influence at the outset of Mikhail's reign.[57]

111

The Soviet specialist on this question, V. A. Figarovskii, links the re-introduction of the time limit with attempts by the government to mollify a horde of nearly twenty thousand cossacks and peasants marching on Moscow from the north.[58] This may have been the moment when the five-year time limit was introduced, and why it was introduced, but we must also bear in mind that this date coincides with the lessening of the influence over the government by the middle service class, which desired no time limit. Simultaneously, the magnates, who desired a short time limit, were consolidating their hold over the government.[59]

Curiously enough, the middle service class was not the first party to request that the traditional five-year time limit be extended. The *dvoriane* and *deti boiarskie* may have been either too euphoric over the end of the Time of Troubles and the illusion of influence over the government through the Assembly of the Land or too fragmented to take any collective action. In any event, the peasant question was reopened by some church magnates. The Troitse Sergiev monastery lands had been devastated during the Time of Troubles (extant records of 1616 indicate that, at the time, from 95 to 98 percent of the monastery's lands were fallow, with only 2 to 5 percent under cultivation, and the number of peasant households on its estates had dropped from 3988 in 1592–94 to 623 in 1614–15, the number of *bobyl'* households from 502 to 426).[60] On February 28, 1614, the monastery received permission to recover peasants who had fled since September 1, 1604.[61] This nine-year period for the recovery of fugitives, which was to become so crucial later, was picked by the monastery to escape reciprocal claims by other lords. In the famine years 1601 and 1602, according to Boris's laws, the monastery had not had the right to accept peasants, but probably had done so anyway. The monastery continued to gain peasants through 1604, but in the years 1605–7 (the period of the Bolotnikov revolt) lost 492 peasant families, and then another 277 in the following seven years, 1608–14 (when the monastery was the scene of many battles between Russian and foreign troops, including the 1608–10 siege of the monastery itself by the Poles).[62] A year later the 1614 grant was renewed.[63] The government provided troops to aid in discovering and recovering the fugitive peasants. Many abuses ensued, and the government ordered the operation completed by August 31, 1615.[64] Nevertheless, the monastery managed to retain an extended nine-year limit which served as a provocative form of discrimination which the middle service class, limited to only five years, could not stand.[65]

The peasant question was relatively quiescent in the 1620s. Peasants still fled from their lords and the latter continued to file suits for their recovery,[66] but no essential changes were made in the institution of the Forbidden Years or in the time limit on the recovery of runaways. A. G. Poliak feels that this was because large numbers of cossacks, made up chiefly of fugitive peasants, posed a threat to the government.[67] He presents no evidence to support this contention, and the reason for the lack of interest in the problem at this time (at least in regard to the time limit) must be sought elsewhere. The first thing to be noted is that Russia was at peace with Sweden (Treaty of Stolbovo, 1617)[68] and Poland (Treaty of Deulino, December, 1618),[69] the Tatar front was quiet, and the country was gradually recovering from the Time of Troubles. The government demands on the middle service class were at a minimum, and its members had every reason to feel content: their peasants were returning, production was increasing, service was not especially onerous; in short, things were getting better. Conditions had so improved by the end of the 1620s that peasants were moving into Russia across the western frontier.[70] Patriarch Filaret, father of Tsar Mikhail and actual head of the government after his return on June 14, 1619, from eight years of Polish captivity in the Marienburg fortress, managed to restrain the rapacity of the magnates as his successors could not and did not want to do. This became particularly evident after 1623, with the fall of the Saltykovs. Filaret, assisted by I. B. Cherkasskii, B. M. Lykov, I. N. Romanov, F. L. Sheremetev and others, held full power.[71] The 1620s were what might be called a period of adjustment to the *urochnye leta,* a time during which the magnates were developing the methods to get around the legal strictures against recruiting others' peasants.

A few cases survive from the 1620s. One is a petition by the *dvoriane, deti boiarskie,* and other petty landholders and citizens of the Elets district against the depredations of Boiarin I. N. Romanov, who was a relative of the tsar and a confidant of Filaret, and who had 3,400 peasant households on his lands. In 1628 the petitioners begged relief, complaining that Romanov and his menials were using every conceivable device to add to the population on his estates.[72] Kidnapping of the petitioners' peasants was extremely well organized by a Romanov steward: gangs of thirty to forty Romanov slaves and peasants would sweep down on a service estate, plunder and burn it, and then carry off the peasants living there and their property. The peasants would be invited to move to Romanov's estates voluntarily and would be kidnapped only if they did not respond favorably to the invitation. (The majority of his labor force was voluntary, and only a small percentage was actually kidnapped.) The government conducted an investigation of the complaints against I. N. Romanov, decided that the accusations were all slanderous, and ordered the accusers flogged.[73] The whole case is another sign that during this period, until after the Smolensk War, there was no change in many

113

of the essential aspects of the peasant question—flight, kidnapping, relief against the depredations of the magnates valuing peasant mobility, the time limit on returning fugitives.

Why the binding of the peasants to the land made no progress during the hegemony of Filaret is worth consideration. He may have realized that peasant labor was flowing toward the larger estates, and so did nothing which would give the lesser lords a greater chance to recover their peasants. Filaret judiciously cultivated the magnates in order to consolidate the new Romanov dynasty.[74] He also purchased the silence of the middle service class by initiating in 1620 a distribution of peasant black lands to servicemen which was to continue through the second quarter of the seventeenth century.[75]

One aspect of Russian serfdom made great progress at this time, particularly during the period between the end of the Time of Troubles and the Smolensk War. Earlier we discussed the issue of the judicial privileges and whether the peasant was subject to the authority of the lord on whose land he was residing. The conclusions reached were that no residual powers remained after the privileges were annulled; that landholders who never had such charters did not gain such rights over their peasants in the various documents connected with landholding; and that judicial power resided in the state, its agents, local authorities, and the peasant commune, at least until the Oprichnina.[76] While the immunities were not crucial in degrading the peasants, other documents that began to be issued in the 1540s did in time abase them.

The reversal of the process of making each free citizen subject solely to state jurisdiction can be traced to documents called *vvoznye, poslushnye,* and *otdel'nye gramoty,* in which peasants were directed by the government to obey their lords (if the lords were in good standing with the government).[77] These documents first appeared in the 1540s. A typical formula was: "The peasants must obey them [their lords], cultivate the land, and provide the income of the landowners" ("krest'ianom ikh sluzhati, pashniu pakhati i dokhod votchinnikov platiti").[78] Peasants who did not obey were subject to call before their lords and threatened with jail, beating, exile, fines, and other penalties.[79] The state authorities might step in, should the lord be unable to make the peasants obey.[80] These provisions did not mean, however, that the peasants had become completely dependent upon their lords. The provisions probably applied simply to the payment of traditional rent, for there is no record of an increase in the level of exploitation at this time.[81] And the peasant could still move.

It is difficult to explain the cause of this development.[82] The new formula was relatively innocuous, and probably was only a verbal expression of the current lord-peasant relationship. If the peasant wanted to use a lord's land, he had to heed the reasonable requests of its owner and pay his rent. One can imagine that during the chaos of the 1540s some peasants, deciding they could ignore their customary inferior place in society, refused to pay rent. The lord then decided he could better convince the peasants to pay without forcing them to leave by waving a government decree in their faces. Those ruling in Ivan IV's name were delighted to fulfill requests which might gain them support. It may not be accidental that the first known such document, dated 1541, was granted to a converted Tatar serviceman.[83] Special provisions were often made for such people, whom the Russian government wanted to remain both Orthodox and in Muscovite service. It is entirely possible, of course, that the religious element of the 1541 grant is accidental and that the crucial factor is that the form was invented for service lands. Peasants in the 1540s may have desired to reassert their claim to expropriated black or to seignorial lands and to refuse to pay rent. This was a period of institutional innovation, and, as discussed in chapter 2, the recently initiated *guba* system had just turned the problem of order in the provinces over to the middle service class. The government analogously may have decided to try to instil order on a particular serviceman's estate by decreeing that his peasants should obey him. Be that as it may, the whole procedure probably seemed fairly harmless to all concerned.

Nevertheless, this was a bad precedent from the point of view of peasant freedom. In the 1550s some lords were allowed to ignore tradition and set the rent at a level to their liking ("pashniu na nikh pakhali, gde sobe oni uchiniat, i obrok im platili, chem vas izobrochat").[84] The form of the *poslushnaia* became more severe and socially degrading in the 1570s. It may be fair to say that the old *pomest'e* lord-peasant customary relations were decisively destroyed at this time.[85] To gain the support of his servitors Ivan IV made each *oprichnik* absolute lord in his domain, in fact if not in law, by transferring to him power over his holdings.[86] The *oprichniki* were given (or assumed) license to do whatever they pleased to the peasants on their lands, including the right to move them out of properties in the Zemshchina into the Oprichnina.[87] A *poslushnaia* of February, 1571, added to the traditional formula the order that peasants had to respect their lord and were subject to his judicial authority ("Vy b, vse krest'iane, Nikitu Oksent'eva *chtili* i slishali, i pashniu na nego pakhali i obrok emu platili i *pod sud emu davalis'* "—the italicized parts were new).[88] The tsar also permitted the *pomeshchiki* to collect the dues in person.[89] The servicemen's new rights over the peasants became more meaningful with the consolidation of the fragmented *pomest'e* parcels, because the lords could exercise their authority on a single holding at times when they were not in service.[90] This was much more difficult, of course, when the service lands were distributed all over Russia. By the 1580s and 1590s the *poslushnye* issued by church institutions to peasants on their lands adopted the new wording of the government charters.[91] This formula was ominous for peasant freedom; it initiated the conversion (consummated in the eighteenth century) of the peasant from a state subject into a near-slave responsible to his lord.

There obviously was a limit to how much real power a lord could have over his peasant if the latter could move when he did not like what the lord might be doing to him. The introduction of the Forbidden Years removed this obstacle to the lords' power, and the lords responded by raising the level of exploitation and introducing more oppressive corvée.[92] So did the government, by gradually equating the judicial status of the bound peasant with that of the slave.[93]

Sixteenth-century Russian law did not equate the peasant and the slave, and in fact even equated the wealthy peasant with the *syn boiarskii* in some respects. In 1506, in the courts run by the great prince's agents, the peasant had a place which was lost by the time of the *Ulozhenie*.[94] In the sixteenth-century court the peasant had all the rights of a free man.[95]

Deterioration of the status of the peasant before the law can be linked with the repeal of the right to move on St. George's Day in the 1580s. This is evident in article 217 of the *Sudebnik* of 1589, which had no precedent in the law code of 1550:

> Boyars, state secretaries, and all chancellery employees must order the peasants on their lands to tell the truth as they know it in investigations [of lawsuits]. If it is found that their peasants lied in the investigations [*obyski*], their boyars shall be in disgrace before the Sovereign for this. The peasants will be punished in the name of the Sovereign as in robbery cases. If boyars and chancellery officials know that peasants have not lied in investigations of suits and have told the truth, they are obliged to inform the Sovereign. Decide the case on the basis of the investigation.

This article bears considerable resemblance to articles 10 and 11 of a decree of 1556,[96] with the crucial difference that Ivan's law concerned only slaves. In the *Sudebnik* article we can see the beginning of the degrading of the juridical personality of the peasant by making his lord, rather than the peasant himself, ultimately responsible for the latter's conduct.

This development took on added dimensions in the seventeenth century, when lords were held responsible for crimes committed by their peasants.[97] The law and practice of the 1620s were that peasants who fled abroad and then returned to Russia were to be interrogated about possible treason; if cleared of suspicion, they were returned (in the same manner as slaves) to their lords, who were held legally and materially responsible for their conduct: they had to guarantee that the peasants would not flee abroad again, spy, "or do anything else illegal."[98] By the middle of the seventeenth century lords and the peasant commune assumed responsibility for misdemeanors and meted out justice in minor civil cases, while the *Ulozhenie,* a fairly complete law code, reserved felonies and more substantial civil matters for the state.[99] The estate correspondence of the great magnate Boris Ivanovich Morozov, who had his own jails, reveals precisely how he directed his bailiffs, working with the elders and representatives of the commune to render justice on his properties, and what types of cases were in his jurisdiction.[100] But the identification of slave and peasant before the law and in common practice was by no means complete by 1649, for the slave was still far more the responsibility of his lord than was the peasant.[101] While a few lords may have issued decrees of a purely police character prior to the promulgation of the *Ulozhenie* of 1649, it is correct to say that the "estate thereby became a state within a state" only in the second half of the century.[102]

The view of the peasant-becoming-slave can be found in a document sent in December, 1606, by Tsar Vasilii Shuiskii to officials in Galich in which the peasants are held responsible for their landlords' conduct. Army officials had observed that the Galich contingents, largely *deti boiarskie,* were absent in large numbers, and the government wanted action taken to stop this. Officials were sent out to round up the absent servicemen, and the expenses of the officials were to be repaid twofold by the *deti boiarskie,* their slaves and peasants. If the servicemen refused to report for duty, their slaves and peasants were to be held in jail until they did.[103] This was to become standard Muscovite practice.[104] Here we see a nearly complete identification of peasants with slaves by the government, which also held the belief that both were equally the property of their lords, who in turn could be punished through their subjects—probably by denying the lords the income which their subjects would have produced had the latter not been in jail.[105] Identification of peasants with slaves can also be found in Tsar Shuiskii's law of March, 1607, on peasants and slaves,[106] and it would be correct to attribute the view that peasants and slaves were nearly the same to the "Boyar Tsar." This was one of his few innovations which was to outlast him.

The practice of making the peasant suffer for his lord's misdeed was extended from army desertion to ordinary criminal practice. When a

117

lord refused to appear for a trial, the agent of the court (*pristav*) was to go to the culprit's estate and take, instead of the landholder, one of his slaves, or a peasant, as his most valuable piece of property.[107] This is an obvious extension to the peasant of the slave's status, although when it occurred is not indicated by available records.[108]

The status of the peasant was lowered still further under Filaret in 1628 with a decree on the disposition of peasants' property by the Robbery Chancellery (*Razboinyi Prikaz*) and the Moscow Administrative Chancellery (*Zemskii Prikaz*) as a part of the new "Decree on Court Cases."[109] If a suit for the return of a fugitive peasant included over fifty rubles worth of property, it was to be decided by a trial. If no value was listed for the property, or the defendant would not testify, the case was to be decided by an oath. A peasant was declared to be worth four rubles and his property five. If a person admitted harboring a fugitive peasant, but denied that the peasant had come to him with property, the matter was to be decided by the taking of oaths. Whichever party dared to swear on the cross (the Muscovite equivalent of the Bible in those times) was assumed to be telling the truth. If the plaintiff listed the property but not its value in the suit, the defendant, if he lost, had to pay five rubles for the property.[110] If a defendant denied having the fugitive, and subsequently the peasant in question showed up on his property, the defendant had to return the peasant plus all the property listed in the plaintiff's suit—without resort to trial. The 1628 decree stated that the tsar would specify further punishment, which the *Ulozhenie* of 1649 subsequently codified. The liar was to be beaten for three days with the knout in the market place, and those looking on were to be told the reasons for the punishment. Then the liar was to be jailed for a year and his word was never again to be believed in a trial.[111] The taking of a false oath was considered one of the most serious crimes in Muscovy, and the penalty for such a transgression was correspondingly severe. Although the upper classes were frequently subject to lesser penalties in Muscovite law than the lower orders, they were not exempted from corporal punishment until the promulgation of the Charter of the Nobility in 1785.[112]

In 1629 another crucial step was taken when the government decreed that debts of a lord were collectable from his peasants.[113] This too became a generalized norm of Russian serfdom, which in a sense limited the right of the peasant to dispose of his own moveable property.[114] Nevertheless, the lord was not given, and did not have, the right to appropriate for his own use the peasant's economic assets—his cattle, inventory, sowings, grain reserves, buildings, and so on. In this sense a basic legal distinction between the peasant and slave was preserved in

118

the first half of the seventeenth century.[115] The peasant also retained throughout most of the first half of the seventeenth century all of his rights as a citizen to enter into contracts and conduct business in his own name.[116] In 1642, however, the peasant was forbidden to contract debts, for it would have been impossible to satisfy defaults by moving the peasant from his plot and converting him into a slave to work them off.[117] Reciprocally, the lord was held materially responsible only for the actions of his slaves, but not for his peasants or slaves who had their own property.[118] This expresses the consistency of Muscovite views on the peasantry.

The peasant was also degraded by the registration procedures evolving at this time, which tended to equate him with a slave. Settlement contracts (*poriadnye*) between landowners and peasants desiring to live on the owners' estates were registered in the same governmental record books which contained slavery contracts (*kabal'nye knigi*).[119] The Service Land Chancellery, responsible for keeping track of peasants on seignorial lands, adopted much of the practice of the Slavery Chancellery in recording where a peasant belonged.[120] Similarly, landowners, by the 1630s, came to enjoy the right to allow their peasants to move.[121] This was expressed in the manumission document (*otpusknaia gramota*), another form borrowed from the institution of slavery. In other cases, however, the Military Chancellery (*Razriad*), learning of an incident where a lord had "manumitted" his peasants, denied that they could be manumitted, and stated repeatedly and explicitly, in a case involving peasants from a service landholding, that "peasants are not set free, but slaves are set free after the owner dies."[122] Nevertheless, manumission was formally codified in the law code of 1649.[123]

Filaret also took measures which tended to degrade the remaining "black" peasants—agriculturalists who owned their own lands. In 1624 the peasants of Sol'vychegodsk were told that they could no longer dispose of their own property. The peasants protested that such transactions were necessary if they were to be able to pay taxes, so the government conceded to them the right to sell or mortgage their property, but only to local fellow-taxpayers. This prohibition was carried further in 1648 and 1649 when the Boyar Duma forbade the sale of black lands in the western Pomor'e region even to local residents; in 1652 the prohibition was strengthened with sanctions and extended to neighboring areas.[124] These measures reflect the compartmentalization and the stratification of society occurring at this time. The vast majority of such edicts resulted in a lessening of peasant freedom.

The year 1625 witnessed the initiation of another practice which further abased the peasant. If a member of the middle service class, his son, or his manager unintentionally killed a peasant living on the estate of another lord, the other lord, by analogy with an earlier decree on slaves, was given the right to claim the richest peasant of the murderer. The peasant was to be transferred to the estate of the deceased peasant's lord with his wife, children, and all his property. The killer also had to pay all the debts of the murdered peasant.[125] Or, if one lord's peasant unintentionally killed another lord's peasant, the culprit was to be beaten with the knout and handed over with his wife, children, and property to the lord of the murdered peasant. If the lord of the murdered peasant did not want the killer and called him a known criminal, he had the right to take his pick of the peasants belonging to the murderer's lord. The preferred peasant was to be transferred to the estate belonging to the lord of the deceased peasant with his wife, children, all his moveable property, and his growing grain.[126] From here it was only a brief logical step to the notion that the lord could transfer his peasant at will from one estate to another, or even manumit (or discharge) a peasant from an hereditary estate.[127] From this point, again, it was not far to the notion that a lord could buy and sell his peasants themselves, who became totally subject to his whim.[128] However, it is questionable whether many, if any, peasants were being sold under various guises at the time of the *Ulozhenie* of 1649.[129]

The result of all this legislation was to convert the peasant into an object akin to the lord's personal property, a position somewhat comparable to that of the slave, to whom similar measures were applicable. There probably was no deliberate political or economic motivation behind the degradation of the person of the peasant. Each step was simply the "logical" answer, given the peasant's abased status, to practical questions as they arose in the chancelleries of Moscow. No direct evidence of borrowing from foreign practice, such as the *Lithuanian Statute* of 1588, has been found, although unquestionably the Muscovites knew of the degraded condition of the peasantry of the Rzeczpospolita. Nevertheless, while the legal abasement of the Russian peasantry seems to have had a purely practical origin, it soon had important political consequences; as will be discussed in greater detail later, it created distinctions not present previously between the average service landholder and his peasants. In all likelihood this in turn made the lord increasingly anxious to preserve his privileged position at the expense of the abased peasant, when the status of the lord was threatened by military reforms.

The measures equating the peasant with the slave had little impact unless the peasant was legally bound to the land (or the person of his lord) and sanctions existed to enforce such a status. The existence of the statute of limitations on the recovery of fugitive peasants caused the middle service class to feel that the peasant was in fact not a serf because he could flee rather easily into the vast spaces of Russia, thereby denying the serviceman his support. The *deti boiarskie* and *dvoriane* resolved to agitate until their plight was remedied—until the peasantry was finally enserfed.

Another phenomenon of this period, the communal system of taxation with its mutual responsibility for the payment of what was due the state (and also the lord), has sometimes been assigned major responsibility for the enserfment of the Russian peasantry.[130] The system worked as follows: the government registered each commune as a unit in the land cadastres and then assigned each one a portion of the amount the government wanted to raise from the country as a whole. (A modern analogy would be the millage rate set by local governments using a property tax in the United States.) The commune apportioned the tax burden among its members on the basis of ability to pay. As a result of this system each peasant had a financial interest in the continued presence of each one of his fellows. If some of the members of a commune moved without finding replacements,[131] each of those who remained had to assume responsibility for a larger share of the allotted tax burden. Cadastres were not compiled frequently, and so the tax burden assigned to a particular commune sometimes bore little relation to those present and able to pay it.

The surviving records of Muscovy vividly portray the awareness by the Russian commune of its members' plight as a result of this type of taxation. The peasants remaining in a tax commune after a fire, plague, or crop failure would bewail their fate to the government and plead for the government to return their members who had fled the disaster "so that the tax burden will not force the rest of us to flee."[132] For some reason this seemed a much more realistic approach than to ask that the tax burden be reduced by conducting a new census. After the Time of Troubles the government gave its consent to the traditional request and ordered the fugitive peasants returned to their communes. A document of 1621 instructed the military governor of Cherdyn to return fugitive peasants to their old plots. No time limit was mentioned. The reason given was that the peasants should be returned to equalize the burden of paying taxes. The military governor also was supposed to try to prevent future flights by the local peasants. This apparently proved to be impossible, for in another Cherdyn case of 1629 the military governor was ordered to search for fugitives who had fled within the past ten years. Here the reason given was that these peasants were not paying taxes at all, contrary to the interests of the government. A mild penalty—disgrace—was stipulated for any lord who received a fugitive peasant.[133]

The time limit for the recovery of taxpaying black land peasants by the remaining members of the commune always outran that for seignorial peasants because the magnates had no personal interest in the matter; few of them had lands in the north, and the peasants simply moved from one commune in the area to another. Therefore the government readily granted petitions for the recovery of fugitives by taxpaying communes. The same more liberal attitude was exhibited toward towns and the problem of fugitive townsmen. The tax issue was, in fact, a minor, secondary factor and had no real impact on the outcome of the enserfment of the peasantry. In the center and most other areas of the Muscovite state, where the issue of the enserfment was resolved, land was viewed primarily as a cash substitute to be used to support social forces valued by the government, not as a direct revenue source for the state treasury. The townsmen were viewed as the government's cash revenue source.[134]

The law of 1592 binding all peasants to the land proved to be a hollow victory for the middle service class because of the statute of limitations applied to violators. As a result, that aspect of enserfment was not yet completed at the time of the Smolensk War. However, the act of binding the peasants to the land seems to have abased them in the eyes of civil authorities. Building on an accretion of innocuous precedents and Ivan IV's total disregard of human dignity, successive administrations for the sake of expediency solved various judicial and other problems by equating the peasants with slaves. This process culminated in the eighteenth century, when lords not only treated, but even sold, their serfs like slaves.

7.
Repeal of the Statute of Limitations

The final period in the history of the enserfment of the Russian peasantry resembles in certain respects the introduction of the Forbidden Years. The origin of this period can be attributed to the Smolensk War. In the Deulino truce Russia had ceded considerable territory to Poland. This was a handicap to Russian merchants, who lost their free access through Smolensk to the west and the Dnepr valley. The truce was humiliating to the Russians. The Poles refused to give up their claims to the Russian throne, which they insultingly continued to insist belonged to Wladyslaw IV as a result of his invitation by the boyars in 1610. Furthermore, the hatred for the Poles by Patriarch Filaret, who had spent about a decade of forced residence in Poland, was fanned by Cyril Lukaris, patriarch of Constantinople and "archfiend of the Catholic Church."[1]

As the truce neared its expiration date, the government began to make plans to retake Smolensk.[2] Because of the death of King Sigismund in April, 1632, and the inevitable ensuing dynastic crisis, Filaret launched an attack on Smolensk prior to the expiration of the truce and prior to the completion of necessary military preparations. This, combined with a lack of enthusiasm for the war within the government and a failure to coordinate a pincer operation on Poland in cooperation with the Swedes, ensured military defeat for the Russians.[3] Filaret died on October 1, 1633, and was followed at the helm of government by a cousin of the tsar, Prince Ivan Borisovich Cherkasskii. The Russians failed to retake Smolensk and its environs, but in the Polianovka Peace Treaty they did induce the Poles to surrender their claims to the Russian throne—while the Russians lost even more territory.[4] The war also revived Tatar attacks on the Ukraine, as the Crimeans, in league with the Poles, tried to take advantage of the concentration of Russian attenion and forces on the western frontier.[5] All of these events combined to cause unrest in the peasant community, unrest which found early expression in a minor uprising in the war zone led by a peasant of the Boldin monastery, Ivan Balash.[6]

During the 1620s Filaret had restored government finances and even succeeded in paying for the first part of the war out of reserves. Soon, however, a Zemskii Sobor had to be called to approve extraordinary levies,[7] and by the end of the war the government was in serious financial straits. This necessitated higher taxes, some of which ultimately fell on the peasant population. Taxes continued to rise after the Smolensk War to support a reorientation of foreign policy toward the southern frontier by the new Cherkasskii government.[8] The peasants began to move about simply to escape the onerous levies.[9]

Tables 2 and 3 show that there was a tremendous rise after the Smolensk War in the level of the two major direct taxes the Russian paid, and that they continued to rise until the end of the period under review (when the household tax replaced the sown-area, or *sokha,* tax). Moreover, at this time (1634–41, and probably in 1640–41) the government changed the relative weight for various categories of the *sokha.* The assessment on towns and *votchina, pomest'e,* and monastery lands was made four times greater than on Pomor'e black lands and on court lands, and remained in this proportion until 1662–63.[10] This measure may have been taken simply for the purpose of raising revenue, or it may reflect recognition that the middle service class, which was financed by these peasants, was rendering less and less useful service and that the revenues should be collected by the government for more effective military utilization. Regardless of the motivation, however, this discriminatory method of taxation created natural conditions for considerable movement, from seignorial land to black and court lands. The enormous rise in taxation proved to be a burden which the peasants could not bear, as witnessed by a great increase in arrears. The government attempted to collect unpaid taxes by nearly every conceivable means, and the ensuing violence was one of the major causes of peasant flight.[11]

This period also witnessed several exceptionally severe winters, bad harvests, and high grain prices in central Russia, although these were as nothing in the eyes of contemporaries compared to the calamities of the reigns of Ivan IV and, especially, Boris Godunov. Nevertheless, the records from the period note that these things were causes of peasant flights.[12]

There is no question that many peasants continued to prefer to live on the estates of the magnates after the Smolensk War.[13] (Opportunities to live on black and court lands, frequently the most favored types of land,[14] were rapidly declining as the government distributed these lands to petitioners.) Life was easier on large estates because the lord could

TABLE 2

Assessment of Taxes to Support the Post System
(Iamskie Den'gi) [15]

YEAR	RUBLES PER SOKHA*
1613–14	105? (35?)
1614–15	?
1615–16	280
1616–17	350
1617–18—1619–20	800
1620–21	584
1621–22—1629–30	468
1630–31—1632–33	400
1633–34—1639–40	534
1640–41—1641–42	726
1642–43	784 ?
1643–44—1659–60	784
1660–61	not collected
1661–62—1679–80	784

Sokha: literally, a two-pronged wooden plow. During the Mongol period the amount of land a man could plow with a *sokha* was converted into a tax unit. In the sixteenth and seventeenth centuries the term became used for much larger units of land or numbers of town houses (the "big sokha") for the purposes of communal taxation by the central government. For agricultural taxation, land was crudely divided into three categories: good, average, and poor. For lands belonging to the service class there were 800 *chetverti* (1 *chetvert'* = about 1-1/3 acres) of good land in a *sokha,* 1000 *chetverti* of average land, or 1200 *chetverti* of poor land. This was for one field; the usual agricultural pattern was the three-field system (fall, spring, and fallow fields), so that a *sokha* tax unit for lands belonging to the service class actually encompassed 2400, 3000, or 3600 *chetverti,* depending on the type of land. The tax burden was greater on lands belonging to the church— lands of monasteries, high church officials, and individual churches— because less land made up one *sokha*: 600 *chetverti* of good land, 700 of average, 800 of poor, and 900 of very poor. On lands belonging to peasants, black lands, the burden was the greatest: 500 *chetverti* of good land, 600 of average, and 700 of poor in one field made a *sokha* tax unit.

In towns the same term, *sokha,* was used for purposes of communal taxation, but the calculation was made in terms of the type and number of houses rather than in terms of arable land. One *sokha* as a taxation unit in a town might be 40 houses belonging to rich people, 60 houses belonging to average people, or 100 houses belonging to poor people. The number of houses comprising a *sokha* of any given type varied widely throughout the Muscovite state.

The intention and purpose of the *sokha* taxation system was to raise revenue from those most able to pay because they had either better land or higher incomes.

125

offer desired loans, overall obligations were probably less onerous (less had to be taken from each of three hundred peasants to support one man than if only six peasants were available for this), and there is some evidence to indicate that output was higher on the larger, better supervised, equipped, and organized estates.[16] In addition, large estates had surpluses with which to lure peasants after a bad harvest.[17] Because

TABLE 3

Assessment of Musketeer Taxes (Streletskii Khleb) [18]

YEAR	GRAIN PER SOKHA	CASH INSTEAD OF GRAIN PER SOKHA
1613–14	100 cheti* rye, groats, and oat flour	175 or 150 R.
1614–15—1616–17	The same, or 80 ch. rye and 40 ch. oats	?
1617–18	200 ch. rye and 200 ch. oats, or 320 ch. rye, 40 ch. groats, and 40 ch. oat flour	800 R.
1618–19	200 ch. rye and oats = 100 iufti	200 R.
1619–20	100 iufti	120 R. from distant towns
1620–21	100 iufti	?
1621–22	200 iufti	150 R. from distant towns
1622–23—1625–26	100 iufti	75 R. from distant towns, 70 R. from nearby towns
1626–27—1628–29	100 iufti	80 R. from distant towns, 76 R. from nearby towns
1629–30	100 iufti	85 R. from distant towns, 80 R. from nearby towns
1630–31—1632–33	100 iufti	80 R. from distant towns
1633–34—1635–36	100 iufti	?
1636–37—1637–38	200 iufti	?
1638–39—1639–40	100 iufti	280 R. from Polish towns of the *Razriad*
1640–41	?	Raised from 120 to 168 R. for Pomor'e towns.
1641–42—1653–54	700 iufti	672 R.
1654–55—1659–60	700 iufti	900 R.
1660–61	Not collected	
1661–62	700 iufti, 175 iufti from Pomor'e towns, which usually paid special cash levy.	Grain only
1662–63—1671–72	1400 iufti	822 R. from Pomor'e towns
1672–73—1678–79	2875 iufti from service-lands, 2506¼ iufti from church lands, 1825 iufti from court lands.	2800 R.

*1 *chet'* (*chetvert'*) = 216 pounds of rye.

of the nature of the tax system, the real per capita burden was probably lower between the census assessments on the more stable estates. Finally, as frequently noted, magnates with estates in several provinces easily could conceal fugitive peasants until the time period for their recovery had expired.[19]

Once a peasant had settled on the estate of a magnate, his opportunities for moving were significantly reduced. This meant that even a lord who was a dreadful exploiter could have a labor force ever increasing in size. He could offer attractive terms to newcomers and then make leaving extremely difficult by expending considerable sums on a repression network. Bailiffs would keep watch over all peasants. Those who fled might be mercilessly beaten at the order of the lord upon capture and returned to the estate. All peasants would be forced to serve as pledges for others, so that guarantors left behind in a pledge would suffer financially or physically because one of their number had fled. Should a member of a family flee individually, the rest would be closely watched so that they could not run away also, and they would be urged to pursuade the runaway to return.[20]

Members of the middle service class could not afford the loss of any peasants, for the flight of even one peasant household usually represented a significant loss of income. Statistical data for the second third of the seventeenth century reveal that members of the middle service class, on the average, had only about five peasant households apiece.[21] Some evidence indicates that this was insufficient to support fully one armed cavalryman. In 1633 the government gave servicemen of the "Moscow register" (discussed in chapter 2 as the "lower upper-service class") who had declared in a petition that they could not serve with only "3, 4, 5, or 6 peasants" supplemental grants of twenty-five rubles to those with fifteen peasants or less, to enable them to render service.[22] Other legislation implies that twenty households was a necessary minimum if the cavalrymen were to render effective service.[23] These facts, probably better than any other, show why the middle service class was so concerned about the peasant question.

In this light, studies which have been made of how peasants "fled" in this period and of which type of peasant was likely to move become especially telling. The first point usually noted is that peasant "flights" usually were not clandestine operations, but open, well planned and organized moves.[24] Frequently the peasant would start off down the road with his family, livestock, agricultural implements, his seed, and all his belongings at the time when his lord was in service. Rarely did a single individual flee.[25] A second important point is that peasants who fled greater distances,[26] whence retrieval was nearly impossible, such as to the southern frontier (which became much safer in the late 1630s and 1640s), were not the destitute, not those in need of loans, but rather the middling and well-to-do—precisely those who were financially able to make meaningful contributions to the support of the middle service class cavalryman.[27] The average value of property seized with fugitive peasants was just under thirty rubles, a significant sum in those days.[28] (By way of comparison, the median value of the property of a group of seventy-seven settled peasants in 1664 was eleven rubles, the average value about twenty rubles.) [29]

Also frustrating to penurious landholders was the practice of some wily peasants of moving from one illegal lord to another every time their rightful lord would file a suit for their recovery.[30] In one such case the peasant Savka Stepanov, with his wife, two daughters, and son-in-law, fled from a village belonging to one F. F. Tinkov. By 1638 Tinkov found out where they were living and procured a document to initiate a trial for their recovery. Savka learned of this and fled again. In 1639 Tinkov got a new document for a trial, whereupon Savka and his family moved once more. By 1641 Tinkov had again located them and filed another suit.[31] The record ends here, but widespread, recurrent instances of this kind consumed to an intolerable degree the energies of the *deti boiarskie.*

There is yet another parallel in the peasant question between the second half of Ivan IV's reign and the end of Mikhail's tenure on the throne. As noted earlier, the conquest of the middle and lower Volga regions served as an outlet for masses of peasants desiring to escape from Ivan's horrors in the central regions of the Muscovite state. Something similar happened after the Smolensk War, when government attention was directed to the Tatar frontier directly south of the Muscovite state. There had been already some population drain into this area from 1619 until the Smolensk War,[32] a period when Tatar raids were generally in abeyance. After the war the government, for reasons to be discussed in chapter 10, decided to fortify the area and moved the actual frontier, and with it the habitable safety zone, hundreds of miles to the south. (The Russian peasant, it should be noted, moved usually to places where security was provided by the government.) [33] As a result of the conditions described above, peasants by the thousands sought freedom in the new frontier area.[34]

The frontier played a complex role in Russian social relations. Briefly stated, it served as an outlet for the tensions of Russian society. The discontented could flee the pressure of a landlord there. Higher incomes from the better chernozem agriculture must have relieved some of the anxieties associated with podzol agriculture in the central regions. Movement south created discontent among the traditional landlords, who tried to convince the government to halt the outflow and return the migrants. The fear of return made the frontier a tinderbox ready to ignite when sufficiently provoked. However, it made the central regions relatively free of discontent until the frontier outlet was closed at the end of the eighteenth century.[35]

The members of the old middle service class were frustrated and angered by the government's decision to leave in the new Ukrainian frontier towns along the Belgorod fortified line (*zasechnaia cherta*) fugitive peasants who had enlisted in the service class there. The return of these runaways would have frustrated efforts to strengthen the defense of the expanded southern frontier. In 1635 and later the government categorically forbade various provincial frontier generals and governors to return fugitives without an order from Moscow—an unprecedented degree of centralization. These measures evoked a massive peasant exodus southward from Voronezh and Riazan' provinces to the new frontier towns. (Some peasants came from even farther away, but the tendency was for peasants to move no further than from one province to the next.) Tambov acquired fame as a new (1636) town "whence no one was returned" to old places of registration. The government in 1636 invited any former serviceman (*syn boiarskii*, musketeer, cossack, and so on) who had become impoverished and entered the peasantry since 1613 to rejoin the service class on the frontier. Officials on the frontier accepted bribes from fugitive peasants not to return them to their lords. The flights to the *cherta* aroused discontent among the northern landholders, who forced the government to slow down its program of fortifying and populating the frontier region.[36]

Life was not stable on the frontier either. A study by E. I. Vainberg followed hundreds of peasants who moved away from Elets and Kursk in the 1630s and 1640s. Many of them went to bordering provinces further south, some moved laterally, a few moved a bit north, but none seem to have returned back north to the area of old Muscovy proper.[37]

All of this Russian expansion south, and especially the cossack's seizure of Azov in the summer of 1637, terrified the Tatars. They feared, correctly, that such expansion would threaten the Crimea. Later, in 1637, the Tatars attacked, and carried away at least 2,250 captives.[38] These events heightened the government's awareness of the defense needs of the southern frontier.

As a result of extra expenses incurred in and losses suffered as a result of the Smolensk War and then in the annual southern frontier service against the Crimean Tatars, the members of the middle service class began a concerted petition campaign for the repeal of the time limit (*urochnye leta*) on the recovery of their fugitive peasants.[39] Experience showed the middle service class that its members needed as much time as possible to recover fugitive peasants. This was much less of an issue for wealthier lords, for their agents were instructed to stop peasant flight before it began, and if peasants did escape, magnates had the resources to keep track of them in flight and then to bring them back to their estates.[40] The *dvoriane* and *deti boiarskie,* with their average of five peasant households each, lacked the resources to compete on these terms with the magnates. Among the causes of their many complaints in the famous petition of February, 1637, the *dvoriane* and *deti boiarskie,* who had gathered for an Assembly of the Land scheduled to convene at the end of 1636,[41] listed prominently "the Moscow strong people," the magnates who were running the government, and the monasteries, which in the fifteenth century had initiated the limitations on peasant mobility:

> We, your slaves, are perishing completely because of Moscow bureaucratism. Our houses have been vacated, and the rest of our peasants and slaves are leaving us, your slaves, for the Moscow strong people, people of all ranks, high church officials, and the monasteries. In the provinces they do not give us, your slaves, trials against high church officials, the monasteries, and the Moscow strong people of all ranks. They rely on your royal charters exempting them from provincial court jurisdiction and on the time limit of five years.

This situation was particularly galling because of the great disparity of wealth in Russia. As mentioned earlier, the petitioners had on an average only about five peasant households each, whereas the members of the Boyar Duma had over five hundred peasant households each, plus an unknown number of slaves.[42]

The solution to this situation, as seen by the petitioners in their complaint to Tsar Mikhail, was the following:

> Grant us, your slaves, your royal decree with your royal grant for our past service and blood, for our poverty, ruin, and never-ending royal service [a return to the situation] as it was during the reigns of former sovereigns [Ivan IV and Fedor Ivanovich]. Order, lord, the five-year time limit [for recovering fugitive peasants] repealed. Order, lord, our fugitive peasants and slaves returned to us, your slaves, on the basis of the land cadastres [*pistsovye knigi*], the books containing the records of land grants [*otdel'nye knigi*], extracts

from official records [*vypisi*], and our documents [*kreposti*], so that our service lands and hereditary lands will not be laid waste and the rest of the peasants and slaves will not leave us, your slaves, and so that we, your slaves, serving in your never-ending royal service from vacant lands and paying your royal taxes, will not perish completely.[43]

The government, which still needed the active, wholehearted military force provided by the middle service class, sent a memorandum to its chancelleries asking what was the special limit for the Troitse Sergiev monastery, and then gave the same length of time, nine years only, to the middle service class.[44]

For some unknown reason both parties in this petition and answer ignored one of the real major issues of the period. Peasants were fleeing not only to the lands of the "strong people," but also, as we have seen, to the frontier. By February of 1637 hundreds of new recruits were reported registered in the *strel'tsy* and cossacks. No doubt most of them were fugitive peasants. Hundreds of others were recruited to build the new Belgorod fortified defense line. The *deti boiarskie* complained bitterly about this loss of peasants, which continued into the 1640s. This may be assumed to have been part of the cause of the anxiety expressed in the 1637 and subsequent petitions.[45]

The extension of the time limit on suits evidently did not become known immediately in all the chancelleries. A decree of October, 1638, from the Moscow Judicial Chancellery stated: "In the Tsar's decree it is written that fugitive peasants who fled not more than five years prior to the petition are to be returned to the servicemen and others; if the case has not been decided in five years, and the petition is registered in the Chancellery, the peasants have not escaped the time limit."[46] The first part of this quotation may simply represent bureaucratic incompetence, or, more likely, a deliberate attempt by the "strong people" to undermine the new gains of the middle service class. The second part is also of interest in that it demonstrates conclusively the importance of the measures taken by those harboring fugitive peasants to conceal them, for once a suit had been initiated, there was nothing which legally could cancel it. (The defendant could, of course, still win by exhausting the plaintiff, bribing the judge, and so on.) [47]

Partial success whetted the appetite of the middle service class. Its members were not to be assuaged by partial concessions. Another petition, submitted four years later, in the summer of 1641, again requested repeal of the time limit, a return to the situation before 1592–93.[48] This petition of the *dvoriane* and *deti boiarskie* was much longer, more elaborate, and explicit than had been the previous one, especially on the issue of where fugitive peasants were going and why:

> Their [those of the *dvoriane* and *deti boiarskie*] hereditary slaves [*kholopi*] and peasants are fleeing from them [in search of] privileges to the large service estates [*pomest'ia*] of various districts and to the hereditary estates [*votchiny*] belonging to the Patriarch, the metropolitans, the archbishops, the Troitse Sergiev and other monasteries; to the Tsar's court villages, to the black land districts, and [to estates belonging to] boyars, *okol'nichie, stol'niki, striapchie,* Moscow *dvoriane,* and other people of various ranks.[49]

The petitioners also raised other points which have been discussed in chapter 3.

Grudgingly, perhaps under pressure from delegates to the 1642 Assembly of the Land convoked to discuss the cossack seizure of Azov,[50] the government, still run by these same boyars and officials, raised the limit another year—to ten—for the recovery of fugitive peasants, and to fifteen for the recovery of peasants who had been taken away by force (*vyvoz*). The kidnapper had to pay the peasant's lawful lord five rubles per year for each year of the peasant's absence.[51] Almost irrelevantly, the government added to this minor concession another which was more meaningful: the members of the middle service class were henceforth freed from having to pay any internal tolls while in government service. Apparently the government hoped to direct the attention of the *dvoriane* and *deti boiarskie* away from their major concern, their labor force, by enacting this measure on tolls—which was to become chapter 9 of the *Ulozhenie* of 1649.

On April 4, 1642, Cherkasskii died and was followed as informal head of government by his brother-in-law, the totally corrupt and incompetent Fedor Ivanovich Sheremetev.[52] During the latter's tenure the pursuit of higher rank and personal wealth by the ruling clique became even more pronounced.[53] This boyar government had no support by any significant segment of the society; it was a time of government prostration and social disorder. A Swedish envoy predicted in 1645 that there would soon be an uprising in Moscow.[54]

On July 13, 1645, Tsar Mikhail died and was followed as sovereign by his son Aleksei Mikhailovich. Aleksei was only sixteen, and his tutor Boris Ivanovich Morozov became "Lord Protector." Boris set about reforming the government by purging his three Sheremetev predecessors from their posts.[55] Of their major lieutenants, B. A. Repnin was sent to Belgorod, G. S. Kurakin to Kazan'. Many others were replaced by Morozov's friends. He also attempted to reform the administration by diminishing the number of the tsar's household servants and cutting in half the wages of those remaining; halving the allowances given ambassadors; and raising the customs.[56]

Morozov was certainly one of the most remarkable men in Muscovy, but his abilities were flawed by an insatiable greed, noted by all contemporaries. His talents netted him an estate of 9,100 taxpaying households.[57] He also used his position to swell his labor force, sending out orders in the name of the tsar to provincial governors to look for fugitive peasants from the Morozov estates.[58] In this respect he personified the fact that in Muscovy there existed no notion that the goal of the state should be to advance the general welfare in preference to private gain.[59] Morozov and his cohorts had set about looting as soon as they gained power.

By 1645 the desired concession of no time limit for the recovery of fugitive peasants had not been granted. The government of Mikhail had failed to complete the process of enserfment, not because it feared the masses, but because it preferred to allow the magnates to fill up their hereditary estates with peasants.[60] The members of the middle service class on duty in Tula tried a third time to get the time limit repealed by submitting a petition in July or August of 1645 to the new tsar, young Aleksei. They noted that they had served Aleksei's father Mikhail in military service, and his predecessors as well, uninterruptedly for thirty-two years. "As a result of these services" they had become "impoverished, burdened with great debts, and had lost their horses." In addition, their labor force had deserted them to live on the lands of the "strong people, the boyars, *okolnichie,* the tsar's advisers, the high church officials, and the monasteries." This lament, never contradicted, gives further evidence that those running the government and the church establishment were profiting from peasant mobility. This petition also indicates that the peasants preferred to live on the larger estates: "The [fugitive] peasants, living on the lands of the 'strong people,' are registering other peasants sight unseen in the land cadastres and [signing their names on] notes for loans, [thereby] befriending those on whose lands they are living while in flight from others."[61] This preference was making the middle service class unable to render military service, which the government still needed.

The new government insisted that the time limit remain ten years for the present, but promised to repeal this limit after the completion of a census which would serve as a source of information on the real condition of the middle service class as well as the documentary basis for the final, complete enserfment of the peasantry. It seems to have been at this time that all of a peasant's relatives (stepchildren, brothers,

133

nephews, and the like) became bound where he was.[62] The census was ordered on October 19, 1645, and was taken in 1646 and 1647.[63]

I doubt whether the time limit ever would have been repealed had it not been for the Moscow riot of the summer of 1648, which forced the government, apprehensive for other reasons as well, to convoke an Assembly of the Land to discuss and approve a new law code, the *Ulozhenie* of 1649. Evidence to support this contention can be found in a supplement to the census directive of 1647. (Three copies of the census directive survive, for the Moscow, Tot'ma, and Kargopol' provinces [*uezdy*]).[64] The directive observed that an earlier order had specified that fugitive peasants, when located, were to be returned to their former lords, regardless of when they had fled. The lords who had harbored the fugitive peasants were supposed to compensate the rightful lords for the loss of their peasants' labor.

But by October, 1647, the middle service class was again quiescent, and the Morozov government obviously hoped that the *dvoriane* and *deti boiarskie* had forgotten the promise made two years earlier. The government ordered its officials to return only peasants who had fled within the last fifteen years, thus restoring the time limit that was anathema to the middle service class. The government also decreed that the church officials and great lords who had received the fugitive peasants did not have to compensate the rightful lords for the loss of the peasants' labor.[65] Another directive noted that many peasants had recently moved from Russia proper to Siberia because of poverty (in large part due to oppressive taxation) and crop failures. These people were to be registered in Siberia, in order to populate it, and no attempt was to be made to return them to their old lords.[66]

Some time between September, 1647, and March, 1648, the government decreed that peasants who had fled to Lithuania over five years ago would be given their freedom if they returned to Russia. Those who had fled less than five years ago were to be returned to their lords. The rationale for the decree is hard to discern, for if it was a device to induce peasants to return to Russia, one wonders why the old five-year limit was chosen. Apparently it had some success, for many old fugitives returned to Russia once the measure became known. On balance, however, the measure failed in its purpose, for the middle service class complained bitterly that masses of peasants were passing over the frontier into Lithuania to put in their five years to gain their freedom. In June, 1648, the government repealed this five-year decree.[67] The whole incident leads one to believe that the government expected the returning peasants to settle on estates belonging to the magnates, and gave no thought to the decree's consequences for the middle service class. Support for this supposition is furnished by the fact that the order was issued from the Chancellery of Foreign Affairs (*Posol'skii Prikaz*), which from January 6 to June 2 was run by the notorious Nazar Chistoi of the Morozov clique. The crucial point for us here, however, is that this incident demonstrates once again that the Morozov government was by no means committed to repealing the time limit on the recovery of fugitive peasants.

In the spring of 1648 not all was going well for young Aleksei and the Morozov government. Aleksei's legitimacy as tsar was being questioned, largely because he had not been installed by an Assembly of the Land.[68] Since January, news of an impending great attack by the Crimean and Nogai Tatars had been filtering into Moscow, and in April the army was alerted for possible duty. The Crimean Khan was demanding triple the usual tribute. The cossacks in the Ukraine were rebelling against Polish hegemony, and the Russians may have been reluctant to support them for fear the rebellion would infect the Russian masses and a new Time of Troubles would result.[69]

A crucial event occurred on Thursday, June 1, 1648, when the people of Moscow began to riot after they were prevented by those surrounding the tsar from presenting a petition to him that contained their grievances against various government officials (particularly L. S. Pleshcheev).[70] The petitioners noted that a commission had been appointed to investigate abuses committed by government officials, but nothing had come of it because the people who were supposed to make the report to the tsar were the very ones committing the abuses. "They, no less than others, were participants in this illegality and [they] concealed all wrongdoing until it seemed as though this were being done for the profit and benefit of the tsar." The petitioners made some very interesting comments on the role of the tsar in Russian society: he was the righter of injustice and internal disorders, a suppressor of wrongdoing officials, a likeness of King Solomon and Emperor Justinian. But Aleksei had not been fulfilling his role, and consequently

> people of all ranks are lamenting and complaining against your royal majesty. [They say] that you pay no heed to those who are poor, lowly, and defenseless, that you do not stand up for us against our oppressors and destroyers, but you permit the rich to continue their plundering.[71]

The petition ended with a plea for the appointment of just officials. If this proved to be impossible, the tsar should permit the people to elect their own officials.[72]

The dispersion of the petitioners by the *strel'tsy* was followed by riots in Moscow and a dozen other towns. The musketeers, responsible for maintaining order in Moscow, then mutinied and refused to obey their commander, Morozov.[73] On June 2 a mob of several thousand gathered in the Kremlin and demanded that the government heed the request for reforming itself. The mob, with the musketeers, plundered the houses of Morozov and his cronies, P. T. Trakhaniotov, L. S. Pleshcheev, and N. I. Chistoi. Chistoi was torn to bits by the mob. On Saturday, June 3, the scale of the disorders expanded, the government lost control of the city, the houses of the wealthy were looted, and a fire broke out in Moscow which burned 24,000 houses, half of the total.[74] The mob petitioned against Pleshcheev and Trakhaniotov. The former was handed over to the mob and stoned to death; the latter, a brother-in-law of Morozov and commander of the artillery, was beheaded at the townsmen's behest on the fifth. Morozov was saved only by the personal intercession of the tsar.[75] On June 3 the Tsar replaced the administration of Morozov and Miloslavskii with another faction, headed by the Cherkasskiis, N. I. Romanov, and the Sheremetevs, which began a gigantic distribution of lands and cash to gain wider support from the service class.[76] During these months the faction headed by Morozov (and containing Tsar Aleksei and Patriarch Iosif [1642–1652]) hoped to gain the support of the townsmen and *strel'tsy* by granting desired concessions. The Cherkasskii faction, on the other hand, cultivated the provincial middle service class.[77]

Sometime during this period the members of the middle service class, discontented because Morozov had refused to pay them,[78] again presented a petition to the government in which they noted the disappearance of their labor force. In its commentary on the petition the government noted that the official time limit for recovering fugitives was ten years.[79] One wonders what had become of the promise of 1645 to return all peasants, without any time limit, upon completion of the census.

The new Cherkasskii government, helpless after the middle service class and the *strel'tsy* joined the uprising against it,[80] convoked by popular request an Assembly of the Land that represented all classes except the peasants and slaves.[81] Patriarch Nikon subsequently observed that it had been convoked "not willingly, but out of fear of the rebellion of the common people."[82] The majority of the Assembly of the Land delegates were from the townspeople and the middle service class, whose members were most responsible for forcing the government to act.[83] Their presence left a lasting imprint on the product of the convocation, the law code known as the *Ulozhenie* of 1649.

Morozov, saved by the tsar from the mob, was sent to the Kirillov monastery in Beloozero on June 12 at the request of the townsmen. His exile did not last long. He soon left the monastery for his estate, Goroden', near Tver', and from there went to his Moscow-area estate, Pavlovskoe. On October 26 he returned to Moscow. Five days later a dispute was contrived between Tsar Aleksei and Ia. K. Cherkasskii, who was placed under house arrest. His post as head of the Musketeer Chancellery (*Streletskii Prikaz*), formerly a major branch of the army but now reduced to an internal police force (see chapter 12), was assumed by Il'ia Danilovich Miloslavskii, a brother-in-law of both Aleksei and Morozov.[84] Miloslavskii in essence became head of state and shepherded the Assembly of the Land through its compilation of the *Ulozhenie*.

The new law code contained a number of concessions to the townsmen (see chapter 14) as well as to the middle service class. The major concession was the removal of the time limit for suing for the recovery of fugitive peasants. The move instituted the final enserfment of the Russian peasantry.[85] By no means whatsoever (with one exception)[86] could a peasant (or his descendants), either seignorial or nonseignorial, legally escape from the place where he was registered in the census of 1646–47.[87] The law code deprived the peasant of the last remnants of the right to move, and converted him into an appendage of landed property. This had also been the goal of the Forbidden Years. These measures did not convert him into a slave bound to the person of an individual.[88] If he was not registered in the census (or in any other valid document, such as the cadastres compiled at the end of the 1620s), then he would be bound to the land whenever he signed a contract with a lord to use his land.[89] The *Ulozhenie* continued the seventeenth-century stipulation that all the property belonging to a fugitive peasant should be returned with him.[90]

The compilers of the *Ulozhenie* put no sanctions in the law code against peasants who fled, as there were against lords who received them.[91] Perhaps this omission was an oversight. Perhaps it was part of the general abasement of the peasant; a slave was not held legally responsible for his actions, and in this case a peasant was not either. Or perhaps nothing was done so that peasants would not be discouraged from fleeing.[92]

The peasant question was nearly the last item of business acted on by the Assembly of the Land, for the decree binding the peasants to the land by repealing the time limit on the recovery of fugitives was not promulgated until January 2, 1649.[93] This serves as additional evidence that the government held out until the last moment and acted only under duress. Further evidence may be found in the important point introduced into the law code at the insistence of the delegates to the Assembly of the Land that owners of hereditary lands had the right to "free" their peasants, who then could go wherever they chose. Holders of service lands, however, could not do this, and any peasants illegally "manumitted" had to be returned to the *pomest'e*.[94] This measure, which indicates as well as anything the bias of the Assembly of the Land, reflected the interests of the members of the middle service class—landholders who did not want to permit their own peasants to move about, but who were more than willing to make provision for the peasants on the estates of the "strong people" (who also ran the government) to do so.

The government[95] did everything in its power to avoid the final concession to the middle service class. The problem was not so much that the leaders, after a realistic appraisal, feared to make the move because of the possibility of a peasant uprising once the final step of enserfment had been taken. It was, rather, that the leading figures in the government personally found even the slightest remnant of peasant mobility very profitable.[96] There is little evidence to support the view that the government had failed to act earlier out of fear of a peasant uprising, but a great deal to support the other hypothesis. Boris Ivanovich Morozov, Tsar Aleksei's tutor and actual head of state until he was forced out in June of 1648, was receiving fugitive peasants on his estates and concealing them there as long as he could, in deliberate violation of the law. Only after he had nearly lost his life did Morozov send eighty-five orders in June, July, and August telling his stewards to return to their rightful lords over two hundred peasant families. From September, 1648, to June, 1649, another 115 peasant families were returned from the Morozov estates to 73 former lords.[97] Another leading figure in Morozov's faction[98] was Patriarch Iosif, who represented the church in all matters, lay as well as spiritual.[99] The leading monastery in his sphere of control, the Troitse Sergiev, recovered 387 fugitive peasants in the few months from December, 1649, through May, 1650.[100] If this monastery, portrayed by contemporaries as the champion seducer of others' peasants, recovered this many fugitives from its own lands, one can only imagine how many peasants subject to other lords must have been living on its estates! It probably was not accidental that the Troitse Sergiev monastery did not file its claims until about ten months after the Zemskii Sobor had adjourned, for claiming such a large number of fugitives would have been provocative and might well have produced a reaction hardly desired by the monastery while the members of the middle service class were still victorious. Most other monasteries, too, had been receiving (if not actually recruiting) all the working hands coming their way, regardless of whether they were fugitives or not.[101]

In spite of the desires of the magnates who controlled the government, the supreme power finally had to capitulate to the demands of the middle service class.[102] The major motivating force behind the magnates' capitulation at the Zemskii Sobor to the demands of the combined forces of the middle service class and the townsmen (allied since the Sobor of 1642 on the Azov question) was unquestionably fear of the mob, augmented when the *strel'tsy* and some members of the middle service class joined the rebels.[103] When the Assembly of the Land convened in September to discuss the draft of the new law code, the government was arming the wealthy boyars, while some people were fleeing Moscow out of fear of another uprising.[104] Although the government figures personally involved left no memoirs on their state of mind in the second half of 1648,[105] other contemporaries did. In January, 1649, the top corporation merchants (*gosti*) and merchants of the second corporation (*gostinaia sotnia*) noted that they had been unable "out of fear" to protest any earlier the course of events in the last six months.[106] This is the same mood described by Nikon.

The frightened government desperately needed the support of the middle service class, for at the moment it had no other force for internal repression or for an instrument of foreign policy.[107] The members of the government were conscious not only of the recent Time of Troubles, but also of the revolutions going on in Western Europe. The protectorate in England was the prime example of what could happen to a monarch and his courtiers should they find themselves isolated and lacking even the support of the army. The initial Russian governmental attempts to gain this support by means of land grants and doles of cash had not been successful, for the petitions on the peasant question continued to come in to the government from members of the middle service class. Not sure even by the end of the year how reliable the potentially mutinous middle service class was, the government decreed that *deti boiarskie* could not come to Moscow to collect their pay.[108] To gain support, the government, whose leading figures felt peasant mobility was profitable to themselves, was compelled to grant the demand of the *dvoriane* and *deti boiarskie* that the time limit on the recovery of fugitive peasants be removed.

To summarize, the Smolensk War and the decision to secure the southern frontier caused renewed turmoil in the peasant community. The middle service class, insecure because of its precarious financial position and because of the technological threat to its social status posed by the gunpowder revolution, pressured the government to complete the enserfment of the increasingly abased peasantry by repealing the statute of limitations on the recovery of fugitives. The government resisted the pressure because it attached more importance to populating the frontier regions and the estates of the ruling magnates than to supporting the obsolescent middle service class cavalry. However, the civil disorders of 1648 forced the oligarchs ruling the country to capitulate to the demand for enserfment in order to save the regime.

8.

Consequences of the Repeal of the Statute of Limitations

The question has been raised as to how important the *Ulozhenie* of 1649 really was in the history of serfdom in Russia. Was it, as Kliuchevskii and his followers believed, simply the belated legislative recognition of what had already been enacted by life itself? Or was the Slavophile Beliaev correct in asserting that the binding of the peasant to the land changed neither his meaning nor position; that the bound peasant lost only the right to wander from one end of Russia to another and that he gained the right to belong to a class and a stationary holding?[1] Or, was the removal of the time limit on the recovery of fugitive peasants something which had to be fought for over a long period of time, and, once achieved, was it something which effected a profound break in the minds and lives of contemporaries and even of future generations?

My study of the evolution of serfdom has led me to the conclusion that Kliuchevskii's interpretation of the social developments of late Muscovy was a brilliant attempt to explain the development of an observed phenomenon. However, utilization of sources brought to light since that great historian's time renders his nondecree theory superfluous and permits another explanation which is a consistent one and takes cognizance of all relevant observed phenomena. The Beliaev interpretation is tied up with the Slavophile conception of the idyllic, organic nature of Russian society before the destructive Petrine reforms and simply flies in the face of reality.

The information now available indicates that the *Ulozhenie* was indeed a profound development in the history of the peasantry, "the greatest legal act directed toward the final enserfment of the peasants."[2] The institution of serfdom codified in the *Ulozhenie* was the basis of the institution which was repealed in 1861. Of course the institution evolved during the two centuries of its existence, but nevertheless it is traceable to the Moscow riots of the summer of 1648, the campaign of the middle service class, and the ultimate victory in the *Ulozhenie*.

Were contemporaries aware that a momentous, even cataclysmic, event had occurred? All signs indicate that in fact they were. First of all, the government sent out a memorandum that provincial officials should be ready for any disturbances which might occur as a result of the repeal of the time limit on the recovery of fugitive peasants.[3] The Moscow government felt that this news might alarm the peasant community and wanted local authorities to prepare for any eventuality. However, the government was to have to wait a few years for the fulfillment of its expectations of peasant uprisings.[4]

Prior to the *Ulozhenie* the government, lords, and peasants all tended to believe that agriculture could be a free, voluntary, and even temporary occupation. After 1649 this view quickly passed away.[5] The peasantry became a rigidly stratified caste. Prior to the new law code, some peasant settlement contracts with lords viewed the repeal by Boris of the right to move on St. George's Day as temporary (*do gosudareva ukaza*), but this phrase no longer was written after that time. Peasants caught by a census-taker knew they could not move legally of their own volition, and those not yet registered on a parcel of land knew their only hope of avoiding enserfment was to keep moving—which some of them did.[6]

The *Ulozhenie* proved to have a deleterious effect on peasant trade and industry when peasants were banned from engaging in what were deemed "urban occupations."[7] Many wealthy peasants were ruined financially when they were forced by the law code to sell their enterprises for very little.[8] This in turn curtailed economic differentiation among the peasantry, as the various legal restrictions combined with the communal system of mutual responsibility for the paying of taxes and dues and for rendering obligations to enforce a greater degree of equality among bound peasants in the countryside.[9] The claim also has been advanced that serfdom hindered the development of peasant handicraft and agricultural technique, neither of which was "backward" by world standards until Russian initiative was stifled by the new social and political conditions.[10] The binding of the peasants unquestionably had a harmful effect on the development of urban industry, as the curtailment of migration to towns created an "unnatural" shortage of labor there.[11]

The year 1649 also proved to be a watershed for the middle service class. As will be shown later, binding the peasants permanently to the land did little or nothing to improve the ability of the middle service class to render service. Having sought and achieved a panacea, the middle service class realized full well that it was wanting and tried other tactics to attempt to cope with problems. Never again was ink put to paper to demand the repeal of the limitations on the right to recover fugitive peasants. After the *Ulozhenie* the demand shifted to attempts to get the law enforced, but even more important became the issue of a cash salary to supplement or replace inadequate incomes derived from peasant serfs.[12]

The *Ulozhenie* also had a great impact on the return of fugitive peasants.[13] The circle of relatives to be returned with a fugitive head of a family was widened.[14] Lords submitted a mass of petitions on peasants whose labor they had assumed was lost to them forever.[15] The state's police powers (and accompanying inhumanity and violence) were injected into the issue as never before. The result was that tens of thousands of fugitives were returned, thousands right after the promulgation of the law code,[16] even more later. The *Ulozhenie* was used as the basis for returning these fugitives.[17] Prior to 1649 each peasant was returned individually after the filing of a suit by a lord.[18] The Service Land Chancellery (*Pomestnyi Prikaz*) received the complaints from lords about fugitive peasants, including (if possible) the whereabouts of the runaways. This information was then transmitted to the Military Chancellery (*Razriad*), which would in turn send the information to a governor (*voevoda*) in the province where the peasant was living. The governor would be ordered to find the fugitive, to get bail for him (*poruchnaia zapis'*—a guarantee by several individuals), and, if the matter was contested, to produce him for trial in the *Razriad* in Moscow on a future date, perhaps nine to eleven months hence, to determine to whom the peasant belonged.[19] But in the 1650s and 1660s, when peasants were again fleeing en masse because of the pressure of taxes resulting from the Thirteen Years War,[20] state agents went out and surveyed the entire population of a given area and returned to their former locales all those not belonging in the area under review.[21] This had been done for townsmen, but never for peasants.

The massive returning of peasants from the rich frontier lands to the poorer plots whence they had come delayed the development of these lands. This was hardly desirable from the treasury's point of view because the peasants could have been expected to pay more taxes from the better frontier lands at a time when the government was relying increasingly on direct taxes to support the army.

The landlord class was not slow to react to the new condition of the peasant prescribed by the 1649 law code. The law allowed no way for the peasant to escape, a situation analogous to the period after the introduction of the Forbidden Years. As in the reign of Fedor Ivanovich, so in the 1650s at least some lords decided to take advantage of the peasant's disability by increasing the level of exploitation. This was done either by raising the rent (*obrok*) or adding to the corvée obligations (*barshchina, barskoe delo*).[22]

The most noticeable impact of the enserfment was on the settlement contracts between lord and peasant.[23] Prior to the *Ulozhenie* a peasant usually received a two- or three-year exemption from paying dues (and often taxes as well) from the lord on whose land he settled, but these exemptions diminished rapidly and then disappeared after 1649.[24] Also, lords sometimes subsidized peasants who settled on their lands (to induce settlement and to help put an economy into production), and prior to the *Ulozhenie* some of these loans (in cash or in kind) were repaid by peasants hoping to move. After 1649 there is not extant even one such repayment, for the peasant knew he could not leave his lord legally, and so made no effort to repay such loans.[25] The enserfment of the peasantry was also recognized in loan contracts by the fact that after 1649 these contracts no longer contained forfeits, payments, or other penalties for nonfulfillment, since legally the peasant had no option but to stay and do what the lord ordered.[26] Finally, the lord-peasant contracts in the second half of the seventeenth century no longer contained the phrases present as late as the 1640s, representing hope for the restoration of the right to move on St. George's Day.[27] Beginning in 1619 a few peasants agreed in their settlement contracts not to move,[28] but after 1649 all knew that a peasant could not legally quit a lord's lands—a realization reflected in the *poriadnye*.[29] The only way a bound peasant could move was to flee illegally, which tens of thousands of them did. By 1700 not only was it clear that peasants registered on an estate would never be able to move in the future, but also that there were few "free peasants" left; nearly all peasants were registered somewhere and the issue of moving legally no longer existed.[30]

It is also probable that the definitive binding of the peasant weakened the commune and lessened its jurisdiction. Until 1649 much punishment was left in the hands of the commune; perhaps the lord gave orders not to the individual peasant but only to the commune. Prior to 1649 the lord could evict unruly peasants from his lands, but after the promulgation of the new law code some lords (owners of estates, not holders of service lands) legally could "manumit" undesired peasants. The tendency was for the lord to punish (or torture) the serf himself corporally, or else fine the now weakened commune for its members' offenses.[31] The individual peasant, as well as his commune, was further abased by the *Ulozhenie*. Article 7 of chapter 16 of the new law code permitted a lord to move peasants (apparently without their consent) from *votchina* and *pomest'e* estates to vacant *pomest'e* lands. When news got out in 1652 that Boiarin Morozov was going to do this, a number of his peasants fled, some of them even out of Russia.[32] In the mind of the peasants the enactment of the *Ulozhenie* legitimized the violence done to them by lords, and they ceased to complain to the government about being mistreated, as they had done even as late as the 1640s.[33] In time the submitting of petitions by peasants against their lords was forbidden by law.[34]

The enserfment of the peasantry also created a sharp distinction between "state" ("court" and "black") peasants and "seignorial" peasants. A minor difference had existed prior to 1649, but this was greatly accentuated by the *Ulozhenie*. State peasants were bound to the land and their taxpaying status, but seignorial peasants were obliged to work for lords, with many of the consequences discussed above. Seignorial peasants, in the labor-short economy, became part of the value of an estate and in essence were sold along with it.[35] In the eighteenth century the difference became all the more noticeable. The seignorial peasants were essentially converted into slaves who also paid taxes, while the state peasants' position was much envied because they retained a considerable degree of human dignity. The immediate cause of the lamentable status of the seignorial peasantry can be traced to the abasement enforced by the 1649 law code.

The *Ulozhenie* of 1649 was the product of the Assembly of the Land convoked by the government in response to the dissidents' demands in the summer of 1648. The Odoevskii commission that drafted the code heeded the cry of the middle service class and repealed the loophole in the Forbidden Years decree of 1592 by making all fugitive peasants returnable to their lawfully prescribed domiciles at any time. In the wake of this development the now totally bound peasant was further degraded, became increasingly dependent on his lord, and was restricted to those few pursuits, mainly agricultural ones, which other castes of society had not reserved for themselves. This was a logical consequence of the stratification of society prescribed by the *Ulozhenie*. The enserfment was a series of conscious acts by the centralized power which by the middle of the seventeenth century had the resources to enforce the binding of the peasant to the land (when it wanted to) and which was sufficiently confident of its own strength to turn jurisdiction over the seignorial peasantry back to the landowners. In this way the legal person of the primary agricultural producer was abased for the sake of administrative expediency.

Peasants comprised about 90 percent of the Russian population. Nearly three-quarters of the total population was finally enserfed by the

Ulozhenie,[36] which established permanent and hereditary serfdom based on the land cadastres and censuses. This was the conclusion of the process begun over two centuries earlier during the civil war in the reign of Vasilii II. No one would want to romanticize the condition of the peasant, whose life was indubitably hard, brutal, and short throughout the period under review, but the decline in his legal and social status is unquestionable. The government never seems to have been enthusiastic about limiting the peasant's right to move, but rather responded to different pressure groups. Large monasteries were the first pressure group, then the middle service class took up the issue. After the Time of Troubles monasteries renewed the pressure, and the middle service class finally brought it to a climax. At first the peasant lost the right to move, then the right to call his person his own. Not accidentally, serfdom was repealed in the reverse order; the later part of serfdom was annulled first, then the older. In 1861–63 the lord lost his police rights over the person of his serfs, but only at the beginning of the twentieth century was the peasant's full freedom to move whenever and wherever he desired restored. This symmetry in the building up and tearing down of an institution is what we might expect.

The government, consisting of the great prince-tsar, noble magnates, and a few lesser but still powerful adviser-officials, functioned for two purposes: for what might be termed the preservation of the monarch's patrimony against external and internal threats, and for the personal aggrandizement of the indivduals who happened to be the sovereign's favorites. The restriction of the peasantry's mobility never seems to have operated much to the advancement of the personal well-being of the magnates, who profitted more from a system of at least semifree labor which they could recruit and retain with comparative ease. In this context the grants to selected monastic institutions must be viewed simply as favors to friends in the church establishment.

Another motivation behind the enserfment of the peasantry was the realization that the conservation of the realm (or the preservation of the fruits of holding a government post) required an adequately supported army. At times of economic dislocation the only means of satisfying the needs of the army, the backbone of which was the middle service class cavalry, seemed to be to limit the movement of the primary producers capable of rendering this support. This understanding was based on an unwillingness to reduce the army to a size the country could afford. Any reduction was impossible, for it would have forced the admission that Russia was indefensible or that its military aspirations were too grandiose. Since neither of these admissions was possible, reducing the size of the army was impossible. The only solution was to cut off shrinkage of support of the army by curtailing peasant removal from the lands of the middle service class to the estates of the magnates and the frontiers. This was effected by binding the peasantry to the land. However, the well-being of the army was not always the primary motive. The government in the 1590s and in 1649 curtailed peasant freedom to garner middle service class support in moments of political crisis.

Part III

*The Gunpowder Revolution
in Muscovy*

9.
The Beginnings

The Muscovite period of Russian history witnessed fundamental changes in military technology, technique, and strategy. In the fifteenth century the major military figure was a cavalryman, armed with bow and arrows, fighting on two fronts, in the south and east against the nomadic Tatars, in the west against the settled Lithuanians, Poles, Livonian Knights, and Swedes. By the end of the seventeenth century this warrior had been replaced by an infantryman armed with a flintlock musket and accompanied by heavy cannon in contests with Sweden, Poland, or Turkey for the possession of heavily fortified towns. This military revolution had a lasting impact on both the peasantry and the middle service class.

In Western Europe, with the growth of towns (which provided both soldiers and taxes to pay them), interest existed in infantry by the end of the thirteenth century. The crossbow, which fired a bolt that could penetrate a knight's armor at 150 paces, began to put an end to heavy cavalry.[1] Western rulers also took advantage of the importation of gunpowder from the Orient in the thirteenth century[2] and the perfection of various types of firearms (and also the pike) to discover by the beginning of the sixteenth century that expensive, capricious, unreliable upper class cavalry could be dispensed with.[3] Consequently, they began to shift from mounted cavalry to infantry. In 1439 Charles VII took a big step in this direction in France at Orleans with his introduction of the *compagnie d'ordonnance* and the *gens d'armes*. He discharged his mercenaries and introduced a national army in 1445.[4] The Swiss infantry proved its superiority over the Burgundian cavalry at Murten in 1476, giving the future military preponderance to infantry until the advent of mechanized warfare in the twentieth century.[5] In the West in the sixteenth century the ratio of infantry to cavalry rose, with some fluctuations, from three infantrymen to one cavalryman to a maximum of eight infantrymen to one cavalryman.[6]

A leading advocate of this change in the West was Machiavelli (1469–1527), who in his *Arte Della Guerra* placed prime importance on the infantry in warfare. He noted that cavalry (cuirassiers and dragoons) was good for spying, sudden attacks, devastating enemy country, interrupting supplies, and pursuing a defeated enemy, but nevertheless the main brunt of military activity had to be borne by the infantry.[7]

Russia, because of the nature of the enemy (until the end of the sixteenth century) and limited resources and imagination (after that time), was unable to adapt itself fully to the Western gunpowder revolution until the second half of the seventeenth century. Russia had a long frontier contiguous with Western powers who were not as interested in captives, booty, and tribute as were the Tatars, but preferred to contend with Russia for real estate. The technological advances made in the West, especially in Poland and Sweden, could not be ignored forever if Russia hoped to survive. Most of these technological advances were connected with gunpowder, and Russia eventually copied them. The Russian army rarely exercised any initiative in its choice of weapons and tactics, usually adapting itself to the conditions imposed by the enemies it had to contend with.[8]

The first recorded use of gunpowder in Russia was in 1382 when Muscovites, defending themselves against a Tatar siege, are reported to have fired cannon from the Kremlin at the troops of Tokhtamysh. Neither the origin of these first cannon nor the time of their arrival in Russia has yet been determined. Russia's immediate neighbors to the east began using gunpowder weapons later than 1382—the Tatars around 1400 and the Persians in the sixteenth century. Firearms were known in Central Asia in the 1370s, but it is doubtful that they leaped from there, over the Tatars, to Moscow. It has been suggested that the Russians may have obtained the recipe for gunpowder either from China via the Mongols or from India, where the first firearms appeared in the middle of the thirteenth century.[9] Or, Russia may have borrowed from the West. Western Europe became acquainted with gunpowder in the second half of the thirteenth century; it was first used for explosive purposes sometime between 1270 and 1320. A type of cannon may have been invented in Germany at the beginning of the fourteenth century.[10]

In any case, gunpowder was in Russia to stay. In 1389 cannon are reported to have been used in Pskov, Novgorod, and Tver'. All available evidence indicates that these weapons were imported from the West, and it is conceivable that the contemporary ones in Moscow were too.[11] Tver', for over a century a leading rival of Moscow, had the closest links with the West at this time; Western technology probably arrived there first and thence spread throughout Russia, for Tverian artillery was usually the most advanced in the country.

The early weapons were used for town defense. Soon, however, artillery began to be moved around as an offensive weapon. These cannon were mainly instruments of terror, to frighten the inhabitants of a fortified town, not offensive weapons as we think of them. They were forged in one or two pieces of rolled up sheet iron, and reinforced by metal straps around the barrel.[12] The weapons were usually of two parts, with the barrel being fastened to the chamber with wedges; they were charged either from the breech or the muzzle. The instrument did not exceed a calibre of 110 mm. The whole piece was set in a hollowed-out log.[13] The charge of the earliest artillery pieces was rather insignificant; when a missile was fired, it was usually a rock that was propelled through the air a hundred or a hundred and fifty yards by an explosion of a pulp form of gunpowder. This early, highly immobile cannon was as likely to explode as to discharge because the missile and the charge often were not in the correct proportions. This cannon was not much of an improvement over the simpler and safer catapult, which continued to be used until at least the second quarter of the fifteenth century. The early cannon also made little impression on the art of war through the first half of the fifteenth century, and the defenders inside a fortress usually had the advantage because the penetration power of artillery was insufficient to damage stone walls. This weakness is reflected in the fact that artillery was not used in all battles for towns until the beginning of the reign of Ivan III. The chronicles mention the use of artillery in twenty-two battles prior to the 1470s, and in only four or five instances did the use of firearms influence the outcome of the battle.[14]

The massive introduction of more penetrating artillery into the armies of Russia began in the 1470s. It was accompanied by significant technological advances. By this time artillery pieces were being manufactured in Russia.[15] There were basically three kinds of artillery: the *pushka* (a mortar-type weapon), the *pishchal'* (a cannon, in the sixteenth century called *pushka* to avoid confusion with the musket-*pishchal'*), and the *tiufiak* (from Turkish *tiufeng*, "weapon," an antipersonnel weapon of the howitzer type firing buckshot). The fifteenth-century *pushka* was about a meter long, had a calibre of 58 to 60 millimeters, and weighed 128 to 279 kilograms; the *pishchal'* was 1.4 to 1.7 meters long, had a calibre of 30 to 40 millimeters, and weighed 39 to 50 kilograms; the *tiufiak* was about a meter long, had a calibre of 50-75 millimeters, and weighed 57–113 kilograms.[16]

The chronicles make twenty references to the use of artillery in the half century from 1470 to 1520, and even though cannons could only get off about four shots a day, firearms had an influence on the outcome of the battle in sixteen of the instances. Artillery was becoming an effective weapon. In 1478 the people of Novgorod were terrified by the fact that Ivan III had brought along artillery, and this undoubtedly contributed to their decision to submit to Moscow. Ivan also used cannon to annex Moscow's old rival, Tver', in 1485. Some other instances were the campaigns of 1481 against the Livonian fortress Valiad (Fellin), of 1493 against Serpensk, of 1495 against Vyborg, and of 1514 against Smolensk.[17]

One of the most important technological advances that contributed to the increased value of artillery was the invention at the end of the fifteenth century of granular gunpowder to replace the powder pulp used earlier. The powder was dried and rolled into small grains, which were then dried once more. The air spaces between the grains caused much faster ignition than had been possible with powder pulp. It also permitted the missile and wad to be placed directly on the charge without an air space, thus considerably facilitating firing[18] A special gunpowder factory (the *Porokhovyi Dvor*) existed at least as early as 1494 in Moscow. Judging by the fact that over two hundred men were killed there in an explosion in 1532, the production of gun powder must have been a large business in the Muscovite state. A special tax was introduced to pay for gunpowder.[19] Nearly every new advance in the application of gunpowder technology was accompanied by new taxes which the populace found hard to bear, with the consequences discussed above in Part 2.

Another significant innovation was the development of casting in bronze, which is more resilient than iron. As a result of the increased durability of the bronze cannon, a larger charge was possible so that missiles would go farther and penetrate deeper than when fired from an iron weapon of the same weight. The organization in Russia of effective bronze casting, which required less work than earlier forging and welding and thus shortened the production cycle, was associated with the arrival in Moscow about 1475 of the Italian (Bolognan) military engineer and architect Aristotel Fioravante, considered the best craftsman in Europe. He participated in the campaigns against Novgorod and Tver' and also against Kazan' in 1482.[20] No later than 1488 a special arsenal, the *Pushechnaia Izba* (renamed the *Pushechnyi Dvor* in 1547), was founded in Moscow.[21] The calibre of these early cannon, cast in bronze, was 90 millimeters, or about 3.5 inches.[22] When Ivan IV rebuilt Moscow's fortifications, he stocked them with brass ordnance.[23]

This early cast-bronze artillery was of high quality and was still used in the second half of the seventeenth century. It did not drive out forged iron artillery in the sixteenth century, for iron was far cheaper than bronze, which had to be imported. Forged iron cannon were made in many towns besides Moscow—Novgorod, Pskov, Ustiuzhna, and others.

The earliest cannons were stationary, and therefore useful for siege defense from a town's walls or for dragging up to a town and using against a town's inhabitants; they were of little value as field weapons. Artillery was used by the Russians for the first time in the field in 1399 in a battle on the river Vorskla, a tributary of the Dnepr.[24] The appearance of the caisson, or gun carriage, at the turn of the fifteenth century permitted light cannon to take to the field as a regular part of warfare. Their use against field formations was greatly facilitated by the invention of trunnions (balancing pins) for the artillery of Charles VIII of France (1483–98). This innovation quickly spread to Russia, as did other Western European advances, such as those made in the first decade of the sixteenth century by the artillery of the Holy Roman emperor Maximilian (1493–1519), who had the best artillery of the time (that is, strengthened in the muzzle and chamber parts of the barrel).[25] The falconet was invented by the Italians in 1536, and eleven years later the Russians were casting them in the *Pushechnyi Dvor*.[26] But because of the nature of Russia's major enemies prior to the reign of Ivan IV, Herberstein was able to report, no doubt with some accuracy, that

> in battle they [the Russians] never use artillery and infantry. Whatever they did, whether they were attacking, pursuing, or fleeing from the enemy, they did it quickly. Therefore neither artillery nor infantry could keep up with them. . . . [The Russians have cannon cast by Germans and Italians] of the same type as our rulers use. Nevertheless, they don't know how, or cannot use them in battle because they have everything arranged for speed.[27]

During his stay in Russia he reported that Vasilii used 15,000 infantry and, for the first time, artillery against the Perekop (Crimean) and Kazan' Tatars at a camp near the Oka river.[28]

The missiles of the earliest cannons were often pieces of stone, which frequently shattered upon impact. But by the 1480s twenty-pound lead cannon balls were in use.[29] In 1495 a major advance was made in Italy with the casting of iron cannon balls; iron has a density two and a half times greater than that of stone, so that a missile of equal weight to one of stone could be of considerably smaller calibre, and the length of flight would be increased. Cast iron cannon balls were in use in Russia by the

1510s.[30] Nevertheless, stone and lead balls continued to be used by Russian artillery until the second half of the sixteenth century.

This chapter is not a military history of Muscovy, but we should bear in mind that Russia was forced to join the gunpowder revolution by its neighbors, who otherwise certainly would have dismembered the newly consolidated state. In 1501, because of a lack of firearms, Russia was defeated by the Livonians on the river Siritsa, ten kilometers from Izborsk, and on Lake Smolino, thirty kilometers from Pskov. In 1514 the Russian army suffered a major defeat at Orsha by Lithuanian artillery.[31] It was events such as these which propelled Russia into the modern era.

Significant improvements in artillery were made during the reign of Ivan IV. The iron industry was well developed. In the sixteenth century Russian industry knew and used most of the advanced technological methods available in the West, and therefore was able to copy, and at times even surpass, any manufactured item brought in from abroad.[32] Russian artillery became very powerful, with the weight of the charge equalling the weight of the missile itself. The ratio between charge-weight and missile-weight was constantly improving in favor of the latter, indicating the strength of the cannon themselves and providing very significant penetrating power.[33] Often incendiary shells were fired. Aiming was improved—without, however, the use of the sight, which had not been invented—and more advanced artillery had a range of up to a kilometer. These cannon could get off up to ten or twelve shots a day, but in time interchangeable powder chambers were used so that two shots a minute could be fired. Loading from the chamber part of the cannon was known earlier in Russia than in the West.[34]

Russia did not have a special branch of the army devoted solely to artillery until the reign of Peter the Great, but Ivan introduced regimental artillery into the Russian army in 1552.[35] He gave each regiment two to four light (6 to 8 pound) cannon (95 to 106 mm.) with a range of 500 meters. The gun carriage was widely used in the second half of the sixteenth century.[36] He also divided artillery into types: fortress (for defense), siege (to take a fortress), and field (mobile antipersonnel pieces), each with a practical range of from 500 meters to a kilometer. Each type of artillery had a definite calibre. Attempts were made to extend the range of artillery, which could fire only two to eight shots per day, by considerably lengthening the barrel and also by casting balls in specially calibrated molds (1555). Native Russian cannon masters began to work during Ivan's reign.[37] The most famous artillery designer of the period was Andrei. Chokhov, whose career spanned the years 1568–1632, during which time he made guns with calibres of 92 to 470 mm., up to 6 meters in length, and weighing 1.2 to 7.2 tons. His masterpiece was the monstrous Tsar Pushka, made in 1585–86 to frighten the Tatars; it weighed 40 tons, had a barrel over 5 meters long, and a calibre of 89 cm.[38]

Ivan took 150 heavy and medium artillery pieces with him to Kazan' in 1552, plus an unknown number of light ones.[39] By 1576, according to the Austrian diplomat Hans Kobenzl von Prosseg, Russia had at least two thousand artillery weapons.[40] By the end of the century the number had increased to thirty-five hundred.[41] In the war with Sweden, during the reign of Fedor Ivanovich, Russia used three hundred pieces of heavy artillery.[42] Russian military successes in the second half of the sixteenth century can be attributed in large part to skilful use of artillery.[43] In the reign of Ivan IV artillerymen, who both made and fired their own pieces, were paid 2 rubles 10 kopeks per year; a century later (during the reign of Aleksei) these valued military servitors got 5 rubles plus cloth worth 2 rubles.[44] Much of the lead and gunpowder Russia used was imported, and foreign suppliers could use this dependence as a club in foreign policy.[45] Weapons also were imported, and Russia had to live in constant fear of an embargo from some quarter.[46]

The earliest cannon caused no change in fortification technology. Fortresses were usually built following the terrain in the bend of a river or on a cliff, so the attack was usually made from the field side; an artificial moat or earthen fortification could more easily be overcome than the natural obstacle provided by the site.

Around the year 1400 changes were made to accommodate defensive artillery. The form of the fortress's turrets was modified, as was the placement of the holes in the turrets to facilitate the use of cannon. By the middle of the century the fortress itself began to change. The increased penetrating power of offensive cannon demanded that the stone walls of fortresses be thickened and that those of wood be made double, with earth in between. Until the middle of the fifteenth century the town benefited by the invention of artillery, for the besieging enemy could be held at a distance of one to two hundred yards by the use of fragmentation cannon placed on top of the thicker walls.[47]

The progress made in artillery during the reign of Ivan III led to radical changes in fortress design and construction. The Moscow kremlin was rebuilt in 1485–95, and the Novgorod kremlin was rebuilt, by order from Moscow, in 1484–90. Almost all fortresses were rebuilt by the end of the fifteenth century, especially in the frontier regions—in Pskov, Ladoga, Ostrov, Kopor'e, and Iam.[48] On the southern frontier Tula was rebuilt in the reign of Vasilii III.[49] From such fortifications, control of the entire surrounding area was possible. Peasants, artisans, and merchants could find refuge there against invaders, and the government in turn used the fortresses as bases from which taxes could be collected and the population otherwise controlled.

When fortresses were rebuilt or constructed anew, the walls were much thicker than earlier. The design was also changed; all walls had to be straight so that no blind area would protect the attacker against defensive fire from the fortress. The earlier practice of building on a good natural site and following its contours was replaced by that of erecting polygonal structures on the plain. Natural barriers and the relief of a locale, such as rivers and cliffs, no longer provided defense against attack, for when cannon succeeded in replacing catapults the range of fire was extended to such an extent that firing on a fortress was no longer confined to the field side; the attack could be launched from any place around the fortress.[50]

The turrets became the central point of the defense. They were equally spaced along the walls so that artillery in them could rake the field in front. They were also lowered so that the attacker would have more difficulty in hitting them; when the turrets, especially the corner ones where the artillery was concentrated, were knocked out, the fortress usually fell. Special niches[51] were also built in the walls and in the turrets for small arms, which began to be used at this time. The new technology and tactics meant that the defense and siege of towns and fortresses became the major form of warfare, at first on the western frontier, and eventually in the south as well.[52]

The first new rectangular fortress to be built was Ivangorod (Ivan's fortress) on the bank of the Narva River opposite a castle of the Teutonic Order. Built in three to five months in 1492, Ivangorod guarded Russia's outlet to the Baltic until it fell to the Swedes in 1581. (Russian troops recaptured it in 1590, only to lose it again, in 1612, until 1704.) Later, in the sixteenth century, thirty major fortresses were constructed, including Nizhnii Novgorod in 1500–1511, Tula in 1514–21, Zaraisk in 1531, Kolomna in 1525–33, Mokhanka in 1535, Samara, and others.[53]

The culmination of the new fortification projects was also the greatest construction project in the world in the sixteenth century: the Smolensk fortress built in 1595–1602 under the direction of the brilliant architect Fedor Savel'ev Kon'.[54] Boris Godunov himself assisted in the overall direction of the massive project.[55] Ten thousand free hired laborers worked on the walls alone, which consumed 150 million bricks. Also used in the construction of the fortress were: 61,160 cubic meters of crushed rock fill, 320,000 piles, 620,000 large white facing stones, 1 million loads of sand, 5,760 tons of lime, 150,000 logs, 50,000 boards, 5,760 tons of strap iron, 2,700 tons of round bar iron, and over 1 million large nails.[56] The fruit of this expenditure was 6.5 kilometers around, 13 to 19 meters high, and 5 to 6 meters thick. The foundation was 4 meters deep and 6.5 meters thick.[57] This was by far the largest fortress built in Russia, and gives some idea of the stimulus given to the economy by the construction that resulted from the introduction of gunpowder technology into Russia.

The remarkable economic upsurge of the first half of the sixteenth century, which helped to prevent further erosion of the peasant's right of free movement, has been partly attributed to this vast program of fortress construction. Thus the initial stages of the gunpowder revolution did not harm the mass of the Russian peasantry, although those living in critical frontier areas sometimes were burdened by corvée obligations (*gorodovoe delo*) connected with the construction of the new fortifications. While corvée for state purposes was not new,[58] an unfortunate precedent was set with this initial advancement of military technology. In 1513, during the struggle for Smolensk, the government introduced a new tax, *primet,* to pay for the building of siege constructions before enemy walls.[59] This new levy probably antedated the gunpowder tax.[60]

Along with the construction of fortresses came another feature of the gunpowder revolution, the art of military mining. The first Russian encounter with mining was in 1535, when the Lithuanians were besieging Starodub. The most notable success was at Kazan' in 1552, when the Lithuanian emigré Razmysl Petrov (later executed by Ivan IV) directed the digging under the Volga and the explosions which preceded the Russian storm of the Tatar stronghold.[61]

With a shift in warfare to the control of heavily fortified places and lines, an army which relied on cavalry was at a disadvantage on many counts. Cavalry was suited for warfare as practiced by the Tatars—largely raiding and looting.[62] With fortification warfare, cavalry became less desirable. The only ways a fortress could be taken were by battering down its walls with artillery, starving out its defenders in a siege, or by introducing a traitor within it. Cavalry could do none of these, and in fact were a great distraction because the horses as well as the men had to be fed. In a siege, cavalrymen spent most of their time plundering the surrounding countryside in search of food and fodder, and usually were the first to desert. This happened inevitably in any protracted encounter involving the *pomest'e* cavalry, which always converted the country into a desert, where no one could survive, once their own supplies had been exhausted.[63] Infantry were much better, for they could continuously harrass the besieged at low cost while denying them succor. Patient besiegers usually had the advantage over the fortress defenders, unless the latter could somehow drive away the attackers. This fact of life became apparent to all in the sixteenth century on the western frontier, but had to wait until slightly later on the Tatar front.

Another aspect of gunpowder technology was the development of hand firearms. The problem of setting off an explosion in a chamber smaller than that of a cannon presented difficulties which took some time to overcome, so that hand firearms appeared later than artillery. The arquebus, a heavy matchlock gun, spread through Germany into Switzerland, Italy, and elsewhere after the middle of the fourteenth century.[64] According to the surviving records, hand guns were first used in Russia almost exactly a century later than cannon: in 1480, in the battle on the Ugra River that symbolically ended the hegemony of the Tatars over the Russians. The chronicles tell of the Russians using arquebuses against the bows and arrows of the Tatars in this encounter, and an illuminated chronicle of the third quarter of the sixteenth century vividly portrays this event.[65]

These early handguns were smoothbore weapons, loaded from the muzzle, weighing eight to ten kilograms. Their roughly .22 calibre shot could be fired from 200 to 300 meters. They were imported from various countries and made by Russians as well, so there was no standardization.[66] This primitive weapon was of the wick, or slow-match, type, meaning that each shot required a light from a campfire or a smoldering wick. Shooting these matchlock weapons was a tedious process which required considerable skill and experience. Firing the matchlock was so complicated that each soldier could shoot only twelve to sixteen times during a battle.[67] The arquebus, which was so heavy that it had to be rested on a stand for firing, was not a suitable weapon for a large army of infantry recruited solely for a major war and then discharged upon the war's completion. This suitability awaited the development of the flintlock musket.

The early matchlock was not suitable for use by cavalry of the Russian type. In steppe warfare, as described in chapter 2, the Russian horseman relied by and large on the bow and arrow. Apparently the arbalest, a terrifyingly powerful and deadly weapon in Western hands, never was used by the Russians to any meaningful extent.[68]

In spite of the drawbacks of the early matchlock (*pishchal'*), the Russian government soon after its introduction began to adapt its military thinking to this new weapon. Having first appeared in 1508, in 1510 a detachment of one thousand infantry arquebusiers (*pishchal'niki*) was outfitted at treasury expense for the campaign to complete the annexation of Pskov to the Muscovite state. They were also used in 1512 to conquer Smolensk. After the campaigns they were disbanded.

The *pishchal'niki* were revived in 1545, when two thousand (half on foot, half on horseback for greater mobility, thus ancestors of the dragoons) were levied from the towns and equipped by the treasury.[69] A new tax was introduced to pay them. It is generally assumed that the *pishchal'niki* are in some respects ancestors of the *strel'tsy*, the standing corps of arquebusiers which functioned together with the middle service class cavalry until the final demise of both at the end of the seventeenth century.[70]

An important step taken by Ivan IV's government was the establishment of the infantry (*strel'tsy*) musketeer corps (or arquebusiers) of three thousand men in 1550.[71] The Soviet military historian E. A. Razin warns against identifying the *strel'tsy* too closely with the *pishchal'niki*, for their methods of recruitment as well as the character of their organization differed fundamentally.[72] Until the *strel'tsy* were formed only foreign mercenaries (with the exceptions listed above) served as infantry in the Russian army. The corps was founded because the middle service class cavalry alone could not fight successfully against the Polish and Swedish infantry.[73] This was Russia's first regular standing army corps, with the number of officers usually corresponding to the number of men and uniforms whose colors are known (for Moscow regiments).[74] The *strel'tsy* were not disbanded in peacetime and consequently were available immediately for service. They had uniform weapons, a definite organization, and underwent regular training. They did not, however, have military regulations spelling out their rights and duties in times of war and peace.[75] It is likely that the corps was formed in light of suggestions made by Ivan Peresvetov, who was familiar with Turkish practices, or by someone else with this knowledge.[76] Numerous foreigners compared the *strel'tsy* with the Turkish Janissaries.[77] Manstein noted that the *strel'tsy* and Janissaries had the same battle formation.[78] Much later, Peter the Great observed that the *strel'tsy* were created on the model of the Turkish Janissaries.[79] Since Lithuania did not establish a standing infantry corps until 1551, Poland until 1562, Russia had to borrow the idea for such a corps from someone other than its immediate neighbor and frequent model.[80]

Initially the entire corps lived just outside of Moscow in the Vorob'evo settlement (later known as Sparrow Hills, now Lenin Hills, the site of Moscow University) where the members underwent military training. As their numbers increased, there were settlements all over Moscow. The *strel'tsy*, armed with heavy axes in the shape of half-moons (*berdyshes*) and sabres, in addition to their arquebuses, learned how to fire their slow-match weapons with relative precision.[81] (A few also carried lances, which could be used as offensive weapons or in defense against cavalry,

161

a sort of cheval de frise or Spanish knife rest.) [82] At least partly because guns did not have sights, great precision in firing was impossible and the most effective uses of arquebuses was the volley over a range of fifty to sixty meters.[83] The gun rested on the musketeer's *berdysh* or a stand (*soshka*). When a campfire was not present, the wick had to be lit with a flint.[84] The Englishman Robert Best, commenting on the annual review of the forces by Ivan IV in the 1550s, noted that "there [were] 5,000 harquebuzzers [sic], which went 5 and 5 in a ranke in a very good order, every of them carrying his gunne vpon his left shoulder, and his match in his right hand. . . . The harquebuzzers began to shoot of [sic] at the banke of ice [set up as a target for the review] as though it had bene in any skirmish or battel, who ceased not shooting vntil they had beaten all the ice flat on the ground."[85] They probably rotated firing in caracole fashion, the front row firing and then stepping to the rear to reload while the second row moved forward to fire a volley.[86]

The *strel'tsy,* wearing no armor and relying on some type of fortification but especially on the cavalry for protection, learned how to function with the middle service class cavalry; in time the two became rather dependent upon one another.

The major function of the *strel'tsy* was to deliver massed firepower. They were protected either by cavalry forces, moats, fascines (specially constructed parapets made of sticks from which they could shoot at the enemy), or the famous "moveable fortress" (*guliai gorod*) discussed below. They never intentionally engaged in hand-to-hand combat, the storming of a fortress, or street fighting. This was left to the *deti boiarskie* cavalry, as during the taking of Kazan' in 1552.[87]

The government realized the worth of the *strel'tsy* and took measures to expand their numbers. By the end of the sixteenth century there were probably seven to ten thousand Moscow *strel'tsy,* of whom two thousand were mounted. (The mounted *strel'tsy* were essentially infantry on horseback, for they could not fire their rifles without the stand.) [88] In addition there were *strel'tsy* who were garrisoned in the provinces, largely on the frontier. For example, in 1574 the government, desiring a standing army and massed firepower, stationed in the Smolensk garrison 519 middle service class servicemen and about 2,800 (twenty-eight companies, *sotni*) *strel'tsy.*[89] The purpose of these frontier forces was to delay enemy attacks while the main body of the middle service class cavalry was being assembled. Then the cavalry, along with the Moscow *strel'tsy,* which served as a mobile reserve, would go off for the major encounter. In offensive operations the cavalry and Moscow *strel'tsy* initiated the actions themselves.[90] All together, there were probably twenty to twenty-five thousand *strel'tsy* in Muscovy by the end of the sixteenth century. In spite of their numbers, the *strel'tsy* were a secondary part of the Muscovite army in the sixteenth century. Only in the Livonian campaign of 1577 did their numbers amount to a significant part of the total armed forces.[91] They often reached their battle destinations by boat, along with the artillery and supplies. The army as a whole, slowed down by the baggage train, usually moved about ten miles a day, although it sometimes traveled at twice that speed.[92]

Each *strelets*, usually a free volunteer who was a good shot, was given a garden plot, cloth, and 4 rubles per year. This salary remained about the same for over a century, as the value of money fell. In the middle of the seventeenth century subcenturions (commanders of fifty men), decurions (in charge of ten men), and the rank and file of the Moscow *strel'tsy* were paid 7, 6, and 5 rubles per year, plus 9, 8⅜, and 7¾ *chetverti* of rye and the same of oats per year, respectively. Provincial *strel'tsy* got 3½, 3¼, and 3 rubles per year and 7, 6½, and 6 *cheti* of rye and the same of oats per year, respectively.[93] This in time meant that the *strel'tsy* could not support themselves on their annual wage, and, as we shall see, they were forced to engage in tax-exempt trade and manufacturing—limiting their military effectiveness. These problems were compounded by the fact that the government had no provisioning network. Each *strelets*, much like each member of the middle service class, was expected to provide for himself in the battle theatre, either out of his grain allotment or his cash salary. The salary was inadequate for peacetime, and probably never sufficed to buy needed supplies at inflated prices in a war zone.[94]

Tactically, the musketeer corps functioned with the middle service class cavalry, in large part because Russia never developed corps of pikemen to protect infantry from enemy cavalry. The commanders (*golovy*) of the *strel'tsy* were appointed from the membership of the middle service class and were responsible to the Musketeers Chancellery (*Streletskii Prikaz*). The vice-commanders (*polugolovy*) and centurions (*sotniki*) also were *deti boiarskie* by origin.[95] The commanders were compensated not only with cash (up to 200 rubles per year) and grain, as were their men, but were awarded service lands as well. The commanding officer of each five hundred or a thousand men was responsible for training and keeping his regiment up to strength and had the right and duty to punish his men for misdemeanors and infringements of the rules.[96]

The *strel'tsy* were significantly more expensive for the treasury than the middle service class cavalry.[97] They were largely paid by the state with a new tax which, as was shown in chapter 7, was the most onerous of all Muscovite levies. This tax had to be paid by the relatively few

163

taxpaying townsmen (2 or 3 percent of the populace) and by the peasants, who experienced no increase in grain yields in this period (see chapter 14). The result was peasant flight to escape the added tax burden. This deprived the members of the middle service class of their labor force and evoked their petition campaign which culminated in the repeal of the time limit on the recovery of fugitives. Thus the expense of the new military technology contributed to the rigid stratification of Russian society.

The Russians created a special branch of service to protect their infantry. This was the so-called *guliai gorod,* or "mobile fortress," first mentioned in 1522 in a Tatar-Russian encounter on the Oka. Walls over six feet high were constructed of planks or logs and mounted on wheels or skiis. Holes were placed in each section of wall for firing handguns and small artillery. In battle sections were placed adjacent to one another to form two parallel lines about three meters apart and from two to ten kilometers in length. The *strel'tsy* and artillerymen fired from within this enclosure at the enemy and the mounted cavalry could regroup behind it after each charge. On major campaigns the general in charge of the *guliai gorod* had one thousand armed cavalrymen assigned to him to protect it. Most field defeats of the Russian army in the sixteenth century were attributed to malfunction of the *guliai gorod* branch of service.[98] The *guliai gorod* was also used by Russians in the seventeenth century, and it was frequently used by the cossacks against the Poles in the struggle for hegemony over the Ukraine in 1648–53.[99] In addition to the *guliai gorod,* which was particularly effective against Tatars firing bows and arrows, the Russian army sometimes (particularly on the western front) drew up its massive quantity of supply carts into a circle and used this as a fortification (*oboz*).[100]

Russia, with an army of perhaps 110,000 men at the end of the sixteenth century,[101] was still using tactics adopted in the fourteenth and fifteenth centuries: the army fought in two to three echelons, with the tsar's regiment and the *strel'tsy* as the core, the others surrounding them. Such structure was susceptible to annihilation by artillery.[102] The favorite cavalry tactic was encirclement combined with an attack on the enemy's rear. Another tactic was the feigned retreat.[103]

In Western Europe (especially Holland and Sweden), on the other hand, significant changes in military tactics were introduced in the sixteenth century and at the turn of the seventeenth. Great military reforms were introduced in the Netherlands by Maurits van Oranje of Nassau (1567–1625). Under his supervision the principles of drill and the tactical training of troops were developed which were used by all of Europe in the seventeenth century.[104] Western armies adopted a linear formation to take advantage of newly perfected hand firearms and to escape devastation by artillery. Instead of the deep-echelon formation, one or two long lines (sometimes rotating in caracole fashion) would be set up to maximize firepower. This new, essentially defensive tactic, was first used by the Dutch against the Spaniards at Newport in 1600, for the Dutch had greater firepower than other armies. The idea spread rapidly, and the Russians first used it in 1605 when the *strel'tsy* faced Polish cavalry supporting False Dmitrii I at Dobrinichie.[105] (It should be remembered, however, that one of the major purposes of the long, narrow *guliai gorod* was to maximize firepower across a broad front.)

During the Thirty Years War, the Swedes greatly refined linear tactics. The two lines of musketeers were about 150 to 200 meters apart and minimized losses from enemy artillery. Lighter muskets of 5 to 6 kilograms were developed which could be fired without a stand. Musketeers began to play a decisive role in battle. In addition, Gustavus Adolphus (1611–1632) of Sweden, using Dutch experience, created a standing army, well-trained and disciplined, and levied on the basis of a recruiting system.[106]

The Russians were aware of the shortcomings of the *pomest'e* cavalry. As early as 1546–49 Ivan Peresvetov submitted petitions to Ivan IV suggesting various reforms, among them that Russia should form a standing army of twenty thousand well-trained infantry soldiers with firearms who would be paid by the Treasury to defend the southern frontier against the Tatars. He also recommended building mobile fortifications which arquebusiers could use as shields—an obvious reference to the *guliai gorod*.[107] He based his recommendations largely on what he had learned about the Turks in six years of service in Hungary and Poland. He claimed that an army of slaves, as supplied by the boyars and also the middle service class, was unfit because slaves were not brave.[108] The *strelets* corps seems to have been the immediate fruit of his suggestion. Throughout the sixteenth century, however, slaves continued to fight on horseback alongside their owners, and this system was not discarded until the seventeenth century, when most slaves were ultimately relegated to guarding the baggage train. The middle service class cavalry remained the nucleus of the Russian army for over a century after Peresvetov wrote.

Gunpowder technology made a significant impact on warfare during its first two centuries in Rus'. Muscovite artillery was the equal of any in the world, yet it was insufficient to give victory to the Russians in the Livonian War. Thousands of foot soldiers were hired at government expense and outfitted with handguns. Nevertheless, at the end of the sixteenth century Russia's basic orientation was still toward steppe warfare, with horsemen and bows and arrows. No doubt this was because the Tatar light cavalry could reach the capital, whereas the Poles and Swedes, in this respect, seemed to pose less of a threat. At the time when the Forbidden Years were introduced, Muscovy had not yet made a full commitment to the gunpowder revolution.

10.
Major Reform Aborted

The Livonian War clearly demonstrated that Rus' soon would be forced to reorientate its military thinking away from the Tatars, and it is highly probable that by the end of the sixteenth century at least some Russians realized that the Poles and Swedes posed the greater military threat.[1] It took the Time of Troubles, and especially encounters with the Swedes, really to bring home to Russian leaders that reforms were necessary if another defeat by the West, which was threatening Russia with trained, regular military forces using advanced firearms,[2] was to be avoided. The fact of national humiliation during the Time of Troubles probably made the completion of the gunpowder revolution much easier because the Muscovites had been unable to resist initially the Swedish and Rzeczpospolita forces. While the post-1613 period was a xenophobic era and a few clerics protested turning the army over to foreign mercenaries, as we shall see, there was remarkably little overt resistance to the new military system. There probably would have been more had it not been for the Polish occupation of Moscow, which revealed to all the weakness of the traditional army.[3]

During the Time of Troubles False Dmitrii I took a number of measures to increase the effectiveness of the middle service class, the production of Russian artillery, and siege techniques. He also asked the pope for military specialists and contemplated asking England for them.[4] Russia also began to become familiar with the more advanced military knowledge possessed by Sweden in order to defeat the mutual enemy of the two countries, Catholic Poland. In 1607 Charles IX sent Tsar Vasilii Shuiskii a copy of Fronsperger's *Kriegsbuch* (published in three parts in 1566, 1573, and 1575 in Frankfurt am Main), which served to acquaint the Russians with Northern European military developments.[5] From this work the court translators Mikhail Iur'ev and Ivan Fomin compiled a so-called *Military Book* (*Voinskaia kniga*),

which adapted the *Kriegsbuch* to Russian needs.[6] About the same time
A. M. Radishevskii (Anisim Mikhailov) began his famous *Regulations*
(*Ustav ratnykh i pushechnykh del*), a work based on Fronsperger plus
other German and Italian sources. The document, which was finished in
1621, consists of 663 articles and is notable for its emphasis on foreign
procedures and on offensive action in foreign territory.[7]

A noteworthy attempt to modernize the Russian forces occurred
during the Time of Troubles. In February, 1609, Tsar Shuiskii concluded an agreement with Sweden in which Russia ceded Korela (Kex-
holm) in exchange for military assistance. In April over fifteen thousand
mercenaries came to Russia under the command of Jakob de la Gardie,
who had been trained in the Netherlands. The mercenaries introduced
the use of infantry lancers, which spread to some Russian forces in
the summer. Swedish Marshall Christernus Some introduced the use of
the portable palisade, which was used in the West to overcome the antipathy of soldiers to constructing earthen works. The palisades were
more durable than the traditional Russian *guliai gorod,* and caused
consternation among opposing Polish forces. However, General Prince
M. V. Skopin-Shuiskii, who had been in charge of the innovations, died
in April, 1610, and the westernization of the army was postponed.[8]

The Time of Troubles forced the Russians to understand that "the
pomest'e system of raising an army served as a brake on the development
of military art."[9] During this time the middle service class, along with
the boyars, could not adapt itself to combat with the Poles and Swedes.[10]
In fact, the middle service class cavalry was completely shattered by the
experience.[11] In the open field it was no match for either the rebel
cossacks or the troops of the Rzeczpospolita.[12] To drive out the invaders,
the Russians were forced to resort to the untrained, inexperienced popular
militia, much of it from urban areas.[13] The twenty to thirty thousand
troops who gathered in Iaroslavl' were armed with lances, spears, berdyshes and artillery, as had been their forebears in the sixteenth century.
Only a few had handguns.[14] Furthermore, the armed recruits (*datochnye
liudi*), sent into the army by the rural and urban communes, performed
absolutely the identical service as the *dvoriane* and *deti boiarskie*. In
1617 they all served in the same army units (*sotni*).[15] Sometimes peasants explicitly replaced *dvoriane* and *deti boiarskie* in service, as when
someone retired and had no son who could replace him: "When [a
serviceman retires], his son must serve; if he has no son, then a [peasant]
recruit [must be furnished to replace him]."[16] All of these facts con-
tribute to the impression that the middle service class was on the verge
of losing its place as the major military force of the Muscovite state.

The recorded disposition of 23,049 servicemen in 1616 gives an idea of the military priorities of the Time of Troubles era. Along the western frontier 1,327 men were opposite Smolensk, which was in the hands of the Poles; 4,215 were facing a Polish army under General Losowski; and 1,927 were in Briansk. There were 850 in Ustiuzhna Zhelezopol'skaia and 2,524 in other northern towns. Three regiments totalling 2,427 troops were listed as directly facing the Crimean Tatars and another 10,227 were garrisoned in southern towns to ward off their incursions. Lastly, 386 were with various embassies.[17] These were not all the forces of Muscovy, but only those on active duty, mainly against the Poles, Swedes, and Tatars.

Filaret's major foreign policy goals were to retake Smolensk (240 miles west of Moscow, Russia's gateway to the west and southwest), lost to Poland during the Time of Troubles, and to liquidate the claims of Wladislaw Wasa to the Muscovite throne.[18] His first step was to restore the financial condition of the government.[19] While this was under way, plans to draw Muscovy into an anti-Hapsburg coalition were proposed by a French embassy in 1625, and again in late 1629.[20] In 1626 Filaret exiled the pro-Polish head of the Chancellery of Foreign Affairs, I. T. Gramotin, and replaced him with E. G. Telepnev, who began a foreign policy offensive against Poland. Then Filaret turned his attention to the backward army. In 1630, with an eye toward attacking Smolensk in late 1632 after the expiration of the Deulino Truce, Filaret began to hire Western Protestant mercenaries, who were available in abundance during the Thirty Years War then in progress.[21]

This was not the first time Russia had hired Western mercenaries. In the beginning of the sixteenth century there was a regiment of fifteen hundred foreigners, largely artillery specialists, in Moscow. Foreigners (such as the Lithuanian mining specialist Razmysl Petrov and the Danish engineer Rasmussen) also participated in the taking of Kazan' in 1552.[22] For the rest of the century there were usually up to one hundred Westerners in Kazan' alone, primarily artillery specialists. After the defeats which Russia suffered in the Livonian War, Boris Godunov, in the reign of Fedor Ivanovich, had recruited twenty-five hundred mercenaries (mainly Poles and Livonians, but also Scots, Danes, Swedes, Austrians, French, and Greeks) under the French captain Margaret and the Livonian Walter von Rosen.[23] Their numbers increased to forty-three hundred infantrymen by the end of the century.[24] During the Time of Troubles, in a famous battle at Klushino in 1610, the Polish forces were outnumbered by the Russians at least six to one, but won the engagement largely because Russia's Swedish mercenaries (who, incidentally, also outnumbered the Poles present) went over to the enemy.

This soured the Russians on mercenaries.[25] Anisim Mikhailov, the author of the *Regulations* mentioned above, opposed the hiring of foreign mercenaries and advocated the development of native cadres.[26]

Most of the foreigners left Russia by the end of the Time of Troubles, and Filaret set about replacing them with men who knew the latest Western technology and tactics. He was aided in his reform of the army by his brother-in-law, Ivan Borisovich Cherkasskii, who had become acquainted with the Swedish mercenary general de la Gardie during the Time of Troubles and shared with Filaret an antipathy toward the Catholic Poles. A great friend of the Swedes and also the Dutch, Cherkasskii used his positions, from 1622, as head of the Treasury (*Bol'shaia Kazna*), the Musketeer Chancellery, and the Foreign Mercenary Chancellery (*Inozemskii Prikaz*) to modernize the Russian army by hiring foreign mercenaries.[27]

In 1631 the Russian government sent recruiters to all the European countries (except France, which was assumed to favor Catholic Poland) to hire mercenary officers. These new mercenaries were to recruit and set up, at the expense of the state treasury, a standing army "based on foreign formation."[28] (This meant the new army was to drill and fight, using the new linear tactics, like Western armies. Also, they were to have a rationalized command structure, which will be discussed below.) By the end of 1631, 190 foreigners were in Russian service as commanders.[29] Filaret also tried to hire seven thousand mercenary footsoldiers in the West, but had little success.[30] In January, 1631, the Russian government asked for permission to hire five thousand mercenaries in Denmark and to buy supplies for them from King Christian IV's treasury. In September, 1631, the Danes agreed, but in October, 1632, a Captain Adam Kohlase was sent back to Christian because he had not brought to Russia the three thousand troops he had promised.[31] Some success was obtained in the recruitment of foreigners by other foreigners: the Scot Alexander Lesly and the Dutchman Indrik van Dam recruited five regiments in the West. Lesly himself hired 7,539 men, of whom 4,633 came to Russia (of these, 214 died from 1632 to 1633 in Russian service).[32] Those hired pledged not to desert.[33]

Recruiting was relatively easy because of the enormous salaries Russia offered the mercenaries to come east. (See table 4.)

These wages were offered for combat service. Those defending a fortress received two-thirds of these sums, those rendering neither were paid one-third the base pay. The munificence of these wages can be gathered by remembering that rank-and-file troops got about 5 rubles a year.

The major task, of course, was to train the Russians themselves to fight in the more modern way. The training of these so-called "new

TABLE 4

1634 MONTHLY PAY RATE FOR FOREIGN OFFICERS[34]
(IN RUBLES)

RANK	CAVALRY	INFANTRY
Colonel (*polkovnik*)	400	250
Lieutenant Colonel (*podpolkovnik*)	133	100
Major (*maior*)	150	50
Captain (*kapitan*)	100	75
Lieutenant (*poruchik*)	40	22½
Second Lieutenant (*praporshchik*)	30	17½

formation regiments" was entrusted from 1630 to 1632 to Alexander Lesly, Franz Pentzner, and Indrik van Dam. Earlier Lesly had served in the Swedish army, but van Dam seems to have been most influential, for the new regiments were created after the Dutch model.[35] The Poles referred to the "Dutch skill" of the Russian troops.[36]

There is a certain paradox in these developments. As will be discussed further below, a situation was created whereby the officer corps was being democratized while Russian society at large was becoming more rigidly stratified. Both tendencies were to reach their extremes during the 1640s and 1650s. For one small sector of society the idea was cast aside that specific classes had exclusive rights to specific positions. Ability and experience, not birth and connections, became the criteria for position and reward in the new army.

In 1630, two thousand *deti boiarskie* who possessed no service lands were invited to come to Moscow for military training as infantry soldiers (*soldaty*), the most desired type of troops in up-to-date European armies. Each was promised five rubles plus a food allowance. This was to be the first time in Russian history that *deti boiarskie* were placed under the command of foreigners, who heretofore had directed only companies of other foreigners. However, the members of the middle service class felt that serving as infantry under foreigners was an insult to their station, and by September, 1630, no more than sixty had registered as soldiers. Stefan Batory had had a similar experience about half a century earlier in Poland.[37] After this failure, Filaret allowed Tatars, cossacks, and other "free people" (those not bound to a town or rural estate or commune) to join the new formation infantry regiments. His action debased service in the *soldaty* in the eyes of the middle service class, and the government made the matter worse by sending *deti boiarskie* there as a punishment.[38] By December, 1631, 3,323 men had been recruited in two regiments. A regiment consisted of 1,600 men and 176 officers. Each regiment was divided into eight companies. By the beginning of 1632 the infantry soldier regiments had been increased to six in number, and all of them fought at Smolensk.[39] While the war was in progress, the government forcibly levied two more regiments plus a company of soldiers from the taxpaying (*tiaglo*) population.

In the middle of 1632 the government decided to form a cavalry regiment (*reitarskii polk*) of two thousand men.[40] The impoverished *dvoriane* and *deti boiarskie* more readily joined this organization. At first an attempt had been made to recruit enough foreigners for such a regiment, but mercenaries in sufficient numbers were unwilling to come to Russia.[41] This could have been fortunate in the long run for Russia, for it might have forced the country to develop its own cadres and, equally important, might have saved great amounts of foreign exchange.[42] Soon these two thousand cavalrymen were increased to twenty-four hundred. Four hundred dragoons, light cavalrymen who also could double as infantry, were recruited.[43] A dragoon regiment consisted of twelve companies of 120 men each, with 160 officers assigned to the regiment. Each regiment was supplied with artillery by the state: twelve small cannons and twenty-four balls per cannon. The pay of cavalrymen was twice that of soldiers. During the war the government formed another cavalry regiment.[44] As was noted in chapter 7, it was necessary to add new taxes to pay the troops. The annual cost of maintaining 6,610 of the troops of the new regiments was nearly 129,000 rubles.[45]

In the entire period from 1630 to 1634 the government formed ten foreign formation regiments with a total of 17,400 men—about half of the 34,500 men sent to Smolensk (along with an unknown number of slaves belonging to the landed part of the army). Although they probably surpassed the middle service class cavalry in military capability, these troops were not yet decisive. There were 11,688 *dvoriane* and *deti boiarskie* at Smolensk; the rest were *strel'tsy*, cossacks, and Tatars. Thus half of the forces at Smolensk were traditional Muscovite forces, the other half were men of the new formation regiments.[46] Shein's forces at Smolensk were, overall, "vastly superior in numbers, armaments, and miltary art to the Polish forces."[47]

Unfortunately for Russia, Filaret died during the war. Moscow lost the contest as far as the goal of recovering Smolensk was concerned, but did manage to get the Poles to give up their claims to the Muscovite throne.[48] Filaret was succeeded by less competent individuals. In 1633 Prince Ivan Borisovich Cherkasskii assumed the helm of government. After the war was over he dismissed Filaret's new semiregular standing army. On June 17, 1634, foreign mercenaries were ordered to leave Russia.[49] In July and August, the traveler Adam Olearius encountered numbers of dismissed foreign soldiers leaving Russia—and committing depredations while leaving.[50] A few officers remained, and were granted service lands if they became Orthodox. This initiated what was to become a tradition—service as an officer opened access to the upper classes and to the prerogative of owning land.[51]

The dismissal of the new army regiments meant that Russia again had to rely on the middle service class cavalry. Here and there, as we shall see, new formation regiments continued to be formed and then dissolved in the rest of the first half of the seventeenth century, but they fundamentally went out of business.

Why the new structure regiments were disbanded is unknown, but the following may be some of the reasons. During the Smolensk War the Balash peasant uprising broke out. It was rapidly crushed, diverting energies from Smolensk, but individual outbursts continued for awhile afterwards. Apparently some of the rebels were soldiers from Smolensk. In spite of the fact that most of the nonpeasant participants in the Balash uprising were members of the "old formation regiments,"[52] it is conceivable that the government may have decided that the new formation regiments should be liquidated as soon as possible to dissolve potentially mutinous concentrations of members of the lower classes.[53] Thus the government may have decided not to risk retaining the new formation infantry regiments, but to rely on the middle service class.[54]

Another consideration may have been that the government was ambivalent about the mercenaries. It knew it needed their skill, but was shocked by their lack of fidelity. Again the truth was revealed that the mercenary fights for cash, not for principle. In one galling case, an Englishman by the name of Richard Stevens changed employers five times—he served the Russians thrice, the enemy twice.[55] In a period of xenophobia such behavior instilled no confidence or enthusiasm in the government for mercenaries.[56]

A major consideration in the dismissal of the new army was simply that the war was over, so the forces could be discharged. Foresight was not a major Muscovite trait. Because the Russians' time horizon was so short, they could only act on an ad hoc basis. At this time it would have been asking too much for the government to comprehend fully that national survival depended on adapting to the qualitative change occurring in the nature of warfare, that the military facts of international life would soon demand the creation of a standing army, and that no state could rely solely on its gentry militia, even if augmented by foreign mercenaries hired for the occasion. The Cherkasskii government lacked such foresight as well as an appreciation of the nature of the military revolution which was in process. This did not mean that the government failed to sense that the old army was obsolete, but that it did fail to comprehend the full significance of this fact, and what should be done about it. Instead of retaining a small cadre to train Russian officer candidates, Cherkasskii told all the foreigners they were free to leave Russia.

The new government, whose members were not imbued with Filaret's hatred of Poland, desired the vast empty lands in the south rather than the far more expensive ancestral territory under Polish hegemony, and so turned its gaze from the western frontier to the areas roamed by the Crimean Tatar light cavalry.[57] Notices were sent to frontier posts that Western mercenaries were not wanted by the army and were not to be admitted to Russia to batten off the country, which was at peace on all frontiers as the bloody Thirty Years War was still raging in the West.[58] Perhaps the government thought that Western mercenaries and infantry armies might be useful against the Poles, but not worth the expense against the mounted Tatars. This would have been in spite of foreign observation made during the reign of Ivan IV that twelve hundred Swedes outfitted with firearms who enlisted in the Russian army "did better service against the Tatars than 12,000 Russians with their short bow and arrows."[59] Besides, the government's finances and administration were in complete disarray, so that retaining the mercenaries needed to train and hold together the new regiments would have been difficult.[60]

Effecting the new southern strategy meant for the ruling elite a redirection of resources from the new army to a rebuilding of the frontier defensive system—a course which led to the obsolescence of the middle service class. While the trans-Oka militia had grown in numbers from five thousand in 1616 to thirteen thousand in 1635, the southern frontier defense system (the *zasechnaia cherta, zaseka*) had been neglected for decades, and the government thought that it was in great need of repair to keep out the Tatars.[61] A look at the *zaseka* system at this moment is in order, for it plays an important role in our story of the relationship between serfdom and the military system. For an historical analogy, the Limes Romanus defensive line constructed by Emperor Hadrian (A.D. 76–138) to hold back the barbarians might be remembered.

Initial efforts to build defensive barriers to keep out the steppe hordes were made by Russians as early as the tenth century around Kiev, by the twelfth in the north, but these efforts had to be abandoned after the imposition of the Mongol yoke. As the Tatar domination began to weaken, the Russian government revived the idea of building a fortified line across the southern frontier to keep the Tatars out of the heartland of Muscovy. Until this was done, the Oka River was the first line of defense, just fifty miles south of Moscow, where the army gathered annually to meet the Tatars—irregularly beginning in 1472, regularly from 1569 to 1599.[62] In the fifteenth century the oldest *cherta* stretched from Kozel'sk through Tula and Serpukhov to Nizhnii Novgorod. This is a distance of over a thousand kilometers, and the line was not as secure as one that was built later.[63] In 1533 the known line was at least 250 kilometers long, running through Kolomna, Kashira, Serkin, Serpukhov, Kaluga, and Ugra. Firearms were employed there to keep out the Tatars.[64] Ivan IV strengthened the ancient *cherta* through Tula, which became the major frontier defense coordinating center, and built a second one from Putivl' through Ryl'sk (1557), Novgorod Severskii (1557), Orel (1567), Novosil' (1565), Dankov, Riazhsk (1558), Shatsk (1553) to Alatyr' on the Sura River (1565 to 1575).[65] By the 1560s a tight system had been constructed in the forest belt south of the Oka six hundred versts long, from Riazan' to the upper reaches of the Zhizdra River. It was supplemented by branches to the south and southeast, from Krapivna to Belev and from Shatsk to Riazhsk and Skopin.[66] The total system was about one thousand kilometers long.[67] This was the system which was supposed to be protected by the first military regulations drawn up in 1571.[68]

Until 1577 the Army Chancellery (the *Razriad*) directed the *zaseka* system. Then a special chancellery was formed, the *Zasechnyi Prikaz*, to run it. This institution was short-lived, for after 1580 the *zaseka* was under the jurisdiction of the Artillery Chancellery (*Pushkarskii Prikaz*).[69] These bodies probably were also entrusted with collecting the special tax to pay for the *zaseka*.

At the end of the sixteenth century a third *cherta* was constructed consisting of two segments: (1) Kromy (1594), Livny (1585), and Elets (1592); (2) Kursk (1596), Oskol, Volovonezh.[70] The lines were populated by the government with townsmen, cossacks, and *strel'tsy*. In 1599, and until 1637, the army met south of the Oka in Odoev, Krapivna, Tula, Dedilov, and Mtsensk, and, to the east, in Riazan', Mikhailov, and Pronsk.[71] In 1599 Boris ordered a town built and named it after himself, Tsarev-Borisov.[72] With the construction of this town Russia's outposts reached the middle of the Northern Donets. In fifteen years after the death of Ivan IV the frontier had moved south five hundred to six hundred kilometers.[73]

The purpose of this fortified line system was to keep out the Tatars, who, out of fear of wearying their horses, nearly always followed the same well-broken routes into Muscovy, called *shliakhi*, which avoided crossing deep and wide rivers. These routes and their river fords were well known to the Russians, but nevertheless they felt they could not rely simply on cutting off just the *shliakhi*, so they tried to wall off the entire southern frontier against incursion.[74] In forested areas the lines

175

were built of felled trees some distance inside a forest. Trees were cut down to about two yards above the ground, with the felled portions pointing south. The six-foot tree stumps were left in the ground to provide additional obstacles. These bands of felled-tree obstacles were from 20–40 to 110–130 yards wide. Initially the Russians felled the trees solely to be obstacles, and only later, in the fifteenth or sixteenth century, did they serve as a basis for an entire system of fortified frontier defense lines.[75] Where the forests were not wide enough for such lines, oak logs were pounded into the ground to form a palisade.[76] The forests were allowed to grow thickly along the fortified lines and peasants were strictly forbidden to cut the trees or pass through the lines; the hope was that an obstacle would be presented which would break up the Tatar cavalry hordes and delay or prevent their gaining further access to the north or returning south with captives, booty, and cattle. In some places there were no breaks in the *zaseka* for tens or even hundreds of versts. The grass on the steppe side of the line was burned after the frost in October or November to deny fodder to the Tatar horses and to prevent the Tatars from lighting counter fires intended to burn down the *zaseka* fortifications.[77] Rivers, such as the Oka, Vazha, Osetr, and Upa, were utilized wherever possible to serve as obstacles to the Tatar cavalry. In nonforested areas moats over four yards wide and deep were dug, and the earth then piled up behind them, in an attempt to thwart the Tatar horsemen. There were fortified garrisons or block houses along and inside (if possible) the line at regular intervals. Their locations were chosen to thwart known Tatar tactics.[78]

During the early years of the Livonian War Russia neglected the Crimean Tatars, who, together with the Turks, waged a campaign against Astrakhan' in 1569. This brought them to Ivan's attention, so in January of 1571 the service patrolling the frontier was reorganized by Prince Mikhail I. Vorotynskii, who was shortly thereafter purged and executed, a victim of the Oprichnina.[79] Thanks to the chaos created by the Oprichnina and the ineptitude of the Oprichnina army, the Tatars succeeded in burning Moscow in May of 1571, but after that time the *zaseka* service seems to have functioned effectively enough so that Moscow was never caught completely unawares again by a Tatar raid.

The frontier service was extraordinarily well organized after 1571. Detachments went out into the steppe at semimonthly intervals, beginning on April 1, according to the military regulations drawn up for the Donets system service by Vorotynskii.[80] There were eight shifts, and the first one began patrol a second time on August 1. The eighth shift went out last, on November 15, but when there was no snow to hinder

Tatar raiders, shifts continued to go out at semimonthly intervals. Each patrol, staffed by local cossacks, petty *deti boiarskie,* and some Tatars, Chuvashi, and Mordva,[81] had to arrive at its command center two weeks before it was scheduled to go on duty, so that if the preceding unit was destroyed it could be replaced immediately. The patrols went out at one-and-a-half-day intervals from settled points and then returned, so that nearly every day someone went by each segment of the frontier (a segment was 5 to 70 versts, usually 15–30 versts),[82] looking for telltale clouds of dust raised by a Tatar band or hoof prints indicating the recent passage of horsemen. The functioning of these patrols, which were always moving to avoid detection, was, first, to sound the alarm that the Tatars might be coming (often there were false alarms caused by sightings of clouds of dust raised by wild animals, but all had to be reported and absolutely no sanctions were imposed for mistakes) and, second, to give exact details of the Tatar movements or to notify the authorities that a false alarm had been raised. Penalties for violation of the rules were severe: death for leaving a post if an enemy got through the *zaseka* as a result, the knout for infractions when no enemy was present. Teams consisted of two men, one to sound the alarm, the second to stay at the post until the enemy was actually sighted. At the end of the sixteenth century such patrols effectively covered the entire southern frontier and were usually able to alert Moscow and the army before the Tatars had reached the *cherta;* the army was then supposed to rout the Tatars before they reached the fortified line and began plundering on the Russian side of it.[83]

In 1592, while the bulk of the Russian forces were fighting the Swedes in the northwest, the Tatars again reached Moscow and burned the suburbs for the last time.[84] This event contributed to the unrest in Russia at the time of the promulgation of the decree binding all peasants to the land until further notice, the decree that was coupled with the five-year time limit on the recovery of fugitive violators. The raid itself no doubt gave added impetus to the building of a series of frontier towns by Boris Godunov—the aim was to keep the Tatars away from the center while effort was being expended to recover a Baltic outlet.[85] (The town-building program caused additional unrest.) The last great raid into the Muscovite state was in 1618, when the Tatars reached Belev and Odoev.[86] During the Time of Troubles and the hegemony of Filaret the southern frontier was neglected. The twenties were generally peaceful, but in the thirties, in connection with the Smolensk War, when Russia reduced its forces on the frontier from twelve to five thousand, the Tatars began to threaten the frontier and made minor, then major incursions.[87] This, plus the fact that the post-Filaret administrations

177

desired to possess the lands in the area, led first to a restoration of the prewar complement of troops on the frontier, then to new construction and rebuilding of the frontier defensive lines in the next two decades. By 1635 there were 13,991 troops in standing garrisons in eleven of the frontier towns for which figures are available.[88]

To protect the south after the Smolensk War the government began to build in 1635 the Belgorod fortified line where the forest zone meets the steppe, roughly on a southwest to northeast axis, through present-day Khar'kov, Ostrogozhsk, and Tambov.[89] A spurt of energy devoted to building the *zaseka* at the end of the 1630s was an unintended consequence of the capture of Azov by the cossacks in 1637. The Tatars, experiencing famine in the Crimea, became frightened that the status quo was being upset, that Muscovy was about to push further south; they began raiding in a combined search for food and a vain attempt to stop the Russian expansion.[90] The attacks alarmed the members of the government ruling clique, both in their roles as governors and as large landholders on the frontier.[91] They began a massive rebuilding of the decayed Oka *zaseka* and budgeted 111,574 rubles for work on the Belgorod fortified line, which was completed in 1653. The length of the entire *cherta* in 1638 was about 730 kilometers. The Belgorod line was 800 kilometers long.[92]

To strengthen the *zaseka* after the Smolensk War the government hired French Huguenot fortification specialists. They, along with Dutch engineers, were probably responsible for the bastions, ravelins, and other innovations introduced along the *cherta* in 1638.[93] In 1638 the Fortress Construction Chancellery (*Prikaz Gorodovogo Dela*) was revived to build forts along the southern frontier. It remained in existence until 1644. Also in 1638 other measures were taken. The affairs of the *cherta* were taken out of the jurisdiction of the secondary Artillery Chancellery (*Pushkarskii Prikaz*) and given to the important Military Chancellery (*Razriad*), which energetically pushed construction in expectation of Tatar attacks. In 1641 the *zaseka* management was returned to the *Pushkarskii Prikaz*.[94] In the late 1630s, the 1640s, and into the 1650s, the government tried to protect the southern frontier and reinforce the *zaseka* system of settling the area with lower service class detachments of troops, often runaway peasants.[95] Thousands were drafted into the dragoons and soldiery to serve as frontier troops during the invasion season, then were discharged, to report the next year.[96] This did not recreate the new formation standing army, but it did effectively remove from the middle service class much of its earlier burden of defending the frontier.[97] Upon completion of the first stage of the construction of the Belgorod fortified line in 1646, the army ceased its usual practice of gathering along the Tula line and moved south, sometimes to meet an expected enemy attack in the towns of the new frontier, in Belgorod, Karpov, and Iablonov.[98] This change reflected a realization by the new Morozov government that the Tatars could no longer threaten the heartland of Muscovy.

The expansion of Muscovy into the steppe can be divided into three periods: to the mid-sixteenth century, 1550–1650, and 1651–1750. By the end of the second period, the construction of the *zaseka* system had so fortified the frontier that the Tatars no longer threatened the major Russian population concentrations.[99] The forces permanently garrisoned along the edge of the state were able to cope with the occasional forays of Tatars north of the fortified lines. When the Tatars did penetrate through the system, they had lost most of their energy and were relatively harmless.[100] Thanks to the Belgorod fortified line, the southern frontier was secure by the outset of Tsar Aleksei's reign, which meant that the middle service class had relatively little to do.[101] After the mid-seventeenth century, the line became obsolete as the frontier moved further south, a fact the government tacitly recognized by letting the line fall into decay. Repair efforts were instituted in 1659, 1666, and from 1676 to 1679, but they were insignificant by comparison with the major efforts of the sixteenth century and the 1640s, and have left almost no trace in the historical record.[102]

The Tatar frontier presented the Muscovite government with a classic dilemma. Not fortifying it at all left the very heartland of Russia open to Tatar invasion and spoliation. The Muscovite policy-makers, unlike the Poles, who unsuccessfully relied on large troop concentrations to keep the Tatars at bay, decided this was an intolerable situation, and fortified the entire frontier with the *zaseka*. The center was thus protected to some extent. Then the government decided further protection could be obtained by advancing the fortified lines. But this led directly to a lessening of the population needing protection in the heartland, for, as was shown in chapter 7, the peasants fled to the relatively secure frontier to escape the chaotic and oppressive center and to avoid the taxes being collected to secure the frontier. The government was then forced to devote a great deal of effort to keep the peasants of the center from taking advantage of the security of the frontier. The problems inherent in this paradoxical dilemma were a decisive element in the last stage of the enserfment which led to the repeal in early 1649 of the time limit on the recovery of fugitive peasants.

During the fourteen-year interval between the conclusion of the Smolensk War and the convoking of the Assembly of the Land in 1648 taxes went up, not down, as one would expect with the conclusion of the war and the dismissal of the standing infantry army which had been maintained at Treasury expense. The demand for increased tax revenues caused great unrest among the peasants and, as was discussed in chapter 7, stimulated them to move to avoid payment—adding to the woes of the middle service class. The government did not keep a budget after Filaret's death, so where the monies went can only be a matter of conjecture. One may assume that the funds which were not stolen by the very corrupt government officials were spent on rebuilding the southern defense network. In any case, we know that the funds were not spent on maintaining a standing infantry army.

In the period from the middle of the reign of Tsar Mikhail to the middle of the reign of Tsar Aleksei the traditional military forces of Muscovy became obsolescent. Western mercenaries and their style of warfare were introduced during the Smolensk War, and both were incompatible with the middle service class cavalry and the musketeers and their more primitive technology. Initially, this step was only temporary, but it presaged a complete reorganization of the army. After the Smolensk War the southern frontier defense was thoroughly overhauled with the construction of the Belgorod fortified line and the formation of local military cadres to ward off the Tatar raids. This deprived the middle service class of its traditional task—protecting the settled Russians against the Crimeans' depredations. The new formation regiments and the *zasechnaia cherta* not only revealed the technological obsolescence of the old forces, but were also expensive innovations which oppressed the taxpaying population. The resulting social discontent produced the completion of the rigid stratification of Russian society.

11.

The Triumph of Reform

Before we turn to the reintroduction of the "new Western formation regiments" in the 1650s and the demise of the middle service class cavalry and the *strel'tsy*, let us first review the changes in military technology which made this possible. In 1632 a modern arms plant and arsenal were constructed in Tula by the Dutch. The Kremlin armory was reconstructed simultaneously and large-scale domestic production of armaments was undertaken.[1] In the 1630s, at the latest, a major technological improvement, the flintlock (invented in Germany at the beginning of the sixteenth century), was being adopted; this weapon later would greatly facilitate the introduction of infantry into the Russian army. The invention of the flintlock also permitted cavalrymen to use firearms much more easily than with the old slow-match guns, which forced the rider to dismount in order to fire. It will be remembered that the *pishchal'niki* and *strel'tsy* of the sixteenth century used matchlock arquebuses which took a great deal of training to master. Another drawback of the matchlock was that it often would not work in damp weather, since the wick had to be kept smoldering all during a battle. When the matchlock began to be replaced by the flintlock is a matter of debate,[2] but it is fairly clear that flintlock handguns were used on a large scale in 1637 during the construction of the *zaseka*. A large distribution of flintlock muskets was made in 1651 (thirty flints cost one altyn). Not all troops were rearmed immediately. The matchlock musket continued to be used in the second half of the seventeenth century, and it predominated among the *strel'tsy* until the 1670s.[3] Nevertheless, by the second half of the seventeenth century even provincial cossacks and *deti boiarskie* were armed chiefly with flintlock muskets. By 1652 the eastern and southern frontiers, facing the Tatars, were fairly well modernized so that the army there, as well as that in the west, was equipped with firearms.[4]

181

There were several types of firearms in use in the seventeenth century: the *pishchal'* or *samopal,* the musket, the carbine, and the pistol. *Pishchal'* (along with *samopal*) was the generic name for any handgun. It was first applied to the heavy slow-match instrument used in the sixteenth century and still manufactured in the seventeenth, but it was also the general name for any handgun when no more specific name was applied.[5] The musket was a long, heavy, smooth-barrelled, large-calibre weapon which had to be fired on a stand, much like the *pishchal'.*[6] In a battle lasting all day, a man firing a musket was expected to get off twelve shots; he was supposed to fire the same number in a month of practice shooting.[7] The musket, introduced around 1630, was associated with the Western formation regiments.[8]

The carbine, introduced during the Time of Troubles, was a shorter, lighter flintlock weapon weighing about 60 percent as much as a musket. The killing power of the carbine was significantly greater than that of the old arquebus.[9] The carbine was more of a precision instrument than the musket and therefore cost more. In 1637 at Rugodiv (Narva) 7,000 muskets with stands, cartridges, and belts, were purchased at a cost of 2½ efimki each, whereas 300 carbines cost 4 efimki each. In still another recorded transaction, muskets cost 1 ruble 23 altyns 1 denga each, carbines cost 4 rubles 30 altyns each.[10] All of these weapons existed in several calibres and weights.[11]

The pistol, also introduced during the Smutnoe Vremia, had a very short range and was considered only a supplementary weapon for a cavalryman—the bow and arrow was necessary if a cavalryman had only a pistol.[12] A pair of pistols cost more than a good carbine. In 1661 firearms were sold to the *dvoriane* and *deti boiarskie* of Pskov who did not have any. Five hundred pairs of foreign pistols with Dutch locks in holsters were sold for 2 rubles 16 altyns 4 dengas each, and five hundred foreign-made carbines, also with Dutch locks, cost 2 rubles each.[13]

The seventeenth century witnessed a rapid growth in the production of firearms in Russia, and, as mentioned, in time all branches of service, including the *pomest'e* cavalry, were equipped with firearms, although not all with arms of Russian make. In the first half of the seventeenth century arms were manufactured mainly in Moscow (in the *Oruzheinaia Palata,* the *Barkhatnyi Dvor,* and the *Stvol'naia Mel'nitsa* on the Yauza), and also in Tula, where manufacture had commenced in 1595.[14] The Time of Troubles cut Russia off from foreign supplies, and the new Romanov government, finding itself short of cash to make foreign purchases, began in earnest to develop domestic manufacture.[15] In 1614 twenty craftsmen were at work in the *Oruzheinaia,* and by 1627 their number had increased to sixty-six. About two hundred craftsmen of various specialties worked round the clock in the Kremlin *Barkhatnyi Dvor* turning out arms as an auxiliary to the *Oruzheinaia*. The number of artisans making handguns in Tula increased from twenty-six in 1630 to seventy-five in 1642, plus seventy-seven assistants.[16]

In the years 1614[17] to 1652 the following were made in the *Barkhatnyi Dvor*, in addition to sabres, armor, and other cold weapons: 2,430 musket barrels,[18] 4,685 locks of the matchlock type (*zhagry*), 695 carbines for cavalrymen of the Western style regiments (*reitary*), 2,351 pairs of pistols, and smaller quantities of other items.[19] These were small quantities, admittedly, but nevertheless a good beginning.

A big push was made precisely at the middle of the seventeenth century to modernize the army in terms of small-arms firepower. In the years before the war with Poland for the Ukraine, from 1647 to 1653, the *Oruzheinyi Prikaz* turned over to the army 10,172 matchlock muskets and 26,609 more modern muskets and carbines with flintlocks. Another 10,076 muskets and 12,998 musket barrels remained in the Armory.[20]

Progress was also made in the technological sphere. In 1644 Nikita Davydov, an employee of the *Oruzheinaia Palata,* invented a new type of gun (*pishchal' vintovannaia*), and in 1659 a "rapid firing" model (*pishchal' vintovannaia skorostrel'naia*).[21] Advances in the manufacture of firearms to equip the new formation regiments were also made in the second half of the seventeenth century. The armories of Moscow continued to produce fairly large numbers of arms and other towns were turning out considerable quantities as well. In 1662 the Tula and Kashira arms factories alone produced five to six thousand muskets.[22]

Yet in spite of this considerable metallurgical progress, the industrial base of Russia was not yet large enough to outfit, out of domestic manufacture alone, the huge army of over 120,000 men in the second half of the seventeenth century. Commencing almost immediately after Aleksei's accession, large imports of firearms were made from Sweden, Holland, England, France, and elsewhere—even Turkey. In 1653 agents were sent abroad to buy twenty thousand muskets in Holland, and the same number in Sweden.[23] Paul of Aleppo, in Russia in 1654–56, wrote that Patriarch Nikon had shown him fifty thousand muskets he had bought from Sweden.[24] As additional preparation for the 1654–1667 war with Poland and Sweden, large quantities of material were purchased from the Dutch: 20,000 muskets and 540 tons of powder and lead in 1653, 20,000 muskets in 1655, 2,000 pairs of pistols and 1,000 carbines in 1660.[25] In 1659–62 37,000 muskets were imported from the West via the port of Arkhangel'sk at a cost of 1 ruble 70 kopeks each.[26] In addition to whole weapons, Russia imported parts, including almost all the weapon locks, which were then fitted to rifle and pistol barrels made in Russia.[27]

Almost all armor was imported, although some was made in Kashira by Peter Marselis.[28] The results of these efforts can be seen in the remark of a German visitor to Russia in the 1680s, who reported that the Muscovites were armed as were other peoples.[29]

Russian artillery, which had not developed during the Time of Troubles,[30] made significant progress in the seventeenth century.[31] In the first half of the century two-thirds of all cannon were made of bronze; by the second quarter standardization had progressed to such a degree that the number of calibres being manufactured was down to thirteen (for weapons using half- to twenty-six-pound balls). In addition, small-calibre weapons were replaced by larger ones.[32] Nevertheless, one of the major problems for Russia in this period remained insufficient standardization. "Until the reign of Peter the Great, the casting and construction of weapons always depended on the whim of the founder."[33] The country was not wealthy enough to discard old weapons when newer, better models appeared. This was evident in an artillery inventory taken at Smolensk in 1670. Of the 377 weapons in the fortress, 93 were made of Tula iron, 62 of Lithuanian bronze, and 92 of Russian bronze. Some of these had been cast as long ago as the reigns of Ivan III and Ivan IV. Some were huge, with barrels nearly 4 arshins long (arshin = 28 inches), others were shorter and of varying weights and calibres.[34] The greatest problem inherent in this variance, which was typical for Russia, was that it greatly hindered the training of artillery specialists; whatever weapon a man might be trained on, he would likely end up in charge of a very different model demanding different ballistics calculations, different charge-to-missile ratios, and so on. Only Peter was able to build factories to equip the army with weapons of Russian make, standardized to the extent that uniform training became possible.[35]

Iron weapons of various calibres were made at the iron works in Tula, Gorodishche, and Pavlov. They produced cannon balls, hand grenades, bombs, iron parts for gun carriages. Cannon of small calibre and balls were made in putting-out (*kustar'*) shops.[36]

The major center of manufacture of heavy armament was the *Pushechnyi Dvor* in Moscow. Whereas there were only twenty to twenty-five cannon masters in Russia in the sixteenth century, there were at least two hundred in the following century.[37] In the 1686–96 period from four to five hundred workers representing thirty-two professions labored in the *Pushechnyi Dvor*.[38] In a very short time they, along with the Moscow artillerymen who also worked there, could turn out comparatively large quantities of weapons of the same type, as during the Thirteen Years War when large orders were filled. Surviving records show that in 1664 the *Pushechnyi Dvor* cast sixty regimental cannons 3 arshins 7 vershki

(96¼ inches) in length, 37 calibre, with a weight of 18–24 poods (648–864 pounds) each; in 1671 another sixty were cast, and at the same time they received yet another order for one hundred of the same length.[39] Large numbers of weapons also were made before and during the Russo-Turkish War of 1676–81.[40] As a result of this large manufacturing capacity and activity, in the second half of the seventeenth century Russia had four to five thousand pieces of artillery.[41]

As in the field of hand firearms, considerable technological progress was made in artillery. One important innovator was Kh. Ivanov, who in 1661 cast fourteen small cannon which could be fired from horseback (*pishchali, chto s loshadei streliaiut*). In the following year he cast two rapid-firing cannon and six regimental cannon with conic powder chambers which were 2 arshins (56 inches) long and which fired a ball of about 3 grivenki (2.7 pounds). The latter weapon was adopted in 1699 as the regimental artillery piece of the regular army.[42]

This artillery was of fairly high quality. In the last half or third of the seventeenth century orders could be placed and filled for cannon of specified calibre and length with the basic parameters of each weapon calculated to some degree of accuracy.[43] The manufacture of cannon balls was also being perfected, and by no later than 1690 the factories at Tula and Kashira used iron forms instead of clay ones for casting shells. (Other factories did not make the switch until Peter forced them to by a decree of 1709.) [44] Headway was also made in the development of mortars, especially in reducing their weights; in the last third of the seventeenth century the weight of the average mortar was reduced by one-third.[45] Another indicator of the expansion of the Russian artillery in the second half of the seventeenth century is the rise of the number of men in the artillery service from 4,250 in 1651 to 7,000 in the 1680s.[46] Significant progress was also made in the 1690s, but that lies beyond the general chronological limits of this discussion.

The spreading use of firearms and the advances made in artillery demonstrate that Muscovy was making a full commitment to the gunpowder revolution. Russia had to make this commitment because it was being drawn or entering—the choice of words depends upon one's view of international relations at the time—ever more regularly into the European theater of warfare in which a nation-state had to meet the competition or else face possible extermination by its more advanced neighbors.

Finally, long after Western Europe had done so, ground was laid for the infantry to become the major element of the army. In the two decades between the Smolensk War and the war with Poland for the Ukraine the government made various halfhearted attempts to revive one or another of the new formation regiments. In the spring of 1638 the government, concerned about renewed Tatar raids, tried to hire free soldiers again, but had no success and had to turn to forced levies. By the autumn of 1638, 8,658 soldiers and 5,055 dragoons had been drafted for service on the southern frontier under the direction of the few mercenaries who had remained in Russia after the conclusion of the Smolensk War, but these new troops were discharged on November 1.[47] This procedure was repeated in the spring and fall of 1639 and in some of the ensuing years. Such forces had little training or discipline and got no battle experience in those years of peace, so they were generally considered to be utterly worthless.[48]

Two regiments of *soldaty* were formed in 1642, when there was danger of war with Turkey over Azov. They were soon disbanded when the cossacks returned the fortress to the Crimean Tatars. In the years 1642–48 the peasants of some villages were drafted into the dragoons, where they were trained in alternate weeks in shifts while continuing to farm. They received no treasury support and became tax-exempt farmer-soldiers. Such units could only serve locally, as in the frontier *zaseka* service, not far away on distant campaigns.[49]

The death of Tsar Mikhail in 1645 was a signal for a changing of the guard. The young Tsar Aleksei brought his tutor into the government, and this remarkable man, Boris Ivanovich Morozov, proceeded to cashier the corrupt and inept officials who had charge of the government at the end of Mikhail's reign. Morozov and his clique began to loot the country too, but they also restored order to the government as a whole. This was not done, however, without a considerable amount of vacillation and uncertainty. Morozov ran everything, but on one day was wont to repeal what he had initiated the day before.

Aleksei's former tutor, who could be called a "Westernizer" in his passion for "modernity," reorientated Russia's foreign policy away from the southern frontier and the steppes, which had been made much more secure by the construction of the *cherty*, toward the western frontier and a conflict with Poland to regain Smolensk and its environs and the Ukraine.[50] It was only too obvious even to the young and inexperienced men of the tsar's council, particularly Morozov and Chistoi, that the training, discipline, and armament of the middle service class cavalry were quite insufficient to cope wth another conflict with Poland.

They knew, for example, that in spite of orders that all *dvoriane* and *deti boiarskie* were to carry carbines into combat, from 75 to 90 percent had only pistols. Such a cavalry was suited only for hand-to-hand combat, and the Polish army of the late 1640s was not the Tatar army of Kazan', the army the cavalry had mopped up in 1552 after the walls of the city

186

had been blown up.[51] Therefore the government imported huge stocks of arms to Novgorod and Pskov and, more important, decided to revive the new formation regiments.[52] It might be noted that by 1649, when the peasants were finally enserfed, no decisive action had yet been taken. The old-style army based on the middle service class cavalry and the *strel'tsy* still dominated the Muscovite military picture, as is evident in the *Ulozhenie,* which refers almost exclusively to the old army. Nevertheless, the new Morozov government was highly conscious of the need for a totally reformed army to fight its more technically advanced enemies.

The Russian government was well qualified to initiate reforms with little or no opposition because of its "incredibly high degree of centralization."[53] Nowhere was this more true than in the military sphere, in both war- and peace-time. Until the very end of this period, when some military districts were created on the frontier, all decisions, minor and major, were made in Moscow. This meant that all assignments, compensation rates, promotions, battle plans, fortifications, materiel and general military hardware allotments, and nearly anything else imaginable were programmed in the capital *Razriad* and a dozen or more other military chancelleries by bureaucrats who had no connection with the military and no qualifications for their posts other than a relatively high level of education. No initiative, ordinarily, was left to the local commander.[54] This situation permitted the introduction and institutionalization of changes, but also led to disasters. Some of the unfortunate consequences of centralization were the Shein campaign to take Smolensk in 1632-34 (left on his own, he could have taken the objective without difficulty), and, even more specifically, the "Sheremetev War" (see p. 217 below), when from Moscow the *Razriad* directed the Russian army into a massacre.[55] Excessive centralized control in the hands of nonspecialists also led to personnel decisions of dubious merit, such as promoting an infantry officer to a cavalry post, and then back again.[56] Nevertheless, in spite of shortcomings, highly centralized control and direction of the Russian army usually worked quite well. Because even the most trivial matters were often decided in Moscow, the rank and file, and even the officer corps, were undoubtedly used to obeying orders from the central chancelleries even more than is the case in most armies. This may help explain why there was so little opposition to the new military system once it was introduced.

There is an abundance of evidence to show that the Morozov administration took steps to revive the new formation regiments which had been abolished, for all practical purposes, at the close of the largely unsuccessful Smolensk War.[57] In 1647 the government ordered translated in the Foreign Affairs Chancellery or in the Moscow Printing Office a volume of infantry regulations entitled *The Drill and Art of the Military Administration of Infantry (Uchen'e i khitrost' ratnago stroeniia pekhotnykh liudei)* from a work by Johann Jacob von Wallhausen, published in 1615 in Oppenheim under the title *Kriegskunst zu Fuss*. (A second edition was published in 1620 in Danzig.) It was based primarily on the work of Prince Maurits van Oranje (Nassau), the leading European military theoretician of the beginning of the seventeenth century, with some new material by Wallhausen. There were eight parts to the book with sections on arms, drill, rank-and-file firing tactics, tactics in general, drummers, supplies, and proper respect for officers. The text was printed in Russia in 1647. The plates and drawings were printed in the Netherlands and the book, the first in Russia to use copper engravings, came out in 1649 when these inserts were received.[58] This was only the third civil book to be published in Russia, and the government certainly would not have expended the effort had not the creation of new infantry regiments been uppermost on its mind. (The effort in fact was wasted to a degree because the book was intended for infantry firing the outdated matchlock rifle, not the more modern flintlock. This was probably one of the reasons why only 134 copies of the printing of 1,200 were sold in ten years.) [59] Peter the Great, writing a manifesto on military regulations published on March 30, 1716, noted that his father had published military regulations in 1647 (sic) and connected this with the initiation of the regular army in Russia.[60] There is no doubt that in the eyes of contemporaries crucial military innovations were being made in the first few years of Aleksei's reign.

In the administration itself new chancelleries were founded by Morozov with jurisdiction over various branches of the new formation regiments. The Dragoons Chancellery (*Prikaz Dragunskogo Stroia*) was founded in 1646 and the Cavalry Chancellery (*Reitarskii Prikaz*) in 1649. In recognition of the ever-increasing significance of firearms the Artillery Barrel Manufacturing Chancellery (*Prikaz Stvol'nogo Dela, Stvol'nyi Prikaz*) was founded in 1647.[61] The day of the bow and arrow was waning fast and the government was highly conscious of the need for innovation.

Another Morozov measure certainly launched with an eye toward the new army was the ill-fated indirect tax on salt of February 7, 1646. This was an attempt to rationalize the revenue system by repealing the two major direct taxes, which supported the army (the musketeers) and the post system, in favor of one source of revenue going directly into the Treasury.[62] As is known, this measure failed. The people ceased to buy salt and revenue fell drastically. The government learned rapidly that the demand for salt could be highly elastic, and repealed the measure on December 10, 1647. The salt tax was not directly responsible for the urban riots of 1648, as is sometimes supposed, although it did linger in the popular mind as an example of the oppressiveness of the Morozov administration.[63]

In 1647 the government utilized another military reform, one which was to endure. It began to draft recruits for the army (*datochnye*) on a very limited basis from a specific number of houses, based on the new census. This meant discarding forever the old system of drafting on the basis of land area (the *sokha*). The draft was one recruit for ten to twenty houses. The draftees served the artillery as drivers, in engineering battalions, in other noncombat roles, and as infantry soldiers (*soldaty*).[64] A decade later the draft became crucial in creating the new army.

Morozov did not have the opportunity to carry to their full conclusion the innovations he initiated, for he was purged as head of government after the Moscow riots in the summer of 1648. Nevertheless, he must be given credit for setting in motion the steps which led to the substantial reform of the army within the next decade.

Undoubtedly the governmental changes paralyzed the work Morozov had begun. But after Miloslavskii took over, the Morozov course continued to prevail. This was true particularly in the area of foreign policy, where the Russian government had three alternatives after the liquidation of the internal disorders. (I have no evidence of awareness of the logical fourth alternative—acceptance of the status quo. Russians who spoke for the historical record seem to have felt that warfare was always desirable, providing Muscovy was strong and ready or an enemy was weak and vulnerable.) An attempt could have been made to annex the Black Sea littoral to liquidate the Tatar menace. Russia was not ready for such a conflict, which would have meant fighting Turkey at a great distance. Another possible choice would have been an attack against Sweden to regain an outlet to the Baltic. This would have pitted the backward Russian army against the' best army in Europe. The third alternative was an attack against the Rzeczpospolita to attain the goals of the unsuccessful Smolensk War and to annex the Ukraine.

Russia was dragged at least partly in spite of itself toward the third alternative by the populace of the Ukraine. Bogdan Khmel'nitskii and his cossacks offered to help Russia annex the Ukraine, but even after the cossacks had taken Kiev in May and June of 1648 this move was impossible to contemplate because of the civil disorders plaguing Muscovy.[65] Once the riots had been suppressed, however, the government, aware of the internal weakness of Poland, was free to accept Khmel'nitskii's offer. Nikon, a rising figure in the Muscovite state and soon to become patriarch, opposed initiating a war with Orthodox Poland.[66]

Nevertheless, those favoring attacking the Rzeczpospolita prevailed in the government and at the lengthy Assembly of the Land of 1653.[67] The tensions between the two countries were such that any other course would have been difficult to maintain.

Concluding that war was likely, the government had to recruit foreign officer-cadres to train the troops to fight the Rzeczpospolita. In 1646 I. D. Miloslavskii, soon to be Morozov's father-in-law, went to Holland to hire infantry officers skilled in the new military techniques. Soon Moscow was teeming with mercenaries. Tsar Aleksei was personally aware of the need for them at least as early as 1647.[68] He ordered foreign officers to train Russians, and in the wake of the 1648 disturbances some members of the middle service class revolted against their new leaders. Massive hiring was absolutely essential, for officers familiar with the new tactics and technology were in short supply after most had been sent home in 1634.[69]

Because of the peace in the West after Westphalia, many mercenaries were willingly recruited into the Russian forces in their continued search for high pay, loot, glory, and excitement.[70] The unemployed free booters (and political refugees) of Scotland, England, France, Germany, Poland, Sweden, Denmark, Austria, and other countries poured into Russia to aid the government in its goal of modernizing its army along Western lines. Officers often brought whole groups of subordinate officers and men with them, as in 1661, when Colonel Shein, Lieutenant Colonel Kreits, and Major Wenstendorf came from the Holy Roman Empire to Russia with thirty-nine corporals and cavalrymen; Colonel Egerat and Lieutenant Colonel Strobel came from Denmark with 136 officers and cavalrymen; and a host of others came in the same year from many lands.[71] In 1661 the Imperial diplomat August Meyerberg reported hordes of mercenaries from Germany, Batavia, England, Scotland, and other countries in Moscow.[72] Not only soldiers came to Russia, but all kinds of dregs (business failures, wife deserters, vagabonds, and criminals) flowed east. In Moscow they forged papers, claiming to have been officers at home, and were given commissions in the new Russian army.[73] This was probably one of the major reasons why the new army was not as effective as it should have been.[74] Still, they and the army they created were better than the old, totally untrained *pomest'e* militia.[75] A noticeable portion of the Russian army of the 1660s consisted of mercenaries hired from northern European Protestant countries.[76] The numbers were so large, as the Thirteen Years War dragged on, that the government, instead of begging each ambassador going abroad to recruit officers to come to Russia, as had been the practice, began to turn away foreigners seeking to enter Russian service.[77]

190

Foreigners usually came to Russia under a contract for a specified time, after which, in theory, they could stay or leave. Sometimes the foreigners, not knowing Russian, signed contracts to serve for life.[78] Unknowingly they became part of the rigidly stratified Muscovite society, although they remained a distinct caste in that they were tried according to their own laws while in Russian service. The government was loath to let people leave the country, and often detained them with the promise of rewards or threats of exile to Siberia.[79] With the conclusion of the Thirteen Years War in 1667, however, a number of foreign officers were dismissed and sent out of Russia.[80]

The financial rewards to foreigners entering Russian service were enormous, many times higher than those they could "earn" elsewhere, or that Russians were paid. A regimental commander was paid from 250 to 400 rubles a month, a major from 100 to 225 rubles, and so on.[81] Additional sums were given those who converted to Orthodoxy.[82] In peacetime, when the army was not convoked, the officers lived in Moscow at half pay. All of this cost the Muscovite treasury dearly, although in the 1680s the munificent sums paid to foreigners were reduced considerably.[83]

In exchange for their compensation foreign officers were expected to train their troops, to tend to discipline, and to try and to punish their troops for infringements and violations.[84] This at times led to tyranny and abuse. Sometimes the soldiers rebelled against their officers' cruelty, and then the mercenaries executed their men illegally without permission of Moscow.[85] A regimental commander had charge of fifty-two to sixty companies of about one hundred men each. In battle, higher officers carried a protozan, a broad spear with a handle about 70 inches long, (2½ arshins) decorated with silver and a tassel, and costing 6 to 8 rubles. Lower officers carried a halberd—an ax on a long handle with a rounded blade and with the butt in the form of a long, sharp tongue, also decorated and expensive.[86]

While all of this was a great expense, any government bent on recovering the Ukraine and the headwaters of the Dnepr or an outlet to the Baltic could hardly have done otherwise. Either project involved obvious long conflicts with advanced military powers, so Russia was obliged to rationalize its army. With this in mind, the government completed the process begun during the Smolensk War and made the holding of officer positions contingent upon experience, knowledge, ability, and proved talent. In so doing, the caste prerogatives of the old service classes were ignored, particularly as nearly all the posts of authority in the new army were granted to foreigners.[87] The comments of the traveler Baron August Meyerberg reveal what an enormous task this was: he

191

observed that the Russians were prone to have confidence not in military experience, but noble origin.[88] The military reform resulted in a modest democratization of the Muscovite power elite, as Western hoi poloi running the army rubbed shoulders and shared prestige, influence, and remuneration with the Muscovites comprising the traditional court and governmental hierarchies.[89] The rewards given to the new elite were commensurate with its responsibilities, for revolutionizing an army during a period of domestic unrest while fighting on several fronts was a difficult task. An unwonted degree of rationality was introduced into the Russian army and Russian life itself. Not only was it now government policy that knowledge and intelligence were prerequisites for command, but each rank in the army was assigned specific tasks.[90] The new, much larger army had at least the organizational possibility of functioning effectively. The necessary tasks each regiment was required to perform were anticipated, and (at least in theory) each task had a person automatically assigned to carry it out. This greatly simplified the problems of commanding the huge masses of troops about to appear under the Russian banner.

These foreign mercenary officers were the men responsible for reviving at the beginning of the 1650s all of the new formation regiments: the soldiers (*soldaty*), who were the infantry; the cavalrymen (*reitary*); and the dragoons (*draguny*), who were both.[91] These new (or revived) branches of service were commanded almost exclusively by foreigners.[92] Less than 20 percent of the officers were Russians, at least partially because Russians who by social origin might have been officer candidates scorned the new army.[93] Until the repeal of the "system of places" in 1682, service in the new officer corps was considered socially degrading, an insult to the officers themselves and to their entire families as well.[94]

A few precedent-setting moves were made before the war with the Rzeczpospolita. In 1649 the government tried to extend its experience with the dragoons on the *zaseka* in the south to soldiers on the northwestern frontier opposite the Swedes. It decreed that the town of Olonets should be built and that all the peasants and *bobyli* (landless peasants) of the trans-Onega and Lopskie rural districts (*pogosty*) should be registered in service as soldiers. These peasants were then exempted from taxation in lieu of payment by the treasury for their military services, and each peasant household had to supply one man. About seventy-nine hundred men were registered in two regiments. Another thousand soldiers were raised in similar fashion from the Sumera and Staropol'skaia districts (*volosti*).

These soldiers were intended solely for frontier service, but they were drawn into the wars with Poland and nearby Sweden, particularly during the war for the Ukraine, when all the taxpaying population became continually liable for service as infantry soldiers. Because the peasants had not yet learned how to pack several generations and families into each household (as they were to later), many peasants were ruined when the sole worker from each household was called into service. The situation became so serious that in October, 1662, the government decreed that peasants should not be drafted as soldiers (*v soldaty*) and after the war discharged those who had been taken into service.

With an eye toward the coming war with Poland or for general service in the Ukraine, Russia at least as early as 1652 initiated steps to modernize its native forces. In October of that year one of the mercenaries told the Military Chancellery what supplies would be necessary to fortify a camp (*oboz*) of four regiments of infantry soldiers: 1,100 spades, 1,000 iron shovels, 200 picks, 8,000 large and medium nails, and many other items.[95] About the same time an order went out to draft or recruit eight thousand men from among the nontaxpaying population of eighteen specified towns for service in Iablonov, the southern frontier coordinating center.[96] A document dated a year later brings up the issue of outfitting four regiments of eight thousand soldiers with firearms and other supplies. All the tortuous calculations are put down as to how much powder, lead, and wick will be necessary to outfit this many men to get off three or four shots in a battle; how to provide for sentry duty is indicated, how to train minimally, and to establish a reserve. Also detailed are the number of carts, horse collars, and other supplies required.[97]

Less than a month later, 6,834 of the 8,000 infantry soldiers reported for duty in Iablonov. They outnumbered the 4,650 (of an intended 6,000) *dvoriane* and *deti boiarskie* who reported for service.[98] This represents perhaps the first sign that the middle service class was about to be permanently eclipsed by the new army. It is also instructive that a considerably higher percentage of the infantry soldiers appeared for service than did the members of the middle service class. This also represented a permanent trend. By November of 1653 infantry soldiers were also in service near Smolensk.[99] The demand of the commanders in the Smolensk theater was for infantry troops to fight the Poles.[100] The *soldaty* played a role, at first secondary, then ever more important, in the early phases of Russia's struggle with its western neighbors.[101]

The war with Poland, which was to be known as the Thirteen Years War, began in 1654. At first it went well. Much of the left bank of the upper Dnepr and the Western Dvina was recovered, and Smolensk fell to the Russians in 1654 along with thirty-two other major towns.[102] The Muscovites were so confident that Tsar Aleksei moved his operations to a camp near Smolensk and ran the government by corresponding with B. I. Morozov and I. D. Miloslavskii in Moscow.[103] The Poles were at a disadvantage because they did not believe in fortified towns, so the population was relatively defenseless and the country open to any invader if he had a stronger army.[104] In 1655 the Russians took Minsk and Vil'no, most of Belorussia, and much of the Ukraine. This brought Sweden into the war, and the northerners took much of the rest of Poland, including Warsaw, Cracow, and Poznan. In 1656 Russia and Poland signed a truce. Then Russia and Sweden fought for two years. Russia took much Swedish territory and almost reached the Baltic. But international developments forced Russia to sign the Valiesari truce with Sweden in 1658. War recommenced with Poland. As was usually the case, the Rzecz-pospolita fought the war largely with cavalry, often with up to ten times as many horsemen as infantry.[105] The latter were often mercenaries.

In the early years of the war, Russian field commanders pointed out to Moscow that the Poles were at a disadvantage when they did not have infantry.[106] They also listed times when the Russian forces were at a disadvantage for lack of infantry.[107] (Such laments are also recorded for lack of cavalry.) [108] In the autumn of 1656 a Russian who had escaped from slavery in a Turkish galley by murdering his captors reported to Moscow that the Austrians were drafting infantry soldiers everywhere in the empire, and that these troops were being used to aid the Poles.[109] By the autumn of 1658 the war was going badly for Russia in nearly all respects, including the international situation and the army itself, which was disintegrating in the face of enormous casualties.[110]

As always, the old Muscovite army, based on the middle service class and the *strel'tsy*, could not stand a prolonged conflict.[111] This proved once again the necessity of modernizing the army.[112] During the Thirty Years War most of the participants had established a ratio of infantry to cavalry of two to one or three to one. Russia, however, had not yet made the change.[113]

The setbacks, combined with the field and intelligence reports, forced Russia's military planners to conclude that the ongoing gradual conversion of the army was insufficient, that a crash program was necessary to change decisively the character of the army. A. L. Ordin-Nashchokin was among the leading advocates of the change to a new army.[114] The decision to make a dramatic investment in the infantry was effected by annual recruiting in the years 1658–63. Most of the burden of the levies fell of necessity on the peasantry because of the population distribution, and besides many of the towns had nearly been wiped out by the recent plague.[115] Before the recruiting levies were completed, they proved to be such a burden on the peasantry that even the avaricious B. I. Morozov was forced to reduce his rent collections from some peasants.[116] The draft rivalled the increased tax burden as the major cause of peasant flights during the Thirteen Years War.[117] By 1660 the government observed that recruiting was destroying the peasantry and ordered measures taken to lessen the impact.[118]

The first levy was in November, 1658, from the entire Muscovite state (except on the southern Tatar and northwestern Swedish frontiers) of one infantry soldier from each twenty-five households, sometimes one soldier from each three adult males. In the Novgorod corps area the draft call was one from each ten households; there also were other exceptions elsewhere from the general norm.[119] The draft yielded eighteen thousand men, plus 10,300 rubles collected at the rate of a ruble per household from areas having less than the ten necessary to supply a soldier.[120] Legally, service in the infantry was for life, although the draftees were usually discharged in peacetime. The service requirement must have been instituted by analogy with that for the *pomest'e* cavalry.

A second levy was made in July, 1659, on the same basis as the one of 1658. It yielded 15,577 men plus 1,830 rubles. A third levy was made in December, 1660. It yielded 17,423 men, plus 13,700 rubles and 43,557 *cheti* of grain. The general norm was one man from each twenty households, but one from each thirty houses on lands belonging to provincial *dvoriane* and *deti boiarskie,* widows, and minors; one per twelve households belonging to court villages; and a grivna per merchant of the *gostinaia* and *sukonnaia sotni.* All three levies brought in fifty-one thousand recruits. These infantrymen were levied by the Kostroma Taxation Chancellery *(Kostromskaia Chet')* . Another 5,117 were drafted from areas subject to the jurisdiction of the Great Court *(Bol'shoi Dvorets)* .[121] A levy of one man per twenty households was also announced on December 18, 1661, and there was yet another in 1663.[122] During the war with Poland (1654–67) over one hundred thousand men were drafted in the provinces. These draft calls, necessitated by very high losses as well as a desire to modernize the military establishment, constituted a step forward in the recruiting system toward a regular army. In 1659 a rebel cossack noted the enormous recruiting program under way, but predicted the Muscovites would be defeated anyway.[123] Subsequent events show that he was right in observing that a new force was being created, but wrong in his forecasting of failure. By 1660, it would be fair to say, the new formation regiments had taken over the Smolensk front, with the infantry predominating.[124]

Having resolved to create the new army, the government ran into an obstacle of its own making. Rationality dictated drafting whatever percentage of the male population was necessary to obtain the desired number of recruits. But, as might be expected, vestiges of the past remained in this sphere and the government soon introduced a discriminatory draft. It was somewhat like the discriminatory tax system discussed in chapter 7, whereby the peasant's tax burden depended on what type of land he was living on. In the tax structure the fundamental assumption was that land bore burdens besides payment of taxes. The same assumption came to be applied to military recruiting, so that lay seignorial lands had to furnish the least percentage of peasants, and court lands the highest.[125] The assumption was that lay seignorial serfs also had to support their lords in service. The dead hand of the past restrained the system which was intended to overcome the past.

As always, the masses paid for the advancement of military technology. However, for the first time since the rise of Moscow they paid not in corvée or taxes, but with extended service; after centuries of leaving warfare to the upper classes and slaves, they became personally involved in it. Recruiting proved to be perhaps an even worse scourge than the increasing taxes and caused great discontent.

In 1663 there were fifty to sixty thousand men in fifty-five infantry regiments. In peace time the number was reduced to twenty-five to thirty thousand soldiers under arms in twenty to twenty-five regiments. The soldiers were outfitted at Treasury expense and equipped with muskets, first of the matchlock type, then flintlock weapons. In addition soldiers were armed with rapiers, berdyshes, long and short pikes, hand grenades, and armor covering the whole trunk (although armor was by no means supplied to every soldier).[126] Pains were taken to outfit them with fur coats in the winter time.[127] They were given an annual cash and grain payment, or else settled on the land.[128] In 1663 their prescribed pay was 2 or 3 kopeks per day, or $7\frac{1}{4}$ to 11 rubles per year.[129] In 1663 a crisis came to a head in the financing of the new army, when the government realized that a cash salary which would buy nothing would not keep an army together. Thereupon it founded a special Grain Chancellery (*Khlebnyi Prikaz,* 1663–83) whose task was to provision the army at the front.[130] In combat areas the government even earlier had regularly concerned itself about feeding the infantry.[131] Tsar Aleksei, a very "economic" individual, even made the sage remark, when telling his officers not to stint on feeding the infantry, that "fortresses are made firm against enemies by people, not grain."[132] While the Grain Chancellery was an interesting innovation, a regular provisioning service was not set up until the beginning of the eighteenth century.[133]

When the government was short on funds and supplies, lords were obliged to send recruits equipped with weapons, supplies, and horses. Each recruit had to have two pounds of lead and the same amount of powder. The amount of clothing was also stipulated.[134] In reality, of course, the costs of outfitting the peasant recruits were borne by their fellows who remained behind.[135]

Two of the new formation regiments of soldiers were garrisoned in Moscow and were virtually regular, standing troops. The men lived with their families in the Butyrki settlement in their own houses and had garden plots. They underwent regular training under their foreign officers.[136] The latter lived in private apartments in Moscow or on their own service lands.[137] Unfortunately the soldiers were permitted to conduct outside businesses which distracted them from their military training, as had occurred earlier with their immediate infantry predecessors, the *strel'tsy*. Nevertheless, these were the most respected, highly prized troops in Muscovy. The officers for the entire army were usually chosen from among these *soldaty*.[138]

Most of the soldiers were quartered in the provinces because the government could not afford to maintain them in Moscow. They were paid by the Treasury while they were in actual service, but had to support themselves in peacetime. Thus conditions were not ideal. Training and morale suffered as the soldiers of the new semistanding army tried to make a living by farming, and their agriculture suffered when they had to go on active service. These soldiers even had to pay taxes from their agriculture equal to those paid by the peasants. In the second half of the seventeenth century they became similar in some ways to the *strel'tsy*, although they did not enjoy the latter's privileges; on the other hand, they were commanded by better officers than the *strel'tsy* had, trained more frequently, and in general were much more effective as a military force.[139] Life in peacetime was better for the soldiers than for the musketeers, who had more arduous police functions, but their positions were reversed in wartime as the soldiers bore the brunt of the fighting.[140]

Perhaps the most interesting branch of the Russian infantry were the ski-troop units. They aided Skopin-Shuiskii against the Polish cavalry during the Time of Troubles.[141] During the Thirteen Years War they frequently struck terror into the hearts of the Polish cavalrymen, particularly when the snow was deep and covered with a hardened layer, perhaps of ice.[142] Under such conditions the cavalryman was at the mercy of the foot soldier. For this reason some advocated fighting the Poles, who relied much too heavily on cavalry, in the winter.[143]

In time, service as a soldier became hereditary in the rigidly stratified Muscovite state, and children were registered in a regiment upon reaching their majority. In spite of all these shortcomings, the striking growth of the relative weight and military significance of the infantry equipped with firearms was a decisive improvement in the second half of the seventeenth century over the old Muscovite army. The infantry, the most onerous branch of service, supplanted the cavalry in the army. The figures tell the tale: campaigning against the combined forces of rebelling cossacks and Crimean Tatars in 1668, the army numbered 40,000 cavalry and 24,000 infantry; in 1681 the ratios were reversed in an army alerted for service under N. I. Odoevskii—81,000 infantry and 45,000 cavalry.[144]

The new formation cavalry regiments (*reitarskie polky*) were also revived for the war to recover the Ukraine.[145] In August, 1653, consideration was given to forming and outfitting two thousand cavalrymen.[146] The *reitary* were soon active in the Thirteen Years War, sometimes together with the old units (*sotni*) of *dvoriane* and *deti boiarskie*.[147] At other times they had to remain in service while the old units were discharged.[148] In March, 1654, *deti boiarskie* who had no pay scale or service lands and were not in service were drafted into the cavalry. Then in 1659–60 2,050 *dvoriane* and *deti boiarskie* were taken out of the *pomest'e* cavalry and put into the new cavalry, which was considered more effective than its predecessor. Up until this time the cavalry had been considered the domain solely of *deti boiarskie* and *dvoriane,* but now cossacks, experienced infantry soldiers, peasants (*datochnye lyudi*—the draft calls usually were for one recruit per hundred households), slaves, and monastery servants were taken in.[149] (After the war, however, all these were purged and sent to the infantry or into the town garrison service.)[150] The numbers of the new formation cavalrymen rose from two thousand in 1653 to eighteen thousand in 1663. A decree of 1660 specified that there should be one thousand men in a regiment consisting of ten companies.[151] There were thirty to forty officers (a colonel, majors, captains, lieutenants, and ensigns)[152] per regiment, who always were on duty and usually were foreigners.[153]

The rank-and-file cavalrymen were called only for war or for training, and thus those who had service lands did not break their ties with their *pomest'e* economies.[154] The new formation cavalrymen were recruited from those who had small or no service lands.[155] Among those who had service lands, especially in the south, service was considered an intolerable burden because, having few or no serfs, these servicemen themselves had to farm; they often transferred half of their lands to another person, usually one who had no lands, in exchange for rendering half of the required service. Sometimes one-third was given to someone else. Then the cavalryman would be replaced in service every year or two. The government, realizing that these frequent breaks in service were deleterious to military efficiency, tried to change the replacement system to one of aid: one would till the land and supply money and materiel while the other served. While there were serious shortcomings in the new formation cavalry service, it should be pointed out that training seems to have been rather regular; during peacetime, the cavalrymen usually trained for not over a month in the autumn after the harvest was in.[156] Furthermore, it must be remembered that the army of the second half of the seventeenth century was based largely on the infantry, and no longer on cavalry. The quality of the cavalry forces was increasingly of secondary importance, and seems in any case not to have hindered the Muscovite state in its expansion at the expense of Poland and the Crimean Tatars.

It must be granted that the reality of the new service cavalry did not match the theory behind its creation, namely, uniformly well-trained men equipped at government expense ready for service at any time. In the first place, there was no manual, no regulations for cavalry in the seventeenth century, so each unit was trained much as the old *pomest'e* cavalry had been—as the officer saw fit. Moreover, the government expected the members of the new cavalry to equip themselves, as had the members of the *pomest'e* cavalry. Each came to service with his own horse, musket (later carbine), pair of pistols, rapier, plate armor covering his upper trunk (*laty*), and an iron hat on his head.[157] The armor plate was regarded as absolutely crucial for the cavalryman.[158] How much the cavalrymen used their firearms is a matter of question. Later, during the reign of Peter the Great, the cavalry used basically cold weapons.[159] The government, as a general rule, outfitted the cavalryman only when he was very poor or had suffered a disaster, such as a fire which had destroyed his battle gear.[160] The number of cavalrymen who had service lands adequate to support them and the number who had to live off the rather generous pay of 15, 12, 10, 8, or 6 rubles per year is unknown. At the end of the 1680s, according to the Bohemian Jesuit Jiri David, the cavalry was below the infantry in prestige, and even lower than the dragoons.[161] If this was indeed the fact, then Muscovy had certainly caught up with the reality of Western military practice, which emphasized the infantry. Another contemporary, Iurii Krizhanich, said that this type of cavalry was worthless for Russia, because it was too slow and could be defeated easily by the Tatars. He recommended using dragoons against the latter.[162]

A special category of cavalrymen were the lancers (*kopeishchiki*). The first group was formed prior to 1658, its members armed with lances and pistols. In 1660 a special squadron of lancers was formed. Sometimes they fought as separate units, other times with the soldiers.[163]

Another category of horsemen were the hussars (*gusary*), who were separate from the cavalry (*reitary*). They were primarily lancers. They were armed with pikes and pistols in addition to their lances, which were longer than those of the lancers and were called *kopeitsy.* Their armor was in some ways different from that of the ordinary cavalrymen, perhaps lighter. Also hussars were all of upper class origin, whereas we have seen that cavalrymen could be recruited from any milieu.[164] In 1681 there were five companies of hussars with 465 men in each.[165]

During the war to recover Smolensk and the Ukraine the dragoons also were effectively revived, their numbers significantly increased, and their status and conditions considerably revised.[166] The dragoons were initially armed like the infantry, with heavy muskets, which forced them to dismount to fire. However, by the time the war for the Ukraine broke out, attempts were being made to rearm them with carbines, but they had the lowest priority of the new formation regiments.[167] It was assumed their horses were better than those of the middle service class.[168] They also were armed with a rapier, an axe, or berdysh. Whether they had armor is doubtful—another way in which they were like perhaps the majority of the soldiers.[169] A number of them were recruited from impoverished *deti boiarskie.*[170] Their pay was three and four rubles per year, or only slightly higher than the two and three rubles per year prescribed for the *strel'tsy* and considerably lower than the pay of the other members of the new formation regiments.[171] In law the dragoons were much like the provincial *strel'tsy,* and like them they were settled on the land, mostly in the Ukraine. After the war, during which they had suffered heavy losses, each dragoon was given twenty-five *chetverti* of land and expected to support himself; that is, the Treasury no longer supported him, as it had his predecessor at Smolensk.[172] The Treasury also did not maintain the dragoons' horses. All cavalry forces—the *pomest'e* cavalrymen, the new formation cavalrymen, hussars, and dragoons—were expected to provide their own fodder during wartime, and all but the dragoons kept their horses at home in peacetime. The horses of the dragoons, however, were fed by monasteries and peasants.[173] Each horse was to be kept by four peasant households.[174] At the beginning of the 1680s the dragoons disappeared.

We are now in a position to draw some conclusions about the radical changes in the size and composition of the Russian army in the second half of the seventeenth century. The major change was the sudden rise to predominance of the new formation regiments: from nothing in 1650 to sixty thousand men in 1663, to eighty thousand men (plus twenty-five hundred officers) in the infantry and cavalry in 1681.[175] The ratio of infantry to cavalry troops was dramatically reversed in favor of the former. The ratio was exactly the same as that in the Polish army which was sent in vain in the summer of 1648 to quell the Khmel'nitskii cossack uprising in the Ukraine: forty thousand cavalrymen and eighty thousand infantry (including nine thousand German and French mercenaries) .[176]

It should also be remembered that the army might have been even larger in 1663 had not the Russians suffered serious defeats and tremendous manpower losses almost continuously for the four previous years. In 1659 Russia was defeated at Konotop; in June of 1660 General Khovanskii was decisively defeated at Polonnye (near Liakhovichi in Belorussia) with the loss of five thousand men; then the Russian army at Chudnovo was annihilated, and this was followed by a defeat at Kushliki (near Polotsk) in October, 1661, in which nineteen thousand Russians perished. Ten thousand more died in August, 1662, at a battle at Buzhin.[177] Many, probably the majority, of the troops killed in these battles were men of the new formation regiments, which already held the "chief place in significance and number of troops as half of the active army."[178] Had these losses not occurred, either the army would have been significantly larger than it was in 1663 or the recruiting levies in these years could have been much smaller. Losses in these years probably exceeded the number recruited.[179] The government was conscious of the fact that enormous numbers were being killed, and it issued orders that the style of combat should be changed to reduce the casualties.[180] Yet the bloodletting continued, probably because the officers, schooled in the slaughter of the Thirty Years War, knew no alternatives. The virtue of the new system was that it permitted the army to continue functioning in spite of the massacres in a way which would never have been possible had the old "Russian formation" army continued to dominate the scene.

The Thirteen Years War witnessed the triumph of the gunpowder revolution in Muscovy. The weak metallurgical base was improved and sufficient numbers of mercenaries were hired to direct the transition of the Russian army to a force capable of coping with its Western competition. The new army was based on the infantry, while the cavalry for the first time in nearly half a millennium became secondary. This new semistanding, semiregular army was not an ideal one, but it proved capable of handling the major military exigencies of the second half of the seventeenth century.

12.

The Old Army
after the Reform

The effectiveness of the new army was disputed by the leading authority on the *strel'tsy,* who claimed that "the new formation regiments satisfied the new military, administrative, and tactical demands [of the second half of the seventeenth century] little more than did the *strel'tsy.*"[1] We shall now, with this suggestion in mind, examine the old part of the army upon which Russia relied until the 1650s. We shall commence our examination of the impact of the gunpowder revolution on the various parts of the traditional army from the point where we left them after the end of the Smolensk War in 1634 until their virtual abolition in the 1680s. The two major components of the traditional Muscovite army were the *strel'tsy* and the middle service class cavalry. We shall also take a look at the cossacks, that group of frontier freemen and criminals who made their living by plundering, fishing, and fighting.

Ever since the middle of the sixteenth century the middle service class cavalry had functioned with the musketeers (*strel'tsy*). Therefore one might expect their fate to coincide with that of the *deti boiarskie* cavalry, and this is precisely what happened. In the first half of the seventeenth century the numbers of the *strel'tsy* increased, especially following the Balash uprising during the Smolensk War, when they were used to combat internal disorders. Their numbers rose in this period, when service became hereditary, from 33,775 in 1632 to over 50,000 in 1681 (about 5,000 cavalry and 45,000 infantry).[2] Much of the increase occurred prior to the introduction of the new formation regiments. The number of provincial *strel'tsy* remained constant in this period, about 30,000 men. The increase took place among those stationed in Moscow when, after the 1648 uprising, a new elite palace guard was created.[3] This increase had to be largely by means of self-reproduction because explicit orders were issued[4] not to permit peasants and townsmen to join the *strel'tsy* (although some did anyway), except when they were drafted, as they were in 1633, 1658, 1664, and 1676.[5] The end for most *strel'tsy* came when in 1680 those in regimental service and capable of rendering service were ordered (along with the artillerymen and some of the cossacks) to register as infantry soldiers in the new formation regiments. The Moscow *strel'tsy* were preserved for awhile, but were split up into regiments of one thousand and distributed throughout Russia's nine military corps districts.[6]

The important thing to notice here, however, is not the increase in the absolute number of *strel'tsy* from 1632 to 1681, but their drastic decline after the middle of the seventeenth century as an effective military force. Only 5 to 10 percent of the *strel'tsy* participated in campaigns, and their major function became that of internal policemen, particularly after the Balash rebellion.[7] During the crisis months of 1648 command of the Musketeer Chancellery was the most critical post in the government, for whoever was in charge of the *strel'tsy* controlled Moscow and Russia. This importance is reflected in a contemporary supplement to the *New Chronicler,* a chronicle of Russia from the 1580s through the 1620s, where the replacement of Morozov by Ia. K. Cherkasskii and then the latter's removal in favor of I. D. Miloslavskii as head of the office is noted.[8]

When Boiarin B. I. Morozov had difficulties with the peasants on his estates, his response was to call for the musketeers.[9] Conversely, when "strong people" refused to obey the law, the *strel'tsy* were called in by police officers or provincial governors who were trying to make these capricious individuals obey their edicts.[10] *Strel'tsy* were also employed to force people living on the southern frontier to take cover when information about a possible Tatar raid had been received.[11] (The Muscovite government expended an enormous amount of effort trying to get people living along the *zaseka* to take precautions against being killed or kidnapped, but the provincials often resisted mightily.)[12] Another one of their frequent tasks was to force others to report for military service.[13] They supplied the necessary force to return fugitive serfs after 1649 and suppressed the Moscow "copper riots" in 1662.[14] The *strel'tsy* also protected the tsar's court, accompanied him and members of his family and higher church officials on their pilgrimages, and performed weekly guard duty at the Moscow chancelleries. Some were assigned to purchase cranes and swans for Tsar Aleksei. Several hundred musketeers always accompanied foreign ambassadors in their travels to and from the frontiers and about Moscow, much to their annoyance. They delivered messages throughout Muscovy for the chancelleries. They were assigned to protect commerce on the Volga against the depredations of the cossacks, Tatars, and Kalmyks. They performed jail guard-duty, enforced the strictures against tobacco, watched over taverns to protect the government's interest in full revenues and in uncovering bootlegging, and even served as firemen.[15]

The *strel'tsy*, still armed much as they had been in the sixteenth century, protested against these "arduous" police duties, but much preferred them to serving on military campaigns. Rank-and-file *strel'tsy* who were engaged in business would complain to the tsar when a commander elevated one of them to a more responsible position such as that of decurion or subcenturion, for that would necessitate paying regular attention to military service and thus distract from business.[16] As the leading specialist on the *strel'tsy*, the late S. L. Margolin, put it, they protested against all military training—which was required anyway. The new infantry tactics of the seventeenth century were alien to the *strelets*, regardless of attempts to train him anew.[17] The great discrepancy between police and military functions must have made it doubly difficult, if not impossible, for the constabulary musketeers to adapt to the new army.[18]

The government seems to have realized soon after the initial experiment with the new formation regiments that the *strel'tsy* no longer were very effective militarily, even though their organization and armaments were consistently better than those of the middle service class.[19] For example, in 1638 a group of *strel'tsy* were sent to Aleksin to protect the builders of the *zaseka*. They were given old-fashioned matchlock muskets which they could not fire because they were used to shooting only the newer flintlock weapons. This indicates that the government cared so little for these forces that it was not even aware of their capacities.[20] In another instance, in June of 1642, out of despair over the poor performance of at least one regiment of musketeers, the government pushed aside the Russian commander and assigned a foreigner to instruct the men.[21] Recognizing that this might be insufficient, the government in the same year formed two regiments of infantry soldiers (*soldaty*) out of the best Moscow *strel'tsy*.[22]

Perhaps the greatest sign of recognition by the government of the obsolescence of the *strel'tsy* was the fact that it cut off their pay and forced them to farm or engage in petty trade and industry to gain a livelihood.[23] In 1636 *strel'tsy* had land grants in 35 of the 110 towns in which they were garrisoned, mainly in the south. In certain of the 35 towns, only part of them lived off the land. At that time only about 12 to 13 percent of the 23,500 provincial *strel'tsy* were forced to make their own living, but their numbers grew substantially (along with the desertion rate) in the course of the seventeenth century, especially as the government cut their pay in the second half of the century.[24] Usually only the

Moscow *strel'tsy* got the annual grain payment.[25] Service in the *strel'tsy* became hereditary and lifelong; some are known to have been under arms as long as seventy years.[26] The lands belonging to the *strel'tsy* were passed from father to son and, like service lands (*pomest'ia*) belonging to members of the middle service class, were sold and exchanged when their holders moved around in service.[27] As time wore on and they tended to perform little or no military service, they moved about less and lived as settled homeowners in the same place for a long time, often for decades.[28]

Nearly from the moment of their creation the musketeers had engaged in trade and manufacturing, much like the townsmen.[29] The role of the *strel'tsy* in urban businesses seems not to have been very significant, in spite of the laments of the townsmen.[30] Participation in urban businesses ranged from an exceptional 25 percent in frontier Riazan' in 1595–97 to the more typical 3 of 260 shops in Viaz'ma in 1627 or the 5 of 791 in Iaroslavl' in 1630. There seems to have been little change in the course of the rest of the century.[31]

The *strel'tsy* were still treated as a privileged caste in the *Ulozhenie* of 1649. This would seem difficult to square with the fact that the townsmen triumphed at the Assembly of the Land of 1648–49 (urban merchants were perturbed by the fact that other elements of society could compete with them unfairly because of privileged position). At the Zemskii Sobor the townsmen gained a near monopoly on the ownership of town property and the conduct of urban trade and industry.[32] And although the *strel'tsy* retained certain of their former privileges,[33] which had originally been granted in lieu of wages, they now lost some of them. For the first time they had to pay duties and taxes on their enterprises, and remained exempt only from regular urban taxes and corvée obligations.[34] Moreover, the first two sons of any *strel'tsy* who had been townsmen had to be returned to the urban tax rolls along with their fathers.[35] Such treatment was a significant concession to the townsmen, for the *strel'tsy* thereby lost much of their competitive advantage. These measures may also explain why more *strel'tsy* did not go into business after the promulgation of the *Ulozhenie*.

The government was willing to appease the urban caste in this way at least partially because everyone, from their former commander Morozov on down, knew that the day of the *strel'tsy* as a useful military arm or reliable internal police force was passing. The government partially sacrificed the *strel'tsy* to win the support of the townsmen. Nevertheless, the privileges the *strel'tsy* did retain were "too mediaeval" and were inconsistent with modern notions of a standing army always subject to call to arms.[36] No doubt the musketeers were allowed to retain some privileges because neither of Aleksei's governmental factions was secure enough to be able to risk alienating any part of the army or its internal police force, as abolition of all *strel'tsy* privileges would have done.[37]

Forcing the *strel'tsy* to seek their own livelihoods as farmers, merchants, contractors, or craftsmen,[38] destroyed much of their remaining military effectiveness. An additional step vitiating their military usefulness was the breaking up of the settlements where they had held regular drill and whence they had always been ready to go to war immediately, like a true standing army corps. The *strel'tsy* came to have no time left for military education. The settlements themselves were in fact in the process of disintegrating anyway as more and more *strel'tsy* sold their houses to outsiders and left the settlements to live elsewhere. As a result, large numbers of them were always absent without leave.[39]

In all probability the Moscow riots of June, 1648, shook the confidence of the government in the *strel'tsy*. Rather than coming to the aid of the government, they threatened their commander Morozov, devastated his house in the kremlin, and joined the mob.[40] Recognizing the military obsolescence of the *strel'tsy,* the government in 1653 ordered the supply of future recruits (children, brothers, nephews, and others living with them) drafted as soldiers, rather than left to become, as they would in the natural course of things in this rigidly stratified society, the next generation of musketeers.[41] The record of the *strel'tsy* during the Thirteen Years War can be summarized briefly. Relatively few of them participated, and those who did revealed their incapacity for a prolonged war; it was just as expensive for the *strelets* to be away from his source of livelihood as it was for the *pomest'e* cavalryman. Only 126 of the required 180 musketeers even bothered to appear in the spring of 1656 to help build the great flotilla of two hundred boats for an attack on Riga.[42] The discipline of the musketeers collapsed, and ultimately they were replaced by *soldaty*.[43] They were to be heard of in Muscovite military annals in 1695 at Azov, where they again failed to distinguish themselves.[44]

In the second half of the seventeenth century the government neglected the *strel'tsy* even to the point that the government no longer paid for their weapons. The result, of course, was that not all of them even had guns—some only had halberds.[45] By the 1670s the situation had deteriorated in the provinces to the point where the musketeers were armed no better than the indigenous population. In 1674 about half of a group of several hundred *strel'tsy* at Sumskii Ostrog was armed with various types of firearms, the other half with cold weapons, mostly various types of lances and some bows and arrows.[46]

Not only the government but the *strel'tsy* themselves knew that their period of effectiveness had come to an end. In the first half of the seventeenth century they continued to be willing tools of the government, but after 1648 the two parties gradually fell out with one another. (Those converted into an elite palace guard were an exception.) The *strel'tsy* merged with the urban population and assumed much of its ethos. The musketeers' awareness of their own obsolescence undoubtedly explains their fervent adherence to the eschatological Old Believer movement, for indeed their world was coming to an end.[47] The same reason certainly explains what is even more striking: the fact that the *strel'tsy* were on the side of the rebels in most of the antigovernment uprisings and demonstrations in the second half of the seventeenth century.[48]

After the Razin uprising (1666–71) the government decided that it had taken enough. It reviewed the *strel'tsy*, reduced them in numbers, and relocated them into new settlements.[49] In the 1670s the government merged some of them with the regiments of foreign formation. An order of March 25, 1680, partially reformed the *strel'tsy* along Western lines, their officers receiving titles like those of the heads of the other new regiments.[50] Decrees of 1681 and 1682 planned to cut off the inadequate cash pay of most of the remaining *strel'tsy* and ordered vacant land to be given to them as compensation. The musketeers had to find the vacant lands for themselves.[51] The heads *(golovy)* of the *strel'tsy* passionately opposed the military reorganization at the beginning of the 1680s.[52] By the end of the 1680s even foreigners observed that the *strel'tsy* had far less prestige than the new infantry troops.[53]

This is how Peter I found the surviving *strel'tsy*—in a condition suitable for terrorizing civilians and participating in palace coup attempts (1682, 1698), but good for little more.[54] It was at no loss to the government that he liquidated many of them in 1698 after their armed uprising.[55] Peter equated the *strel'tsy* with the Janissaries, and properly so, for not only did both become involved in palace politics and urban riots, but the decline of the Russian troops paralleled to a remarkable degree that of their Turkish models.[56] The musketeers were last mentioned in 1710.

In deciding to abolish the *strel'tsy*, Peter also may have been influenced by the fact that in the West, before the introduction of the bayonet at the end of the seventeenth century, musketeers fought together with pikemen, who defended them with mass formations. In Russia this never had been the case, for the *strel'tsy* were always protected by the cavalry, either the middle service class cavalry or later the cavalrymen *(reitary)* and dragoons of the new formation regiments.[57] Peter, who had been enraged by the musketeers' performance at Azov in 1695, learned from

207

his travels in the West that troops such as the *strel'tsy* had no place in a modern army.[58]

Another of the military forces of the traditional "Russian formation" present in the second half of the seventeenth century were the cossacks. They consisted of numerous, very heterogeneous elements. Dating back to the fourteenth century, around the reign of Dmitrii Donskoi or earlier, some cossacks served the Tatars as an advance guard. Others served the Tatar agents in Russia, then later changed over to Russian princes. These cossacks settled in the Murom Land on the tributaries of the Oka and rendered guard service to warn of Tatar attacks on Russia. They were the ancestors of the "fortress" cossacks later serving in the *zaseka* service. Their numbers increased substantially during the reign of Vasilii II, probably as a consequence of the civil war dislocation.[59]

Most of the cossacks were Russians, often runaways from poverty and oppression in Russia proper. They considered that a year or two in the cossacks freed them from all ties they had left behind. For their service they were granted land, sometimes a cash grant, and exemption from taxation. They had to provide their own horses and weapons. Cossacks were first mentioned in military action with the Russian army in 1444 as a free, light-cavalry band.[60] In the reign of Ivan IV the "fortress" cossacks were placed in the jurisdiction of the Musketeers Chancellery. Soon, however, they were assigned to the Military Chancellery.

Distinct from these service cossacks were the free cossacks who were subject to no government, had no definite loyalties, and made their living by piracy, highway robbery, fishing, and warfare. The Zaporozh'e Rapids cossacks appeared soon after 1471, when Poland dramatically changed the status of the Kiev principality.[61] Probably many of them originally had been Ukrainian cossacks before they served in the Rzecz-pospolita army. Tens of thousands of them fought in the battle of Tannenberg in 1410.[62] In the sixteenth century the Zaporozh'e cossacks served Poland as border guards and on campaigns. They became subordinate to Muscovy only in 1686. The Don cossacks were first mentioned in 1502, as fugitives from the Riazan' area.[63] After the conquest of Kazan' and Astrakhan' non-Russians joined the cossacks, who were concentrated in various regional, democratic, free associations. In addition to the Zaporozh'e (or Dnepr) and Don cossacks, there were others, such as the Volga, Iaik, and Terek (Caucasus) groupings. These groups were independent of the government, unlike the fortress and frontier-service cossacks, and lived by fishing and plundering.

In the 1570s the Russian army began to use Don cossacks, although they remained completely independent of Moscow until the last quarter of the seventeenth century.[64] By 1591 the Volga cossacks sometimes joined the regular Russian forces.[65] About this time the fortress cossacks were used to garrison Siberia, which was in the process of being annexed by Muscovy. In the later part of the sixteenth century the cossacks were oppressed by the government, which feared them, and forbidden to come to Moscow and the provincial towns. They took revenge during the Time of Troubles, when they ran wild, looting and destroying everywhere.[66]

Because of the antigovernment role of most of the cossacks in the Time of Troubles, which contributed enormously to the growth of the freebooters, the government took measures to reduce their numbers. Some were sent to the provincial towns, others were converted into *pomeshchiki* in the south. A special chancellery (the *Kazachii Prikaz*) was established after the Time of Troubles which had jurisdiction over the cossacks to the middle of the 1640s. By the beginning of the 1630s there were only about eleven thousand cossacks in Russian service.[67] After the cossacks took Azov in 1637, the government saw some positive value in them and began courting them. An apparent promise not to take fugitive peasants out of the ranks of the cossacks was a recognition of their military utility.[68] As we have seen so often, frontier defense, even if provided by runaway peasants, nearly always had priority over the claims of middle service class landholders. As a result, by 1651 the numbers of the cossacks had doubled. Some of them were so-called "settlement cossacks" who had left areas controlled by the Rzeczpospolita because of religious and other forms of repression.[69] The Muscovites used them as spies against their homeland.[70] Many of them settled in the no-man's-land of the Ukraine along the Northern Donets, Sula, Psel, and Vorskla rivers. For use of the land they agreed to defend the southern frontier against Tatar raids. This added thousands of men to the frontier defense force of Muscovy in the mid-seventeenth century.[71] This was yet another reason why defense of the frontier ceased to be a major obligation of the middle service class cavalry. In small outposts the same officer sometimes was in charge of both the *strel'tsy* and the cossack troops.[72]

In the second half of the seventeenth century many of the cossacks were converted to police functions along with the *strel'tsy*,[73] but many of them proved much more adaptable than the traditionalist musketeers. Judging by compensation, it is evident that the government valued the cossacks more highly than it did other members of the old lower service class and equated them with the dragoons.[74] About twenty thousand service cossacks were absorbed into the new formation regiments, particularly in the early 1650s.[75] The Ukrainian cossacks, *cherkasy*, about 13,500 mounted men, participated in all the great campaigns of the

Russian army in the second half of the seventeenth century.[76] The ability of the cossacks, who in the first half of the seventeenth century were frequently armed only with a lance (*rogatina*),[77] to adapt to the military reality of the second half of the seventeenth century is not difficult to understand, for they were further down the social ladder than the *strel'tsy* and had everything to gain (improved status, social acceptability, more regular compensation) by assimilating with the new formation regiments.[78] It might be said that until this time the cossacks—runaway peasants and slaves living outside the frontiers of the Muscovite state—had irregular relations with the government and only now, in the middle third of the seventeenth century, did the government begin to exert direct control over them. Therefore it was comparatively easy, at least initially, for the government to direct them into the desired channels.[79] (Frequently, however, the cossacks betrayed the Russians and would join, for awhile, the Tatars, Poles, or Swedes.) [80]

Russia was a poor country, and this was reflected in its management of the cossack regiments. The problem of supply remained crucial in the Thirteen Years War, and before it was over supplies ran out. The first servicemen to be cut off were the cossacks. Moscow had strict rules of behavior in occupied territory.[81] However, once the cossacks' incomes and supplies were not forthcoming (and doubtless even at times when they were), they turned to looting and plundering the population of the occupied territories.[82] Such behavior caused bitterness among the occupied peoples, who turned against the Russians and joined Belorussian and Lithuanian resistance movements.[83] This reaction was responsible for many of the reverses the Russians suffered in the 1660s.[84] The government should have retained its earlier wariness of the freebooters. A wiser policy would have been to draft and train more soldiers, and keep the cossacks in the Ukraine. This may not have been a real option, for the soldier pipelines at the end of the 1650s may have been full, while the number of draftable peasants was diminishing; the only option open to a government seeking more troops was to accept the cossack volunteers, in spite of the known drawbacks stemming from such a course.[85] By the end of the reign of Aleksei, however, the provincial cossacks were in the process of being phased out and were being replaced primarily by dragoons. By the time of Peter cossacks comprised an insignificant part of the armed forces.[86] In the eighteenth century all the cossacks were brought under direct governmental control; some were phased out, others were reorganized into units (largely noncombat) which lasted until 1917.

Besides the *strel'tsy* and cossacks, there were other members of the lower service class (*sluzhilye liudi po priboru*) . These included the men who fired and maintained large and small artillery pieces (*pushkari* or *zatinshchiki*), the gatemen (*vorotniki*), treasury masons and smiths (who mainly built and maintained fortifications), postmen (*iamskie okhotniki*), and others. They appeared as special categories in the armed forces during the reign of Ivan IV and often lived in special settlements.[87] Much like the *strel'tsy*, these members also had privileges which set them apart from the majority of the populace. These privileges, however, were reduced considerably by the *Ulozhenie* of 1649 in favor of the townsmen.[88] Until 1675 these members could become *deti boiarskie*, whose ranks had been closed to all others at the beginning of the century, but finally this avenue of mobility became closed as society became ever more rigidly stratified.[89] Whether many of them did rise into the ranks of the middle service class in the seventeenth century is unknown, but it certainly is doubtful. Some may have, for the numbers of the *deti boiarskie* increased considerably after the Smolensk War, but most of this rise was probably due to natural population growth.

Now we shall turn to an examination of the middle service class, made up of *deti boiarskie* and *dvoriane*, whose rise we studied earlier. In the sixteenth century they were the mainstay of the Muscovite state, and their reaction to the gunpowder revolution is very interesting.

One of the major problems of the Russian army in the second third of the seventeenth century was how to adapt the middle service class "old formation" cavalry, which weakened progressively in the course of the century, to the reality of firearms.[90] The leading tsarist specialist on the cavalry made the following observation: "Hand firearms were almost never used by the *dvoriane* and *deti boiarskie* comprising the militia cavalry."[91] This obviously led to difficulties in an era when those in charge of the government were becoming increasingly aware of the need to adapt to the realities of gunpowder technology.

The government made an attempt in 1643 to tell the members of the middle service class how they were to be armed. In the first place, all were required to have pistols and muskets. A concession was made to those whose major weapon was still the bow and arrow: they were to have either a pistol or a carbine. Those, mostly slaves, accompanying the members of the upper and middle service classes could be equipped with bows and arrows only if they were expert marksmen; if they were not, or did not have these weapons, they were obliged to carry muskets or carbines. An exception was made for the very poor *pomeshchiki*, of whom there were vast numbers, in the 1643 rules: they were allowed to carry spears and axes instead of firearms.[92] The arms carried by those who possessed them were of the most diverse sort, as the cavalrymen

211

were required to outfit themselves.[93] Apparently some could shoot from the saddle, but most had to dismount to fire because the weapons were too heavy to manage without a stationary support. In reality, little distinguished these troops from ordinary infantry except for the fact that they were more mobile than a regular foot soldier, the latter was equipped by the government rather than from his own means, and the middle service class continued to wear the same armor they had in the sixteenth century (except the *tegiliai*), whereas the infantry usually had none.[94] In fact, the cavalry, when mounted, only could use cold weapons on the attack, and because the government realized that this cavalry was basically suited only for hand-to-hand combat, it required each cavalryman to wear the old defensive armor: chain mail, helmets, and the rest.[95] Somewhat later, in the 1663 review of the military forces, many of the *dvoriane* and *deti boiarskie* in the Novgorod area did not even have horses, which may well have been typical for all of Russia at the time.[96] The service requirements of the seventeenth century are unknown. The requirements seem to have been set by the locally elected *okladchiki* as they saw fit.[97]

The amount of effort the government was willing to invest in attempting to adapt the middle service class cavalry to firearm technology depended largely on where the members were situated. The rearmament of this cavalry proceeded considerably slower on the southern than on the western frontier. In 1649 in the Riazan' frontier area, where the Tatar horseman was the major enemy, only 38 percent had firearms, the rest had bows and arrows and sabres.[98] But where the Poles were the enemy, as many as 87 percent had firearms (in a typical instance), 10 percent had bows and arrows, and 3 percent had only a sabre, an ax, or spear (*rogatina*).[99] The government commitment to rearming the middle service class cavalry was not very strong. At the very beginning of the 1650s the *deti boiarskie* were regarded so poorly in the army that muskets were taken away from those who had them to arm the *strel'tsy* and the regiments of foreign formation.[100]

There were at least two reasons why the government was unwilling to expend scarce resources arming the middle service class on the southern frontier. For one, nearly enough lower service class members could be found there or drafted, outfitted with firearms, and assigned to the frontier to fulfill the manpower requirements of twelve to seventeen thousand men necessary to handle routine security matters, chiefly Tatar raids.[101] Secondly, the fortifying of the frontier with the *zaseka,* largely completed in 1646, finally in 1653, combined with the reduced Crimean activity, lessened greatly the entire problem of the Tatar front. Nevertheless, the middle service class cavalry continued going out to frontier posts annually in shifts to await a Tatar invasion, as it had done for decades. Actually this was unnecessary, except when a major invasion was expected. The Poles had to send out a large army because they did not have a fortified line, and their strategy was to encounter the Tatars and put them to flight. This proved not to be very successful, with the result that enormous numbers of captives were taken from the Polish Ukraine and sold by the Crimeans every year.[102] The Muscovite defensive line was more effective, so that the Tatars did not threaten the Russians as much. The frontier was so quiet in the middle of the century that the prerevolutionary historian Iu. V. Got'e reported that the Muscovite government ceased calling out the militia in many of the years after 1638.[103] However, the Soviet historian A. A. Novosel'skii discovered that the Muscovites were creatures of habit who continued to call up the militia for service on the frontier in at least most of the 1640s and into the 1650s. He remarked that this was a transitional period, when the government was becoming accustomed to the Belgorod fortified line.[104]

There was little point in gathering annually in Tula, for by the middle of the century it had lost its former significance as a frontier fortress.[105] The frontier had moved so far south that it was no longer rational to send men there from the old Muscovite heartland on the chance that the Tatars might invade.[106] In spite of this fact, until 1646, out of inertia, the old army gathered in Tula whether or not an invasion was expected.[107] In reality, of course, the middle service class had lost its function as a frontier patrol and defense force to lower service class elements, such as cossacks, dragoons, and soldiers, who were stationed on the frontier permanently or brought there in expectation of an invasion.[108] After the completion of the Belgorod fortified line in 1653, the middle service class cavalry ceased being sent to the frontier. In 1661 G. G. Romodanovskii's army guarding the southern and southwestern frontier consisted of 46 members of the middle service class, 1,800 new-style cavalrymen (*reitary*), 855 soldiers (*soldaty*), 52 dragoons, and 313 Donets and Oreshkovo cossacks.[109]

By the beginning of the reign of Aleksei it must have been apparent to at least some figures in the Muscovite government that the relevance of the middle service class cavalry in the military establishment of Muscovy deserved questioning. This class was of marginal utility not only on the southern frontier but elsewhere as well.[110] Only the recently acquired status and accompanying arrogance of the middle service class could have convinced even its own members that they deserved, as late as 1648, to have a good share of the labor force put at their nearly exclusive disposal. Nevertheless, until the reforms were made, this illusion was possible, for the *pomest'e* militia continued to be the basis of

213

the only army Russia had. If danger threatened, the government could only call on the middle service class.[111]

Perhaps the arrogance of the middle service class found its supreme expression at the Assembly of the Land called in 1642 to discuss the problem of Azov. The Don cossacks had taken Azov by surprise in 1637 and offered it to the Russian government. Had Tsar Mikhail accepted the gift, war with Turkey would have followed, for Azov belonged to Turkey's vassal state, the Crimean Khanate. In the 1642 conference the middle service class, supposedly the military backbone of Muscovy, said war would be all right—if the other military groups would do the fighting and the other classes would furnish the soldiers.[112] Later on, in the second half of the century, the members of the class recognized their military shortcomings and proposed to the government that huge armies should be created out of peasant recruits.[113] Obviously it was much easier for the serf-owners, who had no love of warfare, to send some of their peasants as substitutes, or to pay cash in lieu of serving (in spite of the cost in both cases), than to go to war themselves in the face of the very high casualties that seemed to result from the new style of warfare. They adopted such alternatives ever more frequently after the middle of the century.[114] They did not propose, however, that serfdom be abolished, for this would have deprived them of much of their recently acquired social status as well as their livelihoods.

The middle service class reached its peak size in the early 1650s, precisely at the time of its greatest political influence in the Muscovite state. In 1651 there were 39,408 members (adult males) of the middle service class. Only 4.5 percent were serving in the Western formation regiments.[115] At this time the ineffectiveness of this privileged group was becoming ever more apparent. In 1647, for example, *deti boiarskie* prepared for service who had neither peasants nor *bobyli*, *pomest'ia* nor *votchiny*.[116] Getting members of the class to serve at all was an increasing problem. In April and May of 1648 the *dvoriane* and *deti boiarskie* of Arzamas refused to serve on the new Simbirsk *zaseka*. They beat members of the lower service class (gunners and *strel'tsy*) who were sent out as policemen to force them to report for duty.[117] This reluctance to leave the estate became more common as time progressed, particularly during wartime. The members of the middle service class considered war a cause of personal ruin, and so tried to avoid it by all possible means. But if they could not avoid service, they fought as an untrained, unorganized, undisciplined mob.[118] Their presence in battle was a questionable advantage.

Evidence showing that the government was conscious of the obsolescence of the middle service class immediately after the enserfment of the peasantry is to be found in a decree of August, 1653. Here the ultimate demise of the *pomest'e* cavalry was foreseen in the invitation to all children, brothers, and nephews of *dvoriane* and *deti boiarskie* not in service and who had not yet been allotted lands to join the soldiers, the most despised (but necessary) branch of service. They were promised pay for their service, and threatened with degradation to the status of peasant and expulsion from the service class if they found the offer not to their liking. (As if to add insult to injury, the same document discusses recruiting nonagricultural peasants and household servants who were not slaves into the ranks of the infantry.) [119] This document may have been a response to a July 30 report from the general in Iablonov, the leading frontier town. Part of the report detailed the incapacity of the *deti boiarskie* to render military service. He recommended enrolling one thousand criminals in the dragoons for training by the foreign commander.[120] This would seem to be a recognition by a man in the field that dealing with the middle service class was a thankless and hopeless task.

Similar steps were taken subsequently. In October of 1656 *deti boiarskie* were ordered to serve in the infantry. They resisted, so the commander ordered the other soldiers to watch them so that they would not flee.[121] In 1658 more *deti boiarskie* were assigned to serve as *soldaty* in Lithuania.[122] Some *deti boiarskie* were told to be infantry soldiers on the southern frontier and were given virgin lands.[123] A logical consequence of this step was the making of at least a few *soldaty* on the frontier into *deti boiarskie*. These were the forerunners of the *odnodvortsy* (landowners possessing no serfs) who had little resemblance to the old middle service class.[124] Still others were assigned to serve as dragoons against the Tatars on the southern frontier.[125] *Deti boiarskie* violently objected to this also, and some tried to escape serving as dragoons by claiming they were new formation cavalrymen (*reitary*).[126] Those who were ordered to draft *deti boiarskie* into the dragoons were able to fill only one-third of their quota. Their explanation of their failure reveals what was happening to the middle service class. Many of the *deti boiarskie*, their children, brothers, and nephews had already been drafted into the infantry and dragoons. Others had enlisted in the new formation cavalry or in the Moscow regiments of the new infantry. Still others simply refused to be drafted into the dragoons and hid in the forests.[127] Despite resistance, however, the days of the middle service class cavalry were numbered.

The relative numerical weakness of the middle service class was apparent in 1658 when the Belgorod corps was formed on the southern frontier. Of the 19,252 troops, only 2,050 were *dvoriane* and *deti boiarskie*.

Almost immediately they were converted into new formation cavalry-men (*reitary*), who were considered much better in battle than troops of the old order.[128]

On February 21, 1659, the government appointed, without their consent, 350 middle service class youths who were old enough for service but had no lands or pay to permanent service with foreign mercenaries in the new formation cavalry (*reitary*) in Smolensk and its recaptured environs. They were given a free lot in the recently recaptured town and twenty rubles with which to build a house. They were also to be given ten peasant households or ten rubles as an annual salary if there happened not to be any such service estates available.[129] A decree of October 9, 1659, ordered the paying of thirty rubles to each *dvorianin* and *syn boiarskii* in the new formation cavalry service.[130] Of course this was easy while the government was minting vast quantities of copper money. A further step was taken in 1660 when half of the three thousand *deti boiarskie* children who were not yet serving in the army that was assembled in Pereslavl' Zalesskii and the Riazan' area were registered in the soldiers regiments and given five rubles each.[131] An order of June, 1660, specified that new formation cavalrymen who had been killed were to be replaced by *deti boiarskie* who had not yet been given a rank in the middle service class (*neverstanye*).[132] Socially and politically this was a brilliant strategy, for it phased out the old army with a minimum of damage to the feelings of the old servicemen; it left them untouched, but sent their children in another direction. One must imagine that the reform was effected in this manner as a calculated maneuver to raise minimum opposition.

Evidence justifying the government's lack of confidence in the middle service class was revealed in the Thirteen Years War.[133] While rates of failure to report for service or of desertion were high for all categories of servicemen by modern standards, they were far higher for members of the middle service class than for the other military groups.[134] Recognizing this, the government told them that "your ancestors were not insubordinate" and that "you are forgetting the honor of past generations."[135] Every conceivable stratagem was devised and implemented to avoid service: illness, destruction of the serviceman's estate, even the hiding of service-age children.[136] The government, in an attempt to get the middle service class to the front, even resorted to the device of giving bonuses to those who appeared for service on time.[137]

During the war the old truths about the middle service class became ever more apparent. The cavalrymen had to bring their own supplies to the front months in advance, usually in the winter, when travel was easier.[138] After several months of service the supplies ran out. Then the men turned to plundering the war zone.[139] When there was nothing left to loot, chaos prevailed, and they fled.[140] Sometimes, in anticipation of this situation, the government discharged the middle service class, but kept the new formation regiments to continue siege and combat operations through the winter.[141] Another alternative, used more frequently as the war wore on, was to support them, usually on a cash basis, out of government funds, like the members of the new formation regiments.[142] This violated the spirit and purpose of the *pomest'e* system, for which the peasants had been enserfed. Some *dvoriane* and *deti boiarskie* even said that the *pomest'e* system had ceased to function.[143] By 1662 some commanders reported that no one would report for service, in spite of all threats and enticements. They said they could not go to war because they had no troops.[144]

Members of the middle service class increasingly resorted to sending others to fulfill their military obligations. They sent their brothers, sons, or other relatives who had no service lands. Or, as noted earlier, they sent their own serfs or slaves. They also could pay money instead of sending a substitute. Legally, this was possible only when the landholder was physically unable to serve. Practically, it was used as a device by those who simply preferred not to serve at all.[145] In either case, whether the serviceman was genuinely incapacitated or faking, the fact that substitutes could be and were sent revealed to all that the peasant was the military equal of his master. To some it may have indicated that the social order was somewhat askew.

Another point worth noting is that during the Thirteen Years War "the flower of the middle service class cavalry perished."[146] The war turned into a bloody horror in 1657, and remained so for a decade. Two major battles nearly wiped out the *pomest'e* servicemen. The first was the notorious battle of Konotop on June 28, 1659, when an army under Prince A. N. Trubetskoi was massacred by the traitorous cossack Hetman Vygovskii.[147] The following year (after a desperate, abortive attempt by Moscow to end the war) [148] there was the so-called "Sheremetev War," when for nearly two months without respite one hundred fifty to two hundred thousand Poles, Tatars, Muscovites, and cossacks massacred each other.[149] The Russian army of about forty thousand men (plus ten thousand servants and slaves and a baggage train of at least three thousand carts) under V. B. Sheremetev consisted largely of cavalry and had thirty-five thousand horses which had to be fed. The Polish general Potocki finished the "war" in October, 1660, at Chudnovo, when the tsar's entire army of thirty-six thousand men was killed or taken prisoner.[150] Sheremetev himself remained in captivity for twenty-two years.[151] The 1660 catastrophe was a sign that the old army "had outlived its age, was in the need of renewal."[152] The catastrophes also removed from the scene many of the men who had demanded that the peasants be enserfed.

From 1661 on the middle service class ceased to appear in independent organized units in the theater of military operations.[153] The Muscovite autocracy used the opportunity presented by the physical extermination of a good part of the old army to get rid of the obsolete mechanism entirely and replace it with an improvement, as we have seen above in our discussion of the new formation regiments. Simply to have renewed the old middle service class cavalry would have brought additional disasters.

The demise of the middle service class was reflected in the activities of the administration. During the rise of the *pomest'e* cavalry, so-called army offices (*razriadnye izby*) were created in the provinces to handle relations between the middle service class and the central government's Army Chancellery. In the middle of the seventeenth century these offices were converted into centers of general military administration for all types of servicemen. This parallelled the evolution of the Moscow *Razriad* itself, which became sort of a super chancellery, almost a chief of staff, supervising all governmental appointments and personnel in the Muscovite state.[154]

After the disasters in the middle of the Thirteen Years War the numbers of the members of the middle service class rendering military service continued to decline. "The historical role of the *pomest'e* cavalry was completed by the end of the Thirteen Years War."[155] In 1668–69, after the conclusion of the Treaty of Andrusovo (1667), *dvoriane* and *deti boiarskie* no longer were even the major cavalry force of the Muscovite state, for they were only 19,000 out of a total of 42,500. Later, in the Chigirin campaign of 1674, the relative insignificance of the old middle service class cavalry was even more striking: they were only 28,000 out of a total cavalry force of 71,088 men.[56]

The condition of the middle service class military forces continued to deteriorate. A decree of December, 1675, observed the very high rate of inexcusable absenteeism from service for every conceivable reason by *dvoriane* and *deti boiarskie*. Others came to service for a short time and then deserted to live on their estates. The boyars and generals were helpless to do anything about it. The *pomeshchiki* often claimed to be sick or injured when they were not; or, if they had been, their sick leave had expired long ago. Others claimed to be in other branches of service, or to be serving from other towns, which they were not. Minors grew up with lands but did not register for service. Instructions were issued for correcting the situation, among them an order to collect an unspecified number of peasant recruits from the estates of retired, wounded, and ill members of the middle service class who had no heirs to replace them—an explicit reminder that there was no mystique about riding a horse, that any able-bodied person could render service. More important, no one was to be shifted under any circumstances from service as an officer in the new army, as cavalryman (reitar) or soldier, back to the old service. Any disobedience was to be punished by a mercilessly severe public beating and confiscation of all property.[157] As is known, however, the ferocious penalties of Muscovite law were rarely carried out,[158] and the government was loath to use violence to instill discipline in its troops. The Englishman Samuel Collins recorded that Tsar Aleksei responded to a proposal by a foreigner to execute deserters with the comment that "it is hard to do that, for God has not given courage to all men alike."[159] By the end of our period possessors of serfs were frequently absent from service by the thousands. The dvoriane and deti boiarskie were absent without leave from the army in higher percentages— from 13 to 57 percent—than any other category of servicemen.[160]

In the 1670s, a very late date, 75 to 90 percent of the members of the middle service class had only pistols and were fit for no more than hand-to-hand combat. In 1675, 92 percent of the members of the middle service class cavalry from the Kostroma region were armed only with pistols and sabres; most of the remaining 8 percent had carbines and handguns (pishchali), but several were armed only with sabres.[161] Thus the dvoriane and deti boiarskie of the old Muscovite service (sotennaia sluzhba) gradually lost their military significance. This had already been noticed in a 1663 military review. At that time the number of dvoriane and deti boiarskie absent without leave from service was extraordinarily high, whereas a century earlier it had been relatively insignificant.[162] The government, realizing that the time was running out on the traditional cavalry forces, refused anyone who had been in the new regiments permission to return to the old sotennaia sluzhba.

By 1672 50.3 percent (19,003) of the 37,859 dvoriane and deti boiarskie in 77 southern towns were in new formation regiments, compared with only 4.5 percent of 39,408 in 1651. In 1672 the rest of them were in town defensive service (14,935, or 39.4 percent), and only a handful, 3,921 (10.3 percent) were in the old regimental sotennaia sluzhba, which was becoming extinct.[163] In 1678 the government ordered all deti boiarskie and dvoriane who had no serfs to join the new formation cavalry at a pay rate of twenty-four rubles per year. Those with peasants were to have their pay cut at the rate of one ruble per household. All deti boiarskie and dvoriane who had less than twenty-three peasant households had the option of serving in the old formation regiments, but would henceforth receive no pay unless they enlisted in the new cavalry.[164]

We see once again that the government clearly realized the old middle service class cavalry was obsolete and was attempting, gently, to put to the best possible use the *dvoriane* and *deti boiarskie* inherited from an earlier era.

More than a century ago the historian of Peter the Great, N. G. Ustrialov, portrayed superbly the life style and military utility of the old cavalrymen on the eve of the Petrine era:

> In peace time *pomeshchiki* and *votchinniki* who were not on official duty calmly lived in their own villages, engaging in law suits, their economies, trade, and hunting, and least of all thinking about military matters. When the musketeer messenger arrived from the general with a decree from the Tsar, "Prepare for service, get ready supplies to feed the horses," they reached for their grandfathers' rusty armor, got ready a bag of food for the trip, and loaded up several wagons with as many provisions as they had: dried and salted meat, fish, oat flour, buckwheat, butter, and grain. They took with them their own slaves on the campaign, appointing some to fight, others to the wagons. Many showed up late, or not at all. It was best to be sick so as not [to run the risk] of losing one's service lands.[165]

One of the traditional signs of the middle service class cavalry was the body of slaves which accompanied it. The law of 1556 on service specified how many slaves the serviceman had to bring with him. Although no known specific requirements existed in the seventeenth century, the available evidence indicates that about the same ratio of slaves accompanied their masters to war in both periods. The *pomeshchiki* from the south usually brought no slaves; those from the north did. For example, in 1577 the 277 cavalrymen of Kolomna brought 147 armed and mounted slaves. A century later, in 1675, 433 *pomeshchiki* of Kostroma brought 188 men, although with one crucial change: only 42 of them were on horseback. Over two-thirds were infantry, armed usually with lances (*rogatiny*) and berdyshes, assigned to guard the baggage train.[166]

The slaves who were equipped for combat were better armed, on the average, than the *pomeshchiki* themselves. In 1659, only one-third of the landholders of the Riazan' military districts had firearms, but two-thirds of their slaves did. This was largely because only the wealthier lords could afford to bring slaves, and they equipped their vassals better than the average cavalryman could outfit himself. Another factor which should not be overlooked is the fact that the cavalryman's psychological makeup was not in tune with the times. Often the lord would outfit

220

his slave with firearms, but would come to service himself armed only with cold weapons, or cold weapons and a pistol, with the result that the master was effective only in hand-to-hand combat in an era when the general use of firearms was causing armies to fight one another at some distance.[167] In the eighteenth century the slaves were displaced by peasant recruits.

Perhaps the best mark of the disintegration of the middle service class as a fighting force is to be found in its attitude toward its military obligation. The morale of the *dvoriane* and *deti boiarskie* in the second half of the seventeenth century was extremely low. One popular saying was, "God, let us serve the Sovereign, but not have to draw our swords from their scabbards." If they could not by any stratagem avoid serving, then, as I. T. Pososhkov observed in 1701, commenting with contempt on the old militia, they prayed to God to be lightly wounded in order to collect disability compensation and then to be discharged.[168] Everyone could see how they hated war. Foreigners observed them with disdain as cowards who would flee the battlefield given the first opportunity, abandoning the braver infantry to captivity or death at the hands of the enemy.[169]

As has been noted, "during the war with Poland the *pomest'e* militia of *dvoriane* and *deti boiarskie* ceased to exist."[170] Military technology had left far behind the archaic middle service class cavalry.[171] In 1680 the wealthier *dvoriane* and *deti boiarskie* were registered mainly as new formation cavalrymen and lancers, groups which were simultaneously purged of nonlanded elements. The poorer *dvoriane* and *deti boiarskie* were registered in the ranks of the soldiers.[172] The old *sotennaia sluzhba* existed longer among the upper service class Moscow ranks in the tsar's regiment as his bodyguard and for ceremonial functions, but in 1682, when the system of places (*mestnichestvo*) was repealed,[173] this group, too, was abolished. Finally, on March 20, 1685, the government decreed that the minor children of members of the middle service class were no longer to be registered in regimental service, but were to serve in the garrison service as a home guard in the towns where their fathers had served or were serving.[174] This removed them from the likelihood of ever seeing combat or rendering genuinely useful military service.

The reforms at the beginning of the 1680s ended the duality which had existed in the Russian army off and on since the first Smolensk War. The old Russian and the new Western systems had been incompatible. The army-wide organization of the old forces existed only during a campaign, that of the new was continuous in both war and peace. It was almost impossible for officers to transfer from one system to the other. The old and the new segments of the Russian army used two organizations responsible to different chancelleries, two systems of train-ing, two different tactics, and two styles of combat.[175] At the moment Peter ascended the throne with his brother Ivan, most of this was a matter of the past. By the end of century Russia ceased imitating the Tatars in favor of imitating the West. But, as the student of Russian his-tory would expect, it never did occur even to the outspoken and flexible Iurii Krizhanich, not to mention anyone else in Russia, that Muscovy might innovate in the military sphere. Even a person such as Krizhanich proposed studying carefully the enemy, and then adapting to him.[176] Russia did manage to adapt quite successfully in the second half of the seventeenth century, when the leaders realized that the main enemy was no longer the Tatar, but the Pole and the Swede.

The military reforms at the beginning of the 1680s were only part of a larger program introduced by Tsar Fedor's government. These whole-sale changes, initiated by I. M. Miloslavskii and other relatives of Fedor's mother who were ruling in his name, presaged the more dramatic re-forms of Peter the Great. In November, 1679, a vast reorganization of provincial administration was undertaken, government was to some extent decentralized, and the old preserve of the middle service class, the *guba* administration, was abolished and merged into the administra-tion of the provincial governor (*voevoda*).[177] In March, 1680, an attempt was made to introduce accounting and a rudimentary budget into the operation of the central chancelleries.[178] Two months later, in May, the Treasury was given the responsibility of collecting all taxes, and of cen-tralizing operations which had been located in the jurisdictions which spent the funds.[179] The tax system was overhauled in 1681.[180] In Novem-ber, 1680, the army was reformed.[181] On January 12, 1682, the hallowed "system of places" (*mestnichestvo*) was abolished.[182] The system of places was blamed, rightfully, for some of the military defeats Russia had suf-fered.[183] This system was abolished chiefly at the insistence of the new upper service class which had taken power in the seventeenth century, whose members' origin, in many cases, was not highly distinguished. The actual repeal had followed the 1681 recommendation of a military reform commission headed by Prince V. V. Golitsyn that officers be appointed from all service families without regard to origin (*bez mest i bez podbora*), as had been the case with the foreign mercenaries for a long time.[184] After 1682 the government for some time was very chary about using its new freedom of appointment.[185] Nevertheless, it may not be too much of an exaggeration to say that "the destruction of *mestnichestvo* destroyed the last shield protecting the old stagnation" in the military sphere.[186] Incidentally, the persistence of *mestnichestvo* through the period of the reform of the army may have facilitated its modernization, for the system of places kept the leading service families so divided in the contest for position that for them to have united to keep control of the officer corps from the foreigners would have been out of the question.[187] This division, coupled with the obvious need for Westernization, gave the central power free rein in hiring the needed mercenaries and turning the army command over to them.

The remaining vestiges of the middle service class cavalry were finally abolished as part of these reforms because it was obsolete on two major counts. For one, the new order demanded the replacement of the old irregular militia of the past. In order to be secure as an independent state, a country was obliged to have a trained army, and the new Western-style army was a major step in the direction of a regular army. Abolition of the old horde-formation militia, which took months to call into being and then was susceptible to annihilation by enemy artillery, was a necessity. Also, steps had to be taken to ensure treasury support of the army, for no individual could be expected to supply himself for long-term siege warfare.

The middle service class cavalry also had to be abolished because of the changed nature of warfare, based largely on the dominance of firearms. Nations could no longer allocate their resources almost entirely to cavalry and survive.[188] As the traveler Baron August Meyerberg observed in 1661, Aleksei learned by experience that infantry armed with guns were more effective than cavalry, and he took steps to reduce the numbers of the latter.[189] This realization was reflected in the dramatic change of emphasis from cavalry to infantry. In 1660 the cavalry was still dominant, but by 1681 it had yielded decisively to infantry.[190] More-over, as has been shown, the old *pomest'e* cavalry was singularly inept at adapting to the use of firearms. "Like the knights of Western Europe, the *pomest'e* army was unfit for the new conditions of a military art based on firepower warfare."[191] The government was aware of the shortcomings of its army and took gradual, yet drastic, steps to correct them. Had these reforms not been instituted, it would have been difficult for the house of Romanov to continue ruling an ever-expanding Russian empire.

The gunpowder revolution delivered a death blow to the middle service class cavalry. It is hard to see how the *dvoriane* and *deti boiarskie* could not have been conscious of the precipitous decline of their social utility in the half century after the Smolensk War. The remark by the Czech Jesuit David about the low status of the *reitary* has already been noted. If this was true, then the status of the middle service class cavalry could only have been lower.

The Smolensk War must have instilled a sense of greater insecurity in an already insecure middle service class, for its members could see the obvious disparities between themselves and the new formation regiments. The partiality of the government toward the new army was also apparent. This may well have led some of the *dvoriane* and *deti boiarskie* to imagine that the government, which had created their elevated position, could reverse its position and take away their privileges.[192]

Evidence of this consciousness of obsolescence and fear of impending dispensability is not easy to find. The only available expressions of middle service class sentiment are in the petitions to the government, and a formula such as "You, Sovereign, no longer need us, so grant us . . ." would hardly have produced concessions. Also, Muscovite petitions did not always contain all the relevant issues, but were restricted to things the government could act on. The middle service class, for example, did not emphasize the flow of peasants to the newly secured lands on the Tatar frontier. In another petition campaign of the second quarter of the seventeenth century, the leading merchants tried to get foreign competitors expelled, but did not mention the most significant source of unfair competition—the tsar and the government.[193]

In spite of these drawbacks, the middle service class petitions do contain "reactionary" expressions which reveal considerable anxiety about the present and the future. Their supplications of the 1630s and 1640s hark back to the golden age of the sixteenth century when there was no time limit on recovering fugitives, when the servicemen were so important that they even had direct access to the tsar, and when they had much greater control over their own lives in the provincial administration.[194] The petitioners desired a restoration of the time when they were crucial to the security of the state; the administration, knowing this was no longer possible and facing no emergencies, could safely ignore their laments. The frustration engendered by these rebuffs must have added to their anxiety and their determination to hold on to their positions, and is reflected in the increasingly strident tone and elaborate content of the successive petitions.[195] The desperate attempts by the *deti boiarskie* to avoid service in the new army and particularly in the infantry (*soldaty*) reflects a status anxiety which certainly was present in other spheres of action as well. The absence of firearms in all probability shows not only poverty and inability to purchase them, but also a general incomprehension of the changing technical world characteristic of a dispossessed social group.[196] The very high rate of absenteeism by members of the middle service class may also have been a symptom of their resistance to the changes introduced into their military routine by the gunpowder revolution.[197] Finally, the frequent petitions on the slavery question were part of the search for a secure identity and the scramble for status in the rapidly changing times of the Smolensk War and the Thirteen Years War.

In the summer of 1648 it was not accidental that the middle service class joined the uprising against the government. For the previous three years Morozov had been hard at work modernizing the army, and in this way effecting the obsolescence of the members of the middle service class. His refusal to pay them may have been a mark not only of his own cupidity, but also of his probable recognition that to do so was throwing away money which could be better spent elsewhere. The rebels focused their aggression on the Morozov clique, the source of the strains resulting from the major structural change represented by the new army.[198] Mercenaries in the new army being formed by Morozov were instrumental in suppressing the Moscow uprising, so it is even less surprising that shortly thereafter some middle service class contingents rebelled when they were put under the command of foreign officers. The insistent demands by the *deti boiarskie* for cash pay could well be interpreted as partially a desire for recognition of their social utility—which in 1648 the rival Cherkasskii-Sheremetev-Romanov faction was willing to pander to in order to gain power and calm the country. The enserfment of the peasantry was the result of a similar recognition.

The sense of obsolescence by the middle service class is even more apparent in the petitions filed during and after the changeover to the new army in the Thirteen Years War. The tone became simply one of pleading. By this time the middle service class was assuming new functions. These functions and the government's response will be discussed in chapter 14.

In the period between the Smolensk War and the coronation of Peter I, the old army, consisting of the middle service class cavalry and the infantry musketeers, was phased out. This was a trying time for the men of both branches of the service. Many of the *strel'tsy* responded to their declining social utility and status by becoming Old Believers. As will be shown in chapter 14, the *dvoriane* and *deti boiarskie,* because of their involvement with the enserfment, were not free to react to their technological, military, and social obsolescence in so dramatic a way as did the musketeers. Of the old military forces the cossacks became integrated most easily into the new order because they had the least interest in or commitment to the traditional system. For many of them, joining the Western style army represented more than adequate compensation, in the form of increased status, for the loss of freedom they were experiencing.

13.

The Legacy of the Reform

The seventeenth century witnessed a great expansion in the size of the Russian army. In 1632 Russia sent 34,588 men to Smolensk; in 1680 129,300 were sent against the Turks. By the end of the 1670s the total forces at the disposal of Moscow exceeded two hundred thousand men, the largest army in Europe by far.[1] In the 1680s this army was sought as an ally by the two great European coalitions, the anti-Turkish and the anti-Swedish forces.[2] The Moscow garrison alone consisted of from thirty-five to forty thousand men.[3]

No material has ever been published, to my knowledge, which tells in what manner the Muscovite government determined how large its army should be. On the basis of comparative figures, which have been noted from time to time, one can assume that there must have been some attempt to match the size and composition of the army of the Rzeczpospolita. The *Razriad* knew fairly well from constant reports the dimensions of the forces of its major enemies and may have attempted to duplicate or better them.[4] It is certain, however, that ability to pay for the army out of a balanced budget was not the determining factor.

At the beginning of the seventeenth century the government contemplated maintaining the army only during wartime. During peacetime the army had to fend for itself according to the principle "the nation [as opposed to the government] maintains the army" (*zemlia soderzhit voiska*).[5] This principle was followed by all of the old Russian formation army, except the *strel'tsy*. As has been shown, the principle definitely lessened the effectiveness of the new formation army when applied to it in the second half of the seventeenth century. The problem of provisioning the army in combat was not "solved" until Peter's time, and, for similar financial reasons, the new army was only semiregular and semistanding until the end of the seventeenth century.

The exact cost of maintaining the Muscovite army cannot be determined because of significant gaps in the information available. For example, the *strel'tsy* were supported by the government, at least in theory, although we have seen that this support decreased as the seventeenth century progressed. What certainly must have been a significant item in the cost of the *strel'tsy* cannot be determined because the number of their officers is unknown.[6]

The expense of maintaining the army (in peacetime) rose approximately three-fold in the seventeenth century, from 275,000 rubles in 1630 to 700,000 rubles in 1670 (from four to twelve million, figured in constant rubles of the beginning of the twentieth century). This was close to half the state budget.[7] The wartime figures are not known as precisely. Had the government been unable to increase its expenditures by such a magnitude the rapid, successful conversion to the new army would have been unthinkable.[8]

Most of the expense was added because of the cost of the new formation regiments. In 1663 the rank and file of the active army should have been paid (including pay for clothing and bonuses) 722,537 rubles, 190 dengi, or a little more. Two *vybornye* regiments (wealthy people selected from crown lands) and the army of foreign formation had 2,524 officers who were paid the enormous sum of 227,160 to 282,688 rubles.[9] (Officer pay averaged around 100 rubles per man per year, ranging from 90 to 112 rubles, with a few colonels and generals making 420, 540, 600, and 1,200 rubles a year. Foreigners were paid 50 to a 100 percent more than Russians of the same rank.) [10]

Adding the pay of the officers to that of the rank and file, the total wage bill for the active army was around one millon rubles per year—from 949,968 to 1,005,225 rubles. The lion's share of this not insignificant sum went to maintain the foreign formation regiments—from 736,672 to 802,200 rubles per year. The rank-and-file *strel'tsy* in 1663 cost the government only 92,903 rubles per year, the cossacks 5,786 rubles, and the *dvoriane* and *deti boiarskie* 81,015 rubles year year.[11]

In addition to cash pay, the troops were supposed to get an annual allowance of rye and oats which depended on their branch of service and rank. (See table 5.) The total grain allotment was 70,000 *chetverti;*[12] whatever could be collected was distributed first to the dragoons, secondly to the soldiers, thirdly to the cavalrymen (*reitary*), fourthly to the Moscow *strel'tsy*, and lastly, if any was left, to the provincial *strel'tsy*.[13] Here we see once again the low priority attached to the musketeers in the distribution of the fruits of the levy which still bore their name, the "grain for the *strel'tsy*" (*streletskii khleb, korm*). Top priority was given to the foreign formation regiments, and there top priority was given to infantry over cavalry forces, which reflected perfectly the interests of the government.

TABLE 5

1663 SCALE OF ANNUAL COMPENSATION TO THE
RANK-AND-FILE FORCES OF THE RUSSIAN ARMY[14]

RANK	CASH	GRAIN
Dvoriane and		
deti boiarskie	15,* 13,* 10, 8, 6 R	
Shliachta (Poles in cavalry)	10, 8 R	
Cossacks	8, 6, 5 R	
Strel'tsy	3,* 2, 1½ R	
Hussars	15, 13 R	
Cavalrymen	15,* 12,* 10, 8, 6 R	2 ch. rye and 2 ch. oats
Lancers	14 R	
Dragoons	4, 3½, 3 R	½ ch. rye +; ½ chet' rye & ¼ ch. oats; ½ ch. rye & 1 ch. oats
Soldiers	10,* 6, 4 dengi/day = 18,* 11, 7¼ R	1½, 1 +, ½, ¼ chet' rye
Strel'tsy		
Moscow		4 ch. rye, 1 ch. oats;
Provincial		2 ch. rye +; 3 ch. rye & 3 ch. oats; 1 ch. rye.

*Paid only to the top members of the Moscow corps
+ Majority compensation

Obviously the total military wage bill was in excess of the government's resources to meet it, and in fact more than the government paid. One of the signs of the financial embarrassment the new army caused the government was the fiscal devices employed in an attempt to pay for it. In the Thirteen Years War, as throughout the seventeenth century, the Russian government was trying to obtain foreign loans, particularly to pay for weapons and powder.[15] Internal loans were also arranged.[16] The most notorious legerdemain, however, was the radical debasement of the coinage beginning in 1654.[17] This caused grave hardship to the troops who were paid in full, but with worthless money which would buy nothing.[18] The government was forced to abandon this expedient by the 1662 copper riots in Moscow.[19] Seeking a new source of funds, the government in 1663 reopened the farming out of tavern concessions, which Aleksei had stopped in 1651 with a burst of righteous indignation.[20] To borrow from a later phrase, the new army was launched first on a flood of debased copper currency, then on a sea of alcohol.[21] Taxes were raised, as shown in chapter 7 above, and twice the government resorted to extraordinary "fifth" levies on the urban population in an attempt to raise funds to pay the army.[22] Finally, in a decree dated September 5, 1679, the government repealed nearly all the old direct taxes and tried to raise the needed revenue from the new consolidated household tax.[23] All arrears were cancelled. As is known, the household tax was introduced at least partially because the tax on cultivated land ignored other sources of peasant income and could be avoided by curtailing farming in favor of other work.

While the government was trying to increase revenues, each peasant was trying to escape the burden. This is presumed to be one of the reasons for the decline in the size of peasant plots. The average size of a peasant plot at the beginning of the seventeenth century was one-third *vyt'*, but this had fallen to one-fourth *vyt'* in the 1660s.[24] The household tax removed the incentive to curtail agricultural production, but the peasants soon learned to lessen their tax burden by combining households. Peter removed this sanctuary by introducing the male head-tax as the basic direct tax.

The government's behavior in the financial sphere proves that it knew definitive changes had taken place. The hegemony of the new semiregular, semistanding army dictated a change of thought patterns on how the army should be paid for. As a result, the relative importance of the Service Land Chancellery (*Pomestnyi Prikaz*) declined as that of the Treasury rose. This in turn meant that the government, to satisfy the desires of the ruling elite, could dispose of its own lands much more freely in the second half of the seventeenth century than earlier because it no longer needed to worry about providing the middle service class cavalry with land grants to enable it to render service. The middle service class was militarily obsolete, and the government recognized this fact.[25] We must further remember that the evolution of service landholding into hereditary property also forced a change in the method of supporting the army because the government could rely no longer on the *pomest'e* to provide the necessary equipped troops. Nearly all authors ascribe part of the reason for the replacement of the middle service class cavalry by the new army to a need to find other means of financing and levying the army, a need which was met by drafting peasant recruits, hiring foreign mercenaries, and paying both with increased tax revenues.[26]

In the course of the second half of the seventeenth century the advances which were being made in all spheres of military technology and organization were fundamentally incompatible with the old Muscovite middle service class. Recognizing this, the government phased the class out militarily in the 1660s and 1670s. According to one specialist, the major weakness of the reforms at the beginning of the 1680s was that they did not get rid completely of the old system (the *sotennaia sluzhba,* the service in units of one hundred which was nearly the sole organizing principle of the traditional Muscovite army), the continued existence of which weakened the military capability of the entire army. The differences between the two incompatible armies extended even to the point that the members of the middle service class gentry were called up for service at different times and in different ways, depending on which army they were in.[27] Apparently the government abstained from liquidating the remnants of the old *pomest'e* cavalry for financial reasons—not for political reasons.[28] In the second Crimean campaign of 1689, which reflected the renewed interest by the Tsarevna Sofia's government in the southern frontier, there were 17,206 men of the old Russian formation regiments present (of whom 7,936 were *dvoriane* and *deti boiarskie*) along with 78,652 men of the new foreign formation regiments. Only at the end of the century did the old *pomest'e* cavalry yield entirely to the new cavalry.[29]

The transformation to a completely "modern army" was not finished in the seventeenth century. As noted, the new regiments of foreign formation made only a semistanding, semiregular army. They were not always on call and lacked many of the elements required of a regular army. Furthermore, the attitudes of the rulers about the army were not rigorous or determined enough to effect the required transformation. This was reflected in the two Crimean campaigns of 1687 and 1689, which Russia failed to win because of flawed leadership, rather than because of any inherent defects in the Russian army itself. The campaigns were a product of the "Eternal Peace" treaty signed by Poland and Russia on May 6, 1686, in Moscow. Russia became part of the Holy League (Poland, Austria, and Venice) against the Turks and agreed to harass the Turks by attacking their vassals, the Crimean Tatars. Another purpose of the campaign was to curtail Crimean attacks, which violated the 1681 treaty of Bakhchisarai between Turkey and Russia, on the ever-southward-moving Russian frontier.[30]

The campaigns were commanded by Tsarevna Sofia's lover V. V. Golitsyn (1643–1714), the actual head of government from 1682 to 1689. (He held the post of head of the Foreign Affairs, Ukraine, Smolensk, Foreign Mercenary Officers, and Cavalry Chancelleries, plus a number of titles Sofia awarded him in 1684.) The overall evaluations of Golitsyn in Russian historiography are contradictory, but there is not the slightest doubt that he was nearly totally incompetent as a military commander. Every detachment of the new style regiments of cavalry and infantry was commanded by foreign officers, but Golitsyn was in overall charge and was responsible personally for the debacles.

It is true that the Tatars harassed the Golitsyn armies and that crossing the steppe (especially when the steppe had been burned over and eaten up by locusts) with a massive army of over 110,000 troops (plus personal slaves and uncounted cossacks) and a train of 20,000 carts was difficult.[31] However, these inherent difficulties were compounded manyfold by Golitsyn's bungling and cowardice. While travelling about six miles a day, he reported making "great speed" toward the Crimea.[32] The first campaign turned back at the river Konskie Vody, a tributary of the Dnepr. Thousands died of disease.

After the first debacle General Patrick Gordon made a number of recommendations to avoid a repetition. Golitsyn ignored them.[33] The second campaign got within sight of Perekop, fortress guardian of the Crimea. Then, much to the amazement of the Tatars, the Muscovites (who lacked fodder, water, food, and the means to attack Perekop) turned back to Russia. Naturally the Crimeans harassed the retreating Russians, decimating Golitsyn's forces.[34]

At the conclusion of both campaigns Golitsyn boasted of his feats and told incredible lies. Sofia gave him presents befitting a hero and proclaimed to the world that glorious victories had been achieved. The triumphal processions afterward failed to reveal one captive.[35] Peter hated Golitsyn and exiled him along with his half-sister when he assumed power in 1689—an action itself motivated partly by the failure of the second Crimean campaign.[36]

The two unsuccessful campaigns undermined the authority of those who lamented the repeal of the system of places and hankered after the old ways. The dramatic revelation of the hopeless backwardness of the old ways made the coming Petrine innovations more credible and acceptable.[37] The second campaign showed that the Tatar cavalry could make no headway against properly operating Russian field artillery and revealed that the Tatars alone would be helpless against a well-commanded force of Muscovites.[38]

For the military historian A. G. Elchaninov the Crimean campaigns represented the ultimate degradation of the Russian army, conclusively demonstrated the inadequacy of the forces put together by Tsar Aleksei, and cried out for reforms and for Peter as the reformer.[39] Elchaninov's view seems slightly exaggerated, for the major defect in the campaigns of 1687 and 1689 was in the command, not in the army itself. Almost without question there would have been success had, for example, Gordon's advice been followed.

While perhaps the Crimean campaigns were the ultimate degradation for the Russian army, it was really the Azov campaigns of 1695 and 1696 which showed that reforms should be undertaken, that a semistanding, semiregular army would soon be inadequate.[40] Many things had to be done, and Peter began to do them almost as soon as he returned from his European trip. Three divisions of regular standing army troops were created in 1699 and 1700.[41] In the recruiting system introduced in the years 1699–1705 the rank-and-file soldiers came from the peasantry and townsmen, a few of the officers from the gentry who were the descendants of the middle service class.

The fate of the middle service class is worth a last look. As has been mentioned, it could have been expected that this class would make up the officer corps of the army created by Aleksei. The members did not become officers because of a combination of prejudice on their part against the new system and their own lack of suitability for the posts. In the 1660s Iurii Krizhanich had cried out against turning the entire army over to the command of foreigners, but at the time he was a voice in the wilderness.[42] In 1688 the patriarch bitterly attacked command by foreigners of the Russian army.[43] Toward the end of the seventeenth century, as a result of military defeats, the Russian government lost its enchantment with foreign officers, blamed them for the setbacks, and was willing once again to entrust officer positions to specific Russians of gentry origin, who were trained by foreigners.[44] These Russians, however, were given only the posts and remuneration left over after all the foreigners had been satisfied.[45] In 1696 there were 954 foreign officers and generals in Russian service, of whom 213 were in the cavalry and 723 in the more important infantry.[46]

From 1705 to 1713, roughly, foreign officers were gradually replaced by Russians.[47] Even during the reign of Peter, however, at least one-third of all officers in every regiment had to be foreigners. During the reign of Anna this requirement was abolished.[48]

Even if faster progress had been made in turning the officer corps over to Russians, not all of the numerous gentry could have been officers. Thus under Peter there were representatives of the thirty thousand gentry among the rank-and-file soldiers. In 1699, for example, General A. I. Repnin drafted *deti boiarskie* from the ages of fifteen to thirty, along with the children of cossacks and *strel'tsy* from the Volga region, to serve in the infantry. The gentry probably made up about 25 percent of the total army. Only 1 percent of the armed forces were in a gentry cavalry unit of 1,180 men. Twelve dragoon regiments were formed in the years 1699 to 1701 with 12,234 men.[49] Peter truly put the gentry back in harness.[50]

The major impetus to reform in Peter's reign was his 1700 defeat by Charles XII of Sweden at Narva. This induced Peter to make the artillery into an independent branch of service.[51] The Narva defeat showed that Russia could not keep abreast of its enemies with Aleksei's new formation regiments. It showed that Russia was once again lagging behind the most modern Western European armies and gave urgency to further reforms.[52]

The Petrine reforms would have been even more difficult had the transitional, yet radical, stage of the Western-style regiments not occurred. The Thirteen Years War and subsequent events "without severity gradually reeducated society in military matters and to military necessity."[53] This reeducation was peaceful because the government managed to effect it without alienating either the upper or middle service classes, both essential elements of support for the Romanov dynasty. This support was retained at a very high price—the enserfment of the peasantry—but it did insure the survival of Russia and its Romanov autocracy.

A final point worthy of consideration is that Russia, like other states, was drifting into a period of absolutism in government. Part of the absolutist system was a bureaucratic and military structure which would carry out unquestioningly the orders of the autocrat. The reforms of Ivan IV had set a trend in this direction in motion, but its consummation was not possible while the old army existed. Ivan had abolished all private armies (except the church's), and introduced a standing army corps, but had been unable to go further. The privileged *pomest'e* militia, led by the capricious and insulated upper service class, could not be manipulated at will by the government: when its members voted with their hands at an Assembly of the Land or with their feet on the battlefield, the government was helpless and could not wage war. The *strel'tsy*, linked physically and emotionally with the townspeople and their concerns, also came to have minds of their own and were hardly suitable as a tool of autocratic power.[54] Only by creating a new army dependent on the treasury and under the command of foreigners from outside the traditional social system, could the government hope to obtain a malleable instrument responsive to its will. In this transitional period before Peter, the absolutist state was still in the process of formation, but the middle service class gentry had largely been displaced; the members of that class had no monopoly of the power positions either in the army or in the state administrative apparatus.[55] Therefore the state power—the tsar and his advisers, the bureaucrats and military officers—was able to proceed with a radical reform of the army which at one stroke reduced the power and influence of a potential rival—the gentry—while simultaneously assuring the survival of the gentry's perquisites and the Russian state. Why this was done at the expense of the peasant will be the major topic of chapter 14.

The gunpowder revolution in Muscovy occurred in three stages. The first saw the development and massive introduction of artillery, which in turn caused the rebuilding of nearly all fortifications and an eventual abolition of massed formations. The second stage witnessed the introduction of the handgun and an elite corps of infantry, the *strel'tsy*. This infantry functioned well with the middle service class cavalry, which had been introduced not as the result of any technological change but rather to gain maximum support from the primitive peasant economy. The "mobile fortress" was particularly important for the joint military operations of the musketeers and cavalry forces. The third stage involved the wholesale importation of Western military technology and tactics. Russia lacked urban middle-class specialists who could effect this revolution, and had to rely on foreign mercenaries to accomplish it. Neither the *strel'tsy* nor the middle service class cavalry could adapt to the changed situation in the third period. The state, however, had to meet the new challenges of the gunpowder revolution by innovation or adaptation, or perish. Muscovy proved to be capable of meeting the Western military challenge, even at the cost of the discomfort of the former military elites which were at least partially dispossessed. Each stage of the increasingly expensive gunpowder revolution had to be paid for by the peasantry in labor services, in taxes in cash and in kind, and finally with recruits. Serfdom was also part of the price of the gunpowder revolution.

14.

The Persistence of Serfdom

The preceding chapters have traced the enserfment of the peasantry, the rise of the middle service class, and the impact of the introduction of gunpowder technology in Muscovite Russia. This chapter will summarize these developments and show why the gunpowder revolution did not put an end to serfdom as it did to the middle service class cavalry.

The enserfment developed in three or four stages. During the quarter-century-long civil war in the reign of Vasilii II (1425–62), selected monasteries which had grown into large economic enterprises needing much manpower were granted the right by the state power to curtail the movement of their peasants to the period around St. George's Day (November 26). This was a political concession in a period of labor disruption for services rendered by a particular monastery; or it was done to gain a monastery's support. The civil war began because no principle existed to decide who should be great prince, whether accession was lateral or vertical. In the past the khan had resolved such issues, but this was no longer realistic with the Tatar hegemony in its decline. The contesting sides could only fight it out. In the process Vasilii II's side gave away some peasant freedom to gain support.

For reasons difficult to determine, this curtailment was applied to all peasants by the law code (*Sudebnik*) of 1497. After 1497 most peasants could move at only one time of year, upon payment of a small fee to the landlord. This by no means enserfed the peasants, who seem not to have protested against the minor restriction and who continued to move freely until the 1570s and even into the 1580s. It can hardly be accidental that peasant mobility was not curtailed completely at this time, for there was no organ to enforce such edicts. So long as free land was accessible, curtailing mobility became possible only with the progressive development of the central administration in the sixteenth century. Lacking

235

an effective centralized system of courts and a developed system of record-keeping, the government could hope to curtail peasant mobility only to the time most convenient for all parties concerned—peasant, lord, and tax collector. Nevertheless, the government was becoming accustomed to the idea that it could limit peasant mobility.

At the end of the fifteenth century the middle service class was forming. It was a new military force of cavalrymen equipped with bows and arrows who were given conditional land grants by the government for their support. In order for this group to function, their lands had to be populated with rent-paying peasants. By the middle of the sixteenth century the middle service class had become the major military force of the Muscovite state. This resulted in a general elevation of the status of the middle service class, whose members came to adopt the values of the magnates along with some of their prerogatives.

In the second half of the reign of Ivan IV (1533–84) a number of disasters befell Muscovy. The major ones were Ivan's Livonian War (1558–83) and his Oprichnina (1565–72). The result was great hardship for the peasants, who deserted certain key areas, particularly the lands assigned to the members of the middle service class. This in turn proved to be a disaster for the middle service class, which could not serve unless the peasant labor force was stabilized. Members of the middle service class had just begun to acquire control over and a personal interest in their service landholdings. The average member of the middle service class had only a half dozen peasant households for his support, and any loss of these dues-payers was a serious financial blow. Had the serviceman not been given a vested interest in six specific peasant households and had some other way been discovered to finance the army, such as on a cash basis, as had been recommended by Ivan Peresvetov, the reaction to the labor shortage on *pomest'e* lands might have been different, or even might not have occurred.

The government, accustomed to regulating peasant mobility, did the only thing it could: it forbade peasants to move at all. This was a "temporary" measure initiated in 1581 in some areas. These "forbidden years," as they were called, spread throughout the 1580s. In 1592 (or 1593) Boris Godunov, who was seeking support in his bid for the throne, promulgated a decree forbidding all peasants to move until further notice. The country's economy was still in a state of disorder, and doubtlessly the middle service class wanted all movement from their lands curtailed, so Boris obliged. As a result, the cavalrymen became even less interested in rendering military service and more concerned with their economies.

Not all groups wanted mobility curtailed, for peasants had a tendency to move to the large estates belonging to the great boyars and the monasteries. Boris also needed their support in his drive for the throne, so he agreed (also in 1592) to place a five-year time limit on the recovery of peasants who moved in violation of the interdiction. This meant that a fugitive peasant who could escape detection by his rightful lord for five years (not too difficult in Russia) became a free man.

The traumatic Time of Troubles had little influence on the enserfment. Most of the draconian measures of Shuiskii had only a short-range impact on the peasantry. While many individuals and institutions were hard hit by the dislocations of the Troubles, two of the wealthy monasteries which had been in the center of the holocaust seem to have been the ones which brought up the peasant question after 1613. The Troitse Sergiev was granted an extraordinary nine-year time limit to recover fugitives. This was the same institution which within the next decades was to benefit significantly from a short time limit to sue for the return of runaways. Had the superiors of the monastery possessed any memory or foresight, they would have realized that the long-term peasant flow was in their direction, that they would soon recover their laborers, and that the extraordinary privilege they were requesting could only work to their ultimate disadvantage. However, a long time-horizon was not common among Muscovites.

The Smolensk War (1632–34), with its concomitant high taxes, caused turmoil in the peasant community, and the agriculturalists began to move in violation of the Forbidden Years. Also important was the fortuitous capture of Azov, the revival of Tatar attacks on the Ukraine, and the rebuilding of the system of fortified lines.[1] The high taxes at the center, combined with the possibility of lower rents and even complete freedom on the frontier, stimulated southward migration. In fortifying the frontier, the government was contributing to a situation leading to the binding of the population to the poor podzolic soils of the center and thus delaying the development of the better chernozem lands further south.[2] Having secured the southern frontier lands, the government found itself unable to let them be populated as rapidly as it would have desired. This deprived the army of manpower to garrison the frontier and the treasury of the additional revenue which taxes on the better farm land would have produced.

The middle service class asked several times in the dozen-year period after the Smolensk War for the time limit on the recovery of fugitive peasants to be repealed. The magnates running the government refused, for in the chronically labor-short economy they valued the movement of peasants to their own estates. No crisis intervened to force them to act contrary to their personal inclinations.

In this period two developments occurred which further undermined the peasants' position and elevated that of the middle service class. For one thing, the peasant's civil status was being degraded so that he began to resemble a slave in the eyes of the law. The importance of the existence of slavery as a model for developing serfdom should be stressed. The legal abasement of the peasantry, originating in the sixteenth century, was particularly noticeable in the 1620s, and continued at a slower pace thereafter. It created a distinction between the peasant and the rank-and-file cavalryman which had been lacking before, and serfdom became an automatic status-elevator in the Russian social edifice. It was also at this time that a purge was begun of some of the grandsons of peasants, slaves, and cossacks who had joined the middle service class in the sixteenth century.

In the same era the gunpowder revolution finally overtook Muscovy almost completely. By this time the Tatars had ceased to be the major threat to the Muscovite state. The result was that, in warfare for the control of huge fortresses, the middle service class cavalryman with his bow and arrow was technologically obsolete in the face of infantry outfitted with firearms. In the Smolensk War the Russian government introduced a new, Western-style army equipped with hand firearms, but disbanded the army after the war. This meant that the middle service class in the relatively peaceful years of the 1630s and 1640s was still the major military force at the disposal of the Muscovite government.

These two developments must have made a dramatic impression on the middle service class. There is an obvious risk in making cross-cultural assumptions, but the following analysis provides a good explanation of some of the phenomena observed in this period.[3] The cavalrymen were conscious of their technological obsolescence and frightened by the gunpowder revolution. On the basis of their social utility alone they would have little right to social prestige. They were also aware of their rising, protected status in society and of the ever-increasing gap between them and the peasantry. Their rise in social position was slow and probably largely accidental while the middle service class was useful; the rise was faster and deliberate when obsolescence began to set in. Beginning in the reign of Boris, the servicemen took advantage of the tsar's weak position to get the government to restrict access to their increasingly privileged position. They also had the government expel individuals of recent lowly origin from their ranks. Multiplying rapidly in peacetime and thus becoming less scarce themselves, they were a group with no technical skill or genuine specialization to support claims to exclusiveness, so they built on their historically legitimate base to achieve privilege. In the dawning era of massive infantry armies using gunpowder technology, the trained peasant or slave infantryman armed with a flintlock handgun under the command of a foreign officer had more intrinsic worth and genuine skill than the archer on horseback from the supposedly elite military caste. This caste had to rule out competition artificially, by having the government codify the caste's privileged position in the law. Only when pressed would the *pomeshchik* join the new army, and then, aping the haughty Poles, only as a cavalryman, in spite of the fact that the day of the cavalry was waning.

For his psychological security the serviceman needed to have the peasant beneath him and, if possible, under his control. When peasants fled, the serviceman lost not only financial support, but also the presence of degraded people under his authority who reminded him daily that he was superior. The loss of prestige must have been particularly poignant when the peasant fled south and joined the frontier forces on the Belgorod *cherta,* which was contributing to the obsolescence of the old cavalry against the Tatars.[4] A closed society, then, was of crucial importance if the middle service class was to preserve its prestige, its limited authority and power, and its perquisites, particularly its claim to the bulk of the peasant labor force.

This also helps to explain the resort to *mestnichestvo* in the 1640s, which previously had been a privilege of the elite, and the frantic petition campaign to make sure the peasantry remained abased. As a gulf began to develop between the peasantry and the middle service class, the latter's views on the lower classes became increasingly more like those of the magnates. In turn, as will be shown below, the peasantry failed to distinguish between the ruling magnates, who set the tone and policies of Russia, and the petty gentry, who had a few serfs each. Having been created by the government, the middle service class grew to proportions certainly never initially envisaged and in time acquired perquisites and an accompanying cast of mind which initially had been the property solely of the magnates of the upper upper-service class. This development was certainly one of the reasons for the continuation of serfdom in the second half of the seventeenth century.

In 1648 civil disorders broke out in Moscow and a dozen other towns. By this time the middle service class was very conscious of its military obsolescence, particularly as Morozov had begun to modernize the army again—which helped stimulate the discontent which caused the uprising. This class knew that it had no technical competence which would either justify its privileges or distinguish it from the mass of the peasantry.

Nevertheless the obsolete cavalrymen placed a high value on their authority over the peasants (from whom they were legally and socially becoming ever more separate) and desired to preserve their status in society and their continued dominance over the recently degraded peasantry. In 1648 the frantic middle service class again demanded the repeal of the time limit, a move which would consolidate the class's privileges and elevated social status and, its members hoped, alleviate its economic plight. The reluctant government, fearing the disorders and hoping to purchase the support of the middle service class in the time of crisis, granted the request in the law code (*Ulozhenie*) of 1649. Heretofore the repeal of the right to move on St. George's Day had been assumed to be temporary. Without explicitly saying so, the *Ulozhenie* in fact made it permanent. As a result, the peasants, unable to move legally and forever subject to return if they moved illegally, were enserfed.

The government was able to create by legislative initiative a rigidly stratified society because of the hypertrophy of the state power in Russia.[5] It was not mainly a fear of a possible peasant uprising which had inhibited the government from consummating the enserfment earlier, but rather the fact that the magnates were looking out for their own best interests, which experience had led them to believe lay in a mobile peasantry.

During the Thirteen Years War (1654–67) with Poland and Sweden the obsolete middle service class military organization was phased out and then abolished in favor of the new Western-style army.[6] As far as I can determine, the members of the middle service class, in large numbers, ceased to serve in the army and took on no new functions in the course of the rest of the seventeenth century. The middle service class was becoming a privileged gentry. The peasants remained enserfed and continued to support a military class which had lost its central position in Muscovy. After 1662 the mutuality of obligations which had featured the peasant-middle service class relationship broke down: the peasants ceased to have rights, and their lords had significantly reduced obligations. Serfdom was seemingly an anachronism.[7] The institution had been created as a political concession to favor selected monasteries and to help support the *pomest'e* cavalry, but in the 1660s the monasteries were prospering and the *pomeshchiki* ceased to make up the backbone of the army.

While the peasants were being enserfed, the rest of society was becoming rigidly stratified as well. Clearly, the conversion of the townsmen into a closed caste followed in the wake of the enserfment. Prior to the Time of Troubles there had been little concern with the status of the townsmen, although there had been some legislation in the 1590s.[8]

The cataclysm had a drastic impact on the towns. Many were destroyed, most were severely depopulated. Servicemen and church institutions with tax privileges had moved in and taken over many towns by 1613. The condition of the towns continued to deteriorate into the 1620s.[9]

The government relied extensively on the towns for revenue to pay for the increasingly expensive military forces required by advancing technology. This was true after 1613, in spite of the destruction of much of urban life during the Smuta. The government tried to collect the taxes on the basis of the old records. The townsmen could not pay, and after 1613 demanded the return to the tax rolls of all who had fled.[10] The government did not object, and methods developed for dealing with fugitive peasants were applied to absent urban taxpayers. By the 1620s the time limit for forcing return to the town tax rolls was ten years.[11] At this time the limit for recovering peasants was five years, which throws additional light on the attitude toward the peasant question of the magnates running the government. Few townsmen were going to work for the magnates (although some townsmen would, the so-called *zakladchiki,* a form of urban slave), so they let the time limit on recovering fugitive urban dwellers run far ahead of that for runaway peasants. Later, in the 1630s, the gap became even more dramatic: townsmen could be recovered for up to twenty-five years, a statute of limitations never attained by the middle service class in the quest for its peasants.[12] In 1642 the time limit for recovering those who had fled from Pskov was abolished completely.[13] The principle was overturned in the *Ulozhenie.* Townsmen were not to be returned to their old places of residence, but were bound where they were at the moment.[14] The government was indifferent to where townspeople lived because they could be taxed anywhere. The same principle, incidentally, applied to the peasantry: it is time to discard the notion that seignorial peasants were enserfed to aid the fisc.[15] By 1649 the townsmen also achieved a near monopoly on urban activities, largely trade and manufacturing, and on the ownership of town property.[16] Thus, at their own request, they became a closed caste.

B. I. Morozov made these concessions to the townsmen because he wanted their support in the summer and autumn of 1648. He could yield to most of the townsmen's requests because they cost his faction practically nothing. The only exception was Patriarch Iosif, who had 710 houses in seven Moscow "settlements" and was upset by the confiscation of church property in and around the towns. Morozov and the rest of his supporters had very little of this type of tax-exempt property.[17] They were also relatively unaffected by the forcing of the tax-exempt *zakladchiki* on to the tax rolls,[18] and by the granting of monopolies on trade and industry to the townsmen. The magnates were hardly concerned by the migration of townsmen because the latter rarely moved from the towns to the estates of the "strong people."

The tide in the direction of a rigidly stratified society was strong. Caught up were nearly all segments of society—the service classes, the townsmen, the peasantry. The *Ulozhenie* of 1649 codified and made more strict the previous governmental pronouncements of social structure. Contemporaries were aware of what had occurred, as revealed in a petition of 1657. The writers noted that there were four basic, rigidly distinct groups in society: the clergy, servicemen, merchants, and the peasants. Each had its assigned place, functions, and duties in the social organism.[19] Nevertheless, the peasant question was the central issue, and the closing off of other social groups followed and was determined by the fate of the mass of the agriculturalists. Throughout the Muscovite period the fate of the peasantry was the crucial variable, chiefly, of course, because the peasants formed the vast majority of the population.

Had the government not completed the enserfment, the rest of society certainly would have gradually become less compartmentalized as well. It is difficult to conceive of rigidly stratified castes of townsmen or service groups continuing to exist very long in the presence of a relatively free peasantry in Russian conditions. While this is only a conjecture which cannot be supported by any facts, a comparison of the subsequent histories of the peasantry and other social groups would tend to support this proposition. The peasantry remained enserfed until the second half of the nineteenth century, but other categories of the rigidly stratified population loosened up much more rapidly after 1649.[20]

Decreasing compartmentalization, however, was not to be Russia's fate. Morozov was unable to move ahead faster with his military reforms to abolish the old army, and it may well be that his reforming zeal should be added to his cupidity as cause of his violent overthrow as head of government. Serfdom became a solidly entrenched institution. A decade after the *Ulozhenie* the middle service class, essential no longer, was eclipsed; within five years more it no longer existed as a military force. Even the landholding servicemen began to rely more on cash payments from the government for their subsistence and military needs, and less on their service lands.[21] The service land system, which the peasants had been enserfed to support, was in the process of being converted into the heritable property of its owners and proved no more capable of supporting them than had the *pomest'e* prior to 1649. In many ways the enserfment turned out not to be the panacea the middle service class thought it would be.[22]

The general course of Russian military development lay in the direction of an army paid for entirely by the state treasury. Logically this would have meant a radical cancellation of the service land system and the conversion of all dues into state taxes to be paid by the government to the servicemen. Such a step had been advocated by Ermolai Erazm in the middle of the sixteenth century. Had his advice been followed, the Russian peasant conceivably might have escaped enserfment. Increased taxes for support of the army played a role in the enserfment, but only secondarily; the turmoil ensuing from peasant flight to escape onerous levies played havoc with the middle service class's ability to support itself, with the consequences which have been shown. The government, however, was nearly always able to levy taxes, regardless of where the populace lived—even in Kievan times. Moreover, had the real inequality of demands on the peasantry associated with the *pomest'e* system not existed, the agriculturalists would have moved much less in their search for temporary relief from the oppressive exactions. (Relatively few peasants, as we have seen, fled abroad or into the Tatar steppe out of reach of the tax collectors. Besides, the government could do little more to prevent such movement by a serf than by a free peasant.)

Muscovy had an opportunity to turn away from the *pomest'e* method of financing the army during the Thirteen Years War. Peasants on conquered territory were ordered to pay their traditional dues in cash and kind to the Russian government for distribution to the troops.[23] The plan failed, however, because it ran head-long into customary beliefs about the political role of land-ownership in occupied territory as well as the fact that one of the goals of warfare in the Muscovite period was the seizure of populated land to support the middle service class cavalry. Beginning at least as early as the annexation of Novgorod at the end of the fifteenth century, Moscow had developed the practice of ensuring an area's loyalty and rewarding its own troops by deporting the indigenous landowners and replacing them with Muscovite servicemen. The same procedure was repeated after the annexation of Pskov, Kazan', and Baltic lands. Therefore it is not at all surprising that during the Thirteen Years War Moscow soon parcelled out conquered territories to its own servitors and to indigenous servicemen who were willing to pledge allegiance to the tsar.[24] This may have been strategically and politically wise, but Russia lost an opportunity to enter a wedge into the *pomest'e* system.

Not all Russians were oblivious of the contradictions inherent in the privileged position of the gentry after the Thirteen Years War. In the 1680s and 1690s Charles XI of Sweden confiscated many estates for the crown (his "reduction"). V. V. Golitsyn, who ran the Russian government from 1682 to 1689 for Tsarevna Sofia, learned of Charles's acts of 1680, 1682, and 1683, and contemplated emulating the northern monarch. He drafted a proposal for the creation of a regular army containing both the gentry and other categories of servicemen. All would receive only cash pay from a peasant head-tax. The gentry were to lose both their land and serfs. Whether a realization of Golitsyn's project would have signified the end of serfdom is debatable, but it certainly would have reduced drastically the number of peasants subject to seignorial control and increased proportionately those who were taxpaying black peasants. The project was not realized because Golitsyn was soon deposed by Peter and those representing traditional Muscovy.[25]

The middle service class itself was treated by the government in a more high-handed manner in the second half of the seventeenth century, in sharp contrast to 1648.[26] Petitions for relief were sometimes rejected out of hand.[27] The members of the middle service class were ordered around after 1648 in a fashion hardly conceivable earlier. The gentry's weak condition, embodied in its minimal social utility, did not allow it to protest such treatment or the consolidation of power by the magnates, for the latter always could simply threaten to free the serfs and thereby divest the *dvoriane* and *deti boiarskie* of their economic support and social status. This weak condition was the consequence of the government's creation of the new army, which prepared the way for the eventual triumph of the Moscow magnates over the rest of society.[28]

Another sign of the decline of the middle service class can be seen in the disappearance of the Assembly of the Land after the commencement of the Thirteen Years War. The Zemskii Sobor after 1613 had developed into one of the forums where the middle service class could express its interests with the assurance that the government would be listening. After the 1648 experience, when the government was forced to make numerous concessions to the elected delegates to the Zemskii Sobor, the power elite, one can be quite sure, desired to get rid of the consultative institution. During the Thirteen Years War this became possible. The central government's information-gathering system was perfected to the point that it did not have to summon representatives from the provinces to learn the condition of the country. This ability stemmed from the development of the *voevoda* provincial administration at the expense of the decaying *guba* system. The fiscal system was organized so that the autocracy was sure it could raise no more revenue by consulting the townsmen and leading merchants of the realm. Also, the government did not have to consult with the foreign mercenary officers or with the troops of the new formation regiments about whether they wanted to fight, as had become customary with the middle service class.

Therefore, after 1653, the state power never again convoked the Assembly of the Land, and Russia lost its chance to have an extended parliamentary experience.[29]

The Assembly of the Land was not the only thing that seemed vital in 1648 but was soon fated to disappear. Along with that institution went many of the concessions which had been granted under duress during the crisis.[30] Probably only their promoters took many of the new laws seriously, and even at the time of their promulgation the government probably had no intention of enforcing many of them. A few examples will suffice. In 1648 all peasant lands in the western Pomor'e region which had been sold were ordered confiscated from the buyers and returned to their former owners. In September of 1649 the government cancelled the provisions for retroactive confiscations.[31] The *Ulozhenie* prescribed that all towns be granted a certain area around them for garden plots and pasture. The lands were to be confiscated for the town or exchanged for court lands elsewhere. After being enforced rigorously for a short while, these provisions were soon emasculated, then ignored.[32] Another major concession to the townsmen was a decree that no tax-exempt party would be allowed to keep properties in town. Endless litigation vitiated much of the effectiveness of this measure. A decree of 1681 reversed this law and allowed tax-exempt parties to keep taxable properties in towns.[33] The monopoly of the townsmen on trade proved to be ephemeral.[34] The futility of the stricture against additional land acquisition by the church has been discussed in chapter 3.[35] The Monastery Chancellery, created under pressure from the delegates to the Assembly of the Land to bring most of the church and its secular subjects under lay control, was abolished at the request of the patriarch and clergy in 1677.[36] The fate of the provisions on serfs who simply fled from their lords will be discussed below. Those who fled and enlisted in the lower service class were supposed to be returned to serf status, according to the *Ulozhenie*. In 1650 and 1651 and later, the government falsely said that, according to the *Ulozhenie*, all such cases had to be tried in Moscow and could not be tried locally by the governor or commander (*voevoda*). Governors were fined significant sums for violating this nonexistent decree.[37] The import of such capricious action is hard to understand with certainty, but the intent probably was to take the decision out of local control, where the local serf-holders had significant influence even with the officials of the central power. Centralizing the judicial process in the Military Chancellery (*Razriad*) in Moscow, the government could decide the suits in light of the military needs of the country. By inventing the decree, the government circumvented the triumph of the middle service class very soon after the event.[38]

It is apparent that many of the concessions granted under duress in 1648 were soon annulled, but serfdom was not. I am sure that the government, had the resolve been present, could have abolished serfdom after 1649, but it did not. Why?

The seignorial peasantry remained enserfed until 1861 (or even to the beginning of the twentieth century) for several reasons. Inertia was only a minor factor, as revealed by the fact that the government deliberately undid many of the other 1648 concessions. The causes for the continuance of serfdom in the reign of Aleksei and later must be sought elsewhere.

Initially the new Miloslavskii government had to get used to ruling, and any abrupt change on the peasant question would have aroused the instant ire of the middle service class. Then the Thirteen Years War preoccupied the government until the Truce of Andrusovo in 1667. As usual, the combatants exhausted each other, and Russia was forced to sue for a peace significantly less favorable than might have been anticipated after the war had been under way only a few years. This peripeteia, along with the plague of the 1650s and the developing church schism and its repression, consumed most of the energy of the ruling elite.[39]

The truce itself was forced at least partly by peasant disorders, which led to the great Stenka Razin uprising. After 1649 serfdom had become increasingly more degrading and severe.[40] While the *pomest'e* was not to be merged completely with the *votchina* until 1714, the service landholders took increasing liberties with the persons of their serfs, even occasionally moving them illegally from the former kind of holding to the latter.[41] In 1658 peasant flight had been made a criminal offense and the apprehended runaway was supposed to be beaten with the knout.[24] In the years 1658–63, a period which saw the phasing out of the middle service class, the government ceaselessly had conducted investigations throughout the territory of Muscovy to discover and return the tens of thousands of serfs who had fled south and east from their lords after the *Ulozhenie* to escape the plague and crop failures, recruiting, mounting taxes, and general oppression. Unprecedented numbers had fled after the outbreak of the Thirteen Years War. Peasants had been returned who had moved as much as fifty years prior to their discovery.[43]

The Razin rebellion, unlike the Time of Troubles with its slave and peasant uprisings at the beginning of the century, was definitely a class war, with the peasants on one side against—indiscriminately—the lords on the other.[44] The peasants were not revolting against the entire system, but against some of its manifestations. They did not possess sufficient political insight to understand what caused their discontent, which in

246

fact was largely the product of the enserfment. Many of the rebels were runaways from the center, further agitated because their rapid accumulation had caused a famine in the Don region.[45] The spark which lit the Razin uprising was a refusal by the bankrupt government to pay the cossacks what they considered their due. As a result, much of the uprising had economic manifestations—the starving rebels tried to make ends meet. Although the rebels' primary purpose was not to overthrow the system, contemporaries in the upper and middle service classes, frightened by the rebels' rhetoric, cannot be blamed for not having appreciated this fact.[46]

In the Time of Troubles, when the prohibition of peasant movement was considered by all to be "temporary," members of both the upper and middle service classes had at one time or another been on the side of the revolting peasants and slaves under Bolotnikov.[47] During the Smolensk War a few members of the middle service class joined the Balash rebellion. In 1648 *deti boiarskie* were to be found among the rebels against the government in Moscow.[48] However, the *Ulozhenie* served as a watershed, with the result that in 1650 and 1662 members of the middle service class participated in those uprisings only on the government side—that is, by repressing them.[49] The new law code created a closer identity of interest between the magnates running the government and the middle service class; both were privileged groups performing less and less necessary state service while simultaneously exploiting the increasingly abased, oppressed, and angry masses. The code also contributed to the opening of the ultimately notorious chasm between the upper and lower classes in Russia.[50]

By the time of the Razin uprising, the peasants had a generalized feeling that serfdom was definitely their lot and the cause of many of their woes. While they did not fully understand the institution and its complexities, the rebels' proclaimed goals were to attain freedom and to kill first the boyars and then all the lords plus all the military officers.[51] This type of talk, plus the rebels' actions, hardened the elite against all the peasants and forged an alliance between the members of the upper and middle service classes (the magnates and gentry) for the common purpose of survival in a new hostile environment.[52] The rebels also brought the wrath of the church on themselves (the Patriarch's anathema, church funds to pay loyal troops who suppressed the rebellion) by mutilating and drowning priests whenever they were encountered.[53]

After the rebellion, in which the political fabric of Muscovy seemed to have been challenged by the peasantry, any actions which might have amounted to concessions to the serfs were out of the question. The *Razinshchina* upset the peasantry wherever it occurred, causing the massive peasant flights which typically accompanied any form of rural chaos in Russia.[54] Certainly most landowners in such a situation would not have tolerated any legal measures which might have caused more unrest in the serf community, as would have happened had the peasants been given the right to move. As in 1607, when the Shuiskii government crushed the Bolotnikov uprising, in the late 1660s and 1670s the government was in a mood only for repression. Like so many others, this rebellion for freedom backfired.[55]

The Razin revolt set off a chain of uprisings leading to the 1682 disturbances in Moscow and other towns.[56] This in turn stimulated serf uprisings in the countryside.[57] The result was that the government saw only uprisings and thought only of repression for much of the time after the introduction of the new army, when logic alone would have dictated rolling back the enserfment. The ruling elite devoted its attention to suppressing the unrest rather than to solving its causes. The rank-and-file gentry had to stomach their superiors' venality while cooperating in "maintaining order" in the provinces and even in Moscow itself.[58] In this light I would speculate that the government's seeming inability to make the members of the gentry serve in the army or to make the *pomest'e* system continue to function as the major financial prop of the military establishment were both reflections of a developing symbiosis between the ruling elite and the gentry. At first glance one might think that the decay of the old service system was a sign that the Muscovite autocracy was inefficient and weak. Yet the facts that foreigners marvelled at the government's ability to keep track of everyone and that it was capable of returning thousands of fugitive serfs alone would tend to belie such a conclusion. The reason for these apparent contradictions must be sought elsewhere. For one, the government may have felt that forcing the *pomest'e* system to continue to function effectively was not worth the effort because the new system was better on all counts. It was easier to construct a new institution than to rejuvenate the old, obsolescent one which had degenerated beyond salvation. More important, I suspect, must have been the consideration that compelling the reluctant gentry to serve would antagonize its members and might drive them to combine with other forces against the regime. While a certain amount of official violence effectively served to intimidate individuals with no fixed notion of their human or functional worth, experience taught the rulers that a massive use of force might lead to an uprising. In this calculation the magnates were correct, for the gentry let them rule and did not rebel or challenge their prerogatives.

In time the mutual interest of the magnates and the gentry in the maintenance of serfdom developed to such an extent that the autocracy felt serfdom to be its "twin pillar" upon which the whole political and social structure was based. The roots of these late eighteenth and early nineteenth century sentiments can be traced back to the Razin uprising. By the end of the seventeenth century the common interest of the upper and middle service classes in the peasant question was embodied in the fact that only they (plus church bodies) could own serfs. With this went a near monopoly on the right to own land, a true tenure, which kept the urban castes out of the countryside.[59]

The personalities of the leaders of Muscovy help explain why serfdom flourished after 1649. Most of them were weak, venal individuals incapable of understanding what would really be in Russia's best interest; or else they were strong-minded men concerned with issues other than serfdom. A representative of the first type was Tsar Aleksei's debauched father-in-law, Boiarin I. D. Miloslavskii, head of government and general-issimo of the army after 1649. He gained his position as a result of the disorders of 1648, and was hardly one to stir up deliberately discontent which would result in another overthrow of the government in an environment of constant fear of another uprising. Like other heads of administration in the seventeenth century, he was concerned largely with enriching himself. Rather than plunder land or labor, he discovered counterfeiting. He minted 120,000 rubles of bogus coin for himself after 1654—leading to the "copper riots" of 1662.[60] Another debauchee was B. M. Khitrovo, whose major interest was his concubines. His rise began in the 1650s under Miloslavskii; before the latter's death in 1668 he assumed a powerful government position which he held, as a favorite of Tsar Aleksei, until the end of the 1670s.[61] The second type can be seen in Nikon, an egomaniac interested in enhancing his own position and that of his office, or in A. L. Ordin-Nashchokin, whose major interest lay in obtaining an outlet to the Baltic during the 1660s. None of these influential men was the type who could or would give much thought to the importance of the enserfment of the peasantry.[62]

There was a link between these types, for they all shared the attitude of the ruling elite that the state power existed in large part to satisfy their own interests. Miloslavskii, Khitrovo, and Nikon used their offices more to satisfy their personal cravings, while Ordin-Nashchokin was more statesmanlike in his attempts to aid the wealthy merchants. V. V. Golitsyn can be included with this group. To enhance his independence from the traditional powers of Muscovy, he gave thought to the problem of the army and serfdom, but he had no opportunity to effect his reforms because he was purged as a result of his fatuous claims of victory in the Crimean campaigns, his vainglory and corruption. Understanding of the Muscovite period is impossible until one comprehends that most policies, particularly internal ones, but also external ones, were conceived and executed almost exclusively in the interests of the magnates.[63] The rare exceptions had to be coerced from the government by the interested parties.

If we read the words of another important personality, Tsar Aleksei Mikhailovich, the persistence of serfdom seems to become immediately intelligible. A statement of the 1660s would indicate that he felt the service state was still functioning. When a group of peasants complained about their obligations, the tsar discussed the obligations of the various estates of Russia "natural to them." As the gentry served annually, so should the peasantry. However, Aleksei's actions indicate that this statement was demagoguery. Reports of gentry military absenteeism poured into his Secret Chancellery (*Tainyi Prikaz*). He himself pressed the creation of the new army to replace the obsolete old one. He even revitalized the Moscow musketeers into an elite, privileged palace guard because he had little faith in the political reliability of the gentry. The gentry and the *strel'tsy* hated each other, and the sovereign openly favored the latter.[64] Thus while considerable numbers of the gentry were still registered in the army (see appendix), Tsar Aleksei knew full well that, while the peasants had been enserfed for the benefit of the middle service class, the latter were no longer the backbone of the state organism.

Finally, the elite running the government learned to live with and even profit from the new restrictions. If need be, the law could be ignored by lords harboring fugitives or remain unenforced by government officials. The servicemen were very conscious of these evasions and entered actively into the issue of who should carry out the investigations for the runaways. Years of experience had taught them that, left to their own devices, the magnates would simply appoint their friends, who would not bother to enforce the law or would do so only selectively.[65]

After 1649, measures were frequently enacted which vitiated the effectiveness of the *Ulozhenie's* provisions on the return of runaways. Nearly any serf had a chance of escaping his lord if he could reach the frontier. In 1653 the government decreed that those who had fled to the Ukraine prior to the *Ulozhenie* were not to be returned. Lords of those peasants who had fled in the four subsequent years were to be paid cash for their lost laborers. This proclamation was confirmed in 1656 with the notice that no peasant who had been in the Ukraine in 1653 or earlier was to be returned to his former lord. In 1675 no former peasant or slave was to be returned who had enlisted in the new formation regiments.[66] As noted earlier, throughout the seventeenth century defense of the southern frontier usually had priority over the desires of the middle service class.[67] A law of 1684, culminating prior "temporary" developments, permitted all peasants who had fled to Moscow to remain there. Subsequently this measure was extended to other central Muscovite towns.[68] As for court and black-land fugitive peasants, after the *Ulozhenie* they were recovered only for a period up to ten years after departure, in spite of the law.[69]

In some cases where the government decided it would return fugitives, the fines for harboring them prescribed in the *Ulozhenie* were cancelled. In such a case in 1652, the government agent responsible for finding and returning runaway serfs wanted to impose financial sanctions on violators. However, Moscow told him to be satisfied with returning peasants who had found refuge on properties of the Novgorod metropolitan and local monasteries.[70]

These measures did not help the mass of the peasants nor did they retard the development of serfdom. Chapter 11 of the *Ulozhenie* remained the fundamental law on the peasantry which, when enforced, served to enserf them. The lapses in enforcement demonstrate that the government was capable of being flexible about enforcing its own laws. At times fugitives were returned by the thousands, even the tens of thousands, but exceptions were made when the government desired to do so.

It took regular reminders in the form of collective petitions from the gentry, reminiscent of those preceding the *Ulozhenie,* to get the reluctant government to enforce the law. The petitions, which used the provisions of the 1649 law code as their point of reference, do not resemble those of the first half of the century in one respect: they are polite, not demanding and threatening as the earlier ones had been.[71] The members of the middle service class had never questioned the right of the magnates to rule, but in the first half of the century they demanded that they be just. After the enserfment, justice and enforcement of the law yielded to the maintenance of order in the face of increasing peasant discontent. In 1677 *dvoriane* and *deti boiarskie* submitted a petition noting earlier measures to enforce the provisions of the *Ulozhenie* and lamenting their absence during Fedor Alekseevich's reign. At this time there was no crisis, so the government took no steps to meet the demands of the obsolete middle service class.[72]

Justice became less of an issue as the government resorted to violence to crush all dissent. The savage vengeance meted out to peasant participants in the Bolotnikov and Razin uprisings is well known. Similar terror on a lesser scale was used at other times to ensure preservation of a climate pleasing to the magnates. The treatment of the complainants against N. I. Romanov in the 1620s was discussed in chapter 6. The system remained equally unjust half a century later. For example, an

Armenian in Russian service, Stolnik V. A. Daudov, was accused of collecting excessive taxes, taking bribes, engaging in sundry cruelties, illegally brewing alcoholic beverages for himself, and in general ruining the population under his jurisdiction. The government decided to investigate, and 1,105 people were interrogated. After intimidation, the accusers broke down and recanted their accusations. Then they were charged with lodging false accusations and publicly beaten with the knout. They were also denied the right to go to Moscow in the future to complain about anything, could not hold any elected public offices, and were forced to pay Daudov 153½ rubles for insulting him.[73] Such a well-developed system of terror intimidated all but the most hardy, with the result that the magnates were usually able to ride roughshod over all other segments of the population. Even the gentry dared to submit complaints only in times of crisis, when they calculated that the government would be receptive to their request. The government's willingness to crush all dissent helps us to understand the otherwise unexplainable passivity of the gentry after the Assembly of the Land of 1653. The resistance of the dispossessed middle service class and even the lower upper-service class to the new army could find no moderate outlet and had to be internally suppressed. The hostility of these classes to the new regime was hardly expressed, except in a refusal to serve and in occasional petitions, and evoked an overcompensation in the form of submissiveness to the autocracy noted by all foreign observers.[74]

Some lords, after 1649, continued to receive, recruit, and even kidnap others' serfs in spite of the law. Church institutions were noted by petitioners as being guilty of such crimes.[75] Nikon purportedly more than doubled the number of serfs living on patriarchal property during his tenure in office.[76] In one instance from 1658, roughly 60 percent of about 150 returned fugitives were recovered from the estates of various magnates after suits had been filed by lesser lords. B. I. Morozov was the leading offender![77] Other lords also violated the law, but the government curtailed such violations by occasional strict enforcement and by raising the penalties for violations. At times when official massive searches for runaways were conducted, lords, frightened by possible penalties, brought all of their peasants in for review.[78] The most successful maneuver was to confiscate additional serfs from lords who harbored runaways. The struggle for labor was so intense, however, that taking away first one, then two, peasants for every fugitive did not curb the practice. When the government raised the penalty to four for every harbored fugitive, lords drove out the runaways they were keeping.[79] This penalty was repealed in 1681; after the Moscow uprising of 1682, when the government wanted to solidify its support among the gentry, the penalty was reenacted and codified in a general law of 1683 on the recovery of fugitives. Stiffer fines were instituted, and ultimately repealed. Another preventive measure called for the knouting of the stewards managing the large estates who took in fugitives.[80] The mass of serf-owners gained concessions on these points from the government, as usual, in times of stress—and then the magnates repealed the concessions as soon as the pressure was off. Nevertheless, serfdom remained, and in the general manhunt of 1692–93 second- and third-generation fugitives were returned to their fathers' and grandfathers' places of residence.[81]

The magnates soon discovered, as they had during the minority of Ivan IV, that, if they could not steal labor to work their own lands, they could steal others' land with the labor on it. In the reign of Fedor Alekseevich, this tactic led to a mass of boundary disputes and demands by the gentry for a surveying of the country. This movement was aborted by resistance of the magnates and Golitsyn's Crimean campaign.[82] Thus while the Razin uprising hardened the upper classes against the peasantry, the former were not frightened enough to give up trying to enrich themselves at the expense of each other.[83]

Other possibilities for the enrichment of the magnates close to the throne were open besides the rather crude expropriation of the lands of lesser lords. One of the most attractive was to raid the fund of court and black lands, whose inhabitants then joined the ranks of the more abased seignorial serfs. Tsar Fedor Alekseevich gave away 2,796 peasant households in this way. Expropriating of peasant and court lands as a favor to individuals was done on a massive scale between 1681 and 1711, when 273 peasant communes (*volosti*) were given to 213 men. The communes contained 43,665 peasant households on 338,960 *chetverti* of arable land.[84] In the period from 1682 to 1700, 26,647 households were given to magnates with court connections, only 388 to lesser servicemen, and 327 to foreigners in the iron business.[85] This development clearly reveals a shift in tactics by magnates on the labor question: having the government assign them (or assigning to themselves—the favored magnates made the policy) nonseignorial peasants was simpler and more profitable than recruiting other lords' peasants one by one. It was also legal. In all likelihood the recipients of these grants did not object to the fact that the peasants were bound by law to their new lands. The government was able to respond favorably to the ruling magnates' greed for labor because the creation of the new army, which was paid in cash, reduced significantly the importance of the *pomest'e* system and the need to mobilize populated land to support the army. As long as the peasants paid taxes and provided recruits, the dues they had formerly paid or might pay to support the middle service class were less important for the military health of Muscovy.

The binding of the peasants to the land seemingly did nothing to alter the proportion of the peasants living on various categories of land in favor of the gentry. In 1699, 342 leading men (members of the upper upper-service class) from 137 families possessed 121,137 peasant households. On the other hand, 15,920 gentry members from 3,264 families had 238,897 households. Another group of seven to fifteen thousand smaller *pomeshchiki* had just over seventy-five thousand peasant households. The great discrepancy of wealth is equally evident in figures of 1710, when members of the upper service class (boyars through *zhil'tsy*) owned 254,000 peasant households, or 71 percent of all those possessed by laymen. The *Ulozhenie* clearly failed to produce an economic triumph for the middle service class; it did not create the base for a "gentry monarchy."[86] The enserfment did not prove harmful to the magnates, as they had feared it would.

Some magnates may have reasoned that, on balance, binding the peasants to the land was to their advantage. With many peasants fleeing from the center to the southern steppes and the Urals during the Thirteen Years War, a number of magnates may have calculated that a permanent enserfment was not such a bad idea after all.[87] Even members of the lower upper-service class unprecedentedly participated in the petition campaigns for the recovery of runaway serfs after the *Ulozhenie*.[88] Wealthy lords benefited from the massive recovery operations. One in the Riazan' region got back 106 serfs. It was not uncommon for lords to have twenty to fifty fugitives returned to them.[89] These lords were not exclusively members of the middle service class.

This new unity between the lower upper-service class and the middle service class may have been prompted not only by a common interest in the peasant question, but also by a new sense of a shared destiny in face of the new army: the middle service class cavalry was made obsolete by the new formation regiments and most of the command posts were taken away from the upper service class by the foreign mercenary officers.[90]

At least some of the magnates, such as B. I. Morozov, and various monasteries saw that they could raise the level of exploitation of a stable, bound population more than enough to compensate for the fact that they could no longer recruit as much additional labor for their estates from other lords as they had done prior to 1649.[91] Raising the level of exploitation on a personal level meant that the peasant had less left for paying taxes (which were not the "first commandment" in Muscovy) or for his personal consumption—and neither result was beneficial for the state. There is no essential contradiction or mystery in this fact, for, as has been stated, what a modern person would regard as the "state interest" was clearly secondary in seventeenth-century Russia to the desires of the individuals in charge of the state power.

There is yet another significant reason why serfdom was not rolled back after 1649. There hardly can be any doubt that Muscovy could not afford the new army. The fact that from 1613 to 1682 Russia was at war for forty years and at peace for only thirty hardly helped matters, for the population almost never had a chance to rest, to catch its breath. Reforms and manipulations, such as those discussed in chapter 13, never could raise enough revenue. Vasilii Shuiskii had been unable to pay his few mercenaries at the beginning of the century, and this was frequently the case throughout the rest of the century.[92] The population did increase during the period under review, and so could turn over more to the treasury.[93] Urbanization made some progress also, but, unlike in the West, the rise of the new army was the consequence of foreign pressure and was not intimately connected with the growth of towns in Muscovy.[94] Also, Russia's colonial profit was not as great as that available to some other nations. Some of what Russia gained in plunder (primarily furs) from Siberian tributaries it lost, on balance, in tribute to the Tatars.[95]

Russia was still predominantly an agrarian nation whose well-being depended on agriculture. By the seventeenth century Rus' had barely passed the Carolingian grain-yield ratios (less than three to one), a stage one would assume had to be reached in order to support either a large urban population or a large standing army without importing food. When yield ratios were less than three, nearly everyone had to farm simply to survive. The average yield of the major crops—rye, oats, and barley—in Russia in this period was between three and four, with a few over four occasionally.[96] Just at the time Russia was trying to modernize the army, the job was made even more difficult by a big drop in yield-ratios in the second half of the seventeenth century.[97] Any increase in agricultural output was due not to improvements in agricultural technique, but to expansion of the sown area.[98] This expansion in turn was attributable to population growth, for, as noted, the average peasant plot decreased in size at this time. Obviously extensive development requires much time, and under such conditions revolutions in military systems cannot be paid for without considerable dislocation. Not only was the peasant troubled by a rise in taxes, but he indubitably found it difficult to make the change from supporting the middle service class by payments in kind to additional cash payments to the treasury to pay for the new army.[99] The financial embarrassment of the government in the second half of the seventeenth century was one sign of the disloca-

255

tion caused by the introduction of the new army; the renewal of massive peasant flights during the Thirteen Years War was another.

If what a preindustrial nation can afford depends on its agricultural output (plus what it can steal from others), then Russia was unquestionably living beyond its means in the military sphere until the 1850s, when a rise in yield-ratios occurred. The facts of the 1686 military campaign demonstrate this graphically. The wage bill for maintaining the foreign officers, plus forty thousand infantry and twenty thousand cavalry and pikemen amounted to about seven hundred thousand rubles. The government, however, could collect only 324,244 rubles in an extraordinary levy. This meant that the army was not paid, and the whole syndrome associated with the old army followed: the troops began to loot, the theater of war was converted into a desert, disorder and mass desertion followed, and the government had to call a halt to the war three or four months after beginning it.[100] The fact that Russia could not afford modern warfare became evident when Peter modernized the army even further, quadrupled the budget (with from two-thirds to four-fifths of all revenue going to maintain the military establishment), fought almost continuously, and nearly destroyed the population in the process.[101]

In the late Muscovite period, as in the Petrine era, the government simply did not have the means to finance its army entirely in cash. Therefore it continued to rely to some extent on old methods of maintaining the military men. This was true for many of the troops of the new formation regiments, who essentially were required to support themselves by farming. The same rationale may have been partly behind the preservation of the serf-*pomest'e* system: the gentry rendered some military service, the government could always hope for more. This was service which was not fully at treasury expense, just as Peter did not pay his army in full either and relied partially on serf support. The government must have felt that converting the rent paid by the peasants into taxes simply would not be worth the social dislocation and political furore which would have resulted. The state power did not fear to make the gentry work. The record contains numerous instances where the *deti boiarskie* were forced to perform manual labor, and in this sense they were in no way "gentle." However, a massive expropriation would have unstuck the gentry-magnate amalgam against the peasantry in what was a time of great civil unrest anyway. This might in turn have caused a downfall of the regime if the mercenaries failed to support their employers in an internecine conflict.

All of these factors indicate that no one in power felt any need to restore any degree of mobility. They also show why there were, apparently, no other proposals besides Golitsyn's for rolling back serfdom in the second half of the seventeenth century. Since Muscovite officials did not attach high priority to personal freedom or human dignity, they had no moral qualms as they gradually enserfed the peasantry.[102] They delayed only because their own crude economic interest dictated such a pattern of behavior. Having been forced to complete the process, they had no internal philosophical motivation to reverse the enserfment. Only after extensive Westernization were some Russians to question the morality of serfdom.

During the Thirteen Years War (1654–1667) the army based on the middle service class cavalrymen archers, led by wellborn men protected by the "system of places," was phased out gradually and without severity in favor of a military force based on peasant infantry soldiers outfitted with firearms and under the nearly exclusive command of foreign officers. While the foreigners frequently were incompetent, their hiring was based on presumed experience and an ability to change the Muscovite army into a force capable of competing with its more advanced enemies to the West. This extremely radical change aroused no apparent opposition from the middle service class, a result totally unlike the storms created in affected groups by subsequent lesser reforms by Peter the Great.[103] (The *strel'tsy*, on the other hand, did revolt and become Old Believers, but their resistance to change was overcome by governmental violence. Most of them, however, joined the new army or merged with the urban population.)

One may imagine that there was no opposition from the gentry (both the former lower upper-service class and the middle service class), whose position and utility in society had been undermined thoroughly, precisely because they were allowed to keep their serfs. Serfdom, as was shown, hindered the creation of the new army. Had the entire system been rationalized and serfdom been abolished, however, the very creation and development of the new army might have been impossible— regardless of how much terror the government was willing to employ. It is hard to conceive the gentry giving up both their role in society and their derived caste privileges in the years of the wars with Poland and Sweden without significant protest—which might have toppled the government. The government on many occasions could deal high-handedly with the gentry in the second half of the seventeenth century, as when it gradually forced them into the new formation regiments under the command of foreign officers. Nevertheless, it had to proceed so as not to alienate or antagonize them totally. This was done by allowing them to keep their service lands as heritable property and their peasants as serfs.[104] It might be correct to generalize that serfdom was the cost of the

257

new army, although it is highly doubtful that the government planned it that way.

The successful introduction of the new army is evidence of the remarkable resilience the Russian state has had since early modern times. For most of this period since the sixteenth century "backwardness" was characteristic of much of the Russian organism. Yet when disaster and potential dismemberment began to loom large, the government intervened dramatically to save the situation, and often the state frontiers expanded before the crisis had been resolved. The state survived, but at a tremendous price. Serfdom was certainly one of the costs of the survival of the Russian state.

Having completed our review of the Muscovite period, let us look briefly at serfdom in the eighteenth and nineteenth centuries, a much better-known era. It is important to bear in mind the continuity of Russian history. The parallels which will be shown between the Muscovite and St. Petersburg periods tell us a great deal about the essence of the last half-millennium of Russian history, and the developments of the imperial period help to confirm retrospectively some of the judgments made about the less well-known pre-Petrine era.

Peter the Great inherited three well-developed strands of the autocratic system, which he was to perfect even further. Ivan IV had a reliable police force, while the seventeenth century witnessed the formation of an army and a bureaucracy almost wholly subservient to the will of the monarch.[105] The existence of such a system permitted the greatest Romanov tsar to reconsider the seventeenth-century heritage of the anomalous imbalance of rights and privileges in Russian society, the paradoxical situation where the gentry had a very high social status but a very low social utility. The result was that Peter, frightened by military setbacks, put the gentry back in harness and thereby restored the service state.[106] He revitalized provincial administration and completely regularized the army. He gave the gentry a specific place in each system.[107] Much of the reformed army was paid for by taxes levied from the urban population, which nearly doubled in size between 1652 and 1722.[108] The peasantry was also heavily taxed as the government made cash the fundamental reward for service.[109] Peter's gadfly, I. T. Pososhkov, recommended confiscating the gentry's land and paying state bills with taxes collected from the peasantry. Peter did not follow this suggestion, apparently because he felt that every active army officer or governmental official should own property as a matter of course.[110] Furthermore, the dues the serfs paid made an important contribution to the support of the new service class; serfdom ceased being an outrage and became an institution useful to the state. Peasant protests diminished practically to nothing. Just as before the *Ulozhenie,* everyone was again in state service. The gentry was unable to oppose the reimposition of service requirements because the minimal service of its members had left them with little influence. They probably were aware also of the actions of Charles XI and of the ever-present possibility of enactment of proposals such as Pososhkov's. This weakness of the gentry allowed Peter to proceed autocratically with his reforms.

Peter's new service class can be seen as a revitalized continuation of that created roughly two centuries earlier by Ivan III. Ivan had to administer and defend the growing Muscovite state, Peter the Russian empire. Each service class was instrumental in creating a form of serfdom. In Muscovy, the serf was bound to the land. In the Empire he was bound to the person of his lord. In 1721 Peter tacitly gave the lord, who was held responsible for the payment of his serf's taxes, the right to sell the peasant and his family. In the Russian context the peasant remained a serf in that, unlike a slave, he had to pay taxes and was to a lessening degree the subject of the law rather than its object. In other respects the status of the Russian serf came to resemble that of a slave. In 1765 and 1767 peasants lost the right even to complain against their lords.[111]

History "repeated itself" in the eighteenth century. As the status of the peasantry deteriorated, that of the gentry improved. In the Muscovite period threatened or would-be rulers offered concessions to gain support. This phenomenon also occurred in the eighteenth century as court cliques jockeyed for position. Somewhat similar situations had occurred in the Time of Troubles and in the summer of 1648, but ordinarily the magnates had presented a relatively united front against the middle service class in the contest for labor. This united front became harder to maintain after the enserfment when both the magnates and the gentry realized that their mutual interest demanded they ally against the peasantry. As Russia entered the era of palace revolutions, the various magnates forgot their own common interest in face of the masses of petty service landholders and began to compete for the favors of this massive group. Part of the competition was at the expense of the peasantry. Most of it involved a series of concessions to the mass of the gentry. The outcome was the formal freeing of the gentry from all compulsory service by Peter III in his search for support in 1762—perhaps a demagogic step, because he and his advisers knew that many of the gentry who could not live without their income from government posts would still have to serve.[112] The sense of shock and disorientation, of frustration and rejection, felt by many of the servicemen at the logical culmination of their diminishing service requirements since the time of Peter the Great, must have been to some degree similar to the feelings of the members of the middle service class who had been dispossessed by the gunpowder revolution and the new formation army in the seventeenth century.[113] After 1762 the situation was such that once again the owners of much of the peasant labor of Russia were rendering service insufficient to justify their privileged status. Once again serfdom became obsolete, a contradiction.[114]

The "enlightened" empress Catherine II, unlike Tsar Aleksei, is known to have been aware of this contradiction. It outraged her "good and honest principles."[115] She could have resolved the dilemma by taking hold of either of its horns. The gentry could have been put back in service, or the peasants could have been emancipated. Because of her precarious position as an upstart foreign princess on the Russian throne, she found it inexpedient to demand service of the gentry. In fact, through the reign of her late dispatched husband Peter III the gentry enjoyed little official preference in state service, and only after the coup did the serf-owning class begin to accumulate legal preferences in this sphere.[116] After 1762 the gentry retained the command posts in the army and in the bureaucracy, but most of the more than one hundred thousand serf-owners rendered very little service in their lifetimes.[117]

The other resolution to the dilemma would have been to free the serfs, a course apparently favored for awhile by Catherine herself. Such a solution demanded careful consideration, for emancipation would have meant tampering with an institution which was considered by some as part of the established order.[118] The issue of serfdom was first debated as an "Enlightenment" issue in 1766 in the Free Economic Society and then at the 1767 Legislative Commission, convoked to compile a new code to update the *Ulozhenie* of 1649. The treatment of the serfs, but not their emancipation, remained a lively issue, largely in the satirical journals, even after Catherine closed the unsuccessful legal commission.[119]

Another recurring pattern in the 1760s and 1770s was the expectation of the peasants, who were waiting to be freed from serfdom after their masters had been freed from service.[120] They became enraged at the fact that they were still enserfed after 1762, much as the Muscovite peasants had been enraged by 1649 and its aftermath. Still believing in the Petrine ideal of the service state rather than the new corporate state, the peasants sensed the contradiction between the position of the gentry freed from service and their own status and rebelled—first after the 1762 decree, then in 1773–75 under Emelian Pugachev. The peasants' sense of frustration was heightened when Peter III, on March 21, 1762, converted about two million abased seignoral serfs under church jurisdiction into state peasants, an action reminiscent of Golitsyn's proposal for all seignoral serfs. The fortunate former church peasants thought they had been freed completely, while the seignorial serfs belonging to lay lords felt similar provisions would be drawn up for them also. Peter III was deposed on June 28, 1762, but remained a popular figure in the peasant mind, and his name was assumed by many subsequent pretenders.[121]

The forces evoking the Pugachev rebellion were similar to those before the Razin outbreak: recent dramatic legal intervention in the social structure, an inconclusive war on foreign territory, high taxes and heavy recruiting in the peasant community, and discontent caused by governmental action among the cossacks. The professed goals of the Pugachev movement were to destroy the gentry and to create a peasant kingdom.[122] While a peasant kingdom has yet to be created, the *Pugachevshchina,* added to previous peasant violence, was responsible for hundreds of landlord deaths and instilled fear in the entire gentry class.[123] Again, concessions to the peasantry became inconceivable as the government and lords, full of hatred for the peasantry, turned to terrorist repression with catastrophic results for the primary agricultural producers.[124] Throughout the first half of the eighteenth century the government had opposed gentry programs to broaden the bounds of serfdom, but in the reign of Catherine the seignorial peasantry became even further dependent upon their lords, and hundreds of thousands of state peasants were abased by conversion into private peasants. A symbiotic relationship between the government and the gentry quickly developed, with survival in an hostile environment the goal of both. This relationship was to carry serfdom for another century.[125] It allowed the gentry to keep its serfs and the oligarchic government to rule with little concern for the wishes of the rest of society.

The catastrophe of the Crimean War forced the autocracy to give serious consideration to what was wrong with backward Russia. Alfred J. Rieber cogently argues that Tsar Aleksandr II considered emancipating the serfs for military reasons: the institution of serfdom did not permit Russia to have an army reserve, and mid-nineteenth-century warfare demanded a larger army than any country could maintain in peacetime. Serf recruits who served out their twenty-five years in the army were automatically freed, and were too old to be called back into service in emergencies. The government felt it could not increase the draft calls (which confiscated the landlords' property), shorten the term of military service to create ready reserves, and send the discharged soldiers, now emancipated, back to the serf villages. The only alternative was to emancipate the serfs to speed up the flow of men through the army to have the necessary pool of ready reserves.[126] In my opinion, a decision could have been made, as Paul decided in 1797 and 1799, to institute a new service class, with a revitalized institution of serfdom.[127] Instead, the decision was made for serfdom to be abolished, beginning ninety-nine years and a day after the gentry had been freed from obligatory service. The state dismantled the institution in the reverse order of its construction. The edict of emancipation in 1861 proscribed the post-*Ulozhenie* accretions which had made Russian serfdom resemble slavery. The lord lost all right to dispose of the persons of his former serfs, and his police powers were transferred to the commune. As the peasant was first bound to the land, so only in the twentieth century was he finally freed from all ties to the land and permitted to go where he wanted when he wanted—a freedom the Russian farmer had not enjoyed since the fifteenth century.

In the Muscovite period of Russian history the enserfment of the peasantry was a governmental reaction to labor dislocation at times of crisis and a second-order consequence of technological change. The catalysts, or immediate causes, of this development were the civil war of the fifteenth century, Ivan IV's Oprichnina and Livonian War, the dynastic crisis after the death of Ivan IV, the Smolensk War, and the civil disorders of 1648. All of the immediate causes were catalysts which, injected into the Muscovite situation, caused the rigidification and severe stratification of Russian society.

One ultimate cause was the general underpopulation of the country, which resulted, during times of disruption, in glaring labor shortages for certain kinds of landholders. Also crucial were the lengthy frontiers, which had to be defended by increasingly expensive armed forces, which in turn had to be supported by a sparse population subsisting on very low-level agriculture. While the new taxes to pay for the gunpowder revolution did not cause the stratification of Russian society, they did accelerate it because the peasants fled the imposts and then their lords demanded that they be returned. In times of political disruption the government, often headed by less than ideal rulers, usually felt it needed support, which regularly could be purchased by granting concessions to powerful interest-groups.[128] There were many concessions which the hypertrophic government could give, as we have seen, but a major one involved control over the peasantry. This concession was attractive both for economic and sociopsychological reasons. Almost all wealth was produced by the peasantry, so that those who were not primary producers had to live indirectly off agriculture, or not at all. Also, Russian society was very status conscious and placed a high value on dominance and authority. This attitude loomed particularly important when the middle service class became aware of its military obsolescence. The series of deliberate concessions granted by the state power to satisfy the economic demands and psychic needs of its constituents resulted in the certainly unintended enserfment of the peasantry.

Concessions to the lower classes as a response to chaos and disorder never seem to have occurred to any Russian rulers, with the exception of False Dmitrii I. Rather than solve the problems of peasant discontent, the ruling group, probably because of limited ability and perception coupled with commitments other than to what we in the twentieth century think of as social justice, preferred to team up with the service class and church to keep the lid on by repression. Mainly because there were few cracks in the upper and middle service class-church alliance, lower-class rebellion had little chance of success.

One might conclude that serfdom was not inevitable in Russia.[129] Had the crises not occurred, then serfdom would not have developed. However, whether for a quarter of a millennium Muscovy could have avoided all crises that might have touched off the "labor shortage-weak government concessions to solve the labor shortage" syndrome is indeed doubtful. Nevertheless, the formation of a deterministic theory on the inevitability of serfdom, simply because of the probable inevitability of the syndrome, would be going too far. The crises had to occur at the "right time." Had Aleksei's reign progressed without riots until the beginning of the 1660s and through the introduction of the new army, chapter 11 of the *Ulozhenie* of 1649 hardly could have been written. This, of course, is all in the realm of speculation.

Once serfdom was consolidated, nearly all forces at work favored its retention in the face of peasant opposition—even in face of the fact that the gunpowder revolution created an army consisting largely of peasant draftees commanded by foreign officers and thus made the old middle service class cavalry, which had demanded the enserfment, obsolete. When the government wanted to, it could simply ignore the enserfment, as in the case of fugitives to the frontier or in urban areas, and even occasionally when runaways appeared on the magnates' own estates. These magnates of limited talents found they could satisfy their greed for the spoils of office by moving boundary markers and looting the court and black-land funds. As it happened, the *Ulozhenie* proved not to cost the magnates much and aided the gentry little in their quest for a larger share of the country's wealth. On the other hand, the enserfment served as social cement between the great and small lords in the hostile peasant environment. While progress in the government administration and tax-collection system as well as in the economy was insufficient to permit a total discarding of the traditional natural support of the army, it was adequate to permit adoption of the new technology and the tactics of gunpowder warfare, enabling Muscovy to survive as a political entity. The continuation of serfdom permitted a peaceful, radical reform of the army in spite of the fact that this reform dispossessed the potentially troublesome and powerful middle service class. The tsar and his favorite oligarchs were able to rule without challenge. The restriction the enserfment placed on their ability to enrich themselves by recruiting additional labor was a small price to pay for the power to rule. In this way part of the groundwork was laid for the autocratic rule in Russia which continued to the 1917 revolution.

The historiography of the enserfment of the Russian peasantry has nearly come full circle. Prior to the emancipation of the serfs in 1861, most historians assumed that the government had enserfed the peasantry, although they could not find specific evidence to prove it. This became known as the "decree" interpretation. After the emanicipation a "nondecree" school held sway from the 1880s through the 1920s. Based on unfortunate analogies with the Lithuanian Russian peasant, the Roman *colonus,* and other Western European examples, the assumption was made that the peasant had lost his right to move and his general freedom without any significant intervention by the state. The agents of enserfment in the fully developed nondecree interpretation were claimed to have been indebtedness and "long-time residency" (*starozhil'stvo*) .

Throughout the hegemony of the nondecree interpretation convincing attacks were made on every part of it, but evidence was lacking for a decisive rebuttal. At the turn of the century documents came to light which weakened the nondecree thesis by indicating that the government had taken some action in the 1580s. A decree interpretation should by now be back in vogue as a result of discoveries made in the late 1950s and published in 1968 by V. I. Koretskii which provide additional proof of the primacy of the role of the state power in the enserfment. I hope that the present work has shed further light on the causes of the enserfment of the peasantry and on the relationship of this process to the military evolution experienced by Muscovy.

Summing up pre-Soviet scholarship, P. E. Mikhailov wrote that "the development and extension of serfdom to the free peasantry is one of the most complex, interesting, alluring, difficult, and little understood problems in the history of Russian law."[130] Thanks to continued work on the subject, the problem of the enserfment hardly seems as confusing as it once was. Serfdom in Russia was created, under favorable conditions, by the rulers of a hypertrophic state power. They reacted to temporary economic and political exigencies by degrading the peasantry. Serfdom persisted until 1861, and really into the twentieth century, because the ruling elite found this institution to be politically and economically expedient. The government repealed serfdom only when it seemed to be a liability.

Appendix

THE MILITARY FORCES OF THE MUSCOVITE STATE

RANK	IVAN IV	END OF SIXTEENTH CENTURY	1625
Upper service class			
Moscow ranks			
Middle service class			
Dvoriane, deti boiarskie	17,500	25,000	
Vybornye			
Regimental			
Garrison			
Foreigners	4,000	4,000	
Officers			
Lower service class			
Strel'tsy	12,000	20,000	20,539
Moscow		7-10,000	
Mounted			2,697
Foot			
Provincial		13-15,000	17,842
Cossacks	6,000		
Artillerymen	3,000		
Ukrainians (Cherkassy)			
Tatars, Mordva, etc.	10,000	10,000	
New formation regiments			
Lancers			
Hussars			
Cavalrymen			
Soldiers			
Dragoons			
Slaves	17,500	50,000 (25,000)	
Total	70,000	109,000 (110,000)	

Appendix

RANK	1630	1632	1634
Upper service class			
Moscow ranks	2,642	2,769	2,697
Middle service class			
Dvoriane, deti boiarskie	24,791	24,714	
Vybornye			
Regimental	15,850		
Garrison	11,583		
Foreigners			
Officers			
Lower service class			
Strel'tsy		33,775	
Moscow	4,000	6,173	
Mounted		1,812	
Foot			
Provincial			22,972
Cossacks	c. 11,000	11,471	
Artillerymen		4,244	
Ukrainians (Cherkassy)		c. 20,000	
Tatars, Mordva, etc.			
New formation regiments		6,118	
Lancers			
Hussars			
Cavalrymen			
Soldiers		3,323	
Dragoons			
Slaves			
Total	95,000 (92,500)	104,714 + Nogai Tatars	

268

1651	1653	1663	1672	1681
		2,963		6,127 (6,385; 8,278)
39,408		21,850	37,859	9,712 (11,216; 12,059)
		3,309		
		9,526		
		5,072		
2,707				
		224 + (410 not in regiments)		
44,486		65,000		55,000
		18,800 (21,685)		20,048 (16,955 in 16 regiments; 19,259 in 16 regiments)
		13,125 (14,563; 14,640)		30,000
21,124		2,822 + 783 officers		14,868 + 50,000 Hetman cossacks
4,245		6,191		7,000
2,371		2,966		14,865
9,113		2,063		
		1,158 + 50 officers		6 regiments
		405 + 21 officers		
	2,000	18,455 + 919 officers	12,000	30,472 (29,636; 29,435; 29,844 in 20 regiments) + 10,000 recruits
		24,958 + 1,262 officers	31,133	61,288 in 55 regiments (59,206 in 48 [41] regiments)
8,107		4,504 + 108 officers		
				11,830
133,210		98,150 + *strel'tsy*		214,600
(7% New Formation)		(79% New Formation)		(49% Infantry)
Formation)		(21% Old Army)		(51% Cavalry)
(93% Old Army)				

Military Forces in Specific Battles or Campaigns

RANK	1514, ORSHA	1552, KAZAN'	1562, MOZHAISK CAMPAIGN AGAINST BELORUSSIA
Upper service class			
Moscow ranks			
Middle service class			
Dvoriane, deti boiarskie			8,998
Vybornye			
Regimental			
Garrison			
Foreigners			
Officers			
Lower service class			
Strel'tsy			
Moscow			
Mounted			
Foot			
Provincial			
Cossacks			6,054
Artillerymen			
Ukrainians (Cherkassy)			
Tatars, Mordva, etc.			5,854
New formation regiments			
Lancers			
Hussars			
Cavalrymen			
Soldiers			
Dragoons			
Slaves			8,997
Other			2,165 townsmen
Total	30-40,000 (Probably excessive)	50,000 (Probably excessive)	33,407

1578, TO LIVONIA	1632, SHEIN'S ARMY AT SMOLENSK	1660, V. B. SHEREMETEV'S ARMY IN THE UKRAINE	1667–68—1668–69, DOROSHENKO CAMPAIGN SEVSK REGIMENTS	BELGOROD REGIMENTS
212 princes		2,700	2,918	
9,200	11,688 (34%)	4,400		
			9,753 6,354	307
	3,744 (11%)			413 (not all foreigners)
		1,000	19,000	653
2,000				
13,119	1,612 (5%) 2,215 (6%)			
		20,000 +		6,497
6,461	1,667 (5%)			
				1,093
	2,400 (6%)	4,100	9,545 + 525 officers	8,838
	10,962 (31%) 400 (2%)	3,000 4,000		4,600 427
		10,000 (in baggage train)		
1,109 servicemen of Novgorod and Iur'ev 7,850 peasants				38,497 reserves in Belgorod
39,681	34,588 (100%)	40,000	48,233	61,362 + 2,467 from Smolensk regiment

112,062

RANK	1679, CHERKASSKII'S ARMY	1680, GOLITSYN'S ARMY	1687, FIRST CRIMEAN CAMPAIGN	1689, SECOND CRIMEAN CAMPAIGN
Upper service class				
Moscow ranks	3,669			3,366
Middle service class			8,712	
Dvoriane, deti boiarskie				
Vybornye				
Regimental	7,250 (+ unknown number)	10,819 (8%)		4,208 + 362 *kormshchiki*
Garrison				
Foreigners				
Officers				
Lower service class				
Strel'tsy	17,010 (+ unknown number)	23,533 (18%)		
Moscow			11,262	9,270 in 11 regiments
Mounted				
Foot				
Provincial				
Cossacks	With Ukrainians	370 (25%)	15,505	
Artillerymen				
Ukrainians				
(Cherkassy)	12,613 (includes Cossacks)	10,530 (8%)		14,471
Tatars, Mordva, etc.				
New formation regiments				
Lancers			⎱ 26,096	247
Hussars			⎰	
Cavalrymen	42,906	34,614 (26.5%)		29,216 in 28 regiments
Soldiers	23,490 (+ unknown number)	43,204 (33.5%)	49,363	49,189 in 35 regiments
Dragoons				
Others			1,964 others	1,737 others
Total	106,938	129,300 (100%)	112,902	112,066 (117,446)

1687 column additional notes:
New Formation 66.9%
Old Army 33.1%
Infantry 53.7%
Cavalry 46.3%

SOURCES—Baiov, *Kurs"*, 1:41, 152. Bobrovskii, *Postoiannyia*, p. 32; idem, *Zachatki*, p. 20. Chernov, *Vooruzhennye*, pp. 167–68, 188–89, 195–96. *DAI*, 9, no. 106. *DRV*, 14: 350. Elchaninov, "Ocherk"," p. 71. Epifanov, " 'Uchenie," pp. 84, 90. Kliuchevskii, *Istoriia soslovii*, p. 144. Maslovskii, *Zapiski*, 1: 50. Mikhnevich and Geisman, "Glavnyi shtab"," pp. 68–69. Myshlaevskii, *Ofitserskii*, p. 29. Razin, *Istoriia*, 2: 330, 332–34, 343, 351, 357, 373–74; ibid., 3: 216–17, 254, 258. Seredonin, *Fletcher*, pp. 337–38, 349, 359. Sh., "Dvorianstvo," no. 2, p. 542; ibid., 3, pp. 209, 427. Stashevskii, "Biudzhet"," pp. 414–16; idem, "Smeta," pp. 5, 8, 13, 49–57. Ustrialov, *Istoriia*, 1:178–79, 186, 292–94; ibid., Appendix 11:385–86. Zimin, *I. S. Peresvetov*, p. 357.

I have considerable confidence in the relative precision of Muscovite statistics after 1560. The Russians were themselves highly conscious of statistical accuracy, as revealed in a remark by Tsar Aleksei to General Lobanov-Rostovskii, whose report revealed a discrepancy of twenty-four casualties: "For ages it has been unheard of for noble slaves to write a falsehood and lie to their own sovereign on military matters, on campaigns, and on casualties" (Maslovskii, *Zapiski*, 1: 33) . Figures given in parentheses are alternatives to those adjacent. I have no way of deciding between the alternatives, which are relatively insignificant in most cases and never affect my overall conclusions.

Notes

1. Introduction

1. M. A. D'iakonov called this problem the "kapital'neishii vopros russkoi istorii" in his "K" voprosu o krest'ianskoi," p. 317. Mikhailov ("Obychnyi," p. 78) attributes this statement to Sergeevich (*Russkiia drevnosti*, 3:449).

2. For a review of the most recent Soviet work on agrarian history in sixteenth-century Russia, see Shmidt, "K izucheniiu," pp. 17–31.

3. Samokvasov, *Krest'iane*, p. 15.

4. This was the view of some of the nineteenth-century Russian Slavophiles (*OIIN*, 1:329). A. S. Lappo-Danilovskii, among others, attributed the formulation of serfdom in Russia to Peter's famous decree on the soul tax ("Ocherk" i istoriia obrazovaniia," pp. 77, 81).

5. A useful survey of pre-Soviet historiography on this question is Michael B. Petrovich, "The Peasant in Nineteenth-Century Historiography," in *The Peasant in Nineteenth-Century Russia*, edited by Wayne S. Vucinich (Stanford University Press, 1968), pp. 192, 218–30. Petrovich's conclusion about the possibility of a synthesis of the different interpretations of the enserfment of the Russian peasantry is unacceptable.

6. Tatishchev, *Sudebnik*", p. 221; *Istoriia rossiiskaia*, 7:163, 366, 387.

7. Karamzin, *Istoriia*, 10: 229–32; Pipes, *Karamzin's Memoir*, p. 164.

8. Solov'ev, *Istoriia*, 4:296–300.

9. Chicherin, *Opyty*, pp. 174–76, 223, 227. Chicherin, one of the founders of the Hegelian "state historical school," based his theory partly on the following syllogism: forbidding peasant movement was a state action; in the early Muscovite period (the "appanage" period) a state did not exist; therefore peasants were not bound. Then the state arose and bound all to service, including the peasants (ibid., pp. 176, 228).

10. Kostomarov, "Dolzhno li," p. 353.

11. Beliaev, *Krest'iane*, pp. 95, 304. A similar view was held by M. I. Gorchakov (*O zemel'nykh*", p. 318). See also Romanovich-Slavatinskii, *Dvorianstvo*, p. 378.

12. Platonov, "O vremeni," p. 19.

13. Sergeevich, *Russkiia*, 1:251–54.

14. Debol'skii, *Grazhdanskaia deesposobnost'*, pp. 141, 147, 152. Under the influence of other views then prevailing, he also claimed that somewhat earlier, in the mid-sixteenth century, the taxpaying population was bound to its status of paying taxes, but still could move legally (ibid., p. 139).

15. Gradovskii, "Vysshaia," 1:53, 60.

16. See, for example, Shapiro, "Ob absoliutizme," p. 77.

17. Those who would like somehow to fuse these mutually incompatible interpretations should read the words of V. I. Sergeevich on this subject (*Russkiia iuridicheskiia drevnosti*, 3:491–94). His sarcasm should serve as a healthy antidote to any seeker of the golden mean who would attempt to reconcile the irreconcilable.

18. Pazhitnov, "Dvorianskaia," p. 82.

19. Ibid., pp. 67–72. See also Samokvasov, *Krest'iane*, p. 60.

20. Kliuchevskii, "Proiskhozhdenie," *Sochineniia*, 7:238–317. See also his *History*, 5 vols. (New York: Russell and Russell, 1960), 2:chaps. 12, 13; ibid., 3: chap. 9. His earlier view is modified here, but not fundamentally changed; cf. *Sochineniia*, 2:287–328; ibid., 3: 162–86.

21. Miliukov, "Krest'iane v" Rossii," p. 679.

22. D'iakonov, "K" voprosu," pp. 328–31; *Ocherki obshchestvennago* (1912), pp. 342–57; *Ocherki iz" istorii*, pp. 9–10, 27, 31.

23. Lappo-Danilevskii, "Razyskaniia," p. 68.

24. Platonov, *Lektsii*, p. 204.

25. Presniakov, *Moskovskoe tsarstvo*, p. 106. He also added causes for the enserfment of the peasantry, including the extension of seignorial power over the peasant (pp. 101–3), taxes (pp. 103–4), and (somewhat confusingly) state action (p. 107).

26. Sergeevich said "the arguments of Pogodin convinced no one" (*Russkiia*, 1:267).

27. One of the most vigorous advocates of the comparative approach now in the USSR is A. M. Sakharov (Shunkov, ed., *Perekhod*, p. 194).

28. Engel'man, *Istoriia*, pp. 32–45, 58–60. The first Russian translation was made in 1884.

29. Kliuchevskii, "Proiskhozhdenie." Kliuchevskii was followed by many of his lesser-known contemporaries, such as the pseudonymous Sh., who found the indebtedness interpretation appealing at least partially for polemical purposes: in Muscovy indebtedness was "legitimate" because the contracts were made between lord and peasant for the prime necessities of life, whereas post-Emancipation indebtedness—reflecting the decline of the well-being of the peasantry—was simply between a peasant and a usurious kulak or merchant ("Dvorianstvo," no. 2, pp. 242–44). Some Soviet historians also have claimed that increasing indebtedness strengthened serfdom (Cherepnin, *Obrazovanie*, p. 245; I. I. Smirnov, "Zametki," p. 152).

30. Mikhailov, "K" voprosu," p. 319; "Obychnyi institut"," pp. 82–83; Picheta, *Belorussiia*, pp. 368–71.

31. Vladimirskii-Budanov, *Obzor*", pp. 134, 139, 141–42.

32. Kashtanov, "K probleme mestnogo," p. 147; "K izucheniiu oprichniny," p. 102. Presniakov looked even further back, to the fourteenth century, to a category of peasants known as *siroty*, semifree descendants of the Kievan *izgoi*, who could not move freely (*Moskovskoe tsarstvo*, p. 100).

33. Cherepnin, "Istoricheskie usloviia," pp. 92–93; idem, "Iz istorii formirovaniia," p. 244.

34. Grekov, *Kratkii ocherk*, pp. 176–78; Zimin, *PRP*, 5:93–96.

35. D'iakonov, *Ocherki iz" istorii sel'skago naseleniia*, pp. 19–20, 23; Miliukov, "Krest'iane v" Rossii," p. 679.

36. Lappo-Danilevskii, "Razyskaniia," pp. 62–76.

37. Kashtanov, "K probleme mestnogo upravleniia," p. 147; Nosov, "Mnogotomnaia," p. 139; I. I. Smirnov, "Zametki," no. 2, pp. 154–61, no. 3, p. 140; Grekov, *Krest'iane*, p. 831.

38. D'iakonov, *Ocherki iz" istorii*, pp. 48, 74, 76–77, 111, and elsewhere; idem, "K" voprosu," p. 317; *Ocherki obshchestvennago* (1912), pp. 320, 345.

39. Liubavskii, *Lektsii*, pp. 276–77. See also Platonov, *Lektsii*, pp. 197, 203–4.

40. Miliukov, "Krest'iane v" Rossii," pp. 679–80; *Ocherki* (1900), 1:180.

41. Cherepnin, "Novye dokumenty," p. 49; *Novgorodskie*, pp. 174–75, 179–82. See articles 42, 44 and 63 of the Pskov Judicial Charter; Mikhailov, "K" voprosu," p. 332; Vernadsky, "Serfdom in Russia," p. 254.

42. Sergeevich, *Russkiia iuridicheskiia drevnosti*, 1:220; Mikhailov, "K" voprosu," p. 338. For specimens of peasant contracts with lords, see M. A. D'iakonov, ed., *Svodnyi*. Only ten of the forty-four documents contain loan provisions (ibid., pp. 14–15).

43. Grekov, "Proiskhozhdenie" (1930), pp. 64–65, 67–68. See also chapter 5 below.

44. Tkhorzhevskii, "Pomest'e," pp. 79–80. In 1568 the Oprichnina government transferred peasant debts owed to the executed boyar I. P. Fedorov (who had been denounced by V. A. Staritskii) to new lords who were given his lands (Kashtanov, "K izucheniiu oprichniny," p. 109).

45. Makovskii, *Razvitie*, p. 202. L. S. Prokof'eva maintains that all peasants without exception who lived on the lands of the Kirill monastery of Belozero took loans and that these interest-free loans deprived the peasants of freedom of movement (" 'Khlebnyi biudzhet'," pp. 103–4). This contention is open to criticism on a number of grounds, and we can be sure in any case that most landholders were in no condition to give loans. For another example of the current Soviet treatment of the indebtedness

issue, see the article by Pobedimova, "O nekotorykh," which correctly recognizes the obvious presence of indebtedness in Muscovy, but does not attribute to it a significant role in the general enserfment of the peasantry. See also A. N. Sakharov, "O dialektike," p. 38. N. A. Rozhkov said peasant indebtedness was not great ("Sel'skoe khoziaistvo," p. 176). However, elsewhere he contradicted this ("Istoriia krepostnogo prava," p. 116; idem., *Gorod,* p. 46). K. N. Shchepetov shows how the Iosif monastery of Volokolamsk in the 1590s, in order to make money from interest charges, encouraged borrowing by peasants who could repay. Most borrowers repaid the loans. This indicates that most peasants were not permanently in debt and that the monastery officials were interested in loaning only to those who could repay, not in enslaving the agriculturalists with debt ("Sel'skoe," pp. 103–5).

46. Volkov, "Problema," p. 11.
47. Sergeevich, *Russkiia iuridicheskiia drevnosti,* 1:268; Adrianov, "K" voprosu," p. 240.
48. Paneiakh, "O sotsial'nom sostave kabal'nykh kholopov v kontse XVI v.," *Trudy LOII,* 9 (1967): 173; Doroshenko, "Zametki," p. 153.
49. Obraztsov, "Iz istorii zakreposhcheniia," pp. 345–46.
50. Tkhorzhevskii, "Pomest'e," p. 81.
51. Lappo-Danilevskii, "Razyskaniia," p. 59.
52. D'iakonov, *Ocherki obshchestvennogo* (1926), p. 271; Odinets, "Poteria," pp. 221–22.
53. Sergeevich, *Russkiia iuridicheskiia drevnosti,* 3:457–62.
54. Kochin, *Sel'skoe,* pp. 395–427; Volkov, "Problema," p. 16; A. N. Sakharov, "O dialektike," p. 35.
55. Mikhailov, "K" voprosu," pp. 321–22, 327, 337–38, 350, 353.
56. Ibid., p. 324.
57. Ibid., pp. 328, 336, 344.
58. Mikhailov, "Obychnyi institut"," pp. 82, 97. In fact, documents of the fifteenth century indicate that the right of peasants to move was nearly universal. In practice no category of peasants was restricted throughout Russia, as the *starozhil'stvo* theoreticians would have one believe (I. I. Smirnov, "Zametki," no. 3, pp. 144–45).
59. Mikhailov, "Obychnyi institut"," p. 89. This "good life" interpretation was subsequently criticized, not entirely convincingly, by I. M. Kulisher ("Nesvobodnoe," p. 188) and N. A. Rozhkov (*Russkaia istoriia,* 4:111).
60. Mikhailov, "Obychnyi institut"," pp. 113, 115–16. B. D. Grekov later ridiculed the notion that the heart of the Russian peasant thirsted for serfdom, which he viewed as his natural status ("Opyt," p. 4).
61. Mikhailov, "Obychnyi institut"," p. 83; Platonov, "O vremeni," p. 20; I. I. Smirnov, "Problemy," p. 91.
62. The following representative works convey to American students the "nondecree interpretation": Michael T. Florinsky, *Russia. A History and an Interpretation,* 2 vols. (New York: Macmillan, 1953), 1: 215; idem, *Russia. A Short History* (New York: Macmillan, 1969), emphasizes both the decree and the nondecree interpretations (pp. 70, 85, 146); Richard Freeborn, *A Short History of Modern Russia* (New York: William Morrow, 1966), p. 23; Anatole G. Mazour, *Russia. Tsarist and Communist* (New York: D. Van Nostrand, 1962), pp. 73–74; Herbert J. Ellison, *History of Russia* (New York: Holt, Rinehart and Winston, 1964), p. 58; Nicholas V. Riasanovsky, *A History of Russia* (New York: Oxford University Press, 1969), pp. 204–5; Jesse D. Clarkson, *A History of Russia* (New York: Random House, 1969), pp. 95–96.
The same is true for other non-Soviet works: Alexandre Eck, *Le Moyen Age Russe* (Paris: Maison du Livre Etranger, 1933), pp. 318–19; V. B. El'iashevich, *Istoriia prava pozemel'noi sobstvennosti v Rossii,* 2 vols. (Paris, 1948–51), 1:147. Neither of these authors, however, attributed serfdom solely to indebtedness. Note also J. L. H. Keep, "The Regime of Filaret, 1619–1633," *The Slavonic and East European Review* 38, no. 91 (June 1969): 352–53. Even George Vernadsky, who denies that the peasants were enserfed until the second half of the sixteenth century (or even 1649), attributes sig-

nificance to indebtedness and long-time residency in abasing the peasantry ("Feudalism in Russia," in Thomas Riha, ed., *Readings in Russian Civilization* [Chicago: University of Chicago Press, 1964], pp. 82–83). These aspects of the nondecree interpretation are also incorporated in Jerome Blum's superb survey, *Lord and Peasant in Russia* (pp. 98, 116).

63. Odynets, "K" istorii," pp. 136–38, cited by Mikhailov, "Novootkrytye," p. 393.
64. Adrianov, "K" voprosu," p. 244.
65. Mikhailov, "Novootkrytye dokumenty," pp. 398, 401, 408–9. A similar view seems to be held by the Soviet historian N. E. Nosov (*Stanovlenie*, pp. 180, 494).
66. D'iakonov, *Zapovednye*, pp. 7–8, 19.
67. Platonov, *Boris Godunov*, pp. 76–78; idem, *Smutnoe vremia* (1923), p. 31.
68. Platonov, "O vremeni," p. 21.
69. Veselovskii, "Iz istorii," pp. 206–9, 212–17; Polosin, "Pomestnoe," p. 55.
70. Got'e, *Smutnoe vremia*, pp. 15, 25.
71. Tkhorzhevskii, "Pomest'e," pp. 81, 86–88.
72. Kulisher, "Nesvobodnoe," pp. 181–82, 185, 188–90, 197.
73. Rozhkov, *Russkaia istoriia*, 4:102, 107, 110–12, 227–33; idem, "Istoriia krepostnogo prava," pp. 116, 118; idem, "Sel'skoe khoziaistvo," p. 181; *Gorod*, pp. 46–48.
74. M. N. Pokrovskii, *Russkaia istoriia s drevneishikh vremen*, 4 vols. (Moscow: Gosizdat, 1922), 1:286–88.
75. Volkov, "Problema," pp. 8, 15.
76. Grekov, "Iur'ev den'," pp. 67–72. This essay was not included in Grekov's posthumous four-volume *Selected Works* (in Russian), 1957–60.
77. Ibid., pp. 71–72, 75, 77–78.
78. The notion of conquest as the agent of social transformation, especially for the change to feudalism, was popular among some early Soviet historians (Danilova, "Stanovlenie," pp. 79, 101). Vernadsky also attributes some serfdom to conquest— what he calls "state serfdom"—as when Slavic communes were conquered by Alans, Goths, and Magyars ("Serfdom in Russia," pp. 250–51).
79. Samokvasov, *Krest'iane*, pp. 15–16, 21–22, 88. This conclusion is indeed strange, in fact contradictory, coming as it does from the person whose archival discoveries did the most to prove the theory that the peasants were enserfed by state actions through laws. He vigorously denied that such decrees ever had been promulgated, and stated that there was no need for a public decree binding the peasants because new cadastres compiled in the 1580s served as the legal means for accomplishing this (ibid., p. 89). Samokvasov's interpretation is something akin to Vernadsky's notion that Kievan peasants (*smerdy*) were "serfs of the state" ("Feudalism," p. 310; "Serfdom," pp. 250–51). See also B. A. Rybakov's thoughts in *Istoriia SSSR s drevneishikh*, 1:535. M. M. Speranskii earlier had claimed that some peasants had been enserfed when the Mongols imposed taxes on them. Tatishchev had toyed with the same idea in the mid-eighteenth century.
80. I. I. Smirnov, "Problemy," p. 94.
81. Kulisher, "Nesvobodnoe sostoianie," pp. 184–85.
82. Obraztsov, "Iz istorii zakreposhcheniia," p. 333.
83. Shmidt, "V. I. Lenin," pp. 332, 334; Bulygin et al., "Nachal'nyi," p. 70.
84. Zimin, "Problemy," p. 319; Chistiakova, "Narodnye dvizheniia," pp. 190–91; A. M. Sakharov, "V. I. Lenin o sotsial'no-ekonomicheskom razvitii feodal'noi Rossii," *Voprosy istorii* 35, no. 4 (April 1960) : 77–93; idem, "Rabota," p. 153.
85. Shmidt, "V. I. Lenin," p. 340.
86. Barg, "Kontseptsiia," pp. 83, 88, 93, 97; Kachanovskii, "O poniatiiakh," pp. 130–32; A. P. Kazhdan, "Traditsiia i novizna," p. 271. The recent book on feudalism by A. Ia. Gurevich (*Problemy genezisa feodalizma v Zapadnoi Evrope* [Moscow: Vysshaia shkola, 1970]) was attacked at a special assembly held at Moscow University on May 22, 1970, largely for underestimating the economic causes of feudalism. On July 13, 1970, the Ministry of Higher Education removed from the book its certification as a text (*Voprosy istorii* 45, no. 9 [September 1970]:154–67).

87. N. P. Pavlov-Sil'vanskii, *Feodalizm v drevnei Rusi*, 2d. ed. (Moscow-Petrograd: Gosizdat, 1923) ; ibid., with a foreword by M. N. Pokrovskii (Petrograd: Priboi, 1924). The original articles appeared in 1897–1902.

88. Danilova, "Stanovlenie," p. 83.

89. Froianov, "Sovetskaia," pp. 20–21; *OIIN*, 4:272–73.

90. I. I. Smirnov, "Problema," p. 98.

91. Danilova, "Stanovlenie," p. 71.

92. Alekseeva, *Oktiabr'skaia*, pp. 148, 246.

93. Danilova, "Stanovlenie," p. 118; Black, ed., *Rewriting*, p. 54.

94. Danilova, "Stanovlenie," pp. 101, 103–4, 108.

95. Iakovlev, "Ocherk" istorii krepostnago prava," p. 3. For a recent Soviet discussion of the importance of slavery for the development of serfdom, see A. P. P'iankov, "Kholopstvo na Rusi do obrazovaniia tsentralizovannogo gosudarstva," *Ezhegodnik po agrarnoi istorii Vostochnoi Evropy 1965 g.* (Moscow: Moskovskii Universitet, 1970), pp. 42–48.

96. Udal'tsova, "Problemy," p. 146.

97. Cherepnin, "Istoricheskie usloviia," pp. 9–10; idem, "Iz istorii formirovaniia," p. 235; *Istoriia SSSR s drevneishikh vremen do nashikh dnei*, 1:365–76, 476.

98. Valk, "I. I. Smirnov," pp. 37–38.

99. Makovskii, *Razvitie*. See chapter 4 below for more on this thesis, its adherents and opponents. Makovskii summarizes his views in Shunkov, ed., *Perekhod*, pp. 159–65.

100. Bromlei, "Izuchenie," pp. 114–15.

101. Kachanovskii, "O poniatiiakh," pp. 130, 132; *OIIN*, 4:281; Cherepnin, *Obrazovanie*, pp. 182–83. Shunkov, ed., *Perekhod*, p. 161.

102. Vainshtein, "Stanovlenie," pp. 46–47; Danilova, "Stanovlenie," p. 89. For the 1930 and 1933 debates on this issue, see ibid., pp. 89–92, 94–95, 100. L. V. Volkov credits S. V. Voznesenskii with the observation that serfdom must be sought in a feudal epoch ("Problema," p. 16).

103. Danilova, "Stanovlenie," p. 89.

104. Danilova "K itogam," p. 46.

105. I. I. Smirnov, "Problemy," pp. 94–95; A. M. Sakharov, "Rabota," p. 152; Mavrodin, "Feodal'naia," p. 167. For a recent discussion of the problem of the peasant in the "feudal" period for the Soviet historian, see Barg and Skazkin, "Istoriia," pp. 65–67.

106. Zimin, "Problemy," p. 328; Volkov, "Problema," pp. 18–19; Bromlei, Buganov, and Koretskii, "Tsennoe issledovanie," p. 165.

107. Froianov, "Sovetskaia," pp. 29–30, 35. See also *Sudebniki*, p. 91.

108. Man'kov, *Razvitie*, p. 3.

109. Nosov, "Mnogotomnaia," p. 138.

110. Danilova, "Stanovlenie," p. 108; I. I. Smirnov, "Problemy," pp. 95, 97, 99. In the 1920s many historians, among them P. I. Liashchenko, maintained that the Russian peasants were free until the sixteenth century (Volkov, "Problema," p. 15). A. M. Sakharov, stating that "serfdom . . . was established in the time of Kievan Rus'," represents the Leninist position today (*Obrazovanie*, p. 115). For a recent article on Lenin's views on the enserfment, see A. G. Man'kov, "Voprosy krepostnogo prava i krepostnichestva v Rossii v trudakh V. I. Lenina," in N. E. Nosov, ed., *V. I. Lenin i problemy istorii* (Leningrad: Nauka, 1970), pp. 311–44.

111. I. I. Smirnov, "Problemy," p. 102.

112. Cherepnin, "Iz istorii," p. 250.

113. Doroshenko and Ianel', "Zametki," p. 151; Volkov, "Problema," p. 18; Shunkov, ed., *Perekhod*, p. 192.

114. *Ocherki istorii SSSR . . .—konets XV v . . .* , pp. 39, 44–45, 93.

115. Kochin, *Sel'skoe*, p. 380. A recent article on the enserfment of the West-Russian (Lithuanian) peasantry similarly takes the position that there were both free and enserfed peasants at the beginning of the sixteenth century, which was part of the feudal epoch (E. Gudavichius and S. Lazutka, "Protsess zakreposhcheniia

krest'ianstva Litvy i ego otrazhenie v I Litovskom statute 1529 g.," *Istoriia SSSR,* no. 3, 15 [May-June 1970]: 79–81, 87–88, 90) .

116. Doroshenko and Ianel', "Zametki," p. 155; Kashtanov and Klokman, "Sovetskaia," pp. 162–64. See chapter 4, note 75.

117. Grekov, "Opyt," pp. 8–12.

118. Danilova, "Stanovlenie," pp. 99, 104–5.

119. Cherepnin, "Problema," pp. 56, 82, 85; Nosov, "Mnogotomnaia," p. 138.

120. Kulisher, "Nesvobodnoe," p. 178.

121. Danilova, "Stanovlenie," p. 95.

122. Cherepnin, "Problema," p. 58; Danilova, "K itogam," p. 67; Kashtanov, "K izucheniiu oprichniny," p. 102.

123. Makovskii, *Razvitie,* pp. 202–3, 320; "feudally dependent" may not have been a synonym for "enserfed" in Makovskii's lexicon.

124. Nosov, "Mnogotomnaia," p. 139. M. Ia. Volkov dates the introduction of serfdom in the late sixteenth century ("O stanovlenii," pp. 91, 95) . A. N. Sakharov has written that the current "majority" position of Soviet historiography is that free agriculturalists predominated in Russia until the sixteenth century ("O dialektike," pp. 28, 36) .

125. Koretskii, "Novgorodskie." His monograph (*Zakreposhchenie krest'ian i klassovaia bor'ba v Rossii vo vtoroi polovine XVI v.* [Moscow: Nauka, 1970]) reached me as this manuscript was about to be set in type.

126. See Blum's remarks on this subject on pp. 6–8 of *Lord and Peasant.* See also Pipes, *Karamzin's Memoir,* p. 165. S. B. Veselovskii attempted to trace serfdom back to the judicial and fiscal immunities held by landowners (*votchinniki*) in the fourteenth, fifteenth, and first half of the sixteenth centuries (*K voprosu o proiskhozhdenii,* p. 102) . A. E. Presniakov took issue with this interpretation and noted the lack of continuity between the disappearance of immunity documents and serfdom ("Votchinnyi," p. 191) . (This issue will be discussed further in chapters 5 and 6 below) . Presniakov himself in an earlier work expressed the view that the Muscovite service landholder (*pomeshchik*) enjoyed authority over his peasants, an authority acquired as the communes were broken up into service estates, and that this was the key to serfdom (*Moskovskoe tsarstvo,* pp. 102, 104) . On the French serf, see Bloch, *French Rural History,* p. 86.

127. Unlike most scholars, Koretskii says there was little difference in the position of the peasant and agricultural slave in the sixteenth century (*Zakreposhchenie,* p. 189) .

128. The Mongols may have partially limited mobility by attaching each peasant to a tax unit, which he could leave legally only upon finding a substitute. Whether this system continued to prevail, and if so, what its significance in the Muscovite period was, have been matters of considerable dispute (Rozhdestvenskii, "Sel'skoe," pp. 48–49) .

129. See, for example, *GVNP,* nos. 9, 10, 70.

130. M. M. Tsvibak expressed similar convictions in 1934 about the role of the centralized Russian state, which he called "the prison of the people," in the development of serfdom. This position found little support among subsequent Soviet historians, except during the 1956 "thaw" (Sheviakov, "K voprosu," p. 71; Danilova, "Stanovlenie," p. 111; Grekov, *Krest'iane,* p. 732; Zimin, "Problemy istorii," p. 323) . However, A. M. Sakharov noted in 1969 that the state in the first half of the sixteenth century "lacked the force to bind the peasants to the land" (*Obrazovanie,* pp. 87, 115) . Cherepnin's dogmatic assertions against the need for a consolidated state to effect serfdom are hardly convincing ("Problema," pp. 80, 105–6) . Elsewhere he does go so far as to say that "class contradictions were made more intense by the process of the formation of the centralized state" ("Novye dokumenty," p. 52) . See also his *Novgorodskie,* p. 164. The real issue for Soviet historians concerns the interaction between the base and superstructure. The issue of state intervention in social relations has been discussed elsewhere. Another crucial matter for the Soviet historian is how a highly centralized state can arise in conditions of much more primitive economic

conditions. The current answer for the Russian example is that a centralized state was necessary to cope with the problems of the Tatars and other external enemies (A. M. Sakharov, "Lenin ob osnovnykh," pp. 306–8; idem, *Obrazovanie*, p. 92). As has been frequently pointed out, however, this fails to account for the absence of centralization when the threat was greatest, and an ever-increasing degree of centralization once the threat had passed. Another possible Marxist explanation might be that the ruling class of landowners felt the need to create a centralized state in order to bridle the peasantry more effectively (Zimin, "Problemy istorii Rossii XVI v.," p. 317).

131. See Eck for the assertion that the peasant was bound to state obligations, not to the land or the person of a lord (*Le Moyen*, p. 318). This interpretation was initiated by Boris Chicherin in 1856 and continued by M. A. D'iakonov in 1898, only to be very convincingly refuted by V. I. Sergeevich shortly thereafter (*Russkiia . . . drevnosti*, 3:449–57).

132 The amount of scholarship on the middle service class was minimal before the Revolution as well (Novitskii, *Vybornoe*, p. 106).

133. Pipes, *Karamzin's Memoir*, p. 164; Romanovich-Slavatinskii, *Dvorianstvo*, p. 277.

134. Volkov, "Problema," pp. 9–10, 17.

135. This has been a minor issue of Soviet historiography, with frequent references to the Lenin canon (Chistiakova, "Narodnye dvizheniia," pp. 191, 198–99, 201–2, 204).

136. See Barg and Skazkin, "Istoriia," p. 62.

2. The Creation of the Middle Service Class

1. The expansion of Muscovy can be followed in the testaments of its princes (Howes, *The Testaments*). The figures for 1462, 1533, and the end of the sixteenth century are from Kopanev, "Naselenie," pp. 235, 246; that for 1688 is my own. Kopanev noted that P. I. Liashchenko used 37,500 square kilometers for 1462, 110,000 for 1532, and 195,000 for 1584 ("Naselenie," p. 235). While Kopanev's figures may be a bit too large (Moscow may not have controlled all the area he included), Liashchenko's are certainly too small.

2. Jerome Horsey, an Englishman who lived for years in Russia and who ordinarily was well informed, made an observation about the nature of the Muscovite forces on these two frontiers. He said that in fact there were two armies in Muscovy. One consisted "mostly of Tatars" and was used on the western frontier, against Poland and Sweden. The other army consisted "mostly of Russians, except some Poles, Swedes, Dutch, and Scots" and was used against the Crimean Tatars (Hakluyt Society, *Russia at the Close*, p. 181; see also Burdei, "Molodinskaia bitva," p. 59). The report contradicts the general assumption that there was "racial color blindness" in Muscovy. The fact may have been that Ivan IV gave the Tatars encouragement to attack in the west to divert them from his southern flank. A foreigner also could easily get the impression that the southern flank was of greater concern to Moscow than the western: the Tatars were able to sack Moscow, something no Western power could do in the sixteenth century. The record books of the military campaigns (the *razriadnye knigi*) contradict the statement that the Russians fought largely in the south. In the Kievan period the Russians used the Turkic Black Hoods to hold out other nomads; the Muscovites employed the Kasimov Tatars for the same purpose. The well-informed French mercenary Jacques Margeret noted that the Poles in the Russian army in the reign of Boris Godunov were assigned to the southern Tatar frontier out of fear that they would betray Muscovy elsewhere (*Sostoianie*, p. 28). The same principle may have dictated the assignment of Tatars. For a contemporary remark on the necessity of cavalry, rather than infantry, during the reign of Vasilii III (1505–1533), see Denisova, "Pomestnaia," p. 31.

3. Sh., "Dvorianstvo," no. 2, p. 269; Alef, "Reflections," pp. 79–80. Also included in this top group in the *boiarskaia kniga* from 1616 to 1687 (*PSZ*, 2, no. 1243) were *kravchie* (after *okol'nichie*), *chashnik, kaznachei, postel'nich'i* (before *dymnye dvoriane*), then *dumnye d'iaki*, and the *striapchie s kliuchem* (in charge of the wardrobe) (Sh., "Dvorianstvo," no. 3, p. 422; Zagorovskii, *Belgorodskaia*, pp. 26–32). According to M. V. Dovnar-Zapol'skii, in the 1550s these ranks, which conferred the right to sit in the Boyar Council, no longer were bestowed by birth, but only by appointment. As a result the Tsar's Council "lost its aristocratic coloring" ("Vremia Ivana Groznago," pp. 197–98).

4. Zimin, *Reformy*, pp. 168–71, 317–19, 412–14; *Oprichnina*, pp. 107, 364–66. An incomplete list of the men in the upper upper-service class for the last century of the period under review can be found in Glebov-Streshnev, "Spisok", " pp. 130–41. The boyars and *okol'nichie* only went to battle with the ruler, as commanders of his part of the army (Maslovskii, *Zapiski*, 1:7).

5. Gradovskii, "Vysshaia," p. 54. The Oprichnina was one of the most traumatizing phenomena in Muscovy; it played an important role not only in diminishing the political weight of the old upper upper-service class in favor of parvenues and the middle service class, but also in binding the peasant to the land and abasing his person. Orthodox historicist Soviet scholars have reached a crisis in their attempts to rationalize the Oprichnina. A. A. Zimin has tried to palm off Ivan's adventure as rationally necessary to curb Prince Staritskii, the church, and Novgorod, all of which putatively desired to decentralize the Muscovite state (*Oprichnina*, pp. 477–80; "O politicheskikh," p. 41; "Osnovnye etapy," pp. 47, 49). Zimin emphasizes the fragility of the centralization in the sixteenth century. His position represents a triumph of dogma over reason and historical truth: Lenin included the "Moscovite tsardom" of the sixteenth century in the medieval period of Russian history and opposed a centralized state to medieval political fragmentation; therefore there was little centralization in sixteenth-century Moscovy ("Problemy istorii," pp. 323, 329).

R. G. Skrynnikov has shown the utter bankruptcy of the Zimin thesis, and then has created another, equally untenable one. Following the schemes of S. F. Platonov, N. A. Rozhkov, and S. V. Bakhrushin, Skrynnikov has tried to show the Oprichnina as necessarily useful in neutralizing various aristocratic and boyar magnates who desired to fragment the centralized authority (*Nachalo*, pp. 411–12; "Oprichnina i poslednie," pp. 154–60, 170; "Samoderzhavie," pp. 69–75). See also Shapiro, "Ob absoliutizme," p. 71.

At the moment, the notion that the Oprichnina was historically progressive, necessary to liquidate "feudal fragmentation"—which has its origins in S. M. Solov'ev's century-old theory that Ivan's reign represented the triumph of the "state principle" over the "clan principle" and therefore embodied great tension—is the position of official Soviet historiography (Nosov, "Mnogotomnaia," p. 141; *Stanovlenie*, p. 10 [Nosov disassociates himself from this position]; Valk, "I. I. Smirnov," p. 36). Part of the rigidity of this position stems from Stalin's personal emphasis in 1947 on this aspect of Ivan IV's career (Dubrovskii, "Protiv idealizatsii," p. 128).

Zimin and others have shown convincingly that the magnates had no desire to see a fragmentation of the Russian state, but were quite content to vie for power within the centralized framework (*Reformy*, pp. 223–24; "O politicheskikh predposylkakh," pp. 20, 23; "Problemy istorii Rossii XVI v.," p. 327; Volkov, "O stanovlenii," p. 101; Nosov, *Stanovlenie*, p. 199; Shapiro, "Ob absoliutizme," p. 79; Nazarov, "Iz istorii agrarnoi," p. 108). At the height of the anti-Stalin campaign in 1956, V. N. Sheviakov pointed out the absurdity of the claims that the Oprichnina was necessary to centralize and strengthen the Russian national state. There was not even any hint of dismantling the state during Ivan's minority, when the only contention was among various factions for control ("K voprosu," pp. 71–73). S. M. Kashtanov has shown that the Oprichnina, "to avoid conflict," incorporated mainly those lands where boyar land-ownership was not prevailing, rather than annexed boyar lands, in order to curtail "feudal fragmentation" and to liquidate the boyars personally. Perhaps as a sop to the Leninist-Stalinist heritage, Kashtanov says that "subjectively" the goal of the government was to destroy the last *udely* and root out separatism. He then goes on to claim that the Oprichnina was not directed against the boyars, but rather against the peasants, with the goal of enserfing them, mainly in favor of the middle service class. ("K izucheniiu oprichniny," pp. 105–6, 108–9, 116–17).

There can hardly be any question that a relatively high degree of centralization had been achieved in Muscovy by the 1560s (Shmidt, "K izucheniiu," p. 24). A. M. Sakharov's comment that there was not so much centralization in Russia as caprice, despotism, and omnipotence of the bureaucracy is hardly convincing ("Lenin ob osnovnykh," pp. 309–10). Neither is his contention that there is "an objective contradiction between a centralization of power and the preservation of power by the hereditary aristocracy" in the sixteenth century ("V. I. Lenin o sotsial'no-ekonomicheskom razvitii feodal'noi Rossii," *Voprosy istorii* 49, no. 4 [April 1960]:328. The fact of the matter was that many of the objective criteria of centralization were present. There was one army and foreign policy, one judicial system, one system of weights, measures, and currency, a highly developed post communications system linking the whole country with Moscow. There was no longer any struggle over sovereignty among competing political jurisdictions, but rather over a division of the spoils of privilege in Moscow itself. The apparatus of the chancellery (*prikaz*) system was becoming depersonalized, developing a distinctness from the traditional kinship loyalties inherent in the "system of places" (*mestnichestvo*) which was to occur only a century later in the army. Even legal formulations in documents, which had varied widely at the end of the fifteenth century, were much more uniform half a century later (Pokrovskii, "Kupchie," p. 80; A. M. Sakharov, *Obrazovanie*, p. 62).

All attempts at turning the Oprichnina into a rational tool of policy have failed. More moderate historicists try to save the position with statements such as this: "The real substance of the Oprichnina was included in the development of autocratic forms of administration and in the weakening (but not in the elimination) of the boyar aristocracy as a ruling force. In this respect success was achieved" (Shapiro, "Ob absoliutizme," p. 79).

This by no means proves, however, that Ivan had either of these unquestioned achievements in mind as long-range goals when he founded the Oprichnina in 1565. Shapiro's portrayal of Ivan's terror casts doubt on the rationality of his actions, even in Shapiro's own eyes (ibid., p. 74). On the same theme, V. I. Koretskii implies that Ivan consciously used the antagonisms between and among various social elements to weaken them all, thereby increasing his own power ("Zemskii sobor," p. 48). Again, however, this can be stated, but not proved. Given the tendentiousness of Soviet historiography on Ivan IV, it is not surprising that its creators have ignored Herberstein's observation that, with the seizure of Vasilii Ivanovich Shemiachich in 1523 by Vasilii III, there were no lords left who possessed their own castles and principalities (*Commentaries*, p. 81). While one could quibble that *udely* did exist after this time, Herberstein's point is nevertheless well taken: no longer did any Russian lord have a base from which he could threaten the Muscovite autocrat.

V. N. Sheviakov correctly characterized the Oprichnina as a senseless, paranoid destruction of the representatives of all classes of Russian society, boyars, merchants, peasants, artisans, slaves, and others ("K voprosu ob oprichnine," pp. 74–75). D. P. Makovskii also views the Oprichnina as a mad debauch (*Razvitie*, p. 468). Even the classic idealizer of Ivan, the monarchist who in time was to turn Stalinist, R. Iu. Vipper, had to admit, after all was said and done, that the penultimate Riurikovich ruler was insane (*Ivan Groznyi* [Moscow: Dal'fin, 1922], p. 106). So has A. M. Sakharov (*Obrazovanie*, pp. 92, 100, 104–5, 108, 112).

6. Presniakov, "Moskovskoe," 1:10, 28; Veselovskii, *Issledovaniia*, p. 506. Study of the ruling elite has been grossly neglected, for understandable reasons, in the Soviet period. Only one solid book has been published on the subject, a group of posthumous essays on boyar families by S. B. Veselovskii (1876–1952): *Issledovaniia po istorii klassa sluzhilykh zemlevladel'tsev* (Moscow: Nauka, 1969).

7. Pavlov-Sil'vanskii, *Gosudarevy* (1898), p. 165.

8. Iakovlev, *Prikaz"*, p. 259; "Sluzhiloe zemlevladenie," p. 450; Tikhomirov, *Rossiia*, pp. 99–105. Boyars on an average had 852 peasant households, *okol'nichie* had 263 (Keep, "Filaret," p. 350).

9. Barsukov, "Dokladnaia," pp. 1–4. For a fairly complete list of the holdings of the members of the upper service class just before the *Ulozhenie*, see S. V. Rozhdestvenskii, "Rospis' zemel'nykh" vladenii Moskovskago boiarstva 1647–8 goda," *Drevnosti. Trudy Arkheograficheskoi kommissii imp. Moskovskago arkheologicheskago obshchestva* 3 (1913) :193–238. The list reveals, for example, that B. I. Morozov had 6,034 peasant households at the time, his archrival F. I. Sheremetev only 2,791 (ibid., pp. 196, 198). About fifty thousand serfs lived on the lands of Ia. K. Cherkasskii at the end of the 1660s. Their numbers increased by roughly 15 percent in the 1660s (Shchepetov, "Pomeshchich'e," pp. 20, 22).

In 1661 the boyars, *okol'nichie*, and other members of the *Duma* possessed 49,212 inhabited households in the countryside, another 10,375 in towns. This represents about one-eighth of the population in this document—460,297 households (*AMG*, 3, no. 504). Ia. E. Vodarskii has found over 900,000 peasant households in the 1678 census, of which 435,924 belonged to lay lords, 148,799 to church lords, and 110,107 to the court. The rest were subject to no lord ("Chislennost'," p. 229).

10. Novosel'skii, "Rospis'," pp. 88, 149.

11. Sh., "Dvorianstvo," no. 2, p. 269; no. 3, pp. 422–23. Boris Godunov was the last person to hold the rank of *koniushii*.

12. Kliuchevskii, *Istoriia soslovii*, p. 142. A list of over five hundred members of the upper service class (through *dvoriane*) in good standing in 1610–11 can be found in Storozhev, "Materialy," pp. 73–94. A 1621–22 list contains roughly the same number (ibid., pp. 104–20). In 1686 there were 3,233 *stol'niki* and 1,893 *striapchie* (Mikhnevich and Il'enko, "Glavnyi shtab"," p. 6).

13. Iakovlev, *Prikaz"*, p. 259; D'iachenko, *Polnyi*, p. 679.

14. Kliuchevskii, *Istoriia soslovii*, p. 143.

15. The tsar's regiment was sometimes over six thousand strong (ibid.; Burdei, "Molodinskaia," p. 59). The *stol'niki, striapchie*, Moscow *dvoriane*, and *zhil'tsy* were divided into shifts for service purposes. At first there were four shifts, then five by a decree of June 17, 1683, still serving by quarters (*PSZ*, 2, no. 1023). Although they were called the sovereign's regiment, in reality they did not form a general military unit.

16. Myshlaevskii, *Ofitserskii*, pp. 16–17.

17. Chernov, *Vooruzhennye*, p. 125.

18. Sh., "Dvorianstvo," no. 2, p. 269; Bogoiavlenskii, "Voisko," p. 63.

19. *AMG*, 2, no. 424.

20. Novitskii, *Vybornoe*, p. 80; Kliuchevskii, *Istoriia*, p. 142; Sh., "Dvorianskaia," no. 3, p. 423; *AMG*, 2, no. 443. This 1650 document also lists 393 *stol'niki*, 308 *striapchie*, and 1,288 Moscow *dvoriane*.

In the second half of the century the numbers of the lower upper-service class rose rapidly. In 1686 there were over 3,000 *stol'niki*, about 800 *striapchie*, and perhaps 3,000 *zhil'tsy* (Bogoiavlenskii, "Voisko," p. 63; Maslovskii, *Zapiski*, 1:7–8).

21. Kliuchevskii, *Istoriia soslovii*, p. 144. For the numbers at the time of the first and second Crimean campaigns and the first and second Azov campaigns (1687, 1689, 1695, and 1696), see Bobrovskii, *Postoiannyia*, p. 10. For the statistics during the reign of Peter, see Romanovich-Slavatinskii, *Dvorianstvo*, pp. 6–8.

22. Romanovich-Slavatinskii, *Dvorianstvo*, pp. 11–13; Sh., "Dvorianstvo," no. 3, pp. 194–98; Stashevskii, "Sluzhiloe," pp. 10–13.

23. Romanovich-Slavatinskii, *Dvorianstvo*, p. 9.

24. See Appendix, on the military forces of the Muscovite state. The terms *deti boiarskie* and *dvoriane* began to be used systematically about 1433 to refer to military servitors (Cherepnin, *Obrazovanie*, p. 756). In the fifteenth century the terms *dvoriane* and *deti boiarskie* were sometimes used interchangeably. Thus under the year 1462 the first Sofia chronicle speaks of the princely *dvoriane* of Yaroslavl', the Voskresen-

skaia chronicle calls the same people *deti boiarskie* (Sh., "Dvorianstvo," no. 2, p. 561) . Until the mid-sixteenth century *deti boiarskie* were above *dvoriane*. See grant to the Kirillo-Belozerskii monastery, *AAE*, 1, no. 65 (1460) , and first Sofia chronicle, 1433 (Sh., "Dvorianstvo," no. 2, p. 561; Novitskii, *Vybornoe*, p. 10 and elsewhere) .

25. Iakovlev, *Prikaz"*, p. 260.

26. Novitskii, *Vybornye*, pp. 79–80.

27. *Ulozhenie*, 21:47 (all citations of the *Ulozhenie* are by chapter and article numbers) . A somewhat similar categorization was made by E. D. Stashevskii: the boyars, the Moscow gentry, and the provincial *deti boiarskie* ("Sluzhiloe soslovie," p. 8) .

28. Kolesnikova, "Obshchestvenno-politicheskie," p. 258.

29. Vostokov, "Russkoe sluzhiloe," pp. 266, 271.

30. Geisman, *Kratkii*, 1:124, 128; Mikhnevich and Geisman, "Glavnyi shtab"," pp. 18–19, 34. The Soviet historian A. N. Kirpichnikov has portrayed a different military evolution. He says that in the eleventh century in southern Rus' the cavalry became the major armed force in an attempt to hold off the Turkic nomads. Infantry served only as auxiliaries. However, this transition seems not to have occurred in the Volga-Oka basin until after the coming of the Mongols, who were the first steppe horsemen to harry northeastern Rus' ("Vooruzhenie," pp. 45–46, 53) . He also discusses the issue of borrowing enemy tactics and technology and arrives at a "compromise" solution: the borrowing was conscious, selective, adaptive, and necessary (ibid., pp. 51–52) .

31. Elchaninov, "Ocherk"," pp. 47–48; Gorskii, *Ocherki*, pp. 220–22. The Soviet military historian E. A. Razin paints a different picture. He claims there were three parts of the Muscovite army at the end of the fifteenth century: contingents organized around the court at Moscow; units of townsmen; units levied from the peasantry (*Istoriia*, 2: 303–5, 313) . See also Maslovskii, *Zapiski*, 1:6; Bobrovskii, *Perekhod"*, p. 94.

32. Staden, *Land*, p. 88.

33. *PSRL*, 9: 251. Initially the *dvoriane* may have had no right to possess lands and lived off what the court provided (Novitskii, *Dvorianstvo*, p. 4) .

34. Private armies were retained until the reign of Ivan IV by the Bel'skii and Odoevskii princes, who commanded them independently of the Moscow generals (Kliuchevskii, *Istoriia soslovii*, p. 133) .

35. Bogoiavlenskii, "Vooruzhenie," p. 264.

36. Leont'ev, *Obrazovanie*, pp. 78–79; Buganov, " 'Gosudarev razriad' 1556 g.," p. 221. A. A. Zimin opts for a later date, 1531 (*Reformy*, p. 450) . On the early history of the *mestnichestvo* system, see A. A. Zimin, "Istochniki po istorii mestnichestva v XV-pervoi treti XVI v.," *Arkheograficheskii ezhegodnik za 1968 god* (Moscow: Nauka, 1970) :109–18.

37. The origin of the Russian *pomest'e* has been debated by historians for decades (Makovskii, *Razvitie*, pp. 175–77) . The assumption has usually been that the Russians could not have come up with the idea themselves and so must have borrowed it from some place else. Some have compared it with the Western European benefice (Rozhkov, "Sel'skoe," 1:177) . Others have related it to the Byzantine *pronoia*, the Moslem *iqta*, or the Ottoman military fief, the *timar* (Szeftel, "Aspects," p. 182) . The term *pomest'e* has long been considered by some as a translation of the Greek word *topion* (El'iashevich, *Istoriia*, 1:369) . The notion of borrowing was questioned by S. V. Rozhdestvenskii (*Sluzhiloe*, pp. iii, 3–6) . S. B. Veselovskii rejected it entirely (*Feodal'noe*, p. 282) . A useful discussion of the *pomest'e* in comparison with the fief can be found in George Vernadsky, "Feudalism in Russia," *Speculum* 14:302–23.

38. Such people were called *slugi pod dvorskim*, or *slugi dvortsovye* (Kliuchevskii, *Istoriia soslovii*, p. 85; Cherepnin, "Usloviia," p. 91) .

39. *SGGD*, 1, no. 22; *DDG*, no. 1; Howes, *Testaments*, pp. 186–87. On other possible antecedents of the *pomest'e*, see the monastery life grants (*AIuB*, 2, no. 147-I; *AIu*, no. 8; *AAE*, 1, no. 74-I) . See also Cherepnin, *Obrazovanie*, pp. 195–96.

40. Gradovskii, "Vysshaia," p. 57; Miliukov, *Ocherki* (1900) , 1:178. Some historians have sensed that the conditional land grants were made only to court servants who

were dependent on the prince. Free people, boyars, and *deti boiarski* had a right to income-producing administrative and court posts in the thirteenth through fifteenth centuries (Nosov, "Boiarskaia kniga," p. 213). A slightly different analysis of the role of land-ownership is offered by V. B. El'iashevich *(Istoriia,* 1:234–47).

41. See *SGGD,* 1, nos. 139–43; *AAE,* 1, no. 141 (Vasilii III, in 1505, freed the peasants from *namestnik* and *tiun* jurisdiction except in murder and robbery cases). See also *PSRL,* 4: 158, under "1500." On service boyars settled in Novgorod in 1476, see the *Razriadnaia Kniga Beketova* (Karamzin, *Istoriia,* 6:n. 201; Cherepnin, *Obrazovanie,* pp. 197–205). See also the *Sudebnik* of 1497, arts. 62, 63; Stashevskii, "Sluzhiloe soslovie," p. 18; El'iashevich, *Istoriia,* 1:373. The nineteenth-century historian V. N. Storozhev placed the beginning of the *pomest'e* system operations at the beginning of the sixteenth century *(Istoriko,* p. 10).

42. Kliuchevskii, *Istoriia soslovii,* pp. 150–51; Bernadskii, *Novgorod,* pp. 320–22; Polosin, "Pomestnoe pravo," p. 38; Bazilevich, "Novgorodskie pomeshchiki," pp. 62–78; Novitskii, *Vybornoe,* p. 6. L. V. Cherepnin gives a lesser number of one thousand landowners exiled from Novgorod ("Usloviia," p. 92). L. V. Danilova says that traces of the old Novgorodian dialect, customs, and dress can be found more in certain districts of the north (Pomor'e) and Siberia than in the Novgorod region itself because of the massive number of exiles at the end of the fifteenth century ("Usloviia," p. 133).

43 Denisova, "Pomestnaia konnitsa," p. 29.

44. Veselovskii, *Feodal'noe,* pp. 283–99. One of the tenets of what might be termed today's official Soviet historiography is that the service land system was created by the confiscation of princely holdings and the giving of them as military fiefs to the former slaves of these princes and boyars. N. E. Nosov has correctly criticized this notion of the "democratization" of landholding and the landholding class as not corresponding to the facts ("Mnogotomnaia," p. 141).

45. Platonov, *Lektsii,* p. 195. This assumes the "black lands" of the Pomor'e would not have been tapped until sometime in the second half of the sixteenth century, when the *pomeshchiki* had control of their land grants and lived in the provinces.

46. Makovskii, *Razvitie,* p. 178. See, for example, Tikhomirov and Floria, "Toropetskaia," pp. 318–57. A publicist in the time of Ivan IV's minority recommended an extension of this system. The rents should be collected and delivered to the serviceman in town, so that he would always be immediately available for service (Kolesnikova, "Obshchestvenno-politicheskaia," p. 259). S. B. Veselovskii took the position that the *pomeshchik* no later than the beginning of the sixteenth century had the right to change and increase the obligations of his peasants, so long as he did not destroy them. He seems, however, to have believed that most *pomeshchiki* simply collected the traditional rents, much like the *kormlenshchiki* *(Feodal'noe,* pp. 309–10). Whether the lord would dare abuse his free peasants at this time is not discussed. The surviving evidence hints that those who did abuse their peasants were sadists or insane.

47. Makovskii, *Razvitie,* pp. 179-83; Polosin, "Pomestnoe pravo," pp. 36, 45; Veselovskii, *Feodal'noe,* p. 263.

48. Gradovskii, "Vysshaia," p. 57. On the income of a *kormlenie,* see Nosov, *Stanovlenie,* pp. 331–33.

49. Herberstein, *Commentaries,* p. 56. See Zimin, *Reformy,* pp. 445–48, for other estimates of the size of the Russian army. See also Denisova, "Pomestnaia," p. 31.

50. Kliuchevskii, *Istoriia soslovii,* p. 76. The origin of the term *deti boiarskie* is unclear. The problem is whether they were real children of boyars, as the term literally implies, or whether the term represents a survival of patriarchalism and therefore means the servicemen of a boyar's estate. As the rank of boyar was never herditary, the latter possibility seems more likely (Makovskii, *Razvitie,* p. 286; Pavlov-Sil'vanskii, *Feodalism,* pp. 112–13).

51. In 1638 and 1640 the government permitted *deti boiarskie* of peasant origin who also had been musketeers to remain in the middle service class (Novosel'skii, "Dela," p. 151; idem, "Vol'nye," pp. 62–63).

286

52. In 1585 in the town of Epifan' cossacks were converted into *deti boiarskie* and given service land grants of thirty to forty *chetverti* of land (D'iakonov, *Ocherki obshchestvennago* [1912], p. 265; Makovskii, *Razvitie*, pp. 190–91).

53. Zimin, *Oprichnina*, p. 206. In 1476 servants from boyar households were made into *pomeshchiki*. In 1489 townsmen exiled from Viatka were made *pomeshchiki* in Borovsk and Kremenets (Nosov, "Mnogotomnaia," p. 141, citing Veselovskii, *Feodal'noe*, pp. 288–99; Sh., "Dvorianstvo," no. 3, p. 201; Makovskii, *Razvitie*, p. 185). Boris Godunov enrolled slaves in the *deti boiarskie* (Diakonov [1912], p. 265). After the annexation of Novgorod in the sixteenth century, the percentage of persons receiving *pomest'e* lands who were former boyar slaves was smaller than it had been in the last quarter of the sixteenth century (Nosov, "Mnogotomnaia," p. 141). For a discussion of how many peasants and slaves were in the ranks of the *deti boiarskie*, see Vladimirskii-Budanov, *Obzor*", p. 119.

54. Platonov, *Lektsii*, p. 194. See the tables in Makovskii, *Razvitie*, pp. 186, 370, on the social origin of the 519 members of the middle service class at Smolensk in 1574. There is not one recognizable noble name in the list. As A. M. Sakharov has expressed it, "any personally free man could become a serviceman" in the sixteenth century (*Obrazovanie*, p. 95).

55. D'iakonov, *Ocherki* (1912), p. 259.

56. Burdei, "Molodinskaia," p. 58; Markov, *Istoriia*, 3:120; Chernov, "TsGADA," p. 138.

Prior to the consolidation of the Muscovite state the great prince's court made up the center unit, and the right and left regiments represented provincial princes' courts and allied armies. Mercenary nomads made up the rear guard. "Appanage" princes were an ambush or reserve unit (Geisman, *Kratkii*, 1:130).

57. Bogoiavlenskii, "Vooruzhenie," p. 260; Geisman, *Kratkii*, 1:131.

58. Kirpichnikov, "Voennoe," p. 74.

59. *AMG*, 1, no. 85; ibid., 2, nos. 420, 559, 564, 587; Staden, *Land*, pp. 60, 73, 76.

60. Burdei, "Molodinskaia," pp. 60–61.

61. Maslovskii, *Zapiski*, 1:56; Denisova, "Pomestnaia," p. 42. This subject will also be discussed in chapter 12 below.

62. Zagorovskii, *Belgorodskaia*, p. 53; Snegirov, "Storozhaia sluzhba," pp. 29–31. On Tatar tactics, see Nikitin, "Oboronitel'nye," p. 202; Novosel'skii, *Bor'ba*, p. 211; Hakluyt Society, *Russia at the Close*, p. 183.

63. Beskrovnyi, *Khrestomatiia*, pp. 45–46; Herberstein, *Commentaries*, p. 56 (cf. his description of Tatar horsemen on p. 103). Similar observations were made by Englishmen (Hakluyt Society, *Early Voyages*, 1:39–40). See also Podobedova, *Miniatiury*, p. 237.

64. Denisova, "Pomestnaia," pp. 38–39; Markov, *Istoriia*, 3:116.

65. On the production of iron weapons (swords, lances, arrow heads, war axes, helmets, shields, and mail) in the Kievan period of Russian history, see Kolchin, "Chernaia metallurgiia," pp. 130–50. For detailed information with many illustrations of this weaponry, see A. N. Kirpichnikov, "Drevnerusskoe oruzhie," *Arkheologiia SSSR. Svod arkheologicheskikh istochnikov*, E1–36 (1966), 2 vols. For a summary of this evidence, see Kirpichnikov's article, "Vooruzhenie," pp. 42–55.

66. Chernov, "TsGADA," p. 127; Razin, *Istoriia*, 2:311; Bogoiavlenskii, "Vooruzhenie," p. 259. Herberstein listed the bow, javelin, hatchet, a staff like a caestus (*kisten*), swords for the wealthy (cuirasses for them, too), quilted jacket (*tegiliai*), light spears (*Commentaries*, p. 56).

67. Bogoiavlenskii, "Vooruzhenie," p. 266; Kirpichnikov, "Vooruzhenie," p. 51.

68. Denisova, "Pomestnaia," p. 38. Bogoiavlenskii says an oriental sabre cost several hundred rubles ("Vooruzhenie," p. 266).

69. Chernov, "TsGADA," p. 128.

70. *Arkhiv*" *istoriko-iuridicheskikh*", *izd. Kalachovym*", 3 (1861), otd. 2, pp. 25–88. Nosov ("Boiarskaia kniga," p. 204) says armaments must have cost about six rubles. See also Kirpichnikov, "Voennoe," p. 72. For a list of the approximately twenty occu-

pations of the 115 professionals employed in Ivan IV's armory (*Bronnyi prikaz*) in 1573, see Al'shits, "Novyi," pp. 14, 40–42.

71. Denisova, "Pomestnaia," pp. 32–38. According to this author, those who have contended that the Russian army was little more than a horde at this time are mistaken because the facts indicate that there was a great deal of uniformity in arms and armor dictated by the government (ibid., p. 38).

72. *AMG*, 2, no. 85.

73. Sergeevich, "Voennyia," p. 63.

74. See the *Ulozhenie* of 1649, 16: 61; Sergeevich, "Voennyia sily," p. 46.

75. Sh., "Dvorianstvo," no. 2, p. 257.

76. Denisova, "Pomestnaia," p. 41; Sergeevich, "Voennyia sily," p. 63.

77. Baiov, *Kurs*", 1:43; Myshlaevskii, *Ofitserskii*, p. 16.

78. Bogoiavlenskii, "Voisko," p. 63; Buganov, "Gosudarev razriad 1556 g.," p. 225; Razin, *Istoriia*, 2:307; Buganov, "Istochniki," pp. 219–20; Zimin, *Reformy*, pp. 196, 334, 342, 344–45; idem, *Oprichnina*, p. 156; idem, "K istorii voennykh," pp. 345–48. N. E. Nosov is no doubt correct in saying that there was no antiboyar bias in the 1549–50 moves (*Stanovlenie*, pp. 30, 38–43).

79. *Opisanie MAMIu*, 17:245, 283. This problem will be discussed in greater detail in chapter 12.

80. Bobrovskii, *Perekhod*", pp. 110–11; Shelekhov, "Glavnoe intendantskoe," p. 1. The result was that the Russian army almost never pursued and decisively annihilated a defeated enemy because the troops were too busy scrambling for what the vanquished had left behind. An exception to this was the active pursuit after the 1572 Molodi victory over the Tatars (Burdei, "Molodinskaia bitva," p. 74).

81. Sh., "Dvorianstvo," no. 2, p. 538.

82. *Sudebnik* 1550, art. 26; *MS*, p. 4.

83. "Until the seventeenth century the [middle service class] cavalry was the main army bearing all the burdens of war, both offensive and defensive" (Bogoiavlenskii, "Vooruzhenie," p. 259).

84. Russian historiography contains considerable discussion about the forces advocating expansion at the expense of the Tatars in the south and those desiring an outlet on the Baltic, the latter being those who desired the Livonian War. Unfortunately most of this discussion remains in the realm of speculation (Shmidt, "Voprosy," p. 132).

85. See chapter 5 below.

86. Rozhkov, *Russkaia istoriia*, 4:5.

87. Sometimes the collective that ruled Muscovy in the period 1547–60 is called the "Selected" or "Chosen" Council (*Izbrannaia rada*). Upon occasion I shall use this term, aware of the fact that A. M. Grobovsky has argued that the "selected council" was a moral abstraction created by Prince Kurbskii in his polemics with Ivan IV to symbolize the men in the Tsar's government prior to the Oprichnina; that is, there was not any particular inner circle or ruling group, as has been argued by some historians (*The "Chosen Council" of Ivan IV: A Reinterpretation* [Brooklyn, N. Y.: Theo. Gaus' Sons, 1969]). I think my use of the term is consistent with this view: those making government policy for and/or with Ivan from 1547 to 1560. See also G. I. Belozertsov, "O formirovanii znacheniia ad"ektivirovannoi formy prichastiia *izbrannyi* 'luchshii, otbornyi'," *Issledovaniia po slovoobrazovaniiu i leksikologii drevnerusskogo iazyka* (Moscow: Nauka, 1969), pp. 296–304.

88. *Khrestomatiia . . . XVI-XVII*, pp. 72–73.

89. Nosov, *Stanovlenie*, pp. 16–23; *Sudebniki*, pp. 162, 176–77, 260–64; Dovnar-Zapol'skii, "Vremia," pp. 167–68, 187–92; Zimin, *Reformy*, pp. 325–26; Shmidt, "Pravitel'stvennaia," pp. 28, 41; Presniakov, "Votchinnyi," p. 190. Not all historians agree that there was a 1549 meeting, but the current consensus is that something did transpire similar to what I have described (Hulbert, "Sixteenth Century," chap. 4). The *Sudebnik* of 1550 formalized the limitations on the competence of the *namestniki* (A. M. Sakharov, *Obrazovanie*, pp. 96–97; *Sudebniki*, arts. 62, 64, 68; pp. 191, 251).

90. Nosov, *Stanovlenie*, p. 72.

91. This was recommended by the monk Ermolai Erazm (Makovskii, *Razvitie*, p. 511). N. E. Nosov refutes A. A. Zimin's contention (*Reformy*, pp. 429–36) that there was no decree repealing *kormlenie* ("Zemskaia reforma," p. 155, idem, *Stanovlenie*, pp. 375, 421–526). See also Shmidt, "K istorii zemskoi," p. 125.

92. Staden, *The Land*, p. 8; Hakluyt Society, *Early Voyages*, 1:38–39.

93. Zimin, "Osnovnye etapy," p. 44; idem, *Reformy*, pp. 329–30, 398, 401, 418–36; idem, *Oprichnina*, p. 386; Tkhorzhevskii, "Pomest'e," p. 73; Shmidt, "K istorii zemskoi," pp. 132–33; Nosov, "Belozerskaia," pp. 50–53; idem, "Gubnaia reforma," p. 233; idem, *Ocherki po istorii mestnogo upravleniia russkogo gosudarstva pervoi poloviny XVI veka* (Moscow-Leningrad: AN SSSR, 1957).

94. Nosov, *Stanovlenie*, p. 60; Veselovskii, *Feodal'noe*, p. 274–80. S. M. Kashtanov's notion of the origin of the *gorodovoi prikazchik* differs from the exposition of N. E. Nosov, which is presented here. However, there is no doubt that the officials were middle service class *pomeshchiki* (Kashtanov, "K probleme mestnogo," pp. 137–38; Zimin, *Reformy*, pp. 191–94, 254–55, 258, 357–60). My mind balks at the current Soviet dogma that the robbery and theft (*razboi, tat'ba*) dealt with by the *guba* officials were "anti-feudal uprisings" (see Zimin, "Osnovnye etapy," pp. 48, 52). S. M. Kashtanov goes even further and claims that the *guba* reform was instituted to "suppress the class struggle of a population resisting enserfment" ("K probleme mestnogo," p. 147). His definition of "serfdom" is discussed in chapter 4 below.

95. Norretranders, *Shaping of Czardom*, pp. 124, 179; Nosov, "Gubnaia reforma."

96. N. E. Nosov has argued that provincial self-administration was sold to the townsmen, members of the middle service class, and wealthy peasants, all of whom were willing to pay more for the right to govern themselves than the central government, facing heavy military expenditures, could garner from the old *kormlenie* system (*Stanovlenie*, pp. 361, 381).

97. N. E. Nosov correctly points out that the *komlenshchiki-namestniki* were not the bearers of feudal reaction and separatism in the 1550s and notes that the Soviet view of the interests that were served by the reforms of the mid-1550s needs correction ("Boiarskaia kniga," p. 227). See also A. M. Sakharov, *Obrazovanie*, p. 100. The Soviet historian A. A. Zimin has maintained that the functions of the *guba* officials were broadened considerably during the Oprichnina ("Osnovnye etapy," p. 48; *Oprichnina*, pp. 386–87, 427). This would be a logical concomitant of the increasing authority which lords were granted over their peasants at this time, but unfortunately Zimin's notions about the *guba* are not supported by the evidence. He cites a 1571 document, which differs hardly at all from another one of 1555, long before the Oprichnina (Dewey, *Muscovite*, pp. 36–40; *AAE*, 1, no. 281; *PRP*, 4:179–85).

98. See chapter 5 below.

99. *AAE*, 1, no. 225; A. A. Zimin, ed., *Tysiachnaia kniga 1550 g. i dvorovaia tetrad' 50-kh godov XVI v.* (Moscow-Leningrad: Akademiia Nauk SSSR, 1950), pp. 51–108; Novitskii, *Vybornoe*, p. 7.

100. Veselovskii, *Feodal'noe*, p. 320.

101. Note also the laws of August 31, 1587, and 1622, which went into the *Ulozhenie* of 1649, 16:1.

102. Veselovskii, *Feodal'noe*, pp. 314–19; I. I. Smirnov, *Ocherki*, pp. 407–22. The measure to create the "selected thousand" may not have been fully effected (Zimin, "K istorii voennykh reform," pp. 348–51; idem, *Reformy*, pp. 366–67, 371, 375; *Tysiachnaia kniga*, pp. 5–6, 53–103). If the "selected thousand" existed only on paper, problems arise in other areas. Peasant black land is assumed to have been present even in the center of Muscovy until the 1550s. S. F. Platonov attributed peasant mobility and the chaos it caused in Ivan's reign mainly to the conversion of black land into service land. He considered this factor more unsettling than the Oprichnina and far more so than the 1571 Tatar raid and the plagues and famines of the period (*Lektsii*, p. 198). The expropriation of the peasant black land in favor of the *pomeshchiki* may well have begun with the creation of the "selected thousand." Reviewing the evidence,

N. E. Nosov agrees with I. I. Smirnov that the "selected thousand" project was largely carried out (*Stanovlenie*, p. 392).

103. Nosov, "Boiarskaia kniga 1556 g.," pp. 202–4, 211. Many compensation books have survived. See, for example, Al'shits, "Novyi"; Zimin, *Tysiachnaia kniga*, pp. 220–46.

104. Sergeevich, "Voennyia," p. 24. There seems to have been no universal system of compensation in Muscovy. The number of grades varied from place to place, as did the compensation attached to each grade. There seems to have been only one cash value in a given locale for each grade, but there might be several land compensation figures for each grade. In 1584 in Pereiaslavl' the third grade was worth 10 rubles and 250, 200, or 150 *cheti* of land; the fourth grade was worth 9 rubles and 150 *cheti*, and so on (Storozhev, *Materialy*, p. 20).

105. Kliuchevskii, *Istoriia*, p. 159; Vostokov, "Russkoe," pp. 269–72: Storozhev, "Materialy," p. 4.

106. Makovskii, *Razvitie*, pp. 191–92. In the seventeenth century the percentages were even lower—from 5 to 40 (Chernov, *Vooruzhennye*, pp. 157–58; Stashevskii, "Sluzhiloe soslovie," p. 21; Sergeevich, "Voennyia sily," pp. 38–43).

107. Makovskii, *Razvitie*, pp. 180, 189.

108. Storozhev, *Istoriko*, p. 173; *Ulozhenie*, 16:42.

109. Sergeevich, "Voennyia sily," pp. 29–32; Samokvasov, *Krest'iane*, p. 32; Novitskii, *Vybornoe*, p. 84. The monk-publicist of the 1540s, Ermolai Erazm, considered that necessity was a virtue. He recommended giving servicemen only land and no cash (Kolesnikova, "Obshchestvenno-politicheskie," p. 258).

110. Makovskii, *Razvitie*, pp. 177, 189.

111. See also laws of 1551 and 1552 (Makovskii, *Razvitie*, p. 183). The principle that everyone who owned land had to render service was repeated in the *Ulozhenie* of 1649, 17:37. If someone bought an hereditary estate (*votchina*) but did not want to serve, it was to be confiscated: see ibid., 17:41, 45–55 for exceptions.

112. *PSRL*, 13:269 (translated in Kliuchevskii, *Istoriia soslovii*, p. 155); Veselovskii, *Soshnoe*, 2:347–57. An arrangement similar to this one was suggested by Ermolai Erazm in the 1540s (Kolesnikova, "Obshchestvenno-politicheskie," p. 259).

113. In 1625 the government decreed that servicemen could not mortgage their clothing and weapons for drink (*AMG*, 1, no. 199). That this was a hazard can be seen in the travel accounts of Olearius, pp. 142–46, and Maierberg, p. 79.

114. A lord was paid two rubles for each fully-armed slave, five rubles for those above the required norm (Nosov, "Boiarskaia kniga," p. 203). The text is in Tatishchev, *Sudebnik*", p. 141.

115. Denisova, "Pomestnaia," p. 32. It should be remembered that at this same time the *pomeshchiki* obtained the right to litigate directly before the tsar in their own cases, rather than before a bureaucrat, except for cases involving robbery, theft, and murder.

116. Veselovskii, *Feodal'noe*, pp. 89, 308–9; Storozhev, *Istoriko*, p. 201. Elsewhere, V. N. Storozhev has said that confiscation of land for failure to report for service or to perform it was introduced only in 1604; Ivan simply fined the delinquent (*Istoriko*, p. 24).

117. Zimin, *Reformy*, pp. 438–40.

118. Sergeevich, "Voennyia," p. 61; Denisova, "Pomestnaia," pp. 32–33.

119. Zimin, *Peresvetov*, p. 356; *Reformy*, p. 448; "Nekotorye voprosy," p. 108. This is one of the disputed issues of Russian historiography. Others have maintained that the slaves brought by *dvoriane* and *deti boiarskie* played no active role in combat, but rather guarded the baggage train, collected supplies, cared for the horses, and otherwise were engaged in auxiliary activities (Elchaninov, "Ocherk"," p. 47). On the other hand, A. V. Chernov maintained that "it is not true that slaves did not fight, but only defended their lords. They were armed better than their owners, fulfilled the most dangerous operations, and in fact went ahead of the middle service class cavalry in such operations" ("TsGADA," p. 129).

120. Denisova, "Pomestnaia," p. 33.

121. See chapter 5 below.

122. Zimin, *Reformy*, p. 356.

123. On the *krugovaia poruka*, see Horace W. Dewey and Ann M. Kleimola, "Suretyship and Collective Responsibility in pre-Petrine Russia," *Jahrbucher fur Geschichte Osteuropas* 18, no. 3 (September 1970) :337–54.

124. *Sudebnik*, art. 81; *AI*, 1, no. 154-XII.

125. Sh., "Dvorianstvo," no. 2, p. 568 (from *DRV*, 20:171) ; Dovnar-Zapol'skii, "Vremia," pp. 193–95.

126. *AI*, 1, no. 154-VII; *PRP*, 4:525-26.

127. Zimin, *Reformy*, pp. 462–63, 467.

128. *Sudebnik* of 1589, art. 146.

129. *PRP*, 4:524, 529–32, 560–62; Kliuchevskii, *Istoriia soslovii*, p. 205; Nosov, *Stanovlenie*, pp. 111, 147; Sh., "Dvorianstvo," no. 3, p. 190; Storozhev, *Istoriko*, pp. 12–14, 18–20; Veselovskii, *Feodal'noe*, pp. 47–50; Skrynnikov, "Oprichnina," pp. 154, 173; Skrynnikov, "Oprichnaia," p. 223; El'iashevich, *Istoriia*, 2:34–38; Zimin, *Oprichnina*, pp. 93–94.

130. Kliuchevskii, *Istoriia*, p. 204; *Sudebnik*, art. 85. A. A. Zimin sees article 85 as being of a "compromise" character, rather than a specific favor to the middle service class, a position which I. I. Smirnov had held (*Reformy*, pp. 350–52, 469–70) . N. E. Nosov sensibly portrays article 85 as being directed not against the princes and boyars, but in defense of private, lay land-ownership against outsiders, mainly the church (*Stanovlenie*, p. 35) . See also Shigeto Toriyama, "Character of the Reforms Under the Reign of Ivan IV. On the Interpretations of Article 85 of the Sudebnik (1550) ," *Slavic Studies* (Hokkaido) , no. 5 (1961) :17–31; ibid., no. 6 (1961) :1–26.

131. Zimin, *Reformy*, pp. 252, 340; Sheviakov, "K voprosu," p. 72. See also article 73 ,of the *Sudebnik* of 1550 which regulates the claiming of lands held under trusteeship. This was a new article in the code and may reflect partially the struggle for lands which had occurred in the 1530s and 1540s: magnates could appropriate others' lands and claim they were holding them in trust. This would also explain the interest of Ermolai Erazm in a general survey of the land in the 1540s (Kolesnikova, "Obshchestvenno-politicheskie," p. 255) .

132. Valk, "I. I. Smirnov," p. 26; Nosov, *Stanovlenie*, p. 26.

133. Sadikov, *Ocherki*, pp. 50–52, 54; Polosin, "Pomestnoe pravo," p. 55; A. M. Sakharov, *Obrazovanie*, p. 106.

134. A. A. Zimin, on the other hand, seems to think that this was the case (*Oprichnina*, pp. 312–13) . Skrynnikov, "Samoderzhavie," p. 82; El'iashevich, *Istoriia*, 2:46; Nosov, *Stanovlenie*, pp. 112- 15. It is also highly unlikely that such measures were viewed as a specific alternative to binding the peasants to the land. The reasoning might have been as follows: the peasants prefer to live on large estates; we can either forbid them from moving to the large estates by binding them to the small service landholdings, or else subdivide the estates so the alternative of living on large estates or small service holdings will not exist. We know that the peasants were bound to the land beginning in 1581, but there is no evidence that the earlier land legislation was an attempt to effect the same goal of stabilizing the population (Stashevskii, "K" istorii kolonizatsii," p. 246) .

135. Veselovskii, *Oprichnina*, pp. 145–55, 354–478.

136. Burdei, "Molodinskaia bitva," p. 75; Veselovskii, *Feodal'noe*, p. 97; Alekseev, *Agrarnaia*, p. 221. This obviously goes counter to the view held by such Soviet historians as I. I. Smirnov and S. N. Bakhrushin that the Oprichnina was a middle service class reform directed at the final destruction of the boyars, liquidation of boyar landownership, and replacement of hereditary estates by service landholding. S. M. Kashtanov, varying the interpretation of these two, has written that "the basic task of the Oprichnina was the guaranteeing of the middle service class with land and peasants." However, he says that the Oprichnina was directed more against the peasantry than the boyars ("K izucheniiu," pp. 98, 105, 108; Skrynnikov, "Oprichnina," pp. 152, 173–74; Danilova, "Usloviia," p. 118; Zimin, *Oprichnina*, pp. 340–41; Kobrin, "Istoch-

niki," p. 124). R. G. Skrynnikov views the Oprichnina as a mechanism to crush the aristocracy in favor of absolutism. But instead of organizing the middle service class as a whole for this purpose, the government organized, according to Skrynnikov, a privileged middle service class guard, the Oprichnina ("Samoderzhavie," pp. 78, 94).

137. Zimin, *Oprichnina*, pp. 140–43, 146, 150–51, 209, 354; Skrynnikov, "Oprichnaia," pp. 231–32, 236–39, 248.

138. Polosin, "Pomestnoe pravo," p. 53; Shmidt, "Voprosy," p. 123; Zimin, *Reformy*, p. 339.

139. Skrynnikov, "Samoderzhavie," p. 97; Zimin, *Oprichnina*, pp. 166–76, 202; Shapiro, "Ob absoliutizme," p. 73.

140. Skrynnikov, "Samoderzhavie," p. 90.

141. Shapiro, "Ob asoliutizme," p. 73.

142. Zimin, *Reformy*, p. 224.

143. *PRP*, 5:461–62. The 1572–73 law was renewed by Filaret's government in 1628 when it was trying to raise funds for the projected war to recover Smolensk. The devastation in the center of Muscovy after the Time of Troubles was similar to that after the Oprichnina.

144. Koretskii, "Zemskii sobor," p. 34. G. D. Burdei offered the alternative suggestion that this measure was a reward to the middle service class for the 1572 victory over the Crimean Tatars at Molodi ("Molodinskaia bitva," pp. 74–75).

145. Soviet historiography frequently has difficulty with issues involving religion as in the question of whether the church should own land and in general be involved in the "world." Many boyars opposed church land-ownership and were in favor of liquidating it. Some Soviet materialist historians have attributed this phenomenon solely to a desire on the part of lay magnates to conserve their own latifundia by liquidating those of the monasteries. Others have said that the Trans-Volga Elder "Non-possessor" ideology expressed the sentiments of the free peasants who were worried about potential takeover of their lands (Zimin, "Osnovnye etapy," p. 42).

146. Kashtanov, "Ogranichenie," p. 284; Budovnits, *Monastyri*, pp. 259, 336.

147. Nosov, *Stanovlenie*, pp. 30, 133; Makovskii, *Razvitie*, p. 245; Platonov, *Lektsii*, p. 199; Koretskii, "Bor'ba," p. 169; Hakluyt Society, *Early Voyages*, 1:37; El'iashevich, *Istoriia*, 1:270. A 1535 measure forbade monastery purchase of land from servicemen (*deti boiarskie*) without government consent so that land would not go "out of service" (I. I. Smirnov, *Ocherki*, pp. 46–47; A. M. Sakharov, *Obrazovanie*, p. 89).

148. Storozhev, *Istoriko*, pp. 16–17; Zimin, *Reformy*, pp. 320–21, 375–85; Nosov, *Stanovlenie*, pp. 108–9; Zimin, *Peresvetov*, pp. 80, 91, 95, 101; *Stoglav*, questions 16, 56, 101; *AAE*, 1, no. 227; *PRP*, 4:523, 555. On the background of the 1551 legislation, see Moiseeva, *Valaamskaia beseda*, pp. 15–50, 162–63.

M. Gorchakov observed a century ago that the Church Council of 1551 had little or no impact (*Monastyrskii*, pp. 49–51). However, the subsequent law of May 11, 1551, curtailed purchase of land by great monasteries (Zimin, *Reformy*, pp. 389–90; Zaustsinkii, "Makarii," 218: 6–11; El'iashevich, *Istoriia*, 2:21–23, 34, 41–42; Veselovskii, *Feodal'noe*, pp. 33–35, 91–93; Skrynnikov, "Oprichnaia zemel'naia," p. 223).

149. *AI*, 1, no. 154-XIX, with the explicit provision "so that land won't go out of service"; *PRP*, 4:531–32. The 1572 decree could be seen as Ivan IV's answer to Kurbskii, who had complained that the growth of monastery landholding was impoverishing the military class. D'iakonov, *Ocherki* (1912), p. 265; El'iashevich, *Istoriia*, 2:42.

150. *SGGD*, 1, no. 200. It was reaffirmed on January 15, 1581. *AAE*, 1, no. 308; *PRP*, 4:528; El'iashevich, *Istoriia*, 2:42–44; Veselovskii, *Feodal'noe*, p. 35.

151. *SGGD*, 1, no. 202. This temporary *(do gosudareva ukazu*—like the "forbidden years") decree noted that the prohibition had been promulgated "because of the impoverishment of the army" (D'iakonov [1912], p. 266; Veselovskii, *Feodal'noe*, p. 101). See the article by V. A. Petrov, "Sobornoe ulozhenie 1584 goda ob otmene tarkhanov," *Sbornik statei posv. S. F. Platonovu* (Peterburg, 1922), pp. 191–201; Kulisher,

"Nesvobodnoe," p. 196; Gorchakov, *O zemel'nykh*", p. 165; Veselovskii, *Feodal'noe*, pp. 99–107.

152. Zimin, *Oprichnina*, p. 114; Koretskii, *Zakreposhchenie*, pp. 74–75, 86–88, 91.

153. Makovskii, *Razvitie*, pp. 246–49, 253, 271–72.

154. Lappo-Danilevskii, *Organizatsiia*, p. 61. See also the works by S. M. Kashtanov in the Bibliography for many other examples.

155. Chistozvonov, "Nekotorye aspekty," p. 56; A. M. Sakharov, *Obrazovanie*, p. 92. See also Michael Cherniavsky, "Ivan the Terrible as Renaissance Prince," *Slavic Review* 27, no. 2 (June 1968):195–211.

156. Gorfunkel', "Rost," p. 222; *PRP*, 4:528; Zimin, *Reformy*, p. 470. A. A. Zimin attributes this reticence to fear of the "reformation movement," which was supposedly strong among the townsmen and some members of the middle service class ("Osnovnye etapy," p. 46; *Reformy*, pp. 329, 405–6; *Oprichnina*, p. 213). However, the "reformation movement" was hardly very strong in Russia, so that a better reason would be simply the general innate conservatism and religiosity of Ivan and his ministers. The legislation of the second half of Ivan's reign did make it almost impossible for an insignificant retreat to grow into a large monastery. In general, monasteries could grow in the sixteenth century in areas unsuitable for service landholding, such as the north (Budovnits, *Monastyri*, pp. 348, 357; Rozhdestvenskii, "Dvinskie," p. 144).

157. Gnevushev, "Zemlevladenie," p. 287. According to Ellerd Hulbert, the failure of the government's apparent designs on church lands in 1550 and 1551 may help to account for the "failure to realize the 'selected thousand'" ("The Sixteenth Century Assemblies of the Land"). However, it has yet to be proved that the project failed, even without the church lands.

·158. Grekov, "Iur'ev," p. 74; Nazarov, "Iz istorii agrarnoi," p. 106.

159. Sadikov, *Ocherki*, p. 58.

160. Storozhev, *Istoriko*, pp. 158–59; Gorfunkel', "Rost," pp. 223–24; Alekseev, *Agrarnaia*, pp. 196–97; Koretskii, "Pravaia," p. 195; Sadikov, *Ocherki*, pp. 90–104; Kashtanov, "K izucheniiu," pp. 112–13; Nazarov, "Iz istorii agrarnoi," p. 108; El'iashevich, *Istoriia*, 2:41; Veselovskii, *Issledovaniia*, pp. 181–85; idem, *Feodal'noe*, pp. 95–96; Zimin, *Oprichnina*, p. 411. In the period 1552–82 there were 621 donations and sales of land to monasteries (Veselovskii, *Feodal'noe*, p. 96).

161. Gorfunkel', "Rost," p. 221.

162. *SGGD*, 1, no. 202; Chicherin, *Opyty*, pp. 224, 228. S. F. Platonov saw this as one of the ways the government hindered population mobility, other than by binding the peasants to the land. Additional measures were those forbidding the taking of "dependents" (*zakladchiki*) and the keeping of servants without going through legal procedures which essentially enslaved them, limitations on the moving of peasants, and the census of the early 1590s (*Lektsii*, p. 200). Koretskii has noted that the abolition was retroactive to 1581, when the new cadastral survey was initiated which had an important role in the enserfment (*Zakreposhchenie*, pp. 96–97, 119–24).

163. Zimin, *Reformy*, pp. 390–91; Nosov, *Stanovlenie*, pp. 116–17, 128.

164. Zimin, *Oprichnina*, pp. 106–7, 257–58.

165. Pazhitnov, "Dvorianskaia," p. 67; El'iashevich, *Istoriia*, 1:295.

166. Koretskii, "Zemskii sobor," p. 34.

167. Zimin, *Oprichnina*, pp. 213–14; Veselovskii, *Feodal'noe*, p. 231; Makovskii, *Razvitie*, p. 275; Gorchakov, *O zemel'nykh*", pp. 240–43; *AAE*, 3, no. 110.

168. Olearius, *Travels*, p. 52. This may have been the monasteries' response to Patriarch Filaret's proposal at the 1632 Assembly of the Land that they give half of their capital to support the army in the Smolensk War (M. K. Liubavskii, *Russkaia istoriia*, 1:148).

169. Liubavskii, *Russkaia istoriia*, p. 268; Arkhangel'skii, *O sobornom*", p. 74; Man'kov, "Sel'skie," p. 216.

170. *AAE*, 1, no. 7; Koretskii, "Pravaia," pp. 173–93.

171. Koretskii, "Bor'ba krest'ian," pp. 195–96; Nazarov, "Iz istorii agrarnoi," pp. 109–14.

172. Gnevushev, "Zemlevladenie," p. 288.

173. Makovskii, *Razvitie*, p. 234.

174. Ibid., 179. For more on this topic, see chapter 6 below.

175. Makovskii, *Razvitie*, pp. 210, 385. In 1550 the *pomeshchik* was definitely not a landowner *(Sudebnik,* art. 87). Even after the Oprichnina many *deti boiarskie* received *kormlenie po knigam,* the old-style grants over which they had no control (ibid., p. 354).

176. Rozhkov, "Sel'skoe," p. 172.

177. Makovskii, *Razvitie*, p. 493.

178. Shepelev, *Osvoboditel'naia,* p. 118. The Soviet military historian I. M. Kravchenko is correct in maintaining that "certainly it was the granting by Ivan IV to the *pomeshchiki* of the right to supervise their economies which distracted them from their service obligations, not any spurious development of the money exchange economy" (Rotmistrov, ed., *Istoriia,* 1:84).

179. Sh., "Dvorianstvo," no. 3, p. 426.

180. Novosel'skii, "Raspad," p. 248; Koretskii, "Zemskii sobor," p. 47; Samgina, "Sluzhiloe," p. 269; Storozhev, *Istoriko,* p. 23.

181. This legal institution originated at least as early as the fifteenth century and reached the peak of its development around the end of the seventeenth century (Shumakov, "Mena," pp. 125–26; Samgina, "Sluzhiloe" p. 270).

182. Koretskii, "K istorii" (1964), p. 87.

183. Soviet scholars suggest that the middle service class members may have formally protested against the repressions of the Oprichnina at the Assembly of the Land in 1566 (Zimin, *Oprichnina,* p. 211; Sadikov, *Ocherki,* p. 129; Skrynnikov, "Oprichnaia," p. 250). However, the fact that they subsequently did not unanimously suffer the same fate would indicate that Ivan did not take any such representation as a class action. Moreover, there were members of the middle service class in the Zemshchina, and they were joined in their protest by the old Moscow boyars. As R. G. Skrynnikov has observed, in the sixteenth century the middle service class was atomized and played a secondary role in the state administration. But nevertheless, the pressure of the middle service class interests on state policy was very great ("Samoderzhavie," p. 94; A. M. Sakharov, *Obrazovanie,* p. 91).

184. For one collective petition of the 1590s, see Koretskii, *Zakreposhchenie,* pp. 150–51.

3. The Conscious Rise of the Middle Service Class

1. Makovskii, *Razvitie*, pp. 195, 495; Koretskii, "Iz istorii" (1957), p. 183; idem, *Zakreposhchenie,* pp. 149–50. Boris also exempted the middle service class from payment of taxes to maintain jails. "The petty middling *pomeshchiki* formed the social base of Boris's government" (Koretskii, "Iz istorii krest'ianskoi' [1959], p. 124; idem, "K istorii vosstaniia Khlopka," p. 215). V. I. Koretskii has written that the law of 1591 was stimulated by the development of corvée ("K istorii formirovaniia," p. 87). Simultaneously Boris was trying to improve his position among the magnates by showing that his lineage, while it did not go back to Riurik, at least dated from the middle of the thirteenth century (Veselovskii, *Feodal'noe,* p. 23). This seems to have been a century too early, or maybe even more (Veselovskii, *Klass,* pp. 162, 188, 194).

2. Tatishchev, *Sudebnik",* pp. 237–38; Chernov, *Vooruzhennye sily,* p. 125; Storozhev, *Istoriko* pp. 24, 140.

3. *AMG*, 1, no. 40. Boris also recruited significant numbers of slaves into the middle service class (Vostokov, "Russkoe sluzhiloe," p. 266).

4. *AMG*, 1, no. 44.

5. M. A. D'iakonov's attribution of the closing of the middle service class to a shortage of land was perhaps logical, given his view of the functioning of Muscovite society, but I believe this view to be wide of the mark (*Ocherki* [1912]. p. 265). S. F. Platonov attributed the closing of the middle service class to a belief by the government that enough men had been recruited after a period of rapid growth (*Lektsii*, p. 194). In fact, the service class was hardly any larger at this time than earlier, while the available supply of land, resulting from recent annexations, was greater than before.

6. Nazarov, "Iz istorii vnutrennei," p. 103. The French mercenary officer Jacques Margeret noted that the First False Dmitrii had intentions to found a university (*Sostoianie*, p. 114).

7. I. S. Shepelev, "Mesto i kharakter dvizheniia I. M. Zarutskogo v period krest- 'ianskoi voiny i pol'sko-shvedskoi interventsii," *Trudy LOII*, 9 (1967):230, 232; Shmidt, "Lenin," p. 345; Zimin, "Nekotorye voprosy," pp. 106, 109; Zimin and Koroleva, "Dokument," pp. 23–24, 28–29, 36–37; Mavrodin, "Sovetskaia" (1966), pp. 299, 318; idem, "Sovetskaia" (1967), p. 77. Peasants had not participated in the earlier uprising led by Khlopko (Koretskii, "Iz istorii krest'ianskoi," p. 134; idem, "K istorii vosstaniia Khlopka," p. 212).

8. Chernov, "TsGADA," p. 135.

9. Dovnar-Zapol'skii, "Vremia," p. 215. "The members of the service class used the Time of Troubles very well to achieve their own desires" (Veselovskii, *Soshnoe*, 1:318). "The crowning of Mikhail Fedorovich was nothing other than the symbol of the triumph of the gentry and the urban merchant bourgeoisie with a strong preponderance of the former over the latter" (Rozhkov, *Russkaia*, 4:190).

10. Stashevskii, "Sluzhiloe soslovie," pp. 17, 29; Vostokov, "Russkoe sluzhiloe," pp. 269–70; Sergeevich, "Voennyia sily," pp. 58, 61; Novitskii, *Vybornoe*, pp. 100–104, 155–56.

11. Presniakov, "Moskovskoe gosudarstvo," p. 65.

12. *AAE*, 3, no. 222. See *PSZ*, 1, no. 280; ibid., 2, no. 806, for examples of the numbers of soldiers, by households, servicemen had to bring with them to service after 1650.

13. *RIB*, 9:467. For a 1650 case, see *AMG*, 2, no. 433.

14. *AMG*, 2, no. 202.

15. Ibid., no. 113.

16. Ibid., no. 424.

17. Iakovlov, *Zasechnaia;* Nikitin, "Oboronitel'nye," pp. 116–213; Latkin, *Materialy*, pp. 53, 67.

18. *AMG*, 2, no. 113. They claimed to have been ruined by Tatar attacks and consequently claimed "to have no peasants and slaves, and to be impoverished" (Zagorovskii, *Belgorodskaia*, pp. 89, 124–25).

19. *AMG*, 1, no. 108; ibid., no. 959; ibid., 3, nos. 300, 357, 611, 684; Stashevskii, *Zemlevladenie*, pp. 40–237; Iakovlev, *Prikaz*," p. 80, Samgina, "Sluzhiloe," pp. 268–69; Storozhev, *Istoriko*, pp. 149–52, 167.

20. *AMG*, 3, no. 374; Sergeevich, "Voennyia sily," p. 22; Romanovich-Slavatinskii, *Dvorianstvo*, p. 117; Veselovskii, *Feodal'noe*, pp. 306–7.

21. Totally contradictory opinions have been expressed in Russian historiography on the service career pattern of the *syn boiarskii*. E. D. Stashevskii wrote that in the sixteenth century a young man entered service as a *syn boiarskii* in a position determined by his father's service or landholding, but did not depend on his father's family origin. If a father was a "selected" (*vybornyi*) *syn boiarskii*, then so was the son. If the father was on the "court" or "provincial" list, so was the son. In the seventeenth century the career pattern was altered so that all had to start at the bottom, in the provinces ("Sluzhiloe soslovie," pp. 14–16, 27). A. A. Vostokov claimed that there was no material advantage, only prestige, to be gained from serving as a selected, court, or provincial *syn boiarskii* ("Russkoe sluzhiloe," p. 272). V. I. Novitskii convincingly showed that the opposite was true. In the seventeenth century the

title of *syn boiarskii* became hereditary; the man could rise no higher than had his father. It was not hereditary in the sixteenth century. The categories (selected, court, provincial *syn boiarskii*) had differing compensation (Novitskii, *Vybornoe*, pp. 53, 70, 79, 85, 141–48). Essentially the same had been observed by V. I. Sergeevich ("Voennyia sily," pp. 48, 51). See also Nosov, "Boiarskaia," pp. 208–9, 215.

22. *Ulozhenie*, 16:61; Maslovskii, *Zapiski*, 1: appendix 2, pp. 24–26.

23. Storozhev, *Istoriko*, pp. 25, 140, 206–210; Sergeevich, "Voennyia sily," p. 45; El'iashevich, *Istoriia*, 2:170–73; Veselovskii, *Feodal'noe*, p. 88. The subsistence grants were usually concentrated in one place (Samgina, "Sluzhiloe," p. 272).

24. Platonov, "Moskovskoe pravitel'stvo," pp. 383–86.

25. *Ocherki . . . XVII*, p. 337.

26. Stashevskii, *Zemlevladenie*, pp. 25, 198. Lands might have been obtained by accusing someone of treason for having been on the "wrong side" during the political chaos of the Time of Troubles. Platonov was correct, however, in asserting that general revenge was not taken against former enemies in the new Romanov government, that persons of varying factions continued to hold their posts after 1613 (ibid., p. 382). A popular device was court litigation, where friendly judges could always assure the proper outcome. The malfeasance of the magnates in the new Romanov dynasty was powerfully described and condemned by a Pskov chronicler (*PSRL*, 5:63–64).

27. Figarovskii, "Krest'ianskoe vosstanie," p. 202; Gnevushev, "Zemlevladenie," pp. 290–91. A. I. Zaozerskii noted that the delegates to the *Sobor*, on their own initiative, played no role in administration and were concerned mainly with levying extraordinary taxes ("K" voprosu o sostave," pp. 348–49).

28. Veselovskii, "K" voprosu," pp. 26–27; Novosel'skii, "Pobegi," p. 328.

29. Keep, "Filaret," p. 345.

30. Veselovskii, *Soshnoe pis'mo*, 2:188; Liubomirov, *Ocherki*, p. 39. Nevertheless a document of November, 1621, observed that at least some of the census-takers in 1619 had used the occasion to reduce the taxes of the powerful and made up for the loss by increasing those of the small landholders (*AAE*, 3, no. 121).

31. *Ocherki . . . XVII*, p. 149; P. P. Smirnov, *Posadskie*, 2:316–21. These grants were recognized in the *Ulozhenie* of 1649 (16: 46; 17: 24).

32. Sh., "Dvorianstvo," no. 3, p. 201 (see him for exceptions, pp. 201–2).

33. *RIB*, 10:240–41.

34. Vainberg, "Bor'ba krest'ian," pp. 252–53; Zagorovskii, *Belgorodskaia cherta*, pp. 29, 34. See also chapter 7 below.

35. Sergeevich, "Voennyia," p. 16.

36. D'iakonov, *Ocherki* (1912), p. 265. The nineteenth-century historian A. A. Vostokov said that slaves who were converted into *deti boiarskie* were expelled during the following reign, in 1605–6 ("Russkoe sluzhiloe," p. 266).

37. Chistiakova, "Volneniia," p. 256.

38. Mikhenevich and Il'enko, "Glavnyi," p. 7.

39. *PSZ*, 1, nos. 85, 273.

40. *AMG*, 3, no. 355. The same pronouncement was issued in 1662 (*AMG*, 3, no. 611). At this time Grigorii Kotoshikhin observed that the middle service class was closed to outsiders, but that townsmen, peasants, and others could enroll their children in the new army cavalry and infantry and the chancellery service, where they could rise (*O Rossii*, 2:12).

41. *PSZ*, 1, nos. 615, 744. Stashevskii, "Sluzhiloe soslovie," p. 7; A. M. Sakharov, *Obrazovanie*, p. 138. The reasons behind the decrees of the 1670s were different from the previous ones. See chapter 12 below.

42. Liubomirov, *Ocherk istorii nizhegorodskogo*, pp. 38–39; Zimin, "Nekotorye voprosy" (1958), p. 101; A. M. Sakharov, *Obrazovanie*, p. 137.

43. El'iashevich, *Istoriia*, 1:240.

44. A marginal notation next to article 67 of chapter 16 of the manuscript edition of the *Ulozhenie*.

45. *Ulozhenie*, 17:37, 41; Arkhangel'skii, *O sobornom"*, pp. 74–76; Gorchakov, *O*

zemel'nykh", pp. 247–49, 400–2. On the monastery *slugi*, who resembled slaves in certain respects (church institutions could not own actual slaves), see Veselovskii, *Feodal'noe*, p. 231. Of course this provision also reflects the increasing centralization of the Muscovite state, as the possession of armed force became increasingly a prerogative of the government. Such a monopoly position also strengthened the middle class.

46. *Ulozhenie*, 17:41; Stashevskii, "Sluzhiloe soslovie," pp. 2, 5. On land-ownership by slaves, see Veselovskii, *Feodal'noe*, p. 217.

47. *UKPP*, 7:99; *PRP*, 5:469–70. See *Ulozhenie*, 16:40 for land grants in the unpopulated steppe which were available for the asking to the *deti boiarskie* of the southern frontier towns. The free land was there for the asking, but no one was around to farm it.

48. *UKPP*, 7:105; *PRP*, 5:477–78.

49. *UKPP*, 8:118.

50. *Ocherki . . . XVII v.*, p. 159.

51. Chernov, *Vooruzhennye*, p. 158.

52. *PRP*, 5:462. This decree referred to the earlier law of 1573 mentioned above. Got'e, *Zamoskovnyi*, p. 257. Probably because of abuses, the law was repealed in 1629 (*PRP*, 5:466). A decree promulgated by the tsar in 1636 reveals that magnates, mainly, took advantage of the law. The Boyar Council said it could not decide the issue because of possible conflict of interest—its members were involved (*PRP*, 5:471). In another instance, a law of 1627 forbade giving out court lands to servicemen. The court could not pay its bills, had no bread, and could not pay sums it owed monasteries. This measure strengthened the court nobility, who began to give themselves court lands. The *Ulozhenie* of 1649 repealed this law (Gnevushev, "Zemlevladenie," p. 291).

53. *Ulozhenie*, 17:47.

54. *UKPP*, 5:14, 15; ibid., 6:79; *Ulozhenie*, 16:14; *PSZ*, 1 no. 5; *UKPP*, 5:16; ibid., 7:93; *Ulozhenie*, 16:41, 42, 44; Arkangel'skii, *O sobornom" Ulozhenii*, pp. 35–37; Storozhev, *Istoriko*, pp. 175–76.

55. Veselovskii, *Feodal'noe*, p. 88.

56. At first the government ordered the guilty individuals beaten with the knout, then refused to give them new service lands to replace the ones they had destroyed (Stashevskii, "Sluzhiloe soslovie," p. 23). Another way to effect the transfer of peasants was to exchange a *pomest'e* for a *votchina*. The government forbade this also (Storozhev, *Istoriko*, pp. 204–5).

57. A similar process had occurred in the Ottoman Empire in the sixteenth century (McNeill, *Europe's Steppe Frontier*, pp. 56–57, 59–60, 62).

58. For examples of inheritance of *pomest'ia*, see Iakovlev, *Prikaz"*, pp. 187–92. On the free exchange of *votchiny* and *pomest'ia*, see the *Ulozhenie*, 16:4, 5. This was a reversal of *UKPP* of 1636, 7:98. *Pomest'ia* could be converted into *votchiny* for one ruble per *chetvert'*: *PSZ*, 1, nos. 3, 100; ibid., 1:374. See also *PSZ*, 1:nos. 400, 404, 433, 450, 512; ibid., 2: 640, 871, 922, 961, 1079, 1114, 1155, 1177, 1213, 1247, 1291, 1317.

59. *Ulozhenie*, 16:8, 61.

60. Pavlov-Sil'vanskii, *Gosudarevy*, p. 199.

61. *Ulozhenie*, 16:29. Earlier this had been only ten years (*UKPP*, 7:98).

62. Pavlov-Sil'vanskii, *Gosudarevy*, p. 192.

63. *UKPP*, pp. 42–44; Storozhev, *Istoriko*, pp. 177–79. A decree of 1555 stated that a father's service lands were not to be taken away from sons if they were suitable for service (Storozhev, *Istoriko*, pp. 22–23, 193). Nevertheless, some scholars claim that no legislation was enacted in the sixteenth century to legalize what had become custom (Stashevskii, "Sluzhiloe soslovie," pp. 25–26; Gnevushev, "Zemlevladenie," p. 286).

64. *Ulozhenie*, 16:13, 22, 23, 34, 53, 55, 62; Samgina, "Sluzhiloe," pp. 266, 269.

65. Pavlov-Sil'vanskii, *Gosudarevy*, p. 193.

66. Ibid., p. 199; *Ocherki*, p. 145; Storozhev, *Istoriko*, p. 193.

67. Novosel'skii, "Raspad," p. 234.

68. Gvenushev, "Zemlevladenie," p. 294; A. M. Sakharov, *Obrazovanie*, p. 137.

69. Stashevskii, "Sluzhiloe soslovie," p. 26.

70. *PRP*, 7:67, 69, 81–82, 85, 105; El'iashevich, *Istoriia*, 2:146–51. N. A. Rozhkov attributed the conversion of the *pomest'e* into *votchina* in the seventeenth century to a governmental awareness that servicemen had only an attitude of exploitation toward the service holding, which lowered the level of agriculture, and that this attitude could be reversed only by giving them an interest in the land (*Gorod i derevnia*, p. 51). While this may be true, I suspect that the conversion of service lands into hereditary tenure was more a political than an economic phenomenon.

71. Man'kov, "Krest'ianskii," p. 67; *Ulozhenie*, 11:30, 31. Laws of 1676 and as late as 1689 reaffirmed that peasants could not be transferred from service lands to hereditary lands (*PRP*, 7:85).

72. Samokvasov, *Krest'iane*, p. 92; Gnevushev, "Zemlevladenie," p. 295; Romanovich-Slavatinskii, *Dvorianstvo*, pp. 239, 359; *PRP*, 8:247.

73. *PRP*, 5:466–68, 472, 529–30; *Ulozhenie*, 16:13, 30, 31, 32, 33; ibid., 16:17, 18, 19, 20, 56; *PRP*, 7:58–59, 66–67, 69–70, 80; El'iashevich, *Istoriia*, 2:145–46; Veselovskii, *Feodal'noe*, pp. 307–8.

74. *PSZ*, 1, no. 39; ibid., 2, no. 767. But after the 1687 peace with Poland twenty-nine Moscow *gosti* were given *pomest'e* cash *oklady* (*PSZ*, 2, no. 1233).

75. Chernov, *Vooruzhennye sily*, pp. 158–59.

76. Storozhev, *Istoriko*, p. 203; Stashevskii, "Sluzhiloe soslovie," p. 23. See chapter 12 below. Even after retirement the member of the middle service class might be called upon to perform nonmilitary services, such as conducting special criminal investigations (*AMG*, 2, no. 448).

77. *AMG*, 1, nos. 90, 124, 715; ibid., 2, nos. 1, 231; Sergeevich, "Voennyia sily," pp. 38, 54, 62; *Ulozhenie*, 16:24.

78. Iakovlev, *Prikaz*", pp. 162–64.

79. *Ulozhenie*, 21:98. Article 97 says they were to be elected from taxpaying peasants (*soshnye liudi*) from *pomest'e* and *votchina* (and church) lands. *AAE*, 2, no. 19, of November 7, 1601, noted that, earlier, peasants had been ordered taken first from large estates (both *pomest'ia* and *votchiny*), then middling, and lastly small. But henceforth *tseloval'niki* were not to be taken from the middling and small. Certainly this was a concession by Boris Godunov to the middle service class.

80. *Ulozhenie*, 9:6.

81. Veselovskii, *Soshnoe*, 1:317–19, 326.

82. *AI*, 3, no. 107.

83. *AMG*, 1, no. 229.

84. *Ulozhenie*, 8:1.

85. Ibid., 8:4–7. For background information, see *Stoglav*, chaps. 5, 72; Snegirev, *Storozhevaia*, p. 31; Lappo-Danilevskii, *Organizatsiia*, p. 15; *AMG*, 2, no. 91; *AAE*, 3, no. 299; *AI*, 4, no. 43. Ransoming captives became an issue in 1551 at the "Hundred Chapters" church council, which introduced a tax to free them. Prior to the middle of the sixteenth century Moscow sold Christian captives and prisoners of war to the Crimean and Nogai Tatars (Bobrovskii, *Perekhod*", p. 98; Herberstein, *Commentaries*, p. 109). After 1649 Moscow expended considerable resources on the ransoming of captives (Selifontov, *Ocherk*", pp. 3–5).

86. *DAI*, 3, no. 32.

87. *AMG*, 1, no. 375.

88. *AAE*, 3, no. 223. This provision was kept by the *Ulozhenie*, 7:21. The right to buy grain at a set price remained a valued privilege for the middle service class (Preobrazhenskii, "Ural," p. 291).

89. *AAE*, 3, no. 224; cf. *Ulozhenie*, 7:4.

90. *AAE*, 3, no. 234. For all practical purposes there was no real medicine in seventeenth-century Russia. Of course, there was folk medicine, but there were few doctors. The handful of physicians, all foreigners, worked in the Drug Chancellery (*Aptekarskii prikaz*) and looked after the tsar.

91. *AMG*, 1, no. 634; cf. *Ulozhenie*, 7:13.

92. *Ulozhenie*, 21:53. The usual procedure was to pronounce guilty a person without such documents who had a horse; cf. *Sudebnik* of 1589, arts. 195–97.

93. *Ulozhenie*, 7:4.

94. Ibid., 7:5–7. During wartime, provisioners, cooks, bakers, brew-masters, meat men, and all their wares were drafted into service from Moscow and the provincial towns. There were fifty to seventy of these tradesmen per regiment. They received no pay and were ordered to sell to the *sluzhilye liudi* at reasonable prices (Kotoshikhin, *O Rossii*, p. 113).

95. *Ulozhenie*, 7:23.

96. *AAE*, 3, no. 234, 235, 237, 238; Porshnev, "Sotsial'no-politicheskaia obstanovka," p. 132.

97. In the sixteenth century, documents called *srochnye gramoty* fixed the dates, no more than three, when people covered by immunity documents could be called into the court of the great prince to answer suits filed by people outside the jurisdiction of the immunity (Kashtanov, "K probleme," p. 144).

Much legal action had to be undertaken in Moscow. All suits over ten rubles in border towns had to be tried in the capital (*AMG*, 2, no. 173). Cases involving fugitive peasants and slaves often ended up in Moscow (*DAI*, 2, no. 35; *Ulozhenie*, 11:20; ibid., 20:50, 54, 78, 91, 111, 112). Many land cases were handled in Moscow (*Ulozhenie*, 16:39). Suits over twenty rubles and those involving land and slaves could be tried locally only where there were governors with local officials (*d'iaki*) present (*Ulozhenie*, 13:3). This was probably an attempt to limit capricious judgments by magnates who favored one another at the expense of provincial litigants. This is not to say that all important cases were handled in Moscow—far from it. With the development of the central government apparatus in the seventeenth century, its tentacles reached into all towns; major cases could be handled outside of Moscow in the largest provincial towns. Very large suits involving thousands of rubles were tried locally. Governors were required to submit to Moscow only those cases they felt they could not handle (Chicherin, *Oblastnyia*, pp. 136, 139).

98. Cherepnin, *Russkaia khronologiia*, table 16.

99. This was the reason why many petitions from the middle service class originated shortly after Christmas. The servicemen gathered in Moscow, discussed their grievances, and begged relief. For dozens of trial-postponement petitions, see Iakovlev, *Kholopstvo*.

100. In 1627 (*RIB*, 9:469); 1630 (*AMG*, 1, nos. 281, 292, 293); 1631 (ibid., 1, nos. 300, 306); 1633 (*RIB*, 9:530, 531); 1634 (ibid., 9:565); 1650 (*AMG*, 2, no. 420); 1653 (ibid., nos. 559, 567); 1656 (ibid., 2, no. 843).

101. *Ulozhenie*, 16:65.

102. Ibid.

103. Ibid., 11:4; ibid., 15:4.

104. Ibid., 11:4.

105. Smirnov, "Chelobitnye," no. 1; Stashevskii, *K" istorii*, pp. 20–22.

106. Smirnov, "Chelobitnye," p. 7.

107. Lords at this time had five years to hunt down fugitive peasants. Stashevskii discusses a case of 1637–38 in which a lord tried to no avail to recover a peasant kidnapped by another lord (*K" istorii*, pp. 14–17).

108. Smirnov, "Chelobitnye," p. 8.

109. Stashevskii, "Chelobitnye," pp. 20–22.

110. Smirnov, "Chelobitnye," p. 10.

111. *SGGD*, 3, no. 113.

112. On the "joint court," dating from at least the end of the fifteenth century, see Gorchakov, *O zemel'nykh"*, pp. 291–95; El'iashevich, *Istoriia*, 1:261–63.

113. Stashevskii, "Chelobitnye," p. 21. S. F. Platonov naively said the corrupt nature of the government oppressing the middle service class was the result of the fact that the forces which failed to triumph with the second False Dmitrii did succeed

with the installation of the Romanov dynasty ("Moskovskoe pravitel'stvo," *Sochineniia,* 1:402–3).

114. Smirnov, "Chelobitnye," no. 2; *AI,* 3, no. 92-XXXIII.

115. This became article 40 of the Statute Book of the Moscow Administrative Chancellery (*PRP,* 5:373).

116. Chistiakova, "Volneniia," p. 264.

117. *Ulozhenie,* 10:137, 140, 141, 151.

118. Ibid., 10:149.

119. Ibid., 16:55.

120. Ibid., 16:59.

121. Ibid., 16:65.

122. Ibid., 20:109.

123. Ibid., 10:22, 24.

124. In their role as bureaucrats, however, some of the "strong people" who were in government service may have opted for the streamlining of procedures in order to facilitate their work. The balance here is impossible to calculate.

125. In 1653 the matter was again a live issue. See *AMG,* 2, no. 567.

126. Ibid., 1, no. 651. The issue of enslaved captives also arose during the Thirteen Years War (ibid., 2, no. 785).

127. Pavlov-Sil'vanskii, *Gosudarevy,* p. 230.

128. No. 9 of the Slavery Chancellery Statute Book, the *Ukaznaia kniga kholopego prikaza,* published by Vladimirskii-Budanov in his *Khristomatiia,* issue 3.

129. Pavlov-Sil'vanskii, *Gosudarevy,* p. 231.

130. Sergeevich, "Voennyia," p. 19; Stashevskii, "Sluzhiloe soslovie," p. 31. In spite of the laws and familial concern, *deti boiarskie* sometimes did fall into the ranks of cossacks, soldiers, and other groups of the lower service class (Novitskii, *Vybornoe,* pp. 83–84).

131. *AMG,* 2, nos. 41, 153; Smirnov, "Chelobitnye," no. 2. On the very strict 1641 decree, see Iakovlev, *Kholopstvo,* p. 316, and appendix 8; *AI,* 3, no. 92-XXXIII; Smirnov, "Chelobitnye," no. 3.

132. It is extremely difficult to ascertain what the real practice was because the extant documents are very scarce. Most surviving records are either those of the government chancelleries, or are documents written and signed by government officials. Neither were composed when governmental officials themselves or others were engaging in illegal practices.

At first the prohibition was only against taking into slavery *deti boiarskie* who were in service. According to a law of 1621–22, taking into bondage *deti boiarskie* who were not in service was permissible, as in the *Sudebnik* of 1589. But in 1641 all bondage was prohibited for *deti boiarskie,* whether they were in service or not. See P. P. Smirnov, "Chelobitnye," no. 2; Stashevskii, "K" istorii kolonizatsii," p. 246.

133. *Ulozhenie,* 20:1, 2.

134. Ibid., 10:264, 266. Exceptions were made for *deti boiarskie* who were policemen.

135. Chistiakova, "Volneniia," p. 257; Novosel'skii, "Rasprostranenie," p. 23; *Khestomatiia* (1962), no. 102; *MS,* pp. 159–63; Novosel'skii, "Raspad," p. 248.

136. Maierberg, *Puteshestvie,* p. 92; Iakovlev, *Kholopstovo,* pp. 242–44, for individual complaints.

137. P. P. Smirnov, *Posadskie,* 1:411.

138. This law was confirmed by the *Ulozhenie,* 16:39.

139. P. P. Smirnov, "Chelobitnye," no. 2.

140. A. M. Sakharov, *Obrazovanie,* pp. 174–75; Kotoshikhin, *O Rossii,* 7:34; Chicherin, *Oblastnyia,* pp. 184–85, 264, 478–504; Zaozerskii, "K" voprosu," p. 340; Volkov, "O stanovlenii," p. 97.

141. Stashevskii, "K" istorii," p. 11.

142. *Sudebnik* of 1589, arts. 77, 133, 185.

143. Ibid., art. 186.
144. *Ulozhenie*, 10:153. An exception was made for the patriarch, who retained legal jurisdiction over his subjects "because it had been that way during the reign of former tsars" (ibid., 12:1). Anyone who felt he did not get a fair trial from ahe patriarch's judges could appeal to the boyars and tsar (ibid., 12:2).
145. *Ulozhenie*, 19:3, *PSZ*, 2, nos. 507, 699; Gorchakov, *O zemel'nykh"*, p. 256; Arkhangel'skii, *O sobornom"*, pp. 70–71, 142–45. The tax privileges held by the monasteries were more disadvantageous to the treasury through lost revenue than they were to the merchants through a weakened competitive position. As a result there were few complaints about the privileges in the first half of the seventeenth century (P. P. Smirnov, "Ekonomicheskaia politika," p. 399).
146. *DAI*, 3, no. 47-i; *Ulozhenie*, 12; ibid., 13:1; Gorchakov, *Monastyrskii*, pp. 4, 67, 101; Gorchakov, *O zemel'nykh"*, pp. 430–42; Arkhangel'skii, *O sobornom"*, pp. 108–12, 116. For an exception, see *PSZ*, 1, no. 93, which conformed with the *Ulozhenie*. The creation of the Monastery Chancellery was one of the major causes of Nikon's wrath against the *Ulozhenie* (Nikon, "Mneniia," p. 441).
147. Chaev, "Iz istorii," 1936, pp. 25–65.
148. *AAE*, 3, nos. 110, 120; Gorchakov, *O zemel'nykh"*, p. 412; Lappo-Danilevskii, *Organizatsiia*, p. 63. Vasilii Shuiskii had timidly embarked on the path of limiting monastery privileges during the Time of Troubles in an attempt to gain support from the townsmen and perhaps the court peasants (Nosov, "Belozerskaia," p. 52).
149. *AAE*, 3, nos. 175, 178; *PSZ*, 1, nos. 205, 206, and scores of others; Arkhangel'skii, *O sobornom"*, pp. 118–21.
150. Gorfunkel', "Rost," p. 237; El'iashevich, *Istoriia*, 2:185; Storozhev, *Istoriko*, p. 160.
151. *PRP*, 5:439–41.
152. Got'e, *Zamoskovnyi*, p. 212.
153. The 1628 measure was repealed specifically by the *Ulozhenie*, 17:42. Filaret's measure was the logical consequence of a decree of 1620 permitting any form of alienation (including to monasteries) of lands that had been granted for service to Vasilii Shuiskii during the Time of Troubles (Gnevushev, "Zemlevladenie," p. 293).
154. *PRP*, 5:462, 508.
155. Ibid., pp. 468–69.
156. At the same time about 66 percent of the land belonged to lay lords (Vodarskii, "Chislennost' naseleniia," pp. 218–21; Shepukova, "K voprosu," p. 146).
157. Gnevushev, "Zemlevladenie," p. 286.
158. Arkhangel'skii, *O sobornom"*, p. 67.
159. Smirnov, *Posadskie*, 2:224, 229–32. See *AAE*, 4, no. 33. A study was ordered. They also failed in their program to make the monks work and to divide up peasants more equally among all landholders (Iakubov, "Rossiia," 184:431; El'iashevich, *Istoriia*, 2:138–39).
160. *Ulozhenie*, 17:42–44; Arkhangel'skii, *O sobornom"*, p. 46; Gorchakov, *O zemel'nykh"*, pp. 334–35. The prohibition had been repealed again in 1630 (Lappo-Danilevskii, *Organizatsiia*, p. 61).
161. *Ulozhenie*, 16:66; Gorchakov, *O zemel'nykh"*, pp. 247–49, 399–411.
162. Gorchakov, *O zemel'nykh"*, pp. 329–31, 337–41; El'iashevich, *Istoriia*, 2:186–88; Man'kov, "Sel'skie,' p. 218.
163. Collins, *Present State* (1671), p. 124. For other contemporary estimates, see Gorchakov, *Monastyrskii*, p. 21. A Soviet scholar recently noted that in the 1660s 476 monasteries had 87,907 peasant households; 62.8 percent (55,243) of all these peasant households belonged to thirty-two of the largest monasteries (Borisov, "Tserkov' i vosstanie," p. 74).
164. Gorchakov, *O zemel'nykh"*, pp. 342–45, appendix, pp. 97–99, 219–24; *MS*, p. 89; Novosel'skii, "Rospis'," p. 122.
165. Vodarskii, "Chislennost'," pp. 221, 227, 229.

166. Billington, *Icon*, p. 201.

167. Gorfunkel', "Rost," p. 222; Arkhangel'skii, *O sobornom"*, p. 138; El'iashevich, *Istoriia*, 2:193.

168. Novombergskii, *Slovo*, 1, no. 116.

169. According to conventional wisdom, "all the administration of the Muscovite state in all instances was in the hands of the *dvoriane* and *deti boiarskie*—the heads of the chancelleries, the officials appointed by Moscow to govern the provinces, the military governors, the heads of the *guba* system" (Bobrovskii, *Perekhod"*, p. 127).

170. Zimin, *Reformy*, p. 460; *Oprichnina*, p. 181. In 1640 government chancellery service was made hereditary and closed to the children of clergy, townsmen, and peasants (*AI*, 3, no. 92-XXXI; S. K. Bogoiavlenskii, "Prikaznye," p. 221). This had been one of the few remaining paths for nonservice people to rise into the upper service class by gaining the tsar's attention and favor.

171. Stashevskii, *Smeta*, p. 16; *AMG*, 2:406, 467.

172. Demidova, "Biurokratizatsiia," p. 218.

173. Bakhrushin, "Moskovskoe," 2:84–89.

174. Demidova, "Biurokratizatsiia," pp. 215, 217; also Bogoiavlenskii, "Prikaznye," p. 221.

175. Demidova, "Biurokratizatsiia," p. 217. Similarly, clergymen did not work in the church administration. All administrative chores were performed by laymen under the supervision of church hierarchs (Arkhangel'skii, *O sobornom"*, pp. 99–100).

176. Sergeevich, "Voennyia sily," p. 7; Romanovich-Slavatinskii, *Dvorianstvo*, p. 134; Shmidt, "Lenin," pp. 335–36. Members of the middle service class working in the civil service were recorded as absent from military service along with those who were not serving because they were too poor or in jail (Storozhev, "Materialy," p. 23). The method of recording may have been simply a matter of bureaucratic convenience, but nevertheless the servicemen regarded all three reasons for absence as far beneath military service in status.

177. Demidova, "Biurokratizatsiia," p. 213; Novitskii, *Vybornoe*, pp. 78, 95–96. See also *AMG*, 2, no. 443. For an interesting discussion of the role of the *Razriad* in Muscovite military and civil life, see Chernov, "TsGADA," p. 117. For a list of the provincial governors in the seventeenth century, see Aleksandr Barsukov, *Spiski gorodovykh" voevod" i drugikh" lits" voevodskago upravleniia Moskovskago gosudarstva XVII stoletiia* (St. Petersburg, 1902).

178. Demidova, "Biurokratizatsiia," p. 213; *PSZ*, 1, no. 295, pp. 528–29; *AMG*, 3, no. 406.

179. Demidova, "Biurokratizatsiia," pp. 213–14.

180. Bakhrushin, "Moskovskoe," 2:84–89; *Ulozhenie*, 9:6, dating from before 1601–2. See *AAE*, 2, no. 19, which explicitly exempted *dvoriane* and *deti boiarskie* on November 7, 1601 (Kliuchevskii, *Istoriia soslovii*, p. 222). Peter tried to put this burden on retired officers and soldiers in decrees of April 13 and May 11, 1722. The tactic did not work out, so the burden was put back on the townsmen on December 9, 1723 (ibid., p. 223).

181. Demidova, "Biurokratizatsiia," pp. 215, 217.

182. Romanovich-Slavatinskii, *Dvorianstvo*, p. 402.

183. *Ulozhenie*, 21:97. The *Ulozhenie* (21:4) prescribed that literate wounded, superannuated, or retired members of middle service class were to serve as *guba* elders upon election by their neighbors. See also *Ulozhenie*, 20:72; ibid., 21: 3–7, 86. Also, *PRP*, 4:171–226; ibid., 5:262–70; *AMG*, 3, no. 200.

184. *AMG*, 3, nos. 332, 655; Bogoslovskii, *Zemskoe*, 2: 238.

185. However, Shumakov may have exaggerated the degree to which both the *guba* and *zemskaia* systems were the products of local initiative. "Listening to the voice of the Russian land was one of the chief services of Ivan Groznyi. It was not for nothing that the Russian people lamented when hearing of his death" ("Gubnyia," p. 47).

186. *AMG*, 2, no. 568; ibid., 3, nos. 356, 422; Chernov, "TsGADA," p. 116. Aleksei contemplated restoring local self-administration, removing it from the *voevoda*. Peter carried this move out on March 10, 1702. He formed gentry councils to work with the now deflated *voevody* (Kliuchevskii, *Istoriia soslovii*, pp. 224–26; see pp. 225–26 for measures to 1725).

187. *PSZ*, 2, no. 778; *PRP*, 7:365–66. The *guba* elder was revived in 1684, but he was subordinate to the local governor. The office lasted until the beginning of the eighteenth century (*PRP*, 7:383).

188. Platonov, *Lektsii*, p. 196; Miliukov, *Ocherki* (1900), 1:178; Presniakov, *Moskovskoe tsarstvo*, p. 102; Kashtanov, "Otrazhenie," pp. 268–69; Obraztsov, "Iz istorii zakreposhcheniia," p. 339; Iakovlev, "Ocherk"," pp. 6–7; Petrikeev, *Krupnoe*, p. 155. Veselovskii said that lords hired clerks to collect the taxes for them (*Soshnoe pis'mo*, 1:336). But the *guba* officials did collect some taxes (Sadikov, *Ocherki*, pp. 526–27).

This is not the same issue as whether the state held lords responsible for failure by peasants living on their lands to pay their taxes, a phenomenon dating at least from the beginning of the sixteenth century, when the government ordered lords not to exploit their peasants to the degree that the latter could not pay their taxes. When this stricture was violated, or when the government assumed that it had been because peasants had fled, then lords sometimes were required to pay the government the revenues it was expecting. By itself this did not give the landholder any control over his peasant, although it had the obvious impact of making the landholders even more desirous of keeping their peasants (*Sbornik" Khilkova*, no. 59; Koretskii, "Iz istorii" [1964], p. 71; Gnevushev, "Zemlevladenie," p. 275; *AMG*, 3, no. 236; Rozhkov, "Istoriia krepostnogo prava," p. 119; Rozhdestvenskii, "Sel'skoe," p. 83; Kulisher, "Nesvobodnoe sostoianie," p. 178; Samokvasov, *Krest'iane*, p. 43; *AM*, 1 pt. 1, pp. 7, 9). M. I. Gorchakov noticed that lords became responsible for the correct payment of their peasants' taxes as a consequence of the enserfment (*O zemel'nykh"*, p. 320). See, however, Koretskii, *Zakreposhchenie*, pp. 334, 336.

189. Tikhomirov, "Sobornie Ulozhenie," p. 21.

190. *Ulozhenie*, 9:8 (an article which first appeared in this law code); they did not have to pay camping fees when traveling. In 1630, on petition, *deti boiarskie* and *dvoriane* did not have to pay ferry fees (*AMG*, 1, no. 294). In 1641, desiring court reform, the servicemen were given the privilege of not having to pay for the use of roads, ferries, and bridges on their way to service (Smirnov, "Chelobitnye," no. 2). See also *LS*, 1:30; *AMG*, 1, no. 294 (of 1630); *UKZP*, 31:9 (of 1642); *Ulozhenie*, 9:1.

191. *Ulozhenie*, 7:17; ibid., 9:152; ibid., 16:61. V. I. Sergeevich saw in the fact that peasants could substitute for servicemen, about which more will be said in chapter 12 below, evidence of the absence of sharp splits between the lower and upper classes of Muscovy ("Voennyia sily," p. 15).

192. In light of the facts, I have difficulty in accepting P. N. Miliukov's contention that the middle service class was not a privileged estate (*Ocherki* [1900], 1:185–86). A privileged gentry existed already in the seventeenth century; history did not have to wait for the eighteenth century for this phenomenon to develop. Peter appeared and put the gentry "back in harness," but prior to his advent the perquisites of service were not at all in balance with the service performed.

Also, A. V. Romanovich-Slavatinskii's remark that "until the reforms of Peter the Great at the beginning of the eighteenth century Russia did not have a *gentry* in the sense of a separate estate, a social group, whose members were linked by a consciousness of a unity of a general estate interest and who were given special rights distinct from other social classes" is hard to accept in as stark terms as he puts it (*Dvorianstvo*, p. 2).

193. A. M. Gnevushev wrote that "in the seventeenth century a new governing nobility grew up to replace the former one wiped out by Ivan IV and the Time of Troubles. Until the second half of the century the new nobility did not enjoy a privileged position in the state. First place was held without dispute by the service

class" ("Zemlevladenie i sel'skoe khoziaistvo," p. 289). The evidence does not support either such a denigration of the power of the upper service class or an idealization of the middle service class.

194. Koretskii, "K istorii vosstaniia Bolotnikova," p. 142.

195. Miliukov, *Ocherki* (1900), 1:180; Stashevskii, "Sluzhiloe soslovie," p. 30.

4. The Introduction of St. George's Day

1. Kochin, *Sel'skoe khoziaistvo*, pp. 410, 422. D. P. Makovskii found sixty-five princely charters encouraging labor-raiding from other principalities in the fifteenth century. He also examined restrictions on other classes of the population, in addition to thirty-four such restrictions on peasants (*Razvitie*, pp. 206–7, 310; Iakovlev, "Ocherk" istorii," pp. 6–7). George Vernadsky also is of the opinion that the peasant was still personally free in the early post-Mongol period ("Serfdom," p. 252). For some examples, see *MIKR*, nos. 28, 29, 40; Alekseev, "Chernaia volost'," p. 83–84; Mikhailov, "K" voprosu," p. 340.

2. Boris Urlanis, "Time to Live," *Sputnik* (June 1969), p. 11.

3. A. A. Borisov, *Klimaty SSSR* (Moscow: Prosveshchenie, 1967), pp. 164–73, 182–200; I. E. Buchinskii, *O klimate*, pp. 85–86; V. T. Pashuto, "Golodnye gody v Drevnei Rusi," in *Ezhegodnik po agrarnoi istorii vostochnoi Evropy za 1962 g.* (Minsk: Nauka i Tekhnika, 1964), pp. 61–94; Arcadius Kahan, "Natural Calamities and Their Effect Upon the Food Supply in Russia," *Jahrbücher für Geschichte Osteuropas* 16, no. 3 (September 1968): 353–77; Razin, *Istoriia*, 2:308; Michel Roublev, "The Mongol Tribute According to the Wills and Agreements of the Russian Princes," in *The Structure of Russian History. Interpretive Essays*, edited by Michael Cherniavsky (New York: Random House, 1970), pp. 29–64. I also had the privilege of reading Mr. Roublev's 1968 mimeographed paper, "Scope and Frequency of Mongol Raids: 1237–1480."

4. Cherepnin, "Novye dokumenty," pp. 46–48, 51; idem, *Novgorodskie*, pp. 166–74. There are more examples from a period slightly later than the one we are now discussing, but undoubtedly the same type of depredations occurred earlier as well. In the early sixteenth century a Prince Fedor Borisovich plundered his peasants, causing 270 houses to be vacated in Volokolamsk (*Poslaniia Iosifa Volotskogo*, edited by A. A. Zimin and Ia. S. Lur'e [Moscow-Leningrad: Akademiia Nauk SSSR, 1959], pp. 212–14). Sixteenth-century examples can be found in MIKR, nos. 62 (1561), 63 (1564), 68 (1580). A nightmare of the 1630s is described by Vainberg, "Bor'ba," pp. 252–53.

5. *PRP*, 2: 198, ibid., 3:95, 97–99.

6. I would not go so far as to say that this is the key to understanding Muscovite history. P. N. Miliukov went far in this direction with his emphasis on colonization in the posthumous volume of his famous essays (*Ocherki* [1964], 1, pt. 2, pp. 120–225). M. N. Pokrovskii, at the beginning of the 1920s, advanced a serious and convincing critique of the theory of the "struggle with the steppe" (the need for national defense against the nomads) as the major factor in the rise of the Muscovite state. He pointed out that when this defense was necessary, the country fell apart, and might have added that the high points of centralization occurred after the real danger from the steppe had passed (Alekseeva, *Oktiabr'skaia*, p. 240). A. N. Sakharov has observed that "chronologically the apogee of serfdom coincided with the colossal expansion of the state territory of Russia" ("O dialektike," p. 27).

7. David, *Status*, p. 88. In 1670 the government tried to keep the Razin peasant uprising from spreading to Siberia by quarantining the area and ordering sentries posted on all the roads to check everyone coming and going (Preobrazhenskii, "Ural," p. 281).

8. I doubt that the matter of "nationality" played any significant role in determining where a peasant might move. There is considerable evidence that in the seventeenth century the peasant border populace hardly recognized the political frontier between Russia and the Rzeczpospolita and Sweden and moved back and forth at will. See my comments below on the first half of the sixteenth century and articles 33 and 34 of chapter 11 of the *Ulozhenie* of 1649 (Iakubov, "Rossiia," pp. 268–89). Even in the

nineteenth century, Russian peasants were hardly conscious of the concept of nationality. Peasants in the Pripet area in 1934–35 were little more aware of their nationality (Florian Znaniecki, *Modern Nationalities. A Sociological Study* [Urbana: The University of Illinois Press, 1952], pp. 81–82) .

9. ESTIMATES OF THE POPULATION OF MUSCOVY (IN MILLIONS)

	P. P. Smirnov	D. P. Makovskii	V. Ts. Urlanis	A. I. Kopanev	P. N. Miliukov (territory as in 1897	V. I. Kozlov (all of USSR)	V. M. Kabuzan (territory of Petrine census)	Ia. E. Vodarskii
1500			5.8			16		
c. 1550	2 (to 3)		8.8	9-10	10–11½			
1580		4.5						
c. 1600	2.9 (to 4.5)			11-12	15			
1600			11.3					
1620s					12½			
c. 1650	4.9							
1678	6.5				16			9
1719					13		15.578	

SOURCES: Smirnov, "Dvizhenie," 2:69; Makovskii, *Razvitie*, p. iv; Urlanis, *Rost naseleniia v Evrope* (Moscow: Statizdat, 1941) , p. 190; Kopanev, "Naselenie," pp. 245, 254. Miliukov, *Ocherki* (1900), 1:26–31; Kozlov, "Narodonaselenie," *SIE*, 9: 982; Kabuzan, *Narodonaselenie Rossii* (Moscow: Akademiia Nauk SSSR, 1963) , pp. 164, 171; Vodarskii, "Chislennost'," p. 227.

Corrected data on the population of about half of the ninety-three *uezdy* where serfdom predominated indicate that the population rose just slightly between 1678 and 1721. This review also indicates that the error in the taking of the seventeenth-century Muscovite censuses was by no means as large as has been assumed (Vodarskii, "K voprosu," p. 142; idem, "Chislennost' posadskogo," p. 272) .

Considerably larger estimates than the above can be found in table 12 (between pp. 240–41) of V. I. Kozlov's *Dinamika chislennosti narodov. Metodologiia issledovaniia i osnovnye faktory* (Moscow: Nauka, 1969) .

10. Population density per square verst in 1678:

Center (Moscow Province)	39.1
Southwest (Kiev Province)	11.4
West (Smolensk Province)	9.6
South (Azov Province)	4.5
Southeast (Kazan' Province)	2.2
East (Siberia Province)	1.8
North (Arkhangel'sk Province)	1.1

P. N. Miliukov, *Ocherki* (1900) , 1:31. A. M. Gnevushev calculated that the density of the five Novgorod districts varied from 1.2 to 4.9 persons per square verst in 1495–1505 (Kopanev, "Naselenie," p. 244). A verst equals 1.0668 kilometers; a square verst is equivalent to 1.138 square kilometers. For southern frontier densities in the first half of the seventeenth century, see Zagorovskii, *Belgorodskaia*, pp. 42–43.

11. I. I. Smirnov, "Zametki," no. 3, p. 138.

12. Cherepnin, *Obrazovanie*, pp. 149–50, 746.

13. *SGGD*, 1, nos. 34, 41: *DDG*, nos. 12, 21; Howes, *Testaments*, pp. 215, 227; Cherepnin, pp. 748–49. This interpretation has been questioned. See Alef, "A History," pp. 69–72, 117. The Austrian diplomat, Sigismund Herberstein, writing over a century

after the events, reported that Vasilii II, suspecting his wife Anastasia of adultery, had left the principality of Moscow not to their son but to his brother Iurii (*Commentaries*, p. 9).

14. Herberstein reported that Iurii bequeathed Muscovy to his nephew Vasilii II (*Commentaries*, p. 9).

15. Solov'ev, *Istoriia*, 2:393–94.

16. *PSRL*, 11:7; ibid., 12:17–18; Cherepnin, *Obrazovanie*, p. 756.

17. Alef, "A History," p. 126. Solov'ev believed this began the war. *PSRL*, 5:265; ibid., 6:148; ibid., 8:97; ibid., 12:17; ibid., 18:172–73.

18. Solov'ev, 2:393–94; Cherepnin, *Obrazovanie*, p. 756. The war may have been reopened by Vasilii, who took Dmitrov from Iurii; this place had been given to Iurii as a consolation prize at the Horde (Alef, "A History," pp. 118, 121–22, 140). For another interpretation, see Presniakov, *Obrazovanie*, p. 390, where the Dmitrov affair is seen as the cause of the reopening of the war. Vsevolozhskii had defected to Iurii before the wedding, after Sofia had not allowed her son Vasilii II to marry Vsevolozhskii's daughter (Alef, "A History," p. 124). S. B. Veselovskii felt the critical event was the change of brides, from which the enraged Vesvolozhskii's provocation involving the belt followed (*Issledovaniia*, pp. 340–43, 525–26).

19. Alef, "A History," p. 139.

20. Cherepnin, *Obrazovanie*, pp. 155–58, 757–803. One of the most famous pieces of contemporary evidence is the 1452–53 message from the Russian metropolitan to Patriarch Gennadii in Constantinople explaining why the church could send such small donations: "Nasha zemlia ot pogan'stva i mezhdosobnykh branei velmi istoshchala i potomilasia" (*AI*, 1, no. 263).

21. Cherepnin, *Obrazovanie*, p. 809; idem, *Arkhivy*, 2:150–59.

22. Cherepnin, "Istoricheskie usloviia," p. 96; Koretskii, "Pravaia," p. 186. In the fourteenth century, mainly in the second half, 42 monasteries were founded; 57 new ones arose in the fifteenth century. This yielded a total of 150 cenobitic monasteries in the countryside by the end of the sixteenth century (including 51 founded in the sixteenth century). In the same period 104 monasteries, usually of the old idiorhythmic type, were founded in towns (Ivina, "Istochniki," p. 16; Budovnits, *Monastyri*, pp. 201, 216, 223, 234, 239–42, 357, 359).

23. Budovnits, *Monastyri*, pp. 343, 345, 361; Obraztsov, "Iz istorii zakreposhcheniia," p. 334; Rozhdestvenskii, "Dvinskie," p. 143.

24. Cherepnin, "Istoricheskie usloviia," pp. 88, 90.

25. Budovnits, *Monastyri*; Zagorovskii, *Belgorodskaia*, p. 36. A. N. Sakharov has questioned Budnovnits's perhaps exaggerated debunking of the role of monasteries in colonizing Russia ("O dialektike," pp. 24–25). On the issue of monastic colonization, see El'iashevich, *Istoriia*, 1:290. Conclusions on the role of the monasteries in the development of Russian agriculture seem as difficult to arrive at as in the French case: "It is impossible in the present state of our evidence to apportion credit for the great work of clearing the waste between prelates and religious on the one hand and secular lords on the other. But there can be no doubt that the churchmen, with their more consistent habit of thought and wider range of vision, played a very important part" (Bloch, *French Rural History*, p. 15).

26. The landed growth of church institutions can be followed in published collections (*AFZ*; *ASEI*; Veselovskii, "Zhalovannye," pp. 1–81; V. B. Kobrin, "Gramoty XIV-XV vv. iz arkhiva Kirillo-Belozerskogo monastyria," in *Arkheograficheskii ezhegodnik za 1968 god* [1970]: 406-10; Kashtanov, "Kopiinye," pp. 3–47). See also Cherepnin, *Obrazovanie*, p. 179; Makovskii, *Razvitie*, pp. 170–71, 472–73).

Merchants also purchased land in the fifteenth century, but apparently (obviously most records have been lost) on a smaller scale than monasteries and the metropolitan. Boyars and princes were far less active in the land market than even the merchants (Makovskii, *Razvitie*, pp. 230–31; Ivina, "Istochniki," pp. 14–24). The relative absence of the boyars and princes from the land market reflects the fact, which will be noted throughout this essay, that land-ownership held a seemingly minimal attraction for the ruling governmental elite of Muscovy. Probably because of the sparseness of the population, laymen who held real power preferred government posts to land grants, for as officials they could wield authority and collect their fees anywhere (the populace had to live *somewhere*) rather than be restricted to a particular plot whose inhabitants might vanish at any moment. This was basically true until at least the middle of the sixteenth century (and perhaps even later to some degree), and the enserfment may have played a significant role in changing this outlook on the control of land. The old Muscovite attitude probably differed from that found in most other places in the world. For a discussion of the social significance of the control of land, see Edward Shils, *Selected Essays* (Chicago: Center for Social Organization Studies, Department of Sociology of the University of Chicago, 1970), p. 6.

27. Both sides eagerly sought by means of land grants to gain the support of the Troitse Sergiev monastery, already on its way to becoming the country's greatest (Dmitrii Shemiaka: *ASEI*, 1, nos. 101, 164, 165. Vasilii II: *AFZKh*, 1, no. 96. Budnovits, *Monastyri*, p. 202). A somewhat similar situation occurred in 1507. At the time Vasilii III was vigorously curtailing all monastery tax immunities, but he did make a grant to the Belopesotskii monastery of Kashira, which was subject to the Kazan' tsar Mukhammed-Emin, with whom Vasilii had begun open warfare in 1506 (Kashtanov, "Ogranichenie feodal'nogo immuniteta," pp. 275–76).

28. B. D. Grekov believed all lords had a role in the developments of this period (*Krest'iane*, p. 835).

29. Kliuchevskii, *Istoriia soslovii*, p. 88. See *SGGD*, 1, no. 24. *Kormlenie* fees were split half-and-half between the prince and his boyar lieutenant (*namestnik*).

30. Kliuchevskii, *Istoriia soslovii*, pp. 88–89.

31. Ibid., p. 79; Sh., "Dvorianstvo," no. 2, p. 554.

32. Kliuchevskii, *Istoriia soslovii*, pp. 80–81. This was true in the Riazan' principality as late as 1496 (*SGGD*, 1, no. 128).

33. See chapter 2 above for additional information on the early Muscovite army and its compensation.

34. Budovnets, *Monastyri*, pp. 200, 232.

35. *ASEI*, 1, nos. 264 (Bezhetskii Verkh), 265 (Uglich); R. E. F. Smith, *The Enserfment of the Russian Peasantry* (Cambridge: Cambridge University Press, 1968), nos. 22, 23. For my review of this collection of fifty-six translated documents, see *The Journal of Modern History* 41, no. 4 (December 1969): 534–41.

36. Mikhailov, "K" voprosu," pp. 343–49.

37. Kochin, *Sel'skoe khoziaistvo*, p. 410. At the turn of the century, the legal historian V. I. Sergeevich emphasized that this was a special grant which by its very nature deviated from what was obviously, to contemporaries, established custom and law (*Russkiia drevnosti*, 3:464). I. Kulisher also called this "an exclusive privilege" ("Nesvobodnoe," p. 192). On the other hand, P. E. Mikhailov, following M. A. D'iakonov in many respects, incorrectly claimed that the government's response to the monastery's petition was simply a legal sanction to a developing custom ("Obychnyi institut"," p. 100).

38. *MIKR*, no. 30. In 1443 Prince Ivan Andreevich of Mozhaisk granted the long-time residents of the Troitse Sergiev monastery special privileges that freed them from all taxes and customs duties. He also gave exclusive fishing privileges to the long-time residents of the Kirillov monastery of Beloozero (*AAE*, 1: no. 38; Mikhailov, "K" voprosu," p. 339; Nosov, *Stanovlenie*, p. 122). See also Kashtanov, *Ocherki*, pp. 345–47.

Over a century later similar tactics were still being used. In 1569, as Ivan IV was on the verge of executing V. A. Staritskii, he granted the Uspenskii monastery of Staritsa a lucrative charter exempting it from taxation and the civil courts in Staritsa. This was certainly a measure to gain the monastery's support for Ivan (Kashtanov, "K izucheniiu oprichniny," p. 112).

39. *ASEI*, 1, no. 164; Cherepnin, *Obrazovanie*, pp. 806, 813–14. Cherepnin also makes the point that Moscow may have wanted to bind the peasants to the area to

keep them from deserting for nearby Novgorod (*Russkie feodal'nye arkhivy*, 2:158). I find this point less convincing, although it may well have been a minor factor in the government's consideration. If so, it was pointless, for I know of no sanctions the government could have invoked to return fugitives from Novgorod.

40. Mikhailov, "K" voprosu," p. 341, citing *ATN*, 1, no. 1.

41. *MIKR*, no. 36; Solov'ev, *Istoriia*, 2:406, 409, 441. In his will Vasilii gave his third son, Andrei Bol'shoi, both Uglich (where he was born in 1446 and which he received as a *udel* in 1448) and Bezhetskii Verkh. I do not know whether there was any significance in this (Solov'ev, *Istoriia*, 2:446; Howes, *Testaments*, pp. 248–49).

42. In the mid-1450s the government of victorious Vasilii II gave out masses of privilege charters exempting the lords of Shemiaka's provinces from taxation and the judicial authority (except in felony cases) of the Moscow great prince. This was an attempt to gain support in the war-torn areas, particularly Galich and Uglich (Cherepnin, *Russkie feodal'nye arkhivy*, 2:150–58).

43. This date is similar to others chosen elsewhere to restrict peasant mobility. The Pskov Judicial Charter, whose date of origin is unknown, restricted the movement of peasants to around the time of St. Philip's Fast (*Filipovo zagoven'e*), November 14 (arts. 42, 44, 63, 76). This is considered to be after the harvest (Kamentseva, "Usloviia," p. 142).

44. *ASEI*, 1, nos. 338, 359; ibid., 2, nos. 101, 138, 177, 193, 276, 326; *MS*, pp. 97–104. Judging by the generally imitative-adaptive nature of Russian civilization, I would assume that the initial Muscovite restrictions on peasant mobility were modeled on those enacted in Lithuania in 1447 (Vladimirskii-Budanov, *Khristomatiia*, 2: 30–31; Picheta, *Belorussiia*, pp. 305, 315, 383–84; Vernadsky, "Serfdom," p. 252).

45. Cherepnin, *Russkie feodal'nye arkhivy*, 2:374.

46. *ASEI*, 2, nos. 326, 138; Solov'ev, 2:408; Ekzempliarskii, *Velikie*, 2:330–31; Cherepnin, *Obrazovanie*, pp. 802–5, 815.

47. *ASEI*, 2, no. 326. A. A. Zimin has advanced the idea that the *serebrennik* ("silver peasant") was not a debtor, but one who paid his rent in cash (*serebro*) ("A. D. Gorskii. *Ocherki*," p. 173). See also Cherepnin, "Aktovyi material," p. 325. If this hypothesis were correct, a minor revision of my interpretation of the origin of serfdom in Russia would be in order. Two hundred years later the magnate Boris Ivanovich Morozov issued strict instructions that all loans should be collected from the harvest (Petrikeev, *Krupnoe krepostnoe khoziaistvo*, p. 150).

48. Kliuchevskii, *Istoriia soslovii*, pp. 84–85; Cherepnin, "Iz istorii formirovaniia," pp. 252–53.

49. *ASEI*, 2, no. 138.

50. Article 57, *Sudebniki*, p. 27; *MS*, pp. 104–5.

51. Gorskii, "Ob ogranichenii," pp. 132–44.

52. *ASEI*, 2, no. 101. The Muscovites must have known the limitations on peasant mobility which had been introduced in Poland, Lithuania, Transylvania, and elsewhere.

53. Gorskii, p. 143.

54. *ASEI*, 2, nos. 193, 177.

55. Ibid., 1, nos. 338, 359.

56. Ibid., 2, no. 276. In brief, *vykhod* was a peasant's move under his own power, *vyvoz* with someone's aid. For a discussion of *vyvoz* and *vykhod*, see Kliuchevskii, "Proiskhozhdenie," pp. 288–89.

57. Makovskii, *Razvitie*, p. 206. R. E. F. Smith claims that peasants recorded in censuses taken of the grand princely estates in the 1460s were not to be moved. It is not clear how the *Sudebnik* of 1497, which allowed all peasants to move, related to these peasants ("Medieval," p. 545).

58. Kliuchevskii, *Istoriia soslovii*, p. 84. "A boiarom", i detem" boiarskim" i slugam" i khristianom" mezh" nas" volnym" volia," *SGGD*, 1, no. 128. I. M. Kulisher maintained, on the other hand, that the institution of St. George's Day had become a general practice long before it was included in the *Sudebnik* ("Nesvobodnoe sostoianie," p. 184).

59. A. E. Presniakov, who was inclined to call serfdom seignorial power over the peasant, attributed great significance to the rise and expansion of the service land system in enserfing the peasantry (*Moskovskoe tsarstvo,* p. 102). That had nothing to do, however, with the legal developments at the end of the fifteenth century.

60. Cherepnin, "Istoricheskie usloviia," p. 91.

61. Tkhorzhevskii, "Pomest'e," p. 75.

62. Samokvasov, *Krest'iane,* p. 41; Polosin, "Pomestnoe pravo," pp. 40, 42; Makovskii, *Razvitie,* p. 178.

63. Loans and rent were always collected immediately after the harvest (*Ocherki . . . XVII,* p. 183).

64. P. E. Mikhailov claimed that the peasants did not revolt against this universal limitation because they had already become accustomed to it ("Obychnyi institut'," pp. 103, 109). The crucial factor was not that they had become accustomed to the restriction, but that they were accustomed to moving after the agricultural season was over.

Even A. A. Zimin can find no evidence of resistance to the 1497 restriction, even though he assumes it to have been a repressive measure ("Etapy," pp. 40–43). His notions about a "Reformation movement" spreading from town to countryside can hardly be substantiated by the evidence. The absence of peasant participation in the Judaizer and church land controversies becomes especially noticeable when compared with peasant involvement in the Nikon-Old Believer controversy a century and a half later (Bulygin et al., "Nachal'nyi," p. 89).

S. M. Kashtanov claims that peasant flights were reaching massive proportions at this time. (They were not fleeing because of the 1497 decree, which does not figure in Kashtanov's constructions). He arrives at this conclusion from the observation that apparently government grants to a few lords at this time gave them the right to punish peasants engaged in begging ("poproshatai") —and because Engels once wrote that "the numbers of vagabonds were unprecedented in all developed countries in the first half of the sixteenth century" ("Ogranichenie," pp. 279–80).

65. Lappo, "Tverskoi uezd'," p. 48.

66. Presniakov, *Moskovskoe tsarstvo,* pp. 105–6.

67. Some historians have maintained that the Russian peasant possessed a "toiler's right" (*trudovoe pravo*), the right to use a lord's land as long as he continued to farm it (Vernadsky, "Serfdom in Russia," p. 252). It is clear that the relationship was reciprocal in the Pskov Judicial Charter (art. 42): the lord could discharge the peasant and the latter could quit, but only on Philip's Fast Day (*MIKR,* no. 20). This reciprocity was not present in Muscovy.

68. Cherepnin, "Istoricheskie usloviia," p. 90; Zagorovskii, *Belgorodskaia,* p. 22; Alef, "Reflections," p. 103.

69. Kochin, "Razvitie," pp. 278, 284–305, particularly 292–96; idem, *Sel'skoe khoziaistvo,* chap. 2; Kashtanov and Klokman, "Sovetskaia," p. 161; Zimin, "A. D. Gorskii. *Ocherki,*" pp. 171–72. Gorskii tried to show that the three-field system was operative (but not dominant) in the fourteenth century (*Ocherki,* pp. 32–55, especially 34–37). High Stalinist historians sometimes traced the three-field system back to the twelfth century.

70. A. I. Malyshev emphasized the production of grain for the market in this period (Danilova, "Stanovlenie," p. 94). However, this production was for the internal market only. Unlike Poland, Muscovy did not export a significant amount of grain even in the sixteenth century. Therefore the Russian enserfment cannot be explained by demands for a more active participation in foreign trade (Shmidt, "Voprosy," p. 107). A. A. Zimin stresses that Russia was beginning to leave the natural economy era and was entering an era of commodity and money relationships. This led, in Zimin's eyes, to an increase of rent which had to be paid in cash. The peasants were not accustomed to this, and began to flee from what was (or seemed to them) an increase in the level of exploitation. In turn the lords demanded that the government limit peasant mobility ("Osnovnye etapy," p. 40). The Soviet historian L. V. Danilova also

takes at face value the claim in the first half of the sixteenth century by Ermolai Erazm that cash rent was the major enemy of the Russian peasantry ("Istoricheskie usloviia," p. 120). It is true that many rents and taxes formerly paid in kind were converted to cash in this period, but there is no evidence that this was more exploitative or that the peasants objected or resisted (Kashtanov, "Otrazhenie," p. 256).

S. M. Kashtanov views the fact that the lord was collecting more rent (and the state more cash taxes) as in itself giving him more administrative power over the peasant (*Sotsial'no-politicheskaia istoriia*, p. 14; "Otrazhenie," p. 258).

71. The sum was half this in forested regions (*Sudebniki*, p. 27; *MS*, pp. 104–5).

72. Kashtanov, "Otrazhenie," p. 252; idem, "Ogranichenie," p. 294; Geiman, "Neskol'ko," no. 24; D'iakonov, ed., *Svodnyi*, pp. 12–13; Man'kov, ed., *Materialy*, pp. 65, 68, 69.

73. Tkhorzhevskii, "Pomest'e," p. 77.

74. Rozhkov, "Sel'skoe," p. 169. The value of the harvest at the beginning of the sixteenth century was 290 kopeks (ibid.).

75. Gnevushev, "Zemlevladenie," pp. 298–99. For an extensive discussion of the black-land question, see Makovskii, *Razvitie*, pp. 19–20, 37, 140, especially 331–66. See also Miliukov, *Spornye*, pp. 33–34, for a brief discussion of the question in central Russia. His basic opinion was that peasant black land actually belonged to the prince ("Krest'iane," p. 676). See also articles 84 and 87 of the 1550 *Sudebnik* and compare with the comparable articles (157, 173) in the 1589 *Sudebnik* for a current understanding. See also Bogoslovskii, *Zemskoe*, 1:48–61, for additional information on black lands.

Struggle over black lands began at the end of the fifteenth century when state and monasteries were in search of land: expansion to the east and south was blocked by Tatars, westward expansion was very difficult against Poland, Lithuania, and Livonia. So monasteries began to take peasant black lands, especially during the reigns of Ivan III and Vasilii III. This was part of the entire land controversy (Zimin, "Osnovy," pp. 40–41, citing manuscript of L. I. Ivina, "Pravye gramoty i bor'ba za zemliu v Russkom gosudarstve vo vtoroi polovine XV- nachale XVI v.").

Black lands disappeared in the center of the state only with the Oprichnina (Koretskii, "Pravaia," p. 194). This was a consequence of the expansion of the *pomest'e* system in the second half of the sixteenth century (Nosov, "Mnogotomnaia," p. 140; Gnevushev, "Zemlevladenie," pp. 281–82). The isolated black lands remaining by the beginning of the seventeenth century in the center and on the Volga nearly all disappeared in the first quarter of the century (ibid., p. 292). Black lands disappeared entirely in the center, southern, and western parts of the Muscovite state by the end of the seventeenth century (Rozhdestvenskii, "Sel'skoe," pp. 56–57; Samokvasov, *Krest'-iane*, pp. 37–40). The process of usurpation of peasant lands by others is evident in the 1601 census of the properties of the Kirillov monastery of Beloozero, when many lands which formerly had not been monastery property were ascribed to it by the state (Gorfunkel', "Perestroika," p. 109). For numerous documents showing that some "black" peasants continued to buy, sell, redeem, and mortgage their lands throughout the seventeenth century, see Voskoboinikova, "Rodovoi arkhiv."

The issue of black lands has always been one of the interesting secondary disputes of Russian historiography. The answers given often have depended on the author's ideology. Some historians have held that the state owned black lands (Platonov, *Lektsii*, p. 195; Presniakov, *Moskovskoe tsarstvo*, p. 100; Rozhkov, "Sel'skoe khoziaistvo," p. 171). This is also the view held by some Soviet historians (Pokrovskii, "Kupchie," pp. 81, 83, 85). Pokrovskii describes the process of the "feudalization" of black land at the same time that the state is becoming centralized (ibid., p. 90). Recently the Soviet scholar A. D. Gorskii asserted that the state owned black lands because during a feudal period peasants are a dependent class, which means that they could not own landed property—the basic means of production (*Ocherki*, pp. 160–61; Danilova, "K itogam," p. 57). L. V. Cherepnin expresses the Marxist position mixed with that of pre-Soviet scholars: the state owned the land, the peasants possessed it; taxes were rent to the feudal lord, the prince (the state) (*Obrazovanie*, pp. 182–83). See also *Ocherki . . . XVII*, pp. 119–21.

On the other hand, Gnevushev ("Zemlevladenie," p. 268), Kopanev (*Istoriia zemlevladeniia*, pp. 185, 191, 193, 202), Kochin (*Sel'skoe*, pp. 370–88, especially 386), Liashchenko (*Istoriia*, 1:238–39), Makovskii (*Razvitie*, see the above citations), and Alekseev (*Agrarnaia*, p. 23; "Chernaia volost'," pp. 76–84) have all argued for peasant ownership (with differing emphases on whether and how much it was private and/or communal property) of black lands, in spite of the obvious ideological difficulties (Danilova, "K itogam," p. 57). I. I. Smirnov "perverted Marx" to argue that the peasants owned the land (not simply possessed it) through the commune. These black lands were the material basis of the freedom of the peasants inhabiting them ("Zametki," no. 2, 148–52; see also Kashtanov and Klokman, "Sovetskaia," pp. 162–63, 165; A. N. Sakharov, "O dialektike," pp. 27–28). Novosel'skii argued that in a situation where the peasant could sell or otherwise alienate his land allotment, communal agriculture was not being practiced (*Ocherki . . . XVII*, p. 192). The emigré historian V. B. El'iashevich has argued that the "black peasant" was a full owner of his land (*Istoriia prava*, 1:35, 49, 51).

If there is a middle ground on this question, it may be in Rozhdestvenskii's claim that the peasants living in black communes had the full right to dispose of their lands, but were "conscious of a higher right of property belonging to the tsar" ("Sel'skoe," pp. 36–37, 55). This is expressed by saying that the peasant did not have property rights to land, but very broad right of use (Iakovlev, "Ocherk" istorii krepostnago prava," p. 5).

76. Pobedimova, "O nekotorykh," p. 94. I am aware of the calculations showing that twenty-five kopeks was more than a peasant could earn if he sold all the grain he raised in a year (Blum, *Lord*, p. 112). My evidence would seem to show either that something is wrong with the calculations of the price of grain in this period, or that grain was not the sole marketable commodity the peasant had (Rozhkov, "Sel'skoe khoziaistvo," p. 167). The latter would seem more likely.

77. *PRP*, 4:532–33.

78. *MIKR*, no. 95; *MS*, pp. 118–19. There is also evidence indicating that the sum had some relationship to the cost of a house. For example, the Iosif Volokolamsk monastery made loans of from ninety kopeks to two rubles fifteen kopeks for construction in the 1570s (Timofeev, "Krest'ianskie vykhody," p. 66). This contrasts with Giles Fletcher's contemporary observation that a house cost twenty or thirty rubles to build. Perhaps his "fair house" was more elegant than the typical peasant construction (Berry and Crummey, *Rude*, p. 126).

79. Mikhailov, "Obychnyi institut"," p. 108; Kulisher, "Nesvobodnoe," p. 190. I. D. Beliaev, on the other hand, said it was to facilitate movement by requiring the peasant to pay only his rent, not his debts (*Krest'iane*, p. 52).

80. *PRP*, 4:111–12. In 1595 the Iosif Volokolamsk monastery was fining its peasants five rubles apiece for disorders (*MIKR*, no. 78). This would seem to indicate something about the meaning of five rubles in peasant-lord relationships of the time.

81. Timofeev, "Krest'ianskie vykhody," pp. 69, 77–80; *DAI*, 1, no. 51-xxii, xxiv.

82. Olearius, *Travels*, p. 36. See also the frequent references to the ease of winter travel, the *zimnii put'*, in *AMG*, 2, no. 498, and elsewhere; L. N. Godovikova, " 'Moskovskoe posol'stvo' Antonio Possevino," *Vestnik Moskovskogo universiteta. IX. Istoriia* 25, no. 5 (September-October 1970): 98; Rozhkov, "Sel'skoe khoziaistvo," p. 168. The first fall frost now usually hits Novgorod and Moscow about September 21, the Beloozero region to the north in the taiga ten days earlier, the Pskov area to the northwest close to the Baltic ten days later (*Atlas sel'skogo khoziaistva SSSR* [Moscow: GUGK-MGON SSSR, 1960], p. 13; A. A. Borisov, *Klimaty SSSR* [Moscow: Prosveshchenie, 1967], p. 59). The St. George's Day moving date thus gave the peasants about two months in which to harvest and thresh his summer crop (*AMG*, 3, nos. 256, 528) and about the same amount of time for the ground to freeze before he set out for a new home. The average temperature of the air on the earth's surface in November

in the relevant parts of Muscovy was probably about −4°C., which is not very cold (*Fiziko-geograficheskii atlas mira* [Moscow: GUGK GGK SSSR, 1964], p. 209). The climate of Muscovy probably was somewhat different from that of the Russia of today (particularly before the forests were logged over), but the differences cannot have been overwhelmingly great. If the theory advanced by L. N. Gumilev about a periodic ever-changing climate on the East European plain is correct, this statement would have to be revised (*Otkrytie Khazarii* [*Istoriko-geograficheskii etiud*] [Moscow: Nauka, 1966] pp. 28–31).

83. Marija Gimbutas, "Ancient Slavic Religion: A Synopsis," *To Honor Roman Jakobson. Essays on the Occasion of His Seventieth Birthday*, 3 vols. (The Hague: Mouton, 1967), 1:750.

84. Article 88, *Sudebniki*, pp. 172–73; *MS*, pp. 105–6. It is a tenet of Soviet historiography that the *Sudebnik* of 1550 changed nothing on the peasant question (Valk, "I. I. Smirnov," p. 26). The fee to be paid by the departing peasants was hardly significant "compensation to the lord for the labor lost," as claimed by A. M. Sakharov (*Obrazovanie*, p. 97).

85. Rozhkov, "Sel'skoe khoziaistvo," p. 163.

86. Nosov, *Stanovlenie*, p. 107; Makovskii, *Razvitie*, p. 140; Staden, *Land*, pp. 33, 67, especially 69. See specific cases of 1555 in *Khrestomatiia* (1962), no. 8 (*DAI*, 1, no. 56); 1574 in *AI*, 1, no. 191; D'iakonov, *Zapovednyia*, p. 13; 1577 in *MIKR*, no. 56; 1580 in *MIKR*, no. 68. On the struggle for labor, see also *DAI*, 1, no. 51-xxii, xxiv.

87. Zimin, "Osnovnye etapy," pp. 43, 52. P. Mikhailov mistakenly thought that there was a serious economic crisis at the end of the fifteenth century and throughout the sixteenth. He arrived at this conclusion by establishing a fictitious continuum between the economic crises caused by the civil war of Vasilii II and by Ivan IV's Oprichnina and Livonian War ("Obychnyi institut"," pp. 87, 97–98). These crises, in Mikhailov's view, caused the binding of the long-time residents as the lords struggled to hold on to their renters.

88. Herberstein, *Commentaries*, pp. 75–76, 79, 90, 97. Elsewhere, however, he noted that the condition of the peasants was lamentable, that they had to work for their lords six days a week (ibid., p. 62; Rozhdestvenskii, "Sel'skoe," p. 60). This sounds, however, like a description of the slave-agriculturalist rather than the peasant-becoming-serf. Many large estates were farmed by slaves in this period, in spite of the fact that slavery was a dying institution.

89. P. P. Smirnov, "Dvizhenie naseleniia," p. 70.

90. Berry and Crummey, *Rude*, pp. 5, 32, 56, 63, 67; Hakluyt Society, *Early Voyages*, 1:35; ibid., 2:246. For an account of poverty and starvation in the slums, see ibid., 2:376. The comments of the critics of monastery landholding, such as Ermolai Erazm, Maksim Grek, and Vassian Patrikeev, in the first half of the sixteenth, on the miserable condition of the monastery peasantry can be assumed to be largely tendentious rhetoric which hardly represented the conditions of the mass of the peasantry (Koretskii, "Bor'ba krest'ian," pp. 213–14; Shmidt, "K izucheniiu agrarnoi," p. 20). On the other hand, P. E. Mikhailov believed that Vassian Patrikeev and Maksim Grek portrayed correctly the contemporary reality of the peasant condition ("K" voprosu," pp. 324–25).

91. Kopanev, "Naselenie," pp. 237–41.

92. For a lengthy review of this interesting and' provocative work, see my "The Foundations of Russian Capitalism," *Slavic Review* 26, no. 1 (March 1967) : 148–54. A. M. Sakharov, misinterpreting much of what I wrote, claimed my review had the purpose of somehow heating up the Cold War ("O nekotorykh priemakh iskazheniia srednevekovoi istorii Rossii v zarubezhnoi istoricheskoi literature," *Vestnik moskovskogo universiteta. Seriia IX. Istoriia* 24, no. 4 [July-August 1969]: 19–21). Whether there was an "upsurge" and, if so, how significant it was, is one of the hottest issues of contemporary Soviet historiography. Partisans of the view that there was such an upsurge, in addition to Makovskii and S. G. Strumilin, are S. M. Kashtanov (*Sotsial'no-*) and N. E. Nosov. Nosov says that Makovskii exaggerated (*Stanovlenie*, pp. 289–90),

but he takes generally the same position (ibid., pp. 9–10, 193–96, 225, 241–42, 245, 248, 257, 260–61, 265, 271, 274, 276, 279, 283, 285, 307, 312, 325; "Sobor 'primireniia' 1549 goda"). See also Veselovskii, *Feodal'noe*, p. 313. An opposing view can be found in Doroshenko, "Zametki," pp. 158–59, 161. See also Shmidt, "K izucheniiu," pp. 4–25, 29; Chistozvonov, "Nekotorye aspekty," p. 54; A. M. Sakharov, "Lenin ob osnovnykh," p. 309; *Obrazovanie*, pp. 73, 77, 80–81, 83–84, 86, 102, 111, 143, 145. An intermediate position could be attributed to L. V. Danilova, who observes many of the phenomena described by Makovskii, but says they are not of sufficient magnitude to warrant changing the traditional views of Soviet historiography ("Istoricheskie usloviia," pp. 116, 118). A. A. Zimin gives a neutral to positive response to Makovskii's book by terming it "interesting" ("Problemy," p. 325). See also his remark on the development of bourgeois ties in the sixteenth century in "Osnovnye etapy," pp. 40, 43. A conference in the Institute of History of the Academy of Sciences in July, 1965, came to the consensus that "capitalistic relations" exercised no determining influence on the socioeconomic and sociopolitical life of Russia in the sixteenth and seventeenth centuries (Bromlei, "Izuchenie," p. 115). This "consensus" simply upholds the prevailing Soviet notion that this period is one of feudalism. It should be noted that the adherents of this position are "specialists" on the eighteenth century. Pre-Soviet historians were inclined to regard the first half of the sixteenth century as still a period of natural economy, with a change toward a money economy in the second half of the century (Stashevskii, "Ekonomicheskaia politika," p. 345). In fact the situation was the reverse.

93. Makovskii, *Razvitie*, pp. 86, 94, 127; Hakluyt Society, *Russia*, p. 208.

94. Makovskii, *Razvitie*. p. 223.

95. Ibid., pp. 82, 223.

96. Ibid., pp. 158–66.

97. Ibid., p. 87.

98. Ibid., pp. 235–36.

99. Ibid., pp. 20–22, 150, 157, 231–34, 236, 330, 436–37, 446–60, 470.

100. Ibid., p. 237.

101. Ibid., p. 77.

102. Ibid., pp. 74, 156, 223.

103. Ibid., pp. 143–49.

104. Ibid., p. 223.

105. Ibid., p. 113.

106. S. M. Kashtanov claims that serfdom was spreading to the north of Russia and to newly annexed regions at this time, whereas the peasants of the center of the Moscovite state had already been enserfed by the beginning of the fifteenth century ("K probleme mestnogo upravleniia," pp. 145–47; idem, "K izucheniiu oprichniny," p. 105). N. E. Nosov argues convincingly for an opposite interpretation. The liquidation of Novgorod boyar control of the Dvina land at the end of the fifteenth century and the introduction of Muscovite rule established conditions for the flourishing of precapitalism in the region in the sixteenth century (*Stanovlenie*, pp. 242–44, 258, 270, 282–84, 286, 288, 312).

107. *DAI*, 1, no. 51-V, XVIII.

108. Grekov, "Iur'ev den'," pp. 77–78; Koretskii, *Zakreposhchenie*, pp. 64, 103–7.

109. Iakovlev, ed., *Namestnich'i*, pp. 103, 111.

110. Kopanev, "Ustavnaia," pp. 11–12, 19; Dewey *Muscovite*, pp. 77–78, 82.

111. S. Tkhorzhevskii viewed this as a special measure to keep taxpayers on the rolls ("Pomest'e," p. 83). On the other hand, P. E. Mikhailov saw in the Vaga charter confirmation of his view that long-time residents had lost their right to move and that this had become a tradition in the popular mind ("Obychnyi institut"," pp. 106, 108).

112. Nosov, "Zemskaia reforma," p. 144.

113. Sergeevich, *Russkiia*, 3: 453, 464–65. N. E. Nosov portrays these formulas as having effect not only in the Dvina land, but probably throughout Muscovy (*Stanovlenie*, pp. 295, 305, 308).

114. S. M. Kashtanov, following L. V. Cherepnin, defines serfdom as the extra-economic compulsion lords had over their peasants (*Sotsial'no-politicheskaia istoriia*, p. 4; idem, "K izucheniiu oprichniny," pp. 102, 109).

115. A fundamental historical controversy is still raging about the nature of the immunity and its origin in Russia—whether it simply recognized the lord's seignorial power over the peasant derived from land-ownership, or whether it was a princely grant delegating part of the ruler's authority to an agent (Cherepnin, "Problema," p. 64). The emigré historian El'iashevich opts that it was a princely grant (*Istoriia*, 1:391). This follows S. V. Veselovskii's position, based on theories of the state-juridical historical school, that immunities were created by princely grants. Veselovskii saw the forerunner of immunity rights in the personal relations between lord and slave or dependent individual (*zakup, serebrennik*). Presniakov, on the other hand, protested against this construction. Using works of Nevolin and Pavlov-Sil'vanskii, he defended the thesis that the grants were conditioned by common law relations, based on the ownership of land by the lords (*OIIN*, 4:275; Danilova, "Stanovlenie," p. 82; Presniakov, *Moskovskoe tsarstvo*, pp. 101–3). See also I. I. Smirnov, *Ocherki*, pp. 337–52; Dewey, "Immunities"; Kashtanov, "Feudal Immunities."

116. Kashtanov, *Sotsial'no-politicheskaia*, p. 12–13. The compilation of cadastres also cancelled immunity privileges later in the sixteenth century (Kashtanov, "Finansovaia problema," p. 256).

117. Dewey, *Muscovite*, pp. 23–29; Kashtanov, *Sotsial'no-politicheskaia*, pp. 14–15; idem, "Ogranichenie," p. 280; idem, "K probleme mestnogo," p. 143; Smith, *Enserfment*, nos. 14, 26 (murder only), 27–29 (all felonies).

There were exceptions, however, for even as late as the sixteenth century some holders of judicial immunities were granted jurisdiction over felonies. In this case, the peasants were subject solely to the monastery's jurisdiction (Obraztsov, "Iz istorii zakreposhcheniia," p. 336). This did not mean, however, that the peasants could not leave the monastery's jurisdiction.

118. Kashtanov, *Sotsial'no-politicheskaia istoriia*, p. 18; idem, "Feodal'nyi," pp. 250, 253.

119. These privileges, contained in so-called *nesudimye gramoty, obel'nye gramoty,* and *l'gotnye gramoty*, continued to be used by the church institutions and even renewed by the government until the end of the seventeenth century (Kulisher, "Nesvobodnoe," p. 178). There are hundreds of such documents extant, for the institutions concerned were very careful about their preservation. See *SGGD*, 1, no. 128; Nazarov, "Iz istorii agrarnoi politiki," pp. 108, 113–14; *AAE*, 2, nos. 204, 205; ibid., 3, nos. 84, 89, 95, 133, 175; ibid., 4, no. 3; *KOG*, 3. See S. M. Kashtanov's list of over sixteen hundred documents in his "Khronologicheskii perechen' immunitetnykh gramot XVI veka," *Arkheograficheskii ezhegodnik za 1957 god* (Moscow: AN SSSR, 1958), pp. 302–76; idem, *Arkheograficheskii ezhegodnik za 1960 god* (Moscow: AN SSSR, 1962), pp. 129–200; idem (with others), *Arkheograficheskii ezhegodnik za 1966 god* (Moscow: Nauka, 1968), pp. 197–253.

Anyone who still believes that Soviet historical scholarship is monolithic or centrally planned should read the interchange between S. M. Kashtanov and N. E. Nosov on the issue of immunities. Both work in the Institute of History of the Academy of Sciences. Yet Nosov (in Leningrad) did not know that Kashtanov was working (in Moscow) on the third list of immunities until it was published (Nosov, *Stanovlenie*, p. 162).

An especially broad grant was one of 1601 to the Troitse Sergiev monastery renewing earlier ones issued by Ivan IV and Fedor Ivanovich. It specified that the monastery was to run everything on its lands in the Serpukhov and Kolomna provinces (*uezdy*) with its own *guba* officials selected from the peasants according to the law of the state, even including robbery and theft cases. The monastery also was to run its own jail with its own peasant guards. State officials were not allowed to collect local government taxes from the monastery peasants (*AAE*, 2, no. 19).

120. Kashtanov, *Sotsial'no-politicheskaia*; idem, "Otrazhenie," pp. 260–63; idem, "Ogranichenie," pp. 271–73; idem, "Finansovaia problema," p. 253; idem, "Feodal'nyi immunitet"; *Sudebnik* 1550, art. 43 (repeated in the *Ulozhenie* of 1649, 10:153); *Stoglav*, chap. 56.

121. Kashtanov, "Feodal'nyi immunitet v gody boiarskogo pravleniia (1538-1548)," p. 265 (cited by Zimin, "Osnovnye etapy," p. 45). N. E. Nosov feels that Kashtanov's analysis is erroneous, that Kashtanov has mistaken simple acquisitions of land with resultant securing of immunities for a deliberate competitive political policy of granting immunities (*Stanovlenie*, pp. 175, 178). While Nosov's critique of Kashtanov's scholarship and conclusions unquestionably has considerable merit, nevertheless one must bear in mind that his position is based on his interpretation of the "Marxist position on the immunity as an attribute of feudal land property"; thus, for him, this development could not conceivably be regulated primarily by political considerations (ibid., pp. 178–79).

122. For an example of one of the few middle service class grants, see the one of 1546 to a lord with villages in Moscow, Kolomna, and Tula *uezdy (Tul'skii krai,* 1, no. 7.).

123. Kashtanov, "Ogranichenie," p. 280; Nosov, " 'Novoe', " pp. 268–70; *Stanovlenie*, pp. 133–34, 159–61. S. M. Kashtanov has assumed that the basic complex of the immunities granted has survived ("Feodal'nyi," p. 240).

124. Doroshenko, "Zametki," p. 157. N. A. Rozhkov assumed that the boyars had these rights as grants from the state, the *udel* princes as part of their inheritance of sovereign powers from their forebears ("Sel'skoe khoziaistvo," p. 179).

125. Doroshenko, "Zametki," p. 157.

126. Nosov, *Stanovlenie*, pp. 118, 137; Koretskii, "Zemskii sobor," pp. 47–48; Sergeevich, *Russkiia*, 3: 464. The importance of the change of rulers as a time for innovation in Russia has not been sufficiently emphasized. Apparently the Muscovites felt that even treaties with foreign powers had to be reconfirmed when a new monarch assumed the throne (Iakubov, "Rossiia," 184: 410).

127. Kashtanov, "K izucheniiu oprichniny," p. 99. For an opposing argument, see Aleksandrov, *Gosudarstvo*, p. 9.

128. Kashtanov, "Ogranichenie," pp. 275, 281; idem, "Finansovaia problema," pp. 246–47. Holders of immunity documents even lost the rights specified in them if they could not produce them because they had perished in a fire or otherwise been lost. Grantees always hastened to have lost documents renewed. This was also a moment when the government might limit or otherwise change the old privileges (ibid., p. 267).

129. For this reason there is no riddle as to why the privileges progressed from simple stereotypes to complex documents with many distinctions in the period covered by Kashtanov's works. The government was becoming increasingly complex in the first half of the sixteenth century (see Leont'ev, *Obrazovanie*), and, as it did so, its ability to issue more sophisticated documents tailored to meet specific conditions and needs increased. Political factors were more important in the issuance of these immunities than social or economic considerations. The government used the immunities to reward monasteries supporting the state power and to assist in the maintenance of especially needy servicemen. Each grant to a lay lord was individually motivated by political circumstances (Kashtanov, "Ogranichenie," pp. 280, 289–90; idem, "K probleme mestnogo," pp. 136, 146; Budovnits, *Monastyri*, pp. 312–13, 329, 344, 346). This interpretation is hotly contested by N. E. Nosov *(Stanovlenie*, pp. 175, 180, 210).

130. Dewey, "Immunities," pp. 646–56.

131. Kashtanov, "Ogranichenie," p. 296. Vasilii III repealed the right of monasteries and churches to collect customs duties and administrative levies from the population living on seignorial, court, peasant (black) land, and in towns. This state function was transferred to a government official or sold to a tax farmer. (Tax farming of customs revenues had been established in 1497 in Beloozero.) The monasteries complained about this loss of revenue, so the state began the practice of paying cash sub-

sidies (the *ruga*) to these institutions. (This, of course, in the end undermined the independence of these institutions and made them highly subject to state manipulation [Kashtanov, "Otrazhenie," p. 263; A. M. Sakharov, *Obrazovanie*, p. 101].)

132. Makovskii, *Razvitie*, pp. 21, 235; Nosov, "Gubnaia reforma," pp. 218–19. *Guba*-type officials are found nowhere else in Europe in the sixteenth century. Elected members of the middle service class and wealthy peasants participated in the *guba* administration. In the courts of the Solovetskii monastery in the 1560s five or six wealthy and middling peasants had to be on the trial board along with the monastery's judge (*MIKR*, no. 62).

133. Makovskii, *Razvitie*, p. 278.

5. The "Forbidden Years"

1. Polosin, "Pomestnoe pravo," p. 38; Alekseev, *Agrarnaia*, p. 184. See chapter 2 above for more information.

2. Rozhkov, *Sel'skoe khoziaistvo*, pp. 305–17; Zimin, *Oprichnina*, p. 398.

3. D. P. Makovskii correctly cited the Oprichnina as the major cause of the deterioration of life and the economy in the second half of Ivan's reign (*Razvitie*, pp. 210, 216, 383, 461–68, 471). See also Shmidt, "K izucheniiu agrarnoi," p. 25; Zimin, *Oprichnina*, pp. 389–429; I. I. Smirnov, "Problemy," p. 99; idem, "Klassovye protivorechiia," p. 66; Tkhorzhevskii, "Pomest'e," p. 87; Koretskii, *Zakreposhchenie*, p. 78.

Especially graphic contemporary illustrations can be found in Staden, *The Land*, pp. 39, 46, 69, 71, 83, 92, 95, 107, 109, 113–15, 119–22, 126; Hakluyt Society, *Russia at the Close of the Sixteenth Century*, pp. 161–63, 168–79, 185–88. See Veselovskii, "Sinodik," pp. 323–478, for a list of some of those murdered by Ivan. A Danish traveler, Jakob Ulfeldt, visiting Novgorod in 1578 (Makovskii said 1575 [p. 466]), eight years after it had been sacked by Ivan IV, noted that he would have starved to death during his month there had not provisions been imported (Olearius, *Travels*, p. 91). See also Hakluyt Society, *Russia*, p. 208; Kashtanov, "K izucheniiu oprichniny," pp. 106–7; S. V. Bakhrushin, *Ivan Groznyi* (Moscow: Gospolitizdat, 1945), pp. 80–81, 85. I. I. Smirnov saw the Oprichnina as a means of strengthening serfdom. The Oprichnina was created deliberately to destroy the peasant economies and to expropriate their lands for the lords (*Ivan Groznyi* [Leningrad: Gospolitizdat, 1944], pp. 97–98). See also a particularly poignant document of 1568 reviewing the situation and the disorder that caused peasants to flee a monastery in Nazarov ("Iz istorii," p. 111).

4. B. D. Grekov attributed the economic difficulties of Ivan's reign to the Livonian War ("Iur'ev den'," p. 71). See also Perel'man, "Novgorodskaia," pp. 160–86, 197; Koretskii, *Zakreposhchenie*, pp. 75–78, 80, 89. I. I. Smirnov considered it of secondary importance ("Klassovye," p. 68).

5. Veselovskii, *Soshnoe*, 2:360-62. A. A. Zimin claimed oppressive taxation was the major factor ("Khoziaistvennyi," pp. 11–20). See also Kashtanov, "K izucheniiu oprichniny," pp. 110, 114; idem, "Finansovaia problema," p. 265. V. I. Koretskii calculated that peasant obligations rose three-fold from the 1550s to the 1580s ("Pravaia gramota," pp. 195–196, 206–12). See also his "Zemskii sobor," p. 33. This resembles N. A. Rozhkov's prerevolutionary calculations ("Sel'skoe khoziaistvo," p. 168). Samokvasov incorrectly attributed the tax pressure to the abolition of the *kormlenie*, "feeding," system in 1556 in favor of local administration and collection of taxes, rather than to the needs of the Livonian War and the depredations associated with the Oprichnina (*Krest'iane*, pp. 33–34).

6. Buchinskii, *O klimate*, pp. 87–88; Hakluyt Society, *Early Voyages*, 2:307–9, 336–37 (plague of 1570–72), 338–40 (Tatar invasion and fire in Moscow, 1571); Nazarov, "Iz istorii," p. 113; Kashtanov, "K izucheniiu," pp. 107, 114–15; idem, "Finansovaia problema," pp. 268–69; Novosel'skii, *Bor'ba*, pp. 13–33; A. M. Sakharov, *Obrazovanie*, pp. 111–12. The 1571 defeat so traumatized the Russians that Ivan's

government offered to return Astrakhan' to the Tatars and was willing to discuss the return of Kazan' (Burdei, "Molodinskaia bitva," p. 63).

7. Rozhkov, "Istoriia krepostnogo prava," p. 116; Mikhailov, "K" voprosu," p. 326; Samokvasov, *Arkhivnyi*, 2:305, 308.

8. Each court peasant in 1574 was forced to cultivate four *desiatiny* of land for the tsar (*desiatinnaia pashnia*) (Grekov, "Iur'ev den'," p. 71).

9. S. M. Kashtanov has attributed the devastation to the striving of the lords (especially the middle service class) for an increase in rent, and not to the Oprichnina ("K izucheniiu oprichniny," pp. 114, 116). Traditional peasant dues are known to have been raised on service lands at the end of the fifteenth or beginning of the sixteenth century and escalated drastically during the Oprichnina (Danilova, "Istoricheskie usloviia," p. 119). The *oprichniki* Johann Taube and Elert Kruse noted that many *pomeshchiki* collected everything the peasants had: the peasant paid his *oprichnik* lord as much in one year as he was supposed to in ten (Got'e and Roginskii, "Poslanie," p. 36). N. A. Rozhkov, on the other hand, argued that the average real rent may have declined during the sixteenth century. He did, however, insist that exceptionally crude exploitation existed on *pomest'e* and monastery lands in the last three decades of the sixteenth century and attributed the agrarian crisis to the vast expansion of these forms of land tenure at the expense of boyar and peasant black lands ("Sel'skoe khoziaistvo," pp. 168–69, 171–75).

A rise in the level of exploitation was probably the cause for the known peasant protests of the 1570s (Koretskii, "Zemskii sobor," pp. 48–49; idem, "Bor'ba" pp. 171–75). I. I. Polosin stated that the peasant rent was recalculated upward during the Livonian War partly as a result of the European inflation crisis caused by the influx of silver from the New World ("Pomestnoe pravo," p. 54). A. M. Gnevushev observed that the natural wealth of the center of Muscovy was in the process of being exhausted by the second half of the sixteenth century, especially as the forests had all been cut over and the bees and animals in the forests had passed with their habitat ("Zemlevladenie," p. 281). This also should have caused a rise in prices, even more than Western inflation.

10. Danilova, "Istoricheskie usloviia," pp. 114, 117.

11. "Not one peasant would have a pfenning or a horse and cow in a stall" (Staden, *The Land*, p. 67). The magnates, lay and clerical, also could pay the moving fees specified in the *Sudebnik*, as well as offer loans. Monasteries used their fiscal immunity charters to attract peasants (*SGGD*, 1, no. 202; *Khrestomatiia*, no. 52). Monasteries also apparently collected less rent from their peasants (Gnevushev, "Zemlevladenie," p. 272). See *AI*, 1, no. 191, for a 1574 example of peasants moving to monastery estates from lands of *deti boiarskie*.

It must be noted, however, that by this time most monastery lands paid most of the taxes others did. This had been true since the end of the fifteenth century, after the removal of the Mongol yoke, when the government compiled land cadastres for much of the Muscovite state (Kashtanov, "Ogranichenie," pp. 276, 296). In 1534 even the great Troitse Sergiev monastery's peasants had to pay the taxes to maintain the post system (one of the most burdensome taxes, from which they had been freed twenty years earlier), which had been constructed at the end of the fifteenth and beginning of the sixteenth century and which aided considerably in the consolidation of the centralized Muscovite state. These peasants also had to pay the tax to maintain the frontier fortifications and had to render corvée to the local civil authorities. This was the general rule throughout the Muscovite state—nearly all peasants had to pay nearly all taxes by the second half of the sixteenth century (Kashtanov, "Finansovaia problema," pp. 257, 263, 265–67). In 1568 monastery peasants paid the following taxes: post and siege (*iamskie* and *primetnye den'gi*), army engineer (*pososhnyi korm*), fortification, southern frontier defense, and gunpowder (*za gorodovoe, zasechnoe, iamchiuzhnoe delo*) (Nazarov, "Iz istorii," p. 111). In fact, under the developed tax system of the seventeenth century, monastery peasants had to pay taxes at an even higher rate than peasants on lands possessed by lay lords (see above, p. 125).

The peasant did not go off the tax rolls when settling on monastery lands, but rather the institution paid them while the peasant was getting established, temporarily easing the burden on the primary agricultural producer. Monastery estates also offered the advantage of a larger scale and planned production with deliberate management (*MIKR*, no. 62). N. A. Rozhkov, disputing this, attempted to explain the crisis of the last three decades of the sixteenth century by claiming that monastery economies were on a more primitive level than others. He attributed labor flow to monastery lands to a desire by the peasants to gain the spiritual advantages of living on church property (Rozhkov, "Sel'skoe khoziaistvo," p. 175).

See also Obraztsov, "Iz istorii zakreposhcheniia," p. 337. Some peasants refused to pay the onerous levies during the Oprichnina, to which the government (or the *oprichniki*) responded with attempts to collect the taxes by force (*pravezh*) (Zimin, "Osnovnye etapy," p. 48, citing *AM*, 2:305–6; Sadikov, *Ocherki*, p. 191).

12. Samokvasov, *Krest'iane*, p. 45; *AM*, 2: 474–75, 444.

13. Makovskii, *Razvitie*, p. 406.

14. Samokvasov, *Krest'iane*, p. 37.

15. Foreigners reported during the reign of Vasilii III that there was no agriculture in the area between the Dnepr and the Volga, from Kazan' south to Astrakhan' (Herberstein, *Commentaries*, p. 115). In 1558 Anthony Jenkinson reported that there was no settled habitation from Kazan' to Astrakhan' (Hakluyt Society, *Early Voyages*, 1:99). See also note 14, chap. 6 below.

16. P. P. Smirnov, "Dvizhenie naseleniia," p. 75; Makovskii, *Razvitie*, p. 472. In the new regions on the Volga at the end of the sixteenth century, corvée obligations were only half what they were in Old Russia proper (Koretskii, "K istorii," 1964, p. 84; Rozhdestvenskii, "Sel'skoe," p. 61).

17. Kopanev, "Naselenie," p. 251.

18. P. P. Smirnov, "Dvizhenie naseleniia," p. 76.

19. *AMG*, 1, nos. 1, 2; Samokvasov, *Krest'iane*, p. 37. See also chapter 10 below.

20. Kopanev, "Naselenie," pp. 246–47; I. I. Smirnov, "Iz istorii krest'ian," p. 74.

21. Beliaev, *Krest'iane*, p. 106 (1903 ed.); Romanovich-Slavatinskii, *Dvorianstvo*, p. 355; Perel'man, "Novgorodskaia," pp. 186–97; Rozhkov, "Sel'skoe khoziaistvo," p. 173; Mikhailov, "K" voprosu," p. 328; idem, "Obychnyi institut"," p. 89; Pobedimova, "K voprosu," pp. 173–75; Kopanev, "Naselenie," pp. 253–54. Elsewhere, however, Mikhailov placed some credence in the Kliuchevskii "nomadism" theory ("Obychnyi institut"," p. 113). S. I. Tkhorzhevskii pointed out that moving as frequently as Kliuchevskii's theory required would have been absurd in a three-field agricultural system ("Pomest'e," p. 79). N. A. Rozhkov noted the error of the notion that the state had an interest in binding the peasants because collecting taxes from a "nomadic" population was difficult ("Istoriia krepostnogo prava," p. 116).

22. Rozhkov, "Sel'skoe khoziaistvo," pp. 163–64. Rozhkov attributed the decline to a tendency, organically inherent in the *pomest'e* system at a certain stage of its development, to revert to a natural economy. Each small estate supported only its lord, and there was not the tendency, claimed by Rozhkov, of the large *votchina* to venture into the market. The Oprichnina completed the process of destroying the *votchina* and created the hegemony of the *pomest'e* (ibid., pp. 175, 180).

23. Ibid., p. 166. In this light, it does not seem to me to have been an accident that the list of Ivan IV's courtiers compiled in 1573 contained only the record of intended financial compensation and no list of compensation in land at all. By this time the land was worthless, for it would yield almost no rent, so Ivan's 671 military servicemen in the list probably had no interest in such compensation. On the other hand, cash was still coming in from customs revenues, some taxes, sales of court monopoly produce, and so on (Al'shits, "Novyi dokument," pp. 17, 20–30).

24. Makovskii, *Razvitie*, pp. 392, 482; Staden, *Land*, p. 92; Zimin, "Osnovnye etapy," p. 49. Unwilling to admit that Ivan IV destroyed Novgorod for no rational

reason, R. G. Skrynnikov effectively refutes A. A. Zimin's claims that the destruction was because of Novgorod's desire to destroy the unity of the Muscovite state, and then claims that it was partly because of trade and cultural competition between Novgorod and Moscow. Another reason was that the indigenous lower class under the stress of the end of the 1560s rebelled against Moscow ("Oprichnyi razgrom," pp. 158–59, 168–71). Of course this does not explain the similar devastation around Moscow.

25. Pobedimova, "K voprosu o stabil'nosti," pp. 172–90.

26. Kopanev, "Naselenie," p. 246.

27. There hardly can be any doubt that the laws of 1586, March, 1593, February 1, 1597, and January 7, 1606, on slavery are related to the laws of 1580–81, 1592–93, November 24, 1597, and February 1, 1606, on peasants becoming serfs, but their interaction has not been satisfactorily examined or explained to date. Koretskii's analysis is hardly satisfying (*Zakreposhchenie*, pp. 183–234). (Certainly this is the subject of a book I have not seen: E. I. Kolycheva, *Formirovanie klassa krepostnykh krest'ian v Rossii XVI veka. Krepostnichestvo i kholopstvo* [Moscow: Nauka, 1971].) Both institutions finally came together in a law of March 9, 1607. The distinction between agricultural slaves and peasants was wiped out in a law of September 2, 1679 (D'iakonov, *Ocherki iz"*, p. 142).

28. Makovskii, *Razvitie*, pp. 32, 133–35, 140–43, 236, 257, 277, 371, 453, 458–59; Alekseev, "Kholop," p. 438.

29. *Sudebniki*, pp. 172, 322–24; *MS*, p. 105.

30. Polosin, "Pomestnoe pravo," p. 53.

31. Paneiakh, *Kabal'noe*, pp. 34–37; idem, "Iz istorii," p. 100; idem, "Opyt," pp. 546–49. Aspersion has been cast on the conclusion that this process peaked in the 1580s. The conclusion was reached by Paneiakh on the basis of documents registered in 1597, and the objection has been made that the peak of the 1580s may be artificial simply because the documents written earlier may have perished by or been no longer revelant in 1597. There is little dispute that the number of slavery contracts written after the 1580s did decline, however.

32. Geiman, "O nekotorykh svoeobraznykh," p. 191.

33. Rozhdestvenskii, "Sel'skoe," p. 62. See chapter 2 above for evidence on the decline of the quality of the military service which the middle service class was able to offer as a result of the catastrophes outlined above.

34. Kashtanov, "Finansovaia problema," pp. 257, 262, 272.

35. Koretskii, *Zakreposhchenie*, pp. 107, 151–52. L. V. Cherepnin noted that the peasantry was enserfed out of regard for the interests of the middle service class, a new element in Russian society at this time ("Istoricheskie usloviia," p. 91). Of course some monastery lands were depopulated during the late 1560s, 1570s, and 1580s too, but, as is shown in chapter 2 above, the current political climate was definitely hostile to the interests of the great monasteries. The restrictive legislation on church land-ownership was explicitly in favor of the military forces (Koretskii, "Pravaia," pp. 190–91). Chaev was of the opinion that Ivan himself, seeing all in ruins, was the initiator of a general program to "reconstruct" the Muscovite state; forbidding peasant movement was one feature of this reconstruction. He was not, in Chaev's plausible opinion, responding to pressure from any class or group, but rather operating alone above all classes ("K voprosu"). See also Koretskii, "K istorii," p. 87; Polosin, "Pomestnoe," p. 56.

36. Timofeev, "Krest'ianskie vykhody," p. 67.

37. Tikhomirov, "Soslovno-," pp. 15–17. P. P. Smirnov averred that the peasant question was also handled at this "Zemskii Sobor" (*Posadskie liudi*, 1:157).

38. N. I. Pavlenko, "K istorii zemskikh soborov XVI v.," *Voprosy istorii* 43, no. 5 (May 1968): 100–101; Grekov, "Iur'ev den'," pp. 75–76.

39. *SGGD*, 1, no. 200.
Considering the political life of post-Oprichnina Muscovy, a more political interpretation of the Forbidden Years may be warranted than I have advanced here. Many leading figures were disillusioned by Ivan's long Livonian War and wanted it ended.

Some of them may have contemplated replacing Ivan with his son Tsarevich Ivan Ivanovich, who, according to a contemporary, was willing to take the throne. Tsar Ivan upstaged (and outraged) his opposition in 1575 by "resigning" and installing the loyal Christian Kasimov Tatar khan Simeon Bekbulatovich in his stead for eleven months. The tsar also executed some of his opponents. In 1581 Ivan killed his son (Buganov and Koretskii, "Neizvestnyi," pp. 133–34, 145–46). In light of these facts, it is conceivable that Ivan proclaimed the Forbidden Years to win the middle service class to his side in the political struggle, or at least to encourage them not to abandon the war effort.

40. Koretskii, "Iz istorii zakreposhcheniia" (1957) p. 161, (1964) p. 67.

41. *RIB*, 14 (1894), no. 72; *AM*, 2, pt. 2, nos. 16–18, 20, 54; Iakovlev, *Namestnich'i*, pp. 142–47; Geiman, "Neskol'ko," pp. 282, 293, no. 24; Koretskii, *Zakreposhchenie*, pp. 97–100. Writing in 1911, P. E. Mikhailov noted that the discovery of the Forbidden Years documents opened up in a comparatively short time one of the liveliest problems in Russian historical writing, for it cast grave doubts on the nondecree theories of the enserfment of the peasantry ("Novootkrytye dokumenty," pp. 390–91).

A peasant signing a contract with a lord in 1584 agreed not to move until the sovereign's decree: "ne vytti nigde do gosudareva ukazu" (Geiman, "Neskol'ko," p. 293). A 1592 government document to a monastery on the Dvina River said the Forbidden Years were temporary: ". . . v zapovednye leta, do nashego ukaza. . . ." (Veselovskii, "Iz istorii," p. 209, from *RIB*, 14 [1894], no. 72); *MIKR*, no. 72; *MS*, pp. 112–16. Subsequently, in 1608, a document from Tsar Shuiskii to the Zhilant'ev monastery referred to the right to move in noninterdicted years: "vykhod v nezapovednye leta" (I. I. Smirnov, "K kharakteristike," p. 46). Other documents throughout the first half of the seventeenth century contained this or similar phrases (D'iakonov, *Ocherki obshchestvennogo* [1926], p. 277).

42. See chapter 2 above.

43. S. Adrianov offered the proposition that perhaps all peasants had been bound by a decree in 1584–85 ("K" voprosu," p. 245). Samokvasov mistakenly believed that Ivan had promulgated a law in 1582 forbidding all peasants to move, and that after that time all peasants who departed were considered fugitives (*Krest'iane*, pp. 45–46). In 1926 B. D. Grekov followed Samokvasov's idea, but clarified it by claiming adoption of the law in 1580 and its first year of effect in 1581. Grekov was troubled, as had been M. A. D'iakonov, by the fact that peasants were still moving after 1581. The hypothesis of gradual spreading takes care of this objection (Grekov, "Iur'ev den'," pp. 78, 80–83). In his works published in the 1930s and later, he continued his view that the repeal of the right to move had been universal ("Proiskhozhdenie," pp. 67–74; idem, *Krest'iane*, p. 849; I. I. Smirnov, "Problemy," p. 100).

A document of 1592 ordering the return of some peasants, their wives, children, and property to the Nikolaev monastery of Korela implies that the interdiction on movement was particular to that place; there is no hint that it had become universal for all peasants of all lords (*MIKR*, no. 76).

44. I. M. Kulisher, elaborating on ideas of M. A. D'iakonov, offered the alternative hypothesis that the Forbidden Years were at first introduced at the behest of selected small lords ruined by magnates, on their petition, much as St. George's Day had been initiated ("Nesvobodnoe," pp. 192, 194).

45. Samokvasov, *Krest'iane*, p. 79; Koretskii, "Iz istorii zakreposhcheniia krest'ian" (1957), p. 176. Later, in instances where there were no cadastres, the documents granting lands to someone (*otdel'nye gramoty*) were used as evidence to prove where peasants belonged. Peasants were nearly always listed in these documents (ibid., p. 178). I. I. Smirnov calculated that any peasant who had lived on lands given out for service longer than two weeks and a day was bound there regardless of whether he had been registered in a census ("Iz istorii krest'ian," p. 72).

It is regrettable, from the point of view of later historical analysis of what actually happened at the end of the sixteenth century, that the cadastres were used as the basis for deciding where peasants belonged. Cadastres were compiled for tax purposes, which misled historians into believing that the peasants were bound to the land to satisfy fiscal needs (Tkhorzhevskii, "Pomest'e," p. 87).

46. Chaev, "K voprosu o syske," p. 152.

47. Makovskii, *Razvitie*, p. 162.

48. Veselovskii, *Feodal'noe*, p. 35; Zimin, "Osnovnye etapy," p. 50. This has been the general view of Soviet historiography (I. I. Smirnov, "Problemy," p. 99; idem, "Klassovye protivorechiia," p. 68). The notion dates back at least to the 1920s, when B. D. Grekov was the principal advocate of a significant recovery in the 1590s (*OIIN*, 4:278). It was challenged by M. N. Tikhomirov in 1938 ("Monastyr' votchinnik XVI v.," *Istoricheskei zapiski* 3[1938]:159–60). See also Kazakov, "Bor'ba," p. 37.

49. Hakluyt Society, *Russia at the Close*, p. 277.

50. Ibid., pp. 223–24.

51. Marzheret, *Sostoianie*, pp. 8, 40, 42. This was the case in Moscow because of a flood of grain from the southern steppe and a general decline in the demand for agricultural products. In Smolensk, on the other hand, grain prices rose (Makovskii, *Razvitie*, p. 225).

52. Berry and Crummey, *Rude*, p. 140. Professor Crummey belittles the utility for the historian of Fletcher's remark and says that it was a contemporary "conventional moral judgment rather than a political forecast. From his point of view, civil strife probably seemed inevitable for moral, not sociological, reasons: since Ivan IV had not suffered sufficient punishment for the horrors of the oprichnina, his successors had necessarily to taste the bitter fruit of retribution" (ibid., p. 106). This distinction appears to me to be more subtle than real. As will be discussed briefly below, there was already at the time of Fletcher's visit great strife within the ruling class, much of which resulted from the Oprichnina and became an essential ingredient of the Time of Troubles. The fact that there were vast numbers of cossacks, slaves, and other malcontents who played a significant role in the Time of Troubles can also be attributed to the Oprichnina. Fletcher and his observant source, Horsey, knew this as well as the fact that Ivan had been a dreadful tyrant.

53. Makovskii, *Razvitie*, pp. 164, 193, 221, 494.

54. Ibid., p. 194.

55. Shchepetov, "Sel'skoe khoziaistvo," pp. 97–100; A. N. Sakharov, "Evoliutsiia," p. 56. *Bobyli* were usually landless peasants who paid reduced dues, *bobyl'shchina*, to their lords, and little tax (a small quitrent, *obrok*) until the decree on taxable inhabited land, the *zhivushchaia chetvert'*, of 1631–32.

There is a controversy in Soviet historiography over whether a *bobyl'* was a poor peasant or a landless peasant, who escaped most taxation because he was not engaged in agriculture or otherwise somehow avoided the tax rolls. Perhaps he was primarily a landless laborer, but a few peasants who were wealthy merchants and others discovered it as a tax refuge. See Koretskii, *Zakreposhchenie*, pp. 161–83; A. L. Shapiro, "Bobyl'stvo v Rossii v XV-XVII vv.," *Istoriia SSSR* 4, no. 3 (May-June 1960): 49–66; A. N. Sakharov, "Evoliutsiia," pp. 53–60; idem, *Russkaia derevnia*, pp. 157–70. A regular peasant engaged in agriculture was called a *krest'ianin*.

56. Makovskii, *Razvitie*, pp. 222, 260, 269, 281, 399–400.

57. Koretskii, "Iz istorii zakreposhcheniia," pp. 167–68; Timofeev, "Krest'ianskie vykhody," pp. 64–67. (Timofeev's publication reveals the financial resources of a great monastery, the Iosif Volokolamsk, being used to attract peasants.) Makovskii, *Razvitie*, p. 299; D'iakonov, *Ocherki*, 1926, p. 253; *Zapovednyia*, p. 10. All of this information tends to refute decisively notions that the peasants were not moving and were already bound by custom by this time. If there were a shred of truth to this hypothesis, the Forbidden Years would have been totally unnecessary.

58. Koretskii, "Iz istorii zakreposhcheniia," p. 170. A similar observation was made by M. A. D'iakonov, *Zapovednyia*, p. 8.

59. Chapter 1 above discussed the historiography of this crucial issue. Koretskii, "Novgorodskie," pp. 309, 311, 313; idem, *Zakreposhchenie*, pp. 123, 128–34. Koretskii found twenty documents from court cases in the records of the Service Land Chancellery

(*Pomestnyi Prikaz*) ("K istorii formirovaniia," p. 86; *Khrestomatiia*, nos. 51-II, 56-II; *MIKR*, no. 79). Some in the Soviet Union have not yet accepted these new views. See, for example, the section of the Moscow University law history textbook by K. A. Sofronenko, *Istoriia gosudarstva i prava SSSR*, 2 vols. (Moscow: Iuridicheskaia literatura, 1967), 1:299.

60. *AMG*, 1, no. 35; Koretskii, "Iz istorii zakreposhcheniia" (1964), p. 88; idem, "K istorii formirovaniia," p. 87; Starostina, "Shuretskaia volost'," p. 197; Hakluyt Society, *Russia at the Close of the Sixteenth Century*, pp. 203, 218–19, 226–27.

61. *Novyi letopisets*", pp. 24–25. It is possible that Boris even resorted to murdering his opponents and spiriting away their bodies (V. I. Koretskii, "Mazurinskii letopisets kontsa XVII v. i letopisanie smutnogo vremeni," in *Slaviane i Rus'* [Moscow: Nauka, 1968], p. 287).

62. Zimin, "Osnovnye etapy," p. 50. Jerome Horsey credited Boris with substituting more honest men for the corrupt officials of Ivan's reign (Hakluyt Society, *Russia at the Close*, pp. 276–77). Undoubtedly those who had been purged joined the forces against him.

63. Hakluyt, *Russia at the Close*, p. 339.

64. Kashtanov, "Diplomatika," *Voprosy istorii* 40, no. 1 (January 1965): 43–44.

65. Among other favors which were discussed in chapter 3 above, Boris prior to his coronation made a large payment to the troops, which, according to the critical chronicler, corrupted them (*Novyi letopisets*", p. 47; *AMG*, 1, no. 39). Jerome Horsey, on the other hand, felt this was a positive development which would permit the rendering of better service (Hakluyt Society, *Russia at the Close*, p. 277).

66. Presniakov, "Moskovskoe gosudarstvo," p. 12. Compare this with Crummey's comments on Fletcher's millennarianism (Berry and Crummey, *Rude*, p. 106). The compilation of the land cadastres had not been completed by this time, and continued throughout the 1590s. Therefore the denial of the right to move on St. George's Day was definitely not the culmination of a development spreading with the completion of these census records, but rather was evoked by specific developments of the early 1590s.

67. Abramovich, "Novyi istochnik," p. 118.

68. *Novyi letopisets*", p. 39. For a thorough review of the evidence linking Boris with the murder of Dmitrii, see V. I. Koretskii and A. L. Stanislavskii, "Amerikanskii istorik o Lzhedmitrii I," *Istoriia SSSR* 14, no. 2 (February-March 1969): 241–42. K. V. Chistov, on the other hand, remains convinced that Dmitrii's death was an accident (*Russkie narodnye*, p. 35).

69. Koretskii, "Iz istorii krest'ianskoi," p. 121.

70. *Novyi letopisets*", p. 38.

71. Anpilogov, *Novye dokumenty*, pp. 38–44.

72. N. B. Shelamanova, "K voprosu ob izuchenii istochnikov po istorii vneshnei politiki Rossii v kontse XVI v.," *Novoe o proshlom nashei strany* (Moscow: Nauka, 1967), p. 184.

73. According to a Dutch traveler in Russia during the Time of Troubles, the government in 1591, at the time of the Tatar attack on Moscow, accused a group of seventy slaves of wishing to burn the capital during the siege (Isaak Massa, *Kratkoe izvestie o Moskovii v nachale XVII v.* [Moscow: Sotsekgiz, 1937], p. 39). All of this would give credence to Fletcher's foreboding of "civil flame."

74. Anti-Godunov sources state that the Muscovites deceived the Tatars into believing that great reinforcements were coming from Novgorod and elsewhere, whereupon the enemy fled (*Novyi letopisets*", pp. 36–37; Tatishchev, *Istoriia rossiiskaia*, 6:284–85).

75. Zimin, "Osnovnye etapy," p. 51.

76. V. I. Sergeev, "Pravitel'stvennaia politika v Sibiri nakanune i v period osnovaniia pervykh russkikh gorodov," *Novoe o proshlom nashei strany* (Moscow: Nauka, 1967), p. 179.

77. Makovskii, *Razvitie*, pp. 193–94, 196; Koretskii, "Novgorodskie," p. 317; Platonov, *Smutnoe vremia* (1923), p. 30; Gnevushev, "Zemlevladenie," pp. 276–77.

78. *PRP*, 4:586–89. For a discussion of the authenticity of this preamble, see I. I. Smirnov, "Novyi," and his *Vosstanie*, pp. 526–39. Also see Veselovskii, "Iz istorii," pp. 205–6.

79. Abramovich, "Novyi istochnik," p. 118.

80. *Novyi letopisets*", pp. 24–25. These magnates were also upset by Godunov's town-and-fort building program across the southern frontier because of its demands on the peasant population (P. P. Smirnov, *Posadskie liudi*, 1:177, 185).

81. *Khrestomatiia*, no. 58; *AAE*, 2, no. 23; *MS*, pp. 130–34.

82. Shil', "Donesenie," p. 17. V. O. Kliuchevskii claimed that this "view had no foundation in law" (*Istoriia soslovii*, p. 193). Another traveler, Adam Olearius, claimed that Boris Godunov had given a boyar who had "cured" him eighteen peasants as "perpetual and hereditary property" (*The Travels*, p. 135). These sound like slaves, but may have been peasants on an hereditary estate.

Another foreign contemporary, Conrad Busso, used the word "Stande" when discussing Muscovite society, which would indicate that he felt that by the reign of Boris Godunov it was quite rigidly stratified (Konrad Bussov, *Moskovskaia khronika*, p. 206).

83. Danilova, "Stanovlenie," pp. 84, 89–91, 93–96; Koretskii, *Zakreposhchenie*, pp. 18–29.

84. Shmidt, "K izucheniiu," p. 25. For example, V. I. Koretskii has developed a conception of the interaction of serfdom and corvée in the sixteenth century on the basis of Marx. According to Koretskii, corvée was well established by the 1540s, so Ivan's horrors were really of little consequence ("K istorii formirovaniia," pp. 83–84). On the relationship between corvée and the development of serfdom in France, see Bloch, *French Rural History*, p. 91.

85. Shmidt, "V. I. Lenin," p. 332. Lenin even saw corvée in the Kievan *Russkaia pravda* (A. N. Sakharov, "Rabota," p. 160). In his pre-Stalinist period in the 1920s B. D. Grekov held a view developed at the end of the nineteenth century that the origin of serfdom was linked with a change from a natural economy to a capitalistic money economy. Thus in the period of the twelfth-thirteenth to mid-sixteenth centuries most rent was paid in kind. About the middle of the sixteenth century, according to Grekov, rent was converted to cash. At the same time, however, he noted a marked increase in the use of corvée exploitation by lords. Corvée was introduced by lords to get grain to sell on the market, and the resultant cash was used to buy luxury goods to keep up with the high-living court in Moscow and to buy more modern weapons and armor ("Opyt," pp. 8, 15; idem, "Proiskhozhdenie," p. 58). See also N. A. Rozhkov, *Gorod i derevnia v russkoi istorii* (Moscow: Gosizdat, 1920), p. 44. In this scheme corvée itself plays no role in the development of serfdom. For his contemporary, M. N. Pokrovskii, who was attempting to follow Marx, the observed increase in corvée played a crucial role in the genesis of serfdom (Danilova, "Stanovlenie," p. 93). This set the tone for later writers (Bromlei, Buganov, and Koretskii, "Tsennoe," pp. 164–65).

The controversial Soviet historian B. F. Porshnev has added new dimensions to these old theories. He has maintained that lords expanded their sown acreage to produce for market, and the peasant corvée used to work the land is seen as a form of combined rent, a mixture of primitive labor rent and more modern cash form of rent. L. V. Danilova disputes the whole notion by observing that the available facts indicate that produce from the lord's estate was consumed by him, not sold in the market. She notes that the average amount of corvée was barely enough to support a family and animals, and concluded that it showed a lack of development of the cash market. The only entries into the market were accidental and irregular, such as to sell an occasional item in surplus ("Istoricheskie usloviia," pp. 120–23). Danilova has concluded that serfdom developed in Russia prior to a wide-scale use of corvée, which in fact existed as a definite economic system only in the eighteenth and nineteenth centuries ("K itogam," p. 56). See also Kolesnikova, "Obshchestvenno-politicheskie," p. 257.

N. E. Nosov has pointed out the almost incredible contradictions in today's official Soviet history because of the ideological need to find corvée exploitation in the countryside ("Mnogotomnaia," pp. 139–40). A. N. Sakharov has continued Nosov's discussion of the topic ("O dialektike," pp. 20, 28–30). Good examples of the exaggerated emphasis on corvée can be found in the writings of L. V. Cherepnin, "Istoricheskie usloviia," p. 97. See also A. D. Gorskii, *Ocherki*, p. 238; Koretskii, *Zakreposhchenie*, pp. 18–29. This has been observed by L. V. Danilova ("K voprosu," pp. 137, 139).

Correctives are occasionally offered by some Soviet scholars, such as G. E. Kochin, who rightly emphasizes that corvée was insignificant in the fifteenth century (Kashtanov and Klokman, "Sovetskaia," p. 165). A. A. Zimin has also questioned the exaggerated emphasis on corvée in the fifteenth century ("A. D. Gorskii," p. 173). A neutral position is taken by S. O. Shmidt, who notes that the fundamental problem is that no one really knows enough about the dimensions of peasant rent, in labor, in cash, or in kind, in the sixteenth century to make any convincing generalizations ("K izucheniiu agrarnoi," p. 20). S. B. Veselovskii held a similar position (*Feodal'noe*, p. 312).

86. Shmidt, "Voprosy," p. 112; Gnevushev, "Zemlevladenie," p. 303.

87. Rozhkov, "Istoriia krepostnogo prava," p. 116; Zimin, "Osnovnye etapy," p. 49.

88. L. V. Danilova noted that the large monastery estates resorted to corvée only in the second half of the sixteenth century, when the economy had been destroyed ("Istoricheskie usloviia," pp. 121–22).

89. Makovskii, *Razvitie*, pp. 32–33, 213, 278–79, 292, 320, 484, 496–97.

90. Obraztsov, "Iz istorii zakreposhcheniia," p. 341; Koretskii, "Bor'ba krest'ian," pp. 176, 197; idem, "K istorii formirovaniia," p. 84; I. I. Smirnov, *Vosstanie*, pp. 41–42. In the Kirillov monastery in Beloozero corvée commenced in 1577. This resulted from the fact that the monastery's workers had died earlier in a plague. The government wanted to save money on subsidies to the monastery (the *ruga*), so Ivan ordered peasants living on the monastery's lands to work for it to replace the deceased workers. The cultivation norm was one *desiatina* per *vyt'*. A decree of 1601 increased this to two *desiatiny* per *vyt'*. Other obligations were also increased (Gorfunkel', "Perestroika," pp. 100, 106, 107, 110). The introduction of corvée in 1591 or 1592 on the estates of the Iosif monastery of Volokolamsk was a response by enterprising officials to dramatic inflation (Shchepetov, "Sel'skoe khoziaistvo," pp. 101–3).

91. Gnevushev, "Zemlevladenie," p. 300.

92. Chaev, "Iz istorii," p. 31.

93. Ibid.; Obraztsov, "Iz istorii zakreposhcheniia," pp. 339–40; Gorfunkel', "Perestroika," pp. 106–7.

94. A. N. Sakharov, "Evoliutsiia," p. 51; idem, *Russkaia derevnia*, p. 151. Sakharov notes that a similar view was held by M. A. D'iakonov and B. D. Grekov.

95. I. I. Smirnov, "Klassovye protivorechiia," pp. 71–73; Makovskii, *Razvitie*, pp. 484–85; *MIKR*, no. 78; Zimin, "Osnovnye etapy," pp. 49–50; Koretskii, "Iz istorii krest'ianskoi," pp. 119–21; idem, "Bor'ba krest'ian," pp. 194, 197, 199, 202.

96. Mavrodin, "Feodal'naia," p. 179; Iakovlev, " 'Bezumnoe," pp. 664, 678; Chistov, *Russkie narodnye*, pp. 41, 47–48, 54–55, 57–59, 64; *Istoricheskie pesni XVII veka*, edited by O. B. Alekseeva et al. (Moscow-Leningrad: Nauka, 1966), pp. 10, 40, 89–93. The popular reaction to the great Bay of Bengal cyclone and tidal wave catastrophe of the night of November 12, 1970, which caused thousands of fatalities seems to resemble the typical Russian analysis of the Time of Troubles. " 'It is the wish of Allah that this wind and water came,' a fisherman said, in a comment echoed all over the region. 'We have sinned. It would not have happened if we had not sinned' " (*The New York Times*, December 30, 1970, p. 2).

97. Chistov, *Russkie narodnye*, p. 50; I. I. Smirnov, *Vosstanie*, pp. 105, 230, 255.

98. Iakovlev, " 'Bezumnoe," p. 678; Chistov, *Russkie narodnye*, pp. 39, 69; Mavrodin, "Sovetskaia" (1967), 1:70–71, 73, 78; ibid. (1966), pp. 311, 313. See also *Vosstanie I. Bolotnikova. Dokumenty i materialy*, compiled by A. I. Kopanev and A. G. Man'kov

(Moscow: Sotsekgiz, 1959), pp. 197–201; I. I. Smirnov, *Vosstanie*, pp. 282, 495; Makovskii, *Pervaia*, pp. 473, 482.

99. *AAE*, 2, no. 87; Shepelev, *Osvoboditel'naia i klassovaia bor'ba*, p. 127. The question has been raised as to who revolted during the Time of Troubles—the slaves or the peasants who were becoming serfs. Many contemporaries viewed the Smuta as the vengeance of slaves on their boyars (Tikhomirov, "Pskovskie," p. 186). In 1919 V. Firsov denied that the Russian peasants in the seventeenth century fought against serfdom (Mavrodin, "Sovetskaia," [1966], p. 297).

V. I. Koretskii assigned the catalytic role in the Khlopko uprising of 1603–4 to slaves freed during the famine of 1601–3 to shift for themselves by their lords ("K istorii vosstaniia Khlopka," pp. 210–11; idem, "Iz istorii krest'ianskoi," p. 129). See also Shepelev, p. 157. I. I. Smirnov assigned first place in the Bolotnikov uprising to the fugitive slaves (*Vosstanie*, p. 106). A. A. Zimin has questioned this and other positions in some detail and called the uprisings "the answer" to the growing oppression of peasants and slaves ("Nekotorye voprosy," pp. 107–8; "Dokument," p. 28). See also Indova et al., "Narodnye," p. 53. D. P. Makovskii took another position. While he said that slaves had the major role in the Khlopko uprising, he attributed to the urban plebs the chief motive force in the Bolotnikov uprising. Other forces, in descending order of importance, were the "black," free, independent peasants; the petty and middle burghers of the southern frontier; and the enserfed peasantry (*Pervaia*, pp. 468–72). This is an important issue, for it relates directly to the impact made by the repeal of the right to move during the first quarter-century, particularly in light of the limitations placed on the recovery of fugitives which are to be discussed in the next section.

100. If administrative-judicial decisions on privately initiated cases were not heeded, then of course the government was willing to use the police, and even the army, to enforce its edicts (Koretskii, *Zakreposhchenie*, pp. 321–36).

6. *The Statute of Limitations on the Recovery of Fugitive Peasants*

1. Dewey, *Muscovite*, p. 82; Kopanev, "Ustavnaia," p. 31; Iakovlev, *Namestnich'i*, p. 111.

2. This is a period when a number of statutes of limitation appeared in Russian law. In 1588 a fifteen-year limit was established for suits on loans guaranteed by bondage contracts (*AI*, 1, no. 221-I; *MIKR*, no. 70). Local people had one year in which to sue local officials for misconduct, others had eight years (*Sudebnik*, 1589, art. 37). There was a three-year limit on suits between boyars and monasteries over lands, and the same for suits of peasants against each other (*Sudebnik*, 1589, arts. 149, 150). Other suits for lands against boyars and monasteries had to be initiated within six years (ibid., art. 156). Suits had to be initiated within forty years for the return to the family of hereditary estates which had passed out of the family (ibid., art. 164; *Ulozhenie*, 17:40). In 1628 a law decreed that someone who began a suit had to be present for a trial within a week or he would lose the suit. This was repeated in 1629 and 1642 (*AI*, 3, no. 92-XII, XV, XXXIV). In 1648 a victim was given a week for suing a thief who had been caught red-handed for the value of the stolen property (*AI*, 4, no. 6-X).

3. Koretskii, "Novgorodskie," pp. 316, 318, 327–28.

4. Koretskii, "Iz istorii zakreposhcheniia," pp. 179–82.

5. Ibid., p. 180; Koretskii, *Zakreposhchenie*, pp. 140–48.

6. Koretskii, "Iz istorii zakreposhcheniia," p. 182; idem, *Zakreposhchenie*, pp. 154–60; *Khrestomatiia*, no. 54. Both *vyvoz* and *vykhod* were combined later (*AI*, 3, no. 92-XXXIII [1642]). P. N. Miliukov, who did not mention the indebtedness issue in

his discussion of the enserfment of the peasantry, did not speculate on whether a law had been promulgated in 1592, but saw the law of 1597 as a governmental response to the colonization of the steppe and the Volga in an attempt to protect the tax revenues and the rents upon which the middle service class depended (*Ocherki* [1900], 1:211).

7. Koretskii, "Iz istorii zakreposhcheniia" (1957), p. 183.

8. M. M. Speranskii first noted the "completion" of the compilation of the land cadastres in 1593 and connected this with the five-year time limit in the law of 1597. Kulisher agreed ("Nesvobodnoe," p. 197). This was also M. N. Pokrovskii's explanation for the legal binding of peasants—to curtail the legal chaos stemming from suits over fugitive debtors by simply binding them all wherever the putative 1590–93 census caught them. It was also N. A. Rozhkov's explanation—the census was a good basis of information for deciding suits (*Russkaia istoriia*, 4: 102; Pokrovskii, *Russkaia istoriia s drevneishikh vremen*, 4 vols. [Moscow: Gosizdat, 1922], 1:287–88).

9. See chapter 3 above for more detail.

10. Budovnits, *Monastyri*, p. 353; Nazarov, "Iz istorii agrarnoi," p. 106.

11. Platonov, *Ocherki*, p. 169. In 1592, certainly to gain support, Boris Godunov gave an extraordinarily generous donation of 800 rubles to the influential Iosif Volokolamsk monastery (Shchepetov, "Sel'skoe," p. 95).

12. I. E. Engel'man observed the connection between the binding of the peasants and the Time of Troubles discussed above, and went on to note that this aspect of the enserfment of the peasants contributed to the civil disorder of the Smuta because it limited the privileges of the rich, who became enraged (*Istoriia*, p. 45). See also A. M. Sakharov, *Obrazovanie*, p. 115; Nosov, *Stanovlenie*, pp. 11, 90.

13. There is yet another possible explanation. Sometimes Boris is thought to have had one eye on the needs and desires of the lower classes. Koretskii cites the amnesty of January 15, 1598, freeing imprisoned debtors from their obligations, which were assumed by the state ("Iz istorii zakreposhcheniia," p. 188). See also a recent publication of the amnesty document, S. P. Mordovina, ed., "Ukaz ob amnistii 1598 goda," *Sovetskie arkhivy* 5, no. 4 (July-August 1970):84–86. Also, Boris permitted some peasants to move in 1601 and 1602 and took measures to allay popular discontent resulting from the famine of 1601–3 (Khilkov, no. 62). Therefore it is conceivable that a desire to gain lower class support played a role in Boris's curtailing the effectiveness of the Forbidden Years in the 1590s with the introduction of the five-year time limit. I am not aware of any evidence, however, that he was concerned about this constituency at the beginning of the 1590s. Koretskii's hypothesis that the government may have introduced the five-year limit because it somehow felt that it would be unfair to tear a peasant away from a new economy after having developed it for five years seems to me to be simply fanciful.

14. All of these facts are revealed in petitions submitted during the first half of the seventeenth century by members of the middle service class to the government (*Khrestomatiia*, no. 102 [1628]; P. Smirnov, "Chelobitnye," for 1637, 1641, 1635, 1648; *MS*, pp. 159–63, 167–75, 178–96, 198–205, 214).

One of the still unresolved issues of Russian historiography has been how populous the area of the Ukraine south of Russia was after the Mongol invasion. Some have maintained that the invasion, subsequent raids, and perhaps new diseases wiped out all the population that had lived in the heartland of old Kiev Rus'. Subsequently this region was inhabited, or rather traversed, by wandering and marauding Tatars and cossacks. According to this theory, because of the incessant raids, especially by the Crimean Tatars, no settled agriculturalist could live in the middle and lower Dnepr basin until the area was garrisoned by Muscovy. This was the position of most pre-Revolutionary students of the problem—D. I. Bagalei, followed by M. K. Liubavskii, N. D. Chechulin, A. S. Lappo-Danilevskii, G. M. Belotserkovskii, A. A. Kizevetter, et al. (Aleksandrov, "Streletskoe," p. 236; McNeill, *Europe's Steppe Frontier*, pp. 8–9).

Others, especially but not exclusively Ukrainian nationalists, have maintained that this region was never completely devoid of population in spite of the Tatar and cossack depredations. They hold that the "Wild Steppe" territory south of the Oka did not wait until the second half of the sixteenth century for colonization from the center of Muscovy (Tikhomirov, *Rossiia,* p. 422). L. V. Danilova maintains that P. P. Smirnov's 1910 study on the Orel region in the sixteenth century (unavailable to me) does not support his own contention about the absence of population in the Wild Steppe until the end of the sixteenth century. His study of the 1594–96 land cadastres revealed a population density of eight people per square verst. I fail to see how this evidence contradicts his position, or, if it did, why she then had to take pains to show that the economic crisis, the increasing taxes, the Oprichnina, and wars of the second half of the sixteenth century initiated an intensive flow of peasant population out from the center (Danilova, "Istoricheskie usloviia," pp. 134–36, 138). Even a century later, in 1670, the Razin rebels did not march north via the Don "because there was nothing to eat and no supplies could be obtained in the steppe" (Man'kov, "Krugi," pp. 274–75). This would certainly imply that the region was indeed sparsely populated even at that date.

This is of interest because V. I. Koretskii, following A. A. Novosel'skii, claims that members of the middle service class on the largely uninhabited southern frontier sometimes benefited from peasant migration in that direction ("Iz istorii zakreposhcheniia," p. 185). There is little evidence, however, that the members of the middle service class on the southern frontier who, with their few slaves, were the area's first settlers, formed a very effective lobby in the 1590s. The facts show that very few of these persons were in regimental service, the source of power and prestige, such as it was, for the Muscovite service landholders. Sh. presented evidence for the 1615–17 Pskov campaign to back up his point, and then showed that sixty years later, in 1679, only 328 servicemen from the "lower towns" were in Cherkasskii's army in Kiev (Sh., "Dvorianstvo," no. 2, p. 271).

There is also little evidence that peasants who fled to the previously underpopulated frontier settled on the small service estates of the middle service class. In fact, the available evidence indicates strongly that they avoided these estates like the plague. (Of course the government was wont to assign lands being farmed by peasants without lords to any qualified person who asked for them. This was done at the direction of the local military commander [Vainberg, "Bor'ba," p. 255].) Never did the southern frontier *deti boiarskie* succeed in obtaining a significant labor force, nor can there ever have been any realistic hope that they might. As late as 1650 in the Elets district, which is only about 250 miles south of Moscow, there were 415 service landholders— 384 *deti boiarskie,* 21 of their relatives, 3 landholding cossacks, and 7 widows. All of them together had only 190 peasants of the male sex. The richest had only ten such peasants (Chistiakova, "Volneniia," p. 256). Later, as we shall see, the magnates developed an interest in the lands on the southern frontier, and, to a certain extent, their interests coincided with those of the military servitors.

In spite of these facts, however, one cannot deny that the servicemen must have felt that the migration southward somehow benefited them, as seen in the collective petition of 1620 by the servicemen of Elets asking that the five-year limit on hunting down fugitive peasants be strictly observed (*Ocherki . . . XVII,* p. 178). I suspect that this petition was motivated only by a semirational desire to protect what they had (all the peasants would be runaways from the center) rather than a realistic recognition of the possibilities of a future with a longer time-horizon than the immediate present. Unquestionably, many frontier servicemen were former peasants who felt their position in the service class would be more secure with a short time-limit on returning fugitive peasants.

A much more accurate picture of the southern situation is offered by Koretskii. A short time limit was in the interest of the great southern landowners, on whose lands the peasants moving in that direction often settled. After the expiration of the five years, the peasant was bound to the land of his new southern lord ("K istorii formirovaniia," p. 88; idem, *Zakreposhchenie,* pp. 157–58).

327

15. Pavlov-Sil'vanskii, "Liudi kabal'nye," p. 216.

16. There were individual exceptions, such as in 1599 when the Viazhitskii monastery sued to recover peasants who had run away in 1591 (Kliuchevskii, "Proiskhozhdenie," p. 277).

17. Marzheret, *Sostoianie*, p. 73; Konrad Bussov, *Moskovskaia khronika, 1584–1613* (Moscow-Leningrad: Akademiia Nauk, 1961), pp. 97–98, 346–47; Avraamii Palitsyn, *Skazanie* (Moscow-Leningrad: Akademiia Nauk, 1955), pp. 95, 105–6; *Sbornik" Khilkova*, no. 62; Billington, *Icon*, pp. 102, 119, 675; Koretskii, "Iz istorii krest'ianskoi," p. 122; *Novyi letopiset"*, p. 54; Sakharov, *Obrazovanie*, p. 121.

18. *SGGD*, 3, no. 47.

19. I have omitted from my narrative consideration of the decrees of 1601 and 1602 by Boris which permitted a few selected peasants to move (*MS*, pp. 130–34). They were not understood by contemporaries (some of whom felt the right of free movement for all peasants was restored) and have made no sense to modern historians (Koretskii, "Iz istorii zakreposhcheniia" [1964], pp. 69, 77–78). I regard the decrees as having had no real historical significance, except to show government involvement in, and control of, the peasant question. Certainly it was the famine, not the laws of 1601 and 1602 (as Koretskii states, ibid., pp. 82, 86), which led to the emptying of the lands of the small servicemen in favor of the magnates, who had food stores. I would agree that Boris promulgated the law of 1601 to curry favor with the middle service class (Koretskii, "Iz istorii krest'ianskoi," p. 124); the law was issued at the wrong time and under unfavorable conditions rather than simply backfiring.

20. Koretskii, "Vosstanovlenie," pp. 121–22. Elsewhere Koretskii offers the less satisfactory explanation that False Dmitrii I issued the decree to assure the support of the members of the middle service class among his adherents from the south ("Iz istorii zakreposhcheniia" [1957], p. 187). See also Zimin, "Nekotorye voprosy," pp. 99–100, for similar views. My objection that these *pomeshchiki* were not benefiting from the peasant migration south still holds.

21. *AAE*, 2, no. 40.

22. Koretskii, "Vosstanovlenie," p. 124. See also Novosel'skii, "K voprosu," pp. 179–80. My reservations about this still hold, as stated above, in notes 14, 19, 20.

23. *AAE*, 2, no. 40.

24. Koretskii, "K istorii formirovaniia," p. 92.

25. *PRP*, 4:532–33.

26. Koretskii, "K istorii," pp. 92–93.

27. Koretskii, "Vosstanovlenie," pp. 118–30.

28. See I. I. Smirnov, "Novyi spisok," pp. 72–87. Many historians, beginning with Karamzin, have questioned the authenticity of this document. It was first published in the posthumous works of Tatishchev, who, as shown by Grekov, did not hesitate to "modernize" documents (Grekov, "Proiskhozhdenie," pp. 80–81). Few, if any, contemporary historians doubt that a decree close in content to that published by Tatishchev was issued by Tsar Shuiskii (I. I. Smirnov, *Vosstanie*, pp. 526–38). See also Ia. S. Lur'e, "Problems of Source Criticism," *Slavic Review* 27, no. 1 (March 1968): 7–9. For an excellent review of the problem of "Tatishchev evidence," see A. G. Kuz'min, "Byl li V. N. Tatishchev istorikom?" *Russkaia literatura* 14, no. 1 (January-March 1971): 58–63.

29. Kliuchevskii, "Proiskhozhdenie," p. 285. Kliuchevskii said the law also recognized that peasants were attached to the person of a lord, and not strictly to a parcel of land (ibid.).

30. *MS*, pp. 137–38. B. D. Grekov noticed the discrepancy between assigning the initiation of the Forbidden Years to Boris and the documents which indicate that the Forbidden Years already were well known in the 1580s. He explained this by asserting that a part of the introduction to the law of 1607 was commentary introduced by Tatishchev, who did not know of the decrees of the 1580s ("Proiskhozhdenie," p. 83). A much simpler explanation is that Shuiskii hated Godunov and was referring to the universal decree of 1592–93 posited by Koretskii. Tatishchev himself in his *Sudebnik"*

(p. 243) noted that there was confusion in the document and then confused the issue further by interpreting the documents referred to as the head-tax documents of the Tatars. Grekov found comfort in Tatishchev's commentary to the effect that the right of peasants to move was annulled by law and did not by itself die out because of bondage resulting from indebtedness and other factors ("Proiskhozhdenie," p. 84).

31. *MS*, pp. 130–34. These laws excluded half of all peasants from their coverage (D'iakonov, *Zapovednyia*, p. 15).

32. P. N. Miliukov in his article on the peasants saw this as an interpolation by the famous historian Tatishchev referring to the 1601 document (Miliukov, "Krest'iane," 32: 677). I. I. Smirnov convincingly refuted this (*Vosstanie*, pp. 530–32). See also Koretskii, *Zakreposhchenie*, pp. 124–30. Pazhitnov, on the other hand, agrees with Karamzin and Pogodin that at least the whole introduction probably was an interpolation by Tatishchev ("Dvorianskaia," pp. 49, 72). He was writing without the benefit of Koretskii's work. Exceptions in the 1601 and 1602 laws ruled out transfer for a good half of all Russian peasants. This has remained for historians a rather unintelligible interlude (D'iakonov, *Ocherki* [1926], p. 275). The laws of 1601 and 1602 were supposed to be favors by Boris for the members of the middle service class, but Koretskii termed them "simply a demagogic gesture of Boris" ("Iz istorii zakreposhcheniia," 1964, pp. 69).

33. *MS*, p. 139.

34. Shepelev, *Osvoboditel'naia i klassovaia bor'ba*, p. 156; Koretskii, "Iz istorii zakreposhcheniia" (1957), p. 188. Koretskii further hypothesizes that the government would have liked to repeal the time limit entirely, but did not dare to out of fear of provoking still more peasant disturbances (ibid., p. 190).

35. One might think that such an instance would force Soviet historians to revise their generalization that uprisings always bring beneficial reforms. See, for example, Shmidt, "V. I. Lenin," p. 335.

36. I. I. Smirnov, "Iz istorii krest'ian," p. 74.

37. See Olearius's descriptions on how easy it was for Russians to build and move houses (*Travels*, p. 112). See also Schleussinger, "Rasskaz," p. 108.

38. Figarovskii, "Krest'ianskoe," pp. 195–98.

39. The second False Dmitrii, according to the contemporary Conrad Busso, urged the peasants to kill their lords and told them that they could confiscate their lords' land if the latter supported Vasilii Shuiskii (Zimin, "Nekotorye voprosy," p. 101).

40. See chapter 14 below.

41. I. I. Smirnov, "K kharakteristike," pp. 46, 48–49.

42. Veselovskii, "Iz istorii," p. 215; *DAI*, 1, no. 167.

43. *AAE*, 2, no. 164; *SGGD*, 2, no. 200; *Khrestomatiia*, no. 89.

44. Platonov, *Ocherki*, p. 352; Porshnev, "Sotsial'no-," p. 119.

45. *Khrestomatiia*, p. 323.

46. I. I. Smirnov, "K kharakteristike," pp. 46, 48–49.

47. Grekov, "Proiskhozhdenie," p. 86. This was in two grants made by Sigismund III, taking over Russia at this time, to the French captain Jacques Margeret. The grants specifically ruled out *vykhod* and *vyvoz* and allowed for government help in recovering fugitive or absconded peasants should the need arise. No time limit was mentioned for their recovery (*AZR*, 4, no. 183-DCCLXVIII and DCCLXIX). These grants are unique in this collection of more than eight hundred documents, most of them conditional service land grants. In all probability the grants were a special reward for this mercenary, who had served Russia for nearly a decade and knew it well. A grant to another French mercenary simply orders the peasants to obey him—which itself is unusual for this collection (DCCLXXII); a few order the grantee-*pomeshchik* to collect only the traditional dues and not to drive off the peasants or devastate the holding (DCCLXXV, DCCXXX, DCCLXXXIV, DCCLXXXVII, DCCLXXXVIII, DCCXCVIII). Another implies some mobility (CDXXXV).

48. *DAI*, 1, no. 167, p. 296; D'iakonov, *Zapovednyia*, p. 12. He interprets "free people" as meaning sons, brothers, nephews, and other lateral members of a family.

I suspect that it meant those not registered in a census or other official document, and that it might include some of these others. See Koretskii, *Zakreposhchenie*, p. 132.

49. *Khrestomatiia*, no. 91; A. M. Sakharov, *Obrazovanie*, p. 132. N. I. Kazakov has observed that the political program of the first militia reflected the struggle between the middle service class and the boyars for the right to exploit the peasant population ("Bor'ba," p. 42). The document clearly mirrors the interests of the *pomeshchiki* in that struggle (Zimin, "Nekotorye voprosy," p. 103).

50. Platonov, *Ocherki*, pp. 378, 381–90; Zimin, "Nekotorye voprosy," p. 103. The movement under the cossack Ivan Zarutskii (1612–1614) also gathered its forces from the slaves and peasants. Their efforts were directed against the members of the middle service class (ibid., p. 104).

51. Figarovskii, "Krest'ianskoe," pp. 195–98.

52. This was not the view of many pre-Soviet historians, who believed the Smuta had created serfdom (Zaozerskii, "K" voprosu," p. 339). See Mavrodin, "Sovetskaia" (1966), p. 326, nn. 114, 115; "Sovetskaia' (1967), p. 82, nn. 119, 120, for a review of this issue. The traditional Soviet view is that the Time of Troubles (and specifically the Bolotnikov uprising) weakened the institution by frightening the government, and thereby delayed for nearly fifty years the final legal formulation of serfdom (Cherepnin, "Problema," p. 73; idem, " 'Sobornoe Ulozhenie'," p. 63; idem, "Zemskie sobory," pp. 114, 132; Koretskii, "K istorii formirovaniia," p. 95; Zimin, "Nekotorye voprosy," p. 107; Zimin and Preobrazhenskii, "Izuchenie," p. 144; Makovskii, *Pervaia*, p. 490; Novosel'skii, "K voprosu o znachenii," p. 183; Indova et al., "Narodnye," p. 81). This fear was reinforced by the Balash uprising during the Smolensk War (Porshnev, "Sotsial'no-," pp. 119, 139). Porshnev in this case is proving his theories about the nature of absolutism and the "fact" that the constant threat of peasant uprisings demanded centralization of political power. Russia was becoming more centralized, so "therefore" there must have been this constant threat (Chistozvonov, "Nekotorye aspekty," p. 47). Also to be considered is the official Leninist position that peasant wars "undermined, shook" feudalism (Kompan, "V. I. Lenin o klassakh," p. 299). Zimin advances the view that the peasant uprisings were defeated because of the socioeconomic backwardness of the Russian town and the immaturity of the town population, which, because of the backwardness of its development, was unable to take the lead in the peasants' struggle against serfdom. This follows from the Leninist position that peasants cannot lead a social movement—only the bourgeoisie or proletariat can ("Nekotorye voprosy," pp. 105, 113).

Danilova, on the other hand, says the Time of Troubles had no impact because the peasants were already totally enserfed by the end of the sixteenth century ("K itogam," p. 64). Belittling the legislative struggle over the length of time fugitives could be hunted down and returned in the first half of the seventeenth century, Danilova regrettably ignores the fact that effective sanctions and their enforcement were the crucial element in binding the peasant to the land. She also fails to take cognizance of the genuine substantive changes in the peasant's status after he was finally enserfed by the *Ulozhenie* of 1649. In 1954 the Soviet historian V. I. Lebedev advanced the opinion that the peasant uprisings during the Time of Troubles hastened the process of centralization of the state because of their impact on the ruling class and government apparatus, and thereby aided the further growth of production and commodity circulation in Russia (Zimin, "Nekotorye voprosy," p. 107).

Figarovskii says the traditional Soviet view is mistaken and claims that the government of Mikhail immediately set out to restore the system which had been wrecked by the Time of Troubles ("Krest'ianskoe vosstanie," p. 195).

53. The eastern part of the Smolensk fortress was built during the winter and consequently was weak. The traitor Dedevshin pointed this out to the Poles, who were thus able to break through the Kryloshevskie gates and the wall by the Rachevskoe brook with ease and capture the town and its commanding position (Makovskii, *Razvitie*, p. 445).

54. Figarovskii, "Krest'ianskoe," p. 215. See also Novosel'skii, "K voprosu," p. 179, and Grekov, "Proiskhozhdenie," p. 88. In the seventeenth century Moldavia had a ten-year time limit on the recovery of fugitive peasants (Cherepnin, "'Sobornoe Ulozhenie'," p. 64).

55. *AAE*, 3, no. 41. Also in *MIKR*, no. 94.

56. Figarovskii, "Krest'ianskoe vosstanie," p. 196.

57. Ibid., p. 199.

58. Ibid., pp. 212–13, 216.

59. The fact that the boyar magnates actually controlled the government and Mikhail's actions was recognized by contemporaries (Tikhomirov, "Pskovskie povesti," p. 186). See also Chaev, "Iz istorii," p. 32, nos. 3–6. The pre-Soviet historian A. M. Gnevushev advanced another interpretation, that the middle service class dominated state life until the middle of the seventeenth century and that the new nobility did not enjoy a fully privileged position until that time ("Zemlevladenie," p. 289). His contemporary, S. F. Platonov, observed, however, that Mikhail did not have to share his power with any institution (the Assembly of the Land) or estate, that the government was not influenced by any organized social group, but rather by a circle of relatives and individuals who, like the Romanovs, had supported the second pretender during the Time of Troubles ("Moskovskoe pravitel'stvo," pp. 395–406).

60. Got'e, *Zamoskovnyi*, pp. 115–16; Makovskii, *Razvitie*, p. 483. The area in the meridian west of Moscow suffered the most severe devastation during the Time of Troubles (*Ocherki . . . XVII*, p. 31).

61. During this period, the Troitse Sergiev monastery kept very thorough records of all the peasants who fled, where they had fled, and which of them were returned. The average middle service class landholder obviously did not have such resources (see Iakovlev, "Svoznye knigi," pp. 185–260). The introduction to this document contains a decree prescribing the nine-year limit, beginning in 1604–5, the end of the great famine of 1601–3. About 52 percent of the monastery's peasants fled to lands belonging to *deti boiarskie*; only 18 percent to lands of boyars (Man'kov, "Pobegi krest'ian," p. 57). In this situation the monastery accused the members of the middle service class of "becoming strong," that is, of refusing to return fugitive peasants. Later the situation was reversed.

62. Figarovskii, "Krest'ianskoe," p. 198; Man'kov, "Pobegi krest'ian," p. 47. Most of these peasants only moved a comparatively short distance (usually within the province) and settled down again quickly (ibid., p. 56).

63. *DAI*, 2, no. 35; *MS*, pp. 146–50.

64. *AI*, 3, no. 58; *MIKR*, no. 96; *MS*, pp. 150–51. The decree was dated March 10, 1615. Figarovskii sees this as further evidence that the government was preparing to introduce a universal five-year limit ("Krest'ianskoe," p. 216). This seems hardly the case; the decree ordered the monastery to complete its recovery operations simply because, in the words of the decree, "many *dvoriane* and *deti boiarskie* petition to us that their long-time peasants, who have lived on their lands for twenty years and more, are being taken to the estate of the Troitse [monastery]." This was more than the government could allow, especially as Russia was still technically at war with both Poland and Sweden and the services of the middle service class might be needed at any moment. In a census of Moscow-area servicemen taken in 1631–32 (on the eve of the Smolensk War), a man with forty-five years service and a high compensation scale (both in land and cash) reported that his lands were uninhabited because he "had been ruined by the Troitse monastery" (Stashevskii, *Zemlevladenie*, p. 44).

65. *AMG*, 2, no. 143; Novosel'skii, "K voprosu," p. 179.

66. *Opisanie MAMIu*, 17:357, 364, 428.

67. *PRP*, 5:289. This conception of a diabolical government constantly desiring to enslave the entire population, but biding its time before it acted, is perhaps a logical extension of the Soviet notion of the omnipresence of the class struggle, but evidence has yet to be presented to support it. Novosel'skii's view that serfdom did

not always move ahead consistently, but depended on changes of direction in the government's foreign and domestic policy, is more consistent with the facts ("Dela," p. 147).

68. Novgorod, in the hands of the enemy, was returned to Russia, but the Swedes kept Oreshek (Shlissel'burg), Ivangorod, Iam, and Korog, which Tsar Shuiskii had ceded to them. These same towns frequently changed hands at this time. In the Pliusa treaty of 1583 Russia had surrendered Iam, Kopor'e, and Ivangorod to Sweden. They were returned to Russia in the 1595 Tiavzinskii peace (Tikhomirov, *Rossiia v XVI*, p. 19).

69. In exchange for a fourteen-and-a-half-year truce the Russians formally ceded Smolensk and the Seversk district to Poland.

70. *AMG*, 1, no. 259.

71. For example, he curtailed the granting of lands to members of the government, putting an end to the orgy of the 1610s. A law of February 26, 1627, decreed that no more court lands should be distributed to anybody. This law was violated by his successors (P. P. Smirnov, *Posadskie*, 1:411; Got'e, *Zamoskovnyi*, p. 213). Petrikeev, "Zemel'nye," p. 52, citing Got'e, pp. 311–13, says this was repealed by the *Ulozhenie*. The decree itself: *UKPP*, 6: 40, p. 59 (March 8, 1627), repealed by 17: 23, 24. A law of December 19, 1627, forbade the selling and mortgaging of taxpaying properties in Moscow to tax-exempt institutions and individuals (Serbina, "Ukaznye," p. 342). For a discussion of his measures to curtail the financial and judicial privileges of the monasteries, see Keep, "The Regime of Filaret," p. 340, and chapter 3 above.

72. *Khrestomatiia*, no. 102; *MS*, pp. 159–63.

73. Stashevskii, "K istorii kolonizatsii," pp. 242, 244, 290–93. Stashevskii claimed that in the southern frontier area peasants could write into settlement contracts enforceable provisions for leaving upon completion of the contract (ibid., p. 243). I am not aware of any evidence to support this contention.

74. Keep states that Filaret "had no 'peasant policy' as such" ("The Regime of Filaret," p. 352).

75. *Ocherki . . . XVII*, p. 149; *Ulozhenie*, 16:46; 17:24. See chapter 3 above. On black lands, see note 75 in chapter 4 above.

76. One of the assumptions of certain Russian historians has been that somehow the judicial immunities of the fourteenth to sixteenth centuries had connections with the "votchina law" (the rights a landowner had over his peasants) of the seventeenth century (Sh., "Dvorianstvo," no. 3, p. 449).

77. *AMG*, 1, no. 89; Man'kov, *Razvitie*, p. 188.

78. Sadikov, *Ocherki*, p. 426; I. I. Smirnov, "K kharakteristike," p. 48; Vorms, ed., *Pamiatniki*, nos. 19, 24; Koretskii, *Zakreposhchenie*, p. 23.

79. Chaev, "Iz istorii," p. 36; *MIKR*, nos. 52, 63.

80. Nazarov, "Iz istorii agrarnoi," p. 110.

81. V. I. Koretskii relates this to a putative appearance of and increase in corvée at this time ("K istorii formirovaniia," p. 84). This follows from his attempt to create a "Marxist" interpretation of the enserfment of the peasantry. For a critique of Koretskii's interpretation, see Danilova, "K voprosu," pp. 137, 139.

82. S. M. Kashtanov has tried to prove that a change in the formula of the immunity grant in 1522–24 and then widely used after 1538 (when the Elena Glinskaia government yielded to the Shuiskiis) also abased the peasant. In the section of the document on the arrival of new peasants the word "people" (*liudi*) yielded to "peasants" (*krest'iane*). Kashtanov says that *liudi* in the fourteenth century and in the beginning of the fifteenth had meant "long-time residents" (already enserfed) and "newcomers" (*novoprikhodtsy*). In the fifteenth century and particularly in the early sixteenth *liudi* came to mean mainly peasants who were not registered in a census, not on the tax rolls, very poor, and in the process of signing a settlement contract with a lord. By the second third of the sixteenth century these people no longer existed; there remained only *krest'iane*, who were bound to the land and could only move with the aid of another lord (*vyvoz*). The term also, according to Kashtanov, reflects the

spread of corvée (*PRP*, 4:143–44; Kashtanov, "K probleme mestnogo upravleniia," pp. 141, 147; idem, "K izucheniiu oprichniny," pp. 100–106) . The argument impresses me as being totally contrived.

83. *Akty Iushkova*, no. 138.

84. *PRP*, 4:86–87, 65–66. Over a hundred *poslushnye* and similar documents are found in *AM*, 1, pt. 2.

85. Makovskii, *Razvitie*, p. 438; Polosin, "Pomestnoe pravo," pp. 45, 49–51; I. I. Smirnov, *Vosstanie Bolotnikova*, p. 41; Koretskii, *Zakreposhchenie*, pp. 47–54.

86. Polosin, "Pomestnoe pravo," pp. 47–49.

87. Kashtanov, "K izucheniiu oprichniny," p. 106. Koretskii feels such actions were illegal (*Zakreposhchenie*, pp. 66–67) .

88. Kashtanov, "K izucheniiu oprichniny," p. 108; Makovskii, *Razvitie*, p. 438.

89. Polosin, "Pomestnoe pravo," pp. 47–49.

90. Koretskii, "Zemskii sobor," p. 49.

91. Polosin, "Pomestnoe pravo," p. 52.

92. One of the cardinal tenets of Soviet historiography is that labor rent came to prevail over cash or produce rent by the end of the sixteenth century. The giving to the *pomeshchiki* of the right to control their service lands fits in nicely with this scheme, for corvée would pay better when the lord supervised the working of his lands (Liashchenko, *Istoriia*, 1:234) . Whether the serviceman was around enough to do this in fact is another matter, for he spent most of the agricultural season in military service. Another Soviet historian claimed that the sixteenth century witnessed the development of a corvée serf economy with a dictatorship of the middle service class serf-owners over the peasantry (Dubrovskii, "Protiv," p. 125) .

93. P. I. Liashchenko attributed much of the development of serfdom (in the sixteenth century) to the need by *pomeshchiki* for slave labor to farm their estates. The lords converted peasant obligations into corvée, which made the peasant resemble a slave (*Istoriia*, 1:233) .

94. *Sudebnik* (1550) , art. 62. See also Makovskii's citations above in the section on the favorable legal climate of the pre-Oprichnina period (*Razvitie*, p. 21) .

95. Rozhdestvenskii, "Sel'skoe," p. 45.
The Soviet historian N. E. Nosov even argues that the reforms of the 1550s were effected partly out of concern for the interests of at least the wealthy peasants (*Stanovlenie*). Many peasants probably preferred the lord's court to the state courts because the former did not take bribes, was free, and no fees had to be paid to the treasury. Furthermore, justice was much speedier (Engel'man, *Istoriia*, p. 70) .

96. *AI*, 1, no. 154-V; *Sudebniki*, p. 555.

97. *Ulozhenie*, 10:229 (on fugitives) ; ibid., 13:7 ("za krest'ian svoikh ishchut i otvechaiut oni zhe dvoriane i deti boiarskie vo vsiakikh delekh, krome tat'by i razboiu, i polichnogo i smertnykh ubiistv," from a 1642 case [*UKZP*, 31:3; *PRP*, 5:327–425; Vladimirskii-Budanov, *Khristomatiia*, 3: 118–200]) ; ibid., 25:6 (source unknown) . The lord was, furthermore, instructed not to conceal his felonious peasants, but to hand them over to the authorities, at the risk of losing his service lands (ibid., 21:79) . A later decree, of May 2, 1758, prescribed that it was the duty of lords to watch the conduct of their serfs (*PSZ*, 15, no. 10,832) . A decree of 1648 permitted lords to whip peasant debtors (A. M. Sakharov, *Obrazovanie*, p. 168) .

98. *AMG*, 1, no. 259. On the role of the institution of slavery in the abasement of the French peasant, see Bloch, *French Rural History*, pp. 89–90.

99. Alekseev, "Chernaia volost'," p. 78; *AMG*, 3, no. 447. Some commentators have felt that article 13 of chapter 2 of the *Ulozhenie* gave landholders this right, for it denied equally to peasants and slaves the right to testify against their lords in any but treason cases (Sh., "Dvorianstvo," no. 3, p. 205) . Odinets reported that there is no suit extant by a peasant against his lord and said that the filing of such suits had become impossible after the fourteenth century ("Poteria," p. 210) . However, a "unique suit between a lord and former peasant" is reported by V. G. Geiman, "O nekotorykh svoeobraznykh," p. 190. Also see the article by Vainberg, "Bor'ba," which

discusses a suit stretching over years by a group of peasants against a *syn boiarskii.*

100. Petrikeev, *Krupnoe,* pp. 58, 63, 66–68, 77, 159; *Akty* . . . *Morozova,* 1, nos. 41, 60, 79, 80, 86, 94, 96, 97; *Khoziaistvo,* 1, no. 149; *Ocherki* . . . *XVII,* pp. 172–75.

101. *Ulozhenie,* 21:45, 46 (dating from before 1616–17, on slaves) , 66–68 (slaves only, peasants not added, from 1624) .

102. Gnevushev, "Zemlevladenie," p. 305. The right of a lord to administer corporal punishment to his peasants appeared after the *Ulozhenie* of 1649.

The annexation of part of the Rzeczpospolita during the Thirteen Years War (1654–67) presented the Muscovite administration with problems, for the lords of Belorussia and Lithuania had far greater powers over their peasants—up to the right to try and to execute them—than did their Russian counterparts. The lords in the conquered territories demanded they be allowed to retain these rights in exchange for pledging allegiance to Moscow. The Russians agreed, but only for the territory west of the Berezina river (A. N. Mal'tsev, "Nakazy belorusskikh i litovskikh shliakhetskikh seimikov 1657 g.," in *Problemy obshchestvenno-politicheskoi istorii Rossii i slavianskikh stran* [Moscow: IVL, 1963], pp. 262–63) .

103. *Akty Iushkova,* no. 269.

104. *AMG,* 1, no. 233; ibid., 3, nos. 397, 452.

105. Logically enough, a law of 1614 said peasants did not have to obey proscribed landholders (*AMG,* 1, no. 89) .

106. *PRP,* 4:586–89; *MS,* pp. 137–41.

107. *Ulozhenie,* 10:141.

108. See also ibid., 138–40.

109. *PRP,* 5:210, 342.

110. *Ulozhenie,* 11:26.

111. Ibid., 11:27.

112. Romanovich-Slavatinskii, *Dvorianstvo v" Rossii,* pp. 228–38, 269; *Ulozhenie,* 21:41; *MS,* pp. 300–301.

113. *AI,* 3, no. 92-XV. A similar decree was also enacted in 1628 (*UKZP,* 7; ibid., 13: 9; Engel'man, *Istoriia,* p. 73) .

114. *Ulozhenie,* 10:262; *AMG,* 3, no. 279.

115. Kachanovskii, "O poniatiiakh," p. 131. Seemingly, even in the second half of the century a lord could appropriate for himself his serf's property only by resort to violence (Baklanova, "Dela," p. 316; see also Zaozerskii, *Tsar',* pp. 170–72) .

116. Beliaev, *Krest'iane* (1903) , pp. 113, 123; Rozhkov, "Istoriia krepostnogo prava," p. 119. Others emphasize the fact that the property rights of the peasant were not explicitly protected at this time (Rozhdestvenskii, "Sel'skoe," pp. 77, 79) .

117. Engel'man, *Istoriia,* p. 75. See the *Ulozhenie,* 11:32 (compare with 19:16) . On the other hand, Kulisher stated that even in the 1649 *Ulozhenie* peasants had no restrictions on their judicial personalities; they could sue and answer in court, and could engage in any type of financial transaction ("Nesvobodnoe," p. 180) .

The peasant's contracting for his own labor was another matter. A free peasant could do this, but after a brief period of service with someone (six months [1597], *MS,* pp. 253–54; five months [1609], Iakovlev, *Kholopstvo,* p. 52; Pavlov-Sil'vanskii, "Liudi," p. 211; three months [1649], *Ulozhenie,* 20: 16; *MS,* p. 261) he was converted into a slave, if the employer so requested. A seignorial peasant could contract out his labor only with his lord's permission, for laws dating from 1598 said explicitly that a peasant could not become a slave (*Ulozhenie,* 20: 6, 24, 114) . Extant legal cases show that the status of peasant had priority over that of slave (Iakovlev, *Kholopstvo,* p. 121; *AAE,* 2, no. 40) . Peasants continued to contract out their own labor services after the final enserfment in 1649, both individually and in artels (L. L. Murav'eva, "O razvitii krest'ianskogo podriada vo vtoroi polovine XVII v.," *Novoe o proshlom nashei strany* [Moscow: Nauka, 1967], pp. 281–89) .

118. *Ulozhenie,* 21: 45–48 (dating from before 1616–17) and 66–68 (dating from 1624) ; *MS,* pp. 299–301.

119. Samokvasov, *Krest'iane,* p. 76.

120. R. B. Miuller, "Nekotorye zamechaniia ob izdanii zakonodatel'nykh aktov vtoroi poloviny XVI v.," *Problemy istochnikovedeniia* 9 (1961) : 340. Some scholars have attributed the management of cases on peasants to the Slavery Chancellery itself (Samokvasov, *Krest'iane*, p. 125). Later measures developed this practice still further. A law of October 13, 1675, gave the Service Land Chancellery the right to register peasants according to various land transaction documents, without a petition from the peasant or a report to the tsar. In 1681 proprietors engaged in land transactions were ordered to list the peasants on the properties with the Slavery Chancellery. The buyers paid the fee earlier prescribed for the registration of slaves and received a document on the peasant (Rozhdestvenskii, "Sel'skoe," p. 80; Engel'man, *Istoriia*, p. 65; Man'kov, "Zapisnye knigi," pp. 324–26).

121. Novoselskii, "Vol'nye," pp. 71–72.

122. Vainberg, "Bor'ba," pp. 252–53.

123. *Ulozhenie*, 15:3. Only hereditary landowners (*votchinniki*) could manumit peasants, not service landholders. A marginal comment in the manuscript notes that this was a new article in Russian law.

124. Bogoslovskii, *Zemskoe*, 1:58–60; Beliaev, *Krest'iane* (1903), p. 147. Rozhdestvenskii mentions a similar decree of 1626. He thought he saw a precedent in an action of 1388 by Dmitrii Donskoi, who feared lands might end up in the hands of other princes. Rozhdestvenskii saw "the chief goal" of Muscovite legislation of the sixteenth and seventeenth centuries as binding the "black" peasants to their tax status ("Sel'skoe," pp. 45–46, 50).

125. *UKPP*, suppl. 2, in *PRP*, 5: 204–5; *Ulozhenie*, 21: 71. Beliaev attributed this to a decree of January 17, 1615 (*Krest'iane* [1903], p. 117). See also Engel'man, *Istoriia*, p. 72.

126. *Ulozhenie*, 21: 73; 1625, *UKRP*, suppl. 2. See also *AI*, 3, no. 167-XXXIII of 1626. When a murder was not premeditated, or was accidental, the killer was not executed.

127. *Ulozhenie*, 11:20; ibid., 15:3; ibid., 16:7.

128. Certain articles of the *Ulozhenie* (11: 7, 8, 25, 34; ibid., 17: 27, 29; ibid., 20: 27) could be interpreted as giving the lord the right to sell his peasants. A law promulgated a quarter century after the *Ulozhenie*, in 1676, gave the hereditary landowner the right to alienate his lands and to transfer peasants from one estate to another. Frequently this was a form of sale of peasants (Man'kov, "Krest'ianskii," p. 69). Russian civil law permitted out-of-court settlements of suits prior to trial (*Sudebnik* [1550], arts, 9, 10, 31; *Ulozhenie*, 20: 121), and, according to M. A. D'iakonov, this device was used as early as 1598 as a guise for selling peasants: a peasant would flee or be kidnapped, and the rightful lord would take money from the harborer or kidnapper rather than see through a suit to have the fugitive returned (*Ocherki* [1926], pp. 291–93). See also Shilov, "Postupnyia," pp. 268–73; Rozhdestvenskii, "Sel'skoe," p. 77.

129. Man'kov, *Razvitie krepostnogo prava*, p. 212. Petrikeev takes issue with Man'kov's judgment that the selling of peasants only began after the *Ulozhenie* and was developed only in the eighteenth century. Petrikeev claims that the process (illegal until the 1660s) of buying and selling peasants without land began in the first half of the seventeenth century (*Krupnoe krepostnoe khoziaistvo*, pp. 156–57). Samokvasov attributed this phenomenon to the sixteenth century (*Krest'iane*, p. 132). This was also the position of M. A. D'iakonov, who claimed that documents of the last quarter of the sixteenth century show that, at the same time when the peasant's right to move was curtailed, landowners believed they had the right to dispose of the peasant's person (*Ocherki iz" istorii*, pp. 45–46). Now V. I. Koretskii holds this position (*Zakreposhchenie*, pp. 45–47).

130. Lappo-Danilevskii, *Organizatsiia*, pp. 135–37. Miliukov criticized his approach when extended from the free commune to seignorial peasants (*Spornye*, pp. 83–84). Beliaev had a somewhat similar understanding: prior to the *Ulozhenie* of 1649, only peasants with tax responsibilities were bound to the land (*Krest'iane* [1903], p. 105).

See p. 96 above on the reasons for the strong bias in favor of tax reasons for the enserfment. See chapter 3 above for a discussion of the issue of whether lords were responsible for the peasants' taxes levied on seignorial lands.

131. Rozhdestvenskii, "Sel'skoe," p. 49.

132. *MIKR*, no. 98; *AI*, 3, nos. 160, 286; *MS*, pp. 151–56, 166–67.

133. *MS*, pp. 151–56, 166–67.

134. Miliukov, *Spornye*, p. 84. This partially answers S. M. Kashtanov's perplexity over the fact that the Russian government could watch so cavalierly the black-land fund disappear as it recognized monastery seizures of taxpaying peasant lands. Moreover, most monastery lands paid taxes (Kashtanov and Klokman, "Sovetskaia," p. 165). P. N. Miliukov said that the north paid forty times more taxes than the center (*Ocherki* [1900], 1:144). S. B. Veselovskii questioned the size of this figure, but not its general import (*Soshnoe pis'mo*, 2:661–63).

7. Repeal of the Statute of Limitations

1. Billington, *Icon*, p. 108.

2. See chapter 10 below for additional details.

3. P. P. Smirnov states that the army and the merchant class favored the war in order to gain lands and trade routes in the Dnepr region, while the boyars in general were indifferent (*Posadskie*, 1:404). See *AAE*, 3, no. 251.

4. Porshnev, "Sotsial'no-," p. 112.

5. Ibid., p. 114; Novosel'skii, *Bor'ba*, pp. 199–222.

6. *AIuZR*, 3, no. 193; A. M. Sakharov, *Obrazovanie*, pp. 152–53. For more on the Balash affair, see chapter 10 below.

7. *AAE*, 3, no. 242.

8. See chapter 10 for further details.

9. On the impact of the taxes, see *SGGD*, 3, no. 99; *AMG*, 1, nos. 362 ff. See also Porshnev, "Sotsial'no-," p. 121. Man'kov, "Pobegi krest'ian," p. 45. On the other hand, the Holstinian traveler Adam Olearius, visiting Russia in the 1630s, did not feel that the Russians in general paid heavy taxes (*Travels*, p. 198). Several causes may be given to explain his conclusions, but the most likely one is that Russia was probably rather well off by comparison with those areas of Europe directly suffering from the scourge of the Thirty Years War.

10. Veselovskii, *Soshnoe*, 1:187.

11. Ibid., 1:319; Troitskii, "O vliianii," p. 289; Chaev, "Iz istorii," p. 33, no. 7.

12. Kahan, "Natural Calamities," p. 371; Novosel'skii, "Zemskii sobor," p. 28; Buchinskii, *O klimate*, pp. 90–91. *AAE*, 3, no. 322; ibid., 4, no. 30. After 1649 the major cause of peasant flights reverted to the traditional one of food shortage and famine (Obraztsov, "Ulozhenie," pp. 276, 281).

13. Chistiakova, "Volneniia," p. 257; P. P. Smirnov, "Chelobitnye"; Baklanova, "Dela," 313–14.

14. For example, see N. Chaev, "Iz istorii," p. 228, where documents reveal an attempt by peasants to prevent a monastery from taking over black lands. See also Veselovskii, *Soshnoe pis'mo*, 2:205.

15. Veselovskii, *Soshnoe pis'mo*, 1:414; Miliukov, *Spornye*, pp. 90–91. The real value of money fell about 25 percent in the seventeenth century (Troitskii, "O vliianii," p. 289; Shapiro, "Volneniia," p. 312).

16. Ogrizko, "Zernovoe," pp. 20, 27, 29; Prokof'eva, *Votchinnoe*, pp. 9–38, 94–144; *Ocherki . . . XVII*, p. 171; Obraztsov, "Ulozhenie 1649," p. 282; A. M. Sakharov, *Obrazovanie*, p. 136.

17. *AAE*, 3, no. 322 (1643); ibid., 4, no. 30 (August, 1648).

18. Veselovskii, *Soshnoe pis'mo*, 1:415–17. The chart has been abbreviated, with separate assessments for the towns of Novgorod and Ustiug Chancelleries and the Pomor'e towns. The levies for these areas generally followed those of the rest of the state. See also Miliukov, *Spornye*, pp. 92–94, 120.

19. *Ocherki* . . . *XVII*, p. 177.
20. Petrikeev, *Krupnoe krepostnoe khoziaistvo*, pp. 177–78.
21. Iakovlev, *Prikaz*, p. 257.
22. *AAE*, 3, no. 238.
23. *Ulozhenie*, 21:98.
24. Bulygin, "Beglye," pp. 131–49. See also Baranovich, "K voprosu," p. 41.
25. Man'kov, "Pobegi krest'ian," p. 48; Novosel'skii, "Otdatochnye knigi," pp. 151–52; Petrikeev, *Krupnoe krepostnoe khoziaistvo*, p. 177. A. A. Novosel'skii, noted, however, that "peasants felt freer if they fled alone, abandoning their wives and children," because they were thus completely unencumbered ("Pobegi," p. 338).
26. Most peasant migration was by gradual steps; from one province to the next was usually the maximum distance, rather than from the center to the frontier. The obvious difficulties of moving with family, cattle, grain, and general peasant inventory make this observed phenomenon expected (Baklanova, "Dela," pp. 312–13; Novosel'skii, "Otdatochnye knigi," p. 146; Zanicheva, "Krest'ianskie pobegi," pp. 232–33). This fact must limit economic models of the development of Russian serfdom based on "free land." (See, for example, Evsey D. Domar's September, 1967, paper, "The Causes of Slavery: A Hypothesis.") While indeed "free land" was present on the frontiers and in Siberia, this fact diminishes in importance if taking advantage of this "free" commodity was not a real alternative for most individuals. At least some peasants (and presumably most poorer ones) returned to their old dwellings, after moving, to harvest a crop they had planted (Vainberg, "Bor'ba," pp. 252–53). Obviously this was impossible when the peasant moved far away, which often limited this option to those in a three-field system who had reserves sufficient to forego a crop in the ground.
27. Tkhorzhevskii wrote that "only the poor and lucky moved about" ("Pomest'e," p. 82). This was hardly true in the seventeenth century (Baklanova, "Dela," pp. 314–16).
28. Novosel'skii, "K voprosu ob ekonomicheskom," pp. 58–64. This was over eight times the cost of food and fuel for one person for one year—3 rubles 26 kopeks, in the first half of the seventeenth century (Strumilin, *Ocherki* [1960], p. 99). Not surprisingly, it was also the wealthier peasants who led the protests against serfdom (Shapiro, "Volneniia," pp. 313–14).
29. Starostina, "Shueretskaia volost'," pp. 204–5. In Moscow, in 1634, 45 percent of the taxpayers had property valued at less than 5 rubles; 45 percent had from 5 to 50 rubles; 4 percent from 50 to 100 rubles; 2 percent, 100 to 250 rubles; and 2 percent over 250 rubles (A. M. Sakharov, *Obrazovanie*, pp. 149–50).
30. Man'kov, "Pobegi krest'ian," p. 46.
31. Novosel'skii, "Vol'nye," p. 60.
32. Ibid., p. 66.
33. Novosel'skii, "Otdatochnye," pp. 148–49; Man'kov, "Pobegi," p. 57. V. I. Nedosekin denies that the peasant followed the army commander in the settlement of the southern frontier ("Istochniki rosta krupnogo zemlevladeniia na iuge Rossii v XVIII stoletii," *Izvestiia Voronezhskogo gosudarstvennogo pedagogicheskogo instituta* 63[1967]: 263–64). I fail to find his evidence convincing.
34. Novosel'skii, "Otdatochnye," p. 129; P. P. Smirnov, "Dvizheniia naseleniia," p. 77. For the origins of these frontier peasants, see Novosel'skii, *Bor'ba*, pp. 161–66, 293–305; Zagorovskii, *Belgorodskaia*, p. 33.
35. I. G. Rozner, "Antifeodal'nye gosudarstvennye obrazovaniia v Rossii i na Ukraine v XVI-XVIII vv.," *Voprosy istorii* 45, no. 8 (August 1970) :56.
36. Novosel'skii, "Dela," pp. 150–51; idem, "Vol'nye," pp. 75–77; idem, "Otdatochnye," pp. 129, 145–46; idem, *Bor'ba*, pp. 300–5; Zagorovskii, *Belgorodskaia*, pp. 90–91, 99, 101, 129; Latkin, *Materialy*, p. 51.
37. Vainberg, "Bor'ba," pp. 259–61. The maps on pp. 259 and 261 are particularly illuminating.
38. Novosel'skii, "Zemskii sobor," p. 18.

39. Simultaneously certain members of the merchant class were conducting an hysterical petition campaign directed at expelling foreign merchants from Russia. The government was reluctant to yield on this point also, but eventually did so, to the displeasure of both the foreigners and the majority of the lesser Russian merchants. One scholar has discovered that there was a continuity of petitioners in the merchants' campaign, and no doubt there also was in the campaign of the middle service class (K. V. Bazilevich, "Kollektivnye chelobit'ia torgovykh liudei i bor'ba za russkii rynok v pervoi polovine XVII veka," *Izvestiia Akademii nauk SSSR, VII seriia, Otdelenie obshchestvennykh nauk,* no. 2 [1932]: 91–123).

40. Novosel'skii, *Bor'ba*, p. 301; Makovskii, *Razvitie,* p. 277; Chaev, "K voprosu"; Iakovlev, "Svoznye," pp. 185–260; Petrikeev, *Krupnoe,* p. 68.

41. Rozhdestvenskii, "Iz" istorii," p. 156.

42. In the 1630s the 41 members of the Duma had an average of 520 households apiece; in 1678, 97 men had about 480 each (Iakovlev, *Prikaz",* pp. 257–59; Novosel'skii, "Rospis'," pp. 88, 149).

43. Smirnov, "Chelobitnye," no. 1; *MS,* pp. 167–75. On the 1637 petition, see Rozhdestvenskii, "Iz" istorii otmeny," p. 156. See also Stashevskii, *K" istorii,* pp. 20–22. Other issues raised in this and the subsequent petitions have been discussed in chapter 3. A year before this, on December 16, 1636, in an incredible burst of conscience, the boyars asked the tsar to decide an issue because they themselves were involved (*UKPP,* p. 116). To my knowledge, this is the only expression of the notion of conflict of interest, in the modern sense, in all of pre-Petrine Russian history. The ordinary practice was just the opposite: the more influence a person had in the government, the more likely it was that official policy and actions reflected his personal wishes.

44. *AMG,* 2, no. 143; *MS,* pp. 176–78. In 1639 the foreigners in Muscovite military service requested and were granted the same nine-year limit (*AMG,* 2, no. 160).

45. Aleksandrov, "Streletskoe," pp. 239–40.

46. Novosel'skii, "K voprosu o znachenii," p. 181.

47. See chapter 3.

48. Smirnov, "Chelobitnye," no. 2.

49. High service ranks. See chapter 2.

50. Rozhdestvenskii, "Iz" istorii," p. 159.

51. *AI,* 3, no. 92-XXXIII; Vladimirskii-Budanov, *Khristomatiia,* 3: 161–72 (the *Ukaznaia kniga Zemskago prikaza,* no. 31); *PRP,* 5:362–71.

52. S. F. Platonov linked this corruption to the personalities who had supported the second pretender at Tushino during the Time of Troubles. They had failed then, but shortly triumphed with the installation of Mikhail Romanov and set the moral tenor of much of his reign, and of even later times. The implication is that the tone of the seventeenth century would have been much higher had the aristocratic boyar Vasilii Shuiskii not been overthrown in 1610 ("Moskovskoe pravitel'stvo," pp. 402–6).

53. Novosel'skii, "Rasprostranenie," p. 23.

54. P. P. Smirnov, *Posadskie,* 1:486–87.

55. Forsten, "Snosheniia," pp. 368–69; Smirnov, *Posadskie,* 2:19. This was a classical example which would support Lenin's thesis on how simple it was for one group of early modern aristocrats to oust another clique from power before the eighteenth-century era of palace revolutions (Shmidt, "V. I. Lenin," p. 333).

56. Collins, *Present State,* pp. 102–3. Note, however, that both Morozov and F. I. Sheremetev were on the whitewash commission appointed to "investigate" government corruption (P. P. Smirnov, "Chelobitnye," no. 3).

57. Petrikeev, *Krupnoe krepostnoe khoziaistvo,* p. 135. D. I. Petrikeev is the leading contemporary specialist on Morozov. His articles on Morozov and his activities are listed in the Bibliography. For a map of the Morozov holdings, see the insert between pp. 56–57 in Tomsinskii, *Ocherki.*

58. Petrikeev, *Krupnoe,* p. 176.

59. Gradovskii, "Vysshaia administratsiia," pp. 69, 74.

60. Presniakov, "Moskovskoe gosudarstvo," p. 60.

61. P. P. Smirnov, "Chelobitnye," no. 3; *MS*, pp. 191–96.

62. Adherents of the "indebtedness theory" of the enserfment of the peasantry point out that throughout the first half of the seventeenth century children were included with their parents in the settlement contracts peasants made with lords upon taking up residence on the lands of the latter (D'iakonov, *Ocherki iz" istorii*, p. 40). While this is true, it does nothing to advance their argument, for children would almost automatically be covered by the blanket provisions of the Forbidden Years. (A. N. Sakharov has argued that "peasant children" were a separate category of seignorial peasants performing corvée services [*Russkaia derevnia*, pp. 171–77].)

The reinforcement of the clan, or extended family, principle which crept into serfdom in the 1640s flew directly in the face of the budding individualism which can be discerned in other spheres of Muscovite life. The outstanding Soviet literary scholar D. S. Likhachev has pointed out that modern individualism was beginning its triumph in Russian literature in the seventeenth century. Russia had missed the Renaissance because of the church schism, the Mongol yoke, the fall of the Balkans and Constantinople to the Turks, and the decline of Novgorod and Pskov with the rise of Muscovy. However, in the seventeenth century Renaissance themes of personal responsibility and individual dignity were imported into Muscovy through the agency of the Western baroque movement ("Semnadtsatyi vek v russkoi literature," in *XVII vek v mirovom literaturnom razvitii* [Moscow: Nauka, 1969], pp. 299–328; *Chelovek v literature Drevnei Rusi* [Moscow-Leningrad: Akademiia Nauk SSSR, 1958], pp. 151–67; "Budushchee literatury kak predmet izucheniia [Zametki i razmyshleniia]," *Novyi mir* 35, no. 9 [September 1969]:172–73). A similar trend toward emphasis on individualism also occurred in the army officer corps (see chapter 11). Finally, increasing stress on the individual is also demonstrable in the institution of slavery in seventeenth-century Muscovy (*Ulozhenie*, 20:22, 25, 26, 84). These trends running counter to the direction of the enserfment movement are indicative of the tensions present at the time and comprise part of the evidence that serfdom was not "inevitable" in Muscovy.

63. *AAE*, 4, no. 21, of October 30, 1647, referring to a general decree of September 2, 1647, reviews the original instructions and orders corrections made by March 1, 1648, in the completed census; denunciations had revealed that fraud had been committed by concentrating several households in one house for the purpose of evading taxation.

64. Vodarskii, "K voprosu," p. 136. Vodarskii says "undoubtedly" the goal of the census was to bind the taxpaying peasants to their lords (ibid., p. 137).

65. *DAI*, 3, no. 32. See also ibid., no. 33. In this instance a zealous official had believed the government had meant what it had promised the middle service class and consequently had been returning peasants who had fled forty years ago.

66. Ibid., no. 14. Throughout Russian history officials in remote regions resisted returning fugitives to the center of Muscovy. Upon occasion the central authorities collaborated with such officials out of a desire to populate the frontiers (A. N. Sakharov, "O dialektike," p. 25–26). See also chapter 14.

Peasant flights increased significantly in 1646 when the government issued a call for volunteers to join a flotilla of Don cossacks in attacking the Crimea. Indignant landholders complained to the government, which apparently did nothing (Zagorovskii, *Belgorodskaia*, pp. 116–17).

67. *AIuZR*, 3, nos. 192, 193; 3, ibid., suppl., no. 11. This is unquestionably related to the *Ulozhenie's* 11:33 and 34; *MS*, p. 231.

68. In 1645 one Ivan Ushakov informed the government that M. A. Pushkin, who had attended the 1598 and 1613 Assemblies of the Land, had criticized Tsar Aleksei for not having been elected to the throne (*RBS*, 15:319–20, cited in Hulbert, "Assemblies"). Such remarks continued to haunt Aleksei and were considered treasonous (Novembergskii, *Slovo i delo*, 1). On the issue of whether Aleksei was "confirmed" by some assemblage, see Cherepnin, "Zemskie sobory," p. 125. Grigorii Kotoshikhin applied the same phrase to the installation of Aleksei as he did to earlier tsars: *obrali na*

tsarstvo (*O Rossii*, 1:6). Earlier, the legitimacy of Vasilii Shuiskii had been challenged because he had not been elected by a Zemskii Sobor during the Time of Troubles (Tikhomirov, "Pskovskie povesti," p. 185). Aleksei was also haunted by rumors that he was a changeling (Marin, " 'Slovo i delo," p. 218).

69. *AMG*, 2, nos. 310, 312–14, 316, 318–19, 321, 324, 326, 330, 333–34, 336, 337–39, 341, 343; *AIuZR*, 3, nos. 107, 111, 117, 122, 124, 133, 136, 146, 164, 166, 181, 189; Iakovlev, "Rossiia," 184:415; Tikhomirov, "Sobornoe Ulozhenie," p. 20; Buganov, "Osvoboditel'naia," pp. 60–61.

70. P. P. Smirnov, "Chelobitnye," no. 4; *MS*, pp. 198–205. This petition survives only in a version transmitted by the Swedish resident in Moscow, Karl Pommerening, to his government. The original was destroyed by the officials accompanying the tsar. The original of a similar petition a few days later calling for the convocation of a Zemskii Sobor survives (Shakhmatov, "Chelobitnaia").

71. P. P. Smirnov, "Chelobitnye," no. 4; Shakhmatov, "Chelobitnaia," p. 14.

72. *MS*, p. 205. Shakhmatov, "Chelobitnaia," p. 20. On November 13, 1648, the *dvoriane* and *deti boiarskie* of various towns asked for justice against chancellery heads (*d'iaki*) and clerks (*pod'iachie*). They noted that such officials were tried in the very chancelleries where they worked, that they could obtain no justice from them because the officials favored their relatives. They wanted them tried in a separate chancellery. The request was granted (P. P. Smirnov, *Posadskie*, 2:238). As pointed out by Douglas Bennet, the contrast between the contemporary analyses of the causes of the Time of Troubles and of the disorders of 1648 is striking. In the earlier instance, the chaos and strife were seen as divine chastisement for sins and omissions, but during the summer of 1648 people clearly understood and were willing to express the fact that the popular discontent was a product of malpractice by government officials ("The Idea of Kingship in 17th Century Russia," pp. 211–13). Tsar Aleksei, however, seems not to have been as enlightened as some of his critics, for various actions he took in December, 1648, would tend to indicate that he felt that the disorders were divine retribution for the sinfulness of the Russian people in general (ibid., p. 97). See also Chistiakova, "Letopisnye," p. 252.

73. Buganov, "Opisanie," p. 228. This should have come as no surprise to anyone, for *strel'tsy* had participated in the civil disorders during the fire in the Kitaigorod section of Moscow in March, 1636 (Chistiakova, "Moskva," pp. 307–8).

74. Tikhomirov, "Sobornoe," pp. 10–11. Pommerening reported that agents of Morozov had set the fires (Iakubov, "Rossiia," p. 418). The document published by V. I. Buganov contains a list of some of the plundered houses ("Opisanie," pp. 228–29).

75. *Novyi letopisets*", suppl., pp. 5–6. See Olearius, *Travels*, pp. 207–17, for a near-contemporary account of this crucial event. The account is valuable even though it is not entirely accurate. For a contemporary English account, see Loewenson, "The Moscow Rising," pp. 152–56. Pommerening's account is the most accurate (Iakovlev, "Rossiia," 184: 417–20).

76. Bakhrushin, "Moskovskoe," 2:76; P. P. Smirnov, *Posadskie*, 2:165; A. M. Sakharov, *Obrazovanie*, p. 165; P. P. Smirnov, "O nachale," p. 48.

77. P. P. Smirnov, *Posadskie*, 2:197, 208–9, 219–27.

78. Bakhrushin, "Moskovskoe," 2:65; Iakubov, "Rossiia," p. 419.

79. *AI*, 4, no. 30. See *AIuZR*, 3, no. 193, for another postriot petition. The answer of June 12, 1648, prescribed that peasants who had fled to Lithuania and then returned to Muscovy should be given back to their lords regardless of when they had fled (*bezletno*). This certainly was an attempt to mollify, at no cost to the magnates, servicemen living on the western frontier.

80. Bakhrushin, "Moskovskoe," 2:79; Smirnov, "O nachale," p. 45; idem, *Posadskie*, 2: 173, 189–91; Cherepnin, "Zemskie," pp. 126–27; Forsten, "Snosheniia," p. 373. P. P. Smirnov assigned to the servicemen the major role in the uprising of 1648 in Moscow, whereas S. V. Bakhrushin gave this role to the middle stratum of the urban population. The latter point of view has become the accepted one in Soviet historiography (Zimin and Preobrazhenskii, "Izuchenie," p. 145; Tikhomirov, "Sobornoe Ulozhenie," pp.

10, 15). Regardless of which view is "correct," there is no question that the middle service class combined with the townsmen to squeeze concessions out of the magnates running the government at this time (Zimin, "Osnovnye," p. 50).

81. The petition requesting the convocation of an Assembly of the Land was discovered in the Iur'ev-Derpt-Dorpat-Tartu archives and published only at the beginning of the 1930s. It contains much of the same material as the Smirnov no. 4 document, but was written a few days later, for it mentions some of the disorders which occurred after the submission of the initial petition, particularly the firing of several towns (M. V. Shakhmatov, "Chelobitnaia," pp. 1–20).

82. Nikon, "Mnenie," p. 426.

83. Zagoskin, *Ulozhenie*, p. 58; Platonov, "K" istorii," p. 326; Meichik, "Dopolnitel'nyia," pp. 25–26; Tikhomirov and Epifanov, *Sobornoe Ulozhenie 1649 g.*, pp. 425–31; P. P. Smirnov, "O nachale," p. 54.

84. *Novyi letopisets"*, suppl., pp. 6–7.

85. Tikhomirov, "Sobornoe Ulozhenie," p. 26.

86. A peasant who had been captured and taken abroad by an enemy of Russia, and then managed to flee, was not required to return to his old lord. The *Ulozhenie* implies that this custom was still relevant (11:33). Repeating legislation of 1630 (*AMG*, 1, no. 259, which refers back to a decree of May 26, 1624), and perhaps in response to a middle service class petition (*AIuZR*, 3, no. 193), the *Ulozhenie* restated the maxim that peasants could not obtain freedom by fleeing abroad and then returning to Russia (11:33, 34). Some peasants in the north also were exempt from the provisions of the *Ulozhenie* in practice (Ogrizko, *Iz istorii krest'ianstva*).

87. *Ulozhenie*, 11:1,2; ibid., 20:6; Vernadsky, "Serfdom," p. 263.

88. Tkhorzhevskii, "Pomest'e," p. 93; Danilova, "Istoricheskie usloviia," p. 123.

89. This measure was strictly enforced: when peasants complained about their land being turned over to a monastery, the government ordered them to continue to live there and prescribed that each of the plaintiffs should be flogged (Shapiro, "Volneniia," p. 309). The *Ulozhenie* recognized the existence of peasants who were still free, not enserfed (11:20, 21).

90. *Ulozhenie*, 11: 1, 3; *MS*, pp. 215–32. The state followed this law to the letter, even though the lord was really interested only in the labor power of the peasant. His inventory was essential only insofar as it enabled the peasant to work (Man'kov, "Krest'ianskii," p. 44). An exception was made for distant areas such as the Urals. Peasants returned to Russia proper from the Urals were allowed to sell their houses, cattle, and sowings (Preobrazhenskii, "Sysk," p. 97).

91. A fine of ten rubles per year was prescribed for each fugitive harbored (*Ulozhenie*, 11:10). This could, and did, run into enormous sums (Bulygin, "Beglye," p. 137). I do not know whether lords looked on this oversight in the law as a license to impose any sanctions.

92. In 1658, punishment by beating with the knout was decreed for fugitive peasants in Novgorod. In 1683, whipping was made a general rule for all fugitives who were caught. The peasants were beaten, according to the law, because their flights caused quarrels among the landowners (Man'kov, "Krest'ianskii vopros," pp. 45–46; Novosel'skii, "Otdatochnye knigi," p. 136).

93. *AI*, 4, no. 30; *MS*, pp. 213–15. This document states that the law was the result of middle service class petitions.

94. *Ulozhenie*, 15:3.

95. On November 10, 1648, Ia. K. Cherkasskii insulted the tsar and was arrested at home. I. D. Miloslavskii, standing in for Morozov, took all his posts. Subsequently the Cherkasskii clique yielded all posts to the Morozov clique (P. P. Smirnov, *Posadskie*, 2:209–20, 227).

96. This fact has been realized by at least one Soviet historian, A. N. Chistozvonov: "The boyar economies were on firmer foundations economically in the sixteenth and seventeenth centuries. They possessed great possibilities for enticing peasants. . . . They were relatively less interested in establishing severe forms of serfdom" ("Neko-

torye aspekty," p. 55; see also A. M. Sakharov, *Obrazovanie*, pp. 140–41). He does not acknowledge, however, that the government was constituted by the "separate groups of magnates for whom preservation of the old procedures—when they could accept fugitives or even carry off peasants by force—was advantageous."

97. Even as he was being ousted from his posts at mob insistence, Morozov was maintaining that the time limit was ten years. Finally, he ordered his managers not to receive fugitives at all. Never did he order all the fugitives living on his estates to be sent home without their lords having to locate and sue for them (*Akty* . . . *Morozova*, 1, nos. 26, 27, 30, 33, 34, 35, 36, 45; *MS*, pp. 209–13; Petrikeev, *Krupnoe krepostnoe khoziaistvo*, pp. 172–75).

98. At the Assembly of the Land the townsmen and the musketeers (*strel'tsy*) supported a group headed by Morozov, Miloslavskii, Tsar Aleksei, and Patriarch Iosif. The other faction, led by the Cherkasskiis, Sheremetev, and Romanov, had the support of the middle service class (P. P. Smirnov, *Posadskie*, 2:208–9, 219–27).

99. It is significant that Iosif signed the *Ulozhenie*, for the power of the church and especially of the monasteries was considerably restricted by the new law code: all urban tax-exempt enclaves, including those belonging to church institutions, were confiscated, and the monasteries lost most of their judicial power over their subjects (both their peasants and most clerical personnel) to the government (*Ulozhenie*, 13; ibid., 19). Nikon, after becoming patriarch, bitterly attacked the *Ulozhenie* and the Odoevskii commission which had compiled it—even though he had signed the law at the time in his capacity as archimandrite of the Moscow Novyi Spas monastery (Undol'skii, "Otzyv"," pp. 605–20; Nikon, "Mneniia," pp. 423–98).

The church did not surrender completely, however; the church lands were not confiscated and peasants were not divided up equally among all landholders, as the members of the middle service class had wanted. This had been part of the program of the Cherkasskii faction, in addition to forcing the monks to work (P. P. Smirnov, *Posadskie*, 2:229–32).

Iosif probably signed the *Ulozhenie* because he was thankful that the debacle had not been worse for the church at the Assembly of the Land. Giving up fugitive peasants and the right to acquire more lands was not nearly as painful as confiscation of all church lands would have been. See *Ulozhenie*, 17:2, 10, 42; Arkhangel'skii, *O sobornom"*, pp. 136–37. See also chapters 2 and 3 for more information on the problem of church land-ownership.

100. Kashtanov, "Otdatochnye," pp. 198–220. On the *otdatochnye knigi*, see Novosel'skii, "Otdatochnye," pp. 127–52. Curiously enough, the *Ulozhenie* of 1649 did not specifically order the return of peasants who had fled from lands belonging to the clergy, church, and monasteries, even though such flights were numerous. This reflects the obvious anticlerical mood of the delegates to the Assembly of the Land. See Arkhangel'skii, *O sobornom"*, p. 132 (13A); *Ulozhenie*, 11:1, 2. Nevertheless, many monastery peasants were returned in the 1650s and through the 1670s (Obraztsov, "Ulozhenie," p. 275).

101. Obraztsov, "Ulozhenie," pp. 271–74. One way church institutions got around the prohibition against receiving fugitive peasants was by ignoring it, even long after the promulgation of the *Ulozhenie* (Arkhangel'skii, *O sobornom"*, p. 131). See also *PSZ*, 2, no. 731 (1678). See also chapter 14.

102. The non-Marxist reader should be aware that this type of analysis is positively anathema to the ordinary Soviet historian, who regards the middle service class as a ruling class and the government simply as the reflection of this class's desires. A more sophisticated Soviet historian, who refuses to be totally oblivious to the facts of the situation, may attempt to explain the observed phenomenon in the following terms: "In contrast to other forms of state administration, the most important sign of autocratic, absolutist government structure is its relatively greater independence from the ruling class" (Shapiro, "Ob absoliutizme," p. 70).

103. M. N. Tikhomirov questioned P. P. Smirnov's thesis ("O nachale," p. 54) that there was an alliance between the middle service class and the townsmen ("Sobornoe Ulozhenie," pp. 16–18).

104. Iakubov, "Rossiia," 184: 426, 429.

105. Morozov's correspondence with his estate managers does reflect a certain degree of fear when he finally orders them to turn over peasants to their lords if the latter insist (*Akty . . . Morozova*, 1, nos. 30, 33; *MS*, pp. 211–12).

106. *DAI*, 3, no. 47-I; Iakubov, "Rossiia," pp. 426–28. On January 29, 1649, the government beheaded two persons and cut out the tongues of two more who predicted an imminent uprising of greater dimensions than the one the previous summer (Iakubov, pp. 441–42).

107. Rozhdestvenskii, "Sel'skoe," p. 67.

108. Tikhomirov, "Sobornoe Ulozhenie," p. 9. For information on other notable civil disorders of 1648, see Loewenson, "The Moscow Rising of 1648," p. 146; Iakubov, "Rossiia," 184:431, 436, 470; Chistiakova, "Letopisnye," p. 249.

8. Consequences of the Repeal of the Statute of Limitations

1. Beliaev, *Krest'iane* (1903), pp. 164, 179. He saw the "above class state" (as it was called by members of the state historical school) as having bound the peasants for the sake of the treasury. The role of the monasteries and middle service class was ignored. Only in the second half of the seventeenth century and under Peter did the interests of middle service class-gentry diverge from those of the common people (*Krest'iane* [1879], pp. 99, 107).

2. Obraztsov, "Iz istorii," p. 347.

3. *AMG*, 2, no. 439.

4. This will be discussed in chapter 14.

5. Novosel'skii, "Dela," p. 147.

6. Novosel'skii, "Vol'nye," p. 77.

7. *Ulozhenie*, 19:1, 5, 9, 15, 16, 17; *MS*, pp. 51–62. See chapter 14.

8. Makovskii, *Razvitie*, p. 327.

9. L. V. Danilova has observed that serfdom fettered the process, observable in the peasantry, of the development of property differentiation into social differentiation and limited the potential increase in the number of traders and artisans in the population ("Istoricheskie usloviia," pp. 123–24).

S. M. Troitskii emphasizes also the fact that the amount of taxes demanded was growing rapidly and that this braked the growth of differentiation among the peasantry ("O vliianii," pp. 285–86). Petrikeev, while denying the frequent conclusion of Soviet historiography that the rudiments of capitalism were appearing in the second half of the seventeenth century, claims that property differentiation among the peasantry was increasing at this time. He simply relates the phenomenon to the development of commodity money relationships, a current Soviet ideological axiom (*Krupnoe kepostnoe khoziaistyo*, pp. 167, 169). The consolidation of serfdom in 1649 presents Soviet historians with a dilemma. On the one hand, most of them cannot deny that *something* significant occurred in Russian social relations at this time. On the other hand, they are locked into various incompatible ideological positions based on their reading of Lenin. In an off-hand remark, obviously made under the influence of the periodization advanced by pre-Soviet historians such as S. M. Solov'ev and V. O. Kliuchevskii, Lenin said that the last three centuries represented a separate period of Russian history; this new period witnessed the decay of feudalism and the formation of an all-Russian national market with increasing bourgeois capitalistic relations in the seventeenth century (Zimin, "Problemy istorii Rossii," pp. 320–21; Shmidt, "V. I. Lenin," p. 345; A. M. Sakharov, "Lenin ob osnovnykh," p. 308).

However, Sakharov said this is untrue when it comes to governmental structure, which remained "Muscovite" until Peter (ibid., p. 315). This means that serfdom was getting worse, and presumably "feudalism" was *maturing*, precisely at the time when a new era of bourgeois relations was dawning. Thus the economic base and the social superstructure were getting more and more out of phase. One conclusion should be drawn from this: 1649 represents a classical instance of social relations reflecting not at all the economic base, but rather intervention by the governmental part of the superstructure.

10. Shapiro, "Mnogotomnaia," p. 146. In making this affirmation, Shapiro has gone part of the way to effect B. D. Grekov's 1948 dictum that one of the tasks of Soviet historical scholarship was "to destroy one of the firmly held prejudices—that Russia always trailed behind pan-European history" (Schmidt, "K izucheniiu agrarnoi," p. 26). In a survey article, A. N. Chistozvonov limits himself to the generalization that general progress was delayed and deformed for centuries by the system of serfdom and autocratic despotism ("Nekotorye aspekty," p. 61). More solid evidence on this subject is obviously a goal of future research.

11. Baklanova, "Dela," p. 319; Bulygin et al., "Nachal'nyi," p. 84.

12. *AMG*, 2, no. 1004.

13. Preobrazhenskii, "Sysk," p. 90.

14. Man'kov, "Krest'ianskii," p. 60. *Ulozhenie*, 11:9.

15. Novombergskii, "K voprosu," p. 45.

16. Kashtanov, "Otdatochnye"; Novosel'skii, "Otdatochnye," pp. 127–52. See chapter 14 for more information.

17. Bulygin, "Beglye," p. 131; *Tul'skii krai*, 1, no. 30.

18. This of course continued after the *Ulozhenie* too (Baklanova, "Dela," p. 308; *AIuZR*, 3, nos. 348, 362). Some lords even caught their own fugitives (Bulygin, "Beglye," p. 139; *Ocherki . . . XVII*, p. 180).

19. Zertsalov, "O miatezhakh"," p. 7.

20. Bulygin, "Beglye," p. 131.

21. Novosel'skii, "Pobegi krest'ian i kholopov i ikh sysk vo vtoroi polovine XVII st.," *Sbornik trudov nauchnogo Instituta istorii*, 1:327–52; idem, "K voprosu ob ekonomicheskom," p. 58; Bulygin, "Beglye," p. 132; Beliaev, *Krest'iane* (1903), pp. 149–50. Preobrazhenskii shows the difficulties this created for newly developing areas, such as the Urals ("Sysk," esp. p. 94).

22. Got'e, *Zamoskovnyi*, p. 330; *Ocherki . . . XVII*, p. 168; *OIIN*, 4:282; Novosel'skii, *Votchinnik*, pp. 134–35; Bulygin, "Beglye," p. 142; Gorfunkel', "Termin," p. 646; Shapiro, "Volneniia," pp. 301–2; Petrikeev, "Barshchina," pp. 239, 243, 245–48; Petrikeev, *Krupnoe krepostnoe khoziaistvo*, pp. 140, 146; A. N. Sakharov, *Russkaia derevnia*, p. 52; Zaozerskii, *Tsar'*, pp. 68–69, 187; Ogrizko, "Zernovoe," pp. 27, 35. In 1923 V. I. Picheta said in a study of peasant revolts that the worsening economic position of the peasantry was the cause of the uprisings two decades after the *Ulozhenie*, such as that led by Stenka Razin (Alekseeva, *Oktiabr'skaia*, p. 275). Obviously there must have been limits to how far exploitation of the peasantry could be increased, at this or any other time in Russian history. The absurd Soviet position on this point, that somehow exploitation was always increasing and the position of the peasant worsening throughout the centuries of Russian history, has frequently been observed (Shapiro, "Mnogotomnaia," pp. 145–46). See also Cherepnin, *Novgorodskie*, p. 171; A. N. Sakharov, "O dialektike," pp. 18, 33. The present Soviet position should be contrasted with that of the Old Bolshevik M. S. Aleksandrov (Ol'minskii), who generalized that a Muscovite lord did not dare exploit his peasants too much because they could easily run away (*Gosudarstvo*, p. 12).

23. M. A. D'iakonov incorrectly maintained that the settlement contract was in no way changed by the *Ulozhenie* (*Ocherki iz" istorii*, p. 85).

24. Kamentseva, "Usloviia," pp. 132–34; Petrikeev, *Krupnoe*, p. 153. I can hardly agree with A. N. Sakharov's position that the signing of a loan settlement contract

further enslaved the peasant already enslaved by general state decree ("Evoliutsiia," p. 64).

25. Kamentseva, "Usloviia," pp. 142. The role of settlement contracts in the enserfment of the Russian peasantry has been a matter of contention. Samokvasov made the point that they did not serve as the legal basis for the binding of free peasants to an estate, and went on to state that this function belonged to state decrees and to census takers and their resultant cadastres and censuses (*Krest'iane*, p. 75). Geiman makes the point that the *Ulozhenie* did not bind peasants to their *lords*, as some historians have maintained, but rather, if anything did this, it was the loans in the settlement contracts ("O nekotorykh," pp. 185–89).

26. Kamentseva, "Usloviia," p. 152.

27. Ibid., pp. 145, 148. No longer present in the loan contracts (*ssudnye zapisi*) were such words and phrases as *i do vykhodnykh godov, urochnye gody, vykhod, bezvykhodno*, to live with a lord *neprestanno* or *bespovorotno* (Veselovskii, "Iz istorii," pp. 215–16).

28. D'iakonov, *Ocherki iz" istorii*, p. 96. Compare *MS*, pp. 118–19, 120–21.

29. See N. Novombergskii, *Slovo i delo gosudarevy*, 1:71, 198, 249, for other popular notions about the Forbidden Years. D'iakonov at one time averred that the stipulations about nonforbidden years were kept because of memory of the 1601 and 1602 laws of Boris permitting some peasants to move. Later he revised this interpretation to cope with the Forbidden Years. He considered that the peasant masses in the first half of the seventeenth century felt themselves bound only temporarily (*Zapovednyia*, p. 19).

30. The legislative commission of 1700 omitted the *Ulozhenie's* articles on free peasants settling on an estate, the old 11:20, 21 (Man'kov, "Krest'ianskii," p. 77).

31. Kotoshikhin, *O Rossii*, 11:3; Beliaev, *Krest'iane* (1903), pp. 122, 166–67; Rozhdestvenskii, "Sel'skoe," p. 80. About 1653 lords began to enjoy the right to punish peasants corporally for drunkenness and fighting. In 1673 lords began to punish peasants for theft (Engel'man, *Istoriia*, pp. 70, 78). A decree of May 6, 1736, allowed lords to punish fugitive serfs for running away (*PSZ*, 9, no. 6951). On Morozov's estates the commune was especially powerless (Petrikeev, *Krupnoe*, pp. 161, 163). In the second half of the seventeenth century lords were required to pay the taxes of their insolvent peasants; because of the communal nature of taxation, this gave the lord power over not only individual peasants but the entire commune (Rozhkov, "Istoriia krepostnogo prava," p. 119).

32. Petrikeev, *Krupnoe krepostnoe khoziaistvo*, p. 158.

33. Obraztsov, "Ulozhenie 1649," p. 274. In another instance, when the *Ulozhenie* convinced them the matter was hopeless, a group of peasants gave up a suit which had been drawn out for more than a half-century over land seized from them by a monastery (idem, "Iz," p. 338).

34. Lappo-Danilevskii, "Ocherk"," p. 75. This was codified in a law of 1767.

35. Sergeevich, *Russkiia iuridicheskiia drevnosti*, 1:262–63; Man'kov, *Razvitie*, pp. 206–15; Zaozerskii, *Tsar' Aleksei*, p. 165; D'iakonov, *Ocherki obshchestvennago*, pp. 355–57; Lappo-Danilevskii, "Ocherk"," pp. 71–74. See also chapter 6, n. 129.

36. Vodarskii, "Chislennost' naseleniia," pp. 227–30.

9. The Beginnings

1. Denisova, "Pomestnaia," p. 30.

2. Kirpichnikov, "Voennoe," p. 62.

3. Some historians minimize the impact of firearms on cavalry and attribute the gradual decline of horse warfare to other causes (Markov, *Istoriia*, 3:217, 220). Francis R. Allen attributed "the greatest influence in 'unhorsing the knight'" to the English longbow. Firearms "sealed the fate of the knight-in-armor" ("Influence of Technology on War," in *Technology and Social Change*, ed. Francis R. Allen et al. [New York: Appleton-Century Crofts, 1957], p. 359).

4. Bobrovskii, *Postoiannyia*, p. 8; Geisman, *Kratkii*, 1:80–81. This was not the same as the national regular army introduced by Gustavus Adolphus, or before him, in Sweden (Markov, *Istoriia*, 3:222).

5. Geisman, *Kratkii*, 1:91–92.

6. Razin, *Istoriia*, 2:551.

7. Denisova, "Pomestnaia," pp. 30–31.

8. Bogoiavlenskii, "Vooruzhenie," p. 259.

9. Razin, *Istoriia*, 2:309–10.

10. Geisman, *Kratkii*, 1:93; Hall, "Military Technology," 2:726–27; Ayalon, *Gunpowder*, pp. 2, 5. The historiography of the origin of artillery was reviewed by V. V. Arendt, "K istorii," pp. 297, 318.

11. Kirpichnikov, "Voennoe," pp. 62–64. In 1889 Russians celebrated the five hundredth anniversary of their artillery. The artillery historian N. E. Brandenburg (1839–1903) surmised that cannon had been brought to Russia by Hansa League merchants (Beskrovnyi, *Ocherki voennoi istoriografii*, p. 280). See also A. Baiov, *Kurs"*, 1:40; Strukov, "Artilleriia," p. 1. The Soviets have pushed back the initiation of one use of artillery seven years to 1382, or even to 1380 (Kazakov, *Artilleriia*, p. 21; see also Esper, "Military," pp. 187–88). The Soviet medievalist M. N. Tikhomirov claimed that Russian artillery came from the East, maybe Persia (*Russkaia kul'tura X-XVIII vekov* [Moscow: Nauka, 1968], p. 261).

12. Kazakov, *Artilleriia*, p. 11 (see illustration on p. 12); Arendt, "K istorii," p. 300.

13. Arendt, "K istorii," p. 304.

14. Kirpichnikov, "Voennoe," pp. 63–65. Early artillery also made an insignificant impact on warfare elsewhere (Ayalon, *Gunpowder*, pp. 28–29, 46).

15. Baiov, *Kurs"*, 1:74.

16. Razin, *Istoriia*, 2:311.

17. Kirpichnikov, "Voennoe," pp. 67–68. Herberstein reported the use of artillery against Smolensk which "battered much, [but] accomplished nothing." He also reported an artillery siege of Kazan' which also accomplished nothing (*Commentaries*, pp. 57, 82, 106, 113).

18. Arendt, "K istorii," pp. 305; Hall, "Military Technology," 2:382.

19. Kirpichnikov, "Voennoe," p. 70; Kashtanov, "Feodal'nyi," p. 252; idem, "Otrazhenie," p. 260.

20. Kirpichnikov, "Voennoe," p. 68. He had rejected a similar offer to work for the Turks (Strukov, "Artilleriia," p. 3).

21. Kazakov dates the *Pushechnaia izba* to 1479, the *Pushechnyi Dvor* to 1488.

22. Casting of bronze artillery in the West dates at least from 1357 (Arendt, "K istorii," p. 306).

23. Hakluyt Society, *Russia at the Close*, p. 168.

24. Razin, *Istoriia*, 2:311. A. Baiov dated the appearance of field artillery to 1450 (*Kurs"*, 1:74).·

25. Kirpichnikov, "Voennoe," pp. 69–70; Hall, "Military Technology," p. 362.

26. Bogoiavlenskii, "Voisko," p. 81; Baiov, *Kurs"*, 1:74.

27. Herberstein, *Commentaries*, pp. 56–57.

28. Ibid.

29. Kirpichnikov, "Voennoe," p. 68 (twenty pound = "24 funta"). Lead cannon balls appeared in the West in 1373 (Arendt, "K istorii," p. 306).

30. Iron balls were forged in Bologna at least as early as 1381 (Arendt, "K istorii," p. 307).

31. Kirpichnikov, "Voennoe," p. 75; Herberstein, *Commentaries*, p. 15.

32. Kolchin, "Obrabotka"; Makovskii, *Razvitie*, p. 474.

33. Kirpichnikov, "Voennoe," p. 71.

34. Makovskii, *Razvitie*, p. 117. Makovskii, citing N. E. Brandenburg's *500-letie russkoi artillerii* (St. Petersburg, 1889), pp. 13–14, claims that rifling also appeared in Russia earlier than in the West but he does not say when. Strukov says it was in 1615 ("Artilleriia," pp. 8, 13). Rifling appeared in the West about 1525, and for the

first century was confined largely to expensive hunting pieces. Rifles were first used for military purposes in Germany during the Thirty Years War, but did not come into general use until the nineteenth century (Hall, "Military Technology," 3:347, 358).

35. Russian military historians seem to be particularly proud of the fact that the Muscovites had regimental artillery much earlier than Gustavus Adolphus of Sweden (Elchaninov, "Ocherk"," p. 49; Maslovskii, *Zapiski*, 1:44; Baiov, *Kurs*", 1:76).

36. Razin, *Istoriia*, 2:345.

37. Baiov, *Kurs*", 2:74.

38. Razin, *Istoriia*, 2:345. It is now on display in the Kremlin.

39. Baiov, *Kurs*", 1:75.

40. Razin, *Istoriia*, 2:336. Russia in the reign of Ivan had 200 field and 150 siege weapons (Beskrovnyi, *Ocherki voennoi*, p. 281). The exact number of fortress cannon is unknown.

41. Razin, *Istoriia*, 2:346. Maslovskii claimed two thousand pieces before the Time of Troubles—"a huge number of weapons" (*Zapiski*, 1:42).

42. Baiov, *Kurs*", 1:121.

43. Chernov, "TsGADA," p. 147.

44. Bogoiavlenskii, "Voisko," p. 83; Hall, "Military," 3:360.

45. Hakluyt, *Russia at the Close*, pp. 189–90, 348; Hakluyt Society, *Early Voyages*, 1:lix.

46. Hakluyt Society, *Early Voyages*, 1:35; idem, 2:237.

47. Kirpichnikov, "Voennoe," p. 65.

48. Ibid., p. 72.

49. *Tul'skii krai*, 1:27.

50. Rappoport, "Osnovnye etapy," pp. 233–34.

51. Olearius belittled the old Russian fortress, noting that the embrasures were pointed directly ahead and thus were inconvenient to shoot from and not very effective for defense (*Travels*, p. 43).

52. Kirpichnikov, "Voennoe," pp. 73–74; Nikitin, "Oboronitel'nye," pp. 169, 201.

53. Kirpichnikov, "Voennoe," p. 74; Makovskii, *Razvitie*, p. 129. Herberstein observed fortress construction (*Commentaries*, p. 53). During the reign of Ivan IV, 155 town-fortresses were built and equipped (Chernov, "TsGADA," p. 152). Many of them were simply log constructions along the expanding southern frontier.

54. Kostochkin, *Fedor Kon'*, pp. 73–80. He also designed the structures of the Boldin monastery, several churches in Viaz'ma, the walls of Belyi Gorod in Moscow, and a church in the Donskoi monastery (Makovskii, *Razvitie*, p. 122). It would be an exaggeration to call Kon' the Russian Vauban, for he was by no means the theoretician the Frenchman was. Nevertheless, his architectural constructions are without question truly magnificent.

55. *Novyi letopisets*", pp. 42–43.

56. Makovskii, *Razvitie*, pp. 86, 94, 127.

57. Razin, *Istoriia*, 3:159. For a cross-sectional illustration, see Kostochkin, *Fedor Kon'*, p. 86.

58. *NPL*, p. 416; Gorskii, *Ocherki*, p. 220.

59. Kashtanov, "Otrazhenie," pp. 258–59.

60. Chicherin, *Oblastnyia*, pp. 116–20; Lappo-Danilevskii, *Organizatsiia*, pp. 377–89; Veselovskii, *Soshnoe*, 1:325; Nosov, *Stanovlenie*, p. 100.

61. Zimin, "Uchastnik," pp. 273–78; Zheleznykh, ed., *Voenno-inzhenernoe*, pp. 29–32.

62. Bobrovskii, *Postoiannyia*, p. 24. In an earlier military revolution in Russia, in about the second half of the twelfth century, field warfare was largely supplanted by fortress warfare (Kirpichnikov, "Vooruzhenie," p. 49).

63. Bobrovskii, *Perekhod*", p. 83.

64. Geisman, *Kratkii*, 1:96; Stone, *Glossary*, p. 71; Hall, "Military Technology," 2: 727; Ayalon, *Gunpowder*, p. 6.

65. Kirpichnikov, "Voennoe," p. 67. The Egyptian Mamluks first used the arquebus in 1489 or 1490 (Ayalon, *Gunpowder*, pp. 59, 63).

Notes to Pages 160–162

66. Baiov, *Kurs"*, 1:73.

67. Even as late as 1700 a soldier was granted only one pound (*funt*) of powder, three of cotton fuses, and three of lead for his entire training (Rabinovich, "Formirovanie," p. 224).

68. Esper, "Military," p. 204; Bogoiavlenskii, "Vooruzhenie," p. 276. Razin (*Istoriia* 2:350) seems to contradict this, however.

69. Kirpichnikov, "Voennoe," pp. 71–72. The *pishchal'niki* also served the artillery, in addition to being armed infantry. In 1518 *pishchal'niki* accompanied the artillery of Novgorod and Pskov to Polotsk, and in 1535 they are reported to have fired cannon from the walls of Chernigov. Whether they carried arquebuses at these times is unknown. In the first twenty years after its introduction, the arquebus was held in such low esteem by the Egyptian Mamluks that it was issued only to black slaves. The Mamluks raised the first regular unit of arquebusiers only in 1510, and then it was soon disbanded. The Mamluks were decisively defeated by the Ottomans in 1517 because of their failure to come to grips with the new military technology (Ayalon, *Gunpowder*, pp. 65, 71). The Muscovites had more time, and their enemies were less resolute.

70. Chernov, *Vooruzhennye*, p. 33; Kashtanov, "Otrazhenie," p. 259; Zimin, "K istorii voennykh reform," pp. 354–57.

71. Robert Best of the Muscovy Company called them harquebusiers (Hakluyt Society, *Early Voyages*, 2:360). So did other Englishmen (Hakluyt Society, *Russia at the Close*, p. 197). Olearius in the seventeenth century called them musketeers (*Travels*, pp. 45, 216, 315; Margolin, "Vooruzhenie," p. 86).

72. Razin, *Istoriia*, 2:331. A. A. Zimin, on the other hand, sees the *strel'tsy* as the direct descendents of the *pishchal'niki* (*I. S. Peresvetov*, p. 358). He notes a 1598 document which mentioned service of Novgorodians in the *strel'tsy* for fifty years and more ("K istorii voennykh reform," p. 357).

73. Markov, *Istoriia*, 3:110.

74. Margolin, "K voprosu," p. 86; Bogoiavlenskii, "Voisko," p. 69 (see pictures of the regimental banners on p. 65).

75. Razin, *Istoriia*, 2:399.

76. Peresvetov, *Sochineniia*, p. 175. Some have argued that there was no real "Peresvetov."

77. The Janissaries were founded in 1329, completely organized in 1362 (Geisman, *Kratkii*, 1:115; Margolin, "Vooruzhenie," pp. 93–94). See descriptions by Collins in 1671 (*Present State*, p. 111) and Reutenfels (Reitenfel's) at the beginning of the 1670s ("Skazaniia," p. 125). Reutenfels also talks about the middle service class cavalry and the Western formation cavalry and infantry. Krizhanich called Janissaries *strel'tsy*. The Janissaries had been infantry archers centuries before their conversion to handguns. This was not true for the Russians.

78. Margolin, "Vooruzhenie," p. 94, citing Manstein's *Zapiski o Rossii*, p. 309.

79. Beskrovnyi, *Russkaia armiia*, p. 20.

80. Mikhnevich and Geisman, "Glavnyi," p. 25.

81. See illustration in Bogoiavlenskii, "Voisko," p. 67.

82. Margolin, "Vooruzhenie," p. 89; Baiov, *Kurs"*, 1:74.

83. Razin, *Istoriia*, 2:348.

84. Margolin, "Vooruzhenie," pp. 97–98.

85. Hakluyt Society, *Early Voyages*, 2:361–62.

86. Razin, *Istoriia*, 2:548.

87. Margolin, "Vooruzhenie," p. 93. This essentially followed the Western model, although Western musketeers may have had more of an offensive role and the cavalry a greater protective-defensive role, when functioning together, than did their Russian counterparts (Markov, *Istoriia*, 3:221).

88. Margolin, "Vooruzhenie," p. 86.

89. Makovskii, *Razvitie*, p. 184.

90. Mikhnevich and Il'enko, "Glavnyi," pp. 4–5.

91. Miliukov, *Spornye*, p. 15.
92. Razin, *Istoriia*, 2:349.
93. Margolin, "K voprosu," p. 65. These were the wage scales. The amount of grain and cash actually given the musketeer depended on the availability of each, and sometimes he was not paid at all. *Strel'tsy* sometimes were paid other sums, especially after the conclusion of a campaign, as in 1555, 1661, and 1678 (ibid., p. 67).
94. Shelekhov, "Glavnoe intendantskoe," p. 2.
95. Other sources say the commanders were usually appointed from the upper service class *stol'niki* (Mikhnevich and Il'enko, "Glavnyi," p. 9).
96. Bogoiavlenskii, "Voisko," pp. 69–72.
97. Stashevskii, "Ekonomicheskaia politika," p. 345.
98. Razin, *Istoriia*, 2:334, 337, 349, 402; ibid., 3:53–55, 59, 69; Elchaninov, "Ocherk'," p. 52.
99. Buganov, "Osvoboditel'naia," pp. 63, 70. As a rule, the *guliai gorod* was not a reliable defense against European cavalry and infantry attack (Bibikov, "Opyt," p. 5).
100. Maslovskii, *Zapiski*, 1:26–28.
101. Chernov, *Vooruzhennye*, p. 95.
102. Rotmistrov, *Istoriia*, p. 91. See chapter 2.
103. Herberstein, *Commentaries*, p. 58. This was viewed as a national trait of the Russian cavalry (A. Baiov, *Natsional'nyia*, p. 28; idem, *Kurs"*, 1:44).
104. Epifanov, "'Uchenie," p. 91.
105. Kazakov, "Bor'ba," p. 37; Razin, *Istoriia*, 3:68–76. For much of the seventeenth century the Russian army continued to fight as a horde. Only during the Northern War (1700–1721) did the Russians assimilate the linear tactics fully (Klokman, "Severnaia," p. 113).
106. Rotmistrov, *Istoriia*, 1:92–93.
107. Kirpichnikov, "Voennoe," p. 75; Peresvetov, *Sochineniia*, pp. 174–75, 203, 240, 343.
108. Razin, *Istoriia*, 2:395. Zimin, *I. S. Peresvetov*, pp. 354–63; Peresvetov, *Sochineniia*, pp. 174, 256.

10. Major Reform Aborted

1. Hakluyt Society, *Early Voyages*, 1:cx. In spite of the real balance of power, Grigorii Kotoshikhin reported in the 1660s that the Russian troops feared the Crimean Tatars most of all enemies (*O Rossii*, 4:37).
2. Baiov, *Kurs"*, 1:127.
3. Janowitz, *The Military*, pp. 83–84.
4. Nazarov, "O datirovke," pp. 217–18.
5. Billington, *Icon and Axe*, pp. 109, 669. Fronsperger's work was based on an earlier one published in Nuremburg in 1547 by Walter Reiff. It in turn used works of Nikolai Tartali (Zheleznykh, ed., *Voenno-inzhenernoe*, p. 22).
6. Bobrovskii, *Perekhod"*, p. 131.
7. There is some debate in the secondary literature on whether Mikhailov's work was based on Fronsperger or not. He probably used Iur'ev and Fomin's translation. Soviet writers claim that Mikhailov's *Regulations* were far more advanced than contemporary publications in Western Europe (Zheleznykh, ed., *Voenno-inzhenernoe*, pp. 18–24; Nikitin, "Oboronitel'nye," p. 208; Beskrovnyi, *Istochnikovedenie*, p. 61). On the document, see Bobrovskii, *Perekhod"*, p. 131; idem, *Zachatki*, p. 1. V. D. Nazarov says that work on the *Regulations* must have commenced during the reign of False Dmitrii I, rather than on the traditional date of 1607 ("O datirovke," pp. 217–21). A. Baiov said one of the national traits of Russian military strategy was a striving to fight battles outside of Russia (*Natsional'nyia*, p. 24).
8. Bibikov, "Opyt," pp. 6–16; Michael Roberts, *The Early Vasas. A History of Sweden, 1523–1611* (Cambridge: Cambridge University Press, 1968), pp. 453–55.

9. Rotmistrov, *Istoriia*, p. 84.

10. Another view was offered by D. F. Maslovskii, who said the role of the *pomest'e* cavalry in the Time of Troubles was one of the glorious pages in its history, along with the taking of Kazan' in 1552 and the defense of Pskov in 1581 (*Zapiski*, 1:24). In fact, neither was a good example, for at Kazan' the middle service class began disorderly looting before the victory, which was largely attributable to the efforts of foreigners. At Pskov, the townsmen held off Stefan Batory's siege. Maslovskii further generalized that the middle service class cavalry was the best type of armed force for Russia—but only for defending its homeland (ibid., 1:54–55).

11. Bobrovskii, *Perekhod"*, p. 61.

12. Ibid., p. 107.

13. Rotmistrov, *Istoriia*, 1:84, Baiov, *Kurs"*, 1:118. I assume the militia succeeded where the middle service class failed because the former's morale was good. I do not have hard evidence to prove this.

14. Kazakov, "Bor'ba," p. 52.

15. Sergeevich, "Voennyia," p. 10. Remember that the middle service class had been closed to the lower classes in 1601 (*AMG*, 1, no. 40).

16. Sergeevich, "Voennyia," p. 15.

17. Sh., "Dvorianstvo," no. 3, pp. 208–9; *RK*, 1:1616. The recorded total is less than the sum of the figures for the separate units because the Russians were not always careful at addition.

18. B. F. Porshnev, "Sotsial'no-politicheskaia obstanovka v Rossii vo vremia Smolenskoi voiny," *Istoriia SSSR* 1, no. 5 (1957): 112.

19. See chapter 7. J. L. H. Keep, on the other hand, says that Filaret's fiscal policy was a failure ("Filaret," p. 349).

20. Givi Zhordaniia, *Ocherki iz istorii franko-russkikh otnoshenii kontsa XVI i pervoi poloviny XVII vv.*, 2 vols. (Tbilisi: Akademiia Nauk Gruzinskoi SSR, 1959), 2: 151, 401.

21. Billington, *Icon and Axe*, p. 111. I can hardly agree with Porshnev's theory that the government resorted to foreign mercenaries because of internal instability ("Sotsial'no-politicheskaia," p. 120). This fits in with his thesis, discussed in chapter 7, but hardly corresponds to the military facts.

22. Norretranders, *Czardom*, p. 160; Zimin, "Uchastnik," pp. 273–78; Maslovskii, *Zapiski*, 1: 21; Herberstein, *Commentaries*, p. 113. Foreigners always fought in Russian armies, from at least as early as the time of the Varangians. Bands of mercenary Lithuanians, Poles, and Mongols were hired in the fourteenth century and earlier (Baiov, *Kurs"*, 1: 39). There were Westerners fighting in the Russian army also in 1408 and 1447. Whether these were mercenaries is another matter (Myshlaevskii, *Ofitserskii*, p. 18). In 1547 the Livonian Order detained over one hundred Western specialists invited to serve Russia (A. M. Sakharov, *Obrazovanie*, p. 102).

23. Ustrialov, *Istoriia*, 1: 179; Bobrovskii, *Postoiannyia*, p. 12. A Baiov said Boris's contingent of foreign mercenaries may have totalled nine thousand men (*Kurs"*, 1: 119).

24. Bogoiavlenskii, "Voisko" p. 75.

25. Razin, *Istoriia*, 3: 169–75; Myshlaevskii, *Ofitserskii*, p. 18; Mikhnevich and Geisman, "Glavnyi shtab"," p. 55.

26. Zheleznykh, ed., *Voenno-inzhenernoe*, p. 24.

27. Billington, *Icon and Axe*, pp. 112–13, 673; Bogoiavlenskii, *Prikaznye*, p. 308.

28. Writing in 1954, F. I. Kalinychev claimed that the now traditional term for the forces created for the Smolensk War, "the army of foreign formation" (*voisko inozemnogo stroia*), was a retrospective falsification by a Prussian military writer serving Emperor Paul I at the end of the eighteenth century. This writer observed that all the officers were foreigners and that the new forces were managed by the Foreign Officers Chancellery (*Inozemnyi prikaz*). Kalinychev claimed the sole correct term is "regiments of new formation" (*polki novogo stroia*) (*Pravovye*, p. 44).

29. Rotmistrov, *Istoriia*, 1:84.
30. Ustrialov, *Istoriia*, 1:180, 298.
31. "Datskii arkhiv"," *ChOIDR* 164 (1893) :202, 204–5, 208.
32. Ustrialov, *Istoriia*, 1: 180; *SGGD*, 3, no. 81; Liubavskii, *Russkaia*, 1: 146; Inna Lubimenko, "The Correspondence of the First Stuarts with the First Romanovs," *Transactions of the Royal Historical Society*, fourth series, 1 (1918) : 85.
33. Myshlaevskii, *Ofitserskii*, p. 35. I cannot explain the seemingly illogical pay steps in this table.
34. Ibid., pp. 36, 38.
35. Epifanov, " 'Uchenie," p. 91. See also *SGGD*, 3, nos. 82, 83; *AMG*, 1, nos. 267, 276; Maslovskii, *Zapiski*, 1: 21. The Swedes, however, were probably responsible for drawing up the military maps for the Smolensk War. Stefan Batory had just recently begun making military maps (Billington, *Icon and Axe*, pp. 112, 123). In 1632, while Wladyslaw IV was still reigning, Poland also changed its army, or rather its cavalry, from an organization borrowed from the Hungarians to a German prototype. It was called "cudzoziemskii autorament." The officers and men were Poles and Germans (Mikhnevich and Geisman, "Glavnyi shtab"," p. 54).
36. Billington, *Icon and Axe*, p. 112.
37. Mikhnevich and Geisman, "Glavnyi," p. 25. The Mamluk cavalrymen of Egypt also felt that serving in the infantry was beneath their dignity (Ayalon, *Gunpowder*, pp. 76–77, 80–81).
38. Maslovskii, *Zapiski*, 1: 21.
39. Rotmistrov, *Istoriia*, p. 81.
40. By the end of the sixteenth century the "reitar" had begun to disappear in Western Europe. He was replaced by the cuirassier and the dragoon. The former had rather complete armor and was armed with pistols. The dragoon was armed with musket or carbine, and usually was a mobile infantryman on horseback (Markov, *Istoriia*, 3: 220, 222).
41. Denisova, "Pomestnaia," p. 44.
42. See below on the cost of a regiment of mercenaries thirty years later.
43. The troops which were to be called dragoons in the third quarter of the sixteenth century arose in France in the 1530s (Razin, *Istoriia*, 2: 549).
44. Rotmistrov, *Istoriia*, p. 81.
45. Myshlaevskii, *Ofitserskii*, p. 23.
46. Chernov, *Vooruzhennye*, p. 169.
47. Porshnev, "Sotsial'no-politicheskaia," p. 113.
48. See the article by Porshnev for a recent analysis of the purpose of the Smolensk War, a diversion to prepare for a joint Russian-Swedish attack in Silesia (ibid., p. 113). He also notes that the records of this period were subsequently destroyed and that all the archives about the activities of Filaret and about the activities of his successors for several months after his death were systematically purged for internal political reasons so that the patriarch and the Romanov dynasty would not be discredited (ibid., p. 118).
49. Myshlaevskii, *Ofitserskii*, p. 36.
50. Olearius, *Travels*, pp. 51, 53.
51. Myshlaevskii, *Ofitserskii*, p. 51.
52. This is Porshnev's thesis ("Sotsial'no-," p. 128). The fact that some troops joined the Balash rebels was also noted by A. Z. Myshlaevskii (*Ofitserskii*, p. 23). However, Porshnev lists only one instance of members of the new formation regiments joining the rebels, and many cases of members of the old formation regiments (cossacks, *strel'tsy*, even *deti boiarskie*) deserting their posts to join the rebels ("Sotsial'no-," pp. 123, 132, 139). If there is any logic to Porshnev's linking of the dismissal of the new regiments with the Balash rebellion, the conclusion to be reached is just the opposite reached by Porshnev: the government should have cashiered the traditional forces and kept only the new formation regiments.

53. Elchaninov, "Ocherk"," p. 70.

54. The government issued laws to gain support from the middle service class: sick pay for those wounded in the war (November 22, 1633 [*AAE*, 3, no. 234]) and money payments (December 7, 18, 1633 [*AAE*, 3, nos. 237, 238]).

55. *AMG*, 1, nos. 472, 477; Myshlaevskii, *Ofitserskii*, p. 23; Baiov, *Kurs*", 1: 127.

56. On xenophobia, see Myshlaevskii, *Ofitserskii*, pp. 1–2.

57. There is some evidence indicating that the Smolensk War was lost at least partially because of the indifference of the majority of the magnates running the government, who felt that Smolensk was not worth the tribulation. See P. P. Smirnov, *Posadskie liudi*, 1:404. See the following for evidence of a foreign policy shift to the south in 1634 after the signing of the Polianovka treaty with Poland: *AI*, 3, no. 195; *AMG*, 2, nos. 208 ff., 286 ff., 316 ff.; *AAE*, 2: no. 268. On the other hand, the townsmen and the middle service class did not feel that expansion to the south was worth the expense and effort. See their reports at the Assemblies of the Land in 1637 and 1642 on the Azov question: (1637) *AAE*, 3, no. 275; (1642) *AI*, 3, no. 92-XXXIII; *SGGD*, 3, no. 113; *AZS*, pp. 37–40. The order to evacuate Azov is in *SGGD*, 3, no. 114.

On the other hand, V. P. Zagorovskii argues that the Russian government realized it could not retake Smolensk without protecting its southern flank. He cites as evidence a remark at the January, 1634, Assembly of the Land (*SGGD*, 3, no. 99) that Russia lost the war because of Tatar attacks. This certainly was not so.

He goes on to observe that the government began the Thirteen Years War to recover Smolensk and annex the Ukraine only after the Belgorod fortified line had been completed. He also notes, however, the presence of magnate land-ownership in the south, but does not comment on its political significance (*Belgorodskaia*, pp. 49, 67–69, 134–35).

58. *AMG*, 2, no. 171 (1639); *AAE*, 3, no. 315 (1642).

59. Hakluyt Society, *Russia at the Close*, p. 183.

60. Myshlaevskii, *Ofitserskii*, pp. 2, 22. Myshlaevskii conjectures that the new army may have been disbanded because of disillusionment arising out of the lack of military success at Smolensk. However, evidence now available indicates that the loss was "deliberate," the result of a grand power-play which was an integral part of the Thirty Years War but which failed. Therefore, the rulers of Moscow could hardly have rationally blamed the new army, any more than they really could have blamed Shein, who was executed as a scapegoat.

61. *AI*, 3, no. 195; *SGGD*, 3, nos. 107, 124; *AAE*, 3, no. 275; *AMG*, 1, no. 372; ibid., 2, nos. 208 ff., 286 ff., 316 ff.; Novosel'skii, *Bor'ba*, pp. 308–62; Olearius, *Travels*, p. 75.

62. Nikitin. "Oboronitel'nye," p. 121 (see map on p. 126).

63. Razin, *Istoriia*, 2:307; Elchaninov, "Ocherk"," p. 52. The historian of the cavalry, M. I. Markov, wrote that a frontier guard (*zasechnaia strazha*) was first organized in the fourteenth century to defend the southeast frontier. The emphasis changed at the end of the sixteenth century to defense against the Dnepr cossacks on the southwestern frontier (*Istoriia*, 3:112).

64. Kirpichnikov, "Voennoe," p. 72.

65. Razin, *Istoriia*, 2:342; Elchaninov, "Ocherk"," p. 52. The southern border of Muscovy in Ivan's reign ran from Karachev (Orel province) through Orel, Mtsensk, Novosil', Epifan', Dankov, Riazhsk, Shatsk, Temnikov, and Alatyr' to the Volga (Sh., "Dvorianstvo,'" no. 2, p. 269).

66. Zheleznykh, ed., *Voenno-inzheneroe*, p. 7.

67. Margolin, "Oborona," p. 13.

68. *AMG*, 1, no. 1.

69. S. M. Kashtanov, "Izvestie o zasechnom prikaze XVI veka," *Voprosy istorii* 43, no. 7 (July 1968): 204; Buganov, "Zasechnaia," p. 184; Nikitin, "Oboronitel'nye," p. 122.

70. Nikitin. "Oboronitel'nye," p. 126 (map).

71. Ibid., p. 121; Novosel'skii, *Bor'ba*, p. 371.

72. *Novyi letopisets*", pp. 40, 53.

73. Razin, *Istoriia*, 2:342. The dates are from *Razriadnaia kniga*, ed. by Buganov.

74. Marzheret, *Sostoianie*, p. 54. A. V. Nikitin stressed that the major effort was to cut off Tatar passage on the roads and *shliakhi*, that the tree fellings, moats, and so on were just auxiliary efforts ("Oboronitel'nye sooruzheniia," p. 117).

75. Zheleznykh, ed., *Voenno-inzhenernoe*, p. 7.

76. Margolin, "Oborona," p. 13.

77. *AMG*, 1, no. 13. Margolin claimed that the rapid growth of towns and population on the southern frontier in the 1580s and 1590s must have made the burning difficult or impossible ("Oborona," p. 15). This claim assumes that people lived in considerable density on the undefended, steppe side of the line—which seems to have been unlikely, as noted in chapter 5. Moreover, the French mercenary Captain Margeret saw this annual event in the 1590s (*Sostoianie*, p. 54).

78. Nikitin, "Oboronitel'nye," p. 202.

79. Margolin emphasized that a frontier service was mentioned as early as the fourteenth century and that all sixteenth-century chronicles regularly mention intelligence brought in by frontier patrols, *storozhi* and *stanichniki* ("Oborona," p. 5).

80. *AMG*, 1, no. 2.

81. Sh. emphasized the indigenous Tatars and Mordva, plus the cossacks. He also noted the general absence of delegates from southern frontier towns at the *zemskie sobory* of the seventeenth century (exceptions: Alatyr', Ateman, Serpukhov, Starodub, Kasup, Likhvin, and Kozel'sk), indicating that the middle service class did not play a crucial role on the actual frontier itself. He noted also that the western section was guarded by *deti boiarskie*; the middle, near Orel and Riazhsk, by *deti boiarskie* and cossacks; in the region of Temnikov and Kadansk, by Mordva and Tatars; and further east, near Alatyr', by cossacks. The *raz"ezdy* were 1,353 battle-ready servicemen sustained by grants of 50, 70 and 100 *chetverti* of land (Sh., "Dvorianstvo," no. 2, pp. 270–71, 565–66).

82. The *storozh*, who rode around a small area, was supposed to send news to his local military-administrative center; the *stanichnik*, who patrolled large areas of the "wild steppe" overlapping the districts of a number of *storozhi*, had to inform the major town which was threatened. Thus it was assumed both would be informed of the presence of hostile forces (Margolin, "Oborona," p. 7).

83. Snegirev, "Storozhevaia sluzhba," pp. 34–37. Iurii Krizhanich observed in the 1660s that in his homeland, Croatia, sentries stood lookout on top of platforms. If an enemy was sighted, an artillery piece was shot off. Then the second sentry post along the line would relay the message, and so on. "In this way it becomes known in an hour for 35 miles around and more that an enemy is in the country" (*Politika*, p. 425). The Russians were not so efficient. V. P. Zagorovskii questions the efficacy of the southern defensive system prior to the construction of the Belgorod fortified line, 1635–53 (*Belgorodskaia*, pp. 54–55, 60–64).

84. Razin, *Istoriia*, 3:51–58.

85. Ibid., p. 50; P. P. Smirnov, *Posadskie*, 1:160–90.

86. Snegirev, "Storozhevaia sluzhba," p. 44.

87. Zagorovskii, *Belgorodskaia*, pp. 64–69; Porshnev, "Sotsial'no-politicheskaia," p. 137; Novosel'skii, *Bor'ba*, p. 204. It was no doubt because of the weakness of the still uncompleted Belgorod line that Olearius recorded Tula as "on the Tatar frontier" (*Travels*, p. 124).

88. Razin, *Istoriia*, 3:228.

89. Zagorovskii, *Belgorodskaia*, pp. 20, 70–72, 85.

90. Maslovskii, *Zapiski*, 1:47; Nikitin, "Oboronitel'nye," pp. 124–25; Ananiash Zaionchkovskii, " 'Letopis' kipchakskoi stepi' kak istochnik po istorii Kryma," *Vostochnye istochniki po istorii narodov iugo—vostochnoi i tsentral'noi Evropy*, 2 (1969): 16; Zagorovskii, *Belgorodskaia cherta*, pp. 18–19.

91. Buganov, "Zasechnaia kniga," p. 189.

92. *Tul'skii krai*, 1, no. 17; Zagorovskii, *Belgorodskaia*, pp. 94, 104, 239; Buganov, "Zasechnaia kniga," p. 188. Some of the earlier lines had lost their defensive significance (Nikitin, "Oboronitel'nye," p. 118).

93. Billington, *Icon and Axe*, p. 113; Zagorovskii, *Belgorodskaia*, pp. 41, 77, 88, 125, 137; Nikitin, "Oboronitel'nye," pp. 201, 207.

94. Eroshkin and Kulikov, *Gosudarstvennye* (1965), pp. 44, 47.

95. Maslovskii, *Zapiski*, 1:20.

96. Razin, *Istoriia*, 3:214.

97. Baiov, *Kurs"*, 1:113.

98. Novosel'skii, *Bor'ba*, p. 371.

99. Miliukov, *Ocherki* (1964), 1, pt. 2, pp. 160–62, 179; *Ocherki* (1900), 1:56–61. Peter attempted to forestall Charles XII by ordering the construction of a fortified line of walls, moats, and felled trees along the Western frontier, from Pskov to Velikie Luki, Smolensk, and Briansk (Klokman, "Severnaia," p. 87).

100. Iakovlev, *Zasechnaia cherta*, p. 284; Nikitin, "Oboronitel'nye," p. 213.

101. The Tatars also raided in 1643–45 with between fifty and sixty thousand horsemen, but were warded off by the frontier forces alone. V. P. Zagorovskii attributes the resumption of attacks to the evacuation of Azov by the Don cossacks in 1642, thus freeing the Tatar rear from concern (*Belgorodskaia*, pp. 64, 75, 107, 114). I suspect that another reason was that the Tatars knew of the chaos in the Moscow government and hoped to take advantage of it. The Turkic peoples usually took advantage of discord in Kievan Rus', and there is no reason to assume the same situation would not prevail in Muscovy (V. V. Kargalov, *Vneshnepoliticheskie faktory razvitiia feodal'noi Rusi* [Moscow: Vysshaia shkola, 1967], pp. 23–61).

102. Buganov, "Zasechnaia," p. 183; Iakovlev, *Zasechnaia*, p. 288. V. P. Zagorovskii says that the Belgorod line remained functional until the eighteenth century (*Belgorodskaia*, p. 85).

11. The Triumph of Reform

1. Billington, *Icon and Axe*, pp. 113, 123. See also *Krepostnaia manufaktura v Rossii*, 1, *Tul'skie i Kashirskie zheleznye zavody* (Leningrad: Akademiia Nauk SSSR, 1930).

2. Chernov (*Vooruzhennye*, p. 39) and Rotmistrov (*Istoriia*, p. 86) opt for the end of the sixteenth century; Margolin ("Oborona," p. 94) opts for the seventeenth century, as did Strukov ("Artilleriia," p. 15).

3. Margolin, "Vooruzhenie," p. 94.

4. Ibid., p. 101. See the *smetnye spiski gorodov*. The bow was obsolescent in Western warfare by about 1500, but it was still considered a serious weapon in the West for another century (Hall, "Military Technology," 3:351).

5. Bogoiavlenskii, "Vooruzhenie," p. 274.

6. Ibid., pp. 269–70.

7. Ibid., pp. 272–73.

8. Ibid., p. 274.

9. Ibid., p. 278; Elchaninov, "Ocherk"," p. 68; Baiov, *Kurs"*, 1:121; Chernov, "TsGADA," p. 129.

10. Bogoiavlenskii, "Vooruzhenie," p. 279.

11. Maslovskii, *Zapiski*, 1:45.

12. Bogoiavlenskii, "Vooruzhenie," p. 260; Elchaninov, "Ocherk"," p. 68.

13. *AMG*, 3, no. 390.

14. Zaozerskaia, "K istorii," p. 138. B. A. Kolchin linked the rise of Tula as an arms center, on the southern frontier of the Muscovite state, with a need to commence massive manufacture of handguns. This dictated moving the iron-arms business from the north, particularly from Ustiuzhna, to a place more pleasing to masses of workers ("Obrabotka," pp. 200–201). The Tula gunsmiths were freed from all taxation and obligations (*Tul'skii krai*, 1, nos. 13, 14).

15. Zaozerskaia, "K istorii," p. 140.

16. Ibid., pp. 145, 148.

17. The *SIE*, 2: 145, claims the *Barkhatnyi Dvor* was founded by Ivan Dmitriev in 1632.
18. Peter Marselis supplied barrels from Tula factories for sixty kopeks each (Bogoiavlenskii, "Vooruzhenie," p. 269).
19. Epifanov, " 'Uchenie," p. 83.
20. Ibid., p. 85. See also *Tul'skii krai*, 1, no. 18. The Swedish emissary Karl Pommerening wrote his sovereign on September 15, 1647, that "last Easter" the Russians had begun a crash program to manufacture muskets (Iakovlev, "Rossiia," 184: 410). Another Swedish emissary, Johann de Rodes, observed in 1652 that half of the Russian-made muskets exploded when tested (Kurts, "Sostoianie," p. 100).
21. Epifanov, " 'Uchenie," p. 83.
22. Ibid. See also *Krepostnaia manufaktura*, 1 (1930). E. I. Zaozerskaia writes that from 1671 Tula musket production increased to two thousand per year ("K istorii," p. 149). The smiths were paid sixty-seven kopeks per gun for labor. At least some of them tried to avoid working for the government in order to engage in more profitable private business (ibid., pp. 152–56).
23. N. N. Bantysh-Kamenskii, *Obzor" vneshnikh" snoshenii Rossii*, 4 vols. (Moscow, 1894–1902), 1: 184; ibid., 4: 170; Bobrovskii, *Postoiannyia*, p. 32; Iakovlev, "Rossiia," 184: 410.
24. Bogoiavlenskii, "Vooruzhenie," p. 270.
25. Kurts, "Sostoianie," pp. 56, 142, 241–42, 244, 246; Epifanov, " 'Uchenie," p. 85; Esper, "Military," pp. 205–6.
26. Bogoiavlenskii, "Vooruzhenie," p. 269.
27. Ibid., p. 271.
28. Ibid., p. 278. Unquestionably Russia had a considerable deficit in small arms and cold weapons in the seventeenth century which was made up by imports. Russia's inability, before the time of Peter, to organize a completely regular army should not, however, be attributed (as it was by the Moscow University historian P. P. Epifanov) to a lack of self-sufficiency in native arms production, for Russia clearly was able to make up the material deficiencies from abroad. The Marxist base-superstructure argument has considerable validity when applied to an army, because even the simplest maneuvers cannot be executed in practice when the necessary weapons are lacking.

Nevertheless, it should also be borne in mind that Epifanov (" 'Uchenie," p. 85) was not only arguing about the nature of the relationship between the basis and the superstructure of a society, but that he also was trying to restore to Peter his former glorified place as a great reformer. Therefore Epifanov tries to prove wrong those of the great historians, such as Kliuchevskii, Platonov, Miliukov, and Pokrovskii, who "tried to debunk Peter and liquidate his reforms." Epifanov considers the military historians Myshlaevskii (1899) and Maslovskii (1890), who did not see the new formation regiments of soldiers and cavalrymen of the second half of the seventeenth century as a finished regular army, as being closer to the truth. A. A. Zimin also claims that economically Russia was not ready for the new army, for the absence of developed manufacturing hindered the supplying of uniform firearms (*I. S. Peresvetov*, p. 362). Muscovy was also deficient in iron production. Domestic iron was only one-third as expensive as that imported in the first half of the seventeenth century from Sweden, the Netherlands, England, and Germany, but nevertheless foreign metal was needed for domestic arms production (E. I. Zaozerskaia, *U istokov krupnogo proizvodstva v russkoi promyshlennosti XVI-XVII vekov* [Moscow: Nauka, 1970], pp. 334–35).
29. Schleussinger, "Rasskaz," p. 112.
30. See Maksimenkov, "Iz istorii," p. 78, for pictures of seventeenth-century artillery.
31. Maslovskii, *Zapiski*, 1:42.
32. Kolosov, "Razvitie," pp. 259–60.
33. Maslovskii, *Zapiski*, 1:42. See also Strukov, "Artilleriia," p. 6.
34. Epifanov, " 'Uchenie," p. 85. See *DAI*, 5, no. 51-III. In 1664 a census of all the weapons in Moscow was taken and weapons were then distributed by groups of

the same type, in an attempt to make the best of this situation. What was done in the rest of the country is unknown (Kolosov, "Razvitie," p. 262). Descriptions of the Tula fortress of 1625 and 1685 reveal similar diversity (*Tul'skii krai*, 1, no. 19).

35. Epifanov, " 'Uchenie," p. 84. Standardization was achieved by the time of the Poltava battle of 1709 (Klokman, "Severnaia," p. 80).

36. Kolosov, "Razvitie," p. 260.

37. Epifanov, " 'Uchenie," p. 83.

38. Kolosov, "Razvitie," p. 260.

39. Ibid., pp. 260–61.

40. Ibid., p. 261.

41. Epifanov, " 'Uchenie," p. 84. L. G. Beskrovnyi reported that there were 2,730 artillery pieces in Russia outside of Moscow in the middle of the seventeenth century (*Ocherki voennoi*, p. 281). A 1678 census by the *Razriad* discovered 3575 weapons in 150 towns (*DAI*, 9, no. 106).

42. Kolosov, "Razvitie," p. 261. The Egyptian Mamluks employed camels carrying light guns which were fired from above their humps (Ayalon, *Gunpowder*, p. 85).

43. Kolosov, "Razvitie," p. 262.

44. Ibid., p. 261.

45. Ibid., p. 266.

46. Chernov, *Vooruzhennye*, p. 167.

47. Myshlaevskii, *Ofitserskii*, p. 26.

48. Chernov, *Vooruzhennye*, p. 138. A tax of two rubles per household was levied to pay for the forces; it was levied in towns and on "black" peasants (Iakovlev, *Prikaz''*, pp. 394–99).

49. Chernov, *Vooruzhennye*, p. 139.

50. Forsten, "Snosheniia," p. 369; Iakubov, "Rossiia," 184:458; Solov'ev, *Istoriia*, 5:481.

51. Chernov, *Vooruzhennye*, pp. 159–62.

52. Forsten, "Snosheniia," p. 372. The Soviet historian V. P. Zagorovskii denies that there is any fundamental discontinuity between the reigns of Mikhail and Aleksei (*Belgorodskaia*, p. 75). It might be noted that in 1650 the people of Novgorod and Pskov blamed Morozov for exporting such large quantities of grain that a famine ensued. These exports paid for the arms necessary to modernize the army (Iakubov, "Rossiia," 184:472).

53. Maslovskii, *Zapiski*, 1:54.

54. Mikhnevich and Geisman, "Glavnyi shtab'," pp. 36, 67; *AMG*, 2, nos. 425, 434, 877; ibid., 3, no. 690; Bogoiavlenskii, "Voisko," p. 62; Maslovskii, *Zapiski*, 1:52. From time to time there were exceptions: one was right after the Time of Troubles, when order had not yet been fully restored. At that moment the general was allowed to make minor appointments, up to the rank of centurion (*sotnik*). Also, in the early years of the Thirteen Years War the generals had limited power of promotion. This was undoubtedly because the government had not yet become accustomed to running the foreign mercenaries who comprised the officer corps (Myshlaevskii, *Ofitserskii*, pp. 14–15, 39–42, 46–47, 52; Chicherin, *Oblastnyia*, pp. 254–55).

55. Maslovskii, *Zapiski*, 1:37, 52. See also *AMG*, 3, nos. 101, 125.

56. Myshlaevskii, *Ofitserskii*, pp. 48–49.

57. Forsten, "Snosheniia," p. 372.

58. Epifanov, " 'Uchen'e." There is no uniformity in Russian works on the publication date of this work. The latest general work, by Razin, gives both: *Istoriia*, 3: 38 (1649), 212 (1647).

59. Elchaninov, "Ocherk'," p. 75; Myshlaevskii, *Ofitserskii*, pp. 24–25. One might argue that the book never should have been translated because so few Russians could read and they were not destined to be officers in the reformed army anyway. The foreigners who were recruited to head the new army could not read the translation either, so the whole project was simply another overly ambitious attempt of the Morozov administration. However, the sale in the same period of two printings of

1200 copies each of the 1649 Law Code (*Sobornoe Ulozhenie*) shows that a sufficient number of Russians could read and buy books to have purchased all the copies of the *Uchen'e*. Probably the government just did not know in 1647 that the volume was outdated, and Morozov probably did not envisage that Russians, because of resistance and inability, would play as small a leadership role in the new army as they did. It is known to what groups of the population sixty-five of the copies were sold: twenty-seven to nobles, ten to servicemen, three to clergymen, eleven to chancellery officials, five to merchants and townsmen, six to workers in the government printing office, and three to musketeers (S. P. Luppov, *Kniga v Rossii v XVII veke* [Leningrad: Nauka, 1970], p. 93). This evidence indicates that the book enjoyed almost no military application.

60. *PSZ*, 5, no. 3006; Pankov, *Razvitie taktiki*, p. 4. Peter introduced army regulations in 1716, naval in 1720 (Klokman, "Severniaia," p. 80).

61. Bogoiavlenskii, *Prikaznye*, pp. 149, 162; Eroshkin, *Istoriia* (1968), p. 57; Eroshkin, *Istoriia* (1965), p. 44. For some reason Myshlaevskii erroneously dated the founding of the *Reitarskii prikaz* in 1628, along with the Foreign Mercenary Chancellery (*Inozemskii prikaz*) (*Ofitserskii*, p. 44).

62. *DAI*, 3, nos. 38, 66; *SGGD*, 3, 124.

63. P. P. Smirnov, *Posadskie liudi*, 2: 32–33; *Ocherki . . . XVII*, pp. 425–26.

64. Mikhnevich and Il'enko, "Glavnyi," p. 8. Infantry had been drafted on a similar basis in 1637 (Iakovlev, "Sluzhiloe zemlevladenie," p. 450).

65. Buganov, "Osvoboditel'naia," p. 62.

66. Billington, *Icon and Axe*, p. 155.

67. Kozachenko, "Zemskii sobor 1653 goda," pp. 151–58; *Ocherki . . . XVII*, pp. 480–81.

68. Forsten, "Snosheniia," pp. 371–72; Iakubov, "Rossiia," 184: 409. The patriarch and some of the boyars opposed turning the army over to foreigners and wanted to drive out the mercenaries, but Aleksei remained steadfast in his determination to modernize his forces (ibid., p. 430).

69. Olearius, *Travels*, p. 152. Those who remained, and particularly those who became Orthodox, held high positions in the officer corps (ibid., pp. 200–201; Iakubov, "Rossiia," 184: 459, and elsewhere).

70. Gordon, *Passages*, p. 20. For a brief description of the life of foreign officers in Moscow, see David, *Status*, p. 63.

71. Forsten, "Snosheniia," pp. 372–73; Ustrialov, *Istoriia*, 1:181–82.

72. Maierberg, *Puteshestvie*, p. 177.

73. "Veniunt hac praeterea domines pessimi, uxorem desertores, duellatores, profugi et qui propter varia delicta in patriis comperere non audent. Hi testimonia sibi fingunt appressis ficticiis sigillis, quasi his et illis principibus in bello officiales servivissent, ut eiusmodo fraude hic munus aliquod militare ementiantur" (David, *Status*, p. 63).

74. August Meyerberg attributed a number of defeats to the foreign officers' incompetence (*Puteshestvie*, p. 183). See also Schleussinger, "Rasskaz," p. 113.

75. Markov, *Istoriia*, 3:119; Reitenfel's, "Skazaniia," p. 125.

76. Billington, *Icon and Axe*, pp. 67–73, 112. This fact was, incredibly, ignored by some nationalistic military historians, who claimed that "from antiquity the Russian army was completely national" (Maslovskii, *Zapiski*, 1:55). Also, "We always had a national army. Our military history knew neither mercenary armies nor recruiting" (Baiov, *Natsional'nyia*, p. 7). According to one contemporary account, foreigners served only in the officer corps, never as rank and file (Reitenfel's, "Skazaniia," p. 125).

77. Bogoiavlenskii, "Voisko," p. 75; Gordon, *Passages*, p. 104.

78. *AMG*, 3, no. 685; Gordon, *Passages*, p. 53.

79. Ustrialov, *Istoriia*, 1:183; David, *Status*, pp. 82, 95; Gordon, *Passages*, pp. 48, 105, 108–10, 159–63. The situation was different in the sixteenth century, when Ivan IV did not detain any Englishmen who desired to leave Russia (Hakluyt Society,

Early Voyages, 2:331). The Muscovite government also allowed the citizens of lands overwhelmed in the Thirteen Years War to continue to use their own judicial systems (*AMG*, 2, nos. 739, 763, 853, 858, 876, 954).

80. Bobrovskii, *Postoiannyia*, p. 13; Gordon, *Passages*, pp. 62, 104.

81. Foreigners held the following ranks: general, major general, colonel (*polkovnik*, regimental commander), lieutenant colonel (*podpolkovnik*), major (*poruchik maior*), captain, lieutenant (*poruchik*), and second lieutenant (*praporshchik*). David called the "praporshchik" a "vexillifer" (*Status*, p. 87; Elchaninov, "Ocherk"," p. 70). The rank of general was introduced only in the 1670s. In the battle zone, of course, life was not always so pleasant for the mercenary officer (*AMG*, 3, no. 582).

82. Bogoiavlenskii, "Voisko," pp. 77, 80; *AMG*, 3, no. 557. In the late 1640s high sums were paid to petty officers. Three, whose rank is not given, were paid fifty, thirty, and fifteen rubles per month. The first two foreign officers were granted *pomest'ia* from which they could collect the dues instead of cash. The third lived on his cash salary in Moscow (Forsten, "Snosheniia," p. 373).

83. On the cost to the state, see p. 227. At the beginning of the 1660s Moscow had the reputation abroad of paying not handsomely, but regularly—unlike the Swedes (Gordon, *Passages*, p. 42). The Czech Jesuit Irji David noted at the end of the 1680s that officers in the past had received huge salaries, but now had to be content with "modest" ones. He also observed that the officers were paid half in cash, half in sables or other furs. He learned that the price of furs had fallen greatly, so that officers who sold them hardly received half the supposed value for them (*Status*, p. 87; Gordon, *Passages*, pp. 46, 49; *AMG*, 3, no. 488). According to one account, envious Russian merchants forced the government to cut the mercenaries' pay even prior to the 1680s (Reitenfel's, "Skazaniia," p. 125). See the 1670s pay scale in Coyet, *Posol'stvo*, p. 495. Russians were also awarded sables, upon occasion, for their service (*AMG*, 2, no. 937; ibid., 3, nos. 5, 151, 276; *KR*, 2:1028–31; Schleussinger, "Rasskaz," pp. 113–14).

The following was the pay scale in 1696:

MONTHLY PAY RATES, IN RUBLES, OF FOREIGN OFFICERS, 1696

Rank	Cavalry	Infantry
General	120	120
Lieutenant General	100	?
Major General	90	?
Brigadier	45	—
Colonel	50-40	50-25
Lieutenant Colonel	18	15
Major	16	14
Captain	13	11
Lieutenant Captain	9	8
Lieutenant	8	8
Second Lieutenant (*praporshchik*)	7	5

SOURCE: Myshlaevskii, *Ofitserskii*, p. 37. Compare these rates with those on p. 171 above.

84. Bobrovskii, *Zachatki*, p. 6.

85. Ibid., p. 9. Such brutality was typical of mercenary officers in the seventeenth century (Gordon, *Passages*, p. 21). One Thomas Bill, an infantry commander, kept his occupied district quiet by mass hangings, much use of the knout, and the cutting off of ears (*AMG*, 3, no. 45). See also *AMG*, 3, no. 573.

86. Bogoiavlenskii, "Vooruzhenie," pp. 276, 282.

87. Baiov, *Kurs"*, 1: 128, 130; Gordon, *Passages*, p. 24. The government also ignored caste prerogatives in renting out rights to take honey, furs, fish, and so on, from the vacant lands (*ukhozh'i, iurty*) along the southern frontier in the seventeenth century. The highest bidder, regardless of class or estate, won the concessions (Zagorovskii, *Belgorodskaia*, pp. 38–41).

88. Maierberg, *Puteshestvie,* p. 182.
89. Myshlaevskii, *Ofitserskii,* pp. 21, 50–51.
90. Elchaninov, "Ocherk"," p. 70; Mikhnevich and Geisman, "Glavnyi shtab"," pp. 72–73; Myshlaevskii, *Ofitserskii,* p. 24. There were abuses of the pure principles, such as promotion for service rendered by the candidate's father, or appointment to a military position on the basis of court rank, but such exceptions were surprisingly rare (Myshlaevskii, *Ofitserskii,* pp. 47–49). Patrick Gordon wrote that he was offered a higher rank than he deserved if he would join the Russian forces (*Passages,* p. 35).
91. Miliukov, *Ocherki* (1900), 1:130.
92. Bobrovskii, *Zachatki,* p. 21; Zagorovskii, *Belgorodskaia,* pp. 120, 155.
93. Myshlaevskii, *Ofitserskii,* p. 44.
94. Maierberg, *Puteshestvie,* pp. 176–77.
95. *AMG,* 2, no. 482.
96. Ibid., no. 496.
97. Ibid., no. 540.
98. Ibid., no. 542.
99. Ibid., no. 558.
100. Ibid., nos. 612, 696.
101. Ibid., nos. 699, 706, 720, 738, 739, 747, 762, 779, 829, 831, 834, 846, 855, 864, 865, 867, 869, 873, 875, 888, 894, 900, 907, 929, 931, 970, 975, 1008, 1011, 1018, 1020, 1035, 1044.
102. The Poles realized that they were very weak in 1653. The Moscow government was informed in the spring of that year that some Poles were willing to surrender Smolensk on the condition that Rus' would not aid the cossacks struggling to escape Polish rule in the Ukraine (*AMG,* 2, no. 517).
103. *AMG,* 2, nos. 607, 608.
104. Krizhanich, *Politika,* pp. 425–26. The Muscovites observed the lack of fortifications in territory they occupied and proceeded at once to build them (*AMG,* 2, nos. 831, 853; ibid., 3, no. 45).
105. Maslovskii, *Zapiski,* 1: 19.
106. *AMG,* 2, no. 859.
107. Ibid., no. 900.
108. Ibid., no. 939. A 1660 message from Smolensk cried out for both more cavalry and infantry. Cavalry were needed for carrying messages, infantry for warfare (ibid., 3, no. 68). A similar division of labor was noted in 1661 (ibid., nos. 409, 448, 510).
109. *AMG,* 2, no. 922.
110. Ibid., no. 1035.
111. Ibid., 3, nos. 272, 347, 541, 684.
112. Bobrovskii, *Zachatki,* p. 6.
113. Bobrovskii, *Postoianyia,* p. 36.
114. Bobrovskii, *Perekhod",* p. 114.
115. Maierberg, *Puteshestvie,* p. 183.
116. Petrikeev, *Krupnoe,* p. 155.
117. *AMG,* 2, nos. 1095, 1098; ibid., 3, nos. 236, 410, 541, 662, 684.
118. Ibid., 3, no. 101.
119. Sh., "Dvorianstvo," no. 2, pp. 541–42. In 1657 there had been a levy of one peasant from every fifth peasant house in the Novgorod area, also for the infantry (Mikhnevich and Il'enko, "Glavnyi," suppl., pp. 56–57, no. 7).
120. *AMG,* 3, no. 504.
121. Stashevskii, *Smeta,* p. 15; *AMG,* 3, no. 504. This latter document also lists their disposition. For example, 2,634 of the recruits were sent to work for Tsar Aleksei in his Secret Affairs Chancellery (*Prikaz tainykh del*), which largely meant on his estates. Most, however, went into the new infantry regiments.

In 1660 the recruiting from the Novgorod military district was again heavier than normal: one person for every town house, with directions that the poorer people who did not pay much tax or otherwise render much service should be drafted first. Lands belonging to the metropolitan, archbishops, and monasteries were required to furnish one recruit for each five houses, as were the governors (who were "getting rich") and all others, with the exception of widows and minors (one recruit from each ten houses) and *dvoriane* and *deti boiarskie* (one recruit from each twenty-five houses) (Stashevskii, *Smeta*, p. 15). Some exceptions were made in a late 1660 decree (*AMG*, 3, no. 236).

122. Stashevskii, *Smeta*, pp. 14–15; *AMG*, 3, nos. 451, 554, 582. In 1662 there was a draft of one soldier from every fifth house in the Perm area to put down an uprising by dissident Tatars and Bashkirs (Mikhnevich and Il'enko, "Glavnyi shtab"," suppl. pp. 60–61, no. 11).

123. *AMG*, 2, no. 1127.

124. Ibid., 3, nos. 110, 112, 144, 370, 399, 470, 496.

125. Ibid., nos. 582, 588.

126. Bogoiavlenskii, "Vooruzhenie," p. 281. Iurii Krizhanich recommended against using the rapier on the Tatar front because it could easily be broken by a sabre (*Politika*, p. 427). In the West the sole armor was a leather jerkin and a round, open helmet (Hall, "Military," 3: 353).

127. *AMG*, 2, no. 907; ibid., no. 196.

128. Ibid., 3, no. 376.

129. Stashevskii, *Smeta*, p. 1. Moscow artisans were paid about the same, 3 to 5 kopeks per day, or $7\frac{1}{2}$ to $12\frac{1}{2}$ rubles per year for a 250-day year. Out of this they had to pay taxes (Margolin, "K voprosu," p. 67).

130. Shelekhov, "Glavnoe intendantskoe," p. 3; Zaozerskii, *Tsar'*, pp. 231–33.

131. *AMG*, 2, no. 1048; ibid., 3, nos. 77, 191, 320, 377, 445, 461, 472.

132. Ibid., 3, no. 133.

133. Shelekhov, "Glavnoe intendantskoe," pp. 9–11. The Holy Roman Empire planned a provisioning service after Westphalia because of the experience of the Thirty Years War (Bobrovskii, *Perekhod"*, pp. 84–85, 135, 137).

134. Epifanov, "'Uchenie," p. 87. This practice was continued even in the new standing army of Peter the Great, where lords were responsible for equipping and maintaining recruits drafted from among their peasants. Many lords did not fulfill their responsibilities to their former peasants in military service (Rabinovich, "Formirovanie," pp. 230–31).

135. Petrikeev, *Krupnoe*, p. 155.

136. Gordon, *Passages*, p. 49 and elsewhere; Reitenfel's, "Skazaniia," p. 125. In 1681 thirty-four of the colonels commanding the infantry soldiers' regiments were foreigners, and only three were Russians (Ustrialov, *Istoriia*, 1: 302). The German visitor Schleussinger noted in the 1680s that the Russians had no standing army ("Rasskaz," p. 113).

137. Epifanov, "'Uchenie," p. 88.

138. David, *Status*, p. 81.

139. Ustrialov, *Istoriia*, 1:186–87; Bobrovskii, *Perekhod"*, p. 109.

140. Bogoiavlenskii, "Voisko," p. 80.

141. Elchaninov, "Ocherk"," p. 66.

142. *AMG*, 2, no. 640; ibid., 3, nos. 307, 322, 684; Reitenfel's "Skazaniia," p. 126.

143. Ibid., 3, no. 236.

144. Epifanov, "'Uchenie," p. 90; Kalinychev, *Pravovye*, pp. 44–45. The last set of figures is precisely the number and ratio of troops the Rzeczpospolita had when it tried to quell the cossack uprising in the Ukraine in the mid-century.

145. A few *reitary* were formed at the end of the 1640s or in 1650. They were *deti boiarskie* who had served on the frontier and helped build the Belgorod *zaseka* (*AMG*, 2, nos. 440, 443).

146. Ibid., 2, no. 540.

147. Ibid., no. 717.

148. Ibid., nos. 736, 739, 759.

149. This is the claim of Olearius, writing in the beginning of the 1650s (*Travels,* p. 222). Kotoshikhin, writing in the mid-1660s, said lay and clerical lords who were unable to serve for one reason or another sent an equipped slave or monastery lay employee (*sluga*) for each one hundred peasant households (*O Rossii,* pp. 108–9).

150. This fact alone lends considerable support to the view that the Western formation cavalry regiments (along with the lancers) were simply "a modernization of the middle service class-*pomest'e* cavalry, and entirely different from the regular cavalry of Peter I" (Epifanov, p. 86). But the major point as far as the argument here is concerned is that they were supported by the state treasury, not by their peasant serfs (*AMG,* 3, no. 101).

151. This was not heeded, for the regiments seem to have been formed on a territorial basis, and the number of men in each regiment depended on how many there were in each region. For example, during the second Crimean campaign the regiments were as follows:

Oboian regiment		733 men
Livny	"	680 "
Novgorod	"	1791 "
Mozhaisk	"	965 "
Briansk	"	1285 "

(Epifanov, " 'Uchenie," p. 86). See also *DAI,* 8, no. 52 (1679).

152. Ustrialov, *Istoriia,* 1:184.

153. In 1681 five colonels (*polkovniki*) were Russians, twenty were foreigners (Ustrialov, *Istoriia,* 1:301).

154. Epifanov, " 'Uchenie," p. 86.

155. Later on, in 1688, children and relatives of members of the upper service class (*stol'niki, striapchie,* Moscow *dvoriane,* and *zhil'tsy*) who did not appear for regular service were forcibly registered in the *reitary* without cash pay, the assumption being that they could support themselves from their land holdings. Members of the middle service class, however, were enrolled as soldiers, without pay (*PSZ,* 2, no. 1313).

156. Elchaninov, "Ocherk"," p. 75. The nationalist D. F. Maslovskii doubted the reality or efficacy of this prescribed training, saying that the foreign officers were in general so incompetent that they would have been unable to train anyone at any time (*Zapiski,* 1:25). The papal envoy to Moscow at the beginning of the 1670s, Jacob Reutenfels, claimed that the troops trained by the foreign mercenaries had the best theoretical military training and were excellent forces (Reitenfel's, "Skazaniia," p. 125).

157. Bogoiavlenskii, "Vooruzhenie," pp. 278, 280; Markov, *Istoriia,* 3: 114.

158. *AMG,* 3, no. 646.

159. Pankov, *Razvitie taktiki,* p. 6.

160. Epifanov, " 'Uchenie," p. 86. There were exceptions (*AMG,* 3, nos. 190, 390).

161. David, *Status,* p. 81. Reutenfels had reported at the beginning of the 1670s that the Russian infantry was undoubtedly better than the cavalry (Reitenfel's, "Skazaniia," p. 126).

162. Krizhanich, *Politika,* p. 429.

163. Bogoiavlenskii, "Vooruzhenie," p. 280.

164. Ibid. Krizhanich called the hussars "heavy cavalry" (*Politika,* p. 428).

165. Ustrialov, *Istoriia,* 1:186.

166. *AMG,* 2, no. 766.

167. Ibid., no. 905.

168. Ibid., no. 539.

169. Bogoiavlenskii, "Vooruzhenie," pp. 282–83; Elchaninov, "Ocherk"," pp. 73–74. Markov says they had armor (*Istoriia,* 3:114). In general, reliable data on the dragoons is scarcer than for other parts of the army (Mikhnevich and Il'enko, "Glavnyi shtab"," p. 11).

170. Maierberg, *Puteshestvie,* p. 181.

171. Stashevskii, *Smeta,* p. 1; *AMG,* 2, no. 1124.

172. Ustrialov, *Istoriia*, 1:186–87; Chernov, *Vooruzhennye*, p. 139.
173. Beskrovnyi, *Russkaia armiia*, p. 125.
174. Elchaninov, "Ocherk"," p. 74.
175. Stashevskii, *Smeta*, pp. 13–14. See appendix below.
176. Buganov, "Osvoboditel'naia," p. 62.
177. Solov'ev, *Istoriia*, 6: 85, 110, 118; Maierberg, *Puteshestvie*, p. 183; Stashevskii, *Smeta*, p. 14. See above, p. 217. *AMG*, 3, nos. 86, 96, 97, 108, 126, 135, 155, 535, 549, 553, 560.
178. Stashevskii, *Smeta*, p. 18.
179. Ibid., p. 17.
180. *AMG*, 3, no. 58. The government was especially concerned in this decree about the losses of the officers, which it knew from the precise casualty reports submitted. In a 1661 case the government penalized officers whose actions caused needless loss of men (ibid., no. 524).

12. The Old Army after the Reform

1. Margolin, "Vooruzhenie," p. 101.
2. Margolin, "K voprosu," p. 83.
3. Chernov, *Vooruzhennye*, p. 162; Zaozerskii, *Tsar'*, pp. 337–40.
4. *AAE*, 3, no. 199; *DAI*, 3, no. 297; ibid., 4, no. 123; also *Ulozhenie* of 1649.
5. Margolin, "K voprosu," p. 82.
6. Chernov, *Vooruzhennye*, p. 188. Presumably the order had not yet been complied with when the 1681 census of military forces was taken.
7. Ibid., p. 162; Porshnev, "Razvitie" (1963), pp. 225–41.
8. *Novyi letopisets"*, suppl., pp. 6–7.
9. Petrikeev, *Krupnoe*, pp. 180–81; *AMG*, 3, no. 446.
10. *Ulozhenie*, 10: 119, 141.
11. *AMG*, 2, no. 1073.
12. Ibid., 3, nos. 4, 13, 22, 29, 238, 287, 310, 537.
13. Ibid., nos. 560, 587, 588.
14. Baklanova, "Dela," pp. 319–20; Novosel'skii, "Pobegi," p. 346; Buganov, *Moskovskoe vosstanie*, pp. 84–86; *AMG*, 3, no. 626.
15. *Ulozhenie*, 25: 10; *AMG*, 2, nos. 812, 835; ibid., 3, nos. 518, 630, 641, 649; Margolin, "K voprosu," p. 85; Olearius, *Travels*, pp. 310, 314–15; Gordon, *Passages*, pp. 49, 65, 111; Schleussinger, "Rasskaz," pp. 107–8; Kurts, "Sostoianie," pp. 97, 214, 237; Kotoshikhin, *O Rossii*, 4: 25; ibid., 5: 13–15.
16. Bogoiavlenskii, "Voisko," pp. 73–74.
17. Margolin, "K voprosu," pp. 88–89. See also Bogoiavlenskii, who cites a 1639 cry of "ruin" when the Tula *strel'tsy* were ordered to undergo training as soldiers ("Vooruzhenie," p. 277).
18. Janowitz, *The Military*, p. 72.
19. Margolin, "K voprosu," p. 83.
20. Margolin, "Vooruzhenie," p. 97. It is conceivable, of course, that this was simply an oversight, or that it reflects the decline of the government after the death of Filaret in 1633. The *Streletskii Prikaz* was headed by Boiarin Prince Ivan Borisovich Cherkasskii from 1622 until May 26, 1638, when Boiarin Fedor Ivanovich Sheremetev took over. The same *d'iaki* continued to work in and probably actually ran the chancellery. Cherkasskii was back at the helm on November 10, 1638, and stayed there until April 4, 1642. Then Sheremetev took over again until he was purged by Morozov on March 26, 1646 (Bogoiavlenskii, *Prikaznye*, pp. 164–65). Thus the event of 1638 may represent chaos caused in the chancellery by the relatives replacing one another, or more likely, perhaps, simply by their general incompetence. In 1646 an order was issued to make sure that the *strel'tsy* were training constantly and also to train those who were deficient (Margolin, "K voprosu," p. 87). See *DAI*, 3, no. 70; *AI*, 4, no. 560.
21. Bogoiavlenskii, "Voisko," p. 70. See also Gordon, *Passages*, p. 53.

22. Mikhnevich and Il'enko, "Glavnyi shtab"," p. 9. At least once, in 1661, this process was reversed, to the discomfort of the *soldaty*, many of whom fled (Gordon, *Passages*, pp. 52–53).

23. Margolin, "Vooruzhenie," p. 99. One could argue that the government did this because it lacked the funds to pay them. This could well be partly true, but the government probably chose to economize because it realized the *strel'tsy* were a bad investment. Formerly an elite corps, the *strel'tsy* were singularly unable to adapt to the changed conditions presented by the new military technology; the fact that so many of them became Old Believers serves as additional evidence of their traditionalist psychology. Margolin says elsewhere ("K voprosu," p. 69) that the question arose in the seventeenth century of replacing cash pay with a land grant. In some places *strel'tsy* were ordered to put empty lands into production in lieu of pay in cash and kind, but the order was not effected. To their very end they were paid in cash, at least in the Novgorod and Pskov areas. The uprising of 1648 was suppressed only after the government had won over the *strel'tsy* by increasing their pay (A. M. Sakharov, *Obrazovanie*, p. 161).

24. Buganov, "Streletskoe," p. 46.

25. Maslovskii, *Zapiski*, 1: 11.

26. Kozintseva, "Astrakhanskie," pp. 362, 364–66; *Ulozhenie*, 19: 26, 27; *MS*, p. 59; Bogoiavlenskii, "Voisko," p. 71.

27. Margolin, "K voprosu," p. 73.

28. Kozintseva, "Astrakhanskie," pp. 365–66.

29. Kolchin, "Obrabotka," p. 193.

30. P. P. Smirnov, *Posadskie liudi*, 2: 76–77; *AAE*, 4, no. 24.

31. Margolin, "K voprosu," pp. 74–76. The contemporary Englishman Samuel Collins, writing in the 1660s (probably about Moscow), noted that the tsar paid his *strel'tsy* with grain, dried meat, and cloth, "but very little money, for they have all trades and great privileges" (*The Present State*, p. 111).

32. *Ulozhenie*, 19; *MS*, pp. 51–62; see chapter 14.

33. *Ulozhenie*, 19: 4, 11, 27.

34. Ibid., 11; *MS*, p. 55.

35. *Ulozhenie*, 19: 26, 27.

36. Bobrovskii, *Zachatki*, p. 2.

37. K. V. Bazilevich noted the role the *strel'tsy* continued to play during the reign of Aleksei as a valued palace guard (*Denezhnaia reforma*, p. 105). This obviously was a temporary and personal, rather than an institutional, affair, for the musketeers, as such, demonstrated their potential disloyalty in 1648, as they were to do later in the time of Peter the Great. A contemporary who hated them claimed that the Moscow *strel'tsy* were loyal because they were well paid (*AMG*, 3: 626); see also Zaozerskii, *Tsar*, pp. 336–46. The government at least agreed that the capital forces were more reliable than those in the provinces, for it kept them around longer—but largely as policemen, much less so as troops.

38. "Strelcii . . . artes mechanicas exercent" (David, *Status*, p. 87).

39. Margolin, "K voprosu," pp. 80, 92.

40. Bakhrushin, "Moskovskoe vosstanie," 2: 79; Iakubov, "Rossiia," 184: 418.

41. *AI*, 4, no. 70. For a 1660 exception, see *AMG*, 3, no. 201.

42. *AMG*, 2, no. 806 (no. 830 says three hundred were built).

43. Ibid., nos. 699, 704, 830, 834, 846, 973, 1018; ibid., 3 nos. 86 (they arrived late), 448, 497.

44. Bobrovskii, *Postoiannyia*, pp. 11–12.

45. Margolin, "Vooruzhenie," pp. 95–96. Most of the arms the *strel'tsy* had by the 1690s belonged to the men themselves.

46. Bogoiavlenskii, "Vooruzhenie," p. 276.

47. A. V. Kartashev, *Ocherki po istorii russkoi tserkvi*, 2 vols. (Paris: YMCA Press, 1959), 2: 237–39; Michael Cherniavsky, "The Old Believers and the New Religion," *Slavic Review* 25, no. 1 (March 1966): 19–20, 27; A. A. Zimin, "Tserkovnaia reforma

i raskol," in *Tserkov' v istorii Rossii (IX v.—1917 g.)* . *Kriticheskie ocherki* (Moscow: Nauka, 1967) , pp. 153–54.

On the behavior of modern dispossessed social groups with their predictions of the end, see Bell, ed., *Radical Right*, p. 9; Egbert DeVries, *Man in Rapid Social Change* (Garden City, New York: Doubleday, 1961) , p. 97. The church schism also idealized antiquity, which would have appealed to the obsolescent musketeers (Bulygin, "Nachal'nyi etap," p. 89; DeVries, *Man*, pp. 98–99) .

48. Volkov, "O stanovlenii," pp. 98–99; Tikhomirov, "Sobornoe Ulozhenie," p. 13. In January, 1649, the *strel'tsy* expressed a desire to kill Morozov—their commander and the person who, more than any other, represented the innovative spirit in Muscovy. The musketeers were so distrusted that the Swedish resident Pommerening reported a plan to create a special guards regiment of five thousand men commanded by Dutchmen to protect the tsar (Iakubov, "Rossiia," 184: 439–40) .

The *strel'tsy* participated in the 1650 uprisings in Novgorod and Pskov (A. M. Sakharov, *Obrazovanie*, p. 162; M. N. Tikhomirov, *Pskovskoe vosstanie 1650 goda* [Moscow-Leningrad: Akademiia Nauk SSSR, 1935]) . Few *strel'tsy* participated in the 1662 Moscow "copper riots" (Bazilevich, *Denezhnaia*, pp. 96–97; Buganov, *Moskovskoe*, pp. 41–42, 66, 70; idem, "O sotsial'nom sostave," pp. 313–16) . However, the main agitator of the uprising, Kuz'ma Nagaev, was a musketeer (idem, *Moskovskoe*, pp. 43, 48–50, 76; Buganov, ed., *Vosstanie*, pp. 40–43) . Some musketeers also participated in the Razin uprising at the end of the 1660s (Buganov and Chistiakova, "O nekotorykh," pp. 40, 43) .

49. Kozintseva, "Astrakhanskie," p. 361.

50. *PSZ*, 2, no. 812.

51. Margolin, "K voprosu," pp. 69–70.

52. Margolin, "Vooruzhenie," p. 92.

53. David, *Status*, pp. 86–87.

54. "Hi [strelcii] sunt insolentissimi dum occasionem nanciscuntur, maximum timorem Moscuae incutiunt" (David, *Status*, p. 87) ; Gordon, *Passages*, pp. 187–93; V. I. Buganov, *Moskovskie vosstaniia kontsa XVII veka* (Moscow: Nauka, 1969) .

It might be recalled that the *strel'tsy* who revolted in 1682 demanded that those who "had killed" the lately deceased sovereign be punished. They calmed down only after those "responsible" had been executed (Schleussinger, "Rasskaz," pp. 110–11) . I should imagine that this conjuring up of a fictive plot coupled with violent action is precisely the behavior a sociologist would expect from a fallen elite desirous of preserving the old society and its own eroded status and social position (Bell, ed., *Radical Right*, pp. 2, 48, 182) .

55. Mikhenevich and Il'enko, "Glavnyi shtab"," pp. 23–24. V. I. Buganov reviewed the historiography of the 1698 uprising to show how the interpretation of it has changed (and should change) from a plot instigated by Sofia to a popular uprising stemming from discontent over low pay, abuse by foreign officers, and a hard life ("Streletskoe," pp. 45–53) . All of this fails to get at the real issue, the obsolescence of the *strel'tsy*.

56. McNeill, *Steppe Frontier*, pp. 60–61, 63, 133, 150.

57. Epifanov, " 'Uchenie," p. 97.

58. Gordon, *Passages*, p. 184.

59. Nikol'skii, "Glavnoe," pp. 1–4.

60. Geisman, *Kratkii*, 1:128–29; Zagorovskii, *Belgorodskaia*, p. 29.

61. Mikhnevich and Geisman, "Glavnyi," p. 29.

62. Nikol'skii, "Glavnoe," p. 19. B. I. Morozov probably contemplated liquidating the autonomy of the Don cossacks in 1646 while arranging a raid on the Crimea (Zagorovskii, *Belgorodskaia*, p. 115) .

63. Miliukov, *Ocherki* (1964) , 1, pt. 2, 162–63. Maslovskii dated the appearance of the Don cossacks as 1570 (*Zapiski*, 1:40) .

64. Nikol'skii, "Glavnoe," pp. 44, 48, 53. Maslovskii said the Don cossacks entered regular Russian service under oath in 1671 (*Zapiski*, 1:40) .

65. Nikol'skii, "Glavnoe," p. 67; N. I. Kuznetsov, "Razriadnye knigi i ikh znachenie dlia istorii armii perioda ukrepleniia rossiiskogo tsentralizovannogo gosudarstva," *Trudy MGI-AI* 10 (1957) : 400.

66. Platonov, *Ocherki* (1937) , pp. 86–91, 387–92.

67. Zimin and Preobrazhenskii, "Izuchenie," p. 144; Chernov, "TsGADA," p. 132; Chernov, *Vooruzhennye*, p. 128. This fully explains why the government did not accept a 1625 offer from cossack emissaries from Kiev to assume Russian sovereignty, and why Moscow did not aid cossacks headed by Taras Fedorovich (Triasylo) who were rebelling against Polish hegemony in 1630. See Keep, "Filaret," p. 359; Buganov, "Osvoboditel'naia," p. 58. Obviously Filaret was fully aware of the potential fifth column that cossacks might be in a Ukraine annexed by Moscow.

68. Smirnov, *Posadskie liudi*, 1:409–10. Cossacks were also exempted from having to pay court costs (*AMG*, 3, no. 308) .

69. *AMG*, 2, nos. 538, 596, 922; Zagorovskii, *Belgorodskaia*, pp. 142–43. The Polish-Lithuanian authorities tried to curtail the exodus by telling the cossacks that the Muscovites would send them to Siberia if they crossed the frontier (*AMG*, 2, no. 493) .

70. *AMG*, 2, no. 474.

71. Nikol'skii, "Glavnoe," pp. 35–36; *AMG*, 2, no. 477; ibid., 3, no. 201.

72. *AMG*, 2, no. 472. The document also reveals a rather rare instance of a jurisdictional dispute in Muscovy. The officer was getting his orders from the Musketeers Chancellery. Ordinarily the cossacks were subordinate to the Military Chancellery, as was the local general (*voevoda*) . Thus the *voevoda* had no forces at his command to send out on intelligence-gathering missions and asked to be forgiven in advance should the Tatars escape his surveillance. The official government response is not with the document. See also *AMG*, 2, no. 597; ibid., 3, no. 631. In another case, a dispute between the *voevoda* and a *guba* elder, the former won and the government said the *guba* affairs were all subordinate to the *voevoda* (*AMG*, 2, no. 568) . This was the general trend, which meant of course that the middle service class lost any autonomy it might have had in the provinces.

73. Petrikeev, *Krupnoe*, pp. 180–81.

74. Zagorovskii, *Belgorodskaia*, pp. 122, 128.

75. *AMG*, 2, nos. 1103, 1130; ibid., 3, no. 152.

76. Chernov, *Vooruzhennye*, pp. 165–67.
About five thousand cossacks served in fortresses during Aleksei's reign (Nikol'skii, "Glavnoe," p. 6) .

77. Bogoiavlenskii, "Vooruzhenie," p. 266.

78. As noted above, the cossacks in the regimental service in 1680 were forced to join the soldiers (Chernov, *Vooruzhennye*, p. 188) . This weakened the soldiers, for the ex-cossacks, *strel'tsy* and artillerymen served only every other year; they were paid by the treasury one year, and then were released to earn their own livelihoods the second year by farming (ibid., p. 191; Samokvasov, *Krest'iane*, p. 81) .

79. *AMG*, 2, no. 951. On cossack campaigns against the Crimean Tatars in the second half of the seventeenth century, see Iu. P. Tushin, "Iz istorii pokhodov donskogo i zaporozhskogo kazachestva vo vtoroi polovine XVII veka," *Uchenye zapiski Kurskogo gosudarstvennogo pedagogicheskogo instituta* 60 (1969) : 196–203.

80. *AMG*, 2, nos. 1115, 1120, 1128, 1144, 1148; ibid., 3, nos. 160, 188, 203, 212, 248, 254, 266, 321.

81. Ibid., 2, nos. 632, 660, 682, 686, 692, 713, 718, 851, 863, 923; ibid., 3, no. 627.

82. Ibid., 2, nos. 718, 822, 831, 861, 865, 909, 921, 968, 984, 987, 1001; ibid., 3, no. 266.

83. Ibid., 3, nos. 434, 496, 497.

84. Ibid., 2, no. 831.

85. Ibid., 2, no. 987.

86. Maslovskii, *Zapiski*, 1:20, 55.

87. Elchaninov, "Ocherk"," p. 46; Zagorovskii, *Belgorodskaia*, p. 32.

88. *Ulozhenie*, 19: 12, 28; *MS*, pp. 55, 59.

89. Stashevskii, "Sluzhiloe," pp. 4, 7.
90. Margolin, "Vooruzhenie," p. 100; Kalinychev, *Pravovye,* p. 40.
91. Markov, *Istoriia,* 3:114.
92. Denisova, "Pomestnaia," p. 43.
93. Maslovskii, *Zapiski,* 1:23.
94. Bogoiavlenskii, "Vooruzhenie," p. 265.
95. *AAE,* 3, no. 319.
96. Stashevskii, *Smeta,* p. 21. See also a 1661 case (*AMG,* 3, no. 410).
97. Stashevskii, "Sluzhiloe," p. 17. See also *AMG,* 3, no. 548, for an example of different arms and numbers of soldiers furnished by landholders with the same number of peasant households. Also see Bogoiavlenskii, "Vooruzhenie," p. 263.
98. Bogoiavlenskii, "Vooruzhenie," p. 260.
99. Ibid., p. 261. Some Poles were still using bows and arrows (Gordon, *Passages,* p. 28).
100. Bogoiavlenskii, "Vooruzhenie," p. 261.
101. Buganov, "Zasechnaia," pp. 188, 251–52. See this document for the personnel required to repair and man the *cherta.*
102. Novosel'skii, *Bor'ba,* p. 368.
103. Iu. V. Got'e, "Zametki po istorii zashchity iuzhnoi granitsy Moskovskago gosudarstva," *Istoricheskiia izvestiia izd. Istoricheskom" obshchestvom" pri moskovskom" universitete,* no. 2 (1917), p. 51.
104. Novosel'skii, *Bor'ba,* p. 372. For an example of how members of the middle class put pressure on the government to preserve the established ways, see *AMG,* 2, no. 659.
105. *Tul'skii krai,* 1:11.
106. *AMG,* 2, no. 413 (construction). Even as late as 1676, members of the middle service class were supposed to gather for service on the Belgorod *cherta* (*PSZ,* 1, no. 615).
107. *DR,* 3: 95–96, 120, 163, 209, 251; *AMG,* 2, no. 458; Zagorovskii, *Belgorodskaia,* pp. 55, 120.
108. *Tul'skii krai,* 1, no. 20; Gnevushev, "Zemlevladenie," p. 279; Zagorovskii, *Belgorodskaia,* pp. 120, 130, 132, 138, 141, 145.
109. Bogoiavlenskii, "Vooruzhenie," p. 278; *AMG,* 3, no. 318 (also a 1660 case, no. 89); Zagorovskii, *Belgorodskaia,* pp. 73–74. The severe Tatar raids of 1643–45 did not even reach Oka, where the middle service class was waiting for them (ibid., p. 109).
110. *AMG,* 2, nos. 688, 854.
111. Ibid., nos. 445, 495.
112. Bobrovskii, *Perekhod",* p. 107.
113. Ibid., p. 108; *AMG,* 3, no. 236.
114. Bobrovskii, *Postoiannyia,* p. 24; Keep, "Elite," p. 216. In the autumn of 1650 less than half of the members of the lower upper-service class (the *stol'niki, striapchie,* Moscow *dvoriane* and *zhil'tsy*) appeared for the obligatory review. The government ordered those absent without leave to report later. If they hid on their estates, their peasants and slaves were to suffer. The troops themselves were threatened with jail, fining, and a cut in their compensation rates (*AMG,* 2, no. 443). See also Zagorovskii, *Belgorodskaia,* p. 137.
115. Razin, *Istoriia,* 3:215.
116. Sergeevich, "Voennyia," p. 62.
117. *AMG,* 2, no. 335. See a 1638 case of reluctance to serve, but without resort to violence, in Buganov, "Zasechnaia," p. 186.
118. Markov, *Istoriia,* 3:119.
119. *AI,* 4, no. 70; Sh., "Dvorianstvo," no. 2, p. 539; Zagorovskii, *Belgorodskaia,* pp. 145–46. The 1653 technique of reducing the middle service class was subsequently used frequently (ibid., p. 152).
120. *AMG,* 2, no. 539.
121. Ibid., no. 932.

122. Ibid., no. 1027.
123. Ibid., no. 617.
124. Ibid., 3, no. 621. See Thomas Esper, "The *Odnodvortsy* and the Russian Nobility," *The Slavonic and East European Review* 45, no. 104 (January 1967) :124–34.
125. *AMG*, 2, no. 1089; ibid., 3, no. 520.
126. Ibid., 2, no. 1126.
127. Ibid., no. 1130.
128. Zagorovskii, *Belgorodskaia*, pp. 153–57.
129. *PSZ*, 1, no. 246; Sh., "Dvorianstvo," no. 3, p. 206. ,
130. *PSZ*, 1, no. 261. See *AMG*, 3, no. 49, for a 1660 recruiting order. See also ibid., no. 301, which reveals that by 1661 all the old members of the middle service class were serving in the new cavalry under one major commander.
131. Mikhnevich and Il'enko, "Glavnyi shtab"," p. 11; ibid., suppl., p. 58, no. 9.
132. *AMG*, 3, no. 101. Also taken in were some who had already served, but in spite of this had undergone no training (ibid., 3, nos. 170, 190) .
133. *AMG*, 2, nos. 1025, 1042, 1103.
134. Ibid., nos. 655, 672, 854, 1035, 1112, 1113, 1117; ibid., 3, nos. 99, 162, 186, 190, 192, 194, 197, 203, 220, 222, 230, 236, 265, 288, 291, 299, 358, 359, 362, 378, 397, 410, 421, 436, 452, 455, 484, 491, 504, 582, 687, 705. In light of the evidence, I doubt whether D. F. Maslovskii's contention that "discipline was broken primarily by the *strel'tsy* and *soldaty*" in this period can be supported by reference to the facts. Obviously members of the lower service class did flee from service (for example, see ibid., 2, nos. 927, 939, 973, 732, ibid., 3, nos. 53, 107, 236, 473, 552, 582) , but the instances seem to have been no more frequent, in fact less so, than in the case of their "betters."
135. *AMG*, 3, nos. 165, 192.
136. Mikhnevich and Il'enko, "Glavnyi," pp. 16–18; *PSZ*, 1, no. 302; *AMG*, 3, nos. 350, 381, 414, 427, 647, 678, 695.
137. *AMG*, 2, no. 692; ibid., 3, no. 687.
138. Ibid., 2, nos. 420, 559, 564, 587, 736, 940, 945, 1001; ibid., 3, nos. 39, 391.
139. Ibid., 2, no. 912.
140. Ibid. no. 933; ibid., 3, no. 524.
141. Ibid., 2, nos. 736, 768.
142. Ibid., nos. 913-15, 934, 938, 1064; ibid., 3, nos. 52, 125, 127, 159, 170, 174, 177, 178, 193, 297, 314, 334, 355, 358, 359, 365, 387, 407, 410, 452, 484, 490, 541, 582.
143. Ibid., 3, no. 410.
144. Ibid., no. 582.
145. Mikhnevich and Il'enko, "Glavnyi," pp. 18–19, suppl. pp. 56–57, nos. 6, 8; *AMG*, 2, nos. 429, 430, 658, 690, 776; ibid., 3, nos. 258, 601.
146. Bobrovskii, *Perekhod"*, p. 108. In 1662, *dvoriane* and *deti boiarskie* who were still in service began to desert to the Poles (ibid., p. 117) .
147. *AMG*, 2, nos. 1136, 1140, 1144, 1147, 1148, 1152; ibid., 3, nos. 30, 279. Five months later the Muscovites captured Vygovskii in Staryi Bykhov (ibid., 2, no. 1160) . In February of 1660 Trubetskoi's assistant in the Konotop disaster, Prince G. G. Romodanovskii, was handsomely rewarded for his service (ibid., 3, no. 100) . For evidence on the magnitude of the casualties suffered by the middle class as of the summer of 1660, see ibid., 3, no. 126. On the Konotop battle itself, see Yuriy Tys-Krokhmaliuk, "The Victory at Konotop," *The Ukrainian Review* 6, no. 3 (1959) :34–45.
148. *AMG*, 3, nos. 43, 104, 108.
149. Maslovskii, *Zapiski*, 1:26.
150. Gordon, *Passages*, p. 31.
151. 1657 call-up order (*AMG*, 2, no. 961). On the composition of the army, see Mikhnevich and Geisman, "Glavnyi shtab"," p. 61. They compare it with the Rzeczpospolita army of 1621 which fought the Turks (ibid.) . See also Maierberg, *Puteshestvie* p. 183; Bobrovskii, *Perekhod"*, p. 115; Maslovskii, *Zapiski*, 1:26–37; Baiov,

Kurs", 1:152–58; for a map, see ibid., 1, no. 9. A strikingly similar disaster overtook the Rzeczpospolita army in 1652, when at the battle of Batog Field the Polish nobility was exterminated. V. I. Buganov compares Khmel'nitskii's victory over the Poles to Hannibal's massacre at Cannae of the Romans in 216 B.C. ("Osvoboditel'naia," p. 68). Perhaps the real tragedy for Poland was that it did not use this opportunity to form a more centralized state, which could then finance a better and more stable army (*AMG*, 3, nos. 229, 262).

152. Mikhnevich and Geisman, "Glavnyi shtab"," p. 72. One serviceman reported that one of his brothers had been killed at Konotop, three more with Sheremetev (*AMG*, 3, no. 263 [see also nos. 279, 483]).

153. Bobrovskii, *Perekhod"*, pp. 108, 117; *AMG*, 3, nos. 301, 336, 530. Some Soviet historians have failed to recognize this crucial fact and write that on the eve of the Petrine reforms in 1700 "the *pomest'e* gentry cavalry was the basis of the armed forces" (Klokman, "Severnaia," p. 73).

154. N. P. Eroshkin et al., *Istoriia gosudarstvennykh uchrezhdenii Rossii do Velikoi oktiabr'skoi sotsialisticheskoi revoliutsii* (Moscow: Moskovskii gosudarstvennyi istoriko-arkhivnyi institut, 1965), pp. 67–68.

155. Bobrovskii, *Postoiannyia*, p. 10.

156. Denisova, "Pomestnaia," p. 44.

157. *PSZ*, 1, no. 615. This document, which contains great detail on abuses, ordered a census taken of the middle service class. A document of 1679 reveals enormous numbers (over half) of *dvoriane* and *deti boiarskie* absent from service. This was a far higher percentage than for any other category of troops (*KR*, 2:1386). See also Solov'ev, *Istoriia*, 7:67–70; Gradovskii, "Vysshaia," pp. 57–58, 61; Kotoshikhin, *O Rossii*, 2:11.

158. For example, see *AMG*, 2, nos. 450, 681, 684, 902; ibid., 3, no. 282; Stashevskii, "Sluzhiloe soslovie," p. 32; Storozhev, *Istoriko-*, p. 201; Uroff, p. 525, citing N. D. Sergeevskii, *Nakazanie v" russkom" prave XVII veka* (St. Petersburg, 1887), pp. 26–29; and A. I. Markevich, *Istoriia mestnichestva v" Moskovskom" gosudarstve v" XV-XVII veke* (Odessa, 1888), p. 474.

159. Collins, *Present State*, p. 110. The government was capable, however, of ordering the hanging of rich servicemen who refused to report for service (*AMG*, 2, no. 687).

160. Sh., "Dvorianstvo," no. 3, p. 425; *PSZ*, 2, no. 1280; Pavlov-Sil'vanskii, *Gosudarevy*, p. 241; Chernov, "TsGADA," p. 137.

161. Bogoiavlenskii, "Vooruzhenie," p. 262.

162. Chernov, *Vooruzhennye*, p. 160. The review was published by S. B. Veselovskii in *ChOIDR* 238 (1911).

163. Razin, *Istoriia*, 3:215; *PSZ*, 1, no. 522.

164. Sh., "Dvorianstvo," pp. 206–7; Vodarskii, "Sluzhiloe," p. 233.

165. Ustrialov, *Istoriia*, 1:177.

166. Bogoiavlenskii, "Vooruzhenie," pp. 263, 266.

167. Ibid., p. 264; *AMG*, 3, no. 654. One of the minor issues of Russian historiography has been the role played in the army by the slaves brought by their lords. The contemporary Grigorii Kotoshikhin observed that they fought alongside their lords. A few historians have disputed this and claimed that they had largely noncombat, secondary roles, such as accompanying and guarding the baggage train, keeping the horses, getting food and fodder, and so on (Maslovskii, *Zapiski*, 1:9; Baiov, *Kurs"*, 1:72). See also the views of A. A. Zimin, discussed in chapter 2. In Mamluk Egypt black slaves were entrusted with handguns considerably before the traditional forces deigned to use them (Ayalon, *Gunpowder*, pp. 66–71).

168. Pososhkov, *Kniga*, pp. 248, 268; Maslovskii, *Zapiski*, 1:24; Denisova, "Pomestnaia," p. 29. See also *AMG*, 1, no. 1014. The amount a serviceman collected for his wounds depended on his social position (*AMG*, 3, no. 254). See also chapter 3.

169. Maierberg, *Puteshestvie*, p. 181.

170. Chernov, *Vooruzhennye*, pp. 161–62.

171. Miliukov, *Ocherki* (1900), 1:130.

172. Chernov, *Vooruzhennye*, p. 188. For this reason it is hardly surprising that a foreigner would not see the *deti boiarskie* at the end of the 1680s. See A. S. Myl'nikov's note 6 to David, "Sovremennoe," no. 3, p. 97.

173. *PSZ*, 2, no. 904; Myshlaevskii, *Ofitserskii*, p. 33; Bogoiavlenskii, "Voisko," p. 67; Chernov, *Vooruzhennye*, p. 162. The people of the upper service class, or the Moscow ranks, who are not the subject of our major concern, continued to retain their own identity. However, their participation in the major wars continued to decline until the Petrine reforms.

The following figures demonstrate that the power elite of the Muscovite state also was withdrawing from military service and leaving it to others (Bobrovskii, *Posto-iannyia*, p. 9).

CAMPAIGNS		PARTICIPATED IN CAMPAIGN	ABSENT WITHOUT LEAVE ("V NETEKH")	STAYED HOME ("V DOMEKH")
First Crimean	(1687)	6,112 men	719 men	711 men
Second Crimean	(1689)	6,319 ″	618 ″	885 ″
First Azov	(1695)	5,515 ″	1,118 ″	1,329 ″
Second Azov	(1696)	5,528 ″	1,129 ″	1,337 ″

174. *PSZ*, 2, no. 1113. In 1661 the sole surviving son of a widow who had no slaves was exempted from combat service (*AMG*, 3, no. 520).

175. Myshlaevskii, *Ofitserskii*, p. 31; Chernov, "TsGADA," p. 139.

176. Krizhanich, *Politika*, pp. 429, 431, 438.

177. *PSZ*, 1: no. 779. The office of *guba* elder was abolished in 1700 (Bobrovskii, *Perekhod"*, p. 67). It had been subordinate to the voevoda for a long time (*AMG*, 3, no. 356). See also chapter 3.

178. *PSZ*, 2, nos. 802, 842.

179. Ibid., no. 824.

180. Stashevskii, "Ekonomicheskaia," p. 353; A. M. Sakharov, *Obrazovanie*, p. 189; Volkov, "O stanovlenii," p. 100.

181. *PSZ*, 2, no. 844; *DAI*, 8, no. 82. The tsarist military historian P. O. Bobrovskii dated the introduction of the regular army as 1681 (*Perekhod"*, p. 135). Elsewhere he said 1689 (*Postoiannyia*, p. 8).

182. *SGGD*, 4: 298–99. Earlier, *mestnichestvo* had been abolished in religious processions (*PSZ*, 2, no. 775; Bennet, "The Idea," pp. 221–27).

183. Bobrovskii, *Postoiannyia*, pp. 34–35. *Mestnichestvo* disputes also caused disasters in the sixteenth century, such as the defeats in 1578 (at Venden) and 1579 in the Livonian War (Maslovskii, *Zapiski*, 1:44–45).

184. Kliuchevskii, *Istoriia soslovii*, p. 220; Mikhnevich and Geisman, "Glavnyi shtab"," pp. 70–71; Veselovskii, *Feodal'noe*, p. 23; Kotoshikhin, *O Rossii*, 4: 16.

185. Myshlaevskii, *Ofitserskii*, p. 34; Elchaninov, "Ocherk"," p. 73; Epifanov, "'Uchenie," p. 93.

186. Myshlaevskii, *Ofitserskii*, p. 5.

187. Keep, "The Muscovite Elite," p. 217. In the civil sphere, the abolition of *mestnichestvo* is sometimes viewed as a major step in the triumph of the bureaucracy over the old boyars who had run the government (Stashevskii, "Sluzhiloe soslovie," p. 32).

188. Bobrovskii, *Perekhod"*, p. 120. Bobrovskii said that the Russians did not go far enough in this direction because they were enchanted by the Polish cavalry and assumed its haughty attitude toward infantry.

189. Maierberg, *Puteshestvie*, pp. 180–81.

190. Maslovskii, *Zapiski*, 1:10, 55.

191. Bobrovskii, *Zachatki*, p. 2.

192. I am not sure I would go so far as to be tempted to call the middle service class's reaction to the gunpowder revolution an "identity conflict," although traces of

one must have been present. "Some periods in history become identity vacua caused by . . . apprehension: fears aroused by new facts, such as discoveries and inventions (including weapons) which radically expand and change the whole world-image" (Erik H. Erikson, "Autobiographic Notes on the Identity Crisis," *Daedalus* 99, no. 4: 733). The reaction to handguns described by David Ayalon among the Egyptian Mamluk cavalry archers certainly reflected a much greater "identity conflict" than there was in Muscovy (*Gunpowder*, chap. 3). Unlike the Mamluks, the Russians did not, as far as is known, develop any esprit de corps based on cavalry training, horsemanship, the use of sword and bow, and so they may not have been as psychologically bound to the traditional ways as were the Mamluks. Moreover, the enserfment lessened the impact of the technological challenge on the Muscovite cavalryman because his social position as a lord of serfs was enhanced by the abasement of the peasantry.

193. *MS*, pp. 63, 66–91.

194. *MS*, pp. 171, 174, 181, 183, 188, 191, 200, 205; Smirnov, "Chelobitnyia," nos. 1, 2, 4; Shakhmatov, "Chelobitnaia," pp. 16, 20. A similar looking back to the past can be witnessed in the 1650 Pskov uprising, where the people wanted the restoration of the freedom they had before Ivan IV (Iakubov, "Rossiia," 184: 474). On the glorification of the past by those dispossessed by change, see DeVries, *Man*, pp. 98–99.

195. Bell, ed., *Radical Right*, p. 48.

196. Ibid., p. 2.

197. Georges Friedmann, *The Anatomy of Work* (New York: The Free Press, 1961), pp. 16–18.

198. Bell, ed., *Radical Right*, p. 182.

13. The Legacy of the Reform

1. Chernov, *Vooruzhennye*, pp. 168–69. Collins noted that I. D. Miloslavskii was generalissimo of an army 80,000 strong (*The Present State*, p. 165). Billington gives figures of up to 300,000, with a review of the evidence showing that Peter only changed the composition of the army but did not increase its size (*Icon and Axe*, pp. 112, 672). See appendix.

2. Babushkina, "Mezhdunarodnoe," p. 162.

3. Bogoiavlenskii, "Voisko," p. 63.

4. For fairly consistent reports about the dimensions of enemy forces, see the following: (Swedes) *AMG*, 2, nos. 500, 857; (Swedes and Poles) ibid., 2, nos. 750, 790, 793, 820, 842, 859, 955; Gordon, *Passages*, p. 105; (Poles) *AMG*, 2, nos. 504, 517, 573, 590, 638, 837, 986; ibid., 3, nos. 444, 449, 551; (Poles and Tatars) ibid., nos. 186, 230, 249; (Poles, cossacks, and Tatars) ibid., no. 534; (cossacks) ibid., 2, nos. 522, 527, 538; (Tatars) ibid., nos. 505, 531, 605, 606; ibid., 3, nos. 94, 326; (Tatars and cossacks) ibid., 2, nos. 520, 537, 541, 1105, 1111; ibid., 3, no. 329. ("Poles" here means the forces of either the Poles or the Lithuanians, or the mercenaries at the disposal of the Rzeczpospolita.)

In twentieth-century new nations "there is no relationship between per capita gross national product and the size of the military establishment. The size of the military is less related to economic base than to total population" (Janowitz, *The Military*, pp. 17–18). A comparison of the relationship between size of the military and total population in new nations reveals that the Russian military establishment was much larger relative to the size of the population than that in any twentieth-century country. Modern nations in the 9–10 million population-category support armies of from 1,000 to 65,000 men (ibid., pp. 20–21).

5. Beskrovnyi, *Russkaia armiia*, p. 111.

6. Stashevskii, *Smeta*, p. 24.

7. Chernov, *Vooruzhennye*, p. 179; Stashevskii, "Biudzhet"," p. 416. Miliukov gives the rise as from 250,000 to 750,000 rubles in 1680 (*Ocherki* [1900], 1:130).

For the service of 112,062 men in 1667–68 the government paid out from Moscow:

Bonus for service and for food	149,768 R.
Additional	265,037
For muskets and carbines	35,694
	450,499
For wounds of 2,469 men and for the suffering of 171 men in capitivity	45,781
Other disbursements	28,722
	525,002 R.

(Beskrovnyi, *Russkaia armiia*, p. 118).

B. H. Slicher van Bath claims that Poland was "economically more sensible" than Russia in not having a standing infantry army ("The Yields of Different Crops [Mainly Cereals] in Relation to the Seed c. 810–1820," pp. 34–35). This is true only in the crudest possible sense, namely, in terms of treasury outlays. By any other calculation this would be untrue, for the value of the property destroyed in Poland by invading armies must have exceeded manyfold the cost of Russia's successful defense to keep invaders out. Moreover, I doubt whether Poles were happy after the Third Partition that their forebears had saved money by relying on a gentry cavalry and foreign mercenaries.

8. Kalinychev, *Pravovye*, p. 40.

9. Stashevskii, *Smeta*, p. 25.

10. Ibid., p. 27.

11. Ibid., p. 25. In 1679 the Musketeer Chancellery calculated it needed 107,227 rubles to pay its *strel'tsy* (*Ocherki . . . XVII*, p. 423).

12. A *chetvert'* of rye was equal to about 6 poods; of rye flour, about 5 poods. A pood equals 36 pounds (E. I. Kamentseva and N. V. Ustiugov, *Russkaia metrologiia* [Moscow: Vysshaia shkola, 1965], p. 113).

13. Stashevskii, *Smeta*, pp. 20–29.

14. Ibid., pp. 26, 28. See also *AMG*, 3, nos. 340, 702.

15. Bobrovskii, *Perekhod''*, p. 90.

16. *AMG*, 3, no. 641.

17. *Ocherki . . . XVII*, pp. 432–35; P. P. Smirnov, "Ekonomicheskaia," pp. 373, 404–7; Kurts, "Sostoianie," pp. 244–45; Spasskii, "Denezhnoe."

18. *AMG*, 2, no. 861; ibid., 3 nos. 153, 226, 257, 315, 338, 340, 377, 383. In November of 1661 an attempt was made to blame the inflation on a flood of counterfeit copper coinage—much of which was being minted by people in the government (*AMG*, 3, no. 540). In spite of the claim that, with the removal of the counterfeit money, prices had returned to normal, the troops found the situation the same (ibid., nos. 541, 584, 644; Gordon, *Passages*, p. 53).

19. Bazilevich, *Denezhnaia reforma*, p. 85; *AMG*, 3, no. 595.

20. In November of 1654 tavern farming concessions were still being sold (*AMG*, 2, no. 614). In 1658 taverns were being built (ibid., no. 1081). By the end of 1664 military expenses were being paid out of the tavern revenues (ibid., 3, no. 706).

21. P. P. Smirnov, "Ekonomicheskaia," pp. 396–98, 409. Count Witte's expediencies of the 1890s have a familiar ring to the person familiar with the reign of Aleksei. A decree of August 11, 1652, liquidated most taverns completely in favor of package stores (*kruzhechnye dvory*) (*Ocherki . . . XVII*, p. 429). In 1682 Sofia's government again resorted to the expedient of debasing the currency to raise revenues.

22. Troitskii, "O vliianii," p. 286; Miliùkov, *Gosudarstvennoe* (1905), pp. 40–57, 108–12.

23. Miliukov, *Ocherki* (1900), 1:147–49, 160; *Ocherki . . . XVII*, p. 422. Throughout the seventeenth century the government budget relied for the majority of its income on indirect taxes. Even at the beginning of the century these taxes accounted for

from two-thirds to nine-tenths of all income. Although government income tripled in the course of the century, indirect taxes still supplied about half of that income.

GOVERNMENT INCOME FOR 1680

SOURCE		AMOUNT (IN RUBLES)	
Direct taxes			
Strelets tax		101,468	(6.9%)
Post, captive ransom, horse maintenance taxes		53,453	(3.6%)
Extraordinary levies		235,338	(16.1%)
Siberian fur tax (iasak)		103,610	(7.1%)
Total		493,869	(33.7%)
Indirect taxes			
Customs and tavern revenues		650,223	(44.4%)
Crown monopolies and fees			
Coinage debasement in reminting		40,000	(2.7%)
Chancellery revenues		146,150	(10.0%)
Chancellery fees		33,735	(2.3%)
Total		219,885	(15.0%)
Other collections			
Largely from the Monastery			
and Patriarchal Chancelleries,	abt.	100,000	(6.8%)
Total income		1,463,997	

SOURCES: Stashevskii, "Biudzhet"," pp. 414, 417; Miliukov, *Gosudarstvennoe*, p. 118.

For the budget for the year September 1, 1697, through August 31, 1698, see P. N. Petrov, "Rospis' raskhodov" tsarstva Moskovskago," *Zapiski otdeleniia russkoi i slavianskoi arkheologii Russkago arkheologicheskogo obshchestva* 4 (1887):330–51.

24. *Ocherki . . . XVII*, p. 190; Gorfunkel', "Termin," pp. 643, 646; A. M. Sakharov, *Obrazovanie*, p. 138. A *vyt'* was about sixteen acres of good land in one field in a three-field agricultural system, nineteen acres of average land, or twenty-one acres of poor land. In the middle of the sixteenth century each peasant had about one-half *vyt'* of land (Kliuchevskii, "Proiskhozhdenie," p. 279). For the most recent calculations of the amount of arable land per person at the times of the 1678 to 1897 censuses, see Vodarskii, "Kolichestvo."

25. Gnevushev, "Zemlevladenie," p. 292.

26. Kalinychev, *Pravovye*, p. 40.

27. Mikhnevich and Il'enko, "Glavnyi shtab"," p. 6.

28. Chernov, *Vooruzhennye*, p. 190.

29. Denisova, "Pomestnaia," pp. 44–45. Sh. noted that by the end of the century the lower service class made up over four-fifths of the Army ("Dvorianstvo," no. 2, p. 542).

30. Babushkina, "Mezhdunarodnoe," pp. 159–60.

31. Razin, *Istoriia*, 3:254–55; Gordon, *Passages*, p. 164. Babushkina saw the heat and the steppe fires as the cause of the decision to turn back ("Mezhdunarodnoe," p. 166). Note that in 1656 the Moscow government was informed that the Polish king had forces totalling 110,000 men—50,000 Polish cavalry and 60,000 Hungarian mercenary foot soldiers (*AMG*, 2, no. 842). The following year a threat was raised that Russia might be invaded by a force of 120,000 regular troops plus 50,000 cossacks (ibid., no. 963). Thus Moscovy seemed to attempt to equal in numbers the forces of its adversaries.

32. Razin, *Istoriia*, 3:255–56.

33. Ibid., 258.

34. Ibid., 262; Gordon, *Passages,* p. 166. Babushkina blamed the lack of success of the campaigns on the failure by Poland and Austria to fulfill their commitments ("Mezhdunarodnoe," pp. 166–69).

35. David, *Status,* pp. 63–67; Elchaninov, "Ocherk"," pp. 77–79.

36. Babushkina, "Mezhdunarodnoe," p. 172; Gordon, *Passages,* p. 166.

37. Bobrovskii, *Perekhod",* iii.

38. Razin, *Istoriia,* 3:260.

39. Elchaninov, "Ocherk"," p. 79.

40. Klokman, "Severnaia," pp. 75–76. The Azov campaigns caused massive flights to the Don cossacks in the years 1695–99 by persons seeking relief from taxes, civil obligations, and military service (Bovrovskii, *Perekhod",* p. 123). The contemporary descriptions of these campaigns are still extant (Kuznetsov, "Fondy," *Trudy MGIAI* 4 [1948]: 104).

41. Bobrovskii, *Perekhod",* p. 109; Klokman, "Severnaia," p. 78; Rabinovich, "Formirovanie," pp. 221–33. In the new army most of the major officers were foreigners. Of 78 middle officers (a goal of 264 could not be filled), 45 were Russians, 33 were foreigners. The quota of lower officers also was unfilled (Rabinovich, "Formirovanie," p. 225). Austria created a standing army in 1681 at the urging of Field Marshal Raymond Montecuculi (Bobrovskii, *Zachatki,* pp. 17–18).

42. Krizhanich, *Politika,* p. 439.

43. Gordon, *Passages,* p. 164.

44. Bobrovskii, *Perekhod",* p. 119; *Zachatki,* pp. 25–26.

45. Myshlaevskii, *Ofitserskii,* p. 42. The pay of Russian officers was about the same per month as that given foreigners. However, the Russian officer was docked a specific amount, depending on his rank, for every peasant, *bobyl',* and slave household he owned (ibid., p. 43).

46. Razin, *Istoriia,* 3:218.

47. Pankov, *Razvitie taktiki,* pp. 5, 32.

48. Baiov, *Natsional'nyia,* p. 8.

49. Vodarskii, "Sluzhiloe," pp. 233–37; Rabinovich, "Formirovanie," p. 222.

50. See chapter 14.

51. Kirpichnikov, "Voennoe," p. 72; Kolosov, "Razvitie," p. 269; Beskrovnyi, *Russkaia armiia,* p. 21. Klokman entitles the ill-fated attack on Narva which initiated the "inevitable" Northern War (1700–1721) a "preventive war" ("Severnaia," p. 77).

52. Klokman, "Severnaia,' p. 73. It seems to be a cardinal tenet of Soviet faith that Russia's military backwardness at this time was caused by its economic backwardness. The economic backwardness in turn was the result of Russia's isolation, that is lack of warm-water ports. This in turn justified aggression to get the ports (ibid., pp. 73, 75).

M. Ia. Volkov has noted that no regiments of soldiers were formed in the period 1689–98, so that Russia had no infantry on the eve of the war with Sweden. The idea of creating a regular army occurred no earlier than 1700, only after Peter had settled with his internal opponents ("O stanovlenii," p. 103).

53. Myshlaevskii, *Ofitserskii,* p. 50.

54. Shapiro, "Ob absoliutizme," p. 73. M. N. Pokrovskii also appreciated the power which the new army gave the government ("Russkaia istoriia v samom szhatom ocherke," in *Izbrannye proizvedeniia,* 4 vols. [Moscow: Mysl', 1965–67], 3: 77). For a recent lecture on Russian absolutism by L. V. Cherepnin and a discussion of it, see *Dokumenty sovetsko-ital'ianskoi konferentsii istorikov,* edited by S. D. Skazkin et al. (Moscow: Nauka, 1970).

55. E. A. Razin holds precisely the opposite point of view (*Istoriia,* 3:21).

14. The Persistence of Serfdom

1. Novosel'skii, "Zemskii sobor," pp. 16–18.

2. Zanicheva, "Sotsial'no-ekonomicheskoe," p. 204.

3. The terminology of this section is largely from Reinhard Bendix and Seymour Martin Lipset, eds., *Class, Status, and Power. Social Stratification in Comparative Perspective*, 2d. ed. (New York: The Free Press, 1966).

4. Aleksandrov, "Streletskoe," p. 240.

5. How much government can shape society and its practices has long been a matter of contention. The role of government in life has indubitably been larger in Russia than in most other societies. A case in which that role was not large may well have been the rules on the redemption of familial estates, under which members of a clan had the right to buy back alienated property within a specified time, usually forty years. Here the legislation of the sixteenth and seventeenth centuries may simply have followed custom, strengthening those customs which were advantageous for the state. Initially, the system itself was probably not the product of legislative initiative (Storozhev, *Istoriko-*, pp. 162–63). Pre-Soviet historians such as V. O. Kliuchevskii and N. P. Pavlov-Sil'vanskii, reacting against the "state juridical school," did not believe that laws created social relations, but that social relations existed first and then laws followed (N. L. Rubinshtein, *Russkaia istoriografiia* [Moscow: Gospolitizdat, 1941], p. 528). It is hard to understand how they could have developed such a theory after a study of Muscovy or in light of the clear role the state played in the 1861 emancipation. It is more difficult to comprehend how anyone can hold to such notions given all the documents which now exist.

Soviet historians understand the historical reality when they note that the adaptable form of state power existing in Russia permitted the "superstructure to exert effective action on the base to adapt it to the needs of the ruling class"—that serfdom in Russia, in other words, was accomplished with the active participation of the tsarist government (Chistozvonov, "Nekotorye," p. 61; Shapiro, "Ob absoliutizme," p. 77).

6. By the 1680s, the military counterparts of the Russian middle service class, the Tatar cavalrymen, were recognized as militarily obsolete (McNeill, *Steppe Frontier*, p. 176).

7. M. Ia. Volkov also has noted the same phenomenon ("O stanovlenii," p. 92).

8. Iakovlev, *Namestnich'i*, p. 146; *MS*, p. 47; P. P. Smirnov, *Posadskie liudi*, 1:157–58, 172.

9. Smirnov, *Posadskie liudi*, 1:203, 207, 211, 238, 257, 244; ibid., 2:48, 55, 97. Townsmen made up about 3 percent of the population of Muscovy (Vodarskii, "Chislennost' naseleniia," p. 227).

10. *AAE*, 3, no. 55; ibid., 4, no. 6; *AI*, 3, nos. 92–XXV, 160; P. P. Smirnov, *Posadskie liudi*, 2: 114. The essential matter of taxes was referred to in the *Ulozhenie*, 19:14, 34, 35; *MS*, pp. 56–60. On the issue of taxes later in the century, see Man'kov, "Epizod," p. 285.

11. *AAE*, 3, no. 141; *Ocherki . . . XVII*, p. 178; Smirnov, *Posadskie liudi*, 1:353, 384–88.

12. *AAE*, 3, no. 279; Smirnov, *Posadskie liudi*, 1:384–88. It is worth noting that the time limit for recovering fugitive townsmen always referred back to 1613.

13. *AAE*, 3, no. 311.

14. *Ulozhenie*, 19; MS, pp. 51–62. See particularly *Ulozhenie*, 19: 19; Smirnov, *Posadskie liudi*, 2:291; *AAE*, 4, no. 32; *DAI*, 3, no. 47–III.

15. A similar observation was made long ago by N. A. Rozhkov ("Istoriia," 116). The government was not so inefficient that it could not reassess taxes in the rural sector almost immediately to account for population shifts (Vorms, ed., *Pamiatniki*, no. 20; Koretskii, *Zakreposhchenie*, p. 74).

16. On the issue of a monopoly of trade and industry prior to the Time of Troubles, see *Sudebnik* of 1589, art. 189; P. P. Smirnov, *Posadskie liudi*, 1:177, 185. In the 1620s and 1630s, see P. P. Smirnov, *Posadskie liudi*, 1:256–57, 399–400, 447; *AMG*, 2, no. 175. In 1648, *AAE*, 4, no. 24; *Ulozhenie*, 18:23, 29, 30; ibid., 19:1–3, 5, 9, 15, 16, 17.

On the ownership of town property in the sixteenth century, see P. P. Smirnov, *Posadskie liudi*, 1:175. In the 1620s, *AI*, 3, no. 92–IX; *AAE*, 3, no. 138. After the Smolensk

War, *AAE*, 3, no. 267; *AI*, 3, no. 92–XXXV,XXXVII. In 1648, *AAE*, 4, no. 32; Zertsalov, "O miatezhakh"," p. 19; P. P. Smirnov, *Posadskie liudi*, 1:229; *Ulozhenie*, 10:269; ibid., 19: 1, 5–9, 39–40.

It is probably correct to say that the *Ulozhenie* so satisfied the burghers that they did not participate in the Razin rebellion, as they had participated in the Time of Troubles (Makovskii, *Pervaia*, pp. 488–89).

17. Over this issue N. I. Romanov, Ia. K. Cherkasskii, D. M. Cherkasskii, I. A. Golitsyn, the Sheremetevs, and the Kurakins refused to sign the *Ulozhenie* (Smirnov, *Posadskie liudi*, 2: 246, 608).

18. On the evolution of the *zakladnichestvo* question, see *Sudebnik* of 1589, art. 91. For laws of 1584, 1586, 1619, P. P. Smirnov, *Posadskie liudi*, 1: 157–58. In the mid-1630s, P. P. Smirnov, "Chelobitnye," p. 9; *Posadskie liudi*, 1: 273, 424, 428, 430, 440–43. In 1648–49, *AAE*, 4, no. 24; *Ulozhenie*, 19: 13, 18.

19. Stashevskii, "Sluzhiloe," pp. 5–6.

20. Some scholars have contended that the towns were reservoirs of opposition to serfdom after 1649 and that these forces suffered a series of setbacks at the end of the century (Volkov, "O stanovlenii," pp. 98–99, 103). More study is needed on this topic, particularly, I should think, on the question of whether these forces opposed the corporate privileges which went along with the stratified Russian society.

21. *AMG*, 2, no. 1004; Kalinychev, *Pravovye*, p. 121.

22. *AMG*, 3, no. 541.

23. Ibid., 2, nos. 898, 921. For a variation—servicemen being able to collect their renumeration directly from court peasants—see ibid., 3, no. 541.

24. Ibid., 2, nos. 942, 1114.

25. Kliuchevskii, *Sochineniia*, 3: 353–54; Volkov, "O stanovlenii," pp. 101–2.

26. Stashevskii, "Sluzhiloe," pp. 5–6.

27. *AMG*, 3, no. 157.

28. Chernov, *Vooruzhennye*, pp. 157–58.

29. Zaozerskii, "K" voprosu," pp. 340, 349–52. Some Soviet historians offer another explanation for the demise of the Assembly of the Land. "Achieving their goal of enserfing the peasantry, the gentry cooled toward the Zemskii Sobor. They were now much more interested in the strengthening of the central and local power apparatus to guarantee the real fruits of exploiting the enserfed peasantry. Having satisfied the desires of the basic mass of the lay lords and the upper stratum of the urban population, tsarism got the possibility of running the country without the assistance of estate-representative institutions" (Indova et al., "Narodnye," p. 83). See also Cherepnin, "Zemskie," pp. 132–33. I should prefer to emphasize positive government action in recognition of the obsolescence of the middle service class. See Shapiro, "Mnogotomnaia," pp. 147–48.

30. P. P. Smirnov, "Ekonomicheskaia," 3: 409–10.

31. Bogoslovskii, *Zemskoe*, 1: 60.

32. P. P. Smirnov, "Knigi stroel'nye," pp. 109–10; *Posadskie liudi*, 2: 346–50, 371–81, 655, 664.

33. Smirnov, "Ekonomicheskaia," p. 410; Man'kov, *Razvitie*, pp. 261–63.

34. Aleksandrov, *Gosudarstvo*, p. 30.

35. See also Lialina, "K kharakteristike," pp. 400–401; Kapterev, *Istoriia*, 2: 164–68; Arkhangel'skii, *O sobornom" Ulozhenii*, pp. 23, 140–41; Shapiro, "Volneniia," pp. 300, 303; Man'kov, "Epizod," pp. 283, 287; Gnevushev, "Zemlevladenie," p. 294; Ustiugov and Chaev, "Russkaia tserkov'," pp. 300–301.

36. Ustiugov and Chaev, "Russkaia tserkov'," p. 305.

37. Novosel'skii, "Dela," pp. 151–52, 155.

38. Other reforms of the early 1650s, such as the repeal of the vicious farming of taverns, were undone in the 1660s (*SGGD*, 3, no. 173; P. P. Smirnov, "Ekonomicheskaia," pp. 409–10). In general, the Muscovite governments could be flexible, innovative, or reactionary when they wanted to.

39. Ustiugov, "Evoliutsiia," pp. 155–57; Billington, *Icon and Axe*, pp. 675–76; Collins, *Present State*, p. 45; Ustiugov and Chaev, "Russkaia tserkov'," pp. 306–24; Baklanova, "Dela," p. 319; *SGGD*, 3, no. 140.

40. Beliaev, *Krest'iane* (1903), pp. 150–54, 180–82; Tikhonov, "Krest'ianskaia," p. 274. See also chapter 8. The institutional historian A. D. Gradovskii attributed the severity of Russian serfdom to the fact that a provincial gentry with power and interest in the countryside did not develop in Muscovy. Rather, the government based its power on what I have called the Moscow upper service class. The result was that no lord desired to stay in the provinces, because all prestige lay in Moscow service. Lords did not stay in the provinces and cultivate ties and common interests with the peasants, whom the lords were willing to see degraded ("Vysshaia," 1: 58–59). Such a view impresses me as being overly romantic.

41. Lialina, "K kharakteristike," pp. 403–4.

42. Engel'man, *Istoriia*, p. 83; Vorms, ed., *Pamiatniki*, no. 49.

43. Lialina, "K kharakteristike," p. 399; Man'kov, *Razvitie*, pp. 29–34; Zanicheva, "Krest'ianskie pobegi," p. 235; Troitskii, "Finansovaia," p. 283; Zanicheva, "Sotial'no-ekonomicheskoe," p. 205; Novosel'skii, "Pobegi," pp. 329, 332, 336; idem, "Otdatochnye," pp. 130, 133. Government agents returned hundreds, sometimes over a thousand, peasants each in less than a year ("Pobegi," p. 334). They looked for fugitive slaves at the same time. One agent alone caught and returned eight thousand fugitives (Bulygin, "Beglye," pp. 131, 133–34, 149). Other major searches for runaways were conducted in the 1670s, 1683, 1692–94, and in 1698 (Gudzinskaia, "Dokumenty," p. 107). See a list of fugitive serf-hunters, their times and places of activity, in Man'kov, *Razvitie*, pp. 84–89. It can hardly be accidental that practically every one of the above dates coincided with or immediately followed a major crisis.

44. Buganov and Chistiakova, "O nekotorykh voprosakh istorii," pp. 44, 46–47; Koretskii, "K istorii vosstaniia Bolotnikova," p. 128; Buganov and Chistiakova, "O nekotorykh," p. 44. As always, there were exceptions from the general rule. Thus a few *deti boiarskie* with no or very small service estates and no or few serfs in the south continued to resent the activities of the magnates and sided with the rebellious peasants—whom they in many respects resembled anyway (Indova, "Narodnye," p. 63). They also probably were expressing resentment against their low status and army life in general, particularly in the new formation regiments.

45. Aleksandrov, *Gosudarstvo*, p. 43; Pronshtein, "K istorii pokhoda," p. 251.

46. Man'kov, "Krugi," p. 266; Indova et al., "Narodnye," pp. 60–62.

47. Koretskii, "K istorii vosstaniia Bolotnikova," pp. 127, 129; idem, "Novye dokumenty," pp. 68, 79–80; idem, "Novoe o Bolotnikove," p. 101; Indova et al., "Narodnye," pp. 53–54, 83; Kazakov, "Bor'ba," pp. 42, 50, 53; A. M. Sakharov, *Obrazovanie*, pp. 123, 125.

48. Novosel'skii, "Pobegi," p. 328; Indova et al., "Narodnye," pp. 57–58. The hatred which Boris Morozov evoked among the servicemen and others is evident in a legal case of October, 1650, to March, 1651. A *syn boiarskii* and a priest were denounced for referring to the Moscow riot and for speaking ill of the boyars, of Morozov in particular, who was called a "criminal" (*vor*, maybe even "traitor") (*AMG*, 2, no. 444).

49. A. M. Sakharov, *Obrazovanie*, p. 162; Zimin and Preobrazhenskii, "Izuchenie," p. 146; Buganov and Chistiakova, "O nekotorykh," p. 46; Indova et al., "Narodnye," pp. 58–59. For a clear case of class conflict in 1661, see *AMG*, 3 no. 533. The document spells out how peasants deserted their lord at the front, went to Moscow, and there looted and destroyed his home. A. A. Novosel'skii linked the fusion of middle and upper service class interests against the peasantry with the Time of Troubles ("Pobegi," p. 327). This interpretation does not seem to correspond with the facts.

50. Volkov, "O stanovlenii," p. 97. The church schism and Westernization widened the gap even further.

51. Buganov and Chistiakova, "O nekotorykh voprosakh istorii," pp. 42, 44; Mavrodin, "Sovetskaia" (1966), pp. 314, 318; idem, "Sovetskaia" (1967), pp. 71, 76–77;

idem, "Feodal'naia Rossiia," p. 180; *OIIN*, 4:300; Preobrazhenskii, "Ural," p. 289; Tominskii, *Ocherki*, pp. 183–86; Stepanov, *Krest'ianskaia*, pp. 11, 13, 17, 22, 25–31; A. M. Sakharov, *Obrazovanie*, pp. 184–85; Man'kov, "Liudvig Fabritsius," p. 204; idem, "Krugi," pp. 266–73; Buganov and Chistiakova, "O nekotorykh voprosakh," pp. 42, 44; Tikhonov, "Krest'ianskaia," pp. 272, 275; Pronshtein, "K istorii pokhoda," p. 262; Baklanova, "Dela," p. 310. This point is emphasized in a tercentenary biography of Razin (V. I. Buganov, "Stepan Timofeevich Razin," *Istoriia SSSR* 16, no. 2 [March–April 1971]: 67).

52. Shapiro, "Ob absoliutizme," pp. 77, 79; Novosel'skii, "Pobegi," p. 327; *Tul'skii krai*, 1:63–64; Buganov and Chistiakova, "O nekotorykh," p. 47; Pronshtein, "K istorii pokhoda," p. 260; Probrazhenskii, "Ural," pp. 283–84. Occasionally the wealthy peasants joined the government forces against the masses (Tikhonov, "Krest'-ianskaia," pp. 278, 281).

53. Borisov, "Tserkov'," pp. 76–82.

54. Tikhonov, "Krest'ianskaia," p. 276.

55. Novoselskii, "Pobegi," p. 344; Man'kov, *Razvitie*, pp. 50–53, 111. The general Soviet view is that any peasant uprising is an important contribution to progress and the advancement of humanity (Kompan, "V. I. Lenin," pp. 298–99). In light of actual Russian experience, this is hard to believe.

56. Kirillov, "Noveishaia," pp. 133–34; Tomsinskii, *Ocherki*, p. 208.

57. Ustiugov, "Volneniia," pp. 286–88, 290–92; Baklanova, "Dela," p. 320; L. V. Cherepnin, "Klassovaia bor'ba v 1682 g. na iuge Moskovskogo gosudarstva," *Istoricheskie zapiski* 4 (1938): 41–75.

58. The gentry militia played the major role in the suppression of the *strelets* uprising in Moscow in 1682 (Ustiugov, "Volneniia," pp. 290–94). The Leningrad historian A. L. Shapiro sees in this a major cause of the development of "absolutism" in Russia: the gentry supported the central power in exchange for the suppression of protest by the masses ("Mnogotomnaia," p. 147). Similar views are expressed by another writer on "absolutism," A. N. Chistozvonov ("Nekotorye aspekty," p. 57).

59. Sh., "Dvorianstvo," no. 3, p. 204; *PSZ*, 1, no. 39; ibid., 2, nos. 767, 966, 1229.

60. V. I. Buganov, "Kto byl glavnym predvoditelem 'mednogo bunta' 1662 g. v Moskve?" *Voprosy istorii* 40, no. 3 (March 1965):209; Maierberg, *Puteshestvie*, p. 179; Collins, *Present State*, pp. 105–6; Ustiugov, "Evoliutsiia," p. 155; Kurts, "Sostoianie," p. 93. The contemporary Grigorii Kotoshikhin reported that Miloslavskii himself was not counterfeiting, but that he was taking bribes from those who were (*O Rossii*, 7: 9). On the fear of disorder, see Zaozerskii, *Tsar'*, pp. 328, 332–34.

61. Collins, *Present State*, pp. 120–21. For a brief period (1666–70) N. I. Odoevskii assumed a leading position in the government. He was a "man of very limited talents" (Ustiugov, "Evoliutsiia," p. 155; Bakhrushin, "Moskovskoe," 2: 68).

62. Ordin-Nashchokin did curtail in 1667 the manhunts for fugitive peasants so ardently pushed by the gentry (Volkov, "O stanovlenii," p. 100). This temporarily vitiated the effectiveness of the enserfment, but did nothing to roll it back. The Razin uprising renewed the pre-1667 momentum.

63. Gradovskii, "Vysshaia," 1: 69; P. P. Smirnov, "Ekonomicheskaia," p. 404; A. M. Sakharov, *Obrazovanie*, p. 154; Aleksandrov, *Gosudarstvo*, pp. 7, 22; Zagorovskii, *Belgorodskaia*, pp. 95, 102; Kurts, "Sostoianie," p. 92.

64. Zaozerskii, *Tsar'*, pp. 190, 334–45.

65. Novosel'skii, "Pobegi," pp. 346–51; Man'kov, "Krest'ianskii," pp. 14–15, 17, 21–23, 34; Lialina, "K kharakteristike," p. 400.

66. Man'kov, *Razvitie*, pp. 124–27; Novosel'skii, "Dela," p. 154; "Pobegi," pp. 342–43; Bulygin, "Beglye," pp. 134–35. The 1692 response by the new Naryshkin administration to a gentry petition of 1691 for the return of fugitives reconfirmed the 1675 decree (Man'kov, *Razvitie*, pp. 74–76, 150–54).

67. Aleksandrov, "Streletskoe," p. 241.

68. D'iakonov, *Ocherki* (1926), p. 282; Man'kov, *Razvitie*, pp. 271–89.

69. D'iakonov, *Ocherki sel'skago*, pp. 50, 70.

70. *AI*, 4, no. 60.

71. Novosel'skii, "Pobegi," pp. 329–30, 332. Those who served in the army also learned to ask for cash from the state to enable them to serve (*AMG*, 2, no. 1004). This lessened the reliance on peasant support.

72. Man'kov, "Pobegi," p. 56. Yet Man'kov denies there was any substantive divergence of interest between the magnates and the rank-and-file gentry after the *Ulozhenie* (*Razvitie*, pp. 35–36, 53–54, 132). Cf. Volkov, "O stanovlenie," pp. 96–97. In 1682, however, when the surviving gentry forces were the only ones available for suppressing the disorders in Moscow and elsewhere, the government again bowed to demands for renewal of the manhunts for fugitive peasants (ibid., p. 101).

73. Selifontov, *Ocherk"*, pp. 16–18, 84–87.

74. Bell, *Radical Right*, p. 73. The well-known slavish passivity of the members of Muscovite society was commented on by nearly all Western visitors from the sixteenth century on. They particularly marvelled at the willingness of even the most highly placed individuals to abuse themselves as "slaves" before their sovereign— an attitude alien to modern European thought. (For example, see Coyet, *Posol'stvo*, p. 486.) This subservience unquestionably had many causes: the absence of a notion of individualism or human dignity in medieval Russian thought, the willingness of the authorities to mete out violence to deviants, the exaltation of the autocratic power, particularly in the reigns of Vasilii III and Ivan IV. However, the actions of the rising middle service class in the first half of the seventeenth century and the triumph of that class at the Assembly of the Land in 1648–49, combined with the newness of the elected Romanov dynasty and the introduction of at least the rudiments of Western notions of individualism and human dignity (see chapter 7, n. 62), would seem to be grounds for an expectation of the breaklown of the slave mentality, at least among the privileged elements. This did not occur, thanks, I believe, to a combination of the enserfment with the triumph of the magnates over the rest of society and with the other factors discussed here.

75. Novosel'skii, "Pobegi," pp. 333, 335–36; idem, "Otdatochnye," p. 132; Arkhangel'-skii, *O sobornom" Ulozhenii*, pp. 131–32.

76. Billington, *Icon and Axe*, p. 155. A monastery founded by Nikon violated with impunity the laws of the *Ulozhenie* on relations ·with townsmen (Man'kov, "Epizod," pp. 284–85).

77. Lialina, "K kharakteristike," p. 403; Novosel'skii, "Pobegi," p. 337; Baklanova, "Dela," p. 314.

78. Gudzinskaia, "Dokumenty," p. 109.

79. Vorms, ed., *Pamiatniki*, nos. 50, 52, 53; Baklanova, "Dela," p. 317; Man'kov, *Razvitie*, pp. 42–43; Novosel'skii, "Pobegi," pp. 343–45. Novosel'skii claims that the four-for-one fugitive decree was only a tactical move by the government, which was in trouble in 1682 (ibid., p. 344). Neither Novosel'skii nor Man'kov found any instances where the four-for-one provision was enforced ("Otdatochnye," p. 142; *Razvitie*, p. 117). I. A. Bulygin found only one instance of any extra peasants being demanded of lords guilty of harboring fugitives ("Beglye," p. 137). Gudzinskaia found two such instances ("Dokumenty," p. 111).

80. Novosel'skii, "Pobegi," p. 345; Man'kov, *Razvitie*, pp. 42, 55–56, 66–67; Vorms, ed., *Pamiatniki*, no. 54.

81. Zanicheva, "Krest'ianskie pobegi," p. 233.

82. Novosel'skii, "Kollektivnye," pp. 105–8.

83. Shapiro, "Volneniia," p. 318.

84. Ustrialov, *Istoriia*, 1: 399.

85. Gnevushev, "Zemlevladenie," pp. 291–92.

86. Vodarskii, "Sluzhiloe," pp. 234–37; Shepukova, "K voprosu," p. 145.

87. *Tul'skii krai*, 1:62; Man'kov, *Razvitie*, pp. 28–29.

88. Novosel'skii, "Pobegi," pp. 327, 329, 332.

89. Novosel'skii, "Otdatochnye," p. 147.

90. It is difficult to imagine that members of the old service classes "were conscious of their strength and how much the government needed them" in the 1660's and later, as A. A. Novosel'skii maintained ("Pobegi," p. 331).

91. Indova et al., "Narodnye," p. 81; Shapiro, "Volneniia," p. 301; Ustiugov, "Volneniia," pp. 284, 287. In the sixteenth century boyar lands were very fragmented. The process of concentrating them into latifundia began in the seventeenth century, which would have permitted closer supervision of the peasants and a level of exploitation above the traditional and customary (Veselovskii, *Feodal'noe*, pp. 146–50).

92. Bobrovskii, *Perekhod"*, p. 86.

93. The Russian population grew at the rate of about 1 percent per year in the seventeenth century, as it had in the first half of the sixteenth century (Kopanev, "Naselenie," p. 242).

94. In fact, as we know, the plague of 1654 wiped out much of Russia's urban population (*AMG*, 2, nos. 786, 792).

95. The government collected about 60,000 rubles per year in the reign of Mikhail from the *iasak*, the tribute (primarily furs) paid by the subject peoples of Siberia. This figure rose rapidly to about 100,000 rubles per year by the end of his reign and levelled off at that figure in the second half of the century (Miliukov, *Gosudarstvennoe*, p. 113). Roughly similar, if only slightly lower, figures are reported by the Soviet historian P. N. Pavlov, "Vyvoz pushniny," pp. 125, 133. Grigorii Kotoshikhin in the 1660s reported the sum was 600,000 rubles per year (*O Rossii*, 7: 7). For a discussion of this figure, see Uroff, "Kotoshikhin," pp. 460–61.

Soviet historians are wont to overlook the enormous dimensions of the genocidal plunder of the Siberian natives by their Muscovite conquerors and talk of this tribute in terms of "trade" (S. V. Bakhrushin, "Iasak v Sibiri v XVII v.," *Nauchnye Trudy*, 4 vols. in 5 parts [Moscow: Akademiia Nauk SSSR, 1952–59], 3, pt. 2, pp. 75–81). About 25,000 rubles per year had to be expended by the Russian government in an attempt to buy peace in the first half of the seventeenth century with the Crimean Tatars (Novosel'skii, *Bor'ba*, p. 442). Kotoshikhin reported 20,000 rubles (*O Rossii*, 4: 37).

96. Ogrizko, "Zernovoe," p. 31; Prokov'eva, " 'Khlebnyi," p. 106; Indova, "Urozhai," pp. 144–45.

97. In Eastern Europe, including Russia, rye yields dropped 10 percent in the first half of the seventeenth century; in the second half of the century wheat yields dropped 27.8 percent, barley yields 31 percent, and oat yields 25.8 percent. The winters were very cold in the years 1651–80 (B. H. Slicher van Bath, "The Yields of Different Crops [Mainly Cereals] in Relation to the Seed c. 810–1820," *Acta Historiae Neerlandica* [Leiden: E. J. Brill, 1967], pp. 62, 101; on Russia specifically, see p. 61). See also Liashchenko, *Istoriia*, 1:232.

98. Shapiro, "Mnogotomnaia," p. 145; Sakharov, *Obrazovanie*, p. 136. On the other hand, S. M. Troitskii offers the suggestion that the government could increase taxes because of a rise of peasant productivity in this period. He tempers this with the observation that real taxes may not have risen very much in the seventeenth century because of a 25 percent inflation ("O vliianii," p. 289). The seventeenth century also witnessed the development of artificial barriers to increased agricultural output (Z. A. Ogrizko, "Vliianie feodal'no-krepostnicheskoi sistemy na razvitie khoziaistva chernososhnykh krest'ian v XVII veke," in *Voprosy agrarnoi istorii. Materialy nauchnoi konferentsii po istorii sel'skogo khoziaistva i krest'ianstva Evropeiskogo Severa SSSR. Gor. Vologda, 15–17 iunia 1967 g.* [Vologda, 1968], pp. 437, 439–41).

99. Bobrovskii, *Perekhod"*, p. iv. Arms imports were paid for to a considerable extent by grain exports, which Russia could not always afford. Popular resistance to forced grain exporting demanded by foreign customers led to the great uprisings in Pskov and Novgorod in 1649 and 1650 (Iakubov, "Rossiia," 186: 290–387, 405–6, 440, 471–74; M. N. Tikhomirov, *Pskovskoe vosstanie 1650 goda* [Moscow-Leningrad: Akademiia Nauk SSSR, 1935]).

100. Bobrovskii, *Perekhod"*, p. 105.

101. Miliukov, *Ocherki* (1900), 1:131, 134; Bobrovskii, *Perekhod"*, pp. 91–92; Klokman, "Severnaia," p. 77. See S. G. Strumilin's reservations below, note 109.

102. Mavrodin, *Klassovaia*, p. 160. M. S. Aleksandrov said the tsar could not do anything to benefit the peasants because they were subject to their individual lords, of whom the sovereign happened to be only one (*Gosudarstvo*, p. 19). This is part of the theory that the immunity charters only confirmed the obvious and evolved into "votchina law"; that state power did not exist and that the peasants were not enserfed by law.

103. This is not to deny that "the service gentry did not desire an increase of its service burden and therefore hindered attempts of the state to convert it into a standing army" (Volkov, "O stanovlenii," p. 97). This has been discussed in chapter 12.

104. This interpretation does not coincide with the view advanced by some Soviet scholars that "the gentry was the ruling class" (Kagengaus and Preobrazhenskii, "Problemy," p. 157). Such a view is not exactly the same as the contention that "the gentry is the class base of the absolute power, it monopolizes power in the army and in the state administrative apparatus" (Razin, *Istoriia*, 3:21). Certainly the gentry had no such monopoly in Muscovy in the second half of the seventeenth century. It is also difficult to comprehend the contention that "the pre-Petrine army failed to meet the needs of the reigning gentry class" (Klokman, "Severnaia," p. 74). If anything, it was the autocratic state, ruled by the tsar and his advisers, which shortchanged by the new system. The gentry got much of the state labor fund assigned to themselves, a privilege far out of proportion to the services they were providing for the state.

105. Shapiro, "Ob absoliutizme," p. 74. Many Soviet scholars have assumed that there was an identity between serfdom and absolute monarchy (Danilova, "Stanovlenie," pp. 91, 98, 111). A. M. Sakharov ignores the developments of the seventeenth century and does not credit an important role to the bureaucracy until the eighteenth century. "The changes were so significant that the autocracy of the seventeenth century and the autocracy of the eighteenth century were 'not like' one another" ("Lenin ob osnovnykh," p. 312). See a critique of this view by A. A. Zimin ("Problemy," p. 322).

There is no doubt that the state administration did not achieve Weberian bureaucratic perfection in the seventeenth century. A strict system of subordination of lower organs to higher ones was not worked out. The competence of chancelleries was not clearly defined, and officials did not have independence in decision-making (Ustiugov, "Evoliutsiia," p. 167). M. S. Aleksandrov attributed considerable power to the seventeenth-century Muscovite bureacracy, which limited the tsar's power by not submitting everything to him for his decision (*Gosudarstvo*, p. 27). Nevertheless, the government was a very responsive tool in the hands of the autocrat.

106. Marc Raeff, ed., *Peter the Great* (Boston: Heath, 1963), p. 68; Romanovich-Slavatinskii, *Dvorianstvo*, p. 121; Kliuchevskii, *Sochineniia*, 4: 76.

107. Pavlov-Sil'vanskii, *Gosudarevy* (1909), pp. 239–42; *Khrestomatiia . . . XVIII v.*, p. 85; *PSZ*, 4: no. 1900; ibid., 5, nos. 2673, 3245, 3295; Romanovich-Slavatinskii, *Dvorianstvo*, pp. 117, 134. See also chapter 13 above.

108. Vodarskii, "Chislennost' posadskogo," p. 280.

109. Aleksandrov, *Gosudarstvo*, p. 37; Romanovich-Slavatinskii, *Dvorianstvo*, p. 153. Roughly 75 percent of the Petrine budget went to the armed forces (Troitskii, "Finansovaia," pp. 295, 305, 310). S. G. Strumilin recalculated P. N. Miliukov's budget figures for 1680 and 1724 and concluded that expenditures increased was three-fold, but only by 73 percent. Per capita, the burden actually declined by 15 percent in the same period because of the rise in population (*Ocherki ekonomicheskoi istorii Rossii i SSSR* [Moscow: Nauka, 1966], pp. 307, 309). This is not to say, of course, that the populace flourished because of the Petrine reforms.

110. Kliuchevskii, *Sochineniia*, 4:91; *PRP*, 8:247. Other explanations, for which I have no evidence, might be that Peter associated Pososhkov's suggestion with the similar proposal which had been drawn up by Golitsyn, the lover of Peter's discredited and deposed half-sister Sofia. The move might have been considered too radical a break with tradition, a move which would unnecessarily undermine his regime domestically. Also, Peter may have valued the gentry as a police force in the provinces to suppress peasant unrest and Old Believer sentiment, particularly after the Bulavin uprising of 1707–9 (Mavrodin, *Klassovaia*, p. 161; E. P. Pod"iapol'skaia, *Vosstanie Bulavina 1707—1709* [Moscow: Akademiia Nauk SSSR, 1962]). A leader of the Bulavin disturbances had participated in the Razin uprising (Indova et al., "Narodnye," pp. 67–68).

111. Vorms, ed., *Pamiatniki*, no. 89; Romanovich-Slavatinskii, *Dvorianstvo*, p. 299; Makovskii, *Razvitie*, p. 237; Indova et al., "Narodnye," p. 85.

112. Romanovich-Slavatinskii, *Dvorianstvo*, pp. 5–6; Dukes, *Catherine*, p. 134. Another interpretation of the 1762 decree on state service holds that it was not a victory of the nobility over the state, but a declaration of independence by the state from the nobility (Raeff, *Origins*, pp. 94, 109, 113). Professor Raeff views the manifesto of February 18, 1762, as part of the government's desire to regularize the service of civilian officials, to create the basis for a bureaucracy. Rationalizing the state with the aid of Germans and the army required dispensing "with the unwilling services of those nobles who might prefer to mind their estates or to lead a life of cultured leisure" (Raeff, "Domestic," pp. 1293–94, 1309).

There may be some truth in this interpretation, but only with qualifications. I have made similar remarks about the "inability" of the government of Tsar Aleksei to force the old middle service class and the *pomest'e* system to function, once the conversion to the new army under the foreign mercenaries had been fairly well effected; the effort was not worth making. However, I believe I have shown that seventeenth-century developments were largely responses to middle service class desires and pressures.

I should expect the same to be true of the brief reign of Peter III. The problem is lack of evidence. While the "Manifesto on the Freedom of the Nobility" may not have been "a direct response to the demands of the nobility," telling the nobility that they could "continue their service according to their [own] wish for as long and wherever they want [ed] to" can certainly be seen as an attempt to anticipate and pander to the desires of the gentry (quotations from ibid., pp. 1292–93). Peter III was one of the few rulers of eighteenth-century Russia to take the throne legally without the support of a palace clique. He and his advisers must have been aware of his tenuous position. If they had plans to modernize the government, they also should have realized the shock that a rule of rationality and Germans (as in the 1730s) would produce. One way to head off the inevitable opposition would be to give the gentry something, such as the legal exemption from service, that the ruling clique felt was desired and would be appreciated.

We also might remember that Boris Godunov halved the service requirement in 1604 in his search for support. Boris could not abolish it completelv because he had no alternative servicemen. Peter III did. Besides, he knew many Russians would have to continue to serve simply for the income.

113. Raeff, "Domestic," pp. 1291, 1294.

114. Sh., "Dvorianstvo," no. 3, p. 427; Romanovich-Slavatinskii, *Dvorianstvo*, p. 277. Ten to fifteen years of gentry service would hardly seem to justify the continuation of serfdom, especially by comparison with the lifetime service demanded in Muscovy and by Peter I. In 1809 M. M. Speranskii felt that the gentry should render not less than ten years of civil or military service, whichever they chose (*Proekty i zapiski*, ed. S. N. Valk [Moscow-Leningrad: Akademiia Nauk SSSR, 1961], p. 186).

If Professor Raeff's view of the 1762 manifesto were totally correct, then the persistence of serfdom was an even greater contradiction than I assume. If the state power was really so independent, then it also should have reasserted its authority over its peasant subjects and its claim to their surplus product much earlier than it eventually did in the nineteenth century.

115. Mavrodin, *Krest'ianskaia*, 1:524–25. Even some of the gentry delegates at the 1767 Legislative Commission were aware of the contradiction (Dukes, *Catherine*, p. 158).

116. Ibid., p. 159.

117. Kabuzan, *Narodonaselenie*, pp. 153–54; Alexander, *Autocratic*, p. 251.

118. Mavrodin, *Klassovaia*, pp. 162–65; Dukes, *Catherine*, pp. 97, 113, 124; Pipes, *Karamzin's Memoir*, p. 166.

119. Mavrodin, *Klassovaia*, pp. 166–70, 173–76; idem, *Krest'ianskaia*, 1: 529–55; Romanovich-Slavatinskii, *Dvorianstvo*, pp. 372–75; Dukes, *Catherine*, pp. 87, 92, 99, 105, 120, 124, 229–30; Alexander, *Autocratic Politics*, p. 35.

The peasant question on the eve of the *Pugachevshchina* has been the subject of numerous source publications, articles, a doctoral dissertation, and a book by M. T. Beliavskii: *Krest'ianskii vopros v Rossii nakanune vosstaniia E. I. Pugacheva* (*Formirovanie antikrepostnicheskoi mysli*) (Moscow: MGU, 1965); "Novye dokumenty ob obsuzhdenii krest'ianskogo voprosa v 1766–1768 gg.," *Arkheograficheskii ezhegodnik za 1958 god* 2 (1960): 387–430; "Dokumenty ob obsuzhdenii krest'ianskogo voprosa v Vol'nom ekonomicheskom obshchestve v 1767–1768 gg.," *Arkheograficheskii ezhegodnik za 1960 god* 4 (1962): 345–66; "Obsuzhdenie krest'ianskogo voprosa nakanune krest'ianskoi voiny pod predvoditel'stvom E. I. Pugacheva," in *Ezhegodnik po agrarnoi istorii Vostochnoi Evropy za 1960 g.* (Kiev: AN USSR, 1962), pp. 307–19.

Beliavskii's 1964 doctoral defense was an interesting example of the old split between the Petersburg-Leningrad "factual school" and the Moscow "dogma school" of Russian historiography. During the examination, Mavrodin criticized Beliavskii's interpretation on factual grounds. Beliavskii got up, shot his fist into the air, shouted, "Lenin said that was the case, and I'm with Lenin," and sat down.

120. Dukes, *Catherine*, p. 105; Alexander, *Autocratic Politics*, p. 38.

121. Chistov, *Russkie narodnye*, pp. 136–95; Alexander, *Autocratic*, p. 35.

122. Romanovich-Slavatinskii, *Dvorianstvo*, pp. 360–61; Kashtanov, "Krest'ianstvo," pp. 127, 137; Pronshtein, "Reshennye," p. 161. Soviet historians see the uprisings after 1762 only as the climax of a trend beginning in the late 1740s. The trend declined while the peasants waited to see what the Legislative Commission would do (Indova et al., "Narodnye," pp. 74–76). For a recent analysis of the *Pugachevshchina*, see Marc Raeff, "Pugachev's Rebellion," in *Preconditions of Revolution in Early Modern Europe*, edited by Robert Forster and Jack P. Greene (Baltimore: The Johns Hopkins Press, 1970), pp. 161–202.

123. Dukes, *Catherine*, pp. 117, 232; Alexander, *Autocratic*, pp. 196, 202, 209, 211.

124. Romanovich-Slavatinskii, *Dvorianstvo*, pp. 362, 377; Mavrodin, *Klassovaia*, p. 176; Indova et al., "Narodnye," p. 88.

125. Dukes, *Catherine*, pp. 105–6; Alexander, *Autocratic*, p. 34; A. I. Andrushchenko, *Krest'ianskaia voina 1773–1775 gg.* (Moscow: Nauka, 1969), pp. 315, 323. A. V. Romanovich-Slavatinskii offered another explanation, attributing the fact that the peasants were not freed after 1762 to the indecisiveness of the government, the low level of a gentry interested only in its own material interests, and the insufficiency of provincial administration (*Dvorianstvo*, p. 369). Alexander Gerschenkron has offered the hypothesis that the problem of serfdom was not attacked after 1762 at least partially because the institutional legacy of the Petrine reforms proved adequate to maintain Russia's international position until the Crimean War forced a reevaluation by the government of the social order (*Continuity in History and Other Essays* [Cambridge, Massachusetts: Harvard University Press, The Belknap Press, 1968], pp. 143, 146).

126. Alfred J. Rieber, *The Politics of Autocracy* (The Hague: Mouton, 1966), pp. 15–29; idem, "Alexander II: A Revisionist View," *The Journal of Modern History* 43, no. 1 (March 1971) : 47–48.

127. Nicholas I also had ideas about restoring the service state. A new service class was not instituted until after 1917. I am foregoing at this point a discussion of what seems to be a third "service class cycle" because it might lend a political overtone to this work. I do not desire it to have.

128. During the Time of Troubles Vasilii Shuiskii granted concessions to the townsmen, and perhaps the court peasants, to win their support (Nosov, "Belozerskaia," p. 52) . See also *AMG*, 2, no. 695 (1655) .

129. As I understand it, a similar position has been advanced by the Soviet scholar M. Ia. Volkov, "O stanovlenii," p. 91.

130. P. Mikhailov, "Obychnyi institut"," pp. 77–78; "Novootkrytye dokumenty," p. 390.

Abbreviations of Works Cited

AAE. *Akty, sobrannye v" bibliotekakh" i arkhivakh" Rossiiskoi imperii Arkheograficheskoiu ekspeditseiu imp. Akademii nauk".* 4 vols. + index. St. Petersburg, 1836, 1858.

AFZ. *Akty feodal'nogo zemlevladeniia i khoziaistva XIV-XVI vekov.* 3 vols. Moscow: Akademiia Nauk SSSR, 1951–61.

AI. *Akty istoricheskie, sobrannyia i izdannyia Arkheograficheskoiu kommissieiu.* 5 vols. + index. St. Petersburg, 1841–43.

AIu. *Akty iuridicheskie, ili Sobranie form" starinnago deloproizvodstva, izd. Arkheograficheskoi kommissii.* 1 vol. + index. St. Petersburg, 1838, 1840.

AIuB. *Akty, otnosiashchiesia do iuridicheskago byta drevnei Rossii, izdannyia Arkheograficheskoi kommissieiu.* 3 vols. + index. St. Petersburg, 1857, 1864, 1884, 1901.

AIuZR. *Akty, otnosiashchiesia k" istorii Iuzhnoi i Zapadnoi Rossii, sobrannyia i izdannyia Arkheograficheskoiu kommissieiu.* 15 vols. + supplements. St. Petersburg, 1863–92.

Akty Iushkova. *Akty XIII-XVII vv., predstavlennyia v" Razriadnyi prikaz" posle otmeny mestnichestva.* Published by A. Iushkov. Moscow, 1898.

Akty Morozova. *Akty khoziaistva boiarina B. I. Morozova.* Edited by A. I. Iakovlev. 2 vols. Moscow-Leningrad: Akademiia Nauk SSSR, 1940, 1945.

AMG. *Akty Moskovskago gosudarstva, izd. imp. Akademieiu nauk".* Ed. by N. A. Popov. 3 vols. St. Petersburg, 1890–1901.

ASEI. *Akty sotsial'no-ekonomicheskoi istorii Severo-Vostochnoi Rusi kontsa XIV-nachala XVI v.* 3 vols. Moscow-Leningrad: Akademiia Nauk SSSR, 1952–64.

AZR. *Akty, otnosiashchiesia k" istorii Zapadnoi Rossii, sobrannyia i izdannye Arkheograficheskoiu kommissieiu.* 5 vols. St. Petersburg, 1846–53.

ChOIDR. *Chteniia v" Obshchestve istorii i drevnostei rossiiskikh" pri Moskovskom" universitete. Sbornik".* Moscow. 1845–1918.

DAI. *Dopolneniia k" aktam" istoricheskim", sobrannyia i izdannyia Arkheograficheskoiu kommissieiu.* 12 vols. + index. St. Petersburg, 1846–75.

DDG. *Dukhovnye i dogovornye gramoty velikikh i udel'nykh kniazei XIV-XVI vv.* Edited by L. V. Cherepnin and S. V. Bakhrushin. Moscow-Leningrad: Akademiia Nauk SSSR, 1950.

DR. *Dvortsovye razriady, izdannye II-m" otdeleniem" sobstvennoi ego imp. velichestva kantseliarii.* 4 vols. St. Petersburg, 1850–1855.

GVNP. *Gramoty Velikogo Novgoroda i Pskova.* Edited by V. G. Geiman, S. N. Valk, et al. Moscow-Leningrad: Akademiia Nauk SSSR, 1949.

KR. *Knigi razriadnye po offitsial'nym" onykh" spiskam".* 2 vols. + index. St. Petersburg, 1853–56.

LS. *Litovskii Statut" v" moskovskom" perevode-redaktsii.* Edited by I. I. Lappo. Iur'ev, 1916.

LZAK. *Letopis' zaniatii Arkheograficheskoi kommissii.* 35 vols. St. Petersburg-Leningrad, 1862–1929.

Abbreviations

MIKR. *Materialy po istorii krest'ian v Rossii XI-XVII vv. Sbornik dokumentov.* Edited by V. V. Mavrodin. Leningrad: Leningradskii gosudarstvennyi universitet, 1958.

MS. *Muscovite Society.* Readings for Introduction to Russian Civilization, selected, edited, and translated by Richard Hellie. Chicago: Syllabus Division, The College, University of Chicago, 1967.

Ocherki. *Ocherki istorii SSSR.* 8 vols. Moscow: Akademiia Nauk SSSR, 1953–58.

OIIN. *Ocherki istorii istoricheskoi nauki v SSSR.* 5 vols. Moscow: Akademiia Nauk SSSR, 1955–71.

Opisanie MAMIu. *Opisanie dokumentov" i bumag", khraniashchikhsia v" Moskovskom" arkhive ministerstva iustitsii.* 21 vols. St. Petersburg, 1869–1921.

PRP. *Pamiatniki russkogo prava.* 8 vols. Moscow: Gosiurizdat, 1952–63.

PSRL. *Polnoe sobranie russkikh letopisei.* 31 vols. St. Petersburg-Moscow, 1846–1968.

PSZ. *Polnoe sobranie zakonov" Rossiiskoi imperii.* 45 vols. St. Petersburg, 1830.

RIB. *Russkaia istoricheskaia biblioteka.* 39 vols. St. Petersburg-Leningrad, 1872–1927.

RIZh. *Russkii istoricheskii zhurnal".* 8 vols. Petrograd, 1917–22.

RK. *Razriadnaia kniga 1475–1598 gg.* Edited by V. I. Buganov. Moscow: Nauka, 1966.

SGGD. *Sobranie gosudarstvennykh" gramot" i dogovorov".* 5 vols. St. Petersburg, 1813–94.

SIE. *Sovetskaia istoricheskaia entsiklopediia.* Moscow, 1961–.

TODRL. *Trudy Otdela drevnerusskoi literatury Instituta russkoi literatury (Pushkinskogo doma) AN SSSR.* Moscow-Leningrad, 1934–.

Trudy GIM. *Trudy gosudarstvennogo istoricheskogo muzeia.* Moscow, 1926–.

Trudy LOII. *Trudy leningradskogo otdeleniia Instituta istorii ANSSSR.* Leningrad, 1959–.

Trudy MGIAI. *Trudy moskovskogo gosudarstvennogo istoriko-arkhivnogo instituta.* Moscow, 1939–.

Trudy RANION. *Trudy rossiiskoi assotsiatsii nauchno-issledovatel'skikh institutov obshchestvennykh nauk.* 7 vols. Moscow, 1926–29.

UKPP. *Istoriko-iuridicheskie materialy, izd. Moskovskim" arkhivom" ministerstva iustitsii.* Vol. 1. *Ukaznaia kniga pomestnago prikaza.* Moscow, 1889.

Ulozhenie. There are many editions of this fundamental law code, but I prefer the following: M. N. Tikhomirov and P. P. Epifanov, eds. *Sobornoe Ulozhenie 1649 goda.* Moscow: Moskovskii Universitet, 1961.

VIRA. *Voprosy istorii religii i ateizma. Sbornik.* M., 1950–.

VUR. *Vossoedinenie Ukrainy s Rossiei. Dokumenty i materialy k 300-letiiu. 1654–1954.* Edited by P. P. Gudzenko et al. 3 vols. Moscow: Akademiia Nauk SSSR, 1953.

ZhMIu. *Zhurnal" ministerstva iustitsii.* St. Petersburg, 1894–1916.

ZhMNP. *Zhurnal" ministerstva narodnago prosveshcheniia.* St. Petersburg, 1834–1917.

Works Cited

Abramovich, G. V. "Novyi istochnik po istorii khlebnykh tsen v Rossii XVI v." *Istoriia SSSR* 13, no. 2 (March-April 1968) : 116–18.

Adrianov, S. "K" voprosu o krest'ianskom" prikreplenii." *Zhurnal" ministerstva narodnago prosveshcheniia* 297 (January 1895) : 239–51.

Alef, Gustave. "A History of the Muscovite Civil War: The Reign of Vasili II (1425–62) ." Ph.D. dissertation, Princeton University, 1956.

———. "Reflections on the Boyar Duma in the Reign of Ivan III." *The Slavonic and East European Review* 45, no. 104 (January 1967) : 76–123.

Aleksandrov, M. S. *Gosudarstvo, biurokratiia, i absoliutizm" v" istorii Rossii.* St. Petersburg, 1910.

Aleksandrov, V. A. "Streletskoe naselenie iuzhnykh gorodov Rossii v XVII v." *Novoe o proshlom nashei strany.* Moscow: Nauka, 1967, pp. 235–50.

Alekseev, Iu. G. "Chernaia volost' Kostromskogo uezda XV v." In *Krest'ianstvo i klassovaia bor'ba v feodal'noi Rossii.* Leningrad: Nauka, 1967, pp. 72–84.

———. "Kholop na pashne v svete dannykh toponomiki." In *Issledovaniia po otechestvennomu istochnikovedeniiu.* Moscow-Leningrad: Nauka, 1964, pp. 435–38.

Alekseeva, G. D. *Oktiabr'skaia revoliutsiia i istoricheskaia nauka (1917–1923 gg.).* Moscow: Nauka, 1968.

Al'shits, D. N. "Novyi dokument o liudiakh i prikazakh oprichnogo dvora Ivana Groznogo posle 1572 goda." *Istoricheskii arkhiv* 4 (1949) : 3–71.

Alexander, John T. *Autocratic Politics in a National Crisis: The Imperial Russian Government and Pugachev's Revolt. 1773–1775.* Bloomington: Indiana University Press, 1969.

Arendt, V. V. "K istorii srednevekovoi artillerii. (Genezis i razvitie konstruktsii kaznozariadnykh pushek XIV veka.)" *Arkhiv istorii nauki i tekhniki* 7 (1935) : 297–323.

Arkhangel'skii, M. *O sobornom" Ulozhenii Tsaria Alekseia Mikhailovicha 1649 (7158) g. v" otnoshenii k" pravoslavnoi russkoi tserkvi.* St. Petersburg, 1881.

Ayalon, David. *Gunpowder and Firearms in the Mamluk Kingdom. A Challenge to a Mediaeval Society.* London: Vallentine, Mitchel, 1956.

Babushkina, G. K. "Mezhdunarodnoe znachenie krymskikh pokhodov 1687 i 1689 gg." *Istoricheskie zapiski* 33 (1955) : 158–72.

Baiov, A. K. *Kurs" istorii russkago voennago iskusstva.* 7 vols. St. Petersburg, 1909–13.

———. *Natsional'nye cherty russkago voennago iskusstva v" Romanovskii period" nashei istorii.* St. Petersburg, 1913.

Bakhrushin, S. V. "Moskovskoe vosstanie 1648 g.," *Nauchnye trudy.* 4 vols. Moscow: Akademiia Nauk SSSR, 1952–59. 2: 46–91.

Baklanova, N. A. "Dela o syske beglykh krest'ian i kholopov kak istochnik dlia istorii tiaglogo sel'skogo naseleniia v Povolzh'e vo vtoroi polovine XVII v." *Problemy istochnikovedeniia* 11 (1963) : 307–21.

Works Cited

Baranovich, A. I. "K voprosu o zapustenii i zaselenii ukrainskikh zemel' v XVI–nachale XVIII v." In *Voprosy sotsial'no-ekonomicheskoi istorii i istochnikovedeniia perioda feodalizma v Rossii. Sbornik statei k 70-letiiu A. A. Novosel'skogo.* Moscow: Akademiia Nauk SSSR, 1961, pp. 40–42.

Barg, M. A. "Kontseptsiia feodalizma v sovremennoi burzhuaznoi istoriografii." *Voprosy istorii* 40, no. 1, (January 1965) :79–97.

Barg, M. A., and Skazkin, S. D. "Istoriia srednevekovogo krest'ianstva v Evrope i printsipy ee razrabotki." *Voprosy istorii* 42, no. 4 (April 1967) : 59–76.

Barsukov, A. P. "Dokladnaia vypiska 121 (1613) g. o votchinakh" i pomest'iakh"." *ChOIDR* 172, no. 1 (1895) :1–24.

Bazilevich, K. V. *Denezhnaia reforma Alekseia Mikhailovicha i vosstanie v Moskve v 1662 g.* Moscow-Leningrad: Akademiia Nauk SSSR, 1936.

———. "Novgorodskie pomeshchiki iz posluzhil'tsev v kontse XV veka." *Istoricheskie zapiski* 14 (1945) : 62–80.

Beliaev, I. D. *Krest'iane na Rusi. Izsledovanie o postepennom" izmenenii znacheniia krest'ian" v" russkom" obshchestve.* Moscow, 1879.

Bell, Daniel, ed. *The Radical Right.* Garden City, New York: Doubleday & Company, 1963.

Bennet, Douglas Joseph, Jr. "The Idea of Kingship in 17th Century Russia." Ph.D. dissertation, Harvard University, 1967.

Bernadskii, V. N. *Novgorod i Novgorodskaia zemlia v XV veke.* Moscow-Leningrad: Akademiia Nauk SSSR, 1961.

Berry, Lloyd E., and Crummey, Robert O., eds. *Rude & Barbarous Kingdom. Russia in the Accounts of Sixteenth-Century English Voyagers.* Madison: The University of Wisconsin Press, 1968.

Beskrovnyi, L. G. *Atlas kart i skhem po russkoi voennoi istorii.* Moscow: Voenizdat, 1946.

———. *Khrestomatiia po russkoi voennoi istorii.* Moscow: Voenizdat, 1947.

———. *Russkaia armiia i flota v XVIII veke (Ocherki).* Moscow: Voenizdat, 1958.

Bibikov, G. N. "Opyt voennoi reformy 1609–1610 gg." *Istoricheskie zapiski* 19 (1946) : 1–16.

Billington, James H. *The Icon and the Axe. An Interpretive History of Russian Culture.* London: Weidenfeld and Nicolson, 1966.

Black, Cyril E., ed. *Rewriting Russian History.* 2d ed. New York: Vintage Books, 1962.

Bloch, Marc. *French Rural History. An Essay on Its Basic Characteristics.* Berkeley and Los Angeles: University of California Press, 1970.

Blum, Jerome. *Lord and Peasant in Russia. From the Ninth to the Nineteenth Century.* Princeton: Princeton University Press, 1961.

Bobrovskii, P. O. *Perekhod" Rossii k" reguliarnoi armii.* St. Petersburg, 1885.

———. *Postoiannyia voiska i sostoianie voennago prava v" Rossii v" XVII stoletii po russkim" i inostrannym" pamiatnikam".* Moscow, 1882.

———. *Zachatki reform" v" voenno–ugolovnom" zakonodatel'stve v" Rossii.* St. Petersburg, 1882.

Bogoiavlenskii, S. K. *Prikaznye sud'i XVII veka.* Moscow-Leningrad: AN SSSR, 1946.

———. "Voisko v" Moskve v" XVI i XVII vv." in *Moskva v" eia proshlom" i nastoiashchem".* 12 vols. Moscow: Obrazovanie, 1910–1912. 4:62–84.

———. "Vooruzhenie russkikh voisk v XVI–XVII vv." *Istoricheskie zapiski* 4 (1938) :258–83.

Bogoslovskii, M. M. *Zemskoe samoupravlenie na russkom" severe v" XVII v.* 2 vols. Moscow, 1909, 1912.

Borisov, A. M. "Tserkov' i vosstanie pod rukovodstvom S. Razina." *Voprosy istorii* 40, no. 8 (August 1965) :74–83.

Bromlei, Iu. V. "Izuchenie problemy perekhoda ot feodalizma k kapitalizmu v Rossii (Nauchnaia sessiia v Moskve)." *Vestnik Akademii nauk SSSR* 35, no. 9 (September 1965) :114–16.

Bromlei, Iu. V.; Buganov, V. I.; and Koretskii, V. I. "Tsennoe issledovanie po istorii Zapadnoevropeiskogo krest'ianstva i problemy agrarnykh otnoshenii na vostoke Evropy." *Istoriia SSSR* 15, no. 1 (January-February 1970) :162–67.

Buchinskii, I. E. *O klimate proshlogo russkoi ravniny.* 2nd ed. Leningrad: Gidrometizdat, 1957.

Budovnits, I. U. *Monastyri na Rusi i bor'ba s nimi krest'ian v XIV–XVI vekakh (po "zhitiiam sviatykh").* Moscow: Nauka, 1966.

Buganov, V. I. " 'Gosudarev razriad' 1556 g. i. reformy 50-kh godov XVI v." *Istoriia SSSR* 1, no. 5 (1957) :220–31.

———. "Istochniki razriadnykh knig poslednei chetverti XV–nachala XVII v." *Istoricheskie zapiski* 76 (1965) :216–29.

———. *Moskovskoe vosstanie 1662 g.* Moscow: Nauka, 1964.

———. "O sostial'nom sostave uchastnikov Moskovskogo vosstaniia 1662 g." *Istoricheskie zapiski* 66 (1960) : 312–17.

———. "Opisanie moskovskogo vosstaniia 1648 g. v arkhivskom sbornike." *Istoricheskii arkhiv* 3, no. 4 (July-August 1957) :227–30.

———. "Osvoboditel'naia voina ukrainskogo i belorusskogo narodov v seredine XVII v. protiv inozemnogo ugneteniia. Vossoedinenie s Rossiei." In *Stranitsy boevogo proshlogo. Ocherki voennoi istorii Rossii.* Moscow: Nauka, 1968, pp. 56–72.

———. "Streletskoe vosstanie 1698 g. i nachalo likvidatsii streletskogo voiska." In *Voprosy voennoi istorii Rossii. XVIII i pervaia polovina XIX vekov.* Moscow: Nauka, 1969, pp. 45–53.

———. *Vosstanie 1662 g. v Moskve. Sbornik dokumentov.* Moscow: Nauka, 1964.

———. "Zasechnaia kniga 1638 g." *Zapiski otdela rukopisei biblioteki imeni Lenina* 23 (1960) :181–252.

Buganov, V. I., and Chistiakova, E. V. "O nekotorykh voprosakh istorii vtoroi krest'ianskoi voiny v Rossii." *Voprosy istorii* 43, no. 7 (July 1968) :36–51.

Buganov, V. I., and Koretskii, V. I. "Neizvestnyi moskovskii letopisets XVII veka iz muzeinogo sobraniia GBL." *Zapiski otdela rukopisei* 32 (1971) : 127–68.

Bulygin, I. A. "Beglye krest'iane Riazanskogo uezda v 60-e gody XVII v." *Istoricheskie zapiski* 42 (1953) :131–49.

Bulygin. I. A., et al. "Nachal'nyi etap genezisa kapitalizma v Rossii." *Voprosy istorii* 41, no. 10 (October 1966) : 65–90.

Burdei, G. D. "Molodinskaia bitva 1572 goda." *Uchenye zapiski instituta slavianovedeniia* 26 (1963) :48–79.

Chaev, N. S. "Iz istorii krest'ianskoi bor'by za zemliu v votchinakh Antonieva-Siiskogo monastyria v XVII v." *Istoricheskii arkhiv* 1 (1936) :25–65.

———. "K voprosu o syske i prikreplenii krest'ian v Moskovskom gosudarstve v kontse XVI v." *Istoricheskie zapiski* 6 (1940) :149–66.

Cherepnin, L. V. "Istoricheskie usloviia formirovaniia russkoi narodnosti do kontsa XV v." In *Voprosy formirovanii russkoi narodnosti i natsii. Sbornik statei.* Moscow-Leningrad: Akademiia Nauk SSSR, 1958, pp. 7–105.

Works Cited

——. "Iz istorii formirovaniia klassa feodal'no-zavisimogo krest'ianstva na Rusi." *Istoricheskie zapiski* 56 (1956) : 235–64.

——. *Novgorodskie berestianye gramoty kak istoricheskii istochnik.* Moscow: Nauka, 1969.

——. "Novye dokumenty o klassovoi bor'be v Novgorodskoi zemle v XIV-pervoi polovine XV v." In *Krest'ianstvo i klassovaia bor'ba v feodal'noi Rossii.* Leningrad: Nauka, 1967, pp. 42–54.

——. *Obrazovanie russkogo tsentralizovannogo gosudarstva v XIV-XV vekakh. Ocherki sotsial'noekonomicheskoi istorii Rusi.* Moscow: Sotsekgiz, 1960.

——. "Problema krest'ianskogo zakreposhcheniia v Rossii v osveshchenii burzhuaznoi istoriografii." In *Kritika burzhuaznykh kontseptsii istorii Rossii perioda feodalizma.* Moscow: Akademiia Nauk SSSR, 1962, pp. 55–108.

——. *Russkaia khronologiia.* Moscow, 1944.

——. *Russkie feodal'nye arkhivy XIV–XV vekov.* 2 vols. Moscow-Leningrad: AN SSSR, 1948, 1951.

——. " 'Sobornoe Ulozhenie' 1649 goda i 'Pravila' Vasile Lupu 1649 goda kak istochniki po istorii zakreposhcheniia krest'ian v Rossii i v Moldavii." In *O rumiano-russkikh i rumyno-sovetskikh sviaziakh. Sovmestnaia sessiia rumynskikh i sovetskikh istorikov iiun' 1958 goda.* Moscow: Inoslit 1960, pp. 55–70.

——. "Zemskie sobory i utverzhdenie absoliutizma v Rossii." In *Absoliutizm v Rossii (XVII–XVIII vv.).* Moscow: Nauka, 1964, pp. 92–133.

Chernov, A. V. "Tsentral'nyi gosudarstvennyi arkhiv drevnikh aktov, kak istochnik po voennoi istorii Russkogo gosudarstva do XVIII." *Trudy istoriko-arkhivnogo instituta* 4 (1948) :115–60.

——. *Vooruzhennye sily russkogo gosudarstva v XV-XVII vv.* Moscow: Voenizdat, 1954.

Chicherin, B. *Oblastnyia uchrezhdeniia Rossii v" XVII-m" veke.* Moscow, 1856.

——. *Opyty po istorii russkago prava.* Moscow, 1858.

Chistiakov, M. N., ed. *Artilleriia.* Moscow: Voenizdat, 1953.

Chistiakova, E. V. "Moskva v seredine 30-kh godov XVII v." In *Novoe o proshlom nashei strany.* Moscow: Nauka, 1967, pp. 301–9.

——. "Letopisnye zapisi o narodnykh dvizheniiakh serediny XVII v." In *Problemy obshchestvenno-politicheskoi istorii Rossii i slavianskikh stran.* Moscow: IVL, 1963, pp. 242–52.

——. "Volneniia sluzhilykh liudei v iuzhnykh gorodakh Rossii v seredine XVII v." In *Russkoe gosudarstvo v XVII veke. Novye iavleniia v sotsial'noekonomicheskoi, politicheskoi i kul'turnoi zhizni. Sbornik statei.* Moscow: Akademiia nauk SSSR, 1961, pp. 254–71.

Chistov, K. V. *Russkie narodnye sotsial'no–utopicheskie legendy XVII-XIX vv.* Moscow: Nauka, 1967.

Chistozvonov, A. N. "Nekotorye aspekty problemy genezisa absoliutizma." *Voprosy istorii* 43, no. 5 (May 1968) :46–62.

Collins, Samuel. *The Present State of Russia.* London: John Winter, 1671.

Coyet, Balthaser. *Posol'stvo Kunraada fan" -Klenka k" tsariam" Alekseiu Mikhailovichu i Feodoru Alekseevichu.* St. Petersburg, 1900.

Culpepper III, Jack Marcellus. "The Legislative Origins of Peasant Bondage in Muscovy." Ph.D. dissertation, Columbia University, 1965.

Danilova, L. V. "Istoricheskie usloviia razvitiia russkoi narodnosti v period obrazovaniia i ukrepleniia tsentralizovannogo gosudarstva v Rossii." In

Voprosy formirovaniia russkoi narodnosti i natsii. Sbornik statei. Moscow-Leningrad: Akademiia Nauk SSSR, 1958, pp. 106–54.

——. "K itogam izucheniia osnovnykh problem rannego i razvitogo feodalizma v Rossii." In *Sovetskaia istoricheskaia nauka ot XX k XXII s"ezdu KPSS. Istoriia SSSR. Sbornik statei.* Moscow: Akademiia Nauk SSSR, 1962, pp. 37–90.

——. "K voprosu o prichinakh utverzhdeniia krepostnichestva v Rossii." *Ezhegodnik po agrarnoi istorii Vostochnoi Evropy 1965 g.* Moscow: Moskovskii Universitet, 1970, pp. 130–40.

——. "Stanovlenie marksistskogo napravleniia v sovetskoi istoriografii epokhi feodalizma." *Istoricheskie zapiski* 76 (1965) :62–119.

David, Georgius. *Status Modernus Magnae Russiae Seu Moscoviae (1690).* Edited by A. V. Florovskij. The Hague: Mouton & Co., 1965.

David, Irzhi "Sovremennoe sostoianie Velikoi Rossii, ili Moskovii." *Voprosy istorii* 43, no. 1 (January 1968) : 126–31; no. 3 (March 1968) : 92–97; no. 4 (April 1968) : 138–47.

Debol'skii, N. N. *Grazhdanskaia deesposobnost' po russkomu pravu do kontsa XVII veka.* St. Petersburg, 1903.

Demidova, N. F. "Biurokratizatsii gosudarstvennogo apparata absoliutizma v XVII-XVIII v." In *Absoliutizm v Rossii (XVII-XVIII vv.).* Moscow: Nauka, 1964, pp. 206–42.

Denisova, M. M. "Pomestnaia konnitsa i ee vooruzhenie v XVI-XVII vv." *Trudy gosudarstvennago Istoricheskogo muzeia* 20 (1948) : 29–46.

Dewey, Horace W. "Immunities in Old Russia." *Slavic Review* 23, no. 4 (December 1964) : 643–59.

——. *Muscovite Judicial Texts, 1488–1556.* Michigan Slavic Materials, no. 7. Ann Arbor: Department of Slavic Languages and Literatures, University of Michigan, 1966.

D'iachenko, Grigorii. *Polnyi tserkovno-slavianskii slovar'.* Moscow, 1900.

D'iakonov, M. A. "K" voprosu o krest'ianskoi poriadnoi zapisi i sluzhiloi kabale." In *Sbornik" statei, posviashchennykh" Vasiliiu Osipovichu Kliuchevskomu.* Moscow, 1909, pp. 317–31.

——. *Ocherki iz" istorii sel'skago naseleniia v" Moskovskom" gosudarstve (XVI–XVII vv.).* St. Petersburg, 1898.

——. *Ocherki obshchestvennago i gosudarstvennago stroia drevnei Rusi.* St. Petersburg, 1912.

——. *Ocherki obshchestvennogo i gosudarstvennogo stroia drevnei Rusi.* Moscow-Leningrad: Gosizdat, 1926.

——. *Zapovednyia i vykhodnyia leta.* Petrograd, 1915.

D'iakonov, M. A., ed. *Svodnyi tekst" krest'ianskikh" poriadnykh" XVI veka.* St. Petersburg, 1910.

Doroshenko, V. V. and Ianel', Z. K. "Zametki o novoi literature po istorii feodal'noi Rossii." *Istoriia SSSR* 13, no. 5 (September-October 1968) : 147–69.

Dovnar-Zapol'skii, M. V. "Vremia Ivana Groznago." In *Russkaia istoriia v" ocherkakh" i stat'iakh".* Edited by M. V. Dovnar-Zapol'skii. 3 vols. Moscow, 1912. 2: 155–223.

Dubrovskii, S. M. "Protiv idealizatsii deiatel'nosti Ivana IV." *Voprosy istorii* 31, no. 8 (August 1956) : 121–29.

Dukes, Paul. *Catherine the Great and the Russian Nobility. A Study Based on the Materials of the Legislative Commission of 1767.* Cambridge: Cambridge University Press, 1967.

Works Cited

Eck, A. *Le Moyen Age russe*. Paris, 1933.

Ekzempliarskii, A. V. *Velikie i udel'nye kniaz'ia severnoi Rusi v" tatarskii period", s" 1238 po 1505 g. Biograficheskie ocherki*. 2 vols. St. Petersburg, 1889, 1891. (Reprint by Europe Printing, The Hague, 1966.)

Elchaninov, A. G. "Ocherk" istorii voennago iskusstva do Petra Velikago." In *Istoriia russkoi armii i flota*. 15 vols. Moscow: Obrazovanie, 1911–1915. 1: 9–79.

El'iashevich, V. B. *Istoriia prava pozemel'noi sobstvennosti v Rossii*. 2 vols. Paris, 1948, 1951.

Engel'man, I. *Istoriia krepostnogo prava v" Rossii*. Translated from German by V. Shcherba. Edited by A. Kizevetter. Moscow, 1900.

Epifanov, P. P. " 'Uchenie i khitrost' ratnogo stroeniia pekhotnykh liudei' (Iz istorii russkoi armii XVII v.) ." *Uchenye zapiski Moskovskogo gosudarstvennogo universiteta, kafedry istorii SSSR* 167 (1954) : 77–98.

Esper, Thomas. "Military Self-Sufficiency and Weapons Technology in Muscovite Russia." *Slavic Review* 28, no. 2 (June 1969) : 185–208.

Figarovskii, V. A. "Krest'ianskoe vosstanie 1614–1615 gg." *Istoricheskie zapiski* 72 (1962) : 194–218.

Forsten, G. "Snosheniia Shvetsii s" Rossiei v" tsarstvovanie Khristiny." *Zhurnal" Ministerstva narodnago prosveshcheniia* 275 (June 1891) : 348–75.

Froianov, I. Ia. "Sovetskaia istoriografia o formirovanni klassov i klassovoi bor'be v Drevnei Rusi." In *Sovetskaia istoriografiia klassovoi bor'by i revoliutsionnogo dvizheniia v Rossii*. 2 vols. Leningrad: Leningradskii Universitet, 1967. 1: 18–52.

Geiman, V. G. "Neskol'ko novykh dokumentov, kasaiushchikhsia istorii sel'skogo naseleniia Moskovskogo gosudarstva XVI stoletiia." *Sbornik Rossiiskoi publichnoi biblioteki* 2 (1924) : 277–94.

———. "Novoe osveshchenie voprosa o prikreplenii krest'ian"." *Russkii istoricheskii zhurnal"* 8 (1922) : 291–94.

———. "O nekotorykh svoeobraznykh iuridicheskikh dokumentov XVII v." *Istoricheskii arkhiv*, no. 3 (1962) , pp. 185–92.

Geisman, P. A. *Kratkii kurs" istorii voennago iskusstva v" srednie i novye veka*. 3 vols. St. Petersburg, 1893–96.

Glebov-Stretnev, F. P. "Spisok" boiar", okol'nichikh" i drugikh" chinov", s" 1578 goda do tsarstvovaniia Feodora Alekseevicha." In *Arkhiv" istoriko-iuridicheskikh" svedenii, otnosiashchikhsia do Rossii*. Edited by Nikolai Kalachov. 2, part 1 (1855), section II, part 4, pp. 130–41.

Gnevushev, A. M. "Zemlevladenie i sel'skoe khoziaistvo v" Moskovskom" gosudarstve XVI–XVII vv." *Russkaia istoriia v" ocherkakh" i stat'iakh"*. Edited by M. V. Dovnar-Zapol'skii. 3 vols. Kiev, 1912. 3: 267–312.

Gorchakov, M. I. *Monastyrskii prikaz". (1649–1725 g.) Opyt" istoriko-iuridicheskago izsledovaniia*. St. Petersburg, 1868.

———. *O zemel'nykh" vladeniiakh" vserossiiskikh" mitropolitov", patriarkhov" i sv. sinoda. (988–1738 gg.) Iz" opytov" izsledovaniia v" istorii russkago prava*. St. Petersburg, 1871.

Gordon, Patrick. *Passages from the Diary of General Patrick Gordon of Auchleuchries. A. D. 1635–A. D. 1699*. Aberdeen, Scotland: Printed for the Spalding Club, 1859.

Gorfunkel', A. Kh. "Perestroika khoziaistva Kirillo–Belozerskogo monastyria v sviazi s razvitiem tovarno-denezhnykh otnoshenii v XVI veke." *Uchenye zapiski Karelo—finskogo pedagogicheskogo instituta* 2, part 1 (1955): 90–111.

——. "Rost zemlevladeniia Kirillo-Belozerskogo monastyria v kontse XVI i v XVII v." *Istoricheskie zapiski* 73 (1963): 219–48.

——. "Termin 'bobyl' ' v istochnikakh XVII veka (po materialam votchinnogo arkhiva Kirillo-Belozerskogo monastyria)." In *Voprosy istoriografii i istochnikovedeniia istorii SSSR. Sbornik statei.* Moscow-Leningrad: Akademiia Nauk SSSR, 1963, pp. 640–47.

Gorskii, A. D. "Ob ogranichenii krest'ianskikh perekhodov na Rusi v XV v. (K voprosu o Iur'eve dne)." *Ezhegodnik po agrarnoi istorii vostochnoi Evropy 1963 g.* Vilnius: Mintis, 1965, pp. 132–44.

Got'e, Iu. V. *Smutnoe vremia. Ocherk istorii revoliutsionnykh dvizhenii nachala XVII stoletiia.* Moscow: Gosizdat, 1921.

——. "Zametki po istorii zashchity iuzhnoi granitsy Moskovskago gosudarstva." *Istoricheskiia izvestiia izd. Istorich. obshchestvom" pri moskovskom" universitete,* no. 2 (1917), 47–57.

——. *Zamoskovnyi krai v XVII veke. Opyt issledovaniia po istorii ekonomicheskogo byta Moskovskoi Rusi.* Moscow: Sotsekgiz, 1937.

Got'e, Iu. V. and Roginskii, M. G. "Poslanie Ioganna Taube i Elberta Kruze." *Russkii istoricheskii zhurnal"* 8 (1922): 8–59.

Gradovskii, A. D. "Vysshaia administratsiia Rossii XVIII st. i general" prokurory." In *Sobranie sochinenii.* 9 vols. St. Petersburg, 1899–1904.

Grekov, B. D. "Iur'ev den' i zapovednye gody." *Izvestiia Akademii nauk SSSR* 20, nos. 1–2 (January 15-February 1, 1926): 67–84.

——. *Kratkii ocherk istorii russkogo krest'ianstva.* Moscow: Sotsekgiz, 1958.

——. *Krest'iane na Rusi s drevneishikh vremen do XVII veka.* Moscow-Leningrad: AN SSSR, 1946.

——. "Opyt periodizatsii istorii krest'ian v Rossii (s drevneishikh vremen do oformleniia krepostnicheskikh otnoshenii)." *Voprosy istorii* 21, nos. 8–9 (August-September 1946): 3–18.

——. "Proiskhozhdenie krepostnogo prava v Rossii." In *Krepostnaia Rossiia. Sbornik statei.* Leningrad: Priboi, 1930, pp. 45–96.

Grobovsky, Antony N. *The "Chosen Council" of Ivan IV: A Reinterpretation.* Brookyn, N. Y.: Theo. Gaus' Sons, 1969.

Gudzinskaia, A. P. "Dokumenty sysknykh komissii vtoroi poloviny XVII v. kak istoricheskii istochnik." *Arkheograficheskii ezhegodnik za 1967 god* 11 (1969): 107–18.

Hakluyt Society. *Early Voyages and Travels to Russia and Persia, by Anthony Jenkinson and other Englishmen.* Edited by E. Delmar Morgan and C. H. Coote. 2 vols. London, 1886.

——. *Russia at the Close of the Sixteenth Century. Comprising the Treatise "Of the Russe Common Wealth," by Dr. Giles Fletcher, and the Travels of Sir Jerome Horsey, Knt.* Edited by Edward A. Bond. London, 1856.

Hall, A. R. "Military Technology." In *A History of Technology.* Edited by Charles Singer et al. 5 vols. Oxford: Clarendon Press, 1954–1958. 2: 374–82, 695–730; 3: 347–76.

Herberstein, Sigismund Freiherr von, Neyberg and Guettenhag. *Commentaries on Muscovite Affairs.* Edited and translated by Oswald P. Backus III. Lawrence, Kansas: University of Kansas Student Union Bookstore, 1956.

Howes, R. C. *The Testaments of the Grand Princes of Moscow.* Ithaca: Cornell University Press, 1967.

Works Cited

Hulbert, Ellerd Miner. "Sixteenth Century Russian Assemblies of the Land: Their Composition, Organization, and Competence." Ph.D. dissertation, University of Chicago, 1970.

Iakovlev, A. I. " 'Bezumnoe molchanie'. Prichiny Smuty po vzgliadam" russkikh" sovremennikov" eia." In *Sbornik" statei, posviashennykh" Vasiliiu Osipovichu Kliuchevskomu.* Moscow, 1909, pp. 651–78.

———. *Kholopstvo i kholopy v Moskovskom gosudarstve XVII v.* Moscow-Leningrad: Akademiia Nauk SSSR, 1943.

———. *Namestnich'i, gubnyia i zemskiia ustavnyia gramoty Moskovskago gosudarstva.* Moscow, 1909.

———. "Ocherk" istorii krepostnago prava do poloviny XVIII veka." In *Russkaia byl'. Velikaia reforma. 19 fevralia 1861.* n.p., n.d., pp. 3–26.

———. *Prikaz" sbora ratnykh" liudei 1637–1653 gg.* Moscow, 1917.

———. "Sluzhiloe zemlevladenie po dannym" Prikaza sobora ratnykh" liudei (1638 g.) ." In *Sbornik", posviashchennyi S. F. Platonovu.* St. Petersburg, 1911, pp. 450–53.

———. "Svoznye knigi XVII v." In *Pamiatniki sotsial'no-ekonomicheskoi istorii Moskovskogo gosudarstva XIV-XVII vv.* Moscow: Tsentrarkhiv, 1929, pp. 185–260.

———. *Zasechnaia cherta Moskovskago gosudarstva v" XVII v.* Moscow, 1916.

Iakubov, K. I. "Rossiia i Shvetsiia v" pervoi polovine XVII veka." *ChOIDR* 182 (1897, no. 3) , pt. 1: i-x, 1–240; 183 (1897, no. 4) , pt. 1: 241–88; 184 (1898, no. 1) pt. 1: 289–494.

Indova, E. I. "Urozhai v tsentral'noi Rossii za 150 let (vtoraia polovina XVII-XVIII v.) ." *Ezhegodnik po agrarnoi istorii Vostochnoi Evropy 1965 g.* Moscow: Moskovskii Universitet, 1970, pp. 131–55.

Indova, E. I.; Preobrazhenskii, A. A.; and Tikhonov, Iu. A. "Narodnye dvizheniia v Rossii XVII-XVIII vv. i absoliutizm." In *Absoliutizm v Rossii (XVII-XVIII vv.).* Moscow: Nauka, 1964, pp. 50–91.

Ivina, L. I. "Istochniki po istorii formirovaniia monastyrskoi votchiny v kontse XIV–nachale XV v. (na materialakh Moskovskogo Simonova monastyria) ." In *Arkheograficheskii ezhegodnik za 1966 god.* Moscow: Nauka, 1968, pp. 14–24.

Janowitz, Morris. *The Military in the Political Development of New Nations. An Essay in Comparative Analysis.* Chicago: The University of Chicago Press, 1964.

Kachanovskii, Iu. V. "O poniatiiakh 'rabstvo' i 'feodalizm'." *Voprosy istorii* 42, no. 6 (June 1967) : 123–34.

Kafengauz, B. B., and Preobrazhenskii, A. A. "Problemy istorii Rossii XVII-XVIII vv. v trudakh sovetskikh uchenykh." In *Sovetskaia istoricheskaia nauka ot XX k XXII s"ezdu KPSS. Istoriia SSSR. Sbornik statei.* Moscow: Akademiia Nauk SSSR, 1962, pp. 137–86.

Kamentseva, E. I. "Usloviia zakreposhcheniia novoporiadchikov." *Trudy moskovskogo gosudarstvennogo istoriko-arkhivnogo instituta* 7 (1954) : 129–54.

Karamzin, N. M. *Istoriia gosudarstva Rossiiskago.* 3d ed. 12 vols. St. Petersburg, 1830–31.

Kashtanov, S. M. "Diplomatika kak spetsial'naia istoricheskaia distsiplina." *Voprosy istorii* 40, no. 1 (January 1965) : 39–44.

———. "Feodal'nyi immunitet v gody boiarskogo pravleniia (1538–1548 gg.) ." *Istoricheskie zapiski* 66 (1960) : 239–68.

———. "Feudal Immunities in Russia." *The Slavonic and East European Review* 49, no. 115 (April 1971) : 235–54.

———. "Finansovaia problema v period provedeniia Ivanom Groznym politiki 'udela'." *Istoricheskie zapiski* 82 (1968) : 243–72.

———. "K istoriografii krepostnogo prava v Rossii." In *Istoriia i istoriki. Istoriografiia istorii SSSR. Sbornik statei.* Moscow: Nauka, 1965, pp. 270–312.

———. "K izucheniiu oprichniny Ivana Groznogo." *Istoriia SSSR* 7, no. 2 (March-April 1963) : 96–117.

———. "K probleme mestnogo upravleniia v Rossii pervoi poloviny XVI v." *Istoriia SSSR* 3, no. 6 (November-December 1959) : 134–48.

———. "Kopiinye knigi Troitse-Sergieva monastyria XVI veka." *Zapiski otdela rukopisei* 18 (1956) : 3–47.

———. *Ocherki russkoi diplomatiki.* Moscow: Nauka, 1970.

———. "Ogranichenie feodal'nogo immuniteta pravitel'stvom russkogo tsentralizovannogo gosudarstva v l-oi treti XVI veka." *Trudy Moskovskogo gosudarstvennogo istoriko-arkhivnogo instituta* 11 (1958) : 269–96.

———. "Otdatochnye knigi Troitse-Sergieva monastyria 1649–1650 gg." *Istoricheskii arkhiv* 8 (1953) : 198–220.

———. "Otrazhenie v zhalovannykh i ukaznykh gramotakh finansovoi sistemy russkogo gosudarstva pervoi treti XVI v." *Istoricheskie zapiski* 70 (1961) : 251–75.

———. *Sotsial'no-politicheskaia istoriia Rossii kontsa XV-pervoi poloviny XVI veka.* Moscow: Nauka, 1967.

Kashtanov, S. M., and Klokman, Iu. R. "Sovetskaia literatura 1965–1966 gg. po istorii Rossii do XIX veka." *Istoriia SSSR* 12, no. 5 (September-October 1967) : 156–76.

Kazakov, K. P., ed. *Artilleriia i rakety.* Moscow: Voenizdat, 1968.

Kazakov, N. I. "Bor'ba russkogo naroda s pol'sko—shvedskoi interventsiei v nachale XVII v. Minin i Pozharskii." In *Stranitsy boevogo proshlogo. Ocherki voennoi istorii Rossii.* Moscow: Nauka, 1968, pp. 37–55.

Kazhdan, A. P. "Traditsiia i novizna." *Novyi mir* 46, no. 3 (March 1970) : 269–72.

Keep, J. L. H. "The Muscovite Elite and the Approach to Pluralism." *The Slavonic and East European Review* 48, no. 111 (April 1970) : 201–31.

———. "The Regime of Filaret, 1619–1633." *The Slavonic and East European Review* 38, no. 91 (June 1960) : 334–60.

Khoziaistvo krupnogo feodala-krepostnika XVII v. Edited by S. G. Tomsinskii and B. D. Grekov. 2 vols. Moscow-Leningrad: Akademiia Nauk SSSR, 1933, 1936.

Khrestomatiia po istorii SSSR, XVI-XVII vv. Moscow: Sotsekgiz, 1962.

Kirillov, V. I. "Noveishaia sovetskaia literatura o krest'ianskikh i gorodskikh dvizheniiakh v Rossii (XI-XVIII vv.)." *Voprosy istorii* 40, no. 3 (March 1965) : 127–40.

Kirpichnikov, A. N. "Voennoe delo srednevekovoi Rusi i poiavlenie ognestrel'nogo oruzhiia." *Sovetskaia arkheologiia* 1, no. 3 (1957) : 60–76.

———. "Vooruzhenie Rusi v IX-XIII vv." *Voprosy istorii* 45, no. 1 (January 1970) : 42–55.

Kirpichnikov, A. N., and Khlopin, I. N. "Krepost' Kirillo-Belozerskogo mona-styria i ee vooruzhenie v XVI—XVIII vekakh." *Materialy i issledovaniia po arkheologii SSSR* 77 (1958) : 143–99.

Kliuchevskii, V. O. *Istoriia soslovii Rossii.* 3d ed. Petrograd: Lit-Izd. Otdel Komissariata Narodnogo Prosveshcheniia, 1918.

———. "Proiskhozhdenie krepostnogo prava v Rossii." In *Sochineniia.* 8 vols. Moscow: Sotsekgiz, 1956–59. 7: 238–317.

Klokman, Iu. R. "Severnaia voina 1700–1721 gg. Bor'ba Rossii za vykhod k Baltiis-komu moriu i vozvrashchenie russkikh zemel' v Pribaltike." In *Stranitsy boevogo proshlogo. Ocherki voennoi istorii Rossii.* Moscow: Nauka, 1968, pp. 73–114.

Kobrin, V. B. "Istochniki dlia izucheniia chislennosti i istorii formirovaniia oprichnogo dvora." *Arkheograficheskii ezhegodnik za 1962 god* (1963), pp. 121–25.

Kochin, G. E. "Razvitie zemledeliia na Rusi s kontsa XIII po konets XV v." *Trudy LOII* 2 (1960) : 257–305.

———. *Sel'skoe khoziaistvo na Rusi v period obrazovaniia Russkogo tsentralizo-vannogo gosudarstva. Konets XIII—nachalo XVI v.* Moscow-Leningrad: Nauka, 1965.

Kolchin, B. A. "Chernaia metallurgiia i metalloobrabotka v drevnei Rusi (domongol'skii period)." *Materialy i issledovaniia po arkheologii SSSR* 32 (1953).

———. "Obrabotka zheleza v Moskovskom gosudarstve v XVI v." *Materialy i issledovaniia po arkheologii SSSR* 12 (1949) : 192–208.

Kolesnikova, T. A. "Obshchestvenno-politicheskie vzgliady Ermolaia-Erazma." *TODRL* 9 (1953) : 251–65.

Kolosov, E. E. "Razvitie artilleriiskogo vooruzheniia v Rossii vo vtoroi polovine XVII v." *Istoricheskie zapiski* 71 (1962) : 259–69.

Kompan, E. S. "V. I. Lenin o klassakh, sosloviiakh i klassovoi bor'be v feodal'nom obshchestve." In *V. I. Lenin i istoricheskaia nauka.* Moscow: Nauka, 1968, pp. 291–301.

Kopanev, A. I. "Naselenie Russkogo gosudarstva v XVI v." *Istoricheskie zapiski* 64 (1959) : 233–54.

———. "Ustavnaia zemskaia gramota krest'ianam trekh volostei Dvinskogo uezda 25 fevralia 1552 g." *Istoricheskii arkhiv* 8 (1953) : 7–20.

Koretskii, V. I. "Bor'ba krest'ian s monastyriami v Rossii XVI—nachala XVII v." *Voprosy istorii religii i ateizma. Sbornik statei* 6 (1958) : 169–215.

———. "Golod 1601–1603 gg. v Rossii i tserkov'." *Voprosy istorii religii i ateizma* 7 (1959) : 218–56.

———. "Iz istorii krest'ianskoi voiny v Rossii nachala XVII veka." *Voprosy istorii* 15, no. 3 (March 1959) : 118–37.

———. "Iz istorii zakreposhcheniia krest'ian v Rossii v kontse XVI—nachale XVII v. (O prakticheskoi realizatsii ukazov 1601–1602 gg)." *Istoriia SSSR* 8, no. 3 (May-June 1964) : 67–88.

———. "Iz istorii zakreposhcheniia krest'ian v Rossii v kontse XVI—nachale XVII v. (K probleme 'zapovednykh let' i otmeny Iur'eva dnia)." *Istoriia SSSR* 1, no. 1 (1957) : 161–91.

———. "K istorii formirovaniia krepostnogo prava v Rossii." *Voprosy istorii* 20, no. 6 (June 1964) : 77–95.

———. "K istorii politiki Vasiliia Shuiskogo po krest'ianskomu voprosu." *Vnutrenniaia politika tsarizma (seredina XVI—nachalo XX v.)*. Leningrad: Nauka, 1967, pp. 110–26.

———. "K istorii vosstaniia Bolotnikova." *Istoricheskii arkhiv* 2, no. 2 (March-April 1956) : 126–45.

———. "K istorii vosstaniia Khlopka (novye materialy)." In *Krest'ianstvo i klassovaia bor'ba v feodal'noi Rossii*. Leningrad: Nauka, 1967, pp. 209–22.

———. "Novgorodskie dela 90-kh godov XVI v. so ssylkami na neizvestnye ukazy tsaria Fedora Ivanovicha o krest'ianakh." In *Arkheograficheskii ezhegodnik za 1966 god*. Moscow: Nauka, 1968, pp. 306–30.

———. "Novoe o Bolotnikove," *Sovetskie arkhivy* 2, no. 4 (July-August 1967) : 100–103.

———. "Novye dokumenty po istorii vosstaniia I. I. Bolotnikova." *Sovetskie arkhivy* 3, no. 6 (November-December 1968) : 66–83.

———. "Novye dokumenty po istorii russkogo goroda vremeni krest'ianskoi voiny i pol'sko-shvedskoi interventsii." In *Arkheograficheskii ezhegodnik za 1964 god*. Moscow: Nauka, 1965, pp. 316–32.

———. "Ob odnoi 'oshibke' arkhivistov XVIII veka (Lzhedmitrii II i vopros o krest'ianskom vykhode)." In *Arkheograficheskii ezhegodnik za 1962 god*. Moscow: AN SSSR, 1963, pp. 234–43.

———. "Pravaia gramota ot 30 noiabria 1618 g. Troitse-Sergievu monastyriu (Iz istorii monastyrskogo zemlevladeniia XIV-XVI vv.)." *Zapiski otdela rukopisei biblioteki im. Lenina* 21 (1959) : 173–217.

———. "Vosstanovlenie Iur'eva dnia v Rossii Lzhedmitriem I." In *Ezhegodnik po agrarnoi istorii vostochnoi Evropy 1960 g*. Kiev: Akademiia Nauk USSR, 1962, pp. 118–30.

———. *Zakreposhchenie krest'ian i klassovaia bor'ba v Rossii vo vtoroi polovine XVI v*. Moscow: Nauka, 1970.

———. "Zemskii sobor 1575 g. i chastichnoe vozrozhdenie Oprichniny." *Voprosy istorii* 42, no. 5 (May 1967) : 32–50.

Kostochkin, V. V. *Gosudarev master Fedor Kon'*. Moscow: Nauka, 1964.

———. "K kharakteristike pamiatnikov voennogo zodchestva Moskovskoi Rusi kontsa XV v.—nachala XVI v. (Kopor'e, Orekhov i Iam)." *Materialy i issledovaniia po arkheologii SSSR* 67 (1958) : 101–42.

———. "Krepost' Ivangorod." *Materialy i issledovaniia po arkheologii SSSR* 31 (1952) : 224–317.

Kostomarov, N. I. "Dolzhno li schitat' Borisa Godunova osnovatelem" krepostnago prava?" In *Istoricheskiia monografii i izsledovaniia*. 2d ed. 16 vols. St. Petersburg, 1872–1885. 1: 351–84.

Kotoshikhin, G. *O Rossii v" tsarstvovanie Alekseia Mikhailovicha. Sovremennoe sochinenie*. St. Petersburg, 1859.

Kozachenko, A. I. "Zemskii sobor 1653 goda." *Voprosy istorii* 32, no. 5 (May 1957) : 151–58.

Kozintseva, R. I. "Astrakhanskie strel'tsy v poslednie chetverti XVII v. (Opyt izucheniia skazok astrakhantsev)." In *Voprosy voennoi istorii Rossii. XVIII i pervaia polovina XIX vekov*. Moscow: Nauka, 1969, pp. 359–68.

Kulisher, I. "Nesvobodnoe sostoianie krest'ian i odin iz priznakov ego—iuridicheskoe i fakticheskoe prekrashchenie perekhoda v 16–17 st." *Trud v Rossii* 1 (1924) : 178–204.

Works Cited

Kurts, B. G. "Sostoianie Rossii v" 1650–1655 g.g. po doneseniiam" Rodesa."
   ChOIDR 253 (1915, no. 2), part 2, pp. 1–268.
Lappo, I. I. "Tverskoi uezd" v" XVI veke. Ego naselenie i vidy zemel'nago
   vladeniia." *ChOIDR* 171 (1894, no. 4), part 1, pp. 1–238.
Lappo-Danilevskii, A. S. "Ocherk" i istoriia obrazovaniia glavneishikh" razria-
   dov" krest'ianskago naseleniia v" Rossii." In *Krest'ianskii stroi*. Edited by
   S. L. Tolstoi. St. Petersburg: Beseda, 1905. 1: 1–156.
———. *Organizatsiia priamago oblozheniia v" Moskovskom" gosudarstve so vre-
   men" smuty do epokhi preobrazovanii*. St. Petersburg, 1890.
———. "Razyskaniia po istorii prikrepleniia vladel'cheskikh" krest'ian" v" Mos-
   kovskom" gosudarstve XVI–XVII vv." *Zapiski imp. Akademii nauk"*. VIII
   seriia, Po istoriko-filologicheskomu otdeleniiu 5, no. 1 (1901) : 51–175.
Latkin, Vasilii. *Materialy dlia istorii zemskikh" soborov" XVII stoletiia*. St.
   Petersburg, 1884.
Leont'ev, A. K. *Obrazovanie prikaznoi sistemy upravleniia v russkom gosudar-
   stve. Iz istorii sozdaniia tsentralizovannogo gosudarstvennogo apparata v kontse
   XV–pervoi polovine XVI v.* Moscow: Moskovskii Universitet, 1961.
Lialina, G. S. "K kharakteristike feodal'nogo zemlevladeniia vo vtoroi polovine
   XVII v." *Trudy MGIAI* 16 (1961) : 397–407.
Liashchenko, P. I. *Istoriia narodnogo khoziaistva SSSR*. 3 vols. Moscow: Gos-
   politizdat, 1956.
Liubavskii, M. K. *Lektsii po drevnei russkoi istorii do kontsa XVI veka*. Moscow,
   1915.
———. *Russkaia istoriia 17 v. i pervoi chetverti 18 v. Lektsii, chitannyia na Vys-
   shikh" zhenskikh" kursakh" v" 1913–1914 uch. g. (Zapiski slushatel'nits")*.
   2 vols. Moscow, 1913–14.
Liubomirov, P. G. *Ocherk istorii nizhegorodskogo opolcheniia 1611–1613 gg.*
   Moscow: Sotsekgiz, 1939.
Loewenson, Leo. "The Moscow Rising of 1648." *The Slavonic and East European
   Review* 27, no. 68 (December 1948) : 146–56.
Maierberg, Avgustin. *Puteshestvie v" Moskoviiu*. Moscow, 1874.
Makovskii, D. P. *Pervaia krest'ianskaia voina v Rossii*. Smolensk, 1967.
———. *Razvitie tovarno-denezhnykh otnoshenii v sel'skom khoziaistve Russkogo
   gosudarstva v XVI veke*. Smolensk, 1963.
Maksimenkov, G. A. "Iz istorii drevnerusskoi artillerii." *Sovetskaia arkheologiia*
   1, no. 3 (1957) : 77–83.
Man'kov, A. G. "Epizod iz istorii bor'by posada s feodalom vo vtoroi polovine
   XVII v." In *Problemy obshchestvenno-politicheskoi istorii Rossii i slavian-
   skikh stran*. Moscow: IVL, 1963, pp. 283–87.
———. "Krest'ianskii vopros v Palate ob Ulozhenii 1700 g." In *Voprosy ekono-
   miki i klassovykh otnoshenii v Russkom gosudarstve XII-XVII vekov*. Lenin-
   grad: Akademiia Nauk SSSR, 1960, pp. 8–77.
———. "Krugi v razinskom voiske i vopros o putiakh i tseli ego dvizheniia." In
   Krest'ianstvo i klassovaia bor'ba v feodal'noi Rossii. Leningrad: Nauka, 1967,
   pp. 264–79.
———. "Liudvig Fabritsius o krest'ianskoi voine pod predvoditel'stvom S. Razina." *Voprosy istorii* 41, no. 5 (May 1966) : 202–6.
———. "Pobegi krest'ian v votchinakh Troitse-Sergieva monastyria v I-i chetverti XVII v." *Uchenye zapiski Leningradskogo gosudarstvennogo universiteta* no. 80. *Seriia istoricheskikh nauk* 10 (1941) : 45–74.

————. *Razvitie krepostnogo prava v Rossii vo vtoroi polovine XVII veka.* Moscow-Leningrad: Akademiia Nauk SSSR, 1962.

————. "Sel'skie meshchane vtoroi poloviny XVII v." In *Akademiku Borisu Dmitrievichu Grekovu ko dniu semidesiatiletiia. Sbornik statei.* Moscow: Akademiia Nauk SSSR, 1952, pp. 216–20.

————. "Zapisnye knigi krepostei na krest'ian Pomestnogo prikaza vtoroi poloviny XVII v." In *Issledovaniia po otechestvennomu istochnikovedeniiu.* Moscow-Leningrad: Nauka, 1964, pp. 324–30.

Man'kov, A. G., ed. *Materialy po istorii krest'ian v russkom gosudarstve XVI veka. Sbornik dokumentov.* Leningrad: LGU, 1955.

Margolin, S. L. "K voprosu ob organizatsii i sotsial'nom sostave streletskogo voiska v XVII v." *Uchenye zapiski Moskovskogo oblastnogo pedagogicheskogo instituta* 27 (1953) : 63–96.

————. "Oborona russkogo gosudarstva ot tatarskikh nabegov v kontse XVI veka. Storozhevaia i stanichnaia sluzhba i zasechnaia cherta." *Trudy Gosudarstvennogo istoricheskogo muzeia* 20 (1948) : 3–28.

————. "Vooruzhenie streletskogo voiska." *Trudy Gosudarstvennogo istoricheskogo muzeia* 20 (1948) : 85–102.

Marin, V. I. " 'Slovo i delo gosudarevo'." *Voprosy istorii* 41, no. 3 (March 1966) : 215–18.

Markov, M. I. *Istoriia konnitsy.* 5 vols. in 9 parts. Tver', 1886–1896.

Marzheret, Kapitan. *Sostoianie Rossiiskoi derzhavy i velikago kniazhestva Moskovskago s prisovokupleniem" izvestii o dostopamiatnykh" sobytiiakh" sluchivshikhsia v" pravlenie chertyrekh" gosudarei, s" 1590 goda po sentiabr' 1606. Pervod" s" frantsuzskogo.* St. Petersburg, 1830.

Maslovskii, D. F. *Zapiski po istorii voennago iskusstva v" Rossii.* 2 vols. in 3 parts. St. Petersburg, 1891–94.

Massa, Isaak. *Kratkoe izvestie o Moskovii v nachale XVII v.* Moscow: Sotsekgiz, 1937.

Mavrodin, V. V. "Feodal'naia Rossiia v trudakh V. I. Lenina." *Voprosy istorii* 45, no. 4 (April 1970) : 165–82.

————. *Klassovaia bor'ba i obshchestvenno- politicheskaia mysl' v Rossii v XVIII v. (1725–1773 gg.).* Leningrad: LGU, 1964.

————. *Krest'ianskaia voina v Rossii v 1773–1775 godakh. Vosstanie Pugacheva.* 3 vols. Leningrad: LGU, 1961–70.

————. "Sovetskaia istoricheskaia nauka o krest'ianskikh voinakh v Rossii." In *Krest'ianskie voiny v Rossii XVII—XVIII vv.* Moscow-Leningrad: Nauka, 1966, pp. 292–327.

————. "Sovetskaia istoriografiia krest'ianskikh voin v Rossii." In *Sovetskaia istoriografiia klassovoi bor'by i revoliutsionnogo dvizheniia v Rossii.* 2 vols. Leningrad: Leningradskii Universitet, 1967. 1: 53–82.

McNeill, William H. *Europe's Steppe Frontier, 1500–1800.* Chicago and London: The University of Chicago Press, 1964.

Meichik, D. "Dopolnitel'nyia dannyia k" istorii Ulozheniia 1649 g." *Sbornik" Arkheologicheskago instituta,* no. 3 (1880), pp. 1–50.

Mikhailov, P. E. "K" voprosu o proiskhozhdenii zemel'nago starozhil'stva." *Zhurnal" ministerstva narodnago prosveshcheniia* 27 (June 1910) : 318–57.

————. "Novootkrytye dokumenty i 'zapovednyia leta'." *Zhurnal" ministerstva narodnago prosveshcheniia* 31 (February 1911) : 375–410.

———. "Obychnyi institut" starozhil'stva v" protesesse obrazovaniia krepostnogo prava." *Zhurnal" ministerstva narodnago prosveshcheniia* 37 (January 1912) : 75–119.

Mikhnevich, N. P., and Geisman, P. A. "Glavnyi shtab". Istoricheskii ocherk" vozniknoveniia i razvitiia v" Rossii general'nago shtaba do kontsa tsarstvovaniia imperatora Aleksandra I vkliuchitel'no." *Stoletie voennago ministerstva 1802–1902.* Vol. 4, pt. 1, no. 1, sec. 2 (1902).

Mikhnevich, N. P., and Il'enko, A. K. "Glavnyi shtab". Istoricheskii ocherk". Komplektovanie vooruzhennykh" sil" v" Rossii do 1802 g." *Stoletie voennago ministerstva 1802–1902.* Vol. 4, pt. 1, no. 1, sec. 1 (1902).

Miliukov, P. N. *Gosudarstvennoe khoziaistvo Rossii v" pervoi chetverti XVIII stoletiia i reforma Petra Velikago.* St. Petersburg, 1905.

———. "Krest'iane v" Rossii." In *Entsiklopedicheskii slovar'.* Edited by Ivan E. Andreevskii et al. 43 vols. in 86 parts. St. Petersburg, Leipzig: F. A. Brokgauz—I. A. Efron, 1890–1907. 32: 675–714.

———. *Ocherki po istorii russkoi kul'tury.* 3 vols. St. Petersburg, 1900.

———. *Spornye voprosy finansovoi istorii Moskovskago gosudarstva. Retsenziia na sochinenie A. S. Lappo-Danilevskago "Organizatsiia priamago oblozheniia v" Moskovskom" gosudarstve".* St. Petersburg, 1892.

Moiseeva, G. N. *Valaamskaia beseda—pamiatnik russkoi publitsistiki serediny XVI veka.* Moscow-Leningrad: Akademiia Nauk, 1958.

Mongait, A. L. "Oboronitel'nye sooruzheniia Novgoroda Velikogo." *Materialy i issledovaniia po arkheologii SSSR* 31 (1952) : 7–132.

Myshlaevskii, A. Z. *Ofitserskii vopros" v" XVII veke. Ocherki iz" istorii voennago dela v" Rossii.* St. Petersburg, 1899.

Nazarov, V. D. "Iz istorii agrarnoi politiki tsarizma v XVI veke." *Sovetskie arkhivy* 3, no. 3 (May-June 1968) : 106–14.

———. "Iz istorii vnutrennei politiki Rossii nachala XVII v." *Istoriia SSSR* 12, no. 4 (July-August 1967) : 90–103.

———. "O datirovke 'Ustava ratnykh i pushechnykh del'." In *Voprosy voennoi istorii Rossii. XVIII i pervaia polovina XIX vekov.* Moscow: Nauka, 1969, pp. 216–21.

Nikitin, A. V. "Oboronitel'nye sooruzheniia zasechnoi cherty XVI-XVII v." *Materialy i issledovannia po arkheologii SSSR* 44 (1955) : 116–213.

Nikol'skii, A. I. et al. "Glavnoe upravlenie kazach'ikh" voisk". Istoricheskii ocherk"." *Stoletie voennago ministerstva 1802–1902.* Vol. 11, part 1 (1902).

Nikon, Patriarch, "Mneniia patr. Nikona ob" Ulozhenii i proch. (Iz" otvetov" Boiarinu Streshnevu)." *Zapiski otdeleniia russkoi i slavianskoi arkheologii russkago arkheologicheskago obshchestva* 2 (1861) : 423–98.

Norman, A. V. B., and Pottinger, Don. *A History of War and Weapons 449 to 1660. English Warfare from the Anglo-Saxons to Cromwell.* New York: Thomas Y. Crowell Co., 1966.

Nørretranders, Bjarne *The Shaping of Czardom under Ivan Groznyj.* Copenhagen: Munksgaard, 1964.

Nosov, N. E. "Belozerskaia gubnaia izba v nachale XVII v." In *Voprosy sotsial'-no-ekonomicheskoi istorii i istochnikovedeniia perioda feodalizma v Rossii. Sbornik statei k 70-letiiu A. A. Novosel'skogo.* Moscow: Akademiia Nauk SSSR, 1961, pp. 50–53.

WORKS CITED

———. "Boiarskaia kniga 1556 g. (Iz istorii proiskhozhdeniia chetvertchikov)." In *Voprosy ekonomiki i klassovykh otnoshenii v russkom gosudarstve XII-XVII vekov*. Moscow-Leningrad: AN SSSR, 1960, pp. 191–227.

———. "Gubnaia reforma i tsentral'noe pravitel'stvo kontsa 30-kh—nachala 40-kh godov XVI v." *Istoricheskie zapiski* 56 (1956) : 206–34.

———. "'Novoe' napravlenie v aktovom istochnikovedenii." *Problemy istochnikovedeniia* 10 (1962) : 261–348.

———. *Stanovlenie soslovno-predstavitel'nykh uchrezhdenii v Rossii. Izyşkaniia o zemskoi reforme Ivana Groznogo*. Leningrad: Nauka, 1969.

———. "Zemskaia reforma na russkom Severe XVI v. (Ob otmene kormlenii i vvedenii zemskikh uchrezhdenii)." In *Krest'ianstvo i klassovaia bor'ba v feodal'noi Rossii*. Leningrad: Nauka, 1967, pp. 131–56.

Nosov, N. E., et al. "Mnogotomnaia 'Istoriia SSSR'." *Voprosy istorii* 43, no. 3 (March 1968) : 133–55.

Novitskii, V. I. *Vybornoe i bol'shoe dvorianstvo XVI-XVII vekov"*. Kiev, 1915.

Novombergskii, N. Ia. "K voprosu o vneshnei istorii Sobornogo Ulozheniia 1649 goda." *Istoricheskie zapiski* 21 (1947) : 43–50.

———. *Slovo i delo gosudarevy*. 2 vols. Tomsk, 1909.

Novosel'skii, A. A. *Bor'ba moskovskogo gosudarstva s tatarami v pervoi polovine XVII veka*. Moscow-Leningrad: Akademiia Nauk SSSR, 1948.

———. "Dela 'o krest'ianstve' kak istochnik dlia izucheniia istorii zakreposhcheniia svobodnogo sel'skogo naseleniia na iuge Rossii v XVII veke." In *Arkheograficheskii ezhegodnik za 1962 god*. Moscow: Akademiia Nauk SSSR, 1963, pp. 147–55.

———. "Dvortsovye krest'iane Komaritskoi volosti vo vtoroi polovine XVII v." In *Voprosy sel'skogo khoziaistva, krest'ianstva i revoliutsionnogo dvizheniia v Rossii. Sbornik statei k 75 letiiu Akademika Nikolaia Mikhailovicha Druzhinina*. Moscow: Akademiia Nauk SSSR, 1961, pp. 65–80.

———. "K voprosu o znachenii 'urochnykh let' v pervoi polovine XVII v." In *Akademiku Borisu Dmitrievichu Grekovu ko dniu semidesiatiletiia. Sbornik statei*. Moscow: Akademiia Nauk SSSR, 1952, pp. 178–83.

———. "K voprosu ob ekonomicheskom sostoianii beglykh krest'ian na iuge moskovskogo gosudarstva v pervoi polovine XVII v." *Istoricheskie zapiski* 16 (1945) : 58–64.

———. "Kollektivnye dvorianskie chelobit'ia po voprosam mezhevaniia i opisaniia zemel' v 80-kh godakh XVII v." *Uchenye zapiski Instituta istorii RANION* 4 (1929) : 103–8.

———. "Otdatochnye knigi beglykh, kak istochnik dlia izucheniia narodnoi kolonizatsii na Rusi v XVII veke." *Trudy Istoriko-arkhivnogo instituta* 2 (1946) : 124–52.

———. "Pobegi krest'ian i kholopov i ikh sysk v Moskovskom gosudarstve vtoroi poloviny XVII veka." *Trudy Instituta istorii RANION* 1 (1926) : 325–54.

———. "Raspad zemlevladeniia sluzhilogo 'goroda' v XVII v. (po desiatniam)." In *Russkoe gosudarstvo v XVII veke. Novye iavleniia v sotsial'no-ekonomicheskoi, politicheskoi i kul'turnoi zhizni. Sbornik statei*. Moscow: Akademiia Nauk SSSR, 1961, pp. 231–53.

———. "Rasprostranenie krepostnicheskogo zemlevladeniia v iuzhnykh uezdakh Moskovskogo gosudarstva v XVII v." *Istoricheskie zapiski* 4 (1938) : 21–40.

Works Cited

——. "Rospis' krest'ianskikh dvorov, nakhodivshikhsia vo vladenii vysshego dukhovenstva, monastyrei i dumnykh liudei, po perepisnym knigam 1678 g." *Istoricheskii arkhiv* 4 (1949) : 88–149.

——. "Vol'nye i perekhozhie liudi v iuzhnykh uezdakh russkogo gosudarstva v XVII v." *Materialy po istorii sel'skogo khoziaistva i krest'ianstva SSSR* 5 (1962) : 61–77.

——. *Votchinnik i ego khoziaistvo v XVII veke.* Moscow-Leningrad: Gosizdat, 1929.

——. "Zemskii sobor 1639 g." *Istoricheskie zapiski* 24 (1947) : 14–29.

Novyi letopisets", sostavlennyi v" tsarstvovanie Mikhaila Feodorovicha, izdan" po spisku Kniazia Obolenskago. Moscow, 1853.

Obraztsov, G. N. "Ulozhenie 1649 g. i krest'iane votchiny Antonievo-Siiskogo monastyria." *Istoricheskie zapiski* 63 (1958) : 269–82.

——. "Iz istorii zakreposhcheniia krest'ian na Severe (po materialam Antonievo-Siiskogo monastyria) ." In *Krest'ianstvo i klassovaia bor'ba v feodal'noi Rossii.* Leningrad: Nauka, 1967, pp. 333–47.

Ocherki istorii SSSR. Period feodalizma. Konets XV v.–nachalo XVII v. Edited by A. N. Nasonov, L. V. Cherepnin, and A. A. Zimin. Moscow: Akademiia Nauk SSSR, 1955.

Ocherki istorii SSSR. Period feodalizma. XVII v. Edited by A. A. Novosel'skii and N. V. Ustiugov. Moscow: Akademiia Nauk SSSR, 1955.

Odinets, D. M. "Poteria prava perekhoda vladel'cheskimi krest'ianami Moskovskogo gosudarstva." In *Sbornik statei, posviashchennykh Pavlu Nikolaevichu Miliukovu 1859–1929.* Prague, 1929, pp. 205–24.

Odynets, D. M. "K" istorii prikrepleniia vladel'cheskikh" krest'ian"." *Zhurnal" ministerstva iustitsii,* no. 1 (January 1908) , pp. 102–44.

Ogrizko, Z. A. *Iz istorii krest'ianstva na severe feodal'noi Rossii XVII v. (Osobye formy krepostnoi zavisimosti).* Moscow: Sovetskaia Rossiia, 1968.

——. "Vliianie feodalno-krepostnicheskoi sistemy na razvitie khoziaistva chernososhnykh krest'ian v XVII veke." In *Voprosy agrarnoi istorii.* Vologda, 1968, pp. 434–41.

——. "Zernovoe khoziaistvo polovnikov Troitse-Gledenskogo monastyria v XVII veke." *Materialy po istorii sel'skogo khoziaistva i krest'ianstva SSSR* 4 (1960) : 8–37.

Olearius, Adam. *The Travels of Olearius in Seventeenth-Century Russia.* Translated and edited by Samuel H. Baron. Stanford: Stanford University Press, 1967.

Paneiakh, V. M. "Iz istorii politiki tsarizma v kholop'em voprose v konste XVI veka (pomeshchiki-vladel'tsy kabal'nykh kholopov) ." *Vnutrenniaia politika tsarizma (seredina XVI–nachalo XX v.).* Leningrad: Nauka, 1967, pp. 100–9.

——. *Kabal'noe kholopstvo na Rusi v XVI veke.* Leningrad: Nauka, 1967.

——. "Opyt tsifrovoi obrabotki materialov zapisnykh knig starykh krepostei XVI veka." In *Voprosy istoriografii i istochnikovedeniia istorii SSSR. Sbornik statei.* Moscow-Leningrad: AN SSSR, 1963, pp. 542–56.

Pankov, D. V., comp. *Razvitie taktiki russkoi armii XVIII v.–nachalo XX v.* Moscow: Voenizdat, 1957.

Pavlov, P. N. "Vyvoz pushniny iz Sibiri v XVII v." In *Sibir' XVII-XVIII vv.* Novosibirsk: Sibirskoe otdelenie AN SSSR, 1962, pp. 121–38.

Pavlov-Sil'vanskii, N. P. *Feodalizm v drevnei Rusi.* Petrograd: Priboi, 1924.

———. *Gosudarevy sluzhilye liudi. Proiskhozhdenie russkago dvorianstva.* St. Petersburg, 1898.

———. "Liudi kabal'nye i dokladnye." *ZhMNP,* no. 1 (1895), pp. 210–39.

Pazhitnov, K. A. "Dvorianskaia istoriografiia o proiskhozhdenii krepostnogo prava v Rossii (doreformennyi period)." In *Voprosy istorii narodnogo khoziaistva SSSR.* Moscow: Akademiia Nauk SSSR, 1957, pp. 33–84.

Perel'man, I. L. "Novgorodskaia derevnia v XV-XVI vv." *Istoricheskie zapiski* 26 (1948) : 128–97.

Peresvetov, I. S. *Sochineniia I. Peresvetova.* Moscow-Leningrad: Akademiia Nauk SSSR, 1956.

Petrikeev, D. I. "Barshchina na potashnykh predpriiatiiakh boiarina B. I. Morozova." In *Krest'ianstvo i klassovaia bor'ba v feodal'noi Rossii.* Leningrad: Nauka, 1967, pp. 239–49.

———. *Krupnoe krepostnoe khoziaistvo XVII v. Po materialam votchiny boiarina B. I. Morozova.* Leningrad: Nauka, 1967.

———. "O nekotorykh materialakh po istorii votchiny Boiarina B. I. Morozova." In *Issledovaniia po otechestvennomu istochnikovedeniiu.* Moscow-Leningrad: Nauka, 1964, pp. 330–37.

———. "Zemel'nye vladeniia Boiarina B. I. Morozova." *Istoricheskie zapiski* 21 (1947) : 51–104.

Petrovich, Michael B. "The Peasant in Nineteenth-Century Historiography." In *The Peasant in Nineteenth-Century Russia.* Edited by Wayne S. Vucinich. Stanford: Stanford University Press, 1968, pp. 191–230.

Picheta, V. I. *Belorussiia i Litva XV-XVI vv.* Moscow: Akademiia Nauk SSSR, 1961.

Pipes, Richard. *Karamzin's Memoir on Ancient and Modern Russia.* Cambridge, Mass.: Harvard University Press, 1959.

Platonov, S. F. *Boris Godunov.* Petrograd: Ogni, 1921.

———. "K istorii moskovskikh" zemskikh" soborov"." In *Stat'i po russkoi istorii. (1883–1912).* 2d ed. St. Petersburg, 1912, pp. 279–332.

———. *Lektsii po russkoi istorii.* 6th ed. St. Petersburg, 1909.

———. "Moskovskoe pravitel'stvo pri pervykh" Romanovykh"." In *Sochineniia.* 2 vols. St. Petersburg, 1919. 1: 339–406.

———. "O vremeni i merakh prikrepleniia krest'ian k zemle v Moskovskoi Rusi." *Arkhiv istorii truda v Rossii* 3 (1922) : 18–22.

———. *Ocherki po istorii smuty v Moskovskom gosudarstve XVI-XVII vv.* Moscow: Sotsekgiz, 1937.

———. *Smutnoe vremia. Ocherk istorii vnutrennego krizisa i obshchestvennoi bor'by v Moskovskom gosudarstve XVI i XVII vekov.* St. Petersburg: Vremia, 1923.

Pobedimova, G. A. "K voprosu o stabil'nosti sel'skogo naseleniia votchiny v XVI v. (na primere Iosifo-Volokolamskogo monastyria)." In *Voprosy ekonomiki i klassovykh otnoshenii v Russkom gosudarstve XII–XVII vekov.* Moscow-Leningrad: Akademiia Nauk SSSR, 1960, pp. 172–90.

———. "O nekotorykh formakh kreditovaniia krest'ian Iosifovolokolamskogo monastyria v pervoi polovine XVI v." In *Krest'ianstvo i klassovaia bor'ba v feodal'noi Rossii.* Leningrad: Nauka, 1967, pp. 91–97.

Podobedova, O. I. *Miniatiury russkikh istoricheskikh rukopisei. K istorii russkogo litsevogo letopisaniia.* Moscow: Nauka, 1965.

Works Cited

Pokrovskii, N. N. "Kupchie, dannye i menovnye gramoty kak istochnik po istorii chernososhnogo zemlevladeniia Rossii XIV—pervoi chetverti XVI v." *Novoe o proshlom nashei strany.* Moscow: Nauka, 1967, pp. 79–90.

Polosin, I. I. "Pomestnoe pravo i krest'ianskaia krepost'." In *Sotsial'no-politicheskaia istoriia Rossii XVI—nachala XVII v. Sbornik statei.* Moscow: Akademiia Nauk SSSR, 1963, pp. 34–57.

Porshnev, B. F. "Razvitie Balashovskogo dvizheniia v fevrale-marte 1634 g." In *Problemy obshchestvenno-politicheskoi istorii Rossii i slavianskikh stran.* Moscow: Vostlit, 1963, pp. 225–41.

———. "Sotsial'no-politicheskaia obstanovka v Rossii vo vremia Smolenskoi voiny." *Istoriia SSSR* 1, no. 5 (November-December 1957) : 112–40.

Pososhkov, I. T. *Kniga o skudosti i bogatstve i drugie sochineniia.* Edited by B. B. Kafengauz. Moscow. Akademiia Nauk SSSR, 1951.

Preobrazhenskii, A. A. "Sysk beglykh na Urale v 1671 g." In *Iz istorii Urala. Sbornik statei.* Sverdlovsk, 1960, pp. 89–100.

———. "Ural i Zapadnaia Sibir' v gody Krest'ianskoi voiny pod predvoditel'-stvom S. T. Razina." In *Krest'ianstvo i klassovaia bor'ba v feodal'noi Rossii.* Leningrad: Nauka, 1967, pp. 280–93.

Presniakov, A. E. "Moskovskoe gosudarstvo pervoi poloviny XVII veka." In *Tri veka. Rossiia ot smuty do nashego vremeni.* 6 vols. Moscow, 1912–13. 1: 1–84.

———. *Moskovskoe tsarstvo.* Petrograd: Ogni, 1918.

———. *Obrazovanie velikorusskago gosudarstva. Ocherki po istorii XIII—XV stoletii.* Petrograd, 1918.

———. "Votchinnyi rezhim i krest'ianskaia krepost'." *Letopis' zaniatii postoiannoi istoriko-arkheograficheskoi komissii za 1926 god* 34 (1927) : 174–92.

Prokov'eva, L. S. "'Khlebnyi biudzhet' krest'ianskogo khoziaistva Belozerskogo kraia v seredine XVI v." In *Krest'ianstvo i klassovaia bor'ba v feodal'noi Rossii.* Leningrad: Nauka, 1967, pp. 98–113.

———. *Votchinnoe khoziaistvo v XVII veke po materialam Spaso-Prilutskogo monastyria.* Moscow-Leningrad: Akademiia Nauk SSSR, 1959.

Pronshtein, A. P. "K istorii pokhoda otriada Vasiliia Usa k Moskve v 1666 g." In *Krest'ianstvo i klassovaia bor'ba v feodal'noi Rossii.* Leningrad: Nauka, 1967, pp. 250–63.

———. "Reshennye i nereshennye voprosy istorii krest'ianskikh voin v Rossii." *Voprosy istorii* 42, no. 7 (July 1967) : 151–61.

Rabinovich, M. D. "Formirovanie reguliarnoi russkoi armii nakanune Severnoi voiny." In *Voprosy voennoi istorii Rossii. XVIII i pervaia polovina XIX vekov.* Moscow: Nauka, 1969, pp. 221–33.

Raeff, Marc. "The Domestic Policies of Peter III and his Overthrow." *The American Historical Review* 75, no. 5 (June 1970) : 1289–1310.

———. *The Origins of the Russian Intelligentsia. The Eighteenth-Century Nobility.* New York: Harcourt, Brace & World, Inc., 1966.

Rappoport, P. A. "Iz istorii voenno-inzhenernogo iskusstva drevnei Rusi (Staraia Ladoga, Porkhov, Izborsk, Ostrov) ." *Materialy i issledovaniia po arkheologii SSSR* 31 (1952) : 133–201.

———. "Ocherki po istorii russkogo voennogo zodchestva X—XIII vv." *Materialy i issledovaniia po arkheologii SSSR* 52 (1956) .

———. "Ocherki po istorii voennogo zodchestva severo-vostochnoi i severo-zapadnoi Rusi X—XV vv." *Materialy i issledovaniia po arkheologii SSSR* 105 (1961) .

———. "Osnovnye etapy razvitiia drevnerusskogo voennogo zodchestva." In *VII mezhdunarodnyi kongress doistorikov i protoistorikov. Doklady i soobshcheniia arkheologov SSSR.* Moscow: Nauka, 1966, pp. 225–34.

———. "Voennoe zodchestvo zapadnorusskikh zemel' X—XIV vv." *Materialy i issledovaniia po arkheologii SSSR* 140 (1967).

Razin, E. A. *Istoriia voennogo iskusstva.* 3 vols. Moscow: Voenizdat, 1955–61.

Reitenfel's, Iakov. "Skazaniia svetleishemu gertsogu toskanskomu Koz'me tret'-emu o Moskovii. Paduia, 1680 g." *ChOIDR* 214 (1905, no. 3) : i—x,1—128; 218 (1906, no. 3) : 129–228.

Romanovich-Slavatinskii, A. V. *Dvorianstvo v" Rossii ot" nachala XVIII veka do otmeny krepostnago prava.* St. Petersburg, 1870.

Rotmistrov, P. A., ed. *Istoriia voennogo iskusstva.* 2 vols. Moscow: Voenizdat, 1963.

Rozhdestvenskii, S. V. "Dvinskie boiare i dvinskoe khoziaistvo XIV-XVI vekov." *Izvestiia Akademii nauk SSSR, Otdelenie Gumanitarnykh nauk* 2 (1929) : 49–70, 135–54.

———. "Iz" istorii otmeny 'urochnykh" let"' dlia syska beglykh" krest'ian" v" Moskovskom" gosudarstve XVII veka." In *Sbornik" statei, posviashchennykh" Vasiliiu Osipovichu Kliuchevskomu.* Moscow, 1909, pp. 153–63.

———. "Sel'skoe naselenie Moskovskago gosudarstva v" XVI—XVII vekakh"." In *Russkaia istoriia v" ocherkakh" i stat'iakh".* Edited by M. V. Dovnar-Zapol'-skii. 3 vols. Kiev, 1912. 3: 34–84.

———. *Sluzhiloe zemlevladenie v" Moskovskom" gosudarstve XVI veka.* St. Petersburg, 1897.

Rozhkov, N. A. "Istoriia krepostnogo prava v Rossii." In *Iz russkoi istorii. Ocherki i stat'i.* 2 vols. Peterburg: Academia, 1923. 2: 113–37.

———. *Russkaia istoriia v sravnitel'no-istoricheskom osveshchenii (osnovy sotsial'-noi dinamiki).* 12 vols. Leningrad-Moscow: Kniga, 1928.

———. *Sel'skoe khoziaistvo Moskovskoi Rusi v" XVI veke.* Moscow, 1899.

———. "Sel'skoe khoziaistvo Moskovskoi Rusi v XVI v. i ego vliianie na sotsial'-no-politicheskii stroi togo vremeni." In *Iz russkoi istorii. Ocherki i stat'i.* 2 vols. Peterburg: Academia, 1923. 1: 160–82.

Sadikov, P. A. *Ocherki po istorii oprichniny.* Moscow-Leningrad: Akademiia Nauk SSSR, 1950.

Sakharov, A. M. "Lenin ob osnovnykh etapakh razvitiia russkogo gosudarstva (do otmeny krepostnogo prava)." In *V. I. Lenin i istoricheskaia nauka.* Moscow: Nauka, 1968, pp. 302–16.

———. *Obrazovanie i razvitie Rossiiskogo gosudarstva v XIV-XVII vv.* Moscow: Vysshaia shkola, 1969.

———. "Rabota V. I. Lenina nad istochnikami po russkoi istorii." *Voprosy istorii* 45, no. 4 (April 1970) : 152–64.

Sakharov, A. N. "Evoliutsiia kategorii krest'ianstva v XVII v." *Voprosy istorii* 40, no. 9 (September 1965) : 51–67.

———. "O dialektike istoricheskogo razvitiia russkogo krest'ianstva." *Voprosy istorii* 45, no. 1 (January 1970) : 17–41.

———. "Rol' arendy v krest'ianskom khoziaistve XVII v." *Istoriia SSSR* 8, no. 1 (January-February 1964) : 81–93.

———. *Russkaia derevnia XVII v.* Moscow: Nauka, 1966.

Samgina, E. I. "Sluzhiloe zemlevladenie i zemlepol'zovanie v chernskom uezde v pervoi polovine XVII v." In *Novoe o proshlom nashei strany. Pamiati Akademika M. N. Tikhomirova.* Moscow: Nauka, 1967, pp. 264–76.

Samokvasov, D. Ia. *Krest'iane drevnei Rossii po novootkrytym" dokumentam".* Moscow, 1909.

Sbornik" Kniazia Khilkova. St. Petersburg, 1879.

Schleussinger, Georg-Adam. "Rasskaz ochevidtsa o zhizni Moskovii kontsa XVII veka." Introduction by L. P. Lapteva. *Voprosy istorii* 45, no. 1 (January 1970) : 103–26.

Selifontov, N. N. *Ocherk" sluzhebnoi deiatel'nosti i domashnei zhizni stolnika i voevody XVII stoletiia, Vasiliia Aleksandrovicha Daudova.* St. Petersburg, 1871.

Serbina, K. N. "Ukaznye knigi Zemskogo prikaza vtoroi poloviny XVI i pervoi poloviny XVII v." In *Issledovaniia po otechstvennomu istochnikovedeniiu.* Moscow-Leningrad: Nauka, 1964, pp. 337–43.

Sergeeva-Kozina, T. N. "Mozhaiskii kreml' 1624–1626 gg." *Materialy i issledovaniia po arkheologii SSSR* 31 (1952) : 347–75.

Sergeevich, V. I. *Russkiia iuridicheskiia drevnosti.* 3 vols. St. Petersburg, 1901–03.

———. "Voennyia sily moskovskago gosudarstva." *ZhMIu* 11, no. 9 (1905) : 1–66.

Sh. "Dvorianstvo v" Rossii. Istoricheskii i obshchestvennyi ocherk"." *Vestnik" Evropy* 22, nos. 2–3 (March-June 1887) .

Shakhmatov, M. V. "Chelobitnaia 'mira' moskovskago tsariu Alekseiu Mikhailovichu 10. iiunia 1648 g." *Vestnik kralovske cheske spolechnosti nauk. Trida filosoficko-historicka. Rocnik 1933,* no. 4 (1934) : 1–23 + 8 plates.

Shapiro, A. L. "Ob absoliutizme v Rossii." *Istoriia SSSR* 13, no. 5 (September-October 1968) : 69–82.

———. "Volneniia starorusskikh krest'ian v 1671 g." In *Krest'ianstvo i klassovaia bor'ba v feodal'noi Rossii.* Leningrad: Nauka, 1967, pp. 300–318.

Shapiro, A. L. et al. "Mnogotomnaia 'Istoriia SSSR'." *Voprosy istorii* 43, no. 3 (March 1968) : 133–55.

Shchepetov, K. N. "Pomeshchich'e predprinimatel'stvo v XVII v. (Po materialam khoziaistva kniazei Cherkasskikh) ." In *Russkoe gosudarstvo v XVII veke. Novye iavleniia v sotsial'no—ekonomicheskoi, politicheskoi i kul'turnoi zhizni. Sbornik statei.* Moscow: Akademiia Nauk SSSR, 1961, pp. 17–38.

———. "Sel'skoe khoziaistvo v votchinakh Iosifo-Volokolamskogo monastyria v kontse XVI veka." *Istoricheskie zapiski* 18 (1946) : 92–147.

Shelekhov, F. P. "Glavnoe intendantskoe upravlenie. Istoricheskii ocherk". Chast' I. Vvedenie i tsarstvovanie imperatora Aleksandra I." In *Stoletie voennago ministerstva 1802–1902.* Vol. 5, pt. 1 (1903) .

Shepelev, I. S. *Osvoboditel'naia i klassovaia bor'ba v Russkom gosudarstve v 1608–1610 gg.* Piatigorsk, 1957.

Shepukova, N. M. "K voprosu ob itogakh podvornoi perepisi 1678–1679 gg. v Rossiiskom gosudarstve." *Istoriia SSSR* 4, no. 3 (April-May 1960) : 145–47.

Sheviakov, V. N. "K voprosu ob oprichnine pri Ivane IV." *Voprosy istorii* 31, no. 9 (September 1956) : 71–77.

Shil', Mikhail. "Donesenie o poezdke v" Moskvu v" 1598 godu." *ChOIDR* (April-June 1875) pt. 4, pp. 1–22.

Shilov, A. A. "Postupnyia zapisi. (K" istorii krest'ianskago voprosa v" XVII v.) ." In *Sbornik" statei, posviashchennykh" Aleksandru Sergeeevichu Lappo-Danilevskomu.* Petrograd, 1916, pp. 262–311.

Shmidt, S. O. "K istorii zemskoi reformy sobor 1555/56 g.) ." In *Goroda feodal'-noi Rossii. Sbornik statei pamiati N. V. Ustiugova.* Moscow: Nauka, 1966, pp. 125–34.

——. "K izucheniiu agrarnoi istorii Rossii XVI veka." *Voprosy istorii* 43, no. 5 (May 1968) : 17–31.

——. "Pravitel'stvennaia deiatel'nost' A. F. Adasheva." *Uchenye zapiski MGU* 167 (1954) : 25–53.

——. "V. I. Lenin o gosudarstvennom stroe Rossii XVI—XVIII vv. (o metodike izucheniia materialov po teme)." In *V. I. Lenin i istoricheskaia nauka.* Moscow: Nauka, 1968, pp. 330–46.

——. "Voprosy istorii Rossii XVI veka v novoi istoricheskoi literature." In *Sovetskaia istoricheskaia nauka ot XX k XXII s"ezdu KPSS. Istoriia SSSR. Sbornik statei.* Moscow: Akademiia Nauk SSSR, 1962, pp. 91–136.

Shumakov, S. A. "Gubnyia i zemskiia gramoty moskovskago gosudarstva." *ChOIDR* 174 (1895, no. 3) , pt. 4, pp. 1–247.

——. "Mena." *ZhMNP* 6 (November 1906) : 119–54.

Skrynnikov, R. G. *Nachalo Oprichniny.* Leningrad: Leningradskii Universitet, 1966.

——. "Oprichnaia zemel'naia reforma Groznogo 1565 g." *Istoricheskie zapiski* 70 (1961) : 223–50.

——. "Oprichnina i poslednie udel'nye kniazheniia na Rusi." *Istoricheskie zapiski* 76 (1965) : 152–74.

——. "Oprichnyi razgrom Novgoroda." In *Krest'ianstvo i klassovaia bor'ba v feodal'noi Rossii.* Leningrad: Nauka, 1967, pp. 157–71.

——. *Oprichnyi terror.* Leningrad: Leningradskii universitet, 1969.

——. "Samoderzhavie i Oprichnina (Nekotorye itogi politicheskogo razvitiia Rossii v period Oprichniny)." In *Vnutrenniaia politika tsarizma (Seredina XVI—nachalo XX v.).* Leningrad: Nauka, 1967, pp. 69–99.

Smirnov, I. I. "Iz istorii krest'ian v Moskovskom gosudarstve v kontse XVI v." *Uchenye zapiski Leningradskogo gosudarstvennogo universiteta* 32 (1939) : 66–75.

——. "K kharakteristike politiki Lzhedmitriia II po krest'ianskomu voprosu." In *Voprosy sotsial'no-ekonomicheskoi istorii i istochnikovedeniia perioda feodalizma v Rossii. Sbornik statei k 70-letiiu A. A. Novosel'skogo.* Moscow: Akademiia Nauk SSSR, 1961, pp. 43–49.

——. "Klassovye protivorechiia v feodal'noi derevne v Rossii v kontse XVI v." *Problemy istorii material'noi kul'tury* 1, nos. 5–6 (September-December 1933) : 59–73.

——. "Novyi spisok Ulozheniia 9 marta 1607 g." *Istoricheskii arkhiv* 4 (1949) : 72–87.

——. *Ocherki politicheskoi istorii russkogo gosudarstva 30-50-kh godov XVI veka.* Moscow-Leningrad: Akademiia Nauk SSSR, 1958.

——. "Problemy krepostnichestva i feodalizma v sovetskoi istoricheskoi literature." In *Dvadtsat' piat' let istoricheskoi nauki v SSSR.* Moscow-Leningrad: Akademiia Nauk SSSR, 1942, pp. 91–103.

——. *Vosstanie Bolotnikova 1606–1607 gg.* Leningrad: Gospolitizdat, 1951.

——. "Zametki o feodal'noi Rusi XIV-XV vv." *Istoriia SSSR* 6, no. 2 (March-April 1962) : 138–61; 6, no. 3 (May-June 1962) : 137–62.

Smirnov, P. P. "Chelobitnye dvorian" i detei boiarskikh" vsekh" gorodov" v" pervoi polovine XVII v." *ChOIDR* 254 (1915, no. 3) , pt. 1, pp. 1–73.

Works Cited

———. "Dvizhenie naseleniia Moskovskago gosudarstva." In *Russkaia istoriia v'' ocherkakh'' i stat'iakh.''* Edited by M. V. Dovnar-Zapol'skii. 3 vols. Moscow, 1912. 2: 62–80.

———. "Ekonomicheskaia politika Moskovskago gosudarstva v'' XVII v.'' In *Russkaia istoriia v'' ocherkakh'' i stat'iakh''.* Edited by M. V. Dovnar-Zapol'-skii. 3 vols. Kiev, 1912. 3: 369–410.

———. "Knigi stroel'nye." *Trudy Istoriko-arkhivnogo instituta* 2 (1946) : 99–123.

———. "O nachale Sobornago Ulozheniia i Zemskago sobora 1648–1649 gg.'' *Zhurnal'' Ministerstva Narodnago prosveshcheniia* 47, no. 9 (September 1913) : 36–66.

———. *Posadskie liudi i ikh klassovaia bor'ba do serediny XVII veka.* 2 vols. Moscow-Leningrad: Akademiia Nauk SSSR, 1947.

Smith, Robert E. F. "Medieval Agricultural Society in Its Prime: Russia." In *The Cambridge Economic History of Europe* 1 (1966) : 506–47, 818–23.

Snegirev, V. L. *Storozhevaia sluzhba. (Oborona granits gosudarstva v drevnei Rusi.)* Moscow: OGIZ, 1942.

Solov'ev, S. M. *Istoriia Rossii s drevneishikh vremen.* 15 vols. Moscow: Sotsekgiz —Mysl', 1959–66.

Sorokoletov, F. P. *Istoriia voennoi leksiki v russkom iazyke XI—XVII vv.* Leningrad: Nauka, 1970.

Spasskii, I. G. "Denezhnoe khoziaistvo russkogo gosudarstva v seredine XVII v. i reformy 1654–1663 gg.'' *Arkheograficheskii ezhegodnik za 1959 god* (1960) : 103–56.

Staden, Heinrich von. *The Land and Government of Muscovy. A Sixteenth-Century Account.* Translated and edited by Thomas Esper. Stanford: Stanford University Press, 1967.

Starostina, T. V. "Shueretskaia volost' v XVI–XVII vv." In *Krest'ianstvo i klassovaia bor'ba v feodal'noi Rossii.* Leningrad: Nauka, 1967, pp. 195–208.

Stashevskii, E. D. "Biudzhet'' i armiia." In *Russkaia istoriia v'' ocherkakh'' i stat'iakh''.* Edited by M. V. Dovnar-Zapol'skii. Kiev, 1912. 3: 411–17.

———. "Ekonomicheskaia politika Moskovskago gosudarstva v'' XVI-XVII vv.'' In *Russkaia istoriia v'' ocherkakh'' i stat'iakh''.* Edited by M. V. Dovnar-Zapol'-skii. 3 vols. Kiev, 1912. 3: 342–68.

———. *K'' istorii dvorianskikh'' chelobitnykh''.* Moscow, 1915.

———. "K'' istorii kolonizatsii Iuga. (Velikii boiarin'' Ivan'' Nikitich'' Roman-ov'' i ego slobody v'' Eletskom'' uezde) ." *Drevnosti. Trudy Arkheograficheskoi kommissii imp. Moskovskago arkheologicheskago obshchestva* 3 (1913) :239–94.

———. "Sluzhiloe soslovie." In *Russkaia istoriia v'' ocherkakh'' i stat'iakh''.* Edited by M. V. Dovnar-Zapol'skii. Kiev, 1912. 3: 1–33.

———. "Smeta voennykh'' sil'' Moskovskago gosudarstva na 1632 god''." *Voenno-istoricheskii vestnik''* 9–10 (1910) : 49–85.

———. *Smeta voennykh'' sil'' Moskovskago gosudarstva v'' 1663 godu.* Kiev, 1910.

———. *Zemlevladenie Moskovskago dvorianstva v'' pervoi polovine XVII veka.* Moscow, 1911.

Stepanov, I. V. *Krest'ianskaia voina v Rossii v 1670–1671 gg. Vosstanie Stepana Razina.* Leningrad: LGU, 1966.

Storozhev, V. N. *Istoriko-iuridicheskie materialy izdavaemye Moskovskim'' Ministerstvom'' iustitsii.* Vol. 1, *Ukaznaia kniga pomestnago prikaza.* Moscow, 1889.

———. "Materialy dlia istorii russkago dvorianstva." *ChOIDR* 230 (1909, no. 3) , pt. 1, pp. 1–222.

Strukov, D. P. "Artilleriia Drevnei Rusi i sostav" eia material'noi chasti XIV-XVII stol." In *Stoletie voennago ministerstva* 6, pt. 1, bk. 1 (1902) : 1–26.

Strumilin, S. G. *Ocherki ekonomicheskoi istorii Rossii*. Moscow: Sotsekgiz, 1960.

Sudebniki XV-XVI vekov. Moscow-Leningrad: AN SSSR, 1952.

Tatishchev, V. N. *Istoriia rossiiskaia*. 7 vols. Moscow-Leningrad: Akademiia Nauk SSSR—Nauka, 1962–68.

Tatishchev, V. N., ed. *Sudebnik" gosudaria tsaria i velikago kniazia Ioanna Vasil'evicha, i nekotorye sego gosudaria i blizhnikh" ego preemnikov" ukazy, sobrannye i primechaniiami iz"iasnennye . . . Tatishchevym"*. Moscow, 1786.

Tikhomirov, M. N. "Pskovskie povesti o krest'ianskoi voine v Rossii nachala XVII v." In *Iz istorii sotsial'no-politicheskikh idei. Sbornik statei k 70-letiiu Akademiku V. P. Volgina*. Moscow: Akademiia Nauk SSSR, 1955, pp. 181–90.

———. *Rossiia v XVI stoletii*. Moscow: Akademiia Nauk SSSR, 1962.

———. "Sobornoe Ulozhenie i gorodskie vosstaniia serediny XVII v." In *Sobornoe Ulozhenie 1649 goda. Uchebnoe posobie dlia vysshei shkoly*. Edited by M. N. Tikhomirov and P. P. Epifanov. Moscow: Moskovskii Universitet, 1961, pp. 5–26.

———. "Soslovno-predstavitel'nye uchrezhdeniia (zemskie sobory) v Rossii XVI v." *Voprosy istorii* 14, no. 5 (May 1958) : 3–23.

Tikhomirov, M. N., and Floria, B. N. "Toropetskaia kniga 1540 goda." *Arkheograficheskii ezhegodnik za 1963 god*. Moscow: Nauka, 1964, pp. 277–357.

Tikhonov, Iu. A. "Krest'ianskaia voina 1670–1671 gg. v lesnom zavolzh'e." In *Problemy obshchestvenno-politicheskoi istorii Rossii i slavianskikh stran*. Moscow: IVL, 1963, pp. 270–82.

Timofeev, N. "Krest'ianskie vykhody kontsa XVI v." *Istoricheskii arkhiv* 2 (1939) : 61–92.

Tkhorzhevskii, S. "Pomest'e i krest'ianskaia krepost'." *Trud v Rossii* 1 (1924) : 72–97. (*Arkhiv istorii truda v Rossii* 11–12 [1924]: 72–97.)

Tomsinskii, S. G. *Ocherki istorii feodal'no-krepostnoi Rossii*. Vol. 1. *Krest'ianskie voiny v epokhu obrazovaniia imperii*. Moscow-Leningrad: Sotsekgiz, 1934.

Trofimov, I. V., and Kir'ianov, I. A. "Materialy k issledovaniiu Nizhegorodskogo kremlia." *Materialy i issledovaniia po arkheologii SSSR* 31 (1952) : 318–46.

Troitskii, S. M. "Finansovaia politika russkogo absoliutizma vo vtoroi polovine XVII i XVIII vv." In *Absoliutizm v Rossii (XVII—XVIII vv.)*. Moscow: Nauka, 1964, pp. 281–319.

———. "O vliianii fiskal'noi sistemy na polozhenie krest'ian Rossii v XVII-XVIII vv." *Ezhegodnik po agrarnoi istorii vostochnoi Evropy 1963 g*. Vil'nius: Mintis, 1965, pp. 283–95.

Tul'skii krai. Dokumenty i materialy. Compiled by A. P. Bursak et al. 2 vols. Tula: Priokskoe knizhnoe izd-vo, 1966, 1968.

Udal'tsova, Z. V. "Problemy genezisa feodalizma v noveishikh rabotakh uchenykh." *Voprosy istorii* 40, no. 12 (December 1965) : 143–51.

Undol'skii, V. M. "Otzyv" Patriarcha Nikona ob" Ulozhenii Tsaria Alekseia Mikhailovicha. Novyia materialy dlia istorii zakonodatel'stva v" Rossii." *Russkii arkhiv"*, no. 7 (1886) , 605–20.

Uroff, Benjamin Phillip. "Grigorii Karpovich Kotoshikhin, On Russia in the Reign of Alexis Mikhailovich: An Annotated Translation." Ph.D. dissertation, Columbia University, 1970.

Ustiugov, N. V. "Evoliutsiia prikaznogo stroia russkogo gosudarstva v XVII v." In *Absoliutizm v Rossii (XVII—XVIII vv.)*. Moscow: Nauka, 1964, pp. 134–67.

Works Cited

———. "Volneniia krest'ian simonova monastyria v sele Il'inskom Cheremozhskoi volosti Iaroslavskogo uezda v 1682–1683 gg." In *Russkoe gosudarstvo v XVII veke*. Moscow: Akademiia Nauk SSSR, 1961, pp. 284–94.

Ustiugov, N. V., and Chaev, N. S. "Russkaia tserkov' v XVII v." In *Russkoe gosudarstvo v XVII veke*. Moscow: Akademiia Nauk SSSR, 1961, pp. 295–329.

Ustrialov, N. G. *Istoriia tsarstvovaniia Petra Velikago*. 6 vols. St. Petersburg, 1858–64.

Vainberg, E. I. "Bor'ba krest'ian protiv krepostnichestva na iuzhnoi okraine Russkogo gosudarstva v pervoi polovine XVII v." In *Novoe o proshlom nashei strany*. Moscow: Nauka, 1967, pp. 251–63.

Vainshtein, O. L. *Rossiia i tridtsatiletniaia voina*. Moscow: Gospolitizdat, 1947.

Valk, S. N. "Ivan Ivanovich Smirnov." In *Krest'ianstvo i klassovaia bor'ba v feodal'noi Rossii*. Leningrad: Nauka, 1967, pp. 5–41.

Vernadsky, George. "Serfdom in Russia." In *International Congress of Historical Sciences. Relazioni*. Firenze: G. C. Sansoni, 1955. 3: 247–72.

Veselovskii, S. B. *Feodal'noe zemlevladenie v severovostochnoi Rusi*. Moscow-Leningrad: Akademiia Nauk SSSR, 1947.

———. *Issledovaniia po istorii klassa sluzhilykh zemlevladel'tsev*. Moscow: Nauka, 1969.

———. *Issledovaniia po istorii oprichniny*. Moscow: Akademiia Nauk SSSR, 1963.

———. "Iz istorii zakreposhcheniia krest'ian (Otmena Iur'eva dnia)." *Uchenye zapiski Instituta istorii RANION* 5 (1929) : 204–17.

———. "K" voprosu o peresmotre i podtverzhdenii zhalovannykh" gramot" v" 1620–1630 gg. v Sysknykh" prikazakh"." *ChOIDR* 222 (1907, no. 3), pt. 4, pp. 26–27.

———. *K voprosu o proiskhozhdenii votchinnogo rezhima*. Moscow: RANION, 1926.

———. "Sinodik opal'nykh tsaria Ivana kak istoricheskii istochnik." In *Issledovaniia po istorii oprichniny*. Moscow: AN SSSR, 1963.

———. "Smety voennykh sil Moskovskago gosudarstva 1661–1663 gg." *ChOIDR* 238 (1911, no. 3) : 1–60.

———. *Soshnoe pis'mo. Izsledovanie po istorii kadastra i pososhnago oblozheniia moskovskago gosudarstva*. 2 vols. Moscow, 1915–16.

Veselovskii, S. B., ed. "Zhalovannye i ukaznye gramoty XIV-XV vv." In *Pamiatniki sotsial'no-ekonomicheskoi istorii Moskovskogo gosudarstva XIV-XVII vv*. Moscow: Tsentrarkhiv, 1929, pp. 1–81.

Vladimirskii-Budanov, M. F. *Khristomatiia po istorii russkago prava*. 3 parts. Iaroslavl'-St. Petersburg-Kiev, 1875, 1880, 1889.

———. *Obzor" istorii russkago prava*. 6th ed. St. Petersburg and Kiev, 1909.

Vodarskii, Ia. E. "Chislennost' i razmeshchenie posadskogo naseleniia v Rossii vo vtoroi polovine XVII v." In *Goroda feodal'noi Rossii*. Moscow: Nauka, 1966, pp. 271–81.

———. "Chislennost' naseleniia i kolichestvo pomestno-votchinnvkh zemel' v XVII v. (po pistsovym i perepisnvm knigam)." In *Ezhegodnik po agrarnoi istorii vostochnoi Evropy. 1964 god*. Kishinev: Kartia Moldoveniaske, 1966, pp. 217–30.

———. "K voprosu o dostovernosti itogov perepisnykh knig XVII v." *Istoriia SSSR* 14, no. 2 (March-April 1969) : 133–43.

———. "Kolichestvo zemli i pashni na dushu muzhskogo pola v tsentral'no-pro-myshlennom raione v XVII-XIX vv." *Ezhegodnik po agrarnoi istorii Vostochnoi Evropy 1965 g.* Moscow: Moskovskii Universitet, 1970, pp. 237–45.

———. "O dostovernosti pouezdnykh itogov perepisi sel'skogo naseleniia 1678 g. v svodnykh istochnikakh nachala XVIII v." *Arkheograficheskii ezhegodnik za 1967 god* (1969) : 99–106.

———. "Sel'skoe naselenie vologodskogo uezda vo vtoroi polovine XVII v." In *Voprosy agrarnoi istorii.* Vologda, 1968, pp. 426–33.

———. "Sluzhiloe dvorianstvo v Rossii v kontse XVII—nachale XVIII v." In *Voprosy voennoi istorii Rossii. XVIII i pervaia polovina XIX vekov.* Moscow: Nauka, 1969, pp. 233–38.

Volkov, L. V. "Problema zakreposhcheniia krest'ian v Rossii v sovetskoi istoricheskoi nauke [1917 g.—seredina 30-kh godov]." *Trudy MGIAI* 23 (1967) : 5–21.

Volkov, M. Ia. "O stanovlenii absoliutizma v Rossii." *Istoriia SSSR* 15, no. 1 (January-February 1970) : 90–104.

Vorms, A. E., et al., eds., *Pamiatniki istorii krest'ian" XIV-XIX v.v.* Moscow, 1910.

Voskoboinikova, N. P. "Rodovoi arkhiv krest'ianskoi sem'i Artem'evykh-Khlyzovykh." In *Arkheograficheskii ezhegodnik za 1966 god.* Moscow: Nauka, 1968, pp. 384–406.

Vostokov, A. "Russkoe sluzhiloe soslovie po desiatniam" 1577–1608 gg." *Iuridicheskii vestnik"* 28, no. 6–7 (June-July 1888) : 264–78.

Zagorovskii, V. P. *Belgorodskaia cherta.* Voronezh: Voronezhskii Universitet, 1969.

Zagoskin, N. P. *Ulozhenie Tsaria i Velikago Kniazia Alekseia Mikhailovicha i Zemskii sobor" 1648–1649 gg.* Kazan', 1879.

Zanicheva, L. G. "Krest'ianskie pobegi vo vtoroi polovine XVII v." In *Ezhegodnik po agrarnoi istorii Vostochnoi Evropy 1964 god.* Kishinev: Kartia Moldoveniaske, 1966, pp. 231–40.

———. "Sotsial'no-ekonomicheskoe polozhenie krest'ian shatskogo uezda v XVII v." In *Ezhegodnik po agrarnoi istorii Vostochnoi Evropy 1962 g.* Minsk: Nauka i tekhnika, 1964, pp. 202–11.

Zaozerskaia, E. I. "K istorii Tul'skoi oruzheinoi slobody." In *Voprosy voennoi istorii Rossii. XVIII i pervaia polovina XIX vekov.* Moscow: Nauka, 1969, pp. 137–56.

Zaozerskii, A. I. "K" voprosu o sostave i znachenii zemskikh" soborov"." *ZhMNP* 21 (June 1909) : 299–352.

———. *Tsar' Aleksei Mikhailovich" v" svoem" khoziaistve.* Petrograd: Petrogradskii universitet, 1917.

Zertsalov, A. "O miatezhakh" v" gorode Moskve i v" sele Kolomenskom" 1648, 1662, 1771 gg." *ChOIDR* 154 (1890, no. 3) , pt. 1, sec. 2, pp. 1–440.

Zheleznykh, V. I., ed. *Voenno-inzhenernoe iskusstvo i inzhenernye voiska russkoi armii. Sbornik statei.* Moscow: Voenizdat, 1958.

Zimin, A. A. "A. D. Gorskii. *Ocherki ekonomicheskogo polozheniia krest'ian severo-vostochnoi Rusi XIV-XV vv.*" *Istoriia SSSR* 6, no. 4 (July-August 1962) : 170–74.

———. *I. S. Peresvetov i ego sovremenniki. Ocherki po istorii russkoi obshchestvenno-politicheskoi mysli serediny XVI veka.* Moscow: Akademiia Nauk SSSR, 1958.

———. "K istorii voennykh reform 50-kh godov XVI v." *Istoricheskie zapiski* 55 (1956) : 344–59.

———. "Khoziaistvennyi krizis 60–70 godov XVI v. i russkoe krest'ianstvo." *Materialy po istorii sel'skogo khoziaistva i krest'ianstva SSSR* 5 (1962) : 11–20.

———. "Nekotorye voprosy istorii krest'ianskoi voiny v Rossii v nachale XVII veka." *Voprosy istorii* 14, no. 3 (March 1958) : 97–113.

———. "O politicheskikh predosylkakh vozniknoveniia russkogo absoliutizma." In *Absoliutizm v Rossii (XVII-XVIII vv.).* Moscow: Nauka, 1964, pp. 18–49.

———. *Oprichnina Ivana Groznogo.* Moscow: Mysl', 1964.

———. "Osnovnye etapy i formy klassovoi bor'by v Rossii kontsa XV—XVI veka." *Voprosy istorii* 40, no. 3 (March 1965) : 38–52.

———. "Problemy istorii Rossii XVI v. v svete leninskoi kontseptsii istorii russkogo feodalizma." In *V. I. Lenin i istoricheskaia nauka.* Moscow: Nauka, 1968, pp. 317–29.

———. *Reformy Ivana Groznogo. Ocherki sotsial'no-ekonomicheskoi i politicheskoi istorii Rossii serediny XVI v.* Moscow: Sotsekgiz, 1960.

———. "Uchastnik vziatiia Kazani v 1552 g. litvin Razmysl Petrov." In *Voprosy voennoi istorii Rossii. XVIII i pervaia polovina XIX vekov.* Moscow: Nauka, 1969, pp. 273–78.

Zimin, A. A., ed. *Tysiachnaia kniga 1550 g. i dvorovaia tetrad' 50-kh godov XVI v.* Moscow-Leningrad: Akademiia Nauk SSSR, 1950.

Zimin, A. A., and Koroleva, R. G. "Dokument razriadnogo prikaza." *Istoricheskii arkhiv* 8 (1953) : 21–60.

Zimin, A. A., and Preobrazhenskii, A. A. "Izuchenie v sovetskoi istoricheskoi nauke klassovoi bor'by perioda feodalizma v Rossii (do nachala XIX veka)." *Voprosy istorii* 32, no. 12 (December 1957) : 135–59.

Index

concealment of fugitive peasants by, 127, 263 *(see also* Morozov, B. I.) ; in second half of seventeenth century, 229, 244, 247–50, 252, 303 n. 193; usurpation of others' lands by, 67, 253, 263, 291 n. 131; under Vasilii II, 80. *See also* Favorites; Strong people; Upper service class

Makarii, Metropolitan, 34

Makovskii, D. P., 12, 87, 283 n. 5, 304 n. 1, 311 n. 75, 312 n. 92, 316 n. 3, 325 n. 99

Maksim Grek, 312 n. 90

Malaia Penezhka, 89

Malyshev, A. I., 13–14, 309 n. 70

Mamluks, 346 n. 14, 347 n. 65, 348 n. 69, 351 n. 37, 356 n. 42, 368 n. 167, 370 n. 192

Man'kov, A. G., 13–14, 335 n. 129, 378 n. 72

Manumission documents, 119

Margeret, Jacques, 97, 169, 281 n. 2, 295 n. 6, 329 n. 47, 353 n. 77

Margolin, S. L., 204, 353 n. 77, 363 n. 23

Maria Iaroslavna, 79

Markets, 26

Markov, M. I., 352 n. 63

Marselis, Peter, 184, 355 n. 18

Marx, Karl, 101

Maslovskii, D. F., 350 n. 10, 355 n. 28, 361 n. 156, 364 nn. 63, 64, 367 n. 134

Maurits van Oranje, 164, 188

Mavrodin, V. V., 382 n. 119

Maximilian, Austrian Grand Duke, 105

Maximilian, Holy Roman Emperor, 155

Mercenaries, 25, 56, 161, 169, 174, 191, 223, 225, 256, 350 n. 22; in the sixteenth century, 169, 350 n. 23; in the Time of Troubles, 168–70, 255; in the Smolensk War, 169–70, 172–73, 180; in the preparations for the Thirteen Years War, 190; in the Thirteen Years War, 190–91, 201, 216; in the Rzeczpospolita, 194, 201; in Western Europe, 151. *See also* Foreigners, as officers; New formation regiments

Merchant capitalism, 12; role in enserfment of, 9

Merchants, 123, 205, 224, 242, 301 n. 145, 358 n. 83; on 1648 mood, 139; taxation of, 195

Mestnichestvo. See System of places

Meyerberg, August von, 190–91, 223, 357 n. 74

Middle service class: absenteeism of, 29, 38–39, 45, 117, 193, 214, 216–21, 224, 250, 252, 368 n. 157; arms of, 211, 219–21 *(see also* Weapons) ; billetting

obligations, exempt from, 60; and cash remuneration, 143; in central chancelleries, 64, 70–71, 233, 302 nn. 169, 176, 340 n. 72; cohesiveness in, 37, 73; combat role of, 162; common interests of, 33, 46, 52, 294 n. 183; compensation of, 24, 36–37, 49, 51, 217, 219, 225, 227–28, 290 n. 104 (see also *Pomest'e*) ; concessions to, at Smolensk, 61; cossacks in, 28, 209, 238, 287 n. 52; court reform demanded by, 62–63; and decentralization, 62–64, 67; definition of, 22, 24; and discipline, lack of, 32–33, 233; divergent interests of southern and central, 31, 53, 107; and enserfment, 7–9, 17, 39, 45, 84–85, 93, 95, 98, 100, 103, 107, 110, 121, 138, 142–43, 146, 218, 225, 236–37, 319 n. 35, 326 n. 6; favors granted to, 60, 195–96, 216, 303 n. 190, 340 n. 79, 352 n. 54; and gentry, 57, 214, 240; government, beholden to, 27, 33, 46, 70, 73, 215, 224, 239; and grain markets, 59; immunities belonging to, 90; impoverishment of, 39, 62, 65, 97, 99–100, 110, 128, 133, 211–12, 214, 224, 236, 292 n. 151, 295 n. 18, 331 n. 64; under Ivan IV, 34, 43, 95, 100; justice, demanded by, 64–65; labor, struggle for, 47, 54, 66, 113, 136, 236–40; land, struggle for, 37, 42, 47, 52–55, 62, 67, 69, 73, 114; in local provincial administration, 35, 64, 71–72, 222, 224, 233, 302 nn. 169, 176, 365 n. 72; and magnates, upper service class, 17, 34, 40–41, 52, 54, 64, 73, 247, 251, 256, 263, 330 n. 49; materiel of, 37, 216, 220; *mestnichestvo* disputes by, 66, 239; under Mikhail, 111–14, 303 n. 193, 331 n. 59; military reviews of, 31–32, 219; monarch, relationship to, 34, 47, 67, 70, 224, 290 n. 115; and monasteries, 43; morale of, 221, 224; and musketeers, 161–63, 202, 207, 234; and new army, 74, 198; numbers in, 24, 28, 47, 51, 214, 218–19, 267–72; obligations, freed from, 51, 71; obligations of, 33, 50, 298 n. 76; obsolescence of, 17, 56, 73, 124, 168, 179–80, 186, 193, 209, 211, 213–15, 219–21, 223–25, 229, 238–40, 242, 250, 254, 263; obsolescence, reaction to own by, 238–40, 252, 257, 260, 263, 369 n. 192, 376 n. 44; and Oprichnina, 41, 43, 45; and peasantry, 28–29, 45, 71, 115, 239, 280 n. 127, 286 n. 46, 303 n. 188; origin of, 27, 287 n. 153; peasants in, 24, 28, 53, 127, 130, 236, 254, 286

Index

Razin, Stenka, uprising led by, 109, 207, 246–49, 251, 253, 304 n. 7, 327, 344 n. 22, 364 n. 48, 377 n. 62

Recovery and return of fugitive peasants, 81, 88, 105–6, 108, 112, 134, 143, 203, 246, 248, 250–51, 253–54, 376 n. 43. *See also* Government, and recovery of fugitive peasants; Peasants, flight of; Peasants, fugitive

Recruiting, 50, 165, 194–96, 232, 359 n. 119, 359–60 n. 121, 360 n. 122

Recruits *(datochnye liudi)*, 168, 189, 193, 196, 198, 214, 218, 221, 229, 234, 263. *See also* Peasants, in army

Reforms: of Aleksei *(see* Morozov); of Fedor Alekseevich, 222; of Ivan IV, 34–35, 46. *See also* New formation regiments

Regulations, military, 161, 168, 175–76, 188, 199, 357 n. 60

Reitary. See Cavalrymen

Rent, peasant. *See* Peasant rent

Rent fee (prescribed in *Sudebniki)*, 84–85, 87–88, 95, 110, 235, 312 n. 84. *See also* Harvest

Repnin: A. I., 232; B. A., 132

Reutenfels, Jacob, 348 n. 77, 361 nn. 156, 161

Revenues. *See* Government, finances of; Taxes

Review. *See* Middle service class, military reviews of

Riazan', 84, 129, 175, 205, 208, 212, 216, 220, 254

Riazhsk, 175

Rieber, Alfred J., 261

Rifling, 346–47 n. 34

Riga, 206

Rodes, Johann de, 355 n. 20

Roleinyi zakup (debtor), 82

Romanov: dynasty, 51, 73, 114, 296 n. 26, 299–300 n. 113; family, 52; F. N. *(see* Filaret); I. N., 113; N. I., 136, 225, 251, 375 n. 17

Romanovich-Slavatinskii, A. V., 17, 303 n. 192, 382 n. 125

Romanovo, 50

Rosen, Walter von, 169

Rozhdestvenskii, S. V., 311 n. 75, 335 n. 124

Rozhkov, N. A., 8, 34, 93–94, 282 n. 5, 298 n. 70, 310 n. 75, 315 n. 124, 317 n. 9, 318 nn. 11, 21, 22, 326 n. 8

Rudolph II, 101

Rugodiv (Narva), 182

Russkaia Pravda, 82

Russko-Turkish War (1676–81), 185, 226

Ryl'sk, 175

Rzeczpospolita, 99, 120, 168, 189–90, 194, 209, 226, 360 n. 144, 365 n. 69, 368 n. 151. *See also* Lithuania; Poland

Sadchiki, 94

St. George's Day, 87, 311 n. 82; introduction of, 82–87, 235, 308 n. 58; reason for choice of, 86; repeal of, 45, 48, 96, 98, 100–101, 103–5, 116, 142, 322 n. 66, 325 n. 99 *(see also* Forbidden Years); reinstituted, 107

St. Philip's Fast Day, 308 n. 43, 309 n. 67

Sakharov, A. M., 276 n. 27, 279 n. 110, 283 n. 5, 287 n. 54, 312 n. 84, 312–13 n. 92, 344 n. 9, 380 n. 105

Sakharov, A. N., 304 n. 6, 306 n. 25, 324 n. 85, 339 n. 62, 344 n. 24

Salt tax, 71, 188–89

Saltykov family, 113

Samara, 158

Samokvasov, D. Ia., 10, 316 n. 5, 320 n. 43, 335 n. 129, 345 n. 25

Schleussinger, Georg-Adam, 360 n. 136

Scotsmen, 169, 190

Secularization, 89. *See also* Monasteries, land-ownership of

Selected Council, 89, 288 n. 87

Selected Thousand, 36, 289–90 n. 102, 293 n. 157

Serebrennik ("silver peasant"), 308 n. 47, 314 n. 115. *See also* St. George's Day, introduction of

Serfdom: as anachronism, 240, 260; definitions of, 10–15, 309 n. 59, 314 n. 114; Golitsyn proposal to limit, 244, 256, 261; inevitability of, 263, 339 n. 62; peasants rebel against, 102–3 *(see also* Disorders); Petrine, 258–59; Pososhkov proposal to limit, 258–59; sanctions against lords for violation of, 108–9, 122, 132, 134, 137, 251–53, 341 n. 91; sanctions against peasants for violating laws of, 137, 246, 341 n. 92 *(see also* Recovery and return of fugitive peasants); in seventeenth century, 214, 239, 246, 248–49, 253–58, 263. *See also* Emancipation; Enserfment; Peasants; Serfs

Serfs: buying and selling of, 120, 122, 145, 259, 335 nn. 128, 129; obligations of, 196; ownership of, 249; procedures for recovery of, 88; rights of, 15, 107; treatment of, 260. *See also* Corvée; Peasants; Serfdom

428

Index

Vernadsky, George, 277–78 n. 62; 278 nn. 78, 79, 304 n. 1

Veselovskii, S. B., 5, 40, 280 n. 126, 286 n. 45, 314 n. 115, 324 n. 85, 336 n. 134

Viaz'ma, 205; uezd, desolation of, 97, 100

Vil'no, 194

Vipper, R. Iu., 283 n. 5

Vladen'e (possession of peasants), 105

Vladimirskii-Budanov, M. F., 4

Voevoda. See Military governor

Volkov, M. Ia., 280 n. 124, 373 n. 52, 383 n. 129

Volovonezh, 175

Voronezh, 129

Vorotynskii, M. I., 176

Vorskla River, 209; battle on, 155

Vostokov, A. A., 295 n. 21, 296 n. 36

Votchina (hereditary estate), 26; alienable, 68; concentration of, 379 n. 91; and 1556 Decree on Service, 37–38; middle service class ownership of, 57; and Oprichnina, 41; owned by servicemen, 54; preferred to *pomest'e,* 56; properties of, 56; redemption of, 374 n. 5; replaces *pomest'e,* 57; right of middle service class to purchase, 55; right to alienate limited, 40; service required from, 33, 38, 80, 290 n. 111; taxation of, 124

Voznesenskii, S. V., 279 n. 102

Vsevolozhskii, I. D., 79

Vvoznaia gramota. See Poslushnaia gramota

Vyborg, 154

Vybornye dvoriane, 23

Vygovskii, Hetman, 217

Vyia, 89

Vykhod (free peasant moving), 5, 88, 98, 105, 109–10, 308 n. 56, 325 n. 6

Vyt' of land, 372 n. 24

Vyvoz (assisted peasant moving), 5, 83, 88, 94, 105, 109–10, 113, 132, 308 n. 56, 325 n. 6

Wallhausen, Johann Jacob von, *Kriegskunst zu Fuss,* 188, 356–57 n. 59

Weapons, cold: arbalest, 160; axe, 200, 211–12; bayonet, 207; *berdysh,* 161, 168, 196, 200, 220; bow and arrow, 30, 174, 182, 206, 354 n. 4, 366 n. 99; crossbow, 151; halberd, 191, 206; lance, 161, 168, 199–200, 206, 210, 220; pike, 151, 196, 200; rapier, 196, 199–200, 360 n. 126; sabre, 30, 161, 183, 212, 219, 360 n. 126; spear, 30, 168, 191, 211–12; sword, 30

Wergild, 33

Western Dvina River, 193

Western formation regiments. *See* New formation regiments

Western frontier, 281 n. 2

Westernization, 223. *See also* Foreigners; Morozov; New formation regiments

White Sea region, 94; *See also* Northern Dvina; Pomor'e

Widows, 48, 51, 58, 61, 195, 369 n. 174

Wladyslaw IV, 123, 169

Xenophobia, 55–56, 167, 173, 224

Zagorovskii, V. P., 352 n. 57, 353 n. 83, 354 nn. 101, 102, 356 n. 52

Zakladchiki (urban slaves), 241, 293 n. 162

Zakup, 314 n. 115

Zapovednye leta. See Forbidden Years

Zaraisk, 158

Zarutskii, I. M., and peasant-cossack disorders, 103, 330 n. 50

Zaseka, Zasechnaia cherta. See Fortified lines

Zemshchina, 115

Zemskaia provincial administration, 35, 91

Zhil'tsy, 23–24, 29, 71

Zhizdra River, 175

Zimin, A. A., 38, 41, 93, 282 n. 5, 289 nn. 91, 97, 291 n. 130, 293 n. 156, 308 n. 47, 309 nn. 64, 70, 313 n. 92, 314 n. 5, 319 n. 24, 324 n. 85, 325 n. 99, 330 n. 52, 348 n. 72, 355 n. 28, 368 n. 167, 380 n. 105

Znakomtsy, 39